REAL WORLD FREEHAND 8

Real World
FreeHand 8

by
Olav Martin Kvern

macromedia
PRESS

PEACHPIT PRESS

for David Howard & Charlie Spear

REAL WORLD FREEHAND 8
Olav Martin Kvern

Copyright © 1998 by Olav Martin Kvern

PEACHPIT PRESS
1249 Eighth Street
Berkeley, CA 94710
(800) 283-9444
(510) 524-2178
(510) 524-2221(fax)

Find us on the World Wide Web at: http://www.peachpit.com
Peachpit Press is a division of Addison Wesley Longman

 Published by Macromedia Press, in association with Peachpit Press.

Original Developemental Editor & Guiding Light: Stephen F. Roth
Copy Editor: Jon Singer (yes, I know him, too)
Indexer: Jan C. Wright
Cover design: Ted Mader & Associates (TMA)
Cover illustration: Robert Dietz
Interior design, illustration, and production: Olav Martin Kvern, Toby Malina, and Carl Juarez

ISBN 0-201-87485-7

9 8 7 6 5 4 3 2 1

Printed and bound in the United States of America

If I weren't one of the authors of FreeHand, I'd want this book to teach me how to use it. Actually, I'd want Ole to teach me, but he lives two thousand miles away. And he probably would get pretty tired of showing me the tricky parts over and over and over again. With *Real World FreeHand*, I have his advice and insight any time I need them.

When we started working on FreeHand, we had a vision of an easy–to–use, yet extraordinarily powerful graphics program. We wanted it to be usable by both novices and professional designers, and give results limited only by a person's artistic ability. It should be as intuitive as a pencil, but as powerful as a mind link to a hallucination machine. We've come a long way in those years. Of course, we aren't quite up to the level of our vision yet. But it wouldn't have been much of a vision if we could achieve it in just a few years of programming.

We had another vision too—one of talented artists working with computers, multiplying their abilities a hundredfold, and avoiding the dull, routine work of aligning things that simply refused to align; of specifying type, then setting the job aside while waiting for the galleys to come back from the typesetting house; of doing what our first ad agency did—cutting that type apart letter by letter and hand setting it with just the right spacing; of hearing the client ask to change a word in the middle of one of those blocks when the final deadline is tomorrow morning. With FreeHand, everything is malleable until the moment when a scanning laser beam starts to reveal the billions of pixels that make up your page on the drum of a laser printer or to the film of an imagesetter.

I am really happy with what has been achieved in FreeHand 8. The development team worked for months fixing bugs that companies who don't care as much about perfection as Macromedia would have shipped with. They kept improving it even after it was good enough, kept working on it until they were sick of it, in fact. I think there are three factors in FreeHand's success: the team really cares about doing the best job they know how, they have several very smart software engineers working on it, and they have some awesomely talented users who continue to tell them how to make it even better.

Reading the drafts of this book is a lot like reading a biography of your own daughter. The writer talks about her accomplishments. Her beauty. Her charm. Her high-pitched whiny voice. Well, no writer is perfect. Fortunately, Ole laughs with us on those few occasions where the reality differs from the vision. And he goes on to explain those hard parts step by step in a way that almost anybody can understand.

Reader, you've made two good choices. Crank up FreeHand and get started with *Real World FreeHand*. I think you'll have fun with both.

Jim Von Ehr
founder, Altsys Corporation
(original creators of FreeHand,
now part of Macromedia)

If you're new to this book, welcome. If you've read previous editions, welcome back! I hope you think this one's worth the wait. Due to the peculiar speed with which the FreeHand team manages to produce product updates, this edition is late, even though it's only been a year since I sent the last one to the printer. That's life in the computer book publishing "fast lane," I guess.

"Vaikka FreeHandin tuntisi miten hyvin tahansa, löytyy tästä kirjasta silti uutta tietoa," the Finnish text you'll see on the back cover, means, more or less (according to my translator), "Even if you think you know everything about FreeHand, you'll learn something from this book." I hope you agree.

Where I'm Coming From

Why should you listen to what I have to say about working with FreeHand? I've worked as a technical, medical, archaeological, and veterinary illustrator, as well as a general-purpose book and magazine illustrator. I've also worked as a designer, typesetter, paste-up slave, and art director.

More importantly, I bring my experience as a FreeHand user. I really have been through the long shifts (some of them longer than 40 hours) working with FreeHand: drawing, entering text, setting type, importing images, exporting EPS graphics, and trying to get files to print. On most of those late nights and early mornings, I could have been home in bed if I'd known just one key piece of information. But I didn't. There was no one to tell me.

I'm here to tell you.

If some piece of information in this book saves you one late night, one early morning, or gets your file to print on the first pass through the imagesetter instead of the second or third, I will have succeeded in my purpose.

A janitor once found me pounding on a Linotronic film processor (an ML-314, for you hardware tweaks) with a wastebasket. It was 4:00 AM, I'd been up for more than 36 hours, and the processor just shredded a job that had taken more than six hours to print on an imagesetter (an L-300). I wrote this book in the hope that I could save others from repeating this scene.

The Wild Ride

"Adobe's just acquired Aldus."

The news made my head spin. First, it was good news for a product I love. PageMaker, as an entity, would probably benefit. Second, it was very bad news for another product I love. Free-Hand. There was no way that FreeHand would benefit from having its marketer (Aldus) acquired from the maker of its chief competitor (Adobe, and Adobe Illustrator, respectively). I thought, and it seemed likely, that Adobe would do everything they could to hang on to the marketing rights to FreeHand, while, simultaneously, doing very little to sell it. FreeHand would wither and die.

I wasn't the only person thinking this way—Altsys, the software development company that's always written FreeHand, sued immediately to get FreeHand back. And then—to make a long and involved legal story short—something unexpected happened.

They won.

FreeHand went back to Altsys, and Altsys then merged with Macromedia, becoming Macromedia's Graphics Products Division. Which means that the FreeHand team can concentrate on doing what they do best—making FreeHand the best illustration tool on the market. Pushing it farther into new fields, like page layout and Web publishing.

I think we're in for a wonderful ride.

Organization

This book's pretty simple: first, I'll show you how to get things *into* FreeHand; next, I'll talk about how to work with elements in FreeHand; and then I'll tell you how to get things *out* of FreeHand.

Chapter 1: FreeHand Basics. This chapter is your orientation to the world of FreeHand. In it, I describe the publication window, selecting objects, moving objects, working with FreeHand's toolbox, and then I give an overview of the ways that you create and import elements into FreeHand (including basic path drawing).

Chapter 2: Drawing. This is all about using FreeHand's drawing tools—from creating and joining paths to applying strokes and fills, creating graphic styles, working with blends, creating charts and graphs, and drawing using perspective.

Chapter 3: Text and Type. This chapter deals with working with text in FreeHand—how to enter, edit, and format text. It covers wrapping text around graphics, specifying type, FreeHand's type effects, joining text to a path, pasting graphics into text blocks, and converting text into paths.

Chapter 4: Importing and Exporting. FreeHand doesn't exist in a vacuum. You need to be able to import images from image-editing programs, or to be able to import EPS graphics from other PostScript drawing programs. You need to be able to import text from your word processor. This chapter shows you how, and where, FreeHand fits in with your other applications.

Chapter 5: Transforming. This chapter shows you how to manipulate FreeHand elements you've drawn, typed, or imported, and describes how to use the transformation (skewing, scaling, rotation, and reflection) tools.

Chapter 6: Color. In this chapter, I cover creating and applying colors in FreeHand. I also discuss color models, color management, the history of color printing, creating duotones, and controlling the conditions under which you view and create color publications.

Chapter 7: Printing. It don't mean a thing if you can't get it on paper or film (but see Chapter 9 for a dissenting opinion). Here's how to do that, plus a bunch of tips that will save you money at your imagesetting service bureau and at your commercial printer. This chapter is mostly about the options in FreeHand's Print and Print Setup dialog boxes, and how they affect your publications.

Chapter 8: PostScript. I wrote this chapter because I want to try to make PostScript programming more accessible to the average FreeHand user. It's not hard, and it's a great way to add your own unique touch to your FreeHand publications. And it's fun!

Chapter 9: FreeHand and the Web. How to get your FreeHand artwork into our newest publishing medium. This chapter covers exporting GIF images, creating Shockwave Flash graphics and animations, and embedding them in HTML pages.

Disclaimer

Some of the techniques in this book involve modifying either FreeHand's subsidiary files (like PPDs) or modifying FreeHand itself. While I've tried to make the procedures as accurate as possible, you need to be aware that you're proceeding entirely at your own risk. Given that, there are a few things you can do to make everything less risky.

Work on copies of files. If you don't keep your original files in their original state, how can you ever go back to where you started? Always back your files up before you try altering them.

Remember that not everyone will set up their system the way you've set up yours. You can't expect your friends—or your image-setting service bureau—to be absolutely up-to-date with your current modifications if you don't provide them. Therefore, if your publication requires a custom page size you've written into a PPD, make sure that your imagesetting service bureau has the PPD.

Clean up after yourself. If you change any of FreeHand's Post-Script printing routines in a printer's RAM, make sure that you change them back to their original state before anyone else sends a job to that printer. Nothing is worse than having your name and the word "DRAFT" printed across all of the jobs printed on a particular printer because you forgot to change *showpage* back to its original definition. This is a great way to provoke the villagers to come after you with torches and pitchforks.

Don't call Macromedia technical support if something you read in this book doesn't work. They didn't write this book and shouldn't be expected to support it. This book is not a Macromedia product (in spite of their kindly lending me their imprint), and they have no control over its content. I'm not kidding. Write to me, instead. My mail addresses are listed in Appendix B, "About This Book."

Extensis Vector Tools. I designed, and even wrote some code for, some of the plug-ins in VectorTools 2.0, from Extensis. While I think it is an excellent package of add-ons for FreeHand, please don't construe any mention I make of it in the book—or its appearance in some of the illustrations—as an advertisement.

Cross-Platform Notes

This is the second edition of this book to cover both the Macintosh and Windows versions of FreeHand. Windows users, please forgive me for using so many Macintosh screen shots (though you'll note that most of the *new* screen shots are from Windows), and for the number of "Macintosh only" sections.

When I show a keyboard shortcut in the text, the Macintosh shortcut comes first, followed by the Windows shortcut—like this: Command-Option-F/Ctrl-Alt-F.

Acknowledgments

Thanks to the FreeHand engineering team (and related folks at Macromedia), for creating a great product to write about and use. Special thanks to (current and former FreeHand team members) Samantha Seals-Mason and Pete Mason, Steven Johnson, Doug Benson, Katharine Green, Joel Dreskin, Anna Sturdivant, Lorin Rivers, the incomparable Brian Schmidt, the amazing Bentley Wolfe, the astounding Mark Haynes, Kevin Crowder, Rusty Williams, and, especially, to Jim Von Ehr for his inspiring foreword.

Thanks to Harry Edwards, Nick Allison, Karen Fishler, and Tamis Nordling, current and former editors of *Adobe Magazine* (formerly *Aldus Magazine*) for making me a better writer.

Thanks to the Seattle Gilbert and Sullivan Society, and their photographer, Ray O. Welch, for giving me permission to use some of their archival photographs as example images. Special thanks to Ed Poole for the free use and abuse of his moustache.

Thanks to Nancy Ruenzel for being a great publisher, to Ted Nace for founding Peachpit Press, and to Steve Roth, for his editorial vision and assistance with the original manuscript of this book (no one does it better). Thanks to Jeanne Woodward, Cary Norsworthy, and everyone else at Peachpit Press. Thanks to the other sometime denizens of the Seattle Desktop Publishing Commune/Ghetto/Grotto—David Blatner, Krista "no nickname yet" Carreiro, Don "Zap!" Sellers, Steve "thumper" Broback, Glenn Fleishman, the always elegant Michele Dionne, and the numerous other Thunder Lizards. Thanks to Carl Juarez, Toby Malina, Jon Singer, Jan C. Wright—the "Real World FreeHand 8" team (more about them in Appendix B, "About This Book").

Finally, thanks to my wonderful wife, Leslie Renée Simons, and to my son, Max Olav Kvern, for their encouragement, understanding, and support.

Olav Martin Kvern
Republic of Fremont
Seattle, 1998

FreeHand Basics

Start FreeHand, and you enter another world—a software model of a graphic artist's studio. Most programs are based on some real-world model: PageMaker works like a layout board, Excel works like an accountant's worksheet, and Word works like a reasonably intelligent electric typewriter. Metaphors like these make computer software "user-friendly"—partly because they give us an environment we're familiar with, and partly because they give the program an internal logic of its own.

In this chapter, I'll show you around the virtual reality that is FreeHand. There'll be lots of definitions of terms (how can you know what I'm talking about unless we're using the same vocabulary?) and "maps" of FreeHand's screen (how can you tell where you're going unless you know the lay of the land?). Almost all of the concepts and practices covered here are covered in greater depth in other chapters. In those cases, I'll provide a cross reference to the more detailed explanation.

I'll also be going through some techniques for changing the way FreeHand looks and behaves, because I believe that the tools you use should fit your working habits. I'll spend a lot of time discussing the meaning and use of FreeHand's multitudinous preferences and defaults.

At the end of the chapter, I'll run through my list of rules for using FreeHand. You can take them or leave them; there are many different ways to approach FreeHand, and my methods are not necessarily the ones that'll work best for you. Some of my habits are rooted in the dim and primordial past (giant ground sloths, woolly mammoths, and Linotronic L100s roamed the earth), and some, while true today, might not apply when this book reaches your hands. That's the thing about computer software—as soon as you really know something, it's obsolete.

The Publication Window

When you open or create a FreeHand publication, you view and work on the publication in the publication window (see Figure 1-1). FreeHand's publication window gives you a view on FreeHand's pasteboard—the place everything happens in FreeHand.

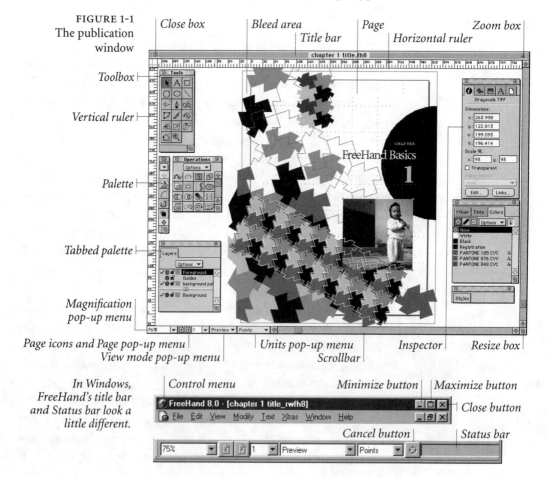

FIGURE 1-1
The publication window

Close box · Bleed area · Page · Zoom box
Title bar · Horizontal ruler

Toolbox

Vertical ruler

Palette

Tabbed palette

Magnification pop-up menu

Page icons and Page pop-up menu · Units pop-up menu · Inspector · Resize box
View mode pop-up menu · Scrollbar

In Windows, FreeHand's title bar and Status bar look a little different.

Control menu · Minimize button · Maximize button
Close button

Cancel button · Status bar

What you see in the title bar differs slightly between Macintosh and Windows versions of FreeHand. On the Macintosh, you'll see the title (the name of your publication file), close box (click it to close the window), and zoom box (click it to make your publication window the size of the screen; click it again to return the publication window to its previous size). In Windows, you'll see the title, control menu, and close/minimize/maximize buttons (click them to close, shrink, or enlarge the window, respectively).

Scroll Bars

The most obvious, least convenient, and slowest way to change your view of your publication is to use a scroll bar (that is, to click in a scroll bar, drag a scroll handle, or click the arrows at either end of a scroll bar). For more on better ways to get around, see "Moving Around in Your Publication," later in this chapter.

Page Icons and the Page Pop-up menu

Now that FreeHand publications can contain multiple pages, you need a way to move from one page to another. One way is to click the left page icon to move to the previous page in your publication, and click the right page icon to move to the next page. If you know which page you want to go to, you can choose the page number from the Page pop-up menu, or enter the page number in the field associated with the pop-up.

There's a better way to get from page to page, however: press Command-Page Up/Ctrl-Page Up to move ahead one page; or press Command-Page Down/Ctrl-Page Down to move back one page (relative to the order in which the pages appear on the pasteboard). If you want to move more than one page at a time, double-click the page you want to move to in the thumbnail view of FreeHand's pasteboard in the Document Inspector (see "Moving Around in Your Publication," later in this chapter).

View Mode Pop-up Menu

Choose a viewing mode from this pop-up menu to switch between FreeHand's four viewing modes. You can also press Command-K/ Ctrl-K to switch between Keyline and Preview.

In either Preview mode, FreeHand renders the objects you've drawn as they'll be printed. In the Keyline modes, FreeHand shows you only the outlines of the objects on the page (see Figure 1-2). FreeHand's new viewing modes, Fast Preview and Fast Keyline, cut

FIGURE 1-2
FreeHand's
viewing modes

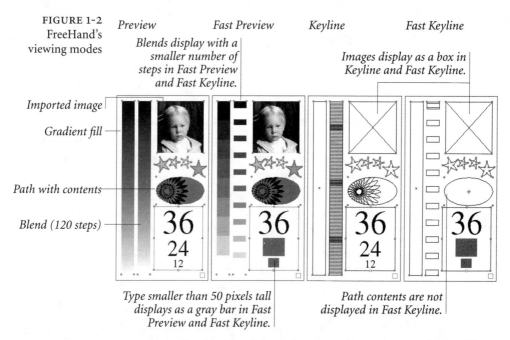

Preview   Fast Preview   Keyline   Fast Keyline

Blends display with a smaller number of steps in Fast Preview and Fast Keyline.

Images display as a box in Keyline and Fast Keyline.

Imported image

Gradient fill

Path with contents

Blend (120 steps)

Type smaller than 50 pixels tall displays as a gray bar in Fast Preview and Fast Keyline.

Path contents are not displayed in Fast Keyline.

corners on the display of slow-drawing objects (text and blends). In addition, Fast Keyline does not display objects pasted inside paths.

Each viewing mode has advantages and disadvantages. In Preview mode, you'll see something resembling your printed publication, but you'll also wait longer for it to display; Keyline mode redraws quickly but doesn't usually resemble the printed publication. It's easier to select points in Keyline mode, and it's easier to select objects in Preview mode. You'll find yourself switching between Preview and Keyline often.

You can also set specific layers to display in either Keyline or Preview mode using the Layers palette. For more on how to do this, see "Working with Layers," later in this chapter.

Magnification Pop-up Menu

Choose a magnification from this pop-up menu, and FreeHand magnifies or reduces the view of the publication you see in the publication window. There are better ways to do this, as shown in "Moving Around in Your Publication," later in this chapter.

Note that these views aren't the only magnifications available—using the magnifying glass, you can achieve any magnification you want. For more on using the magnifying glass, see "Magnifying Glass," later in this chapter.

Note, too, that the maximum magnification cited in the Magnification pop-up menu isn't the ultimate magnification FreeHand's capable of. Without any trickery, you can view your publication at 25,600 times its actual size (256x%); *with* trickery (see "Secret Preferences" later in this chapter), you can get as close as 16,384x% (1,638,400 times actual size). If you need to draw microscopic organisms at their actual size, this magnification is for you.

Units
Pop-up
Menu

Choose your favorite unit of measure from this pop-up menu to set the measurement system FreeHand uses. You can always override the current unit of measure when you're entering values in FreeHand's palettes and dialog boxes, as shown in Table 1-1.

TABLE 1-1
Overriding units of
measurement

If you want this value	Type this in the dialog box
7 inches	7i
22 points	p22
11 picas	11p*
6 picas, 6 points	6p6*
23.4 millimeters	23.4m*

* There are approximately 236,220.4 picas in a kilometer.

Multiple
Windows

If you want to open more than one window on your publication, choose "New Window" from the Window menu (or press Command-Option-N/Ctrl-Alt-N). The new window covers the original window, so you'll have to drag and resize windows to see both views at once (or, in Windows, choose Tile Windows from the Window menu). Alternatively, you can use the Window menu to move from one window to another—each window appears in the list of open publications at the bottom of the menu (see Figure 1-3).

Sometimes, when you're working with a multi-page document, it's easier to display pages in multiple windows than it is to scroll or zoom from page to page. This is especially true when you're copying objects from one page to another (and the pages aren't next to each other on the pasteboard—see Figure 1-4).

FIGURE 1-3
Multiple windows on a
single publication

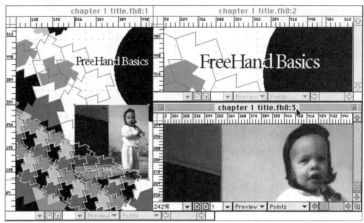

*FreeHand numbers
views as you create
them.*

*Multiple views of a single publication. You can switch among different views
using the Window menu.*

FIGURE 1-4
Dragging objects from
window to window

*Though these pages
couldn't be much
farther apart (as
you can see from the
view of the pasteboard
shown in the Document
Inspector), it's easy to
drag an object from
one page to the other.*

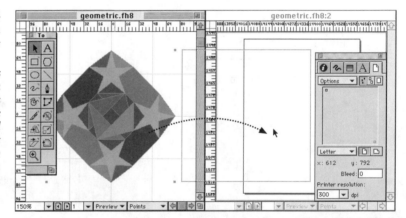

Stop dragging, and FreeHand copies the object to the new window.

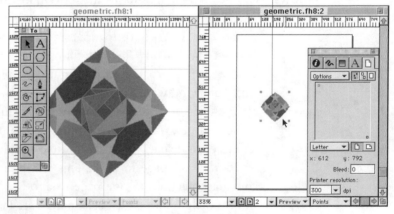

*Note: The size of the
rectangle FreeHand
displays as you drag the
object is determined
by the magnification
of the window you're
dragging out of. This
looks funny, at first.*

Tip:
Closing All
Open Windows

To close all open windows for a publication, hold down Option as you click the Close box (Macintosh) or hold down Shift as you click the Close button (Windows). Or, if you'd rather use a keyboard shortcut, press Command-Option-W/Ctrl-Shift-F4. FreeHand closes all of the open windows, then closes the publication.

Named Views

Do you frequently find yourself moving back and forth between two or more locations and magnifications in a publication? If so, you can create a named view for each location, then flip quickly from one view to another without zooming or scrolling.

To create a named view, set up the view you want, then choose New from the Custom submenu of the View menu FreeHand displays the New View dialog box. Enter a name for your view and click the OK button. FreeHand adds the view to the list of views at the bottom of the Custom submenu (see Figure 1-5).

FIGURE 1-5
Creating a named view

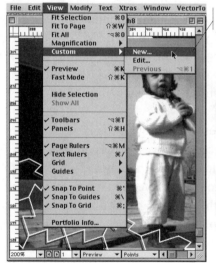

To save a view, choose New from the Custom menu.

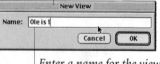

FreeHand displays the New View dialog box.

Enter a name for the view and click the OK button.

Choosing the view name from the Custom submenu of the View menu will zoom and/or scroll your view of the publication to the view you saved.

FreeHand adds the view to the Custom submenu of the View menu.

To delete a named view, choose Edit from the Custom submenu. FreeHand displays the Edit Views dialog box.

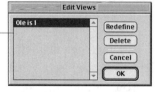

Select the view you want to delete, then click the delete button.

To redefine a named view, display the Edit Views dialog box, select a view, and then click the Redefine button. FreeHand redefines the view using the current state (i.e., magnification and location) of the publication window.

To display a view, choose the name you've assigned to the view, or press Command-Option-1/Ctrl-Alt-1 (to display the previous view) until the view you're looking for appears. Note that changing views does not open a new window—FreeHand's named views are simply a shortcut for navigating (i.e., zooming and/or scrolling) to a particular location and magnification in the current window.

To delete a view, choose Edit from the Custom submenu. Then, in the Edit Views dialog box, select the name of the view and click the Delete button. FreeHand deletes the view from the list.

To redefine a named view, zoom and/or scroll to the view you want, then display the Edit Views dialog box (again, you choose Edit from the Custom submenu of the View menu). In the Edit Views dialog box, select the name of the view you want to change and click the redefine button. FreeHand changes the view to the current magnification and location.

Multiple Open Publications

You can have as many different publications open as FreeHand can fit into your machine's RAM. You move between open publications by choosing their file names from the Window menu, or by clicking on their windows, just as you'd switch among applications (see Figure 1-6).

Page and Pasteboard

Like most other page layout programs, FreeHand is built around the concept of pages—areas on which you place graphic elements. Pages float on the pasteboard—a 222-inch-square area. In Free-Hand you can create as many pages as you want, provided they all fit on the pasteboard. You can use areas of the pasteboard that don't contain pages for temporary storage of the elements you're working with—just drag the elements off the page, and they'll stay on the pasteboard until you need them (again, this is just like an old-fashioned layout board).

Bleed Area, Page Size, and Paper Size

Objects can extend past the edge of the page, into an area of the pasteboard that's defined as the bleed. What's the point of having a "bleed?" Sometimes, you want to print objects that extend beyond the edge of your page (they'll be clipped off at the edge of the page when your commercial printer cuts your pages, but sometimes, that's just the design effect you want).

FIGURE 1-6
Window menu

List of open publications or windows. FreeHand displays a check beside the title of the active window.

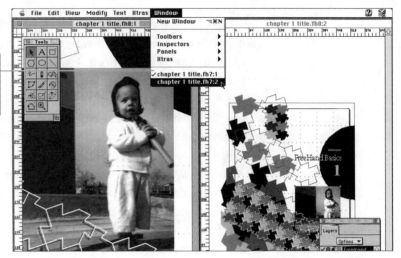

Each page's bleed is shown in the publication window by line (a gray line on color and grayscale monitors, or a dotted line if you're working in black and white) surrounding the page. Different pages can have bleed areas of different sizes.

The size of the bleed, the page size, and the size of the paper (that is, the paper size you want to use when you print your *final* copy) all affect each other. In FreeHand, the page size you define in the Document Inspector should be the same as the final size of the document's page after it's been printed by a commercial printer. You define the paper size—the physical size of the paper in your printer—in the Print Options dialog box. When you're printing to an imagesetter, the paper size is a defined area on the imagesetter's film roll (or sheet, for drum imagesetters).

If your publication's page size (without the bleed) is the same as the paper size you've chosen in the Print Options dialog box, you can expect FreeHand to neatly clip off the bleed area you've specified. Choose a larger paper size in the Print Options dialog box than your publication's page size when you want to print bleeds (choose Letter.Extra when you're printing a letter-size publication with a bleed, for example). If you want to learn how to create new paper sizes for imagesetters (I don't know of any laser printer that can handle custom paper sizes), see "Rewriting PPDs" in Chapter 7, "Printing."

Rulers   Pressing Command-Option-M/Ctrl-Alt-M displays or hides Free-
Hand's rulers—handy measuring tools that appear along the top
and left sides of your publication window (see Figure 1-7). They're
marked off in the units of measurement specified on the Units
pop-up menu. The actual increments shown on the rulers vary
somewhat with the current page view; in general, you'll see finer
increments and more ruler tick marks at 800% size than you'll see
at 12% size.

As you move the cursor, lines in the rulers (called shadow cursors) display the cursor's position relative to the rulers (see Figure
1-8). When you select an object, FreeHand highlights areas on the
rulers that correspond to the size and position of the object (I call
this the "shadow selection").

FIGURE 1-7
FreeHand's rulers

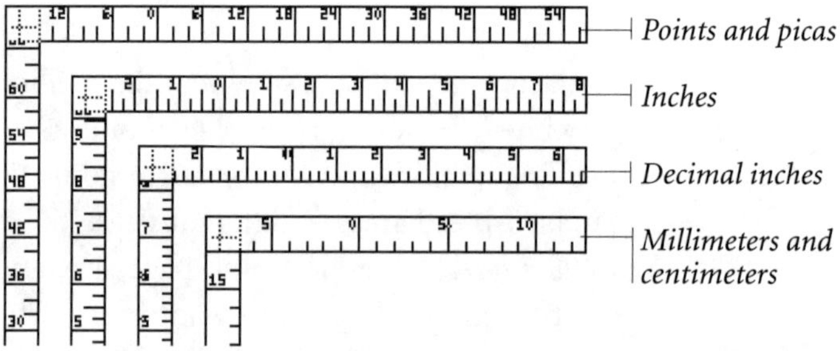

Points and picas

Inches

Decimal inches

Millimeters and
centimeters

FIGURE 1-8
Shadow cursors and
shadow selection

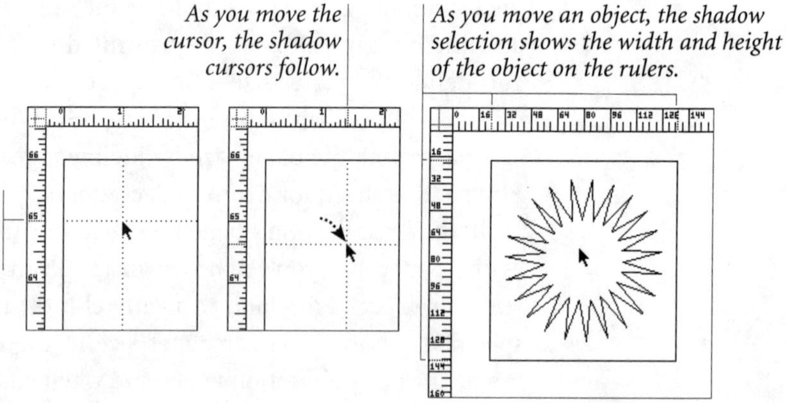

*As you move the
cursor, the shadow
cursors follow.*

*As you move an object, the shadow
selection shows the width and height
of the object on the rulers.*

*Shadow cursors
track your cursor's
position in the rulers.*

Zero Point   The intersection of the zero measurement on both rulers is called
the zero point. In FreeHand, the default location of the zero point
is at the lower-left corner of the current page. To control the location of the zero point, use the zero-point marker (see Figure 1-9),

which you see at the upper-left corner of your screen (when you have the rulers displayed). You can think of it as the point where the two rulers intersect on the page.

To move the zero point, drag the zero-point marker to a new position (see Figure 1-10). As you drag, intersecting dotted lines show you the position of the zero point. When you've moved the zero point to the location you want, stop dragging. The rulers now mark off their increments based on this new zero point.

If you need to reposition only the horizontal or vertical ruler's zero point, drag the zero-point marker along the ruler—the one you want to change—until the zero point is where you want it (see Figure 1-11).

FIGURE 1-9
Zero-point marker

Zero-point marker

FIGURE 1-10
Repositioning
the zero point

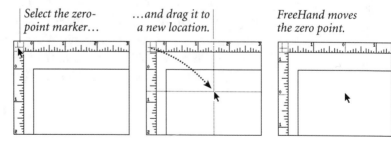

Select the zero-point marker...   ...and drag it to a new location.   FreeHand moves the zero point.

FIGURE 1-11
Repositioning only one
of the zero points

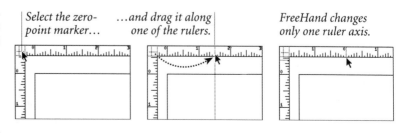

Select the zero-point marker...   ...and drag it along one of the rulers.   FreeHand changes only one ruler axis.

Tip:
Resetting the
Zero Point

To reset the zero point to the lower-left corner of the page, double-click the zero-point marker.

Guides

Guides are nonprinting guidelines you use when you're aligning items on a page. In FreeHand, you'll find two kinds of guides.

◆ Ruler guides are the guides you might remember from earlier versions of FreeHand—or, for that matter, from other programs, such as PageMaker or Quark XPress—they're straight lines that run all of the way across the page. These guides are always either vertical or horizontal (just like the rulers).

◆ Custom guides are paths you've drawn in FreeHand and converted to guides. Custom guides can be any shape, any length, at any angle relative to the page, and can be turned back into paths at any time.

As far as I can tell, there's no limit to the number of guides you can use in a publication.

Adding ruler guides. To add a ruler guide, position the cursor over a ruler and drag the cursor onto the page or pasteboard. As you drag the cursor off the ruler, a line follows the cursor, showing you where your new ruler guide will fall. When you've got the line where you want it, release the mouse button. FreeHand positions a new ruler guide at this location (see Figure 1-12).

Adding custom guides. To add a custom guide, select a path you want to use as a guide and click on the default Guides layer in the

FIGURE 1-12
Positioning
a ruler guide

*Position the
cursor over
a ruler...*

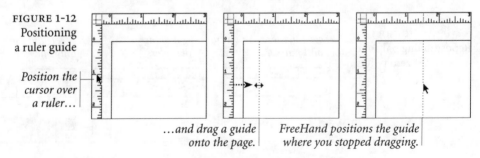

*...and drag a guide
onto the page.*

*FreeHand positions the guide
where you stopped dragging.*

Layers palette (see Figure 1-13). FreeHand converts the selected path into a guide. You'll be able to tell immediately that the path is a guide, because FreeHand changes its color to the Guides color, and because FreeHand removes any formatting that's been applied to the stroke of the path, rendering custom guides as one-pixel wide lines at any screen magnification (don't worry—the path's fill and stroke will reappear when you release the guide).

FIGURE 1-13
Creating a
custom guide

Select the path or paths you want to convert to a guide...

...and click the Guides layer. FreeHand converts the paths to custom guides.

Tip:
When You Want
a Wide Guide

What can you do when you'd like your custom guide to be the same width as the formatted path you've used to create it? Before you convert the path to a guide, select the path and choose "Expand stroke" from the Path Operations submenu of the Arrange menu. FreeHand displays the Expand Stroke dialog box. Enter a value in the Width field that's equal to the stroke weight of the path, and FreeHand creates a composite path that's the width of the formatted path (see Figure 1-14). Once you've done that, you can convert the path to a guide and you'll have the wide guide you were looking for. Though I haven't ever had a need for this, I'm betting some of you will.

Tip:
Custom Guides
and Snap to
Point

When you convert a path into a guide, you lose the ability to snap objects (or other points) to the points in the path using FreeHand's Snap to Point feature (it's on the View menu). If you want to use Snap to Point, consider putting the path on a locked layer rather than turning it into a custom guide (for more on locking layers, see "Locking and Unlocking Layers," later in this chapter).

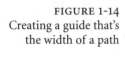

FIGURE 1-14
Creating a guide that's
the width of a path

Select the path you
want to turn into
a guide.

Choose "Expand
Stroke" from the Path
Operations submenu of
the Arrange menu.

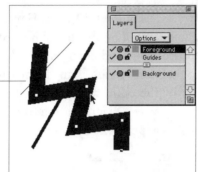

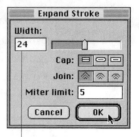

Enter the width of the stroke in
the Expand Stroke dialog box.

FreeHand expands
the path.

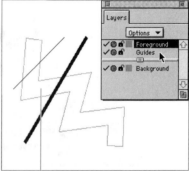

Click the Guides layer.

FreeHand converts the path
to a guide that follows the
outline of the original path.

Adding guides numerically. When you know precisely where you
want a ruler guide to appear, use the Guides dialog box to add the
guide (see Figure 1-15).

1. Choose "Edit Guides" from the View menu. FreeHand
   displays the Guides dialog box.

2. Click the Add button. FreeHand displays the Add Guides
   dialog box.

3. Enter the type of ruler guide you want to add (vertical or
   horizontal), the number of guides you want, and the range
   you want those guides to fill. Use the Count option to enter
   a specific number of guides, or turn on the By Increment
   option to enter the distance you want between guides (in
   this case, the actual number of guides entered depends on
   the values in the First and Last fields—you'll get as many

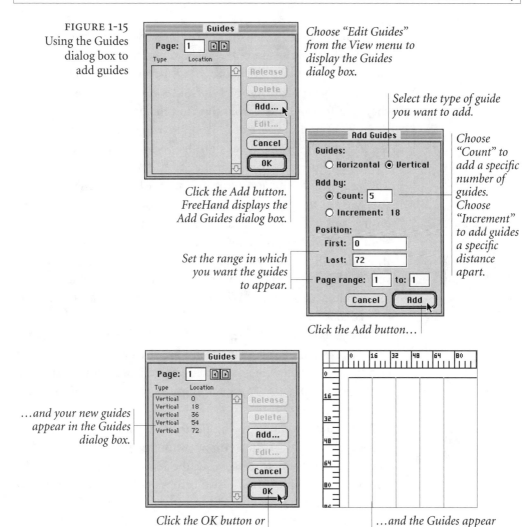

FIGURE 1-15
Using the Guides
dialog box to
add guides

*Choose "Edit Guides"
from the View menu to
display the Guides
dialog box.*

*Select the type of guide
you want to add.*

*Choose
"Count" to
add a specific
number of
guides.
Choose
"Increment"
to add guides
a specific
distance
apart.*

*Click the Add button.
FreeHand displays the
Add Guides dialog box.*

*Set the range in which
you want the guides
to appear.*

Click the Add button…

*…and your new guides
appear in the Guides
dialog box.*

*Click the OK button or
press Return…*

*…and the Guides appear
on your page (or pages).*

guides as will fit in the defined range). These options give
you the ability to create grids of guides. Use the range of
pages you want to apply these guide settings to

4. Press Return to close the Add Guides dialog box. FreeHand
    adds the guides to the list in the Guides dialog box.

5. Press Return (or click the OK button). FreeHand adds the
    guides to your page (or pages, if you specified a range).

Removing Guides. When you want to remove a ruler guide, position the Pointer tool above the ruler guide and drag the ruler guide back onto the ruler (see Figure 1-16). If you can't select the ruler guide, you've probably got Lock Guides turned on. Turn it off by choosing "Lock Guides" from the View menu.

In FreeHand 4, you had to drag the ruler guide all the way off the page to remove it. What did this mean if you couldn't see an edge of the current page? It meant you had to zoom out, then drag the guide off of the page. Or it meant that FreeHand would scroll your view of the page as you dragged a guide. Most FreeHand users didn't want to do either (and I agreed with them), and felt that you shouldn't have to change your view of the page to remove a guide. If, on the other hand, you *liked* the way it worked in FreeHand 4, you can make FreeHand 8 work that way, too—just check Dragging a Guide Scrolls the Window in the General Editing Preferences dialog box, and you can have it your way (you weirdo).

To delete a guide, double-click the guide. FreeHand displays the Edit Guides dialog box, which shows a list of the guides on the current page. The guide you clicked is highlighted in the list. Click the Delete button, and FreeHand removes the guide from the page (see Figure 1-17).

You could, of course, bring up the Edit Guides dialog box by choosing "Edit guides" from the View menu, then locate and select the guide you want to remove in the list of guides. I prefer the double-click technique, because it brings up the Edit Guides dialog box with the guide you clicked selected in the list of guides the dialog box displays. If you don't do this, it's hard to tell which guide is which by looking at the guide positions in the dialog box.

FIGURE 1-16
Removing a
ruler guide

 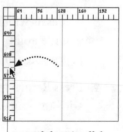 

Position the cursor over a ruler guide… *…and drag it off the page, or onto a ruler.* *FreeHand removes the guide.*

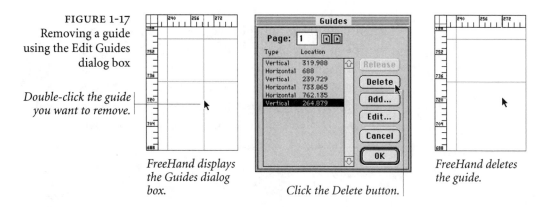

FIGURE 1-17
Removing a guide
using the Edit Guides
dialog box

*Double-click the guide
you want to remove.*

*FreeHand displays
the Guides dialog
box.*

Click the Delete button.

*FreeHand deletes
the guide.*

Removing multiple guides. To remove more than one guide at a time, hold down Command/Control as you select guides from the list of guides displayed in the Edit Guides dialog box, then click the Delete button. Want to get rid of all the guides on the current page? Hold down Shift and drag through the list. Once you've selected all of the guides, click the Delete button.

Converting guides to paths. To convert a guide into a normal path, double-click the guide. FreeHand displays the Edit Guides dialog box and selects the guide you clicked (in the list of guides shown in the dialog box). Click the Release button. FreeHand converts the guide to a path (see Figure 1-18). If you selected a custom guide, any formatting you applied to the path before you turned it into a guide reappears.

FIGURE 1-18
Releasing a
custom guide

*Double-click the guide
you want to release.*

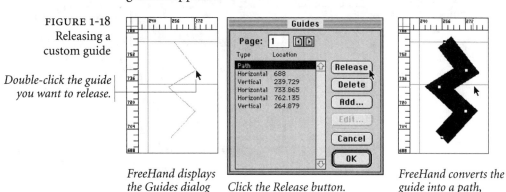

*FreeHand displays
the Guides dialog
box.*

Click the Release button.

*FreeHand converts the
guide into a path,
complete with its
original formatting.*

Tip:
Documenting
Layouts

I often need to document how a particular layout works so that other people can use my design. When I do this, I like to print example pages that show where I placed guides. In the old days, this meant that I had to draw a line wherever a guide appeared. These days I simply convert the guides to paths, then print sample pages for my clients and co-workers to follow (see Figure 1-19).

FIGURE 1-19
Documenting layouts

Business card layout in FreeHand

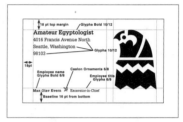

To document the layout, I converted the guides to paths, then added text annotations.

Editing guides. Want to change the location of a guide? Drag the guide to a new position. If you want to move the guide to a specific vertical or horizontal location, double-click the guide and use the Guides dialog box (see Figure 1-20).

1. Double-click the guide you want to change. FreeHand displays the Guides dialog box and selects the guide you double-clicked from the list of guides.

FIGURE 1-20
Editing guide positions

Double-click the guide you want to edit.

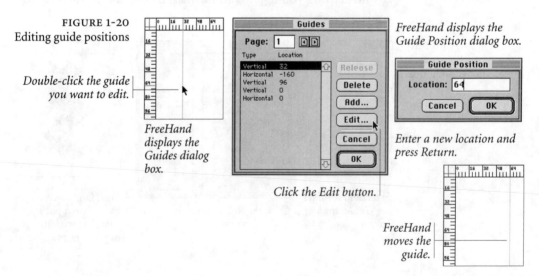

FreeHand displays the Guides dialog box.

Click the Edit button.

FreeHand displays the Guide Position dialog box.

Enter a new location and press Return.

FreeHand moves the guide.

2. Click the Edit button. FreeHand displays the Edit Guide dialog box.

4. Enter the position you want to move the guide to.

5. Press Return to close the Edit Guides dialog box. FreeHand changes the position of the guide in the list of guides in the Guides dialog box.

6. Press Return (or click the OK button). FreeHand moves the guide.

Snap to Guides

Ruler guides are especially useful in conjunction with the Snap to Guides option (toggle this option on and off by pressing Command-;/Ctrl-;). When you've turned on Snap to Guides, objects within the distance you've set (in the Snap Distance field of the Editing Preferences dialog box) automatically snap into alignment with the ruler guide (see Figure 1-21). For more on snapping in general, see "Snap Distance," later in this chapter.

To see how this works, turn on Snap to Guides, draw a box, position a ruler guide, and drag the box toward the guide. When the box gets within the specified distance of the guide, it snaps right to it. You can almost feel the magnetic pull of the guide in the mouse as you move the box closer to the guide. There's nothing

FIGURE 1-21
Snap to Guides

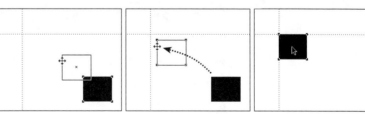

When you're dragging an object with Snap to Guides turned on, nothing happens...

...until you drag the object within a certain distance of a ruler guide. At this point, the guides seem to pull the object toward them...

...until the object snaps to the guide (or guides).

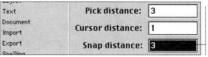

You use the Snap Distance field in the General Editing Preferences dialog box to set the "strength" of the snap.

actually affecting the movement of your mouse, of course, but it's a useful illusion.

FreeHand's Palettes

FreeHand has many different ways of referring to the various floating control panels it displays. Sometimes they're called "panels," sometimes they're called "toolbars," and sometimes they're called "Inspectors." I try to call all of them "palettes," though I refer to each one of them by its given name (i.e., "Fill Inspector"). This lets me differentiate between the Text Inspector and the Text toolbar.

FreeHand's palettes work two ways—they display information on the publication (or about the selected object), and they provide controls for changing the publication and the objects in it. The palettes are an integral part of FreeHand's user interface, and are the key to doing almost everything you can do in FreeHand (see Figure 1-22, on the next page).

- ◆ Toolbox
- ◆ Main toolbar
- ◆ Text toolbar
- ◆ Info toolbar
- ◆ Layers palette
- ◆ Styles palette
- ◆ Halftones palette
- ◆ Colors palette
- ◆ Color Mixer
- ◆ Transform palette
- ◆ Align palette
- ◆ Inspector

In addition, you'll probably see one or more palettes relating to FreeHand Xtras—such as the Xtra Tools palette, Operations palette, URL Editor palette, or the Set Note palette. What and which of these you see depends on the Xtras you've installed.

FIGURE 1-22
FreeHand's palettes

Toolbox

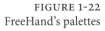

Display different Inspector palettes by clicking these tabs.

Some Inspectors feature multiple panels. When they do, you'll see arrays of buttons like these— click them to display the sub-panels.

Stroke Inspector

Click these buttons to display panels for different color models.

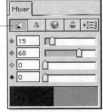

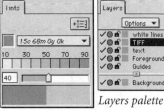

Color mixer   *Colors palette*   *Tints palette*

Layers palette

Click these buttons to display the different panels of the Transform palette.

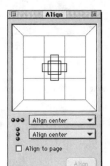

Halftones palette   *Styles palette*

Alignment palette

URL Editor palette   *Operations palette*   *Xtra Tools palette*

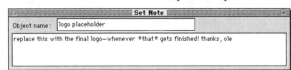

Set Note palette

The toolbars work just like any other palette, except that you can't navigate to the fields in the toolbars using keyboard shortcuts. In general, I work with the Toolbox displayed, and keep the Main and Text toolbars hidden. Why? All of the commands on the Main and Text toolbars are duplicated elsewhere in FreeHand's user interface, and I found that I wasn't using the controls on the toolbars. So I hide them to save precious screen real estate.

Active and Inactive Palettes

When a palette is active, FreeHand tints its title bar (see Figure 1-23). On the Macintosh, this can sometimes be hard to see. For the most part, you don't have to worry about whether a palette is active or not unless you're trying to apply a change you've made in a text field. If the palette has text entry fields, you know that the palette's active when one of its fields is selected.

FIGURE 1-23
Active and
inactive palettes

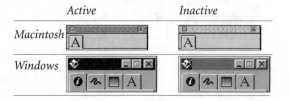

Displaying and Hiding Palettes

You don't have to use the menus to display or hide the palettes—you can use keyboard shortcuts and save yourself lots of mouse movement (see Table 1-2). If a palette's hidden, pressing the keyboard shortcut makes the palette visible; if it's visible, pressing the shortcut hides it.

You can also close palettes using the controls on the palettes themselves. On the Macintosh, click the Close box to close the palette; in Windows, click the Close button.

The Inspector is the palette you'll use most when you work with FreeHand. I refer to each of the subpanels of the Inspector as an Inspector, such as the Paragraph Inspector or the Fill Inspector (see Figure 1-24). This saves me from having to say things like "the Character subpanel of the Text section of the Inspector."

Do you really have to click the different icon buttons in the Inspector to display the different sections of the Inspector? No—you can use keyboard shortcuts for almost all of the Inspectors. Take a look at Table 1-3, on page 27.

TABLE 1-2
Palette keyboard
shortcuts

Palette:	To display or hide the palette, press:
Align palette	Command-Option-A/Ctrl-Alt-A
Colors palette	Command-9/Ctrl-9
Color Mixer	Command-Shift-C/Ctrl-Shift-9
Halftone palette	Command-H/Ctrl-H
Object Inspector*	Command-I/Ctrl-I
Layers palette	Command-6/Ctrl-6
Styles palette	Command-3/Ctrl-3
Toolbox	Command-7/Ctrl-7
Transform palette	Command-M/Ctrl-M
Xtra Tools palette	Command-Shift-K/Ctrl-Alt-X
Operations palette	Command-Shift-I/Ctrl-Alt-O

* Each Inspector has its own keyboard shortcut,
  as shown in Table 1-3, on page 27.

Tip:
Using Standard
Windows
Keyboard
Shortcuts

In the Windows version of FreeHand, you can perform any of the operations controlled by the buttons at the top of a palette using the Control menu attached to the palette—or, more importantly, the keyboard shortcuts shown on that menu. When a palette is active press Alt-spacebar to drop the Control menu, then press the keyboard shortcut for the command you want. To minimize a palette using a keyboard shortcut, for example, you'd press Ctrl-Tab until you select the palette, press Alt-spacebar to display the Control menu, and then press Alt-Z to minimize, or "zip" the palette.

Hiding All Palettes. In FreeHand 4, you couldn't display or hide *all* of the palettes with a single keystroke. In FreeHand 8, press Command-Shift-H/Ctrl-Shift-H ("H" for "hide"), and all of the palettes currently displayed disappear; press it again, and they reappear.

Hiding All Toolbars. To hide or show FreeHand's toolbars (including the Toolbox), press Command-Option-T/Ctrl-Alt-T.

FIGURE 1-24
The many faces
of the Inspector

The Object Inspector displays
different options depending on
the element you've selected.

You use the Fill and Stroke Inspectors
to set the formatting of paths (and
the fill and stroke of text).

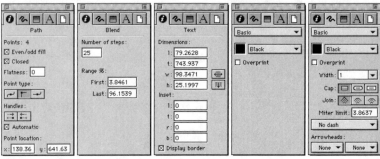

Object Inspector
(point selected)

Object Inspector
(blend selected)

Object Inspector
(text selected)

Fill Inspector
(Basic fill)

Stroke Inspector
(Basic stroke)

You'll find most of FreeHand's type formatting
features in the five panels of the Text Inspector.

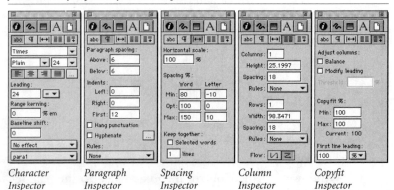

Character
Inspector

Paragraph
Inspector

Spacing
Inspector

Column
Inspector

Copyfit
Inspector

The Document Inspector is where you create,
duplicate, arrange, and delete pages.

Document
Inspector

TABLE 1-3 Inspector keyboard shortcuts	To display the:	Press:
	Document Inspector	Command-Option-D/Ctrl-Alt-D
	Fill Inspector	Command-Option-F/Ctrl-Alt-F
	Object Inspector	Command-Option-I/Ctrl-I
	Stroke Inspector	Command-Option-L/Ctrl-Alt-L
	Character Inspector	Command-T/Ctrl-T
	Paragraph Inspector	Command-Option-P/Ctrl-Alt-P
	Spacing Inspector	Command-Option-K/Ctrl-Alt-K
	Column Inspector	Command-Option-R/Ctrl-Alt-R
	Copyfit Inspector	Command-Option-C/Ctrl-Alt-C

Zipping and Unzipping Palettes. With all these floating palettes, it's easy to run out of room on your screen to see anything but the palettes. While you can use keyboard shortcuts to display or hide all of the palettes, you might like this better: Macintosh users can shrink a palette down to just its title bar by clicking the zoom box at the right end of the title bar; Windows users can click the Mini-mize button to do the same thing. This is called "zipping" a palette (and, at this point, the palette is "zipped"). The title bar stays on the screen (see Figure 1-25). When you want to display the entire palette, click the zoom box again if you're a Macintosh user, or click the Maximize button if you're using Windows. The palette expands to its full size.

FIGURE 1-25
Zipping and
unzipping palettes

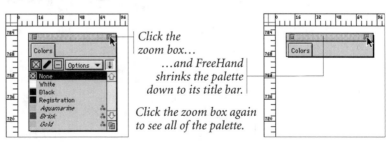

Click the zoom box...
...and FreeHand shrinks the palette down to its title bar.

Click the zoom box again to see all of the palette.

In Windows, click the Minimize button to shrink the palette. To expand the palette, click the Maximize button.

Minimize button | Maximize button

Resizing Palettes. To resize a palette on the Macintosh, drag the Resize box at the palette's lower-right corner. If a palette doesn't have a Resize box, you can't resize it. In Windows, you can drag any side or corner of most of the palettes to resize them (though you can't resize the Color Mixer or any of the Inspectors).

Snapping Palettes into Position. When you drag a palette within 12 pixels of the edge of another palette, FreeHand snaps the edge of the palette you're moving to the nearest edge of the other palette. This also happens when you drag a palette near the edge of the screen, or, in Windows, near the edge of the FreeHand application window. This makes it easy to arrange palettes around the edge of the screen, or to get them ready for docking (see "Docking Palettes," later in this chapter). To turn off this "snap," hold down Shift as you drag a panel.

Combining and Separating Tabbed Palettes. You can rearrange any of the "tabbed" palettes (the Styles palette, Layers palette, Colors palette, Color Mixer, and any of the Inspectors). You can combine many palettes into a single palette, or you can create more palettes than you'll see when you first open FreeHand (this is a mind-boggling concept, I know). Why would you want to do this? You could display the Fill Inspector and the Stroke Inspector at the same time (rather than having them stacked on top of each other, as Free-Hand does by default). Or you could drag the Text Inspector out on its own. It's up to you (see Figure 1-26).

FIGURE 1-26
Working with
tabbed palettes

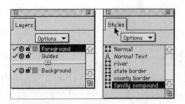 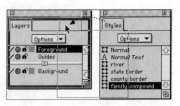

To combine two palettes into one...   *...drag the tab from one palette into the area at the top of the other.*

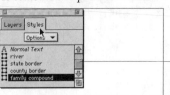

FreeHand combines the two palettes. To see the controls for a palette that's hidden behind another palette, click the appropriate tab.

Docking Palettes. If you want, you can stick two palettes together so that they move, display, hide, or zip and unzip as a single palette. This is called "docking" the palettes. To dock two palettes, hold down Control/Ctrl as you drag one palette close to another. After you stop dragging the palette, Freehand displays a gray bar between the two palettes indicating that they're docked (see Figure 1-27). To separate docked palettes, hold down Control/Ctrl as you drag one of the palettes.

Not all palettes can be docked—on the Macintosh, panels displayed by Xtras can't be docked; in Windows, only tabbed palettes can be docked.

FIGURE 1-27
Docking palettes

*To "dock"
two palettes...*

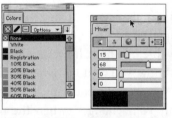

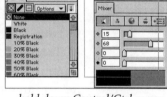

*...hold down Control/Ctrl as you
drag one palette near the other.*

*When palettes are
docked, you'll see a
gray bar joining
them together.*

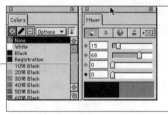

*FreeHand joins the two palettes together.
To "undock" the palettes, hold down
Control/Ctrl and drag one of the palettes.*

**Palette
Navigation**

To move from one field in a palette to the next, press Tab. To move from one field to the previous, press Shift-Tab. Windows users will be able to use these shortcuts to move from one control to another, rather than just moving between fields. This ability does not, unfortunately, extend to pop-up menus (though it will take you to drop-down menus).

To cycle through all of the visible palettes (excluding toolbars), press Command-` (accent grave; it's just below the ~, or tilde, symbol)/Ctrl-Tab. On the Macintosh, each press of this shortcut takes you to the next palette containing a text field; on Windows, pressing this shortcut takes you to the first active control in the palette.

Windows users can also move between controls by pressing the shortcut for the specific control. Like any other Windows program,

Press Alt-L when the Character Inspector is active, and FreeHand selects the contents of the Leading field.

FreeHand shows you the control's shortcut by underlining a letter in the control's name. Hold down Alt and press the shortcut when the dialog box or palette is active, and FreeHand selects the corresponding control. To change the setting for a button or checkbox, press the spacebar. To change the setting for a drop-down menu, press the arrow keys or type the name of the menu choice you want. To change the setting for a slider, press the arrow keys (this doesn't work in the Color Mixer). Strangely enough, the up arrow key *decreases* the value controlled by a slider, and the down arrow key *increases* it (the left and right arrow keys work as you'd expect, respectively decreasing and increasing the value of the slider).

Applying Palette Changes

When you make a change in a palette using a button or a pop-up menu, that change takes effect immediately. When you make a change by entering a value in a field, however, you have to press Return to let FreeHand know you're done entering text. In the Transform palette or the Align palette, you can click the Apply button or press Return to apply your changes (when the palette is active). When you're finished making changes in the Inspector, press Return to apply your changes (there's no Apply button).

Doing Arithmetic in Fields

You can add, subtract, multiply, or divide in any numeric field in any FreeHand palette or dialog box. Want an object to be half its current width? Type "/2" after the value in the W (width) field in the Object Inspector and press Return (see Figure 1-28). Want an object to move two picas to the right? Enter "+2p" (yes, all of the measurement unit overrides shown on page 7 work with these operations) after the value shown in the X field in the Object Inspector. Enter "*" to multiply, or "-" to subtract. You get the idea.

Setting Notes

If you've installed the Set Note Xtra (if you see it on the Xtras submenu of the Windows menu, it's installed), you can add text annotations to elements and/or assign names to objects (see Figure 1-29). To do this, select the object or objects you want to name or annotate, then enter the name and/or annotation in the Set Note palette (if the palette's not visible, choose Set Note from the Xtras submenu of the Windows menu).

FIGURE 1-28
Using fields
to do arithmetic

*Here's a story problem:
You want to shift the
baseline of a drop cap
down three lines. The
paragraph's leading is
14.5 points. What's the
quickest way to get the
baseline shift you need?*

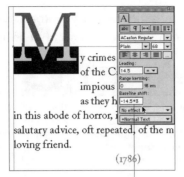

*Enter "-14.5*3" in the
Baseline Shift field…*

…and press Return. Bingo!

Setting notes is a great way to leave messages for yourself or anyone else who might work on the file. I find I often forget what I was doing between FreeHand sessions, and like to leave myself notes just before I go out for more coffee. You can also name objects or classes of objects using the Set Note Xtra. If you do this, you can search for objects of a certain name, which means you can select all of the objects you've named "Delete Before Printing," for example. This also means you can replace the objects you find with some other object (see "Graphic Search and Replace" in Chapter 4, "Transforming").

If you're a PostScript geek (like me), you'll also like the fact that the text you enter as the annotation ends up in the PostScript FreeHand sends to disk when you create an EPS file. But I'm getting way ahead of myself. For more on matters PostScript, and what it has to do with the Set Note Xtra, see Chapter 7, "PostScript."

FIGURE 1-29
Using the
Set Note Xtra

To add a name or note to an object, select the object, then enter the name and/or note in the Set Note palette and press Return.

Use the notes to communicate with your co-workers, or use the object name in conjunction with the FreeHand's Search and Replace feature.

Info Toolbar   FreeHand's Info toolbar displays information about the current state of the cursor or selected object (see Figure 1-30).

FIGURE 1-30
FreeHand's Info Bar

Info Bar showing that you have nothing selected, and that your cursor is off the page. "x" shows the horizontal position of the cursor; "y" shows the vertical position of the cursor.

When you rotate an object, the Info Bar looks like this. "dx" and "dy" show you the point you're rotating around, "x" and "y" show you the cursor's position, and "angle" shows you the angle of rotation.

Finding the Right Mouse Button

Like many other Windows programs, FreeHand displays a menu of options when you click the right mouse button. What, exactly, you see on the menu depends on what's selected in your publication. The right mouse button menu is a great way to do a lot of things—from exporting the selected objects to changing your current view. When your Macintosh-using friends brag about their keyboards having an extra modifier key, show them this menu.

Customizing Toolbars

If you're a fan of toolbars (I'm not, but you might have a larger monitor than I do), you'll be happy to note that FreeHand 8 gives you the ability to modify FreeHand's existing toolbars. This ability comes with a few limitations. You can't create new toolbars of your own—you've got to work with the four FreeHand provides (Text, Main, Info, and Toolbox). In addition, you can't remove some default toolbar features—the fields in the Info toolbar, for example, can't be deleted. Finally, not every command in FreeHand can be put on a toolbar (there's a button for horizontal center alignment, and another for vertical center alignment, but there's no button that simultaneously aligns the horizontal and vertical centers of the objects in a selection).

How do you add a button to a toolbar? Follow these steps (see Figure 1-31).

FIGURE 1-31
Customizing toolbars

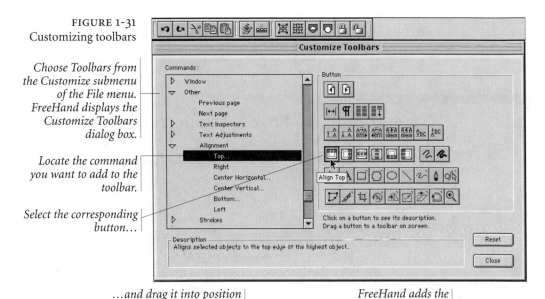

Choose Toolbars from the Customize submenu of the File menu. FreeHand displays the Customize Toolbars dialog box.

Locate the command you want to add to the toolbar.

Select the corresponding button...

...and drag it into position on the toolbar.

FreeHand adds the button to the toolbar.

To remove a button from the toolbar, display the Customize Toolbars dialog box and drag the button off the toolbar. To rearrange buttons on a toolbar, drag them around on the toolbar.

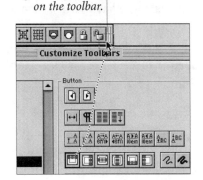

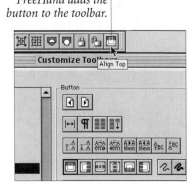

1. Display the toolbar you want to customize, then choose Toolbars from the Customize submenu of the File menu (or choose Customize from the Toolbars submenu of the Window menu). FreeHand displays the Customize Toolbars dialog box.

2. Scroll through the list of commands (at the left side of the dialog box) until you find the button you want to add to the toolbar, then drag the button out of the dialog box and drop it on the toolbar. FreeHand adds the button to the toolbar.

3. Add more buttons, if you want. When you're done adding buttons, close the dialog box.

To remove a button from a toolbar, display the Customize Toolbars dialog box, then drag the button off the toolbar.

Customizing Keyboard Shortcuts

I hate it when software manufacturers change the keyboard shortcuts I know and love. Especially when they change an easy-to-reach, frequently-used shortcut (like Command/Ctrl-W for the "Fit to Page" view) to one that's difficult to use (like Command/Ctrl-0). When FreeHand 7 appeared, I kept closing windows when all I wanted to do was change my view (because "Fit to Page" had changed from Command/Ctrl-W to Command/Ctrl-Shift-W). FreeHand 8 gives me something I think should be in every application—I can make the program's keyboard shortcuts work the way I think they ought to.

For the most part, the keyboard shortcuts you can redefine are those that correspond to menu commands—you can't redefine keyboard shortcuts that modify mouse actions. If you hate having Spacebar be the shortcut to the Grabber Hand tool, you're out of luck—at least this time around.

To define or redefine a keyboard shortcut, follow these steps (see Figure 1-32).

1. Choose Shortcuts from the Customize submenu of the File menu. FreeHand displays the Customize Shortcuts dialog box.

2. Use the list of commands to display the current keyboard shortcut (if any) for a the command you want to change.

3. Highlight the Press New Shortcut Key field (click on the field or press Tab to move the cursor into it), then press the keys you want to use as a shortcut for the selected command. If the shortcut you've entered is the same as an existing shortcut, FreeHand will remove that shortcut (in this case, FreeHand displays the command that will be affected). If you've turned on the Go to Conflict on Assign option, FreeHand will display the command you've just deprived of a keyboard shortcut. This makes it easy to redefine a "chain" of shortcuts.

FIGURE 1-32
Customizing
keyboard shortcuts

*Choose Shortcuts from
the Customize submenu
of the File menu.
FreeHand displays the
Customize Shortcuts
dialog box.*

*Locate the command
you want to add to the
toolbar.*

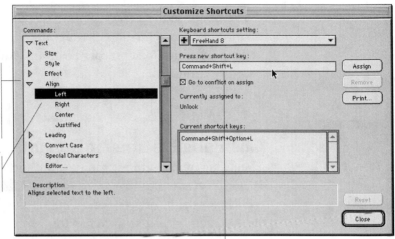

*To make FreeHand's
shortcuts mimic those in
another application,
select the application's
name from the
Keyboard Shortcut
Setting pop-up menu.*

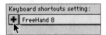

*To save your own set of
keyboard shortcuts, click
the "+" button. Enter a
name for your keyboard
shortcut settings file and
save it.*

*Highlight this field and press
the keyboard shortcut you want
to use for this command.*

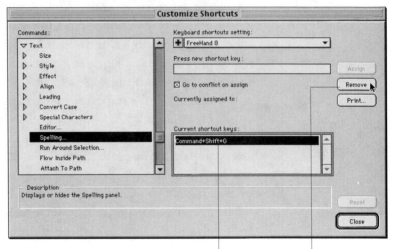

*To remove a keyboard shortcut, select the
shortcut in the Current Shortcuts list...*   *...and click the
Remove button.*

To remove a shortcut, select the command you've assigned the
shortcut to, select the shortcut from the list of shortcuts in the
Current Shortcut Keys field, and then click the Remove button.
FreeHand removes the shortcut.

To save your keyboard shortcut settings, click the "+" button
(to the left of the Keyboard Shortcut Settings pop-up menu). Free-
Hand displays a standard "Save as" dialog box. Enter a name for

the keyboard settings file, then save the file in your keyboard settings folder (~:FreeHand 8:Settings:Keyboard on the Macintosh, ~:\Program Files\Macromedia\FreeHand 8\English\Settings\Keyboard in Windows).

Changing Document Defaults

"Defaults" are the settings you start out with when you start FreeHand. FreeHand has two kinds of defaults—application defaults (which, for the most part, correspond to the settings in the Preferences dialog boxes—see "Preferences," later in this chapter), and document defaults. FreeHand's defaults control page size, fill type and color, available styles, type specifications, and other details.

When you create a new FreeHand document, do you immediately add a set of colors to the Colors palette, change the default line weight, display the rulers, or add styles to the Style palette? If you do, you probably get tired of making those changes over and over again. Wouldn't it be great if you could tell FreeHand to create new documents using those settings?

You can. Open the file named FreeHand Defaults on the Macintosh, or Defaults.ft8 in Windows, that's in the same folder as FreeHand, make the changes you want using FreeHand's dialog boxes and palettes, and save the file (using the same file name) as a FreeHand template. Make sure that the new file replaces the original file, and that you save the file as a template.

The next time you create a new FreeHand document (changing the "FreeHand Defaults" file has no effect on existing documents); it'll appear with the same defaults as you specified in the defaults file (for more on working with defaults files—even working with multiple defaults files, see "Preferences," later in this chapter).

This technique works for objects, as well. If you find you're always copying a corporate logo into your publications, add it to your FreeHand Defaults template, and it'll appear in every new document you create.

To use a different template file, change the file name in the New Document Template field in the Document Preferences dialog box (see "Document Preferences," later in this chapter.)

In FreeHand 5.5, you could use the FreeHand defaults file to set defaults for fills and strokes, but changes you made to any settings for text or type were ignored. It often *looked* like you were changing the default type specifications, but text in your new documents would always default to 24-point Times. In FreeHand 8, almost every specification you set for text and type in the FreeHand defaults file "sticks" and becomes the new default. Which means I can set my default text to 11-point Minion on 14-point leading (using the Fixed leading method). This saves me lots of trips to the Character Inspector.

To set the default for anything you see in the Character, Paragraph, or Spacing Inspectors, all you need to do is change the setting and save the defaults file. To set defaults for tabs, create a text block and set up the tabs the way you want them, then delete the text block and save the defaults file.

Which settings don't become new defaults? The controls found in the Copyfit Inspector (including, unfortunately, the First Line Leading field) and the Column Inspector are ignored. For more on what all of these settings mean, see Chapter 3, "Text and Type."

If you've gotten hopelessly away from FreeHand's original defaults and want to go back to them, move the FreeHand Defaults file out of the folder containing your FreeHand application and put it somewhere else. Or rename the file. When FreeHand can't find the defaults file, it creates a new one using the original default settings (which are stored inside FreeHand).

Setting Up Pages

The first thing you do when creating a publication is to set up your publication's pages using the Document Inspector. You can always make changes in these palettes, if you need to; changing the values here only changes the underlying pages and their associated settings, and won't change anything you've drawn or imported (objects may end up sitting on the pasteboard, but they won't disappear or change shape).

**Working
with Wizards
(Windows only)**

FreeHand's Wizards, like those found in many other Windows applications, guide you through the process of setting up a publication, asking you questions and modifying the publication based on your responses. If you're not a fan of Wizards, you can turn them off by unchecking the Show this Screen When Starting FreeHand option (it's in the Welcome to FreeHand dialog box). You can use FreeHand's Wizards at any time by choosing Wizards from the Help menu. FreeHand displays the Choose a Wizard dialog box (see Figure 1-33).

FIGURE 1-33
FreeHand's Wizards

*You'll see this dialog
box when you first
start FreeHand.*

*Choose Wizards from
the Help menu, and
FreeHand displays this
dialog box.*

*Click this button to
display the Welcome to
FreeHand dialog box.*

*To keep this dialog box from
appearing when you start
FreeHand, turn this option off.*

*The other buttons start Wizards
that guide you through various
page setup tasks.*

*Click the Business
Stationery button, for
example, and FreeHand
leads you through the
process of setting up a
publication file. Note
that this publication
contains pages of
differing sizes and
orientations.*

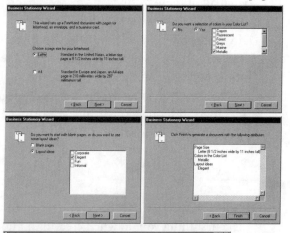

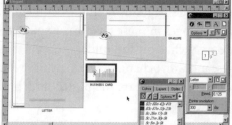

*When you click the Finish
button, FreeHand creates a
new publication based on
the settings you've entered
using the Wizard. In this
example, FreeHand has
added document pages.*

Using the Document Inspector   To display the Document Inspector, click the Document button in the Inspector palette, then click the Pages button (or, better, press Command-Option-D/Ctrl-Alt-D). The Document Inspector displays a window in the middle of the Inspector, showing you a miniaturized view of FreeHand's pasteboard (see Figure 1-34).

FIGURE 1-34
Document Inspector

The Document Inspector displays a thumbnail view of the pasteboard.

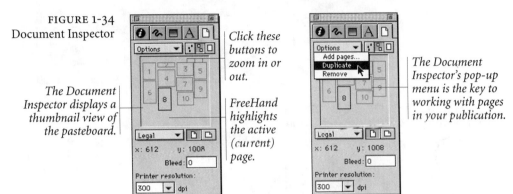

Click these buttons to zoom in or out.

FreeHand highlights the active (current) page.

The Document Inspector's pop-up menu is the key to working with pages in your publication.

Zooming in the Document Inspector. In FreeHand 4, small document pages (say, for example, business cards) could end up being *very* small in the Document Inspector's thumbnail view of the pasteboard. These tiny pages (some not more than one pixel on a side) were very hard to arrange on the pasteboard—there were, after all, only so many pixels to work with in the Inspector's view of the world. Worse yet, in FreeHand 4 you couldn't zoom in to get a better grip on your pages using the Document Inspector.

These days, you can change the view that the Document Inspector uses to display your publication's pages. The buttons above the Inspector's thumbnail view of the pasteboard control the view of the Pasteboard (see Figure 1-35).

Scrolling in the Document Inspector. To change your view of the Pasteboard, position the cursor inside the thumbnail view in the Document Inspector, hold down spacebar, and drag. The cursor turns into the grabber hand, and FreeHand scrolls your view of the pasteboard as you drag (see Figure 1-36).

Adding pages. To add a new page, choose Add Pages from the pop-up menu at the top of the Inspector (see Figure 1-37). FreeHand

FIGURE 1-35
Zooming in the
Document Inspector

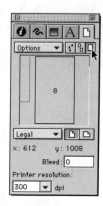

FIGURE 1-36
Scrolling your view
of the Pasteboard

*Position the
cursor inside the
Document Inspector.*

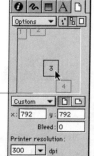

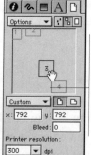

*Hold
down
Spacebar.
The cursor
turns into
the
Grabber
Hand.*

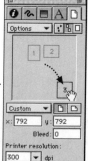

*Drag the
Grabber
Hand. As
you drag,
FreeHand
scrolls the
thumbnail
view of the
pasteboard.*

FIGURE 1-37
Adding pages

*Choose "Add pages"
from the pop-up menu.*

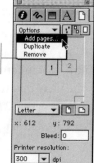

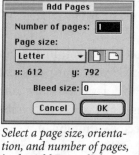

*Select a page size, orienta-
tion, and number of pages,
in the Add Pages dialog
box, then press Return.*

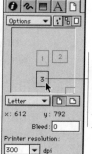

*A new page
(or pages)
appears
in the
Document
Inspector.*

displays the Add Pages dialog box. Choose a page size (the current
page size is the default) and press Return. FreeHand adds a new
page (or pages) to your file, and positions them on the pasteboard.

You can change your page setup at any time by clicking the
page in the Document Inspector—its outline changes to black when
it's the current selection—and choosing a new page size from the
pop-up menu below the window.

Rearranging pages. To rearrange your pages on the pasteboard, drag the page icons around in the Document Inspector. FreeHand won't let you position one page on top of another, so it's easy to get pages to abut perfectly. Bleed areas, on the other hand, do overlap other pages, as they should (see Figure 1-38).

As you move the pages around in the Document Inspector, their page numbers change. FreeHand numbers pages according to their position on the pasteboard—the page closest to the upper-left corner of the pasteboard is always the first page, the next closest is the second page, and so on.

FIGURE 1-38
Rearranging pages

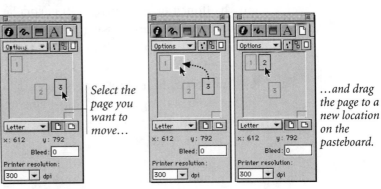

Select the page you want to move...

...and drag the page to a new location on the pasteboard.

Duplicating pages. To duplicate a page, click the page in the Document Inspector and choose Duplicate from the Inspector's pop-up menu. FreeHand adds the duplicated page to your pasteboard, if there's room to add it.

Removing pages. To remove a page, click the page in the Document Inspector and choose Remove from the pop-up menu.

Page size. Generally, you'll want to enter the page size you want for your printed publication. I see far too many people (especially those who should know better) laying out single business cards in the middle of a 51-by-66-pica (that's 8.5-by-11-inch) page. Try not to do this; it wastes film and time when you go to your imagesetting service bureau (if you operate the imagesetter yourself, it's even more important). If your design features elements that extend beyond the edge of the page, use the Bleed option, described later in this section.

You can specify any page size from nine by nine points up to 1,332 by 1,332 picas (222 inches square) As you set up the page size, keep in mind the paper sizes available for the printer you'll be using for your final printing. Linotronic L330s, for example, print on a roll of film that, while very long, is just 11.7 inches (70 picas) wide. When you need the larger page sizes, you can always look for an imagesetter that uses wider film, or you can print tiles (selected parts) of your publication and paste them together (see Chapter 7, "Printing," for more on tiling).

I try to avoid tiling, because it's almost impossible to avoid having halftoned objects (images in particular, or just about any object that's not colored using 100% black) cross tiles. When this happens, it's very difficult to match up the halftone dots perfectly between tiles.

You can print multiple pages on a single sheet of paper or film using manual tiling to print "reader spreads" or "page spreads." For more on printing reader spreads and page spreads (imposition), see Chapter 7, "Printing."

Tip:
Getting That
Big Page to Fit

FreeHand sometimes refuses to create a page or change a page size. When you enter a page size, FreeHand displays the message "Could not complete the 'Set page info' command because an object would be placed off the pasteboard," or "Could not complete the 'Set page info' command because the page would overlap another page." You get these messages even when you know that there's plenty of room on the pasteboard (or between pages) to add the new page or change the page size. What gives?

Here's the deal: FreeHand calculates the space available for the new (or changed) page from that page's lower-left corner. If the page would extend within six picas (one inch) of the edge of the pasteboard, or over another page, in either dimension, measured from the current location of the lower-left corner of the page, FreeHand refuses to create (or change) your page.

The solution? Move the page farther left and/or down on the pasteboard, or move other pages to make room.

Page orientation. If you're using one of the preset page sizes, you can choose a Tall or Wide orientation. If you're creating a custom page size, the measurements you enter in the X and Y fields determine the page's height and width, respectively. If you want a Wide orientation page, enter a larger value in the X field than you've entered in the Y field. It's that simple.

Once again, try to keep in mind the printer you'll be using for your final printing. In some cases, you might find yourself laying things out sideways to get them onto a film roll's limited width (though you can flip the printing orientation of your publication by rewriting the PPD you're using—see "Rewriting PPDs" in Chapter 7, "Printing").

Bleed. Enter the amount of space you want to print that extends beyond the edge of the page. The value you enter here is added to all four sides of the page. Again, keep the page sizes of your final output device in mind as you enter the bleed area. If your publication's page size is 10 by 12 picas and your imagesetter's page size is 11 by 13 picas, the largest bleed area you'd be able to use is 6 points (though you could always rewrite the PPD file you're using to accommodate a larger bleed, provided the imagesetter you're printing to can handle it).

Grid Size   To specify a size for FreeHand's page grid, choose Edit from the Grid submenu of the View menu. FreeHand displays the Edit Grid dialog box. The value you enter in the Grid Size field controls the distance between intersections of a nonprinting grid on each page in your publication (see Figure 1-39). The grid starts at the zero point on the rulers and moves when you move the zero point.

When you choose Show from the Grid submenu of the View menu, FreeHand displays the grid on your screen. The appearance of the grid varies—depending on the size of the grid, the current units of measurement, and the current magnification. At higher magnifications, you'll see a point at each grid intersection. The grid is the same for every page in a publication—you can't use different grids on different pages. When you choose Snap to Grid, objects you're creating, moving, or resizing snap to the grid. Snap to Grid works whether the grid's visible or not.

You can't enter a value smaller than one point or larger than 720 points in the Grid Size field.

FIGURE 1-39
The grid

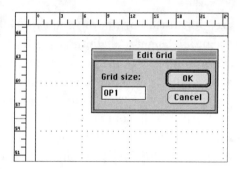

Tip:
Avoiding
Accuracy

Most of the time, I don't want or need to know the location of an object with anything like the kind of accuracy that FreeHand uses, by default, to display information in the Info palette. In fact, the extra decimal places can become downright distracting. Here's an example: you want to position a rule 16 points from the left edge of the page, and no matter how hard you try to match the tick mark on the ruler, the info palette displays the rule's position as 16.0115. Why can't you get the object into the right position?

There are only so many pixels on your screen. At certain views, it might not be possible to "hit" specific coordinates, because that location is "between" two rows of pixels. Zooming in helps, but the best thing to do is to set Grid to a small value, such as one point, and turn on Snap to Grid. Now, when you drag the rule, it snaps to each point location, and the Info toolbar displays coordinates in whole points (see Figure 1-40). Note that the rule still appears at the same screen location, in screen pixel terms, as it was before you turned on Snap to Grid—but it's *really* at the grid location FreeHand snapped it to (which you'll see if you zoom in far enough).

FIGURE 1-40
As accurate as
you want to be

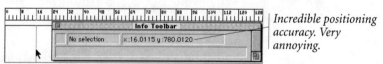

Incredible positioning accuracy. Very annoying.

Dragging a guide with Snap to Grid turned off.

⊢ *Nice round numbers.*

*Dragging a guide, Snap to Grid turned on,
Grid Size set to one point.*

Constraint   When you hold down Shift as you drag a tool or an object across a page, FreeHand limits your movement—this limiting action is called "constraint." You can set the angle used as the basis for this feature by choosing Constrain from the Modify menu. FreeHand displays the Constrain dialog box. The value you enter in the Constrain field controls the angle FreeHand uses when you constrain tools (see "Constraining Tools," later in this chapter).

The angle you enter here also affects how FreeHand draws rectangles and ellipses (see Figure 1-41). If you've entered "30" in the Constrain field, rectangles and ellipses you create are constrained to 30 and 120 degrees (rather than the default 90 and 180 degrees).

FIGURE 1-41
Setting a
constraint angle

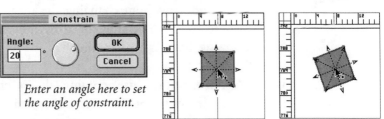

Enter an angle here to set
the angle of constraint.

When the constraint angle is "0" (the default), holding down Shift as you drag an object constrains its movement to 45-degree angles.

If you change the angle, the constraint axes are based on the angle you entered.

The Angle field also affects the way FreeHand draws basic shapes.

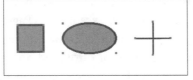

Constraint angle: 0   Constraint angle: 20

Printer Resolution   Enter a value in the Printer Resolution field (at the bottom of the Document Inspector) that corresponds to the resolution of the printer you intend to use for final output of your publication, or choose a value from the defaults listed in the pop-up menu. FreeHand uses this value to calculate the optimum number of steps to use in a graduated fill, a radial fill, or a blend (see Chapter 2, "Drawing"). FreeHand also uses this value for sizing bi-level bitmaps to the resolution of the output device ("magic stretching," to you PageMaker fans out there). For more on stretching bi-level bitmaps to match your printer's resolution, see "Resizing Images to Your Printer's Resolution" in Chapter 4, "Importing and Exporting."

Moving Around in Your Publication

FreeHand offers three ways to change your view of the publication: zooming, scrolling, and moving from page to page. Zooming changes the magnification of the area inside the publication window. Scrolling changes the view of the publication in the publication window without changing the magnification. Moving from page to page can be thought of as either automated scrolling or zooming, but I'm not sure which.

Zooming   Most of the time, I use zooming (that is, changing magnifications of the view of the publication) rather than scrolling (that is, changing the view of the publication without changing magnification) to move from one area of the page or pasteboard to another.

Zooming with the View menu. The View menu offers FreeHand's "standard" magnifications, or views, and provides keyboard shortcuts for most of them (see Table 1-4, on the next page).

All of these commands except Fit to Page center the object you've selected in the publication window. If there's no object selected, these shortcuts zoom in or out based on the center of the current view. Fit to Page centers the publication in the publication window. This makes Fit to Page the perfect "zoom-out" shortcut.

Fit Selection. Another view command I use all of the time is Fit Selection. It does just what it says—zooms (in or out) on the current selection and makes it fill the publication window (see Figure 1-42). Press Command-0/Ctrl-0 to zoom to Fit Selection.

Zooming with the Magnifying Glass. Another zooming method: choose the Magnifying Glass, point at an area in your publication, and click. FreeHand zooms to the next larger view size (based on

TABLE 1-4	To reach this magnification:	Press:
	Fit to Page	Command-Shift-W/Ctrl-Shift-W
	Fit All	Command-Option-0/Ctrl-Alt-0
	Fit Selection	Command-0/Ctrl-0
	6%	None/Alt-V,M,6
	12%	None/Alt-V,M,%
	25%	None/Alt-V,M,5
	50%	Command-5/Ctrl-5
	75%	Command-7/Ctrl-7
	100%	Command-1/Ctrl-1
	200%	Command-2/Ctrl-2
	400%	Command-4/Ctrl-4
	800%	Command-8/Ctrl-8

TABLE 1-4
Magnification
keyboard shortcuts

FIGURE 1-42
Fit Selection

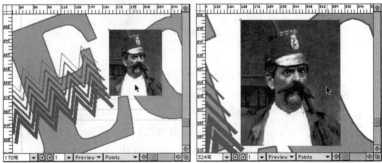

*Select an object and press
Command-0/Ctrl-0...*

*...and FreeHand zooms in (or out),
centering the object in the window.*

your current view—from 100% to 200%, for example), centering the area you clicked on in the publication window. Hold down Option/Alt and the Magnifying Glass tool changes to the Reducing Glass tool. Click the Reducing Glass tool and you'll zoom out.

Tip:
Switching to the
Magnifying Glass

Press Command-spacebar/Ctrl-spacebar to temporarily change any tool into the Magnifying Glass to zoom in; or hold down Command-Option-spacebar/Ctrl-Alt-spacebar to change any tool into the Reducing Glass to zoom out (see Figure 1-43).

FIGURE 1-43
Magnifying Glass

*Press Command-spacebar/
Ctrl-spacebar, and the cursor
turns into the Magnifying
Glass tool.*

*As you zoom,
FreeHand displays
the magnification
percentage.*

*Click the Magnifying Glass,
and FreeHand zooms in to the
next "standard" magnification
level (that is, those seen on the
Magnification submenu of the
View menu).*

*To zoom out, hold down
Command-Option-spacebar/
Ctrl-Alt-spacebar to turn any
tool into the Reducing Glass,
and click again.*

Tip:
The Best Way
to Zoom

To zoom in, press Command/Ctrl and hold down the spacebar to
turn the current tool (whatever it is) into the Magnifying Glass
tool, then drag the Magnifying Glass in the publication window.
As you drag, a rectangle (like a selection rectangle) appears. Drag
the rectangle around the area you want to zoom in on, and release
the mouse button. FreeHand zooms in on the area, magnifying the
area to the largest size that fits in the publication window (see
Figure 1-44).

To zoom out, use one of the keyboard shortcuts—Command-
Shift-W/Ctrl-Shift-W, for Fit Page, is especially handy.

Tip:
Maximum Zoom

Want to zoom in as far as you can go? Hold down Command-
Control-spacebar/Ctrl-Shift-spacebar. The cursor turns into the Magnifying Glass. Click the Magnifying Glass, and you'll zoom in to
256x%—that's 25,600%. If this isn't close enough for you, or if it's
too close, you can increase or decrease the maximum zoom percentage—see "Secret Preferences," later in this chapter.

FIGURE 1-44
Drag magnification

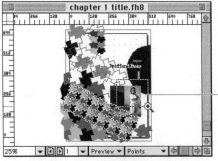

Drag the Magnifying Glass
around the area you want to
zoom in on and release the
mouse button.

FreeHand zooms in on the area
you selected.

You can hold down Option as
you drag the Reducing Glass to
zoom out. I've never found a use
for this technique, myself.

When you use drag
magnification, you can
use percentages other
than those seen on the
Magnification sub-
menu.

Tip:
Minimum Zoom

To zoom out to FreeHand's minimum zoom percentage (6%) hold
down Command-Control-Option-spacebar/Ctrl-Alt-Shift-spacebar
and click. FreeHand zooms out to the 6% view.

Tip:
What's the Most
Accurate View in
FreeHand?

Lots of FreeHand users have noticed that elements seem to shift
slightly as they zoom in and out, and have wondered which magnification is most accurate. It's simple: it's the 256x% view. Inter-
estingly, the Fit to Page view is pretty good, too.

If something's a point off in the 256x% view, it sometimes looks
like it's about a mile away in the Fit to Page view. Which is good.
You want to know when lines aren't where you want them, so a
little exaggeration is a good thing.

The final arbiters of accuracy are the numbers in the Object
Inspector. If points don't seem to line up, select them by turn and
look at their coordinates in the Object Inspector. By comparing
their numeric positions, you'll know exactly where they are, and
whether they're where you want them.

Entering a magnification percentage. To zoom to a specific magnification percentage, enter the percentage in the Magnification field

and press Return/Enter. FreeHand zooms to the percentage you specified.

Scrolling   As I said earlier in this chapter, I rarely use the scroll bars to scroll. So how do I change my view of my publication? I use the Grabber Hand, or I let FreeHand do the scrolling for me as I move objects.

Scrolling with the Grabber Hand. You can also change your view of the publication using the Grabber Hand (see Figure 1-45). Provided you're not editing text, holding down the spacebar turns the cursor into the Grabber Hand (if you *are* editing text, you'll enter spaces, which probably isn't what you want to do). Drag the Grabber Hand, and FreeHand scrolls in the direction you're dragging.

FIGURE 1-45
Grabber Hand

Hold down the spacebar to turn the cursor into the Grabber Hand (it doesn't matter what tool you have selected when you press the spacebar).

Use the Grabber Hand to drag your publication around in the window.

Scrolling as you drag objects. Don't forget that you can change your view by dragging objects off the screen (see Figure 1-46). If you know an object should be moved to some point below your current view, select the object and drag the cursor off the bottom of the publication window. The window scrolls as long as the cursor is off the bottom of the screen and the mouse button is down. Sometimes it's the best way to get something into position.

FIGURE 1-46
Scrolling by dragging

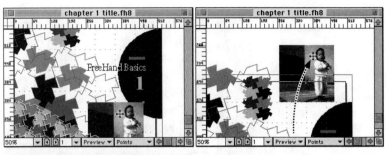

As you drag an object...

... FreeHand scrolls the current window to keep up with your dragging.

Using FreeHand's Toolbox

If FreeHand is your workshop, and the menus and palettes are where you collect the wood, nails, and paint you use, the toolbox is where you keep your saws, hammers, and brushes.

Some of the following descriptions of the tool functions aren't going to make any sense unless you understand how FreeHand's points and paths work, and that discussion falls in "Points and Paths," later in this chapter. You can flip ahead and read that section, or you can plow through this section, get momentarily confused (remember that confusion is a great state for learning), and then become enlightened when you reach the descriptions of points and paths.

Or, you can flip ahead to Chapter 2, "Drawing" for even more on points and paths. It's your choice, and either method works. This is precisely the sort of nonlinear information gathering that hypertext gurus say can't be done in books.

You can break FreeHand's toolbox into four main conceptual sections (as shown in Figure 1-47).

◆ Tools for drawing basic shapes (the Rectangle, Polygon, Ellipse, and Line tools)

FIGURE 1-47
Tools in the toolbox

Toolbox

When you see this symbol on a tool, it means that you can view and set options for the tool by double-clicking on the tool in the Toolbox.

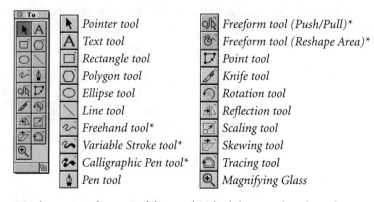

Pointer tool	Freeform tool (Push/Pull)*
Text tool	Freeform tool (Reshape Area)*
Rectangle tool	Point tool
Polygon tool	Knife tool
Ellipse tool	Rotation tool
Line tool	Reflection tool
Freehand tool*	Scaling tool
Variable Stroke tool*	Skewing tool
Calligraphic Pen tool*	Tracing tool
Pen tool	Magnifying Glass

Can't see more than one of these tools? That's because they share the same slot in the Toolbox. Only one of them can be visible at a time—double-click the tool in the Toolbox to display a dialog box, where you can set the options for the tool.

◆ Path-drawing tools (the Point, Freehand, Pen, and Freeform tools, also known as the freeform drawing tools)

◆ Transformation tools (the Rotation, Reflection, Skewing, and Scaling tools)

◆ The Text tool

The basic shape tools draw complete paths containing specific numbers of points in specific positions on the path, while the path-drawing tools draw paths point by point (or, in the case of the Knife tool, delete points or split paths). The transformation tools act on objects you've drawn, typed, or imported, and the Text tool is for entering text.

The two remaining tools don't really fit into a single category—the Pointer tool is for selecting objects, and the Magnifying Glass tool is for changing your view of your publication.

The tool descriptions in the following section are brief and are only intended to give you a feeling for what the different tools are and what they do. For more on drawing objects with the drawing tools, see Chapter 2, "Drawing." To learn more about entering text with the Text tool, see Chapter 3, "Text and Type." For more on working with the Transformation tools, see Chapter 5, "Importing and Exporting."

Talking about FreeHand's tools and their use can get a little confusing. When you select a tool in the toolbox (or press the keyboard shortcut to select a tool), what does the cursor become? In a previous edition of this book, I used the same wording as in FreeHand's documentation: "When you select a tool, the cursor turns into a crosshair." I didn't like that, because I think the cursor remains the cursor (and because we couldn't decide between "cross hair" or "crosshair"—either one sounds uncomfortable). Therefore, in this book, I'll use phrases like "select a tool and drag" or "select a tool and drag the tool."

Toolbox Keyboard Shortcuts. You can choose most of the tools in FreeHand's toolbox through keyboard shortcuts. This is usually faster than going back across the screen to the toolbox (see Table 1-5).

Pointer Tool

You use the Pointer tool to select and transform objects. You can press 0 (zero) to select the Pointer tool. You can temporarily switch to the Pointer tool by holding down Command/Ctrl when any other tool is selected.

Text Tool

You enter and edit text using the Text tool. To create a text block, select the Text tool and click or drag the tool in the publication window; a text block appears with a flashing text-insertion point (or cursor) in its first line. To edit text, select the Text tool and click in a text block. If you want to edit text using the Text Editor, select the text block (using either the text tool or the Pointer tool) and press Command-Option-E/Ctrl-Alt-E. FreeHand opens the story you selected, in the Text Editor. For more on entering, editing, and formatting text, see Chapter 3, "Text and Type." To select the Text tool, press A.

Rectangle Tool

Use the Rectangle tool to draw rectangles. If you hold down Shift as you draw a rectangle, you draw squares.

Note that you can always draw rectangles and squares using the other drawing tools, but that the rectangles drawn using the Rectangle tool have some special capabilities (see Table 1-6, later in this chapter). Press 1 (on either the keyboard or on the numeric keypad) to select the Rectangle tool.

TABLE 1-5
Toolbox keyboard
shortcuts

Tool:	Key:
Pointer tool	0*
Pointer tool (temporary)	Hold down Command and the current tool turns into the Pointer tool. Release Command and the cursor changes back into the selected tool.
Text tool	A
Rectangle tool	1*
Polygon tool	2*
Ellipse tool	3*
Line tool	4*
Freehand tool	5*
Pen tool	6*
Reshape tool	9*
Point tool	8*
Knife tool	7*
Magnifying Glass	Hold down Command-spacebar/Ctrl-spacebar and the current tool turns into the Magnifying Glass. Release Command-spacebar and the Magnifying Glass turns back into the selected tool. If your cursor is inside a text block, make sure you press Command/Ctrl slightly before you press spacebar, or you'll get a bunch of spaces in the text block.
Reducing Glass	Hold down Command-Option-spacebar/Ctrl-Alt-spacebar and the current tool turns into the Reducing Glass. Release the keys and the Reducing Glass turns back into the selected tool.

* The number keys on the numeric keypad work, too.

If you want to draw rectangles with rounded corners, double-click the Rectangle tool. FreeHand displays the Rectangle Tool dialog box. Drag the slider or enter a number to set the corner radius you want to use for your rounded corners (see Figure 1-48).

If you draw a rectangle with square corners and then decide that you'd rather its corners were rounded, you can always change them using the Corner Radius field in the Object Inspector. Until, that is, you ungroup the rectangle—once you do that, the rectangle becomes a normal path (and you'll have to make the corners rounded using path-drawing techniques).

FIGURE 1-48
Specifying rounded corners

Double-click the Rectangle tool to display the Rectangle Tool dialog box. Enter a corner radius and press Return.

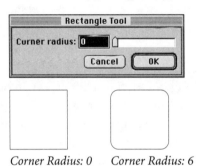

Corner Radius: 0   Corner Radius: 6

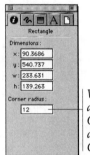

When you select a rectangle, the Object Inspector displays the Corner Radius.

Polygon Tool

The Polygon tool makes it easy to draw equilateral polygons, such as pentagons, hexagons, and dodecagons. (Polygons are closed geometric objects that have at least three sides; they're equilateral if all sides are the same length.) You can also use the Polygon tool to draw stars.

To change which polygon the Polygon tool draws, double-click the tool in the toolbox. FreeHand displays the Polygon Tool dialog box (see Figure 1-49), where you can specify the number of sides you want your star or polygon to have, and how acute (or obtuse) you want the star's interior angles to be. You can drag a slider for polygons or stars from three to 20 sides or points, or enter a larger number.

The preview is dynamically updated as you drag the slider or enter a number. For stars, there's another slider for changing the interior angles of the star from acute to obtuse.

Press 2 (on either the keyboard or on the numeric keypad) to select the Polygon tool.

FIGURE 1-49
Polygon tool controls

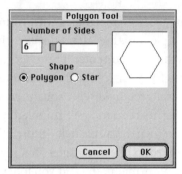 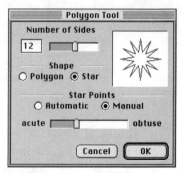

*Double-click the
Polygon tool to define
what kind of polygons
the Polygon tool draws.*

*Drag the slider to set the number of
sides in the polygon, or enter a
number.*

*Click Star, and options appear for
drawing star-shaped polygons.
Enter a number to specify the
number of points you want for the
star, then drag the Star Points
slider to set the sharpness of the
star's points.*

Ellipse Tool

Use the Ellipse tool to draw ellipses. If you hold down Shift as you
draw an ellipse, you draw circles. Note that you can always draw
ellipses and circles using other drawing tools, but that the ellipses
drawn using the Ellipse tool offer some special capabilities (see
Table 1-6, later in this chapter). If you ungroup these ellipses, you
lose those capabilities.

Press 3 (on either the keyboard or on the numeric keypad) to
select the Ellipse tool.

Line Tool

Use the Line tool to draw straight lines. If you hold down Shift as
you drag the Line tool, the lines you draw will be constrained to 0-,
90-, and 45-degree angles (relative to the current default axis—see
"Constrain," earlier in this chapter).

Press 4 (on either the keyboard or the numeric keypad) to select the Line tool.

Freehand Tool

Select the Freehand tool (it's not the "FreeHand" tool), hold down
the mouse button, and scribble. The Freehand tool creates a path
that follows your mouse movements, adding points according to
its settings.

If you double-click the Freehand tool, the Freehand Tool dialog
box appears. This dialog box lets you customize the way the Freehand tool works. The Freehand tool is really three tools—the Freehand, Variable Stroke, and Calligraphic Pen tools. To change from

one tool to another, choose the appropriate option at the top of the Freehand Tool dialog box. The options you see in the dialog box depend on which tool you've selected. Note that the paths you draw using the Freehand tool are open paths (unless you intentionally close them), while the paths drawn using the variable stroke and calligraphic pen tools are closed paths.

Press 5 (on either the keyboard or on the numeric keypad) to select the Freehand tool.

Freehand tool. The Tight fit option draws more points along the path as you draw, and the Draw Dotted Line option controls the way your path appears as you draw it. With Draw Dotted Line on, the Freehand tool simply places a series of dots as you draw and waits until you stop drawing to connect the dots and display the path you've drawn (see Figure 1-50).

FIGURE 1-50
Freehand tool options

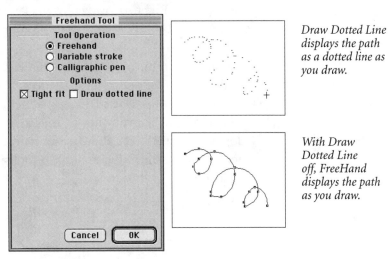

Draw Dotted Line displays the path as a dotted line as you draw.

With Draw Dotted Line off, FreeHand displays the path as you draw.

Variable Stroke tool. The Variable Stroke tool (also known as the "variable blob tool") is good for creating paths that look like brush strokes (see Figure 1-51). Tight fit and Draw Dotted Line are the same as those for the Freehand tool. In the Minimum and Maximum fields, enter the minimum and maximum widths you want for paths you create using the Variable Stroke tool.

If you have a pressure-sensitive drawing tablet (such as those made by Wacom, Calcomp, or others), you can use pressure to control the width of paths you draw using the Variable Stroke tool.

FIGURE 1-51
Variable Stroke
tool options

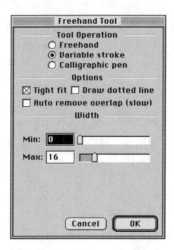

Use the Variable Stroke tool to create paths that look like brushstrokes.

If you don't have a pressure-sensitive tablet, however, you can get similar effects. As you drag the Variable Stroke tool on your page, press 2 (or the Right Arrow key) to make your path get wider, or press 1 (or the Left Arrow key) to make your path narrower.

Calligraphic Pen tool. The Calligraphic Pen tool draws paths that look like they were drawn with a lettering pen (see Figure 1-52). Tight fit and Draw Dotted Line are the same as those for the Freehand tool. When you choose fixed in the Width section of the dialog box, the paths you draw are a single, fixed width. When you choose Variable, the Calligraphic Pen tool simulates a pen with a flexible nib.

FIGURE 1-52
Calligraphic Pen
tool options

Drag the Calligraphic Pen tool to create paths that look like hand lettering.

Like the Variable Stroke tool, the Calligraphic Pen tool is pressure-sensitive and uses the same keyboard shortcuts.

Pen Tool

You use the Pen tool to draw paths containing both straight and curved line segments (that is, paths containing both curve and corner points). Illustrator users will recognize the Pen tool immediately, because it works the same as Illustrator's Pen tool. Click the Pen tool to create a corner point; drag to create a curve point.

Press 6 to select the Pen tool.

Freeform Tool

FreeHand 8's new Freeform tool gives you a way to change the curve of line segments without manipulating control handles (see Figure 1-53). For more on reshaping paths, see Chapter 2, "Drawing."

FIGURE 1-53
Freeform tool

Double-click the Freeform tool to display the Freeform Tool dialog box. Like the Freehand tool, the Freeform tool really comprises two tools: Push/Pull and Reshape Area.

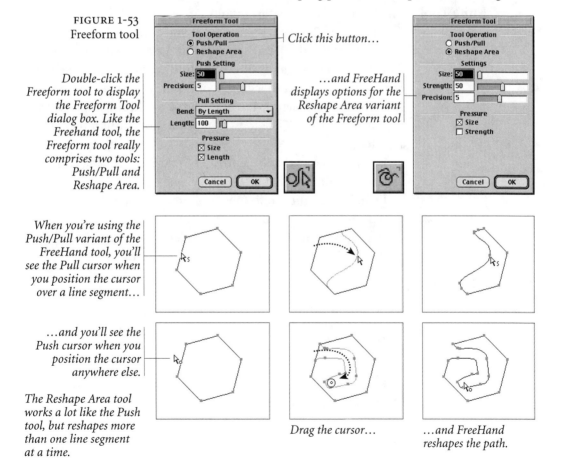

Click this button…

…and FreeHand displays options for the Reshape Area variant of the Freeform tool

When you're using the Push/Pull variant of the FreeHand tool, you'll see the Pull cursor when you position the cursor over a line segment…

…and you'll see the Push cursor when you position the cursor anywhere else.

The Reshape Area tool works a lot like the Push tool, but reshapes more than one line segment at a time.

Drag the cursor…

…and FreeHand reshapes the path.

Point Tool   Use the Point tool to place points on your page (the FreeHand manuals call this tool the "Bezigon" tool, but I find I can't—I just can't—type the word). You can create curve points, corner points, or connector points. To add a corner point, all you need to do is click. To create a curve point, hold down Option/Alt and click. Add a connector point by holding down Control/Ctrl as you click. As you position points, bear in mind that you can always change any kind of point into any other kind of point, and that you can always change the curve of line segments attached to points. For more on corner points, curve points, and connector points, see "Points and Paths," later in this chapter.

Press 8 to select the Point tool.

Knife Tool   The Knife tool splits paths or points. Select a path, choose the Knife tool from the Toolbox (or press 7), and then click on the path. FreeHand splits the path into separate paths where you clicked. *Drag* the Knife tool, and you'll see a line extending from the point at which you started dragging. Don't worry—you're not drawing anything—you're defining a path that cuts through any selected path it encounters. Knife tool? Maybe we should call it the "chain-saw" tool!

Press 7 to select the Knife tool. For more on splitting paths, see "Splitting Paths" in Chapter 2, "Drawing."

Double-click the Knife tool, and FreeHand displays the Knife Tool dialog box (see Figure 1-54).

If you want to cut closed paths using open paths, you should use the Divide path operation (see Chapter 2, "Drawing").

FIGURE 1-54
Knife tool options

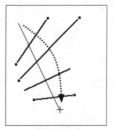

Select the paths you want to cut, then drag the Knife tool over them.

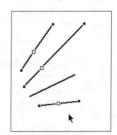

FreeHand cuts the selected paths; other paths are not affected.

Straight or Freehand. When you choose the Straight option, dragging the Knife tool produces a straight "cutting" path. Click the Freehand option, and the Knife tool picks up the current settings of the Freehand tool. That's right—you can cut things with a pressure-sensitive calligraphic knife, if you want. See "Drawing with the Knife tool," in Chapter 2, "Drawing."

Width. The value you enter in the Width field sets the width of the swath you're cutting through things with your Chainsaw—I mean Knife—tool. As you'd expect, entering larger values gives your Knife a thicker blade.

Close Cut Paths. Choose the Close Cut Paths option if you want FreeHand to close the paths you've cut using the Knife tool (if you're cutting closed paths, you'll usually want this turned on; for open paths, you'll probably want it turned off (see "Drawing with the Knife Tool," in Chapter 2, "Drawing").

Tight Fit. When you turn on the Tight Fit option, you're directing FreeHand to more closely monitor the motion of the Knife tool as you drag it on the page. This means that it produces more irregular cuts in paths when you're using the "Freehand" form of the Knife tool.

Rotation Tool

To rotate an object, select the Rotation tool from the toolbox, select the object, and drag the Rotation tool on your page. The point at which you start dragging specifies the center of rotation. On the Macintosh, you can rotate an object around its center, by holding down Control as you drag.

Reflection Tool

The Reflection tool creates a mirror image of an object around the object's vertical or horizontal axis (or both), around an angled axis, or around a fixed location on your page or pasteboard. To reflect an object, select the object, select the Reflection tool, then drag the Reflection tool on the page to flip the object. The point at which you start dragging determines the axis about which you're reflecting the object. On the Macintosh, you can reflect an object around its center if you hold down Control as you drag.

Scaling Tool   To scale (or resize) an object, select the object, select the Scaling tool, and drag the Scaling tool to size the selected object. The point at which you start dragging determines the center point around which you're sizing the object. Hold down Shift as you drag to retain the object's proportions as you scale it. On the Macintosh you can scale an object around its center point, by holding down Control as you drag.

If you want to do your scaling numerically, double-click the Scaling tool—FreeHand will display the Scale section of the Transform palette.

For more about sizing or scaling objects, see "Scaling" in Chapter 5, "Transforming."

Skewing Tool   Skewing alters the vertical or horizontal axes (or both) of objects, which makes them appear as though they're on a plane that's been slanted relative to the plane of the publication. To skew a selected object, select the Skewing tool from the toolbox and drag it on your page. As you drag, FreeHand skews the object. The point at which you start dragging sets the point around which the object skews (this means that the object will move, unless you've started dragging in precisely the center of the object). On the Macintosh, you can skew an object around its center point by holding down Control as you drag the tool.

To use the Skewing section of the Transform palette, double-click the Skewing tool—FreeHand displays the Skewing section of the Transform palette.

For more on skewing elements in FreeHand, see "Skewing" in Chapter 5, "Transforming."

Tracing Tool   To automatically trace objects in your publication, select the Tracing tool and drag a selection rectangle around the objects you want to trace. Many people have the idea that the Tracing tool is only for tracing bitmaps, which isn't true—it'll trace anything.

If you double-click the Tracing tool, the Tracing Tool dialog box appears (see Figure 1-55). For more on using the Tracing tool, see "Tracing" in Chapter 2, "Drawing."

FIGURE 1-55
Tracing tool settings

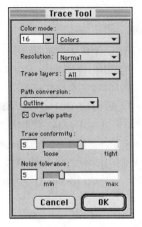

Magnifying Glass   Use the Magnifying Glass to change your view of the publication. Holding down Option/Alt changes the Magnifying Glass tool (which zooms in) into the Reducing Glass (which zooms out). To temporarily switch to the Magnifying Glass, hold down Command-spacebar/Ctrl-spacebar, and then click the area you want to magnify, or drag a selection rectangle around it. To temporarily switch to the Reducing Glass, hold down Command-Option-spacebar/ Ctrl-Alt-spacebar, and then click or drag to zoom out.

For more on using the Magnifying Glass, see "Zooming," earlier in this chapter.

Constraining Tools

Most drawing and page layout applications have the concept of constraint: that holding down some key (usually Shift) makes tools behave differently. Usually, constraint limits movement to vertical and horizontal axes, relative to the sides of your screen (though some applications limit movement to 45-degree tangents of the current location). Table 1-6 (on the next page) shows how constraint works in FreeHand.

Additionally, you should note that constraint (holding down Shift) is affected by the angle you entered in the Constrain angle

TABLE 1-6
Effect of constraint
on tools

Tool:	Constraint:
Pointer tool	If you're moving an object, holding down Shift limits the movement of the object to 45-degree tangents from the point at which you started dragging. You can hold down Shift at any time as you drag the object to get this effect. If you're selecting objects, holding down Shift extends the selection to include the next object or set of objects you click.
Polygon tool	Hold down Shift to constrain the rotation of the polygon's axis to 15-degree increments as you draw it.
Rectangle tool	Hold down Shift to draw squares.
Ellipse tool	Hold down Shift to draw circles.
Line tool	Hold down Shift to constrain the Line tool to draw lines in 45-degree increments (that is, 0, 45, and 90 degrees, where 0 degrees is horizontal and 90 degrees is vertical, relative to your publication).
Freehand tool	Hold down Option/Alt to constrain line segments to straight lines (from the point you held down the key); hold down Option-Shift to constrain line segments to 45-degree angles.
Pen tool	Shift constrains the next point placed to a 45-degree tangent from the previous point on the path.
Knife tool	Same as Line tool.
Point tool	Same as Pen tool.
Magnifying Glass	None
Reducing Glass	None

field of the Constrain dialog box. All constraint, including drawing, is based on the angle you enter (see "Constrain," earlier in this
chapter).

What's on My Page?

A FreeHand page can contain four kinds of objects: paths, basic
shapes, text blocks, and imported graphics.

Points and Paths   Because so much of working with FreeHand depends on understanding the concept of points and paths, I've written about it in
several places in this book. The following section is an overview of
the topic. For more (much more) on points and paths, see "Points
and Paths" in Chapter 2, "Drawing."

In FreeHand, continuous lines are called paths. Paths are made
up of two or more points. Points in a path are connected by line
segments. Paths can be open (which means that there's no line
segment between the ending and starting points on the path) or
closed (see Figure 1-56).

A point can have curve control handles attached to it which
control the curve of the line segments associated with the point
(see Figure 1-57). Many people call these handles "Bezier control
points" (which is the technical, mathematical term for them), or
"Bezier control handles." I find it confusing talking about two different kinds of "points," so I call them "control handles" or "curve

FIGURE 1-56
Paths and points,

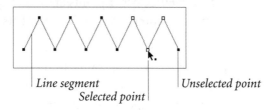

Line segment
Selected point
Unselected point

*Open path. Open paths can be filled,
but they can't have objects pasted
inside them.*

*Closed path. Closed paths can be filled,
or have objects pasted inside them (see
Chapter 2, "Drawing").*

FIGURE 1-57
Points and curve
handles

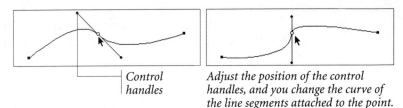

*Control
handles*

*Adjust the position of the control
handles, and you change the curve of
the line segments attached to the point.*

handles," and use "point" to refer to the point on the path. It's simple: there are points, and those points may, or may not, have control handles attached to them.

Points come in three fundamental flavors—curve points, corner points, and connector points. Each type of point has its own special properties.

♦ A curve point adds a curved line segment between the preceding and following points along the path. Curve points are shown onscreen as small circles and have curve control handles placed along a straight line from the curve point itself (see Figure 1-58).

The curve handle following the point controls the curve of the line segment following the curve point on the path; the curve handle preceding the point controls the curve of the line segment preceding the curve point on the path. Curve points are typically used for adding smooth curves to a path (see Figure 1-59).

♦ A corner point adds a straight line segment between the current point and the preceding point on the path (see Figure 1-60). Corner points are typically used to create paths containing straight line segments.

♦ A connector point adds a curved line segment following the point on the path. A connector point is something like a curve or corner point with one curve control handle extended and connects corner points and curve points (see Figure 1-61). I've been using FreeHand for years, and I have yet to use a connector point.

You can always drag curve control handles out of corner and connector points. Select the point, hold down Option/Alt, and drag a curve control point out of the point. The first curve handle con-

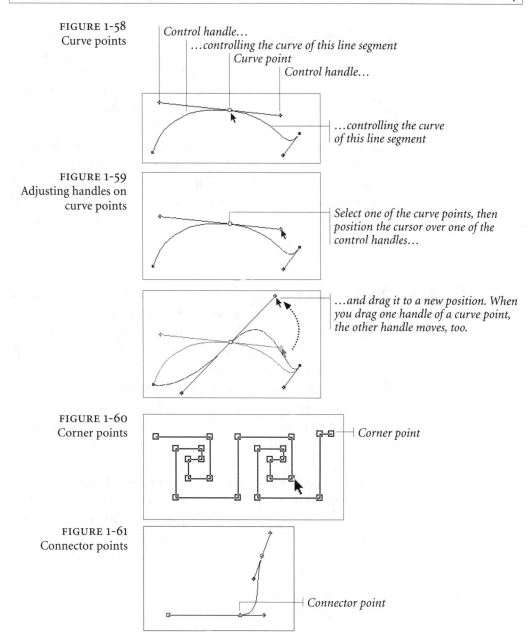

FIGURE 1-58
Curve points

Control handle...
...controlling the curve of this line segment
Curve point
Control handle...
...controlling the curve of this line segment

FIGURE 1-59
Adjusting handles on curve points

Select one of the curve points, then position the cursor over one of the control handles...

...and drag it to a new position. When you drag one handle of a curve point, the other handle moves, too.

FIGURE 1-60
Corner points

Corner point

FIGURE 1-61
Connector points

Connector point

trols the curve of the line segment following the point along the path; the second curve handle controls the curve of the line segment preceding the point along the path.

What points should you use? Any type of point can be turned into any other type of point, and anything you can do with one kind of point can be done with any other kind of point. Given these two points (so to speak), you can use the kinds of points and drawing tools you're happiest with and achieve exactly the results you want. There is no "best way" to draw with FreeHand's free-form drawing tools, but it helps to understand how the particular method you choose works.

I always use the Point tool, and place corner points to draw straight line segments. I add curves later, once I've placed points where I want them along the path. This seems easiest to me; what you like may be different. Experiment until you find what method of drawing suits you best. For more on working with points and paths, see Chapter 2, "Drawing."

Basic Shapes   The Rectangle, Polygon, Ellipse, and Line tools draw basic shapes (that's what I call them, anyway). The Line tool draws a straight line segment between two points, which then behaves exactly as if you'd drawn it by placing two corner points. The other three tools draw paths with specific properties and points in specific places. It's as you'd expect: the Rectangle tool draws rectangles, the Ellipse tool draws ellipses, and the Polygon tool draws polygons. Objects drawn with the Ellipse and Rectangle tools act like grouped paths, but have certain special properties, as shown in Table 1-7.

Text Blocks   FreeHand's text blocks can contain any number of typefaces, paragraph formats, colors, and sizes of type. Text blocks can be linked to each other (so text flows between them as you edit the copy, reshape text blocks, or change formatting), and can be linked across pages. Text can flow along a path (that is, have its baseline follow a path), and can be flowed inside a closed path (see Figure 1-62).

For more on FreeHand's text-handling capabilities, see Chapter 3, "Text and Type."

Imported Graphics   FreeHand can import graphics saved in the many popular graphics file formats. Vector graphics (such as WMF in Windows and vector PICT on the Macintosh) are disassembled into their component objects on import and are converted into FreeHand elements you can edit just as if you'd drawn them in FreeHand. EPS graphics

TABLE 1-7 Special properties of basic shapes	Shape:	Special properties:
	Rectangle	The Object Inspector for rectangles contains fields specifying the object's X and Y (horizontal and vertical) coordinates, W and H (width and height), as well as a field for specifying the rectangle's corner radius. (If you ungroup the rectangle, you won't be able to change its corner radius using the Object Inspector.) If you hold down Option/Alt as you draw a rectangle, FreeHand positions the center of the rectangle at the point where you started dragging, drawing the rectangle out from that point.
	Ellipse	The Object Inspector for ellipses contains fields specifying the object's X and Y (horizontal and vertical) coordinates, W and H (width and height). If you hold down Option/Alt as you draw an ellipse, FreeHand positions the center of the ellipse at the point where you started dragging, drawing the ellipse from that point.
	Polygon	When you select a polygon, the Object Inspector displays the same information as it would if you selected a freeform path. If you hold down Option/Alt as you draw a polygon, FreeHand positions the center of the polygon at the point where you started dragging.

you've opened (as opposed to placed) are also converted into Free-Hand elements (if possible). TIFF, paint, and EPS files you've placed are handled very much like a FreeHand group, except that they cannot be ungrouped. You can use all of FreeHand's transformation tools (for scaling, rotation, reflection, and skewing) to manipulate imported graphics (see Figure 1-63).

FIGURE 1-62
Text blocks

FIGURE 1-63
Imported graphics

For more on working with imported graphics, see Chapter 4, "Importing and Exporting."

Thinking Objectively

FreeHand's world is made up of objects (also called elements)—points, line segments, paths, basic shapes, text blocks, groups, and imported graphics. Each class of object has certain attributes that you can view and edit by selecting the object and looking at the Object Inspector.

The Object Inspector provides an extremely powerful way of editing and examining objects in your publication—by the numbers (see Figure 1-64).

If you know exactly where an object needs to go, or exactly how wide an object should be, try using the Object Inspector. It can beat dragging, measuring, and waiting for the screen to redraw.

FIGURE 1-64
Objects and the
Object Inspector

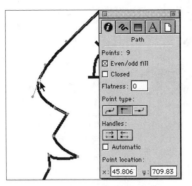

*Object Inspector, point selected.
From here, you can move the point,
change the point type, or retract the
point's control handles.*

*Object Inspector, image selected. The
X and Y fields refer to the lower-left
corner of the object.*

Selecting and Deselecting Elements

Before you can act on an object, you have to select it. You select
objects with the Pointer tool by clicking them, dragging a selection
rectangle over them, or by Shift-selecting (select one object, hold
down Shift, and select another object). You can also choose Select
All from the Edit menu (see Figure 1-65).

When you select an object, FreeHand displays the object's selection handles. FreeHand displays selected objects a little bit differently depending on the method you've used to select them and the
type of object you've selected. If you've turned on the Highlight
Selected Paths option in the General Editing Preferences dialog box,
FreeHand displays a line (in the highlight color of the current layer)
that follows any paths you select (see Figure 1-66).

Most of the time, I leave the Highlight Selected Paths option
turned off. I often work with thin strokes, and find the highlight
line distracting.

To deselect objects, click an uninhabited area of the page or
pasteboard, or, better yet, press Tab.

Tip:
Deselect All

Pressing Tab deselects all selected objects. This can come in handy
when you're having trouble deselecting objects at a high magnification—when you can't see the currently selected objects' selection
handles because they're outside your page view. This shortcut is
easy, fast, and guaranteed to deselect all objects. If you're entering

FIGURE 1-65
Selecting objects

Shift-selecting

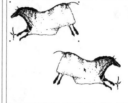

Click on one object
to select it.

Hold down Shift, and
click on another object.

You've selected both
objects.

Drag-selecting

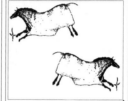

Position the cursor
outside a group of
objects...

...and drag a selection
rectangle over the
objects.

You've selected all of
the objects inside the
rectangle.

FIGURE 1-66
Highlighting

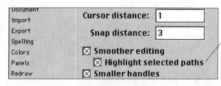

When you turn on the
Highlight Selected Paths option
in the General Preferences
dialog box...

...FreeHand draws a line (in the
highlight color of the current layer)
that follows the path.

Turn the option off, and FreeHand
highlights only the path's points.

text in a text block, press Command-Tab/Alt-E,S,R to deselect all objects (this keeps you from accidentally entering tab characters in the text block).

Tip:
Selecting Parts
of Paths

Sometimes, you only want to work on specific points in a path, rather than working on the path as a whole. To do this, drag a selection rectangle over only the points you want to select. If you want to select several points but can't reach them all with one selection rectangle, select some of the points by dragging a selection rectangle, then hold down Shift and drag more selection rectangles until you've selected all of the points you want.

Tip:
Selecting Paths
Instead of Points

If you've selected a path by dragging a selection rectangle over part of it, you've probably got some points specifically selected. While you sometimes want to do this, it can cause problems—when you drag the path, it's likely that the unselected points on the path stay put while the selected points move. To select the path as a whole when you've selected some of the points on the path, choose Superselect from the Edit menu, or press ` (accent grave),—it's at the upper left of your keyboard, underneath the ~ (tilde) character (see Figure 1-67).

FIGURE 1-67
Selecting paths only

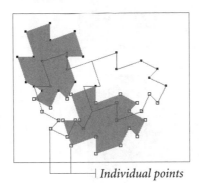 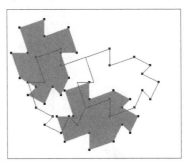

Individual points

Press ` (accent grave) and FreeHand selects the paths as paths, rather than as individual points.

Tip:
Selecting
Through
Objects

To select an object that's behind another object (or objects), hold down Control/Ctrl and click (in Windows, click using the right mouse button) through the stack of objects until the selection handles of the individual object you want to select appear (see Figure 1-68).

FIGURE 1-68
Selecting through
stacks of objects

 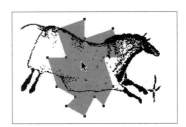

Control-click once to select the object on top of the stack.

Control-click again to select the next object in the stack.

You don't have to ungroup a group of objects to edit the objects in the group—you can select them and work with them just as if they were outside the group. Hold down Option/Alt and click the element that you want to edit, and FreeHand selects the object. While it's selected, you can change its attributes, text, shape, or position. When you deselect the subselected item, it goes back to being part of the group (see Figure 1-69).

FIGURE 1-69
Subselecting items
inside groups

Point at an object inside a group.

Hold down Option and click to select the object.

You can move or edit the object, but it remains inside the group (in this example, I've changed an object's color and position).

If you're trying to select an object in a group that's behind other objects, hold down Option-Control/Ctrl-Alt as you click (in Windows, click using the right mouse button) through the stack of elements. You can also select multiple buried objects this way by holding down Control-Option-Shift/Ctrl-Alt-Shift as you click (again, in Windows use the right mouse button) through the stack of objects.

This set of features is flexible enough that you can select any number of groups or individual objects through a stack of items containing groups or individual elements.

When you have an object inside a group selected, and you want to select and act on the group, press ` (accent grave). FreeHand selects the group. When you're working with groups nested inside other groups, each press of ` selects the next encompassing group.

Moving Elements

You can move individual points, sets of points, paths, groups or imported graphics—or sets of selected points, paths, or objects. Moving any single object is simple: just position the Pointer tool over the object (but not over a point in the path), hold down the mouse button, and drag the object to wherever you want it (see Figure 1-70).

FIGURE 1-70
Moving by dragging

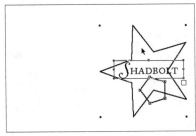

Select the objects you want to move...

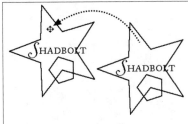

...and drag them to a new position.

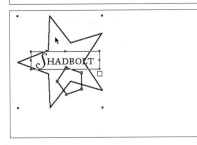

When the objects are where you want them, drop them (that is, stop dragging and release the mouse button).

Okay, I admit that this is pretty basic, but I do get asked, honest.

To move more than one object at once, hold down Shift and click on the objects you want to move. When you reach the last object you want to select, position the Pointer tool over the object, and, while still holding down Shift, press the mouse button. If you want to constrain the object's movement, continue holding down Shift (if not, release the Shift key), and drag the selected objects to where you want them.

Alternatively, you can use the Move palette. Select an object (or group of objects) and press Command-M/Ctrl-M to display the Transform palette (then click the Move icon at the top of the palette if the Move palette's not visible). Use the X and Y fields to enter the horizontal and vertical distances you want to move the selection, then press Return. FreeHand moves the object (see Figure 1-71). For more on moving objects, see "Moving," in Chapter 5, "Transforming."

FIGURE 1-71
Moving objects using
the Move palette

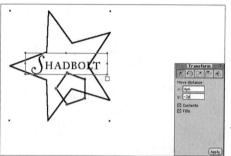

Select the objects you want to move and press Command-M/ Ctrl-M to display the Transform palette (if it's not already visible). Click the Move icon to display the Move palette, type the distance you want to move the objects in the X and Y fields, and press Return (or click the Apply button).

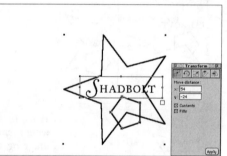

FreeHand moves the objects as you specified.

Working with Layers

Many authors would save the intricacies of working with the Layers palette for later in the book. Sorry. The Layers palette is one of the most important tools at your disposal for speeding up the process of creating publications with FreeHand.

Like many CAD programs, FreeHand uses the concept of layers—transparent planes on which you create and place elements. Once you've gone beyond creating very simple publications, you'll find layers indispensable because they help you organize and control the elements in your publication.

Layers give you control over which parts of your publication redraw while you're working on the file. If, for example, you're correcting text in a publication containing large TIFF images, put the TIFFs on their own layer and make it invisible while you work on the text. Don't spend time displaying things you're not working on and don't need to see.

Default Layers

FreeHand has three default layers: Foreground, Guides, and Background. These layers are representative of the three major types of layers available in FreeHand (see Figure 1-72). You can create or delete any number of background and foreground layers, but you can't create a new, or delete the existing, Guides layer.

◆ Foreground layers are where you do your drawing. In general, they're what you want to print, when you print.

◆ The Guides layer contains FreeHand's guides. Move the layer, and the guides move with it.

◆ Background layers are where you put objects you want to trace. Background layers don't print.

The line in the Layers palette defines the boundary between background and foreground layers. Layers above the line in the palette are foreground layers; layers below are background layers. Objects on the background layers are screened to 50 percent of their original color (this makes it easier to manually trace objects on the background layer).

FIGURE 1-72
Layers palette

The checkmark shows that the layer and its contents are visible.

This line marks the boundary between the foreground and background layers.

The view button shows (and controls) the viewing mode (keyline or preview) for a layer.

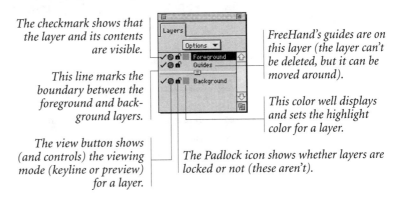

FreeHand's guides are on this layer (the layer can't be deleted, but it can be moved around).

This color well displays and sets the highlight color for a layer.

The Padlock icon shows whether layers are locked or not (these aren't).

Using the Layers Palette

Here are some of the things you can do using the Layers palette.

- ◆ Make the Layers palette visible or invisible
- ◆ Move objects from one layer to another
- ◆ Create new layers
- ◆ Remove layers (and their contents)
- ◆ Make layers visible or invisible
- ◆ Display layers in Preview or Keyline view
- ◆ Change the stacking order of layers
- ◆ Make layers foreground or background
- ◆ Make layers printing or nonprinting
- ◆ Copy the contents of one layer to another
- ◆ Lock layers (objects on locked layers cannot be selected)
- ◆ Rename layers

Displaying the Layers palette. You can display the Layers palette by pressing Command-6/Ctrl-6. If the palette is already visible, pressing Command-6/Ctrl-6 hides it.

Moving objects from one layer to another. To send an object or objects to a specific layer, select the objects and click the name of the layer in the Layers palette. FreeHand moves the selected objects to that layer (see Figure 1-73).

Creating new layers. To create a new layer choose New from the pop-up menu at the top of the Layers palette. FreeHand adds a new layer to the Layers palette. If you want to change the default name FreeHand's assigned to the new layer, double-click on the layer's name in the Layers palette, type a new name for the layer, and press Return (see Figure 1-74).

Removing layers. To remove a layer, select the layer name in the Layers palette and choose Remove from the pop-up menu at the

FIGURE 1-73
Moving objects from
one layer to another

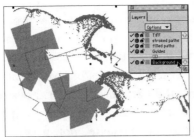 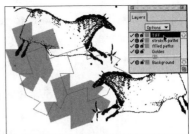

*Select the objects you want to move
(in this example, the objects are on
the background layer).*

*Click on the layer name in the Layers
palette. FreeHand moves the objects to
the layer.*

FIGURE 1-74
Creating and
naming a new layer

 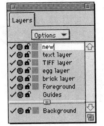 

*Select "New" from the
Layers palette pop-up
menu.*

*Double-click the new
layer's name and type
the name you want
for the layer.*

*Press Return, and
FreeHand adds the new
layer's name to the
Layers palette.*

top of the palette. If there are objects on that layer, FreeHand asks
if you want to remove those objects (see Figure 1-75). If that's
what you want to do, click OK and all of the objects on that layer
will be deleted along with the layer. If you don't want the objects
removed, click Cancel, and move the objects to other layers. Then
try removing the layer again.

FIGURE 1-75
Removing layers

 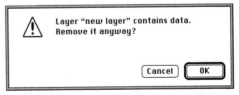

*Select the layer you want
to remove and choose
Remove from the Layers
palette pop-up menu.*

*If there's anything on the layer, FreeHand
displays this message. Click OK (or press
Return) if you want to remove the objects on the
layer. Otherwise, click Cancel and move the
objects to other layers.*

Tip:
Removing
Multiple Layers

Want to remove more than one layer at once? To select a contiguous range of layers (layers adjacent to each other in the Layers palette), hold down Shift and click on the layer names in the Layers palette. To select a series of layers that aren't in a range, hold down Command/Ctrl and click on the layers you want to select. Once you've selected the layers you want to remove, choose Remove from the Layers palette's pop-up menu (see Figure 1-76).

FIGURE 1-76
Selecting and
removing multiple
layers

Select the start of the range...

...then hold down Shift and click the end of the range.

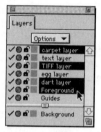

...or hold down Command/ Ctrl and click individual layers.

Once you've chosen the layers you want to delete, choose Remove from the Layers palette's Options menu.

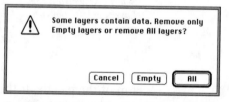

FreeHand displays this alert. Delete all of the selected layers by clicking the All button, or remove only the empty layers in the selection by clicking the Empty button.

Making layers visible or invisible. If you want to make all of the objects on a layer invisible, click the checkmark to the left of the layer's name in the Layers palette. Everything that's on that layer disappears (see Figure 1-77). Don't worry. It's not gone; it's just not visible and can't be selected. To make the layer visible again, click the space to the left of the layer's name. The checkmark reappears, and the objects on the layer become visible.

You can make all layers visible by choosing All On from the pop-up menu at the top of the Layers palette, or make all layers invisible by choosing All Off. When you want to work on just one layer, choose All Off and then make that one layer visible.

FIGURE 1-77
Making layers visible
or invisible

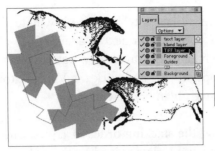

*This figure is on the
layer "TIFF layer."*

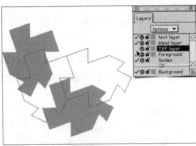

*Click the checkmark to the left of
the layer's name to make the layer
invisible.*

*Hold down Option/Ctrl and click
the checkmark to hide all layers, or
hold down Option/Ctrl and click in
the column to show all layers.*

Tip:
All On/All Off
Shortcuts

To quickly hide all layers, hold down Option/Ctrl and click a check-mark to the left of a layer's name in the Layers palette. FreeHand hides all layers. To show all of the layers again, hold down Option/Ctrl and click to the left of a layer you've turned off. Free-Hand displays all layers.

Changing your view of layers. You can set the viewing mode (Pre-view or Keyline) of a layer by clicking the view button to the left of the layer's name in the Layers palette (see Figure 1-78). When you do this, everything on the layer is displayed in the viewing mode you've chosen.

FIGURE 1-78
Changing the viewing
mode for a layer

 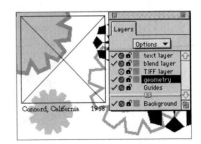

TIFF layer, displayed in preview.   *TIFF layers, in keyline mode.*

Tip:
Keyline/Preview
Shortcut

To switch all layers to keyline view, hold down Option/Ctrl and click the View button next to a layer that's already in keyline view. To switch all of the layers in a publication to preview mode, hold down Option/Ctrl and click the View button to the left of a layer that's currently in preview mode.

Changing the stacking order of layers. The stacking order of the layers you use is determined by the order in which they appear in the Layers palette. Layers nearer to the top of the Layers palette are closer to the front in your publication. If you want to move the contents of a specific layer closer to the front, drag the layer name toward the top of the Layers palette (see Figure 1-79).

FIGURE 1-79
Changing the stacking
order of layers

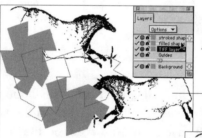

Drag the layer name up or down in the Layers palette.

This image is on the layer named "TIFF layer".

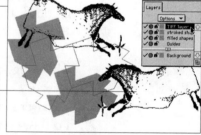

Drop the layer when it's where you want it.

The image comes to the front, along with any other objects on the same layer.

Tip:
Moving the
Guides Layer

To send the guides all the way to the back, drag the Guides layer below the line on the Layers palette. The Guides layer is now behind every foreground layer. If you want to move the Guides layer behind every background layer, drag the Guides layer to the bottom of the list in the Layers palette.

You can also move the Guides layer so that it falls behind one or more foreground layers.

Making layers foreground or background. To make a layer a background layer, drag it below the line in the Layers palette. To make a background layer into a foreground layer, drag it above the line in the Layers palette. You can also drag the line up and down in the palette, making whole ranges of layers foreground or background.

Making layers printing or nonprinting. If you want to print only the visible foreground layers (the layers above the line in the palette with a checkmark to the left of their names), click All Visible Foreground Layers in the Print Options dialog box. If you want to print all foreground layers, whether they're visible or not, click All Foreground Layers. Alternatively, you can make foreground layers into background layers to make them nonprinting, and vice versa.

The default Guides layer cannot be printed. If you want to print guides, see "Documenting Layouts," earlier in this chapter.

Copying layers. To copy all of the objects on a particular layer to a new layer, select the layer and choose Duplicate from the Layers palette's pop-up menu. FreeHand creates a new layer containing copies of all of the objects on the original layer. Your page won't look any different, of course, because the copied objects are exactly on top of the original objects.

Locking and unlocking layers. When you're working on a complex publication, it's too easy to select something you'd rather not—or, worse, delete it. Instead of losing time "undoing" your mistakes, why not put the things you're not currently working with on a layer of their own, and then keep them safe by locking the layer?

To lock a layer, click the Padlock icon to the left of the layer's name in the Layers palette (see Figure 1-80). The objects on the layer remain visible, but you can't select them. You can still change the layer's position in the stacking order when it's locked.

To unlock a layer, click the Padlock icon to the left of the layer's name. When the padlock's open, the layer is unlocked.

Renaming layers. You can rename a layer at any time. Double-click the layer name in the Layers palette, type a new name for the layer and press Return.

Renaming layers makes not a bit of difference to FreeHand, but it might help you remember which layer contains which objects.

FIGURE 1-80
Locking and
unlocking layers

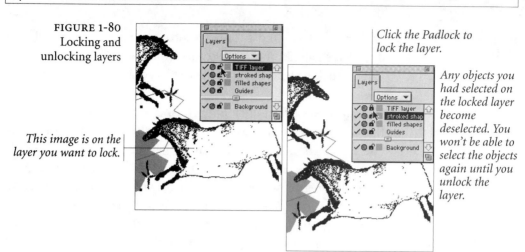

*Click the Padlock to
lock the layer.*

*This image is on the
layer you want to lock.*

*Any objects you
had selected on
the locked layer
become
deselected. You
won't be able to
select the objects
again until you
unlock the
layer.*

Setting highlight colors. When you select an object, FreeHand displays the object's selection handles in the highlight color you've assigned to the layer. If you've turned on the Highlight Selected Paths option in the General Editing Preferences dialog box, and have selected a path, you'll also see a line of the highlight following the path. The color wells to the left of the layer name in the Layers palette show you the highlight color for each layer. To change the highlight color for a layer, drag a color swatch from any other color well (such as those in the Colors palette and Color Mixer) and drop it on the color well next to the name of the layer you want to change (see Figure 1-81).

FIGURE 1-81
Setting a layer's
highlight color

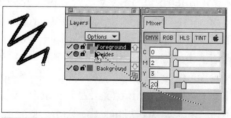

*Drag a color swatch from any
color well…*

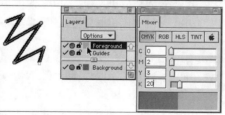

*…and drop it on the color
well next to the layer name.
FreeHand changes the
highlight color of the layer.*

FreeHand and the Edit Menu

FreeHand works a little bit differently than other applications, particularly in that you don't have to go through the Clipboard to copy items in your publication. Instead, you'll typically use Clone and Duplicate (which you'll find on FreeHand's Edit menu) inside a publication (you'll still need to use Cut and Copy to move items from publication to publication). Not only are Clone and Duplicate faster, they use less memory and have some useful features of their own.

Clone

The Clone command, Command-=/Ctrl-Shift-C, creates a copy of the selected object exactly on top of the original (see Figure 1-82). This can be a little confusing at first, because the cloned object's selection handles look just the same as the selection handles of the original object. New FreeHand users sometimes end up with stacks of identical objects in their publications.

Placing the object in the same position, however, offers distinct advantages. If, for example, you know that you want a copy of a specific object two picas to the right and two picas down from the location of the original object, just clone the object, then display the Move palette, and move the object numerically. If you hadn't started in exactly the same position as the original object, you'd have to do a bunch of measuring to figure out where the copied object was supposed to go.

FIGURE 1-82
Cloning

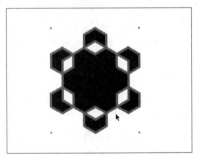

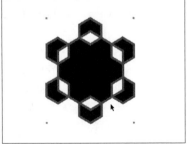

Select an object and press Command-=/Ctrl-Shift-C to clone it.

FreeHand places a copy of the object exactly on top of the original object. It doesn't look like a new object, but it's there.

Duplicate   The Duplicate command (Command-D/Ctrl-D) creates a copy of the object at a slight offset from the selected object (see Figure 1-83), or copies the object and repeats the last series of transformations (that is, the last time you used the Move, Scaling, Rotation, Skewing, or Reflection tools). I'll cover more of the complex uses of the Duplicate command in Chapter 5, "Transforming."

FIGURE 1-83
Duplicating

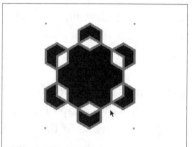

Select an object and press Command-D/Ctrl-D to duplicate it.

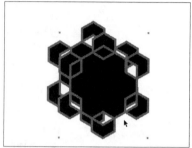

FreeHand places a copy of the object at a slight offset from the original object.

Preferences

My mind still boggles as I look through FreeHand's Preferences dialog boxes—and I expect yours does, too. There are so many different options (and some of them pretty obscure) that you might want to close the dialog box and try not to think about it—Life, after all, is complicated enough. Don't yield to this temptation. FreeHand's Preferences dialog boxes are one place you can really fine-tune FreeHand's performance and behavior. Preference settings are so useful, in fact, that I'm hoping that FreeHand 9 will have a Yet More Preferences dialog box, or a Son of More Preferences dialog box. The possibilities are endless.

When you choose Preferences from the File menu (or press Command-Shift-D/Ctrl-Shift-D), you'll see the Preferences dialog box. On the Macintosh, click an item in the list to display the different panels of the Preferences dialog box; in Windows, click one of the tabs. From now on, I'll refer to each section of this dialog box as if it were a separate dialog box (as, in fact, each is).

General   When you click the General option in the Preferences list (or, in Windows, the General tab), FreeHand displays what I call the General Preferences dialog box (see Figure 1-84). Some of the most important of FreeHand's preferences live here.

Undo's. This option sets the number of actions held in FreeHand's Undo queue. Enter smaller numbers here if you find you don't use that many levels of Undo or want to save memory. Enter larger numbers here if you change your mind a lot and don't like the idea of using Save As and Revert when you're experimenting with possibilities. Remember, however, that each level of Undo adds to the amount of RAM that FreeHand uses (the amount of RAM consumed depends on the action). You can enter any number from one to 100 in this field.

Pick Distance. How close to the edge of an object do you have to click to select the object? How does FreeHand "know" you want to select the object? The value you enter in the Pick Distance field determines how close, in pixels, you can click before FreeHand decides you're trying to select the object. You can enter a value from zero to five pixels in this field—the lower the value, the more accurate your clicks have to be.

FIGURE 1-84
General Preferences
dialog box

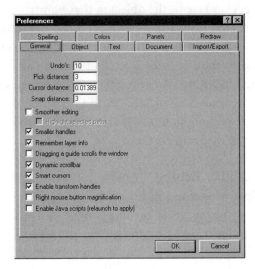

The Pick Distance field also controls how close you have to get to an object to apply a color to it using drag-and-drop color. If you're having trouble dropping color swatches on paths, you might want to increase the value you've entered in the Pick Distance field (see "Drag-and-Drop Color" in Chapter 6, "Color").

Cursor Distance. Enter a number in the Cursor Key Distance field to set the distance a selected object moves when you press the arrow keys to "nudge" an object.

Snap Distance. FreeHand has lots of different "snaps" under the View menu. There's Snap to Guides, Snap to Point, and Snap to Grid. Snap to Point makes FreeHand points snap together when you drag them to within a specified distance of each other. Snap to Guides snaps objects to ruler guides when you drag objects within a specified distance of them. Snap to Grid makes objects snap to an underlying grid, which you define in the Setup Inspector.

The number you enter in the Snap Distance field in the Editing Preferences dialog box sets the distance (in screen pixels) that all of the Snap commands rely on. Set the Snap Distance option to five pixels, and the next time you drag an object within five pixels of an active snap point (point, ruler guide, or grid intersection), FreeHand snaps the object to that point.

If you just can't seem to get one point to land on top of another so that you can close a path or connect the end of one path to the end of another (see "Open and Closed Paths" in Chapter 2, "Drawing," for more on closing paths), try increasing the number in the Snap Distance field. If, on the other hand, you're having a hard time keeping points from snapping together, enter a smaller number in the Snap Distance field.

Smoother Editing. I can't actually think of a reason you'd want "jerkier editing," so I think you should turn this option on (actually, you might try turning it off if you're short on RAM and find that FreeHand's running very slowly). Turn on the Highlight Selected Paths options to have FreeHand display a one-pixel-wide line on top of the path (in the highlight color of the current layer—see "Layers," earlier in this chapter) when you select the path. Some people like this feature because it reminds them which layer the path is on; others (count me in) think it's annoying.

Smaller Handles. If you thought the selection handles displayed by previous versions of FreeHand were too big, turn this option on. If you're having trouble seeing the selection handles, turn this option off (it's on by default).

Remember Layer Info. In FreeHand 3, you'd lose layer information when you cut, copied, or pasted objects, or when you grouped and ungrouped objects. The Remember Layer Info feature, which first appeared in FreeHand 3.1, gives you the option of keeping that layer information. With Remember Layer Info on, you can cut and paste, group and ungroup, as much as you like, and the objects you're working with always appear on their original layers.

If you're copying objects into a publication that doesn't contain the layers, FreeHand adds those layers to the publication. If you've deleted layers, and ungroup a group containing objects originally assigned to those layers, FreeHand adds the layers to the Layers palette.

If, on the other hand, you want to paste objects from other layers into the current layer, turn off Remember Layer Info.

Dragging a Guide Scrolls the Window. If you like to scroll your current view of the publication by dragging ruler guides, turn this option on. Once you do this, you can't remove ruler guides by dragging them to the rulers—you have to drag them all the way off the page (or use the Guides dialog box). This was the way ruler guides worked in FreeHand 4.

Dynamic Scrollbar. When this option is off, FreeHand doesn't redraw the screen as you drag the slider in the scroll bars—it redraws when you stop dragging. If you want to see your publication as you scroll using the slider, check this box. Bear in mind, however, that turning this option on makes scrolling slower. Turn this option off if you're running low on RAM.

Note that both the Dynamic Scrollbar and the Redraw While Scrolling preferences sound like they address the same issue—they don't. The Redraw While Scrolling preference affects all scrolling methods; the Dynamic Scrollbar option applies only to scrolling by dragging the slider in the scroll bar.

Smart Cursors. When you turn this option on, FreeHand changes the appearance of the cursor as you work (see Table 1-8). When you're using the Freehand, Point, and Pen tools, the cursor shows whether you're starting a new path, continuing a path, closing a path, or adding a point to an existing path. When you're using the Pointer tool, FreeHand changes the cursor as you approach a "snap" point (a guide, a point, or a grid intersection). When you're dragging color swatches, FreeHand changes the cursor to indicate what type of fill you're about to apply (basic, graduated, or radial), or whether you're about to apply the color to the stroke of a path.

Enable Transform Handles. Turn this option on, and FreeHand displays transform handles around any object you double-click. (see Figure 1-85) This is a new feature in FreeHand 8. Using the transform handles, you can rotate and scale the object without having to select a transformation tool or enter numbers in the Transform palette. To hide the transform handles again, double-click the object. For more on working with the transform handles, see Chapter 5, "Transforming."

Right Mouse Button Magnification (Windows only). When you turn this option on, clicking the right mouse button won't bring up a menu. Instead, it switches to the Magnifying Glass tool. Click or drag the Magnifying Glass tool, and FreeHand zooms in (or out) and switches back to the Pointer tool. As handy as this option is, I turn it off—after all, there's already a perfectly good shortcut to the Magnifying Glass (Ctrl-Spacebar), and I find the right mouse button menus too useful to do without.

Enable Java Scripts. To run Java scripts you've created using the Macromedia Script Editor, turn this option on and restart Freehand. For more on this topic, see Appendix A, "Scripting."

TABLE 1-8 Smart cursors	What you see	What it's called	What it means
	+	Standard cursor	You're using one of the drawing tools (the Point tool, Freehand tool, or Pen tool), but have not yet started to create a path
	+□	Create path cursor	You're creating a path using one of the drawing tools
	+■	Close path cursor	You're about to close a path you're drawing with one of the drawing tools
	+ʌ	Insert point cursor	You're about to add a point to a path
	+.	Continue path cursor	You're about to add points to the end of an open path
	▶ⱶ	Vertical guide snap	The object you're dragging or creating is about to snap to a vertical guide
	▶≖	Horizontal guide snap	The object you're dragging or creating is about to snap to a horizontal guide
	▶ₒ	Point snap	The object you're dragging or creating is about to snap to a point

Object When you click Object in the Preferences List (or, in Windows, click the Object tab), FreeHand displays the Object Preferences dialog box (see Figure 1-86).

Changing Object Changes Defaults. If you check the Changing Object Changes Defaults box, any changes you make to a selected object's attributes (colors, type specifications, fills, and strokes) are carried over to the next object you create. For example, if you've

FIGURE 1-85
Transform Handles

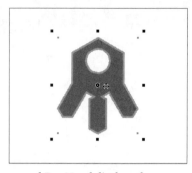

Double-click an object...   *...and FreeHand displays the transform handles.*

To hide the transform handles, double-click the object again.

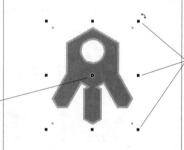

To skew an object, position the cursor over one of the transformation handles and drag.

To move the center of transformation, drag this icon.

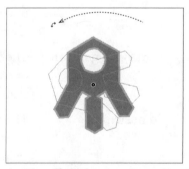
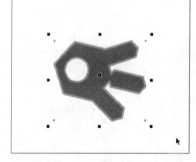

To rotate an object, position the cursor outside one of the transformation handles and drag.   *FreeHand rotates the object around the center of transformation.*

created a stroke and set its width to six points and its color to 20-percent gray, the next path you create has the same stroke width and color.

When this option's unchecked, you set defaults for the entire document by making changes to object attributes (colors, fills, lines, type specifications, and so on) without having any object selected. In this case, each new object you create picks up the publication's

FIGURE 1-86
Object Preferences
dialog box

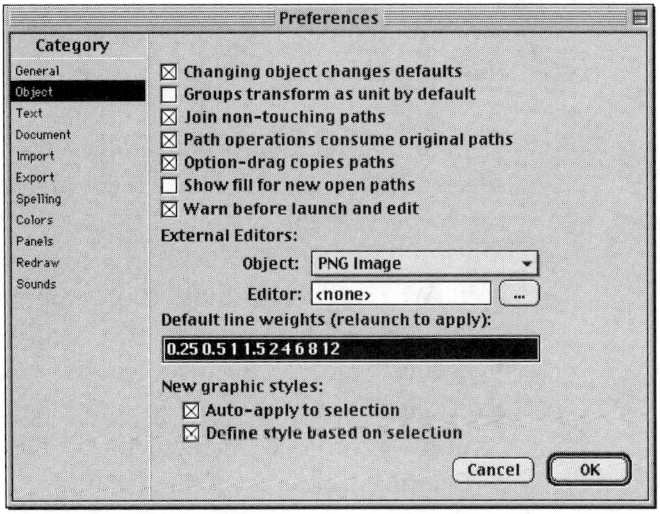

default attributes regardless of what changes have been made to selected objects created or modified previously.

Groups Transform As Unit by Default. When you're transforming (moving, scaling, skewing, or rotating) objects, you can choose to have the transformation affect the line weights and fills of objects in the group. If you don't want this to happen, uncheck this box. For more on Groups Transform as Unit by Default, see Chapter 5, "Transforming."

Join Non-Touching Paths. When Join Non-Touching Paths is on, FreeHand joins the endpoints of open paths when you select the points and press Command-J (or choose Join Elements from the Arrange menu). With Join Non-Touching Paths turned off, Free-Hand only joins the endpoints of paths that you draw or drag to within the distance in pixels you entered in the Pick Distance field.

Path Operations Consume Original Paths. In FreeHand 4, most of the path operations (on the submenu of the same name on the Xtras menu and, on the Combine and Alter Path submenus of the Modify menu) would delete the original paths as they produced new paths from the selected objects. To retain the original paths, you had to clone the paths before running the path operation. You can turn this option off and save your original paths—or you can turn it on and clone any paths you want to keep around before you run any path operations.

Option/Alt-Drag Copies Paths. Many graphics applications clone selected objects when you drag them while holding the Option/Alt key down. Turn this option on to have FreeHand join the club, or, if you feel the Option/Alt key is getting overloaded as it is, turn it off. Why might you think that? Because Option/Alt is used for "Bend-o-matic" path drawing (see "Bend-o-matic" in Chapter 2, "Drawing"), and for forcing a preview drag (see "Preview Drag," earlier in this chapter), *and* for dragging control handles out of points on a path (see "Manipulating Control Handles," in Chapter 2, "Drawing"). Still, I keep this one turned on.

Show Fill for New Open Paths. In FreeHand 8, open paths can be filled. Do you want FreeHand to fill new open paths as you create them? If so, turn this option on. Leave this option off, and you'll be able to work with FreeHand as you did in earlier versions. You'll still be able to use the Fill Inspector to fill any open paths you create.

Warn Before Launch and Edit. If you're a FreeHand 7 user, you *know* what this option is about—I don't know how many times I found myself waiting for FreeHand to launch Photoshop after I'd accidentally double-clicked an imported image. I've found that turning this option on dramatically decreases the number of times I swear at FreeHand. Just turn it on.

External Editors. Since you can double-click an image in a Free-Hand publication to open that image in an image editor, you've got to be able to tell FreeHand *which image editor you want to use.* If you're a Photoshop fan, you'll want to use Photoshop; if you're an xRes user, you'll probably want to use xRes. Or you might want to mix and match—editing TIFFs in Photoshop and LRG images in xRes. Choose a file type from the pop-up menu, then click the "..." button. FreeHand searches your system for applications capable of editing the file type, then displays a list of applications in the Select External Editor dialog box. Choose the application you want to use from this list and click the OK button to set that application as the editor FreeHand launches when you double-click an image of the selected file type.

Default Line Weights. Want different choices on the Stroke Weights pop-up menu in the Stroke Inspector? You can add (or subtract) line weights to this menu by entering (or deleting) them in the Default Line Weights field. If you want to add a stroke weight, type it here (separating it from other weights with a space). Restart Free-Hand, and your new stroke weight will appear on the menu.

New Graphic Styles. Look. I try not to insist that the way I like to work is the best way to work (sometimes, I'm *sure* it's not). I try to present FreeHand's features in a neutral, objective, and fair way, and leave the conclusions up to you. But, in this case, I've got to say that if you want to make your life easier, you'll just leave these two options checked (see Chapter 2, "Drawing" and Chapter 3, "Text and Type").

When the Auto Apply Style to Selection option is on, FreeHand applies a style you've created to the object that's selected when you create it. Ordinarily, you create a style based on an example object, so you definitely *want* the style applied to that object. Or maybe you don't—in which case you can turn this option off. But don't say I didn't warn you.

If you prefer defining styles using the Edit Style dialog box, and *never* want to define styles by example, turn the Define Style Based on Selection option off. If you're like me, and think that defining styles by example is the easiest and quickest way to define styles, you should leave this option turned on.

Text
The controls in the Text Preferences dialog box, as you'd expect, affect the way that you work with text in your FreeHand publications (see Figure 1-87).

Always Use Text Editor. If you always want to use the Text Editor to edit and enter text, turn this option on. Yes, I have met people who want to do this, and no, I don't think they're crazy—though they're mostly cartographers, and that's pretty close. If you prefer

FIGURE 1-87
Text Preferences
dialog box

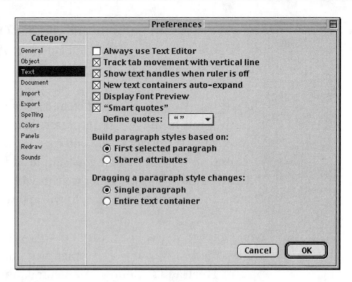

editing text on the page, leave this option turned off—you can always switch to the Text Editor dialog box by selecting a text block and pressing Command-Shift-E/Ctrl-Shift-E.

Track Tab Movement with Vertical Line. Here's one of my favorites: turn this on, and a vertical line appears when you drag a tab marker on the tab ruler (see Figure 1-88). The line runs through the tab marker, through the text, and, in fact, all the way to the horizontal ruler at the top of the page (provided, of course, that you've got FreeHand's rulers turned on). This makes it very easy to see where the tab's going, and even provides this book with a sleazy tip—see "Indent to Here," in Chapter 3, "Text and Type."

FIGURE 1-88
Tracking
tab movement

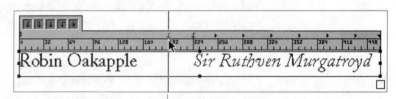

Vertical rule tracks the position of tabs as you drag them on the tab ruler.

Show Text Handles When Ruler Is Off. If you've turned the Text Ruler off (by pressing Command-/ or Ctrl-/), turning this option on displays the selection handles of a text block as you edit the text in that text block (FreeHand always displays text block handles when you select the text block with the Pointer tool). When this option is turned off, and you've turned off the Text Ruler, Free-Hand won't display a text block's selection handles while you're editing text (see Figure 1-89).

FIGURE 1-89
Displaying or hiding
text block handles

Editing text with the Show Text Handles When Text Ruler Is Off option turned on.

Editing text with the Show Text Handles When Text Ruler Is Off option turned off.

If you find you're frequently resizing text block as you edit text, and you prefer to work without displaying the Text Ruler, you might want to turn this option on (see Chapter 3, "Text and Type," for more on working with the Text Ruler).

New Text Containers Auto-Expand. What's a default-sized text container? It's what you get when you *click* (as opposed to *drag*) the Text tool (see "Creating Text Blocks," in Chapter 3, "Text and Type"). If you're typing captions or other one-line blocks of text, and you want the text blocks to be the size of the text, turn this option on, then create text blocks by clicking the Text tool. When you turn this option off, clicking the text tool produces text blocks 18 picas wide by about 12 picas tall. In either case, dragging the Text tool gives you the ability to create text blocks of any width and height.

Display Font Preview. When you turn this option on, FreeHand displays a small preview of the selected text (or a default text string, if no text is selected) when you select a font using the Font pop-up menu in the Character Inspector (see Figure 1-90).

FIGURE 1-90
Font preview

When you turn on the Display Font Preview option, FreeHand shows an example of the font you select from the Font pop-up menu.

Smart Quotes. Using "typewriter" quotation marks and apostrophes (" and ') instead of their "typographic" equivalents is one of the hallmarks of amateur desktop publishing design. On the Macintosh, it's sometimes difficult to remember what keys to press to get the preferred marks (press Option-Shift-] to produce an apostrophe), and on Windows systems it's downright painful (Alt-0144 will give you an apostrophe, for example). When you turn on the Smart Quotes option, and you can have FreeHand enter the correct marks for you as you type. You can also choose from a variety of different "international" styles using the Define Quotes pop-up menu (see Figure 1-91).

FIGURE 1-91
Smart quotes

Choose the quotation marks you want to use.

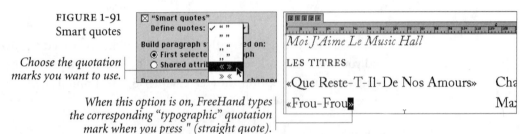

When this option is on, FreeHand types the corresponding "typographic" quotation mark when you press " (straight quote).

Build Paragraph Styles Based On. When you're creating styles, and have multiple paragraphs selected, FreeHand needs to know whether you want to create a style based on all the paragraphs in the selection (turn on the Shared Attributes option), or on only the first paragraph in the selection (use the FreeHand first Selected Paragraph option).

If you choose the Shared Attributes option, you run the risk (or accrue the advantage, depending on your point of view) of creating paragraph styles that lack some attributes—if, for example, the paragraphs in your selection have more than one leading, your style won't include a leading value—which means that applying the style won't affect the leading of the paragraphs you're applying it to. While this has some uses, it might not be what you want (see "Defining Styles" in Chapter 3, "Text and Type").

Dragging a Paragraph Style Changes. If you apply styles by dragging and dropping (see "Applying Styles" in Chapter 3, "Text and Type"), you can choose whether the style you're applying affects only the paragraph you dropped it on (turn on the A Single Paragraph option), or affects all of the paragraphs in the text block (turn on The Entire Text Container option).

Document

The options in the Document Preferences dialog box (see Figure 1-92) change the way FreeHand opens and creates publications.

Restore View When Opening Document. When this option is off, FreeHand displays page one of your publication at fit in Window view when you open it; when it's on, FreeHand returns to the view (or views) you were using when you last saved it (that is, it returns you to the same page and the same zoom level).

FIGURE 1-92
Document Preferences
dialog box

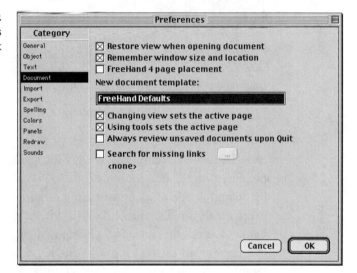

Remember Window Size and Location. This option is a lot like the previous one. Do you want FreeHand to open your documents to a default window size and window position, or do you want your documents opened with windows the same as they were the last time you saved the publication? You choose.

FreeHand 4 Page Placement. FreeHand 8 features a larger pasteboard than FreeHand 4. This is great, until you export a FreeHand 8 publication in the FreeHand 4 format. What happens to all of the extra space on the pasteboard? It goes away, taking with it any pages that won't fit on FreeHand 4's pasteboard. If you plan to export documents in the FreeHand 4 file format, turn this option on—you'll then see an area marked off in the lower-left of the pasteboard (in the Document Inspector's thumbnail view of the pasteboard). This area is the same size as FreeHand 4's pasteboard, and any pages you drag inside this area will appear in any FreeHand 4 document you export (see Figure 1-93).

FIGURE 1-93
FreeHand 4
page placement

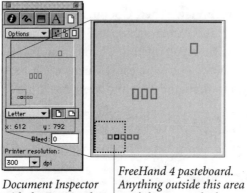

Document Inspector with the FreeHand 4 Page Placement option turned on.

FreeHand 4 pasteboard. Anything outside this area won't be exported when you export a FreeHand 4 publication.

Document Inspector with the FreeHand 4 Page Placement option turned off.

New Document Template. What's the name of the template file FreeHand bases new publications on? Whatever you enter here. By default, FreeHand's template file is named "FreeHand Defaults" (Macintosh) or "Defaults.ft8" (Windows), but you can change that name to anything you want. The name you enter here must match the name of an existing file, and that file must have been saved as a template. If the names don't match, or if FreeHand can't find the file, or if the file wasn't saved as a template, FreeHand will create new publications based on the original, default settings.

Tip:
Oops!

It's driving you crazy. You keep changing the default template, but your new documents don't seem to be picking up the changes! What's going on?

It's likely that the template file's been renamed or deleted—go check the Default Template for New Documents field. Is there a filename in it? If not, enter one. If so, does that filename exactly match what you've been calling your template file? If not, change the name so that it matches, and create a new publication. The new publication appears with your new default settings in effect.

Tip:
Working
with Multiple
Defaults Files

Imagine that you have two clients. Each client has their own set of logos, their own favorite typeface, and their own corporate colors. While you could load your defaults file with everything you need to work on publications for either client, you'll have to make some compromises (do new files start off with the font favored by Client A or Client B?), and it can get confusing (is that a color I use for Client A, or is it Client B's?). Wouldn't it be great if you could have two default files—one for Client A and one for Client B?

Create two template files, each containing the different settings. When you want to change defaults files, enter the new defaults file name in the Default Template for New Documents field of the Expert Document Preferences dialog box. From that point on, each new publication will be based on the template file you specify. Want to change it? Go enter another template name in the field.

The page highlighted in the Document Inspector is the active page.

Changing View Sets the Active Page. The "active page" is the page selected in the thumbnail view of the pasteboard shown in the Document Inspector. When you turn on Changing View Sets the Active Page, FreeHand sets the active page to the page taking up the largest percentage of your publication window—which might or might not be the page you're working on. Since the active page determines the effect of the choices on the Magnification submenu of the View menu (or their keyboard equivalents) and the effect of the "Select All" command, you can end up jumping to some other page—and away from your work—when you have this option turned on.

When this option is turned off, you set the active page by clicking the thumbnail of the page in the Document Inspector.

Using Tools Sets the Active Page. This option, like the last one, controls which page is active. Unlike the last option, this one's pretty useful—it usually makes sense to have FreeHand set the active page to the page you're working on.

Always Review Unsaved Documents Upon Quit. Are you sick of having FreeHand ask if you want to review unsaved publications when you quit? If so, turn this option off.

Search for Missing Links. In FreeHand 5.5, losing a link to an image you stored outside a publication (rather than embedding it in the publication—see Chapter 4, "Importing and Exporting") was a serious problem. Sometimes, you'd have to import the image all over again. These days, you can click the Search for Missing Links button to locate any imported graphics files you've misplaced, and, at the same time, update the publication's links to those images.

Import/Export

On the Macintosh, you'll see two options in the Preferences list—"Import," and "Export," each of which brings up a dialog box. In Windows, you'll see a single tab, "Import/Export." The options in the dialog boxes are about the same, so I'll present them here in the order in which they appear in the Windows version of the dialog box (see Figure 1-94).

FIGURE 1-94
Import/Export
Preferences dialog box

Convert Editable EPS When Imported. FreeHand can open a wide variety of EPS formats and convert their contents to editable FreeHand objects. In general, these converted files print faster than placed EPS files—and they're editable, to boot (see "Importing EPS Graphics," in Chapter 4, "Importing and Exporting"). When you turn on the Convert Editable EPS When Imported option, FreeHand converts the objects in imported EPS files into editable elements, just as it would if you opened the files using the Open command.

What's the difference? You save a step. When you use "Open," FreeHand opens the file as a new, untitled publication—which means you'll have to select, copy, and then paste the objects into your current publication. When you use "Import," the converted objects appear as a group in your current publication.

Embed Images and EPS Upon Import. By default, FreeHand does not store imported images or EPS graphics in your publications when you import them. Instead, FreeHand establishes a link to the file on disk. When the time comes to print or export the file, Free-Hand goes out to the linked file and gets the information it needs. If you'd rather store ("embed") the file in your FreeHand publication, turn this option on. Your publication will increase in size by the size of the files—in effect, you end up storing the files twice. Still, it means you have only one file to worry about.

Save File Thumbnails. Turn this option on, and you'll be able to see small preview images of files when you select them in the Open, Import, or Links Info dialog boxes (see Figure 1-95). Bear in mind, however, that displaying these thumbnails can make for slightly slower scrolling through the lists of files shown in the affected dialog boxes.

FIGURE 1-95
Thumbnail view

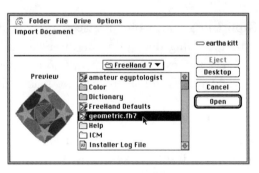

When you turn on the Save File Thumbnails option, you can see a preview of a file before you open or import it.

DXF Import (Macintosh only). The way to import CAD drawings (created by, for example, Autocad) into FreeHand is to save them in the DXF format. When you import a DXF file, you need to have some control over the way that FreeHand interprets the objects in the file. Turn on the Import Invisible Block Attributes option when you want to import DXF objects that have no stroke or fill.

Turn on the Convert White Strokes to Black and the Convert White Fills to Black when you know that the DXF file contains objects containing white strokes and white fills you want to convert to black (you'll use one or both of these settings when the CAD file used to generate the DXF file has been set up for printing blueprints).

Convert PICT Patterns to Grays (Macintosh only). When you import object PICT files, such as those created by MacDraw or Canvas, FreeHand needs to know what to do with any PICT patterns used to represent shades of gray (like those you see when you choose Pattern from the pop-up menu in the fill Inspector). In my opinion, you should turn this preference on—and leave it that way.

PICT patterns are no substitute for real gray shades, and they don't print reliably on imagesetters. If you've just got to have those PICT patterns, go ahead and leave this option unchecked, but don't say I didn't warn you (for more on patterned fills, see "Patterned fills" in Chapter 2, "Drawing").

Note that this option has nothing to do with bitmap PICT files— bitmap PICT files are always converted to TIFF when you import or open them (for more on this conversion, see Chapter 4, "Importing and Exporting").

Export EPS with Color Previews (Windows only). Just as you'd expect, turning this option on gives you color preview images in EPS files you export; with this option turned off, FreeHand's EPS preview images will be bi-level (i.e., black-and-white) bitmaps.

Bitmap PICT Previews (Macintosh only). When this option is off, Macintosh EPS files you export from FreeHand contain object (or vector) PICT previews—almost like using a MacDraw file for a screen preview. Object PICT previews provide more accurate previews than bitmaps—but they can also take substantially longer to draw on your screen (depending on the file), and can be larger than a TIFF preview of the same graphic.

Bitmap Export. If you've exported FreeHand objects as images (by choosing an image format in the Export Document dialog box), you've probably noticed that you can set options for the images as you export them (for more on exporting FreeHand elements as images, see Converting FreeHand Objects to Bitmaps," in Chapter 4, "Importing and Exporting"). If you want, you can set default options for image export by clicking the Bitmap Export button. FreeHand displays the Bitmap Export Defaults dialog box (just as it does when you click the Options button in the Export Document dialog box).

Include Portfolio Preview (Macintosh only). If you want to add your exported FreeHand files to an Extensis Portfolio (formerly called "Fetch") database, check this option. If you don't, leave it unchecked—the previews make your exported files larger.

When you check this option, you can choose how large you want to make the preview—using the Bitmap Portfolio Preview Size option. As you'd expect, larger previews are more accurate representations of your file, and they also take up more space on disk. As you do this, remember that most people look at previews in Portfolio in Thumbnail view, so you can probably get by with a small (say, 25 percent) preview.

Name of UserPrep file. FreeHand's UserPrep files give you the ability to customize your PostScript printing. It's pretty simple—if FreeHand finds the file named in the Name of UserPrep file field inside the FreeHand folder, it sends the contents of the file to your printer prior to sending your print job. Technically speaking, the contents of the UserPrep file are merged into the PostScript output stream immediately after FreeHand downloads FreeHand's user dictionaries, but before FreeHand sends any of the document you're printing. You can control which, if any, UserPrep file gets sent by entering the file's name here. (See Chapter 8, "PostScript," for more on what you can do with a UserPrep file).

Override Output Options when Printing (Macintosh only). Why would you ever want to override the Image Data options you've set in the Output Options dialog box? I don't think you would—but you might if you're printing to a proof printer but exporting EPS files for use on an OPI-compliant prepress system. In this case, you'd probably be using the None (OPI Comments Only) option in the Output Options dialog box. By turning on the Always Binary Image Data option here, you'd be able to print images on your proof printer without changing the settings in the Output Options dialog box. (For more on the Output Options dialog box, see Chapter 9, "Printing.")

Clipboard Output Formats. When you switch to another application, or drag FreeHand elements to another application, or quit FreeHand, you've probably seen the "Converting Clipboard" message go by on your screen. What's going on? FreeHand is rendering the contents of its internal Clipboard to the system's Clipboard. This means that FreeHand has to convert FreeHand's native (AGX2) format into formats other applications can use, such as PICT (Macintosh), BMP (Windows), WMF (Windows), RTF, text-only, and Adobe Illustrator—just in case you want to paste objects you've copied from FreeHand into another application.

If you think this process takes too long, you can turn off some or all of the conversions by checking the corresponding options. Don't turn off the FreeHand option if you're copying FreeHand objects to a library (such as the Macintosh Scrapbook) for future use, and don't turn off the Adobe Illustrator option if you want to copy FreeHand paths to Photoshop.

Spelling

One of the great innovations of the word processing age is the spelling checker. FreeHand has one, and has preference settings to match (see Figure 1-96).

Find Duplicate Words. Do you want FreeHand's spelling checker to let you know when it finds duplicate words in your text? ("He said he had had it up to here," for example, would produce an alert.) If so, turn this option on.

Find Capitalization Errors. You can also ask FreeHand's spelling checker to look for possible errors in the capitalization of characters in your text. When this option is on, FreeHand will warn you if it encounters a lowercase letter at the start of a sentence.

FIGURE 1-96
Spelling Preferences
dialog box

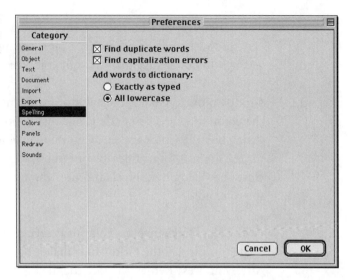

Add Words to Dictionary. You know lots of words that can't be found in FreeHand's spelling dictionary. Your name, for example. Or, almost certainly, *my* name. If you're tired of having FreeHand's spelling checker object to a word you frequently use in your publications, then the thing to do is enter that word in your user dictionary (see "Adding Words to FreeHand's User Dictionary" in Chapter 3, "Text and Type").

But wait—do you want Freehand to consider the case of the word you're entering? That is, do you want FreeHand to alert you to words that have the same spelling, but aren't capitalized in the same way as you entered them? That's where the Exactly as Typed and All Lowercase options come in. If you want FreeHand to check both the spelling and the capitalization of the word you're entering, turn on the Exactly As Typed option (then enter the word as you want it capitalized). If you want FreeHand to ignore the capitalization of the word, use the All Lowercase button.

I know—"all lowercase" sounds like FreeHand's spelling checker will flag a word as misspelled if its first character is capitalized (because it's in a title or at the start of a sentence, for example). That isn't how it works. Try to think of the buttons as "Case sensitive" and "Case insensitive." That makes a little more sense (not that this wording is FreeHand's fault alone—Word, PageMaker, and XPress all say the same thing).

Colors   The options in the Colors Preferences dialog box (see Figure 1-97) control FreeHand's user interface for working with colors—these settings do not change the way your colors are defined.

Guide Color. To change the color of FreeHand's ruler guides, click the color swatch. The Guide Color dialog box appears (I call this dialog box the Color Picker). Choose the color in you want to use for the nonprinting guides in your publication and press Return to close the dialog box. FreeHand uses the new color for displaying the ruler guides.

Grid Color. To change the color of FreeHand's grid, click the color swatch to display the Grid Color dialog box, then choose a color. After you press Return to close the dialog box, FreeHand displays the grid in the new color (when the grid is visible).

Colors List Shows. One of FreeHand's great features—the ability to apply a stroke and/or fill to the background of a text block—ends up causing a some confusion. When you select a text block, should the fill and Stroke buttons at the top of the Colors palette show the colors applied to the text block, or should they show the fill and stroke you've applied to the text itself? In FreeHand 4, the Colors palette settled on the former (the container) rather than

FIGURE 1-97
Colors preferences

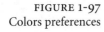

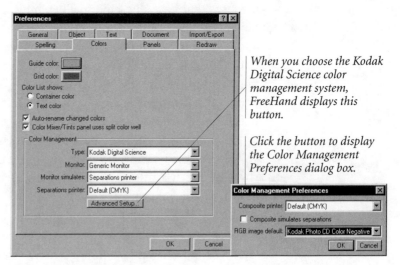

When you choose the Kodak Digital Science color management system, FreeHand displays this button.

Click the button to display the Color Management Preferences dialog box.

the latter (the text). In FreeHand 8, you can decide for yourself. Choose the Container Color option to have the Colors palette show the colors of the fill and stroke applied to the text block; choose Text Color to work with the fill and stroke applied to the text itself (see Figure 1-98).

FIGURE 1-98
Container color
versus text color

When you select the Container Color option, the Colors palette displays the color of the text block when you select the text block with the Pointer tool...

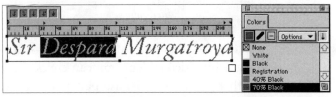

...and displays the color of the text when you select the text with the Text tool.

When you choose the Text Color option, FreeHand displays the color of the text in the Colors palette, regardless of the tool you use to select the text. While this is usually what you want, it makes it impossible to quickly apply a color to the text block's background.

Auto-Rename Colors. If this option were called "Auto-Rename Auto-Named Changed Colors," it'd make (a little) more sense. It'd also be harder to say. If you check this option, FreeHand renames any automatically-named (that is, colors you've created but haven't typed a name for) colors as they're edited. If you add 10% cyan to a color FreeHand named "20C 50M 0Y 10K," FreeHand will change the color's name to "30C 50M 0Y 10K." If you don't want FreeHand to do this, turn this option off—but bear in mind that the names might not reflect the color values.

Color Mixer/Tints Panel Uses Split Color Well. If, as you're editing a color, you'd like to see a swatch of the original color next to a swatch of the edited color, turn this option on. It splits the color well at the bottom of the Color Mixer into two sections—one side showing the original color, the other showing the edited color (see Figure 1-99).

FIGURE 1-99
Split color well

When you turn on the Split Color Well option, the Color Mixer looks like this when you're editing a color.

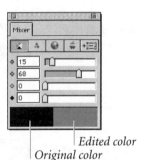 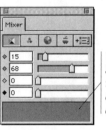

When you turn off the Split Color Well option, the Color Mixer shows only the edited (or current) color.

Edited color
Original color

Dither 8-Bit Colors (Macintosh only). If you're working with an eight-bit video system, you can check this box to make FreeHand dither colors (that is, use patterns of different-colored pixels) to represent the colors in your publication. These dither patterns do not affect printing. Why does FreeHand need to use dithering? Because an eight-bit video system has only 256 colors available—which means it's easy to pick a color your system can't display.

Leave this box unchecked, and FreeHand will use the eight-bit color that's closest to the color you're working with.

This one's up to you—dithered colors more accurately represent the colors you've chosen, but you might not like the pixel patterns it creates. In any case, FreeHand always uses dithering to represent colors in graduated and radial fills on eight-bit systems.

Color Management. Color management systems try to keep track of the differences between the systems you use to produce and print your publication—your scanner, monitor, proofing printers and systems, and the type of printing process you use. Every one of these devices has a different method of reproducing color—and a different range of color it can reproduce—and the job of a color management system is to make the differences between the different rendering devices *predictable*. Note that this doesn't necessarily mean that colors will look the *same* from device to device—while that's the ideal, it's not usually possible given the current state of color technology.

How do color management systems know what the differences are between rendering devices? They use "device profiles," files that describe a device's color characteristics. The Kodak Digital Science color management System included with FreeHand can use device profiles that conform to standards set by the International Color Consortium (ICC). In addition to the device profiles included with FreeHand, you can use Apple's ColorSync device profiles.

Use the options on the Type pop-up menu to choose which type of color management system you want to use, or to turn Free-Hand's color management off altogether.

◆ Adjust Display Colors. Choose this option when you want to make manual adjustments to FreeHand's display of color. This isn't exactly "color management," but it gives you a way to do things you can't ordinarily do—especially with spot colors (see "Adjusting Display Colors," in Chapter 6, "Color").

◆ Kodak Color Tables. A version of the Kodak Digital Science color management system (see below) that doesn't rely on your having the Kodak Digital Science system extensions installed. When you select this option, you won't be able to assign source profiles to imported images, though you can change the default source profile using the Kodak Digital Science color management system.

◆ Kodak Digital Science. A complete color management system for FreeHand. When you choose this option, Free-Hand adjusts the display and printing of colors in your publications (even the colors in imported images) according to a series of device profiles (for image source, monitor, separations printer, and composite printer).

◆ None. Turns color management off.

Turn color management on (choose "Kodak Color Tables" or "Kodak Digital Science") when you want to:

◆ Have FreeHand color-separate imported RGB images (see "Separating Color Images," in Chapter 6, "Color").

◆ Convert FreeHand objects to images (see "Converting FreeHand Objects to Bitmaps," in Chapter 4, "Importing and Exporting").

◆ Use Hexachrome colors or create separations for printing using the Hexachrome HiFi printing process (for more on Hexachrome, see Chapter 7, "Printing").

Turn color management off (choose "None") when you're creating publications that won't be printed in color, or when you're preparing artwork for on-screen use.

For a more complete description of FreeHand's color management features, see Chapter 6, "Color."

Panels The settings in the Panels Preferences dialog box tell FreeHand how you'd like to deal with a few small-but-important issues having to do with FreeHand's user interface (see Figure 1-100).

Remember the Location of Zipped Panels. When you turn this option on, FreeHand keeps track of the location of a palette's title bar when you zip the palette. Unzip the palette, drag it to some new location, and then click the zip box to zip the palette back up again, and the zipped title bar of the palette reappears in the position it was in before you unzipped and moved the palette.

FIGURE 1-100
Panels Preferences
dialog box

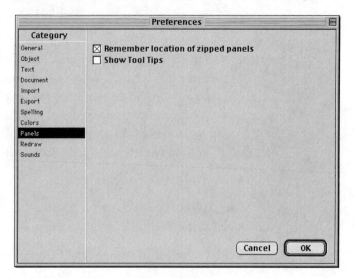

This is useful, because it means you can assign a "storage" area for your palettes, where you keep a stack of zipped title bars, and then set each palette to open to some more useful location on your screen. Park the palettes in some part of the screen that you rarely use, then set the unzipped palettes to appear in the areas you like to work in.

This wouldn't do us much good, of course, if we had to drag our cursor across the screen to unzip the palettes—but you don't have to use the zip box to unzip the palettes. Just press the keyboard shortcut for a particular palette that's zipped, and FreeHand will unzip the palette and move it to the pre-set location.

Use this technique consistently, and you'll always *know* where a particular palette is going to show up when you call for it.

Show Tool Tips. When you turn this option on, FreeHand displays a short description of a user interface feature (a button, field, or other control) when you leave the cursor over the control for a few seconds (see Figure 1-101). Not all tools display a tip.

FIGURE 1-101
Tool tips

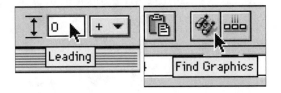

Redraw   The options in the Redraw Preferences dialog box control the way that FreeHand draws objects on your screen (see Figure 1-102). Many of these preferences can speed up—or slow down—the time it takes FreeHand to draw the screen.

Better (but Slower) Display. When the Better (but Slower) Display option is turned off, FreeHand draws graduated and radial fills on screen more rapidly, using fewer gray steps to render them. Turn it on to see a better representation of your fills on screen. This option has no effect on the printing of the fills.

Display Text Effects. Turn this option on to display any of Free-Hand's text effects you've applied to text in your publication. Turn

FIGURE 1-102
Redraw Preferences
dialog box

Preferences

Category

General
Object
Text
Document
Import
Export
Spelling
Colors
Panels
Redraw
Sounds

☒ **Better (but slower) display**
☒ **Display text effects**
☐ **Redraw while scrolling**
☐ **High-resolution image display**
☐ **Display overprinting objects**

Greek type below: 8   pixels
Preview drag: 10   items

Cancel   OK

this option off, and Freehand displays the text at the correct size
and leading, but without the effects. If the text effects extend
beyond the text block (Zoom Text often does, for example), the
selection rectangle shows the extent of the effect when you move
the text block. Turning this option on shows you your text effects,
but slows down your screen display (see Figure 1-103).

FIGURE 1-103
Display Text
Effects option

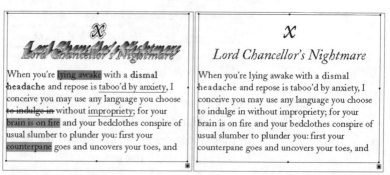

Display Text Effects option on   *Display Text Effects option off*

Redraw While Scrolling. If you want FreeHand to redraw while
you're scrolling, check this option. If you'd rather FreeHand waited
to redraw the screen until you've finished scrolling, leave it unchecked. This option affects both scrolling using the scroll bars
and scrolling using the Grabber Hand (for more on using the Grabber Hand to scroll, see "Moving Around in Your Publication," later
in this chapter). FreeHand always redraws the screen when you

scroll while you're dragging an object. Turning this option on makes scrolling slower.

High-Resolution Image Display. When you turn this option on, FreeHand gets its information about how to render an image (a TIFF, usually) from the original file that's linked to your FreeHand publication, which means that FreeHand renders the best possible display of the image for your current magnification level (see Figure 1-104). With this option turned off, FreeHand constructs a low-resolution screen version of the image and uses it for display at all magnification levels.

The tradeoff is the speed of screen redraw. High-resolution images can take forever to draw on your screen. Given this, it's a good idea to leave this option unchecked until those times when you absolutely must see all of the detail in the image.

FIGURE 1-104
High- and low-
resolution TIFF
display options

Low-resolution TIFF display   *High-resolution TIFF display*

Display Overprinting Objects. When you turn on this option, Free-Hand displays a pattern—a repeated "O"—inside any fill or stroke that's set to overprint. With this option on, you can quickly see what's set to overprint and what's not (see Figure 1-105).

FIGURE 1-105
Displaying
overprinting

*All of the objects shown
are set to overprint.*

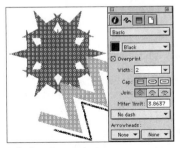 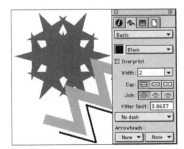

*Display Overprinting
Objects option turned on.*   *Display Overprinting
Objects option turned off.*

I don't leave this option on—I find the pattern distracting, and it looks too much like the pattern of repeating Cs FreeHand uses to denote a Custom fill (see "Custom fills," in Chapter 2, "Drawing"). But it's a great option to turn on just before you send your file out for imagesetting.

Greek Type Below N Pixels. This option displays type as a gray bar if it's shorter, in pixels, than the value you enter. As you zoom close to the text, you'll see the characters in the text block again (see Figure 1-106). This happens because the type's taller, in pixels, at larger magnifications.

FIGURE 1-106
Greeked type

24-point type at 100% view; Greek Type Below set to six pixels.

24-point type at 100% view; Greek Type Below set to 100 pixels.

The advantage of using this option is that greeked type redraws much faster than the actual characters, speeding up your screen display. This option applies to both Preview and Keyline views.

Tip:
Greek All (or
Almost All)

You can always choose to greek all (almost, anyway) of the text in your document at most views by entering "200"—the largest value you can enter—in the Greek Type Below field. This will greek all type below 200 points at 100% view, and all type below 400 points at most Fit to Page views (the exact magnification of the Fit to Page view depends on the size of your page).

Preview Drag. When you drag an object quickly, FreeHand displays only a box showing the general dimensions of the object. If you pause slightly before you drag the object, however, FreeHand displays the object itself as you drag (see Figure 1-107). When the value in the Preview Drag field is one (FreeHand's default), FreeHand always displays a box (that is, not the objects themselves) when you're dragging more than one object. Increase this value,

FIGURE 1-107
Preview Drag

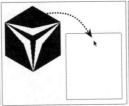
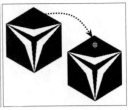

Select the object you want to move.

Drag quickly, and FreeHand displays only the object's bounding box as you drag.

Wait a second (or tap Option/Alt) and Free-Hand displays the object as you move it.

and you'll be able to see more objects as you drag them, but the amount of time you'll have to wait before FreeHand redraws the objects increases commensurately. You can enter values from zero to 32,000 (don't even think about it!) in this field.

Tip:
Viewing
Objects as You
Drag Them

Tap the Option/Alt key as you start to drag an object or objects, and FreeHand displays the objects as you drag them (don't hold down Option/Alt, as this creates a copy of the objects you're dragging). It's a temporary way of turning on Preview Drag. So instead of increasing the value in the Preview Drag field, leave it at one—or even set it to zero—and tap Option/Alt when you want to see objects as you drag them.

Sounds
(Macintosh Only)

Choose Sounds from the Preferences list, and FreeHand displays the Sounds Preferences dialog box (see Figure 1-108). When you check Snap Sounds Enabled, FreeHand plays a sound when a snap happens. When you're dragging an object toward a ruler guide, for example, you might want to hear it snap into position.

Snap to Grid, Snap to Point, Snap to H(orizontal)-Guide, Snap to V(ertical)-Guide. If you want to hear different sounds for different snaps, you can choose the sounds you want here—all of the sounds currently in your system appear in the pop-up menus. If you want to audition a particular sound before committing yourself to hearing it thousands of times, select the sound from the pop-up menu and press the appropriate Play button.

Snap Sounds Enabled. Turn on this checkbox to enable the snap sounds you've selected above.

FIGURE 1-108
Sounds Preferences
dialog box
(Macintosh only)

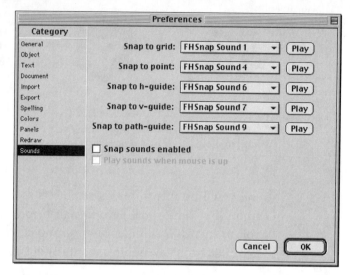

Play Sounds When Mouse Is Up. Turn on this option if you want to hear the snap sounds whenever your cursor crosses a snap point, regardless of whether you're moving or sizing an object. This is actually useful when you're trying to draw something on a grid— you'll hear a sound if you're in the right place to start drawing. Most of the time, however, this makes FreeHand sound like an out-of-control video game.

Secret Preferences

FreeHand keeps track your preferences (all of the options you've chosen in the Preferences dialog box) and the current state of the FreeHand environment (the location of the palettes, dialog boxes, and toolbars appear, for example) in a text file named "FreeHand 8 Preferences" on the Macintosh, "FHprefs" in Windows. On the Macintosh, you'll find the file in the Preferences folder inside your system folder. In Windows, you'll find the file inside your Free-Hand folder.

The FreeHand preferences file is a text-only file, so you can open and edit it with any text editor or word processor. Why would you want to do that? Because you can set "secret" preferences in there that you cannot set any other way. Read on, and you'll see.

To edit the FreeHand preferences file, quit FreeHand, then open the file using your favorite text editor or word processor. When you open the file, you'll see something like the following text (I say "something like this" because your file will probably look different—the order in which the items are written into the file isn't significant, and FreeHand reshuffles items according to its whim).

```
% FreeHand Preferences File
(Modal27320Vis) (No)
(Modal27320ZoomPos) (147 326 243 506)
(Modal27320Pos) (147 326 243 506)
(TabInspMgrDocksTo) ()
(TabInspMgrZoom) (No)
(TabInspMgrZoomPos) (121 652 143 776)
(TabInspMgrVis) (Yes)
(TabInspMgrPos) (121 652 360 776)
(Modal27320Zoom) (No)
```

The file is quite a bit longer than this—I've just shown the first ten lines to give you an idea of what it's like. While the text above looks a bit daunting, it's really pretty simple. The lines starting with "(Modal27320" control the appearances of one of FreeHand's dialog boxes. "(Modal27320Vis) (No)" tells FreeHand that this dialog box isn't currently visible; "(Modal27320ZoomPos) (147 326 243 506)" sets the location of the dialog box when it's "zoomed" (or minimized); and "(Modal27320Pos) (147 326 243 506)" sets the location of the dialog box at its full size (these coordinates and the coordinates for the "zoomed" version of the dialog box are the same because this particular dialog box can't be resized).

Following each preference keyword (such as "(XFishCurrH)"), you'll see a value—it's usually a number (such as "(62)"), or a true/false switch ("(Yes)" or "(No)"). "(XFishCurrH)" means you ordered the fish curry, extra hot (no, not really—it controls one of the Fisheye Lens Xtra's parameters).

There's no need to edit most of the settings in this file—if you want to change the location of a dialog box, you can simply drag it to a new location. If you want to change one of FreeHand's standard preferences, it's easier to do using FreeHand's Preferences dialog box. The reason you might want to open and edit this file are the "hidden" preferences it contains. I don't know all of them, but I've managed to figure a few out.

Beyond the
Maximum Zoom

How close is close enough? FreeHand, by default, can zoom in to a maximum magnification of 256x%—but what if you need to get closer to your work? There's a hidden preference just for you. Scroll through the FreeHand preferences file until you see the following line.

```
(MaxMagnification) (256)
```

Enter a new, larger number in place of "256" to set a new maximum magnification. You can enter values up to 16384—meaning 1,638,400 times actual size. At that magnification, my 832-pixel wide (17") screen covers an area a little smaller than one tenth of a point (see Figure 1-109).

FIGURE 1-109
Secret
Maximum
Zoom

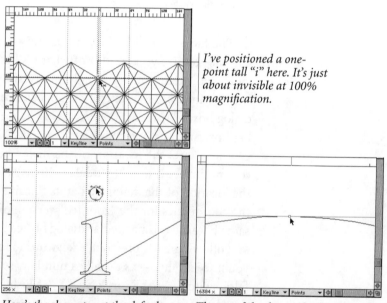

I've positioned a one-point tall "i" here. It's just about invisible at 100% magnification.

Here's the character at the default maximum magnification of 256x (25,600% of actual size).

The top of the dot on the "i" at the "secret" maximum magnification of 16384x (1,638,400 times actual size)!

Converting
Type to Outlines
as You Print

If you need to print to a non-PostScript printer (such as many inexpensive color inkjet printers), you've probably discovered that you can get your PostScript fonts to print by converting them to paths (see "Converting Text to Paths" in Chapter 3, "Text and Type") before you print the file. The only problem with this approach is that you lose the ability to work with the text as text (that is, you won't be able to edit it using the Text tool). To get around this problem, you've probably learned to undo the conversion after you print. It's a bother. Instead of jumping through these hoops, you can have FreeHand convert the type to paths *as you print.* Find the following line in your FreeHand preferences file.

```
(ConvertTextNonPS) (No)
```

Change the "No" to "Yes" and save the file. When you restart FreeHand, any PostScript Type 1 fonts in your publications will be converted to outlines as you print. This process affects only the information that's sent to the printer—nothing in your publication is affected. When you want to print to a PostScript printer, turn this option off (that is, set it back to "No") again.

Changing the Clipboard Import Order (Macintosh Only)

When you copy objects to the Clipboard, your applications usually place their information on the Clipboard in more than one data format. That way, when you paste from one application to another, the application you're pasting into can choose which format it wants to work with. When you copy an object from FreeHand, FreeHand renders the object into AGD2 (FreeHand's native data format), ASCII (text-only), Rich Text Format (RTF), AICB (Adobe Illustrator), PICT (on the Macintosh), and LRG (xRes). When you paste an object from the Clipboard into FreeHand, FreeHand prefers some data formats over others. By default, FreeHand looks first for AGD2, if it finds this format on the Clipboard, that data is what gets pasted. If it doesn't find anything on the Clipboard in its native format, it looks for LRG, AICB, EPS, RTF, PICT, and ASCII, in that order.

```
(PBReadOrder) (DataTypeAGD2 DataTypeLRG DataTypeAICB DataTypeEPS
DataTypeRTF DataTypeMacPICT DataTypeASCII)
```

Why would you want to change the order of preference FreeHand uses when pasting? Because you're not getting the format you want, even though you know it's on the Clipboard. When you copy objects from PageMaker, for example, FreeHand pastes the RTF text PageMaker put on the Clipboard. In many cases, I'd rather have FreeHand convert the PICT PageMaker put on the Clipboard. To get FreeHand to do this, I can rearrange the order of the data types in this line, moving PICT to some point before RTF.

```
(PBReadOrder) (DataTypeAGD2 DataTypeLRG DataTypeAICB DataTypeEPS
DataTypeMacPICT DataTypeRTF DataTypeASCII)
```

The next time you paste objects into FreeHand from PageMaker, you'll get all of the objects (PageMaker-drawn lines, rectangles, ellipses, polygons included), rather than just an incorrectly formatted version of the text (see Figure 1-110).

FIGURE 1-110
Pasting Objects
from PageMaker

Layout in PageMaker.

What you'll get, by default, when you paste the PageMaker objects into FreeHand.

What you'll get when you paste if you change the "PBReadOrder" preference to prefer PICT over RTF.

FreeHand Xtras

Many applications support *plug-ins*, small programs that run inside a "host" program and add features to the program. Plug-ins go by a different names: PageMaker, Illustrator, and Photoshop have all standardized on "plug-ins"; Quark XPress users are familiar with "Xtensions"; FreeHand's plug-ins are called "Xtras." Xtras can add tools, palettes, dialog boxes, and other features to FreeHand.

Unless you specifically direct the FreeHand installation program not to install them, you'll see a variety of "in the box" Xtras on FreeHand's menus. You know that tool you've been drawing arcs with? It's an Xtra. How about the Smudge tool or the Fisheye Lens tool? Or the Set Note palette? Or the Chart tool and Chart dialog box? They're all Xtras. We think of them as integral parts of FreeHand, but they're not.

In this book, I discuss FreeHand's basic set of Xtras according to their category. Does the Xtra create or alter a path? If so, I talk about it in Chapter 2, "Drawing." Does the Xtra change the colors inside your publication? If it does, I talk about it in Chapter 6, "Color." Other Xtras, such as the Set Note Xtra, have a more general use, so I've mentioned them in this chapter.

FreeHand's Xtras are stored in the Xtras folder in your FreeHand folder on the Macintosh; you'll find them in ~/Program Files/ Macromedia/FreeHand 8/Usenglsh/Xtras in Windows. To add a new Xtra when FreeHand isn't running, simply copy the Xtra into this folder. If you find you're not using an Xtra, you can remove it from your set of Xtras by moving it out of this folder. When you restart FreeHand, the features controlled by the Xtra won't appear.

You can use the Xtras Manager to load and unload Xtras while FreeHand is running (you couldn't do this in FreeHand 5.5—to change your set of Xtras, you had to quit, then restart FreeHand).

To load an Xtra you've copied into your Xtras folder, follow these steps (see Figure 1-111 on the following page).

1. Choose Xtras Manager from the Xtras menu. FreeHand displays the Xtras Manager dialog box.

2. Locate the Xtra in the list of Xtras, then click the Xtra's name. FreeHand displays a check mark next to the name.

3. Click the OK button to close the Xtras manager. FreeHand loads the Xtra you selected.

Xtras don't have to come from Macromedia. A growing number of third-party software developers, such as Extensis (see "Disclaimer" in the Introduction) and MetaTools, have produced Xtras for the Macintosh FreeHand (I don't know of any third-party Xtras for Windows FreeHand as I write this, but hope that some will exist by the time you read it).

Getting Help

If you installed FreeHand's online help system, you can display information on the meaning and use of specific FreeHand features.

FIGURE 1-111
Loading and
Unloading Xtras

*Imagine that you've
turned off some of the
color-related Xtras, and
want to load them
again. Choose Xtras
Manager form the
Xtras menu...*

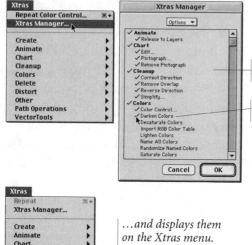

*...and FreeHand displays
the Xtras Manager dialog
box.*

*List of Xtras found in
the Xtras folder.*

*Click the Xtras you
want to load.*

*As you click, FreeHand
displays check marks
next to the Xtra names.*

*After you click the OK
button to close the Xtras
Manager dialog box,
FreeHand loads the
Xtras marked with a
check mark...*

*...and displays them
on the Xtras menu.*

*To unload an Xtra, click
the Xtras name in the
list. The check mark
disappears.*

Press Help/Shift-F1 to display the Help cursor, then click on the item you want explained (see Figure 1-112). FreeHand starts the online help system (it's a separate program) and displays text describing the item you clicked (if any such reference is available).

If you can't find the help you need using this approach, you can always look through the help system's index, or search for a specific topic. To display the help system on the Macintosh, choose Help from the Apple menu (it'll be immediately below About FreeHand). To display the help system in Windows, choose an option from the Help menu.

The Tao of FreeHand

Here are those rules I promised at the beginning of the chapter.

Keep it simple. Every path, text block, or imported object you put on a page makes it harder to print. Every time you use a clipping path, import an image, or use another font, it makes your printer

FIGURE 1-112
FreeHand Help

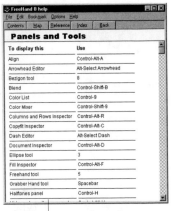

A page from the Shortcuts topic

You can look through the Index for your topic, or click the Find tab to search through the help system's titles.

work harder still. But we can't be happy (or stay employed) creating blank FreeHand pages. What can we do? With practice, we can reach an intuitive understanding of the relative complexities of each type of FreeHand object and effect. Once you have achieved this transcendental state, you will create FreeHand publications that are only as complicated as they need to be—and no more.

One of the purposes of this book is to help you develop an understanding of what's difficult for PostScript printers (especially imagesetters) to do. When you use "Paste Inside," for example, you need to be aware that the complexity (number of points and number of curves) of the enclosing path affects printing—the more complex the path, the longer it'll take to print.

Use styles. Unless you work for people who never change their minds, and you never change your mind yourself, you need the ability to change things quickly and systematically—and that's where styles really shine. If you work for people who never change their minds, and you never change your mind yourself, please give me a call—I've never met anyone like you.

Use layers. And use them systematically. Not only will you find your publications easier to work with if you've spread the publication elements over several logical layers, but you'll be able to speed up your screen display, as well. Layers can speed printing, too.

Use trapping. I can't count the number of color jobs I've seen ruined because of bad or nonexistent trapping (especially around type). See "Trapping" in Chapter 6, "Color."

Make color proofs. If you're working with process colors, it's an absolute necessity to make color proofs (Cromalins, Match Prints, or the equivalent) *from the same negatives you intend to use to print the publication* (proofs printed using composite color printers just won't cut it). Color proofs are expensive, but they're cheaper than thousands of publications printed the wrong way because the film was wrong. Believe me.

Talk to your commercial printer. This can often save you lots of time and money. The thing to remember when you're talking with your printer is that they're the experts. Don't be a jerk. Don't assume you know their job better than they do (you might, but don't assume you do). If possible, work out a printing contract for your job that spells out in exact terms what you expect of them and what they expect of you.

Talk to your imagesetting service bureau. First, ask them how they plan to print your FreeHand file. If they say they'll make an EPS of it, then print it from Quark XPress, you should move on. Once you've found a service bureau that can answer the question correctly, approach them as you would your commercial printer. A good working relationship with an imagesetting service bureau or inhouse imagesetter operator is essential.

CHAPTER

Drawing

2

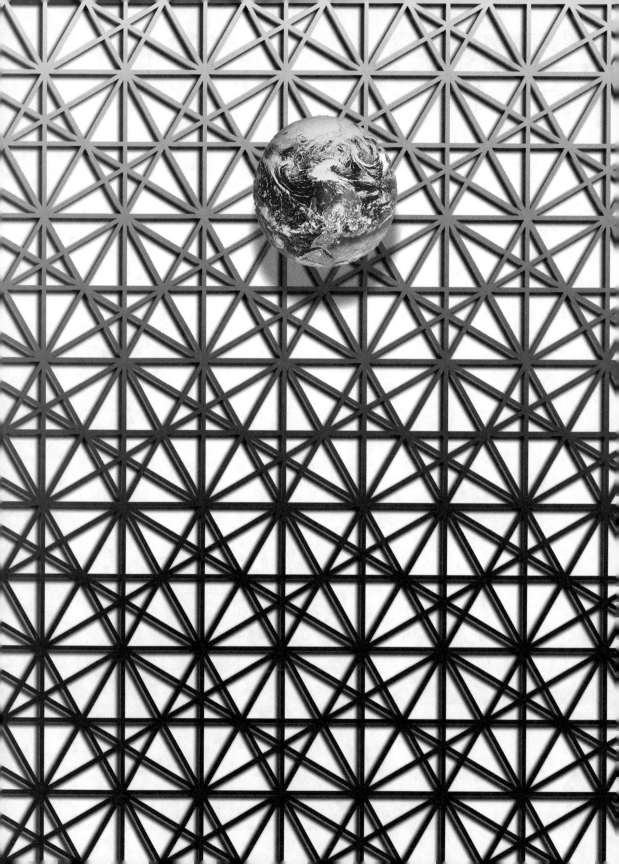

Human

beings draw pictures. The walls of caves inhabited since prehistoric times, the interiors of the tombs of the Pharaohs, and the development of desktop publishing all show that we're a kind of animal that likes to make marks on whatever we find around us. Drawing is at the center of us; it's one of the unique attributes that make us human.

Drawing is also at the heart of FreeHand. Eight of the 17 tools in the FreeHand toolbox are drawing tools, and you'll find (at least) three more in the Xtra Tools palette. Using these tools, you can draw almost anything—from straight lines and boxes to incredibly complex freeform shapes. You can create charts and graphs using the Chart tool, or trace any object using the Trace tool.

As I explained in Chapter 1, "FreeHand Basics," the paths you draw in FreeHand are made up of points, and the points are joined to each other by line segments. A FreeHand path is just like a connect-the-dots puzzle. Connect all the dots together in the right order, and you've made a picture, or part of a picture. Because points along a path have an order, or winding, you can think of each point as a milepost along the path. Or as a sign saying, "Now go this way."

The drawing tools can be divided into three types: the Rectangle, Polygon, Ellipse, Line, Arc, and Spiral tools are for drawing basic shapes; the Freehand, Pen, and Point tools draw more complex, or "freeform," paths; and the Chart, Trace, and Graphic Hose tools automate the process of drawing paths (see Figure 2-1). I'll

FIGURE 2-1
Drawing tools

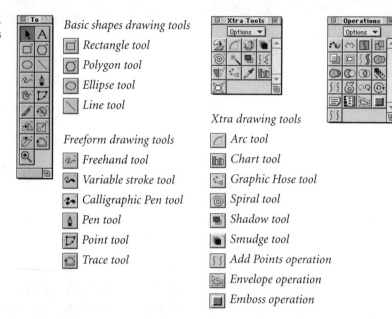

start by talking about the basic shapes tools and the freeform drawing tools, and then cover the others later in the chapter.

FreeHand also features a large number of tools for changing paths once you've drawn them. The Knife tool, Freeform tool, and a number of the Xtra tools are examples of path manipulation tools. Again, I'll cover these tools later in the chapter.

Which path drawing tools should you use? Don't worry too much about it—the basic shapes can be converted into freeform paths, and the freeform drawing tools can be used to draw basic shapes. You can draw any path with any of the drawing tools (I was once stranded on a desert island with nothing but the Polygon tool, and survived), but some tools are better at some tasks.

Basic Shapes

The basic shape tools (the Rectangle, Polygon, Ellipse, Line, Spiral, and Arc tools) don't draw anything you couldn't draw using the freeform drawing tools (discussed later in this chapter); they just make drawing certain types of paths easier. They're shortcuts.

The operation of the basic shapes tools is straightforward, but there are a few details you need to know. If you're a FreeHand ace, you might want to skip the next few paragraphs. It isn't that I'm getting paid by the word to write this (I'm not), but that I'm trying to cover all the bases. It's amazing, too, what people can miss when they're learning a software product; I've seen FreeHand gurus who weren't aware that you could turn a rectangle drawn with the rectangle tool into a rounded-corner rectangle.

You can think of the paths drawn by the Rectangle and Ellipse tools as grouped paths. These paths have a few other special properties, as well, that you can't get by grouping a path drawn with the freeform drawing tools.

◆ You can edit the corner radius of rectangles drawn using the Rectangle tool.

◆ Rectangles and ellipses have a special constraint key you can use when you resize them, as described in the section, "Resizing Rectangles and Ellipses," later in this chapter.

These magical properties disappear when you convert rectangles and ellipses into freeform paths (see "Converting Rectangles and Ellipses into Paths," below), and there's no way to convert the converted path back to its original state (apart from using Undo).

To draw a rectangle, ellipse, or polygon, follow the steps below (see Figure 2-2).

1. Select the appropriate tool (press 1 for the Rectangle tool, 2 for the Polygon tool, or 3 for the Ellipse tool).

    If you want to draw a rectangle with round (rather than square) corners, double-click the Rectangle tool. FreeHand displays the Rectangle dialog box. Set the corner radius you want, then close the dialog box and start drawing.

    To specify what type of polygon you'll be drawing, double-click the Polygon tool and choose the shape you want in the Polygon dialog box before you start drawing.

2. Position the cursor where you want one corner of the shape, or position the cursor where you want the center of the shape and hold down Option/Alt. The first method draws from one corner of the shape, the second method, draws the shape from its center.

FIGURE 2-2
Drawing basic shapes

 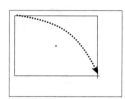 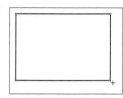

Select the basic shape tool (Rectangle, Polygon, or Ellipse)...

...and drag the tool in the publication window.

When the basic shape looks the way you want it to, stop dragging.

 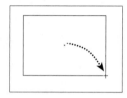 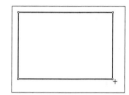

To draw from the center point of the basic shape (rather than from the corner)...

...hold down Option/Alt as you drag the tool. Polygons are always drawn from their center.

Stop dragging when the basic shape looks the way you want it to.

3. Drag. FreeHand draws a path, starting where you first held down the mouse button.

   To draw squares, hold down Shift as you drag the Rectangle tool. To draw circles, hold down Shift as you drag the Ellipse tool.

4. When the rectangle is the size and shape you want it to be, stop dragging and release the mouse button.

Drawing Lines

To draw a straight line (a path containing a single line segment between two corner points), follow these steps (see Figure 2-3).

1. Select the Line tool from the toolbox (or press 2).

2. Position the cursor where you want one end of the line.

3. Drag. FreeHand draws a line, starting where you clicked the mouse button. To constrain your line to 45-degree increments (based on the angle you entered in the Constrain dialog box), hold down Shift as you draw the line.

4. When the line is the length you want, stop dragging and release the mouse button.

FIGURE 2-3
Using the Line tool

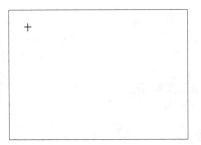

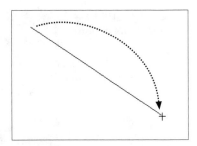

*Position the line tool where you
want one end of the line to start.*

*Drag the line tool across the page.
To constrain the line to 45-degree
angles, hold down Shift as you drag.*

Drawing Spirals

Maybe it's just my clients, but it seems like everyone, all of a sudden, has a use for spirals. I don't know if they're out to hypnotize the world or if it's just some cosmic coincidence, but spirals—especially spirals with text joined to them—seem to be all the rage.

Whatever the case, FreeHand's Xtra Tools palette proudly displays a tool for drawing spirals. Select the Spiral tool from the Xtra Tools palette, then drag the tool on the page, and FreeHand draws a spiral, centered around the point at which you started dragging (see Figure 2-4).

Double-click the Spiral tool in the Xtra Tools palette, and FreeHand displays the Spiral dialog box (see Figure 2-5). I confess, this is one of those points in the book where I'd like to gloss over the controls in this dialog box. Just play with them and see what happens, I'd like to say. But, in the interest of being complete and authoritative, I'll grit my teeth and wade through the options.

FIGURE 2-4
Drawing spirals

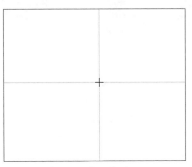

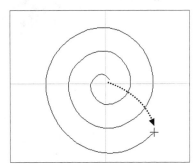

*Position the Spiral tool where you
want to locate the center of the
spiral...*

*...and drag. As you drag, FreeHand
creates a spiral. Stop dragging when
the spiral looks the way you want it to.*

FIGURE 2-5
Spiral tool options

FIGURE 2-5
Spiral tool options

Spiral Type. When you click the button on the right (in this section), the Spiral tool draws concentric spirals—spirals in which each successive rotation of the spiral is a fixed distance from the previous rotation. Clicking the button on the left directs FreeHand to draw "nautilus" spirals, in which each rotation of the spiral is an increasing distance from the previous one (see Figure 2-6).

If you choose the nautilus spiral type, a new control appears in the Spiral dialog box: the Expansion slider/field. Enter a percentage in the field or drag the slider to set the rate of expansion.

FIGURE 2-6
Nautilus and
concentric spirals

*Note: In fact, both spiral
types are concentric (I
can't imagine a non-
concentric spiral), but
only one of them is
called "concentric."*

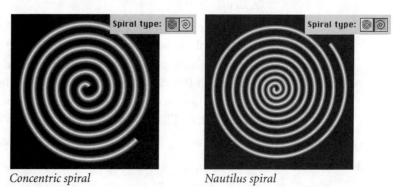

Concentric spiral   Nautilus spiral

Draw By. Choose "Rotation" from the Draw By pop-up menu to specify how many rotations you'd like to have in your spiral (which means that the size of the spiral determines the distance between the rotations of the spiral), or choose "Increments" to control the distance between rotations of the spiral. If you've chosen the nautilus spiral type, you'll see "Rotation" and "Starting Radius" on the pop-up menu; in this case, choosing "Starting Radius" gives you a way to set the initial radius of the spiral.

Draw From. If you want to draw your spirals from somewhere other than their center, choose "Corner" or "Edge" from the Draw From pop-up menu.

Direction. Use these buttons to determine the direction of rotation of the spirals.

If you don't use the Spiral tool, you can keep it from loading by moving or deleting the file "Spiral" from the Xtras folder in your FreeHand folder.

Drawing Arcs

The Arc tool draws—are you ready for this—arcs (quarters of an ellipse). To draw an arc, select the Arc tool and drag it on the page (see Figure 2-7).

To set options for the Arc tool, double-click the tool in the Xtra Tools palette. The Arc dialog box appears (see Figure 2-8).

FIGURE 2-7
Drawing arcs

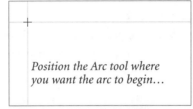

Position the Arc tool where you want the arc to begin…

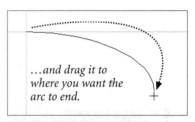

…and drag it to where you want the arc to end.

FIGURE 2-8
Arc tool options

Double-click the Arc tool in the Xtra Tools palette to display the Arc dialog box.

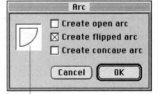

The preview window shows you the effect of the options you've chosen.

Create Open Arc. Turning on the Create Open Arc option makes the Arc tool draw a single curved line segment between two points. Turn "Create Open Arc" off, and you're drawing pie wedges.

Create Flipped Arc. By default, the Arc tool draws the two top quarters of an ellipse—turn on the Create Flipped Arc option when you want to draw either of the bottom two quarters.

Create Concave Arc. Turn on the Create Concave Arc option when you want to create an arc that's on the *inside* of a rectangle (the opposite of a pie wedge).

Like just about every other FreeHand tool, the Arc tool features several keyboard shortcuts.

- ◆ To toggle the Create Open Arc option on and off, hold down Command as you drag the Arc tool (Macintosh only).

- ◆ To constrain the arcs you're drawing to circular arcs, hold down Shift as you drag the Arc tool.

- ◆ To toggle the settings of the Create Convex Arc option in the Arc dialog box, hold down Option/Alt as you drag.

- ◆ To toggle the Create Flipped Arc option in the Arc dialog box, hold down Control as you drag the Arc tool (Macintosh only).

If, at some point, you decide you don't like or aren't using the Arc tool, you can remove it by deleting it or moving it out of the Xtras folder. When you restart FreeHand, the Arc tool will be gone.

Resizing Rectangles and Ellipses

To resize a rectangle or ellipse, use the Pointer tool to select the path you want to resize and then drag any corner handle.

If you hold down Option/Alt as you drag a corner handle, Free-Hand uses a special type of constraint that only works with groups (FreeHand thinks of rectangles and ellipses as groups), and resizes the object around its center point (see Figure 2-9). This is a very handy feature when you need to enlarge an object while leaving its center in the same place.

If you want to resize a rectangle or ellipse proportionally, you'd expect that you could just hold down Shift and drag a corner handle, but you can't—unless you're resizing a circle or a square—because holding down Shift and dragging a corner handle turns the object into a circle or square.

To resize a rectangle or ellipse proportionally, select the shape using the pointer tool, and then press Command-G/Ctrl-G to group the shape. Position the Pointer tool over any corner handle. Hold down Shift and drag the corner handle to resize the shape (see Figure 2-10). Ungroup the shape after you finish resizing it.

FIGURE 2-9
Special constraint for
basic shapes

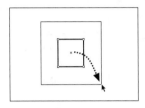 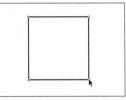

When you hold down Option/Alt as you resize a basic shape, FreeHand resizes the basic shape from its center.

FIGURE 2-10
Proportionally resizing
rectangles and ellipses

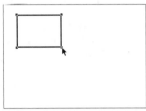 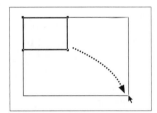

Select a basic shape, group it, hold down Shift…

…and then drag the corner handle to proportionally resize the basic shape.

Changing a Rectangle's Corner Radius

To change a rectangle with square corners into a rectangle with rounded corners, select the rectangle with the Pointer tool and Press Command-I/Ctrl-I to display the Object Inspector (if it's not already visible). Press Command-`\Ctrl-Tab to move your cursor to the Inspector, then tab to the Corner Radius field. After you enter the corner radius you want, press Return to apply your change. Free-Hand converts the rectangle into a rectangle with rounded corners (see Figure 2-11).

To change a rectangle with rounded corners into one with square corners, enter 0 (zero) in the Corner Radius field.

Converting Rectangles and Ellipses into Paths

Why would you want to convert a rectangle or an ellipse into a freeform path? Sometimes you want only part of a basic shape to

FIGURE 2-11
Rounding corners

*Select a rectangle
and press Command-I/
Ctrl-I to display the
Object Inspector.*

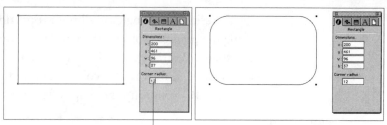

*Enter the corner radius
you want in the Corner
radius field.*

*Press Return. FreeHand rounds the
corners of the rectangle, using the
corner radius you specified.*

connect to a path (see "Adding Round Corners to a Path," later in this chapter, for an example).

To turn a rectangle or an ellipse into a normal path, select the shape, and then press Command-U/Ctrl-U to ungroup it. The rectangle or ellipse becomes a normal path, and can be manipulated as you'd manipulate any other path (see Figure 2-12).

FIGURE 2-12
Converting basic
shapes into paths

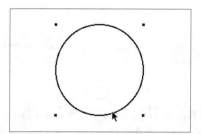

*Select a rectangle or an ellipse and
press Command-U/Ctrl-U.*

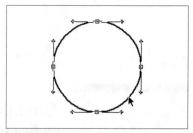

*FreeHand converts the shape into a
freeform path, which you can edit as
you would any freeform path.*

Points and Paths

I briefly covered points and paths in Chapter 1, "FreeHand Basics," but there's still more to explain. Why is it that the most important things are often the most difficult to learn?

When I first approached FreeHand and Illustrator, drawing by constructing paths, placing points, and manipulating control handles struck me as alien, as nothing like drawing at all. Then I started to catch on.

In many ways, when I used pens and rulers to draw I was drawing lines from the point of view of everything *but* the line; in Free-Hand, I draw lines from the point of view of the line itself. This is neither better nor worse; it's just different and takes time to get used to. If you've just glanced at the toolbox and are feeling confused, I urge you to stick with it. Start thinking like a line.

Thinking Like a Line

Imagine that, through the action of some mysterious potion or errant cosmic ray, you've been reduced in size so that you're a little smaller than one of the dots in a connect-the-dots puzzle. For added detail and color, imagine that the puzzle appears in a *Highlights* magazine in a dentist's office.

The only way out is to complete the puzzle. As you walk, a line extends behind you. As you reach each dot in the puzzle, a sign tells you where you are in the puzzle and how to get to the next dot in the path.

Get the idea? The dots in the puzzle are points. The route you walk from one dot to another, as instructed by the signs at each point, is a line segment. Each series of connected dots is a path. As you walk from one dot to another, you're thinking like a line.

Each point—from the first point in the path to the last—carries with it some information about the line segments that attach it to the previous and next points along the path.

Paths are made up of two or more points, connected by line segments, as shown in Figure 2-13. Even if the stroke applied to the path is "None," (and the path doesn't print or show up in Preview mode) there's still a line segment there.

FIGURE 2-13
A path

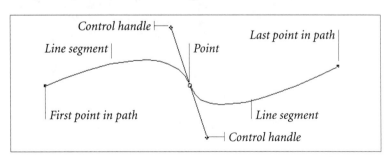

Winding

PostScript paths have a direction, also known as "winding" (as in "winding a clock"—nothing to do with the weather) that generally corresponds to the order and direction in which you place their points (see Figure 2-14). In our connect-the-dots puzzle, winding tells us the order in which we connect the dots.

When you create objects using the basic shapes drawing tools, FreeHand assumes a particular winding (see Figure 2-15). This is a useful thing to know, particularly when you're joining text to a path and want to control where that text begins (or ends) on the path (FreeHand always positions the first character of text in a text block at the path's starting point, unless you're joining text to an object you've drawn with the basic shape tools, in which case it behaves differently; see "Joining Text to a Path," in Chapter 3, "Text and Type").

FIGURE 2-14
The direction of a path

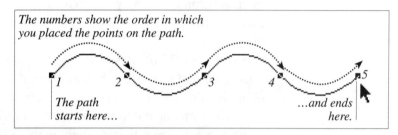

The numbers show the order in which you placed the points on the path.

The path starts here...   *...and ends here.*

FIGURE 2-15
Winding for basic shapes

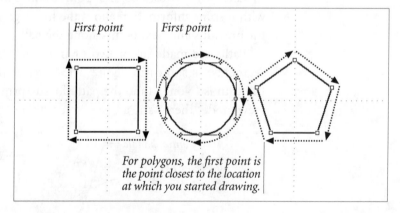

First point   *First point*

For polygons, the first point is the point closest to the location at which you started drawing.

You can use FreeHand's path operation Reverse Direction to reverse the winding of a path. To do this, select the path and choose Reverse Direction from the Alter Path submenu of the Modify menu. FreeHand reverses the direction of the path.

Reflecting paths can also change their direction. You can use Reverse Direction to restore the original winding of the path.

Control Handles   You control the curvature of the line segments before and after each point with control handles. Points can have up to two control handles attached to them. By default, new corner points have none, connector points have one, and curve points have two (for more on the different types of points, see "Types of Points" in Chapter 1, "FreeHand Basics").

The first control handle attached to a point sets the curvature of the *next* line segment in the path along the direction (or winding) of the path. The second control handle sets the curvature of the line segment *before* the point (see Figure 2-16).

FIGURE 2-16
Control handles

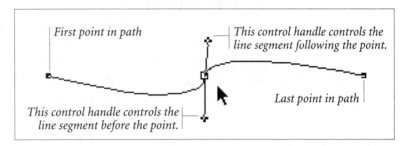

Besides winding, paths also have another property, flatness. Flatness is a PostScript property that controls how accurately curves are rendered on a PostScript printer. What? Can't the printer just print a curve? No. Laser printers, even PostScript laser printers, print by filling in pixels in a grid—just like a black-and-white painting program (like the original MacPaint). Practically, this means that they only print straight lines. If you make the straight lines small enough, or short enough, however, they look like smooth curves. Flatness is PostScript's way of asking "How close is close enough?"

You can think of flatness this way: a flatness setting of one on a 300-dpi printer is equal to an inaccuracy in drawing curves of ⅟₃₀₀ of an inch; or ⅟₂₅₄₀ of an inch on a an imagesetter printing at 2540 dpi. The first is acceptable accuracy for proofing; the second is acceptable resolution for most publications. In fact, I've even gone to flatness settings of 3 without any problems when I knew I was going to be printing color separations at 2540 dpi. You can enter flatness values from 0 to 1000. Figure 2-17 shows the effect of increased flatness setting at 1270 dpi.

Flatness

FIGURE 2-17
Flatness

Flatness of 0   *Flatness of 3*   *Flatness of 50*

If you increase the Flatness setting to a high value—100, for example—you'll see that a smooth curve starts to look like a series of line segments. A flatness setting of 0 ensures that the path prints at the highest level of accuracy possible, given the printer's resolution. This doesn't mean, however, that it's always the best choice.

Lower flatness settings take longer to print and use more of your printer's RAM (which is precious, unless you like PostScript error messages), because the printer has to draw more tiny line segments to render the path's curves. Increasing the flatness sometimes eliminates PostScript errors that make a job unprintable, especially if there are a lot of curved line segments in the illustration you're trying to print.

You can see a path's flatness in the Flatness field of the Object Inspector (select the path and press Command-I/Ctrl-I to bring up the Object Inspector). You can also set the flatness for all of the paths in your publication using the Output Options dialog box (see "Output Options," in Chapter 7, "Printing").

Path-Drawing Tools

You use the freeform drawing tools—the Freehand tool, the Pen tool, and the Point tool—to create paths. The following sections discuss each freeform drawing tool. These tools have already been discussed, briefly, in Chapter 1, "FreeHand Basics," but this section gives you more detailed descriptions of their uses.

Freehand Tool The Freehand tool in the toolbox is actually three different tools: the Freehand tool, the Variable Stroke tool, and the Calligraphic Pen tool. You can switch between these tools by double-clicking the tool in the toolbox.

◆ The Freehand tool draws a single, open path that follows your cursor.

◆ The Variable Stroke tool draws closed paths that look like brush strokes.

◆ The Calligraphic Pen tools draw closed paths that look like they were drawn with a flat-nib lettering pen.

Freehand tool. The simplest, quickest way to create a path on a FreeHand publication page is to use the Freehand tool. Just select the tool and scribble (drag the tool on the page). As you drag the tool across the page, FreeHand creates a path that follows your mouse motion (see Figure 2-18).

FIGURE 2-18
Using the
Freehand tool

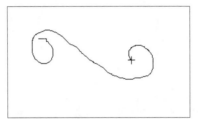 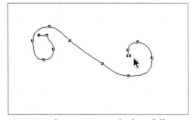

Select the Freehand tool and drag it across the page.

FreeHand creates a path that follows your mouse movements.

As you drag, FreeHand places corner and curve points along the path. You have some control over FreeHand's placement of these points—double-click the Freehand tool to bring up the Freehand dialog box (see Figure 2-19).

The Tight Fit option controls the number of points FreeHand creates to construct the path. Turn off Tight Fit to create a simpler path, but bear in mind that the simplified path follows your mouse movements less accurately.

Draw Dotted Line displays the path you're drawing as a dotted line as you drag the Freehand tool. Turn Draw Dotted Line off to show the path as you draw it. Why would you want to do this? Drawing's a little faster with Draw Dotted Line turned on.

If you need to back up along the path while you're drawing with the Freehand tool, hold down Command/Ctrl, and drag back along the path. To continue drawing the path, let go of Command/Ctrl and continue dragging the tool (see Figure 2-20).

FIGURE 2-19
Freehand Tool
dialog box

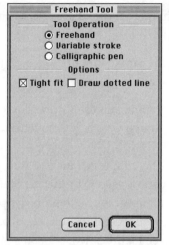

To set options for the Freehand tool's behavior, double-click the Freehand tool in the Toolbox. The FreeHand Tool dialog box appears.

FIGURE 2-20
Erasing part of a
freeform path

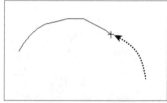

If you don't like what you've drawn with the Freehand tool...

...hold down Command/Ctrl and drag back along the path.

If you need to create a straight line segment while you're drawing a path using the Freehand tool, hold down Option/Alt as you're dragging: each line segment you add forms a straight line from the last point on the path. If you want to constrain the angle of the straight line segment to 45-degree tangents (of the angle set in the Constrain dialog box), hold down Option-Shift/Alt-Shift as you drag the Freehand tool (see Figure 2-21).

FIGURE 2-21
Constraint and the
Freehand tool

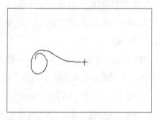

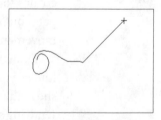

Hold down Option-Shift as you drag the Freehand tool...

...and you constrain the lines you draw to 45-degree angles.

Variable Stroke tool. The introduction of the wacky "variable blob tool" (known to serious persons as the Variable Stroke tool) in

FreeHand 3.1 gave FreeHand users a way to create paths shaped like brush strokes. To see the Variable Stroke tool's controls, double-click the Freehand tool in the toolbox, then click the Variable Stroke option at the top of the Freehand tool dialog box (see Figure 2-22).

If you have a pressure-sensitive tablet (such at those manufactured by Wacom, Calcomp, and others), you can use the pressure of your stylus to change the widths of the path you draw with the Variable Stroke tool.

FIGURE 2-22
Variable
Stroke tool

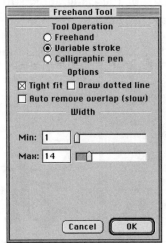

To set options for the Variable Stroke tool's behavior, double-click the Freehand tool and click the Variable Stroke option.

Variable stokes

Tip:
If You Don't
Have a Tablet

What if you don't have a pressure-sensitive tablet? You can still use the tool's pressure-sensitivity. As you draw a path, press 2 (or right arrow) to increase the width of the path, or press 1 (or left arrow) to decrease its width. This technique takes a little practice, but you'll soon be drawing variable blobs just as well as your friends with their fancypants tablets (see Figure 2-23).

FIGURE 2-23
Pressure without
the pen

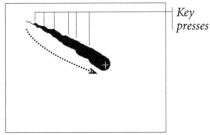

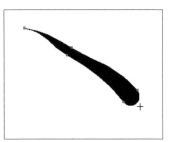

Key presses

As you drag the Variable Stroke tool, press the right arrow key to increase the width of the stroke; press the left arrow key to decrease the width.

Calligraphic Pen tool. Choose the Calligraphic Pen tool when you want to create paths that resemble lines drawn with a pen. To use the Calligraphic Pen tool, double-click the Freehand tool in the toolbox, then click the Calligraphic Pen option. This is also where you set up the Calligraphic Pen's options (see Figure 2-24).

As with the Variable Stroke tool, you can use the Calligraphic Pen tool's pressure-sensitivity even if you don't have a pressure-sensitive tablet—as you draw a path, press 2 (or right arrow) to increase the width of the calligraphic stroke, or press 1 (or left arrow) to decrease its width.

FIGURE 2-24
Calligraphic Pen tool

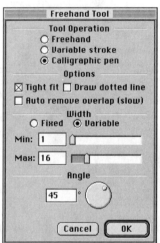

To set options for the Calligraphic Pen tool's behavior, double-click the Freehand tool and click "Calligraphic Pen."

Calligraphic pen strokes

Pen Tool

When you *click* the Pen tool in the publication window, FreeHand places corner points. *Drag* the Pen tool, and FreeHand places a curve point where you first started dragging—you determine the length of the control handles (and, therefore, the shape of the curve) by the distance you drag (see Figure 2-25).

FIGURE 2-25
The Pen tool

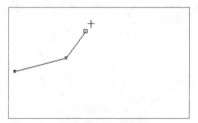

Click to create a corner point.

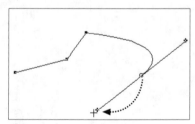

Drag to create a curve point.

To curve the line segment following a corner point, hold down Option/Alt as you place a corner point and drag. The control handle doesn't appear until you place the next point. Once you place the next point, the control handle appears and can be adjusted as you like (see Figure 2-26).

FIGURE 2-26
Dragging a
control handle out
of a corner point

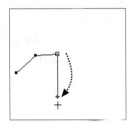 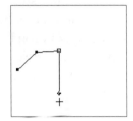 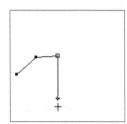

Hold down Option/Alt as you drag...

...and FreeHand creates a corner point with a single control handle.

This control handle applies to the line segment following the corner point.

The trickiest thing about using the Pen tool this way is that you often don't see the effect of the curve manipulation until you've placed the next point. This makes sense in that you don't need a control handle for a line segment that doesn't yet exist, but it can be quite a brain-twister.

To convert a curve point you've just placed to a corner point, tap Option/Alt after you've finished dragging out the curve point's control handles (see Figure 2-27). This creates a corner point with two control handles extended.

FIGURE 2-27
Converting a curve
point to a corner
point (with two
control handles)

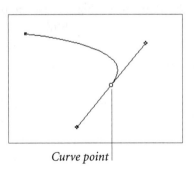 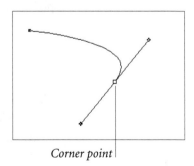

Curve point   *Corner point*

Drag out the curve point's handles as you normally would...

...then tap Option/Alt and stop dragging. FreeHand converts the curve point to a corner point.

To convert a curve point you've just placed to a corner point with one control handle extended, hold down Option/Alt and click the point. Just to make life interesting, this control handle applies to the line segment *before* the corner point along the path. Ordinarily, the first control handle dragged out of a corner point applies to the line segment *after* the point (see Figure 2-28).

You can change the position of points, as you'd expect, by holding down Command/Ctrl (which, as you'll recall, chooses the Pointer tool without deselecting the current tool), selecting the point, and dragging the point to a new location.

FIGURE 2-28
Converting a curve
point to a corner
point (with one
control handle)

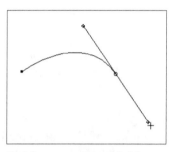
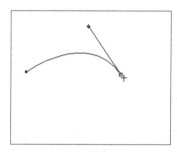

Position a curve point, hold
down Option/Alt...

...and then click the point to
convert it into a corner point.

Point Tool

Use the Point tool when you want to create paths point-by-point. Dragging the Point tool as you place a point moves the point—unlike the Pen tool, where dragging adjusts the curve of the line segments attached to the point you're placing. In general, you place points with the Point tool, then adjust the points' control handles to get the curves you want. Which tool is better—the Point tool or the Pen tool? Your answer depends on who you are and how you like to work. I'm a Point tool kind of guy, myself.

Placing corner points. When you click the Point tool on the page, you're placing corner points—points that have no control handles attached to them. Corner points look like small squares. Because corner points have no curve control handles attached to them (initially), the line segments between corner points are straight (see Figure 2-29).

You can drag curve handles out of corner points: place the corner point as you normally would, then hold down Command/Ctrl (to turn the cursor into the Pointer tool) and Option/Alt, and drag a control handle out of the corner point (see Figure 2-30).

Note that you can also drag a control handle out of a corner point any time by selecting the point with the pointer tool, then holding down Option/Alt, and dragging a control handle out of it.

The most significant difference between corner points and curve points is that the angle of control handles pulled out of corner points can be adjusted independently, while changing the angle of one control handle of a curve point changes the angle of the other control handle (see Figure 2-31). This difference, in my opinion, makes corner points much more useful than curve points—you can do anything with a corner point you could do with a curve point or a connector point.

FIGURE 2-29
Corner points

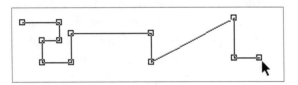

FIGURE 2-30
Dragging control
handles out of
corner points

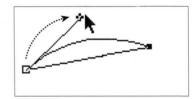

Select a corner point,
hold down Option/Alt…

…and drag a control handle
out of the point.

FIGURE 2-31
Adjusting corner point
control handles

Corner points are more
flexible than curve
points, because you can
adjust their control
handles independently.

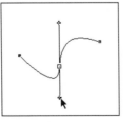
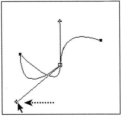
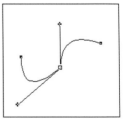

Point at a control
handle…

…and drag.

The handle moves
independently of the
other handle.

To turn a corner point into a curve point, select the corner point, press Command-I/Ctrl-I to display the Object Inspector, and then click the Curve Point button. The corner point you selected becomes a curve point.

Placing curve points. Hold down Option/Alt as you click the Point tool, and you place curve points—points with two control handles pulled out of them. Curve points look like small circles. How far the control handles are extended depends on the curve point's position in the path (see Figure 2-32).

You can increase or decrease the distance from one control handle to its curve point without moving the other control handle, but both handles move if you change the angle one of them presents to the curve point—they always move along the same axis. This makes them somewhat less flexible than corner points (see Figure 2-33).

You can turn a curve point into a corner point by selecting the curve point, pressing Command-I/Ctrl-I (to display the Object Inspector), and clicking the Corner Point button in the Inspector.

FIGURE 2-32
Curve points

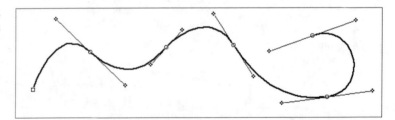

FIGURE 2-33
Manipulating
control handles
on curve points

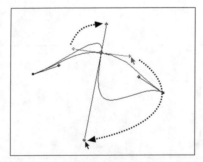
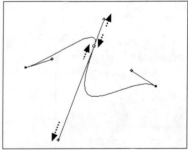

As you drag a control handle attached to a curve point, note that both control handles move as you drag.

Control handles attached to curve points always move along the same axis.

Placing connector points. If you hold down Command-Option/ Ctrl-Alt and click the Point tool, you create connector points— points that may or may not have control handles pulled out of them depending on where they're placed in the path (and, I suspect, depending on their own whim). I never really have figured out connector points. Anyway, they look like little triangles.

When you place a curve point immediately after a connector point, FreeHand extends the control handle for the line segment between the two points from the connector point. This control handle is positioned along the axis formed by the connector point and the point preceding the connector point on the path, and is placed at the same distance from the connector point as the preceding point along this axis. When you drag the control handle, it moves along this axis (see Figure 2-34). If you want to change the curve, convert the connector point into another type of point.

FIGURE 2-34
Connector points

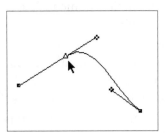

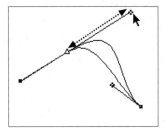

Connector points look like little triangles.

The control handle on a connector point can only move along its original axis.

What's the use of connector points? They create smooth transitions between straight and curved line segments. I think of them as a sort of "half" curve point. They never seem to give me the curve I'm looking for, but you should experiment with them. In spite of my bias, they might be just what you're after.

Manipulating Control Handles

The aspect of drawing in FreeHand that's toughest to understand and master is the care, feeding, and manipulation of control handles. These handles are fundamental to drawing curved lines in Free- Hand, so you'd better learn how to work with them.

To change the shape of a path you've drawn, you can use any or all of the following techniques.

- ◆ Adjust control handles individually by dragging them around with the Pointer tool.

- ◆ Change the curve of line segments using the "Bend-O-Matic" feature (described later in this chapter).

- ◆ Use the Freeform tool to push, pull, or reshape the path.

Which technique should you use? As usual, there's no right or wrong approach. The first method gives you the greatest control, but is also the hardest to master and the least "intuitive." Most of the time, I use the "Bend-O-Matic" technique.

Adjusting Control Handles

To adjust the curve of a line segment, use the Pointer tool to select a point attached to the line segment. The control handles attached to that point appear. If you don't see any control handles, the curve of the line segment is controlled by the point at the other end of the line segment—select that point, and you'll see the control handle (or handles) you're looking for. Position the cursor over one of the control handles and drag. The curve of the line segment associated with that handle changes as you drag. When the curve looks the way you want, stop dragging (see Figure 2-35).

FIGURE 2-35
Manipulating a control handle

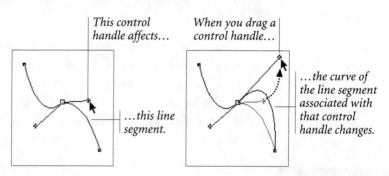

This control handle affects...

...this line segment.

When you drag a control handle...

...the curve of the line segment associated with that control handle changes.

To retract (delete) a control handle, drag the handle inside the point it's attached to, or select the point and use the Retract buttons in the Object Inspector, as described in "Issuing a Retraction," later in this chapter.

Tip:
Adjusting
Multiple Points

You can select multiple points (by dragging a selection rectangle around them, for example), and then adjust the control handles of all of the points in the selection, if necessary (see Figure 2-36).

FIGURE 2-36
Selecting multiple
points and adjusting
curve control handles

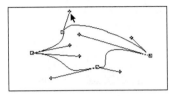

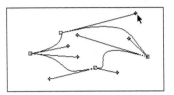

Drag a selection rectangle over a path to select all of the points on the path.

Now you can adjust control handles while looking at the positions of all of the control handles on the path.

Tip:
Converting
Multiple Points

When you want to convert more than one point from one point type to another, select the points you want to convert, then click one of the point type buttons in the Object Inspector (see Figure 2-37). FreeHand converts the selected points to that point type.

FIGURE 2-37
Converting multiple
points from one point
type to another

*This trick only works
for a single path at a
time.*

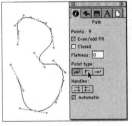

Select a series of points...

...and click one of the Point Type buttons in the Object Inspector. FreeHand converts all of the selected points.

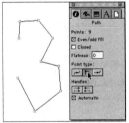

Automatic Curvature. As you place curve or connector points along a path, FreeHand adds and adjusts control handles where it thinks you'd like them. It's actually quite good at guessing. This is Free-Hand's automatic curvature feature, which you can turn on or off for any point in your publication.

To turn automatic curvature on, select a point and press Command-I/Ctrl-I to display the Object Inspector. Turn on the Automatic option, and FreeHand decides how to extend control handles from the point, based on the point's position in the path.

When you adjust a control handle, FreeHand turns automatic curvature off for that point. If you decide you've made an error, and would like to return to FreeHand's automatic curvature, you can display the Object Inspector and turn on the Automatic curvature option (see Figure 2-38).

FIGURE 2-38
Automatic curvature

If you change your mind about an adjustment you've made to a control handle...

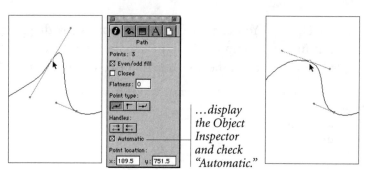

...display the Object Inspector and check "Automatic."

FreeHand returns the point's control handles to their default position.

Issuing a Retraction. Click one of the Retract buttons in the Object Inspector and FreeHand pulls the corresponding control handle back into the point. No more not quite being sure if you've dragged the handle inside the point! Anything you'd ordinarily do by dragging a curve control handle inside a point, you can do using the Retract buttons (see Figure 2-39).

FIGURE 2-39
Retracting control handles

This technique leaves open the question: "Why simply retract what you can plausibly deny?"

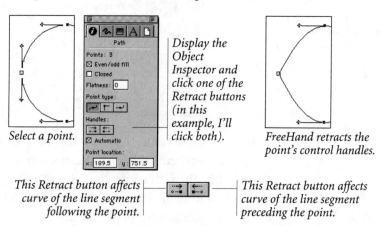

Select a point.

Display the Object Inspector and click one of the Retract buttons (in this example, I'll click both).

FreeHand retracts the point's control handles.

This Retract button affects curve of the line segment following the point.

This Retract button affects curve of the line segment preceding the point.

Bend-O-Matic

What's the easiest way to change the curve of a line segment? Select the Pointer tool, select a path, hold down Option/Alt, and then drag any line segment between any two points. As you drag, FreeHand bends the line segment, automatically adjusting the two control handles (one from either point) that define the curve of the line segment (see Figure 2-40). This is called the "Bend-O-Matic" feature. Use it often enough, and you get a set of steak knives and a bamboo steamer. (But wait! There's more...)

FIGURE 2-40
Bend-O-Matic

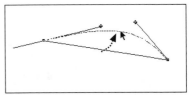

*Select the Pointer tool, then point at
the line segment you want to curve...*

*...hold down Option/Alt, and drag.
FreeHand curves the path.*

Using the Freeform Tools

FreeHand's new Freeform tool is really two tools—the Push/Pull tool and the Reshape Area tool. These two tools give you three ways to reshape the paths in your publications. To change from one Freeform tool to another, double-click the Freeform tool in the Toolbox. FreeHand displays the Freeform Tool dialog box (see Figure 2-41). Choose the type of Freeform tool you want, then specify the settings you want to control the behavior of the tool. You use both tools the same way: select a path, then drag the tool over the path. You can also drag the tool over an unselected path—FreeHand selects the path, then applies the effect of dragging the tool to the path.

FIGURE 2-41
Freeform Tool Options

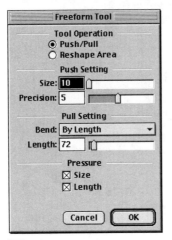

*When you choose Push/Pull,
the Freeform tool looks like
this.*

*When you choose Reshape
Area, the Freeform tool looks
like this.*

Push/Pull Tool

When you choose the Push/Pull option in the Freeform Tool dialog box, FreeHand displays a series of options that define the way the tool works. Before I dive into a description of these options, however, I'd better define some terms.

When you *pull* a path, FreeHand bends the line segment (or an area thereof) below the cursor. It's a bit difficult describing what *pushing* a path actually does. Imagine that you're pushing a piece of string around on a flat surface with your finger, and you'll get an idea of what pushing a path is like (see Figure 2-42).

FIGURE 2-42
Freeform Tool Options

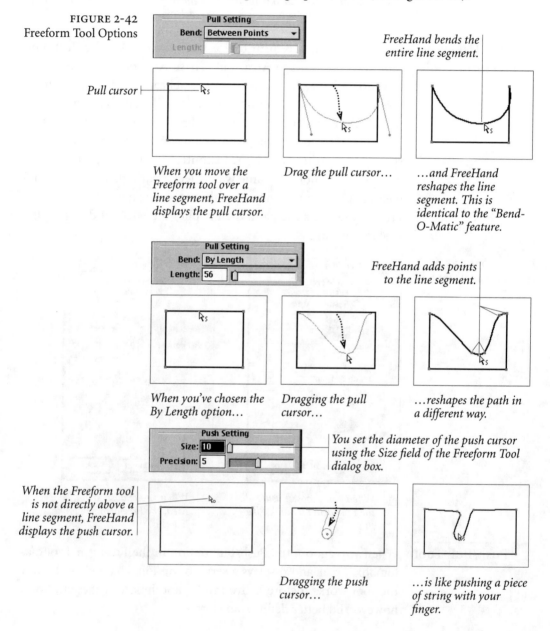

Pull cursor

FreeHand bends the entire line segment.

When you move the Freeform tool over a line segment, FreeHand displays the pull cursor.

Drag the pull cursor…

…and FreeHand reshapes the line segment. This is identical to the "Bend-O-Matic" feature.

FreeHand adds points to the line segment.

When you've chosen the By Length option…

Dragging the pull cursor…

…reshapes the path in a different way.

You set the diameter of the push cursor using the Size field of the Freeform Tool dialog box.

When the Freeform tool is not directly above a line segment, FreeHand displays the push cursor.

Dragging the push cursor…

…is like pushing a piece of string with your finger.

Whether the Push/Pull tool pushes or pulls a path depends on where the cursor is when you start dragging. Luckily, the cursor changes to give you an idea of what's going to happen. If the cursor is touching a path, you'll see the pull cursor. Dragging the tool changes the curve of the line segment the tool is above. If the cursor is inside or outside a path, you'll see the push cursor—dragging the cursor pushes the path.

Size. Sets the diameter of the push cursor—that's the area affected by the tool when you drag it across a path. This value is in *screen pixels* (though it doesn't *say* so)—which means that pushing a path affects areas of different sizes at different screen magnifications. You can enter values from 1 to 1000 pixels.

Precision. When you push a path, FreeHand adds points to the path. The value you enter here affects the accuracy of FreeHand's point-adding behavior. You can enter values from one (least accurate, fewest resulting points) to ten (most accurate, most resulting points) in this field.

Bend. To make pulling a path with the Push/Pull tool work like the Bend-O-Matic feature (described earlier in this chapter), choose Between Points from the Bend pop-up menu. When you choose Between Points, FreeHand bends the entire line segment between two points, rather than adding points as you drag. In my opinion, this is the most useful variant of the Freeform tool.

To limit the length of the area affected by the Push/Pull tool, choose By Length. When you choose By Length, the Length field appears below the pop-up menu. Enter a value from one to 1000 in this field to set the length of a line segment affected by the Push/Pull tool. As in the Size field, this value is in screen pixels.

Size (Pressure) and **Length (Pressure).** You can use pressure sensitivity from a drawing tablet to change the Size setting, the Length setting, or both settings. Even if you don't have a pressure-sensitive drawing tablet, you might want to turn these options on. Like the Freehand tool's pressure-sensitive options, you can simulate the effect of pressure-sensitivity using the keyboard.

Tip:
Switching
Between Bend
Types

To temporarily switch from one bend type (Between Points or By Length) to another, hold down Option/Alt *before* you start pulling a path. This saves you a trip to the Freeform Tool dialog box.

Tip:
Cloning and
Push/Pull

To clone a path as you use the Push/Pull tool, hold down Option/Alt as you *finish* dragging and release the mouse button. Don't hold down Option/Alt *before* you start dragging.

Tip:
Constraining the
Push Cursor

If you hold down Shift as you push a path, FreeHand constrains the cursor's movement to 45-degree tangents from the point at which you held down the key (again, the Freeform tool behaves just like the Freehand tool).

Tip:
Switching to the
Reshape Area
Tool

When you see the push cursor, you can switch to the Reshape Area tool by pressing Option/Alt and then holding down the mouse button. If you want to clone the path as you reshape its area, continue holding the key as you drag the cursor. If you don't want to clone the path, release the key while continuing to hold down the mouse button, then drag the cursor to reshape the path.

**Reshape
Area Tool**

If pushing a path with the Push/Pull tool is something like pushing string with your finger, pushing a path with the Reshape Area tool is like pushing a wall with a wrecking ball (see Figure 2-43). It's a kind of "super push."

FIGURE 2-43
Reshape Area Tool

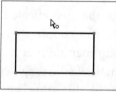

Select a path...

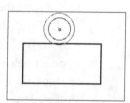

...hold down the mouse button...

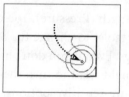

...and drag the cursor into (or out of) the path.

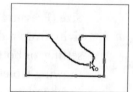

FreeHand reshapes the path.

Reshape Area tool options. The Size, Precision, and Pressure options are the same as those for the Push/Pull tool (see above). The Strength option, however, takes a bit more explaining. When you drag the Reshape Area tool, you'll see two circles—a red circle inside a blue circle (if you don't see two circles, it's because you've turned off the Smoother Editing option in the General Preferences dialog box). The red circle defines the area at which the Reshape Area tool has its maximum effect; the blue circle shows the entire area affected by the tool. The Strength field defines the amount of the blue circle filled by the red circle (see Figure 2-44).

FIGURE 2-44
Size and Strength

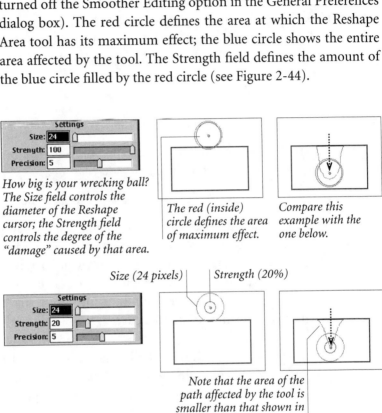

How big is your wrecking ball? The Size field controls the diameter of the Reshape cursor; the Strength field controls the degree of the "damage" caused by that area.

The red (inside) circle defines the area of maximum effect.

Compare this example with the one below.

Size (24 pixels)   *Strength (20%)*

Note that the area of the path affected by the tool is smaller than that shown in the example above.

Tip:
Switching to the
Push/Pull Tool

When you have the Reshape Area tool selected, you can temporarily switch to the Push/Pull tool by pressing Option/Alt and then holding down the mouse button. If you want to clone the path as you push or pull it, continue holding the key as you drag the cursor. If you don't want to clone the path, release the key while continuing to hold down the mouse button, then drag the cursor to push or pull the path.

Drawing Techniques

Now that you know all about the elements that make up paths, let's talk about how you actually use them.

Ways to Draw Paths

When you're drawing paths, don't forget that you can change the path after you've drawn it. I've often seen people delete entire paths and start over because they misplaced the last point on the path. Go ahead and place points in the wrong places; you can always change the position of any point on the path. Also, keep these facts in mind:

◆ You can always split the path.

◆ You can always add points to or subtract points from the path.

◆ You can always change tools while drawing a path.

It's also best to create paths using as few points as you can—but it's not required (after all, you can always use the Simplify path operation). Create paths in whatever way you find works best for you—there's no "right" way to do it. I've talked with dozens of FreeHand users, and each one uses a slightly different method for putting points on a page.

The classical method. Use the Point tool to place curve, corner, and connector points, and place points one at a time. I call this the "classical" method, because it's how people were taught to place points in FreeHand 1.0. To construct a path using this method, you use the Point tool, holding down Option/Alt as you click to produce a curve point, or Option-Shift/Alt-Shift to produce a connector point (see Figure 2-45).

People who use this method of constructing paths keep one hand on the mouse and one hand hovering around the keyboard, because they'll change point type by pressing keys (as described in "Using the Point tool," earlier in this chapter).

The "Illustrator" Method. Use the Pen tool only. I call this method the "Illustrator" method, because I've found that this set of users

FIGURE 2-45
The classical method

Choose the Point tool and click to place a corner point.

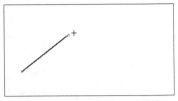

Hold down Control/Alt and click (in Windows, click the right mouse button) to place a connector point.

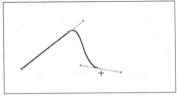

Hold down Option/Alt and click to place a curve point.

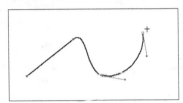

Continue placing points until you've drawn the path you want.

generally learned to use Illustrator before they started using Free-Hand. In this method, you click and drag the Pen tool to create paths containing only curve and corner points (see Figure 2-46).

FIGURE 2-46
The "Illustrator"
method

Choose the Pen tool and click to place a corner point.

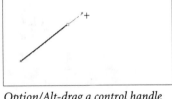

Option/Alt-drag a control handle out of the next corner point.

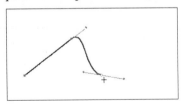

Drag out a curve point.

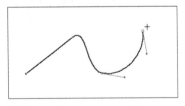

Click to place a corner point.

Drawing paths my way. Place corner points only, then pull control handles out of the points using the Option-Drag technique (see "The Quick Way to Make a Curve," earlier in this chapter). I call this method "my way," because it's how I do it. In this method, you use the Point tool to place corner points defining the path you want to create, then hold down Option/Alt and drag line segments to create the curves you want (see Figure 2-47).

I like this method because I can place points quickly where I know I want them to go, then work on the fine details of the curves when I can actually see the path changing as I drag—unlike using the Pen tool, where you're dragging control handles controlling a line segment you haven't yet placed. The disadvantage of this method is that you need to know where you're going to place points ahead of time, a skill you acquire by using the program a lot (see also "Keeping Paths Simple," below).

All three methods work well, and there's no reason not to mix and match methods in different situations. There's also no reason not to mix these methods with the use of the Freehand tool, the basic shapes tools, autotracing, or blending.

FIGURE 2-47
My way

Click the Point tool to create a corner point.

Click to place more corner points.

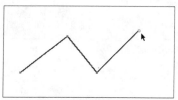

Drag the points into position.

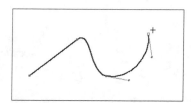

Drag out and adjust control handles, or hold down Option/Alt and bend line segments (see "Bend-O-Matic" earlier in this chapter).

Drawing with the Knife Tool

I've always liked working with scratchboard (or "scraperboard"), and woodcuts—I like the process of taking an area and cutting a drawing out of it. You can do the same with FreeHand's Knife tool. If the Knife tool could only draw straight lines, this wouldn't be so much fun—but the Knife tool can also act like the Freehand tool.

To try this neat technique, follow these steps (see Figure 2-48).

1. Draw a closed path and fill it with a basic fill.

2. Double-click the Knife tool. FreeHand displays the Knife Tool dialog box.

3. Turn on the FreeHand option and the Cut Closed Paths option.

4. Hold down Command/Ctrl (to turn the Knife tool into the Pointer tool) and select the path you drew earlier.

5. Drag the Knife tool through the filled path. As you drag, FreeHand cuts a path out of the filled path.

Bear in mind, as you draw with the Knife tool, that you're creating compound paths. It's pretty easy to create a path that's too complex to print, so don't get carried away—especially if you plan to paste a TIFF inside the path.

FIGURE 2-48
Drawing with the
Knife tool

Double-click the Knife tool in the Toolbox to display the Knife Tool dialog box.

Turn on the Close Cut Paths and Tight Fit options.

Select a filled path, then drag the Knife tool inside the path.

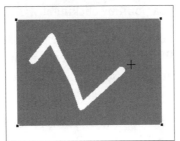

As you drag, the Knife tool cuts a hole in the path.

Drawing with the Knife tool creates composite paths, as you can see from this Keyline view.

Keeping Paths Simple

People who have just started working with FreeHand tend to use more points than are needed to create their paths. Over time, they learn one of FreeHand's basic rules: Any curve can be described by two points and their associated control handles. No more, no less (see Figure 2-49). FreeHand's "Simplify paths" path operator makes a great path-drawing instructor—draw a path and then run Simplify Paths on it (select the path, then select Simplify Paths from the Alter Path submenu of the Modify menu). Notice where Free-Hand deletes and removes points on the path you've drawn, and you'll get a good lesson in path drawing. Note, however, that Simplify Paths is not perfect, and may change the shape of your path (you can always undo the action).

FIGURE 2-49
Any curve can be described by two points

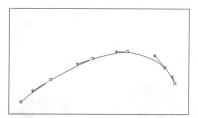

This path uses too many points.

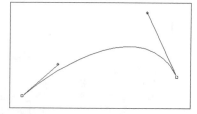

Here's the same curve, using only two points.

Selecting and Moving Points

If you've gotten this far, you probably know how to select points, but here are a few rules to keep in mind.

◆ You select a point by clicking it with the Pointer tool.

◆ You can select more than one point at a time by holding down Shift as you click on each point with the Pointer tool, or you can drag a selection rectangle around a number of points to select them all.

◆ You can select points on paths inside groups or composite paths by holding down Option/Alt as you drag a selection rectangle around the points.

◆ When you move a point, the control handles associated with that point also move, maintaining their positions relative to the point. Note that this means that the curves of the line segments attached to the point change, unless you're also moving the points on the other end of the incoming and outgoing line segments (see Figure 2-50).

FIGURE 2-50
Effect of moving a
point on its attached
line segments

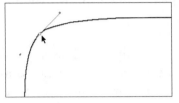
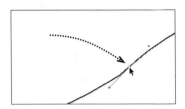

When you select and move a point...   *...the point's attached control handles move with the point.*

Flipping and Flopping

I hate drawing objects from scratch when I don't have to, so I use flipping and flopping to create most of the objects I use in a FreeHand publication. What's flipping and flopping? It's the process of cloning an object and then selecting and moving some—but not all—of the points on the cloned object. Look at Figure 2-51. Flipping and flopping depends on FreeHand's ability to select and move several points on a path without moving the entire path.

Flipping and flopping come in especially handy when you need to create two paths—even paths of different shapes—that share a

FIGURE 2-51
Flipping and flopping

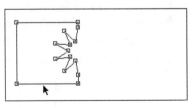
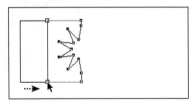

Clone the original object.   *Select individual points on the clone and drag them...*

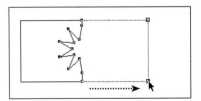
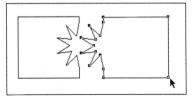

...until they're where you want them.   *You now have two objects with an identical border.*

common boundary. Redrawing the boundary between two paths is not only boring, but can be hard to do if the boundary is complex enough. It isn't that I'm averse to tackling difficult tasks; I just hate to make something more difficult than it has to be, so I use flipping and flopping even when the shapes sharing a boundary are very different.

Open and Closed Paths

You can think of an open path as a line and a closed path as a shape. What's the difference? Less and less, as time goes by. In FreeHand 8, open paths can be filled, or have objects pasted inside them. As in previous versions of FreeHand, open paths can't be manipulated using some path operations (Crop, Union, Punch, and Intersect). You can always join the endpoints of an open path to create a closed path, or split a closed path to create an open path.

To use FreeHand's Object Inspector to close a path, select the path, press Command-I/Ctrl-I to display the Object Inspector (if it's not already visible), and then check the Closed checkbox in the Inspector. FreeHand creates a straight line segment that joins the first point in the path to the last point in the path (see Figure 2-52).

You can use the Object Inspector to change a closed path into an open path by unchecking the Closed option. When you do this, FreeHand removes the line segment connecting the last point in the path to the first point in the path. When you convert a closed path into an open path, any fill you've applied to the path disappears. The fill is still applied to the path—if you convert the open path back into a closed path, the fill will reappear.

FIGURE 2-52
Changing an open
path into a closed path

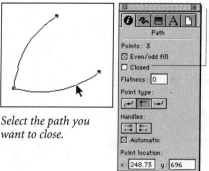

Select the path you
want to close.

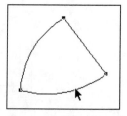

Display the Object
Inspector and click
the Closed checkbox.

FreeHand closes the path with a
straight line segment.

Splitting and Joining Paths

You can always add points to or subtract points from a path in FreeHand. You can split an open or closed path into separate paths, or join paths to each other, or make a single path a closed path.

Splitting Paths

You can split a path in any of three ways.

♦ Select a point (or points) on the path with the Pointer tool, and then choose Split (Command-J/Ctrl-J) from the Modify menu.

♦ Select the path, then click the Knife tool on the path (or on a selected point on the path).

♦ Select the path, then drag the Knife tool over the path.

When you split a path by splitting a point, FreeHand creates a new point on top of the point you selected. This new point is connected to the line segment going to the next point along the path's winding (see Figure 2-53).

FIGURE 2-53
Splitting a path by splitting points

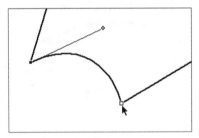
Select a point and choose "Split" from the Element menu.

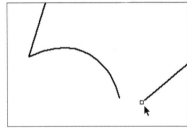
FreeHand splits the path at the point you selected.

When you split a path using the Knife tool, two new points are created (see Figure 2-54).

To select one or the other of the two paths you've created by splitting the path, press Tab (to deselect everything), then click the path you want to select, or press ` (to select both paths), then hold down Shift and click the path you don't want selected.

When you split a path and create two new points, it can be very difficult figuring out which endpoint belongs to which path. It's simple, really. The point closest to the start of the path (following

FIGURE 2-54
Splitting a path by
splitting a line segment

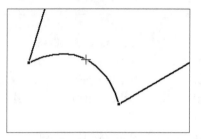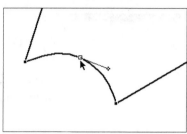

Select a path, select the knife tool, and then click on the path (or drag the knife tool across the path).   *FreeHand splits the path where you clicked.*

the path's winding) becomes the point farther to the back, and the point farthest from the start of the path is on top of it (see Figure 2-55). You can always use Bring To Front and Send To Back to change which point's on top.

You can use the Split command to split any number of points. Drag a selection rectangle over all the points you want to split, choose Split from the Modify menu, and FreeHand splits all the points (see Figure 2-56).

FIGURE 2-55
Which point is on top?

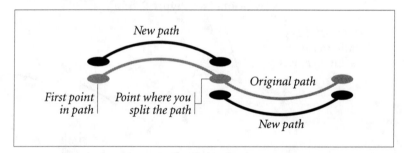

FIGURE 2-56
Splitting several
points at once

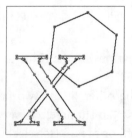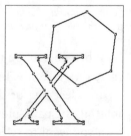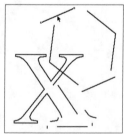

Select the points you want to split (you can drag a selection rectangle over them, if you want).   *Choose Split from the Modify menu. FreeHand splits all of the selected points.*   *Now you can take the objects apart.*

Joining Paths   You can join two open paths to create a single path, or you can join two closed paths to create a composite path. In this section, I'll talk about joining open paths. For more on joining closed paths to create composite paths, see the section "Composite Paths," later in this chapter.

To join points on two open paths and create a single path, drag the endpoints of the two open paths over each other. It's easier to do this when you've turned on Snap To Point (on the View menu). If FreeHand—for whatever reason—won't join the points, drag a selection rectangle over the two points and choose Join from the Modify menu (see Figure 2-57).

FIGURE 2-57
Joining paths

 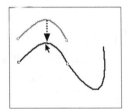 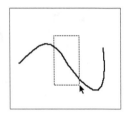

Move the paths so that their endpoints meet.

Drag a selection rectangle around the overlapping endpoints.

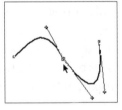

Press Command-J/Ctrl-J to join the points. The two paths become a single path.

If you've turned on the Join Non-Touching Paths option (in the Object Preferences dialog box), you don't have to line up the endpoints of the two paths. Select two paths, then choose Join from the Modify menu (or press Command-J/Ctrl-J). FreeHand joins the endpoints of the paths with a straight line segment (see Figure 2-58). Note that you can select more than two open paths, and FreeHand join all of the paths in the selection.

Tip:
If "Join" Is
Grayed Out

If the Join menu item is grayed out, one or both of the paths containing the points you've selected is probably a closed path. If you're not sure if a path is closed or open, select the path and look at the Closed checkbox in the Object Inspector—if it's checked, the path is closed.

FIGURE 2-58
Joining non-
touching paths

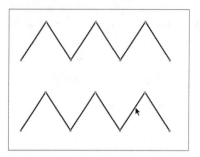 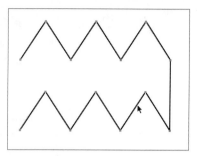

If you've turned on the Join Non-Touching Paths option in the Object Preferences dialog box…

…choosing Join from the Modify menu joins (you guessed it) non-touching paths with a straight line segment.

Composite Paths

In the old days, not only did I have to walk miles to school in freezing cold weather, but I also had to work my way through an impossibly difficult series of steps just to create holes inside closed paths. While the process was kind of fascinating, it did nothing to help me hit my deadlines.

These days, creating holes in paths is easier—just make them into composite paths. Composite paths are made of two or more paths (which must be unlocked, ungrouped, and closed) that have been joined with "Join." Areas between the two paths, or areas where the paths overlap, are transparent (see Figure 2-59).

1. Select the Ellipse tool from the toolbox.

2. Draw two ellipses, one on top of the other.

3. Fill the ellipses with some basic fill.

4. Select both ellipses.

5. Press Command-J/Ctrl-J to join the two ellipses.

What if you don't want transparent areas where the paths overlap? Select the composite path. Press Command-I/Ctrl-I to display the Object Inspector (if it's not already visible). Uncheck the Even/Odd Fill option. This fills all the objects in the composite path with the same fill (see Figure 2-60).

FIGURE 2-59
Creating
composite paths

FIGURE 2-59
Creating
composite paths

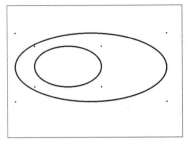

Create two ellipses using the Ellipse tool.

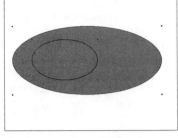

Apply the stroke and fill you want to the ellipses.

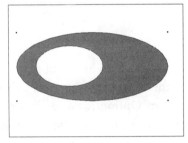

Press Command-J/Ctrl-J to join the ellipses.

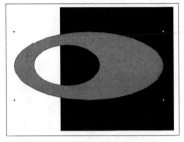

You've just created a composite path. The inside of the shape is transparent.

FIGURE 2-60
Even/Odd fill and
composite paths

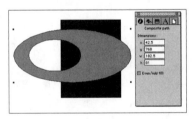

Even/Odd Fill on

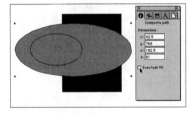

Even/Odd Fill off

If you decide you don't want the paths to be composite paths, you can change them back into individual paths by selecting the composite path and then choosing Split from the Modify menu.

Composite paths can be transformed just as you'd transform any other path.

When you convert characters to paths, FreeHand automatically converts the characters as composite paths (see Figure 2-61). This is great, because you can paste things inside composite paths.

Composite paths work much like groups of objects, in that you can continue joining paths to the composite paths, just as you can group objects together with groups.

FIGURE 2-61
Characters converted
to paths are
composite paths

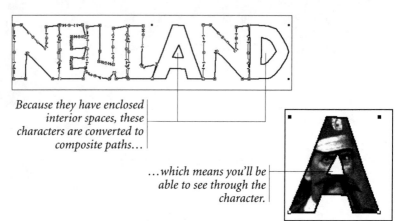

Because they have enclosed
interior spaces, these
characters are converted to
composite paths...

...which means you'll be
able to see through the
character.

Editing Composite Paths

You can subselect the individual subpaths that make up a composite path in the same way that you subselect objects inside a group—hold down Option/Alt and click on the object. Once an object is selected, you can alter the position of the path's points, move or otherwise transform the path, delete points, delete the entire path, or clone the path (see Figure 2-62).

FIGURE 2-62
Subselecting
individual paths inside
composite paths

For clarity, these
two illustrations are
shown in Keyline view.

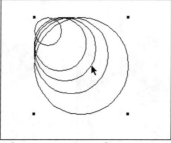

Select a composite path.

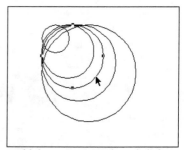

Hold down Option/Alt and click
to select a subpath.

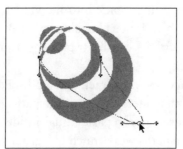

Modify the subpath.

The subpath remains part of the
composite path.

You can subselect multiple subpaths inside a composite path by holding down Shift as you select the subpaths. You can also select through any overlapping subpaths or objects by holding down Command-Option/Ctrl-Alt as you click on the subpaths, just as you can Command/Ctrl-click your way through stacks of objects (click the right mouse button if you're using Windows). You can apply any of FreeHand's transformations to the selected subpath.

When you join paths with different lines and fills, the composite path takes on the stroke and fill attributes of the path that's the farthest to the back.

Path Operations

FreeHand's path operations (the commands on the Combine and Alter Path submenus of the Modify menu) fall into four conceptual groups, which don't necessarily match their grouping on the submenu. The path operations automate path-drawing tasks that would be difficult—if not impossible—to do manually.

- ◆ The path utilities (Correct Direction, Reverse Direction, Remove Overlap, and Simplify) are handy commands for cleaning up paths.

- ◆ The path-generating commands (Blend, Expand Stroke, and Inset Path) create new paths based on existing, selected paths, according to specific rules that differ from command to command.

- ◆ The Join Blend to Path command, which gives you a way of attaching a blend to a path.

- ◆ Intersection operations (Intersect, Crop, Punch, and Union) give you ways of manipulating the areas of intersection between two (or more) closed, overlapping paths. The new Divide operation gives you a way of adding open paths to the mix.

In my opinion, the path operations are some of FreeHand's most important features. Why? First, the path operators make it easy for new users to create shapes they could never draw by hand: they can draw basic shapes (rectangles, polygons, and ellipses) and use the path operations to turn these basic shapes into the shapes they want. Second, illustrators and graphic artists benefit, because they can draw more accurately.

These features can also save you time, regardless of whether you're an amateur or a pro.

Blending

Blending is a way of creating a number of paths, automatically, between two existing paths. Blending is one of FreeHand's most useful tools, especially for creating shaded objects. When Illustrator first introduced the world to blending, all of the marketing materials stressed this great new feature's ability to turn an "S" into a swan, or a "V" into a violin. That's pretty cool, *but how often do you actually need to do that?* Blending's actually a much less glamorous, much more useful tool (see Figure 2-63).

FreeHand doesn't impose too many limitations on what, when, and how you can blend FreeHand objects. FreeHand even lets you blend between more than two objects at once. But there are a few things you've got to keep in mind.

You can blend ungrouped paths having like attributes. What do I mean by "like attributes?" I mean that you can blend a path containing a gradient fill into a path containing another gradient fill,

FIGURE 2-63
Blending

Select two points on two paths and choose Blend from the Path Operations submenu of the Arrange menu.

FreeHand fills in the intermediate blend objects.

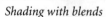
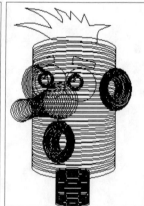

Shading with blends   *Keyline view of shading*

but you can't blend a path containing a gradient fill into a path containing a custom fill (such as "Burlap").

When you try to blend paths having different stroke patterns, or patterned fills, the shapes of the objects blend, but the strokes or fills will flip from one to the other at the halfway point of the blend (see Figure 2-64).

FIGURE 2-64
Blending paths with
differing dashed
strokes

Blending and reference points. When you're blending paths, you have the option of selecting a "reference point." What's a "reference point?" It's a way of telling FreeHand, "Blend these two objects from this point to that point" (see Figure 2-65). Most of the time, you won't have to pick a reference point.

FIGURE 2-65
Reference points

The position of the reference points has a great effect on the blend. Select two reference points—one on either end of two paths...

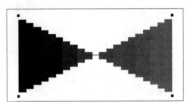

...and blend. In this example, the reference points make the blend flip over at its midpoint.

How many steps do you need? One of the most important parts of creating a blend is the number you enter in the Number of Steps field in the Object Inspector (see Figure 2-66).

♦ The number you enter in the Number of Steps field is the number of steps you want in your blend, not including the original, selected objects.

♦ The number you enter in the First field is the percentage of the distance between the original paths where you want to place the first blended path.

FIGURE 2-66
Blend controls in the
Object Inspector

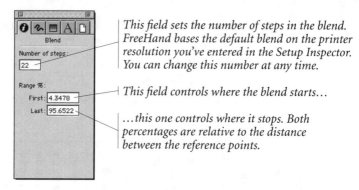

This field sets the number of steps in the blend. FreeHand bases the default blend on the printer resolution you've entered in the Setup Inspector. You can change this number at any time.

This field controls where the blend starts...

...this one controls where it stops. Both percentages are relative to the distance between the reference points.

◆ The number you enter in the Last field is the percentage of the distance between the original paths where you want to place the last blended path.

◆ Most of the time, you'll just type a number in the Number of Steps field and press Return. You can enter numbers in the other fields to create special blend effects (Figure 2-67).

FIGURE 2-67
Special blend effects

Normal blend: 19 blend steps; first blend step 5%; last blend step 95%.

Special blend: 19 blend steps; first blend step 20%; last blend step 80%.

When you're working with blends, you can determine the best number of blend steps to use, based on the length of the blend and the properties of your printer, by solving the following equation.

number of steps = (dpi   lpi)² ¥ % change in color

In this equation, *dpi* is the resolution of your final output device in dots per inch; *lpi* is the screen frequency you'll be using, in lines per inch. The value *% change in color* is just that, and it's easy to figure out if you're using spot colors.

If you're using process colors, figure out which component process color goes through the largest percentage change from one end of the blend to the other, and use that value for the % change in color part of the equation.

The purpose of this equation is to tell you the minimum number of steps you should use. Below this number of steps, you'll start losing gray levels, and bands of gray (or color) will appear in your blend. You can always use more blend steps than this, but you won't gain anything, and each additional blend step increases the complexity of your publication, therefore increasing the time your publication takes to print.

Also be aware that you never need more than 256 steps in a blend (unless you have to fill gaps between blend objects inside the blend), because that's the maximum number of gray levels a PostScript interpreter can render. You might have heard that newer versions of PostScript (known as PostScript Level 2 and PostScript 3) can print smoother blends, and it's true, they can—in theory. I have yet to see an imagesetter print a blend or gradient fill created by a standard graphics program using more than 256 levels of gray. I'll let you know when I do.

What if using the optimum number of blend steps means that gaps appear in your blend? This happens when your original blend objects aren't big enough to cover the distance from one blend step to the next. When this happens, you can either increase the number of blend steps you're using, or you can figure out how much larger you'll have to make your blend objects using the following equation.

distance blend has to cover   number of steps = size of original object

Blends and spot colors. You can blend between two spot-colored objects and get what you'd expect: the intermediate blend steps are rendered in tints of the "parent" spot colors (see Figure 2-68).

Creating a blend. Now that you know the rules, let's create a blend (see Figure 2-69).

1. Select two or more ungrouped paths (with matching or compatible attributes).

2. Choose Blend from the Path operations submenu of the Modify menu (or press Command-Shift-B/Ctrl-Shift-B).

Is Blend grayed out? If it is, your paths may not be of the same type (that is, you might have one open path and one closed path).

FreeHand blends the paths you've selected. The original objects and the newly created paths are grouped together. I refer to the resulting group as a "blend."

If the attributes of the paths you're trying to blend are incompatible, FreeHand displays an alert (shown in Figure 2-70). Sorry, no blend. You'll have to track down what's different between the two paths, make changes, and try again.

You can enter negative numbers (to -100%) in the First and Last fields. You can use this to extend the blend past the original objects by up to the distance between them. Of what possible use is this? I haven't found one yet.

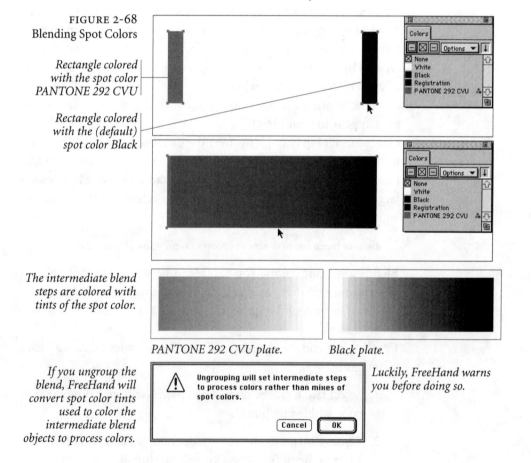

FIGURE 2-68
Blending Spot Colors

Rectangle colored with the spot color PANTONE 292 CVU

Rectangle colored with the (default) spot color Black

The intermediate blend steps are colored with tints of the spot color.

PANTONE 292 CVU plate.   Black plate.

If you ungroup the blend, FreeHand will convert spot color tints used to color the intermediate blend objects to process colors.

Ungrouping will set intermediate steps to process colors rather than mixes of spot colors.

Cancel   OK

Luckily, FreeHand warns you before doing so.

FIGURE 2-69
Creating a blend

Select two reference points and choose Blend from the Path Operations submenu of the Arrange menu.

FreeHand creates your blend.

Enter the number of blend steps you want in the Object Inspector and press Return.

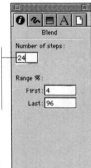

The blended objects are grouped.

Okay, this example's no more typical of the uses of blending than the swan or violin I mentioned earlier.

But it sure is fun!

FIGURE 2-70
What happens when you try blending incompatible objects

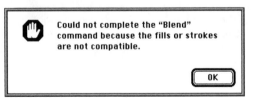

Editing blends. If you want to change the number of steps in your blend, select the blended objects and press Command-I/Ctrl-I to display the Object Inspector. Change the blend by entering new values in the Number of Steps, First Blend, or Last Blend fields, and press Return. FreeHand creates a new blend from the original objects (see Figure 2-71).

FIGURE 2-71
Editing blends

Select a blend. (Press Command-I/Ctrl-I to display the Object Inspector if it's not already visible).

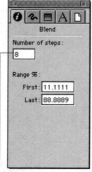

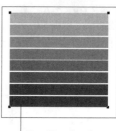

Enter a number in the Number of Steps field and Press Return.

FreeHand redraws your blend.

Changing the shape of the entire blend. You can change the shape and attributes of blended objects to a certain extent by changing the shape, position, and attributes of the original shapes in the blend. Subselect an original path by holding down Option/Alt as you click on the path (to subselect an element in a group). Next, change the path's attributes, position, and/or shape. As you make changes to the path, FreeHand recreates the blend based on the current shape, position, and/or attributes (see Figure 2-72).

FIGURE 2-72
Changing the shape and attributes of blended objects

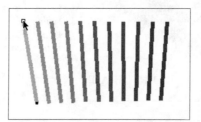

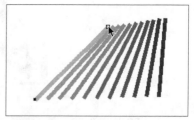

Hold down Option and click on the first or last object in the blend to subselect it.

Reshape the object. FreeHand alters the blend based on the new shape.

Editing an intermediate path in a blend. To edit one or more of the intermediate paths in the blend, ungroup the blend, select the path, and edit away. There's no way to get the changes you make to this intermediate point to ripple through the blend, however. If you want to do that, consider reblending between intermediate objects (see Figure 2-73).

Creating colors based on blend steps. When you create a blend, the colors applied to the intermediate paths in the blend are not automatically added to FreeHand's Colors palette. If you want to

FIGURE 2-73
Editing intermediate
paths in a blend

Select the blend you want to edit...

...and press Command-U/Ctrl-U to ungroup it.

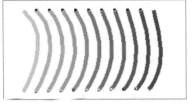

Press Command-U/Ctrl-U again to ungroup the intermediate blend objects.

Now you can edit the intermediate blend objects.

add one or more of the colors created by the blend to your Colors palette, this is the procedure (see Figure 2-74).

1. Select the blend.

2. Press Command-U/Ctrl-U twice to completely ungroup the blend (when you first press the keyboard shortcut, FreeHand ungroups the original objects, but leaves the objects generated by the blend grouped; pressing the shortcut again ungroups all the objects in the blend).

3. Select one of the objects you created by blending.

4. Press Command-Option-F/Ctrl-Alt-F to display the Fill Inspector, then choose Add to Color Palette from the pop-up menu next to the color well. FreeHand adds the path's color to the Color palette.

Tip:
Adding all of the
colors in a blend

When you want to add *all* of the colors in a blend to your publication's Colors palette, ungroup the blend (twice), then choose Name All Colors from the Colors submenu of the Xtras menu. FreeHand adds all of the colors to your Colors palette, automatically assigning a name to each color as it does so. Bear in mind that this will add as many colors to your Colors palette as there are steps in the blend.

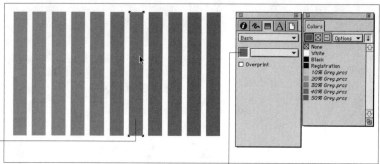

*After ungrouping the
blend, select the object
filled with the color you
want to add to your
Colors palette.*

*When you select the object, its fill
color appears in the color well in
the Fill Inspector.*

*Drag a color swatch
from the color well in
the Fill Inspector to a
blank area in the Colors
palette (or drop it on
the Add Arrow at the
top of the Colors
palette). Or choose Add
to Color List from the
pop-up menu attached
to the color well.*

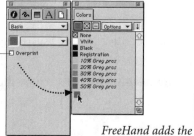

*FreeHand adds the
color to the Colors
palette and automati-
cally assigns a color
name to the new color.*

*To change the
name, double-
click the color
name in the
Colors palette…*

*…and type a name
for the color. When
you're done typing,
press Return.*

Using blend to create gradient fills. If you want total control over
the creation of gradient fills in FreeHand, use blending, rather than
the Gradient fill types. If you use blending, you accrue several significant advantages.

♦ Control over the graduation. FreeHand's Gradient fill type
offers you the choice between Linear and Logarithmic fill
progressions, but blending can give you more control. By
blending objects, you can make the blend go as rapidly or
slowly from color to color as you choose.

♦ Control over trapping. See Chapter 7, "Printing," for more
information on trapping gradient fills.

♦ Optimization of your fill for printing on your final output
device (printer or imagesetter).

♦ Superior screen display of fills.

The only disadvantage I can think of is that you've got many more objects on a page to worry about. Unless you ungroup them, however, they'll be treated as a single group.

Blends also produce very different-looking results. I find that I mix blends and gradient fills inside a publication to get the effects I want. If I want a fill that doesn't follow the shape of an object, I'll often use a gradient fill. But if I want a fill that follows the shape of an object, I'll use a blend. Figure 2-75 shows the difference.

FIGURE 2-75
Blends and
gradient fills

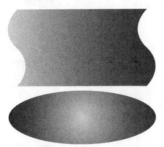 

Gradient fills don't follow the shape of the object.   *Blends follow the shape of the object.*

To create a gradient fill using Blend, follow these steps.

1. Create a path that has the fill attributes you want for one end of the gradient.

2. Create a path that has the fill attributes you want for the other end of the gradient.

3. Select one point from the first path, and then select a point from the second path.

4. Choose Blend from the Combine submenu of the Modify menu (or press Command-Shift-B/Ctrl-Shift-B).

5. Display the Object Inspector, if it's not already visible, by pressing Command-I/Ctrl-I. Type a number in the Number of Steps field and press Return.

Blending with the Smudge Tool. If you've installed the Smudge tool (that is, if the file "Smudge" is in your Xtras folder), you can create a blend by dragging—it's almost like painting with a blend (see Figure 2-76). What do you have to do?

FIGURE 2-76
Creating a blend with
the Smudge tool

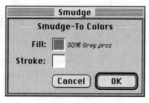

*You'll find the Smudge
tool in the Xtra Tools
palette (if the palette's
not already visible, you
can display it by
pressing Command-
Shift-K/Ctrl-Alt-X).*

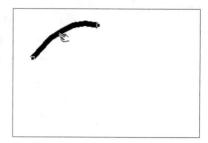

*Double-click the Smudge
tool in the Xtra Tools palette
to display the Smudge dialog
box.*

*Position the Smudge tool over
a path...*

*Note: You can't use the
Object Inspector to
change the number of
steps in a blend you've
created using the
Smudge tool.*

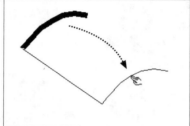

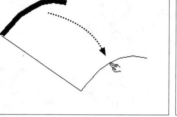

...and drag.

*Stop dragging, and FreeHand creates
a blend.*

1. Display the Xtra Tools palette (press Command-Option-X/Ctrl-Alt-X, if it's not already visible), then select the Smudge tool.

2. Hold down Command/Ctrl (to turn the cursor into the Pointer tool) and select the path you want to "smudge," then release the key and drag the Smudge tool. As you drag, FreeHand extends a line from the original path, showing you the distance and direction of the blend you're creating. Hold down Option/Alt as you drag, and FreeHand bases the blend on the center of the path.

3. Stop dragging, and FreeHand creates the blend.

You can set options for the Smudge tool by double-clicking the tool in the Xtra Tools palette. When you do this, FreeHand displays the Smudge dialog box. You can set the Fill and Stroke colors as you would any other FreeHand colors—drag a color swatch into the color well. Unlike most other color wells, double-clicking these won't bring up the Color Mixer and the Color palette.

Blending Gradient Fills. In FreeHand 8, you can blend gradient fills (or, at least, between gradient fills of the same type and color ramp). The effects are astonishing, as shown in Figure 2-77.

FIGURE 2-77
Blending Gradient Fills

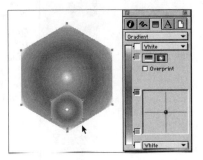 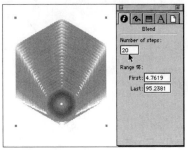

Select two objects formatted with the same gradient fill...

...and blend. Try rotating one of the paths before you blend.

Join Blend to Path

When you join a blend to a path, the objects in the blend space themselves along the path. In effect, the first and last points in the path become the beginning and ending points of the blend. But there's more—you can have the objects in the blend rotate to follow the angle of the part of the path they're on.

To join a blend to a path, select the path and the blend and choose Join Blend to Path from the Combine submenu of the Modify menu. FreeHand joins the blend to the path (see Figure 2-78). When you look at the Object Inspector for the path, you'll see two new options: Show Path, and Rotate Around Path. Turn on the Show Path option to have FreeHand display the path you've joined the blend to (complete with its original formatting, on top of the blend). Turn on the Rotate Around Path option to make FreeHand rotate the objects in the blend to match the angle of the path segment they occupy.

Tip:
Creating
Gradient Fills
That Follow
a Path

Being able to join a blend to a path give us the ability to do something that's always been on my FreeHand wish list—creating gradient fills that run along a path. The trouble is that the edges of the blend you've joined to a path are somewhat jagged—at least when compared to the perfection of the path. What can you do to get a smooth edge? When you want to create a ribbon, or when you want to create a line indicating motion (as on a map), follow these steps (see Figure 2-79).

FIGURE 2-78
Joining a
Blend to a Path

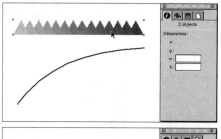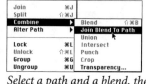

Select a path and a blend, then choose Join Blend to Path from the Combine submenu of the Modify menu.

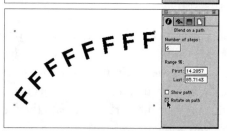

FreeHand joins the blend to the path.

When you turn on the Rotate Around Path option, FreeHand rotates the objects in the blend so that they're rotated at an angle equal to the angle of the line segment they're joined to.

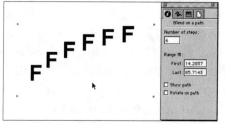

Turn the Rotate Around Path option off, and FreeHand positions the blend on the path without changing the angle of the objects in the blend to match the path.

1. Create a blend.

2. Join the blend to a path.

3. Hold down Option/Alt and click the blend until you've selected the original path.

4. Clone the path.

5. Choose Expand Stroke from the Alter Path submenu of the Modify menu (see "Expand Stroke," later in this chapter). FreeHand displays the Expand Stroke dialog box.

FIGURE 2-79
Creating a
"motion" arrow

These rectangles (in the blend) look pretty smooth here, but they add a jagged edge to the path when you print them.

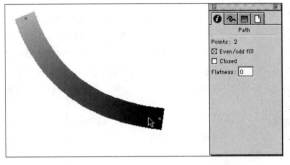

Create a blend between two rectangles, then join the blend to a path.

Hold down Option/ Alt and click the blend to select the path.

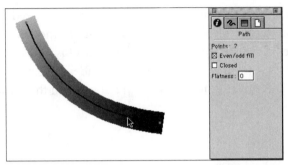

Press Command-=/ Ctrl-= to clone the path. The new path appears on top of the blend.

Choose Expand Stroke from the Alter Path submenu of the Modify menu. Enter the width of the "stroke" you want to create.

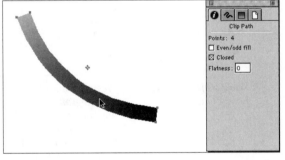

Cut or copy the blend, then select the closed path you created using Expand Stroke. Press Command- Shift-V/Ctrl-Shift- V to paste the blend inside the path. This makes the edges of the blend smooth.

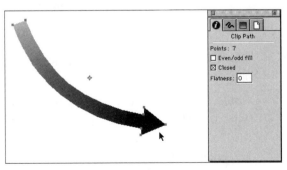

You can add an arrowhead, if you want to.

6. Enter a width for the expanded path. Make sure that the width you choose is narrower than the blend. Set the miter limit and cap type, if necessary, then press Return. Free-Hand creates a new, closed path from the open path you selected.

7. Cut the blend, then paste it into the path you created using Expand Stroke.

Tip:
Ungrouping a
Blend You've
Joined to a Path

When you ungroup a blend you've joined to a path, each object in the blend appears on the page at the same position as it occupied when it was joined to the path (as you'll recall, separating a blend from a path returns the blended objects to their original positions relative to the first and last paths in the blend). See Figure 2-80.

FIGURE 2-80
Ungrouping a blend
joined to a path

Select a blend you've joined to a path.

Press Command-U/Ctrl-U to ungroup. FreeHand ungroups the original objects (in this example, the first and last stars in the blend), but leaves the objects generated by the blend grouped.

Ungroup again, and FreeHand ungroups the blend, placing each object on the page— in exactly the same location it occupied when it was joined to the path.

Union

I often want to create a single path from two or more overlapping closed paths, but I don't want the path to have holes in it, as it would if I made it a composite path using Join. Union does just what I want—it combines paths while removing any areas where they overlap (see Figure 2-81). If the paths I've selected don't overlap, FreeHand creates a composite path.

Union is great for creating complex paths from simple paths, such as rectangles and ellipses.

FIGURE 2-81
Using Union

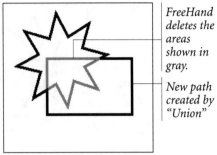

FreeHand deletes the areas shown in gray.

New path created by "Union"

Select two or more closed paths (in this example, the star shape is on top).

Choose Union from the Combine submenu of the Modify menu. FreeHand creates a new path by merging the original paths and removing their areas of intersection.

Divide

While the other path operations (Union, Intersect, Crop, Punch, and Transparency) work their magic on two or more selected closed paths, Divide only becomes available when you select both closed and open paths. In essence, Divide uses each open path in the selection as if it were running the Knife tool along that path. It's a way to use open paths to cut up closed paths (see Figure 2-82).

FIGURE 2-82
Using Divide

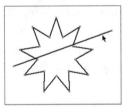

Select an open path and a closed path (or any number of closed and open paths).

Choose Divide from the Combine submenu of the Modify menu. FreeHand splits the closed paths where they intersect the open paths.

In this example, I've dragged the resulting closed paths apart.

Intersect

What do you do when you want to create a path that's defined by the intersection of two (or more) overlapping paths? Select the overlapping objects and choose Intersect from the Path operations submenu, and FreeHand creates the path for you. It's that simple (see Figure 2-83).

FIGURE 2-83
Using Intersect

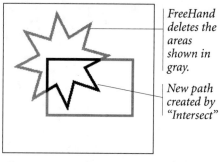

FreeHand deletes the areas shown in gray.

New path created by "Intersect"

Select two or more closed paths (in this example, the star shape is on top).

Choose Intersect from the Combine submenu of the Modify menu. FreeHand creates a new path based on the intersection of the shapes, and deletes the original paths.

Here are a few things to keep in mind when you use Intersect.

◆ The path FreeHand generates takes on the formatting of the original path that's farthest to the back.

◆ If you run Intersect on a set of paths that don't intersect, FreeHand deletes all the paths.

◆ If you've turned on the Path Operations Consume Original Paths option in the Object Editing Preferences dialog box, FreeHand deletes the original paths as it creates the new path. If you want to keep the original paths, clone them before using Intersect, or turn this option off.

Punch   When you want to use one closed path to cut a hole in another closed path, use Punch. Position the path you want to use as the "cookie cutter" above the path you want to use as "cookie dough," and choose Punch from the Combine submenu. FreeHand deletes the area where the two paths overlap from the path that's farthest to the back (see Figure 2-84). When the topmost path is entirely within the path behind it, FreeHand turns the paths into a single composite path.

Crop   Crop is something like the opposite of Punch. Where Punch removes paths or parts of paths *inside* the area of the topmost path (the "cookie cutter"), Crop removes all paths *outside* that area. To use the Crop path operation, follow these steps (see Figure 2-85).

FIGURE 2-84
Punch effect

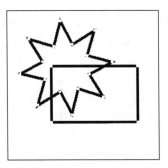

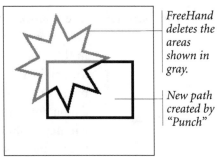

FreeHand deletes the areas shown in gray.

New path created by "Punch"

Select two or more closed paths (in this example, the star shape is on top).

Choose Punch from the Path Operations submenu of the Arrange menu. FreeHand creates a new path by cutting the topmost path out of the paths behind it.

FIGURE 2-85
Using Crop

This polygon is on top of the other selected objects.

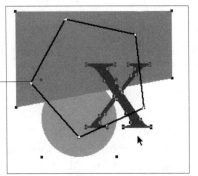

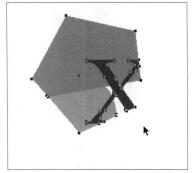

Select some objects and choose Crop from the Path Operations submenu of the Arrange menu.

FreeHand removes the parts of the paths that aren't covered by the polygon.

1. Position a path above some other paths.

2. Select the paths.

3. Choose Crop from the Path Operations submenu of the Modify menu (or choose Crop from the Path Operations submenu of the Xtras menu). FreeHand crops the background paths into the area taken up by the cropping path.

The Crop path operation is nothing like the cropping tool found in other applications. Crop won't crop images unless those images have already been pasted inside a path. If that's the effect you're after, you can paste the image inside the path.

Transparency   The Transparency path operation is a lot like "Intersect," in that it generates a new path where the selected paths overlap, but differs in that the new path is colored with a color based on the colors of the original objects. Choose "Transparency" from the Combine submenu of the Xtras menu, and FreeHand displays the Transparency dialog box. Choose a percentage (0 percent equals complete transparency, 100 percent equals complete opacity—the same color as the topmost path) and press Return, and FreeHand creates a new path (see Figure 2-86).

FIGURE 2-86
Transparency
dialog box

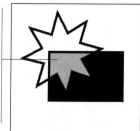

The larger the number you enter in this field (up to 100), the more "opaque" the topmost object becomes.

Transparency creates a new shape and colors it with a new color based on the colors of the original shapes.

Correcting Path Direction   Most of the time, you could call Correct Path Direction, "make clockwise"—because that's what it does. You've probably noticed that you don't always get what you'd expect when you join paths to create a composite path. Sometimes, you'll see gaps in interior areas you'd expect would be filled. You can fix this problem by selecting the composite path and choosing Correct Direction from the Alter Path submenu of the Modify menu (see Figure 2-87). Using Correct Direction has no effect on the shape of your path.

FIGURE 2-87
Correcting path
direction

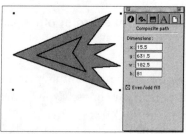

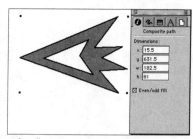

Before choosing Correct Direction—path doesn't fill properly.

After "Correct Direction."

Reversing Path Direction   When you want to change a path's direction (for example, when you want an arrowhead to appear on the other end of an open path), choose Reverse Direction from the Alter Path submenu of the Modify menu. FreeHand reverses the direction of the path (see Figure 2-88). Reverse Direction has no effect on the shape of your path.

FIGURE 2-88
Reversing path
direction

Before "Reverse Direction"   *After "Reverse Direction"*

Removing Overlap

When a single FreeHand path crosses over itself, it becomes more difficult to print (and, to a certain extent, more difficult to edit). It's easy to create self-crossing paths when you're working with the Freehand tool, the Calligraphic Pen tool, or the Variable Stroke tool. It's also easy (it's practically unavoidable) to create composite paths that cross over themselves. Remove Overlap simplifies your paths by turning them into composite paths containing separate, closed paths (see Figure 2-89). It's kind of like a combination of Punch and Union, but works on a single path.

FIGURE 2-89
Removing overlap

Before "Remove overlap"   *After "Remove overlap"*

Simplifying Paths

Okay, confess—here's something we've all done (at least once): we place a TIFF in FreeHand and trace it with the Trace tool, thereby generating a path containing billions and billions of points—and then express surprise when the publication won't print. These days, we don't have to give up our sloppy habits (not that it'd be a bad idea…), provided we remember to select the path and run Simplify on it before we try to print (see Figure 2-90).

Simplify is also a great tool for new users who haven't quite gotten the hang of FreeHand's drawing tools—they can draw a path (new users typically use too many points when drawing), and then see how FreeHand thinks the path should be drawn.

FIGURE 2-90
Simplifying a path

This path went from 177 to 127 points after simplification.

Remember: fewer points = easier printing.

Before "Simplify"   *After "Simplify"*

Expand Stroke

Expand Stroke creates two new paths, where each new path is a specific distance from the center of the original path. One of the generated paths is a specific distance *outside* the original path; the other is the same distance *inside* the original path. Once FreeHand's created the paths, it joins them into a single, compound path (see Figure 2-91).

FIGURE 2-91
Using Expand Stroke

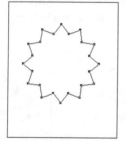

Select a path and choose Expand Stroke from the Path Operations submenu of the Arrange menu.

FreeHand displays the Expand Stroke dialog box. Enter the distance you want between the selected path and the new path in the Width field, and press Return.

FreeHand creates a new path, placing each new point a precise distance from each original point.

Inset Path

Inset Path works like Expand Stroke—but Inset Path only creates one new path, a specific distance inside or outside the original path (Figure 2-92). Note that scaling a path and using Inset Path produce (in most cases) very different results.

When you enter negative numbers in the Inset Path dialog box, FreeHand creates a new path a specific distance *outside* the original path ("inset path" becomes "outset path").

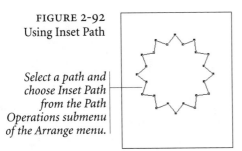

FIGURE 2-92
Using Inset Path

Select a path and choose Inset Path from the Path Operations submenu of the Arrange menu.

Clone the path first, if you want to keep it in its original shape— "Inset path" operates on the current path.

FreeHand displays the Inset Path dialog box. Enter the distance you want between the selected path and the new path in the Width field, and press Return. Enter a negative distance to make the generated path larger than the original path.

FreeHand creates a new path, placing each new point a precise distance from each original point.

Path Operations and Preferences

If you're getting tired of cloning paths before you run path operations on them, there's a preference you should know about. It's the Path Operations Consume Original Paths option in the Object Preferences dialog box (see "Preferences," in Chapter 1, "FreeHand Basics"). When this option is off, FreeHand clones paths as you run path operations—and leaves your original paths alone. Turn this option on to have FreeHand delete the original paths while performing path operations (see Figure 2-93).

FIGURE 2-93
The Path Operations
Consume Original
Paths option

These examples show the effect this option has on the Inset Path path operation.

Object Preferences dialog box.

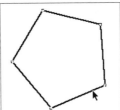

Original path.

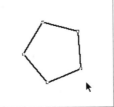

When the Path Operations Consume Original Paths option is on, FreeHand deletes the original path.

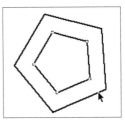

When the Path Operations Consume Original Paths option is off, FreeHand retains the original path.

Another way you can run FreeHand's path operations is to use the Operations palette (see Figure 2-94). To display the Operations palette, press Command-Shift-I/Ctrl-Shift-I. The path operations (and various other FreeHand operations) are represented by buttons in the palette (you can display the palette without labels once you get used to the appearance of the buttons).

FIGURE 2-94
Path operations on the
Operations palette

*The Operations palette
takes up less room with
"Show labels" turned
off—but you've got to
know your icons.*

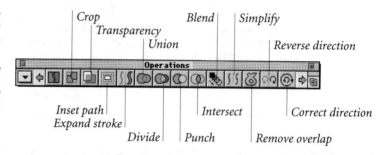

Crop   Blend   Simplify
Transparency
Union   Reverse direction
Inset path   Intersect   Correct direction
Expand stroke
Divide   Punch   Remove overlap

Tracing

When Illustrator 1.0 first appeared, tracing scanned artwork or Mac-Paint images was seen as the major use for the product. People just couldn't imagine creating entire pieces of artwork using a point-and-path drawing program. While times have changed—I think more people now use FreeHand and Illustrator to create illustrations without tracing—tracing is still a powerful option you can use in creating your FreeHand publication.

You can trace any object in FreeHand, and you can trace the object manually or use the Trace tool.

To manually trace an image, follow these steps (see Figure 2-95).

1. Import an image. Make sure you've turned on the High-Resolution Image Display option in the Redraw Preferences dialog box; this way, you'll see the high-resolution display of your imported image rather than a low-resolution rendition.

2. Without deselecting the image, click the Background layer in the Layers palette to send the image to the background. This tints the image and makes it easier to trace.

FIGURE 2-95
Manually tracing an
imported image

Import the image you want to trace.   *Send the image to a background layer.*

Place points and paths until...   *...you've traced the image.*

3. Lock the background layer by clicking the padlock icon next to the layer's name in the Layers palette.

4. Zoom in on some portion of the image and start placing points.

5. When you're through tracing the image, you can delete it.

**Using the
Trace Tool**

I have to confess: in versions of FreeHand prior to version 7, I didn't use the Trace tool much. Most of the time, I found it was quicker to trace objects manually—the old Trace tool didn't do a very good job of tracing anything other than the simplest of objects. In addition, it didn't trace color or grayscale images. The Trace tool is now amazing, and is at least as good as Adobe Streamline (a dedicated tracing program). It's so good, it's downright scary.

In spite of what you might have heard elsewhere, you can use the Trace tool to trace (or "autotrace") *anything* on a FreeHand page. I have to mention this, because many people have gotten the impression that you can only autotrace bitmapped images. You can autotrace text, paths, imported images—and even EPS graphics. Autotracing is a fast and fun way to create new paths from other FreeHand objects.

To set options for the Trace tool, double-click the tool in the Toolbox. FreeHand displays the Trace Tool dialog box (see Figure 2-96). The following sections discuss the Trace tool's options.

FIGURE 2-96
Trace Tool Options

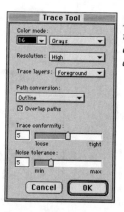

Double-click the Trace tool in the Toolbox. FreeHand displays the Trace Tool dialog box.

Number of Colors. The value you choose from the Number of Colors pop-up menu depends on how many colors are in the object you're trying to trace, and how accurately you want FreeHand to trace that object. It's another balancing act. Choose more colors (up to the number of colors or grays in the object, or 256, whichever comes first), and FreeHand creates a more accurate tracing of the object. At the same time, the more colors you choose, the more paths FreeHand will generate as it traces the object. In general, pick as few colors as produce an accurate tracing of whatever it is you want to trace. If you're tracing a black-and-white image, choose "2" from the Number of Colors pop-up menu (and choose "Grays" from the Color Mode pop-up menu).

Color Mode. The color mode determines the colors FreeHand applies as it creates paths by tracing an object. If you're tracing a color graphic, and want to create paths using those colors, choose "Colors." If you're tracing a black-and-white or grayscale image, choose "Grays." If you're tracing a color image, and want FreeHand to create a grayscale version of the graphic, choose "Grays."

Resolution. Choose "High" from the Resolution pop-up menu, unless you're running out of RAM as you trace. If you do run out of memory, try "Normal." If you're still running out of memory, choose "Low," and think about buying more RAM.

Trace Layers. Use the Trace Layers pop-up menu to tell FreeHand which layers you want to trace.

Path Conversion. You'll just have to experiment with the choices on this pop-up menu to see which option is best for each object you want to trace. Here are a few general guidelines.

◆ If you're tracing grayscale and color images (scanned photographs or artwork you've imported from Painter, for example), choose "Outline." When you choose "Outline," FreeHand displays the Overlap Paths option. Turn it on.

◆ If you're tracing black-and-white line art, choose "Center-line." When you do, FreeHand displays the Uniform Lines option. Turn it on if the strokes in the object you're scanning are of similar width, or turn if off if they're not.

◆ Choose "Centerline/Outline" if the object you're trying to trace contains both shaded (i.e., color and grayscale), and high-contrast (i.e., black-and-white) information.

◆ Choose "Outer Edge" when you're tracing an object that's surrounded by white space (or other solid color) and want to create a clipping path.

Trace Conformity. Enter larger numbers in the Trace Conformity field (or use the slider) to make FreeHand trace more accurately. Enter smaller numbers (zero is as low as you can go) to make it create paths with fewer points (if you're running out of memory as you try to trace an object).

Noise Tolerance. Does FreeHand spend time tracing "noise" pixels in your images that have more to do with all of the dust that's on your scanner than they do with the pictures you're trying to trace? Tell FreeHand to ignore them by setting the value in the Noise

Tolerance field to a higher number. Or, if FreeHand seems to be losing details in your images, decrease the value.

To autotrace an object, select the Trace tool and drag the cursor around the area you want to trace (see Figure 2-97). Keep this area as small as you can—autotracing can take a long time and can generate paths containing lots of points. It's sometimes a little easier to autotrace a complex or large object in several passes, and then join the resultant paths. If you run out of memory while you're autotracing, select a smaller area to trace, or use a lower resolution setting (in the Trace Tool dialog box). If that doesn't work, you can try quitting other programs to free system resources in Windows, or, on the Macintosh, you can increase the amount of RAM dedicated to FreeHand.

After you release the mouse button, FreeHand autotraces the object or objects you dragged a rectangle around. It's a good idea to move the paths you've created to a new layer. Without deselecting the paths, choose New from the pop-up menu in the Layers palette. Click the new layer's name in the Layers palette to move the selected objects to that layer.

The current magnification has no effect on autotracing.

Strokes

Once you've created a path, you'll probably want to give the path some specific line weight, color, or other property. The process of applying formatting to a path is often called "stroking a path," and we refer to a path's appearance as its "stroke." Strokes specify what the outside of the path looks like.

To define a stroke for a path, display the Stroke Inspector by pressing Command-Option-L/Ctrl-Alt-L (see Figure 2-98). Use the Stroke Type pop-up menu (the pop-up menu directly below the Inspector buttons) in the Stroke Inspector to choose the type of stroke you want to use.

Basic Strokes   When you select Basic from the Stroke Type pop-up menu, the Stroke Inspector shows you the basic stroke attributes. Most of the

FIGURE 2-97
Autotracing

Imported TIFF (16 levels of gray).

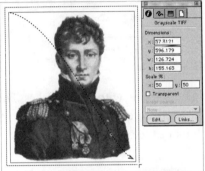

Drag the Trace tool around the object you want to trace.

FreeHand traces the object.

To make things more clear in this screen shot, I've deselected the paths created by the Trace tool, then deleted the original TIFF. What you see here is the result of a quick-and-dirty autotrace—I could probably make it better by adjusting the Trace tool's options. Amazing.

FIGURE 2-98
Stroke Types

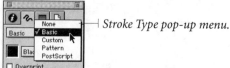

—| *Stroke Type pop-up menu.*

The Stroke Inspector displays different controls as you choose different stroke types from the Stroke Type pop-up menu.

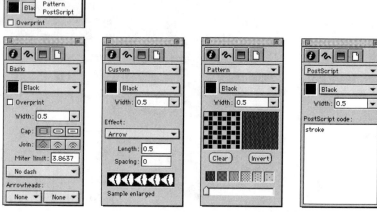

time, you'll be working with basic strokes. Though they're not flashy, there are a few interesting tricks to using them, and a couple of things to look out for.

Color. Drag a color swatch from a color well in the Colors palette (or the Color Mixer, or from any other color well) into the color well in the Stroke Inspector to apply a color to the stroke of your path, or choose a color from the Color pop-up menu (next to the color well). If you're working with a named color, the color's name appears next to the color well in the Stroke Inspector.

Overprint. Checking this option makes the stroke overprint (rather than knock out of) whatever's behind it. This setting overrides any ink-level overprinting settings in the Print options dialog box (see Figure 2-99). This might not seem like much, but if you're creating color publications, you'll find it's one of the most important features in FreeHand (see Chapter 6, "Color").

Width. You can enter a width for the stroke of the selected path using the Stroke Width field, or you can choose a predefined line weight from the Stroke Widths pop-up menu in the Stroke Inspector. You can add new stroke widths to this submenu using the Expert Editing Preferences dialog box (see "Expert Editing Preferences," in Chapter 1, "FreeHand Basics"). Don't type zero, even if

FIGURE 2-99
Overprinting strokes

*You won't see the effect
of overprinting until
you print separations of
your publication. When
you do that, you'll see
something like these
thumbnails.*

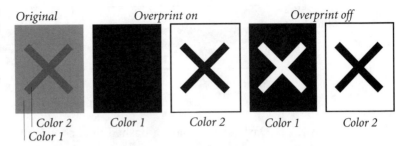

Original · Color 2 / Color 1 · Overprint on · Color 1 · Color 2 · Overprint off · Color 1 · Color 2

it works to produce the finest stroke available on your 300-dpi printer, because a stroke weight of zero on an imagesetter produces an almost invisible line.

Cap. Select one of the Cap options to determine the shape of the end of the stroke (see Figure 2-100). The Cap option you choose has no visible effect on a closed path.

FIGURE 2-100
Line caps

 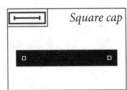 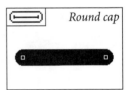

Butt cap · *Square cap* · *Round cap*

Join. The Join option determines the way FreeHand renders corners—the place where two line segments in a path meet in a point (see Figure 2-101).

FIGURE 2-101
Line joins

Miter join · *Round join* · *Beveled join*

Miter Limit. The number you enter in the Miter Limit field (from 2 to 180 degrees) sets the smallest angle for which FreeHand will use a mitered join. If the angle of the line join is less than the number you enter in the Miter limit field, FreeHand renders the corner as a beveled line join (see Figure 2-102).

FIGURE 2-102
Miter limit

Miter limit of 2   *Miter limit of 30*

Dash. If you want a dashed line, choose one of the dash patterns from the Dash pop-up menu—that's the pop-up menu directly below the Miter Limit field (see Figure 2-103).

FIGURE 2-103
Dash patterns

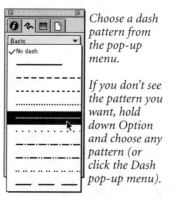

Choose a dash pattern from the pop-up menu.

If you don't see the pattern you want, hold down Option and choose any pattern (or click the Dash pop-up menu).

FreeHand displays the Dash Editor dialog box, where you can create your own dash pattern.

**Tip:
Creating Your
Own Dash
Patterns**

If you've looked at the Dash pop-up menu for a while and still don't see the dash pattern you're looking for, hold down Option/ Alt and click the pop-up menu. The Dash Editor appears. In the Dash Editor, you can create a wide variety of dashed line patterns by entering different values in the Segment Lengths fields.

   If you still can't find the dashed line style you want, you can create one using PostScript. See Chapter 8, "PostScript" for more on creating custom dashed lines.

**Tip:
Editing Your
Custom Dash
Patterns**

Once you've created a custom dash pattern, you can edit it. Hold down Option/Alt and select a dash pattern from the Dash pop-up menu in the Stroke Inspector. FreeHand displays the Dash Editor, where you can edit the pattern.

Arrowheads. You can add arrowheads or (I guess) tailfeathers to any line you want by choosing an arrowhead from the pop-up menus at the bottom of the Stroke Inspector. The leftmost pop-up menu applies to the first point in the path (according to the direction of the path); the rightmost pop-up menu applies to the last point in the path. You don't have to make choices from both of the pop-up menus (see Figure 2-104).

FIGURE 2-104
Arrowheads

Choose an arrowhead
from either (or both)
of the pop-up menus.

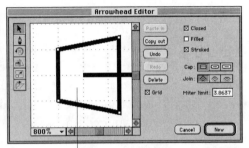

If you want to create your own arrowhead, choose New from the pop-up menu.

FreeHand displays the Arrowhead Editor dialog box.

In the Arrowhead Editor dialog box, you can draw your new arrowhead, or you can paste in an arrowhead that you drew in the Publication window.

What if you can't find the arrowhead you need? You can make your own.

1. Draw the shape you want for your custom arrowhead using any of FreeHand's drawing tools. The shape can be anything you want, but it must be a single path.

2. Select the path you've drawn and press Command-C/Ctrl-C to copy it to the Clipboard.

3. If the Stroke Inspector isn't already visible, display it by pressing Command-Option-L/Ctrl-Alt-L.

4. Choose New from one of the Arrowhead pop-up menus at the bottom of the Stroke Inspector. FreeHand displays the Arrowhead Editor.

5. Click the Paste In button. The path you copied appears in the Arrowhead Editor. Scale it, change its shape, if you want. When the arrowhead looks the way you want it to, click the

New button to create a new arrowhead style. FreeHand adds your arrowhead to the pop-up menus at the bottom of the Stroke Inspector, and you can apply it to any open path in your publication.

You can also draw the arrowhead in the Arrowhead Editor, but I find it easier to draw it on a FreeHand page (where more drawing tools are available).

Tip:
Editing
Arrowheads

You can edit any of the arrowheads shown in the Arrowhead pop-up menus—just hold down Option/Alt and choose the arrowhead you want to edit from the menu. FreeHand displays the Arrowhead Editor dialog box. When you're done editing the arrowhead, Free-Hand changes the arrowhead's appearance in the pop-up menu to reflect your editing.

Custom Strokes

FreeHand's Custom stroke styles are something like the "graphic tapes" from Chartpak and Letraset (for those of you who remember what graphic production was like before computers). Like the graphic tapes, they come in handy when you need to do a custom border for a coupon or flyer.

When you choose a custom stroke from FreeHand's Effect pop-up menu, you'll see a preview of the stroke at the bottom of the Stroke Inspector. The color and width settings for custom strokes all work exactly as described in "Basic Strokes," above.

Enter different values in the Length and Spacing fields, and you can vary the custom stroke's appearance (see Figure 2-105, on the next page). The appearance of the Stroke Inspector for the Neon custom stroke is a little different—it doesn't have fields for Length and Spacing (they're irrelevant to the effect).

These stroke effects are PostScript, so they won't print on a non-PostScript printer.

Patterned Strokes

When you select Patterned from the Stroke Type pop-up menu, the Stroke Inspector fills in with a variety of patterns you can apply to your path (see Figure 2-106). The color and width settings for patterned strokes work exactly as described in "Basic Strokes," above.

FIGURE 2-105
Custom strokes

Here's an example of FreeHand's stock custom strokes. I printed each path using a pattern length of 8, a pattern width of 8, and a spacing of zero (except for "Rectangle," which I printed using a spacing of 3).

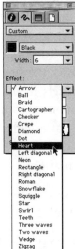
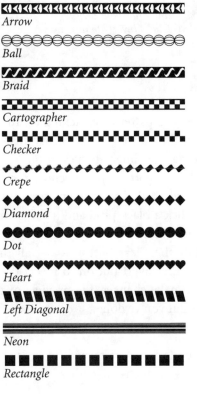

The appearance of custom strokes can vary a great deal, depending on what variables you enter in the Inspector.

Here's what the parameters control.

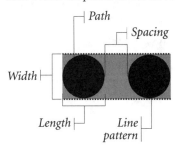

Example settings for the Braid custom stroke

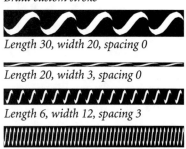

Length 30, width 20, spacing 0

Length 20, width 3, spacing 0

Length 6, width 12, spacing 3

Length 3, width 16, spacing 0

FIGURE 2-106
Patterned strokes

Choose a pattern from the scrolling display at the bottom of the dialog box, or click "Clear" to clear the current pattern and draw your own. Click "Invert" to invert the current pattern.

You choose a pattern by clicking on the swatch of the pattern you want in the bottom of the Stroke Inspector (to display other patterns, drag the slider at the bottom of the Inspector). If you want to edit the pattern you've chosen, click inside the cell containing the enlarged view of the pattern. It's like a miniature paint program—click a black pixel and it turns white; click a white pixel and it turns black. If you want to create a pattern entirely from scratch, click the Clear button to set all the pixels in the cell to white. Click the Invert button to invert the pattern shown in the cell. As you make changes, the preview of the pattern changes to show you what you've done.

Patterned strokes have several significant limitations.

♦ The pattern in a patterned stroke is always the same size—72 dots per inch—regardless of the weight of the stroke.

♦ Patterned strokes won't separate into process colors unless you're printing to a PostScript Level 2 printer.

♦ Patterned strokes can take a long time to print.

♦ Patterned strokes have an opaque background, so the pattern won't knock out of whatever's behind them. The entire path will, instead.

♦ You can't apply a halftone screen to patterned strokes.

♦ Patterned strokes are kinda ugly.

Patterned strokes are really intended to provide compatibility for imported PICTs drawn in MacDraw II (FreeHand's competition, way back when). Some people feel more comfortable working with the patterned strokes than with the PostScript or custom stroke types, which is (in my opinion) unfortunate. If you're trying to make a stroke gray, apply a tint of black to the stroke. If you want to apply a stroke with a pattern to a path, use a custom stroke.

PostScript Strokes

When you choose PostScript from the Stroke Type pop-up menu in the Stroke Inspector, a large field appears at the bottom of the Inspector. In this field, you can enter up to 255 characters of PostScript code (you can also paste text into the field).

Don't press Return to break lines—FreeHand will think you're trying to apply the effect to the path (and won't enter a carriage return in the field, in any case). Separate your entries with spaces instead; PostScript doesn't need carriage returns to understand the code (see Figure 2-107).

Similarly, don't include the character "%" in your code—PostScript uses this character to denote comments, and will ignore any text following it (if you enter this character in the middle of your code, you'll probably cause a PostScript error).

PostScript strokes display on screen as a basic stroke of the width and color you specify. Your PostScript code can, of course, change the width or color of the stroke, if that's what you want.

FIGURE 2-107
PostScript strokes

FreeHand enters this code by default; delete it before you type your code.

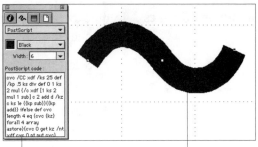

Note: You can't see the complete code for this PostScript stroke in this screen shot (some of it has scrolled out of the field). For a complete code listing, see Chapter 8, "PostScript."

Type up to 255 characters of PostScript code in this field.

PostScript strokes look like this on your screen...

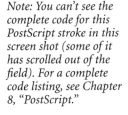

...but print according to the code you enter.

While you can enter complete descriptions of PostScript strokes in this dialog box, you'll usually use it to call PostScript routines in external UserPrep files. See Chapter 8, "PostScript," for more on passing values to external routines.

Editing Strokes

Once you've applied a stroke to a particular path, you can change the stroke using any of the following methods. Again, there's no "right" way to edit a stroke—which method is best and quickest depends on how you work and which palettes you have open at the time you want to change the stroke.

- ◆ Press Command-Option-L/Ctrl-Alt-L to display the Stroke Inspector, then make changes in the Inspector.

- ◆ Use the Color palette to apply a color to the path (see Chapter 6, "Color," for more on applying colors using the Colors palette).

- ◆ Drag and drop a color swatch (from the Colors palette, the Color Mixer, or the Inspector) onto the path (see Chapter 6, "Color," for more on drag-and-drop color).

- ◆ Click on a style name in the Styles palette.

Removing Strokes

To quickly remove a stroke from a path, use one of the following techniques.

- ◆ Select the path, then click the Stroke selector (at the top of the Colors palette), then click None.

- ◆ Drag a color swatch from None in the Colors palette and drop it on the Stroke selector.

- ◆ Drag a color swatch from None in the Colors palette and drop it on the path (see Chapter 6, "Color").

- ◆ Select the path, then display the Stroke Inspector and choose None from the Stroke Type pop-up menu.

Fills

Just as strokes determine what the *outside* of a path looks like, fills specify the appearance of the *inside* of a path. Fills can make the inside of a path a solid color, or a graduated fill, or a pattern of tiny faces. Any path you create can be filled.

You set up fills using the Fill Inspector. To display the Fill Inspector, press Command-Option-F/Command-Alt-F. FreeHand features eight different fill types, which you can choose from the Fill Type pop-up menu—the (conveniently unlabeled) pop-up menu at the top of the Fill Inspector (see Figure 2-108).

FIGURE 2-108
Fill Types

The Fill Inspector displays different controls as you choose different fill types from the Fill Type pop-up menu.

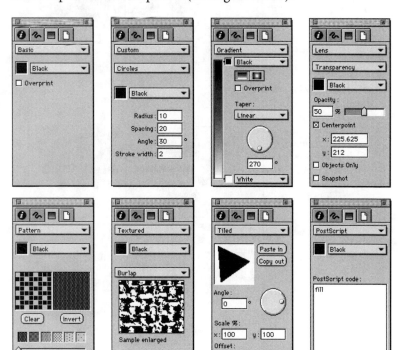

Fill Type pop-up menu.

Basic Fills   Choose Basic from the Fill Type pop-up menu when you want to fill an object with a solid color (see Figure 2-109). Apply the color to your path by dragging a color swatch from the Colors palette (or the Color Mixer) into the color well in the Fill Inspector (for more on applying colors to objects, see Chapter 6, "Color").

FIGURE 2-109
Applying basic fills

Select the path you want to fill, then choose Basic from the Fill Type pop-up menu.

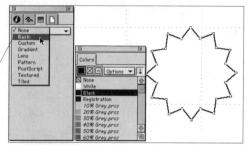

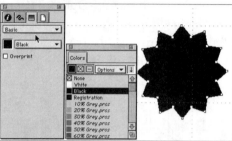

FreeHand fills the path with a basic fill of the current default color (in this example, Black).

To change the color of the fill, drag a color swatch from one of the color wells in the Colors palette (or from the Color Mixer or the Tints palette) and drop it in the color well in the Fill Inspector.

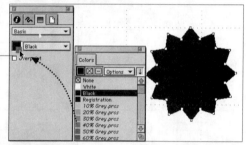

Alternatively, you could click the color name in the Colors palette, or drag a color swatch onto the Fill button at the top of the Colors palette.

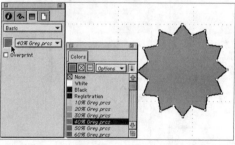

FreeHand applies the fill to the selected path.

Check the Overprint checkbox if you want to make that this fill overprint any underlying objects. If you don't check Overprint, the object will be knocked out of any underlying objects unless its ink color has been set to overprint. Depending on the colors you're using in your publication and the printing process you intend to use, this might not be what you want (see Figure 2-110).

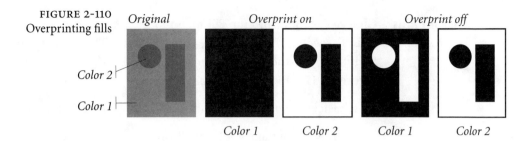

FIGURE 2-110
Overprinting fills

Original   Overprint on   Overprint off

Color 2

Color 1

Color 1   Color 2   Color 1   Color 2

Tip:
Dragging
and Dropping
Basic Fills

To change any fill to a basic fill, hold down Shift as you drop a color swatch into a path. FreeHand fills the path with a basic fill of the color you dropped on the path (see Figure 2-111).

FIGURE 2-111
"Drag and drop"
basic fills

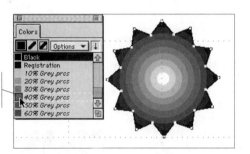

Position the cursor over the color you want to apply...

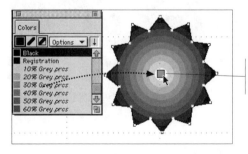

...and drag a color swatch over a path. Hold down Shift...

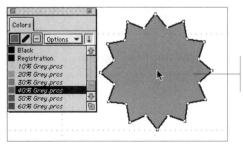

...and drop the color swatch into the path. FreeHand applies a basic fill to the path.

Custom Fills   Choose Custom from the Fill menu to use one of FreeHand's special fills, such as Bricks, Noise, or Tiger Teeth. These fills are PostScript, so you they won't print on a non-PostScript printer (see Figure 2-112). To apply a custom fill, follow these steps.

1. Select the path you want to apply the custom fill to.

2. Press Command-Option-F/Command-Alt-F to display the Fill Inspector, if it's not already visible. Choose Custom from the Fill Type pop-up menu.

3. Choose a fill from the Effect pop-up menu in the Fill Inspector. Options for the fill you've chosen appear. The number of parameters you can change varies from fill to fill.

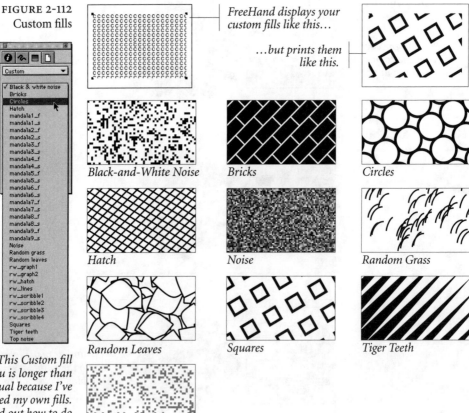

FIGURE 2-112
Custom fills

FreeHand displays your custom fills like this...

...but prints them like this.

Black-and-White Noise   Bricks   Circles

Hatch   Noise   Random Grass

Random Leaves   Squares   Tiger Teeth

Top Noise

Note: This Custom fill menu is longer than usual because I've added my own fills. To find out how to do that, see Chapter 8, "PostScript."

4. Set the parameters for the fill (using the controls in the Inspector).

Custom fills appear on screen as patterns of little Cs.

You can vary the appearance of the custom fills to a tremendous degree. For the Bricks fill, for example, you can specify the color, width, height, and angle of the "bricks" in the fill, as well as setting the color of the "mortar." Figure 2-113 shows how variables can dramatically change the appearance of a custom fill.

FIGURE 2-113
Changing variables
of custom fills

Variations on "Bricks"

Gradient Fills   Choose Gradient to fill an object with a graduation from one color to another—an effect also known as a "fountain" or a "vignette." FreeHand offers two types of Gradient fills: "Graduated" and "Radial" fills (in previous versions of FreeHand, these were separate fill types). Use the Gradient Type buttons to choose the type of fill you want. For either type of gradient fill, you can set the colors used in the gradient, and you can specify the taper of the graduation (linear or logarithmic). For Graduated fills, you can set the angle that the graduation is to follow.

Graduated fills create a smooth color transition (or series of transitions) from one end of a path to another (see Figure 2-114).

A radial fill creates a concentric graduated fill from the center of an object to the outside of the object. By default, the center of a radial fill is placed at the center of the two most distant points in the object (see Figure 2-115). You can control the location of the center of a radial fill using the Locate Center control in the Fill Inspector—drag the handle around, and FreeHand repositions the center of the radial fill. Radial fills are subject to the same limitations as graduated fills.

The key to working with either type of gradient fill is the Color Ramp, which you'll see at the left of the Fill Inspector. You can add

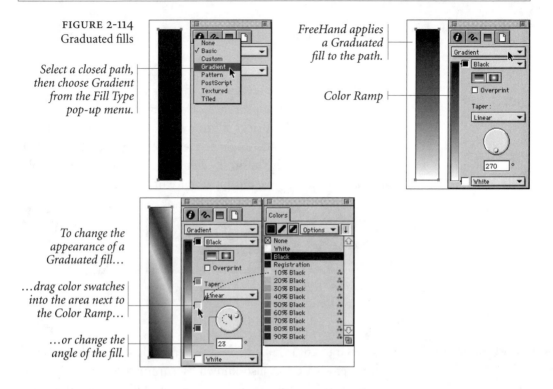

FIGURE 2-114
Graduated fills

Select a closed path,
then choose Gradient
from the Fill Type
pop-up menu.

FreeHand applies
a Graduated
fill to the path.

Color Ramp

To change the
appearance of a
Graduated fill...

...drag color swatches
into the area next to
the Color Ramp...

...or change the
angle of the fill.

or remove colors from the gradient fill, change the position of colors in the gradient, or change colors inside the gradient .

To add colors, drag a color swatch to the right of the Color Ramp and drop it. FreeHand adds the color to the gradient. To remove a color, drag a color swatch away from the Color Ramp. To change a color that's already in use in the gradient, drop another color swatch on top of the existing color swatch. To change the position of a color inside a gradient, drag the corresponding color swatch up and down next to the Color Ramp.

Tip:
Copying Color
Ramp Colors

To duplicate a color swatch that's already in use in a gradient fill, hold down Control/Alt and drag the swatch you see to the right of the Color Ramp. FreeHand creates a duplicate of the color swatch.

Tip:
Dragging and
Dropping
Graduated Fills

To change any fill to a Graduated fill, hold down Control/Ctrl as you drop a color swatch on a path. FreeHand applies a graduated fill, and sets the To color to the color of the swatch. FreeHand sets the From color to the original color applied to the path. FreeHand

FIGURE 2-115
Radial fills

*Click the Radial button
to apply a Radial fill to
a closed path.*

*FreeHand positions the
center point of the fill at
the geometric center of
the path you selected.*

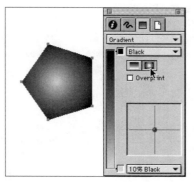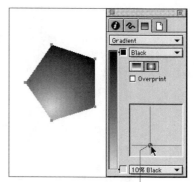

*Change the location of the center point of the
radial fill by dragging this control around.*

*To change the colors
used in a radial fill,
drag color swatches
into the area to the
right of the Color Ramp.*

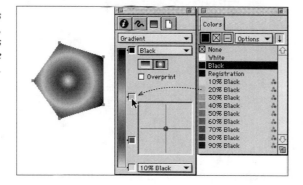

determines the angle of the graduation from the point at which you
drop the color swatch (see Figure 2-116).

Tip:
Dragging and
Dropping
Radial Fills

To change any fill to a Radial fill, hold down Option/Alt as you
drop a color swatch onto the path containing the fill. FreeHand
fills the path with a radial fill, and sets the Inside color of the radial
fill to the color of the swatch you dropped on the path. FreeHand
sets the Outside color to the original color applied to the path.
FreeHand positions the center point of the radial fill at the point at
which you dropped the color swatch (see Figure 2-117).

Tip:
Resetting the
Center Point

To reset the center point of a radial fill to the center of the path,
hold down Shift as you click inside the Locate Center control.

FIGURE 2-116
"Drag and drop"
graduated fills

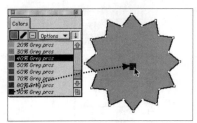 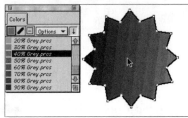

Hold down Control/Ctrl as you drop a color swatch into a path...

...and FreeHand applies a Graduated fill to the path, using the color you dropped to set the fill's "To" color.

FIGURE 2-117
"Drag and drop"
radial fills

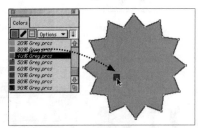 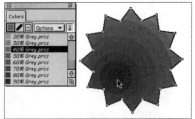

Hold down Option/Alt as you drop a color swatch inside a path...

...and FreeHand applies a Radial fill to the path, the color you dropped becomes the fill's Inside color. The point at which you dropped the swatch becomes the center point of the fill.

Lens Fills

Lenses—pieces of glass ground and polished to produce specific optical effects—have a way of upsetting the established order of things. When Galileo looked at the heavens with his telescope, or when Leeuwenhoek observed microscopic organisms with his magnifying glasses, the things they saw changed the way that we think about the universe, and our place in it. I can't say that FreeHand's new "Lens" feature is revolutionary in the same sense, but it's sure changed the way I work with FreeHand.

Like the physical lenses they emulate, FreeHand's Lens fills alter the appearance of objects viewed through them. Some lenses enlarge, some reduce, and some alter the colors you see through them (see Figure 2-118).

Transparency. Transparency, translucency, and opacity. These aren't exact terms—the same object could be described as being "partially transparent," or "nearly opaque." When you apply a transparent Lens fill to a path, FreeHand adds a tint of a color you specify to the objects behind the fill. You define the tint using the Opacity

FIGURE 2-118
Lens Fills

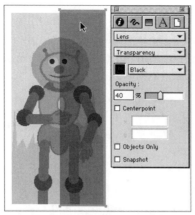

The Transparent Lens fill adds tints of a color to the objects behind the path.

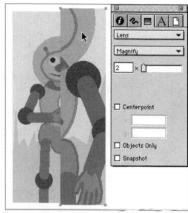

The Magnify Lens fill magnifies (or reduces) the objects behind the path.

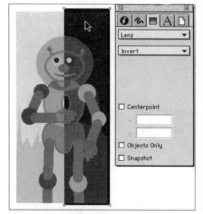

The Invert Lens fill inverts the colors in any objects behind the path.

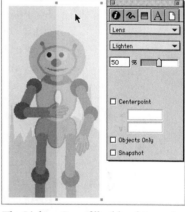

The Lighten Lens fill adds white to the objects behind the path.

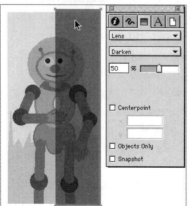

The Darken Lens fill adds black to the colors of any objects behind the path.

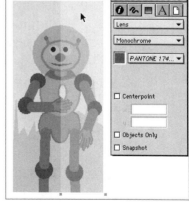

The Monochrome Lens fill converts the colors behind the path to tints of the selected color.

slider. Applying a transparent Lens fill with an Opacity setting of 100 percent is exactly the same as applying a Basic fill of the color you've chosen. Moving the slider to zero percent produces a fill that's completely transparent.

Monochrome. Converts the colors in any objects behind the path to a tint of the color you've applied to the Lens fill.

Magnify. Scales the objects behind the lens. When you're creating an inset view of a map or technical drawing, you can use a magnifying Lens fill to pull out an area to display in greater detail (particularly if you use the Snapshot option—see below).

Lighten. Adds white to the colors behind the Lens fill. In the CMYK color model, this means decreasing the value of each ink by the percentage you enter; for RGB colors, this means increasing each color value.

Darken. Increases the amount of black in the objects behind the Lens fill (in the CMYK color model, this adds more black ink; for RGB colors, this decreases each color value by the percentage you entered).

Invert. It's clear enough what inverting black objects does (it turns them white), but what happens when you invert a tint of black? FreeHand subtracts the original tint percentage from 100 to create the inverted color (if the tint is 80 percent black, FreeHand will turn it to 20 percent black). What does it mean to invert a color? When you're using the CMYK model, FreeHand uses new ink values equal to 100 minus the original ink percentage (so 40 percent cyan becomes 60 percent cyan). If you're using the RGB color model, FreeHand changes each color component to a value equal to 255 minus the original color value (so a Red value of 50 becomes a Red value of 205, for example).

Lens fill controls. Most of the Lens fill types display several controls in addition to the fill's color and transparency. Here's what the options you see in the Fill Inspector mean.

♦ **Centerpoint.** Often, objects seen through transparent surfaces appear to shift from their original positions—think about what happens when you see an object behind a glass full of water. That's just what FreeHand's Centerpoint control does—it moves the objects you see through the Lens fill (it doesn't move the objects on the page, it moves the *copies* of the objects inside the path you've filled with the Lens). Turn on the Center Point option, and FreeHand displays the Centerpoint Handle in the center of the Lens fill. Drag the Centerpoint Handle or enter new coordinates in the X and Y fields to move the center point of the Lens fill to a new location (see Figure 2-119).

FIGURE 2-119
Centerpoint

When you turn on the
Centerpoint option,
FreeHand displays the
center point of the Lens
fill (it's the little
cloverleaf in the center
of the path).

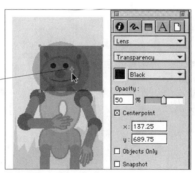

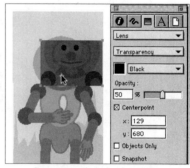

Drag the center point…   *…and FreeHand shifts the objects in the Lens fill.*

♦ **Objects Only.** When you turn on the Objects Only option, FreeHand applies the effect of the Lens fill to any objects behind the filled path, but leaves the page background unaffected (see Figure 2-120). This comes in handy when you're creating shadows—you want the shadow to fall on objects, not on empty space.

♦ **Snapshot.** When you turn on the Snapshot option, Free-Hand "freezes" any objects inside the Lens fill. Move the path, and the objects inside the Lens fill move along with the path (see Figure 2-121). Used with a Magnifying Lens fill, this makes it easy to create inset views for maps and technical illustrations.

FIGURE 2-120
Objects Only

*Lens fill applied to
empty space.*

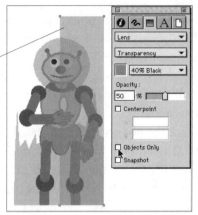
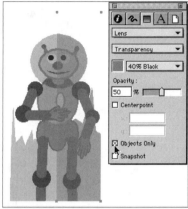

*When you turn on the Objects Only
option…*

*…FreeHand applies the Lens fill to
paths, type, or images—not to empty
space.*

FIGURE 2-121
Snapshot

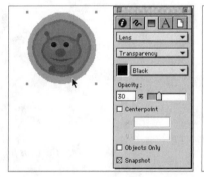
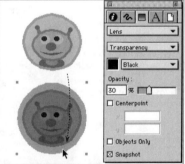

*When you turn on the Snapshot
option, FreeHand "freezes" the
contents of the Lens fill.*

*Drag the path away from the original
objects, and you'll see that a copy of
the objects travels with the path.*

The fine print. Lens fills have some limitations, as described below.

◆ Lens fills don't work with spot colors. When you try to
apply a Lens fill to a path that's over an area of spot color,
FreeHand warns you that the colors inside the path will be
converted to process colors.

◆ You can't apply Lens fills to type—you'll have to convert the
text to paths, then apply the fill to the paths. You can place
Lens fills over type, however.

◆ You can't blend paths you've formatted using Lens fills.

◆ You can't apply Lens fills to imported bitmap images to make the images transparent (though you can always apply Lens fills to paths that pass over the images). To make an imported grayscale image transparent, apply a Basic fill to the image and turn on the Transparent option. You won't see any difference on screen, but the image will now print over anything that's behind it, rather than knocking it out.

◆ Lens fills have no effect on imported EPS graphics.

How Lens fills really work. FreeHand is not magic (though it sometimes seems it must be). It can't go faster than the speed of light, travel through time, or make transparency a feature of your Post-Script printer. Given this last limitation, how does FreeHand get its transparent Lens fills to print? It's simple: it cheats.

In previous versions of FreeHand, you could create the illusion of transparency by changing the color of objects where they happened to intersect other objects. Using the Paste Inside feature, and some or all of FreeHand's path operations (Union, Intersect, Punch, etc.), you could do a good job of making things look transparent. FreeHand 8, as it turns out, does pretty much the same thing. When you print or export a path filled with a Lens fill, Free-Hand creates copies of the objects that appear inside the path, then pastes these copied objects inside the path. These additional objects aren't added to your FreeHand publication—they're added to the PostScript FreeHand sends to your printer or to an EPS file.

This approach means that your "transparent" fills have a good chance of printing, because FreeHand isn't relying on arcane Post-Script techniques to create the illusion of transparency using your printer's PostScript interpreter (an approach that's theoretically possible, but probably impractical). A drawback to this approach, however, is that FreeHand can end up adding *lots* of new objects to your print job or EPS file. How many more objects? That depends on the way you've used Lens fills in the publication. Count on FreeHand adding a copy of every path, text block, or imported image that touches a Lens fill. If an object crosses two paths formatted using Lens fills, you'll get two new copies of the object—one pasted inside of each of path. You get the idea.

With power comes responsibility. Use restraint with Lens fills—especially when you're placing them over imported images or over other Lens fills. Is it worth doubling the size of an EPS to put an image inside a Lens fill? This doesn't mean that you shouldn't use Lens fills—but it does mean you should use them with some caution—just as you should when using the Paste Inside feature.

Finally, FreeHand's approach to creating transparent fills means that they behave just like clipping paths. Increasing the flatness of a path you've filled with a Lens fill will make it print faster (if the path contains curved line segments—see the discussion of flatness at the beginning of this chapter).

Tip:
Rasterizing
Lens Fills

Here's a rule of thumb: if your pages are taking forever to print, or if your EPS files containing Lens fills are huge, try rasterizing the paths in the document that use any of the Lens fills (in a copy of the publication)—especially paths over imported images. Rasterize at two times the resolution of the halftone screen frequency you intend to use to print the document (see Figure 2-122). You might find that the size of your EPS file actually decreases—which means it'll print faster, too. Whether or not you can get away with this depends on your artwork—in some cases (such as magnifying Lens fills used on black-and-white line art), the rasterized paths won't look as smooth as they would had you not rasterized them.

FIGURE 2-122
Rasterizing Lens Fills

EPS version: 1 MB. In this example, each composite path has been filled with a transparent Lens fill.

Rasterized version, 300 dpi, saved as TIFF and converted to grayscale in Photoshop: 363 KB.

Tip:
Using Lens Fills
to Duplicate
Objects

If, like me, you were wondering why you'd ever want to use an entirely transparent Lens fill (i.e., one with an Opacity setting of zero percent), I've got (at least) one reason: you can use the Lens fill to duplicate objects, as shown in Figure 2-123. The cool thing about doing this is that the link between the original object and the objects in the Lens fills remains "live"—change the original object, and all of the duplicates change, too.

You can simulate the "master pages" found in other page layout programs using this technique.

FIGURE 2-123
Duplicating Objects
Using Lenses
(continued on
next page)

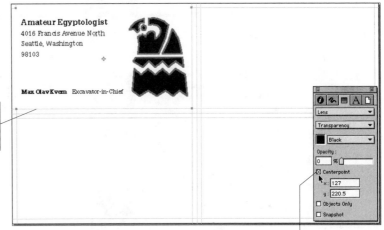

Draw a path (in this example, a rectangle) around the objects you want to duplicate.

Apply a transparent Lens fill to the path, then turn on the Centerpoint option.

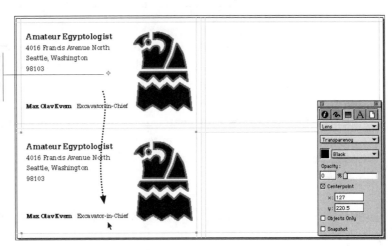

Drag the path to a new location. Note that the center point of the Lens fill stays behind.

FIGURE 2-123
Duplicating Objects
Using Lenses
(continued from
previous page)

*Duplicate the path
containing the Lens
fill as many times
as you want.*

*When you make
changes in the area
under the center
point...*

*...FreeHand applies
those changes to all of
the copies of the path.*

This trick won't work if you use the Snapshot option—when you use "Snapshot," the items inside the duplicated paths do not change when you change the original objects.

Tip:
Resetting the
Center Point

To reset the center point of a Lens fill to the geometric center of a path, turn the Centerpoint option off, then on again.

Patterned Fills

Patterned fills have the same problems and limitations as patterned lines, discussed in "Patterned Lines," earlier in this chapter. I recommend that you don't use them.

PostScript Fills   When you choose PostScript from the Fill menu, FreeHand displays a large field at the bottom of the Fill Inspector. PostScript fills work just like PostScript lines, described earlier in this chapter (see Figure 2-124). For more on working with PostScript fills, see Chapter 8, "PostScript."

FIGURE 2-124
PostScript fills

FreeHand enters this code by default; delete it before you type your code.

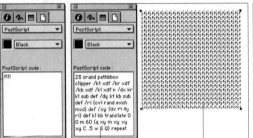

Type up to 255 characters of PostScript code in this field.

PostScript fills look like this on your screen…

…but print according to the code you entered in the Fill Inspector.

Tiled Fills   Tiled fills repeat a pattern of FreeHand objects inside a path; they're like the tiles you see in your kitchen or bathroom. Here's how to create a tiled fill (see Figure 2-125).

1. Create the objects you want to have repeated inside a path. You're creating one of the tiles you'll have in your tiled fill.

2. Copy the FreeHand objects.

3. Select the path you want to apply the tiled fill to.

4. Press Command-Option-F/Ctrl-Alt-F to display the Fill Inspector. Choose Tiled from the Fill Type pop-up menu.

5. Click the Paste In button in the Fill Inspector. This pastes the objects you copied into the window next to the button.

6. Adjust the scale, offset, and angle of the tiles. If you want the objects in the fill to be rotated, skewed, scaled, or otherwise transformed, remember to check the Contents option in the Transform palette.

Offset doesn't change the distance between tiles in a tiled fill—it changes the position at which FreeHand starts drawing the tiles

FIGURE 2-125
Creating a tiled fill

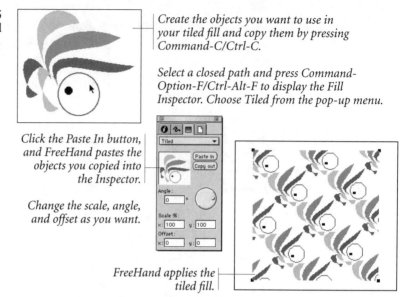

Create the objects you want to use in your tiled fill and copy them by pressing Command-C/Ctrl-C.

Select a closed path and press Command-Option-F/Ctrl-Alt-F to display the Fill Inspector. Choose Tiled from the pop-up menu.

Click the Paste In button, and FreeHand pastes the objects you copied into the Inspector.

Change the scale, angle, and offset as you want.

FreeHand applies the tiled fill.

(ordinarily, FreeHand calculates tile positions based on the lower-left corner of a page). Values you enter in the X field move the horizontal starting point of the tiled fill (positive numbers move the starting point to the right; negative values move it to the left); values you enter in the Y field move the vertical starting point up (positive numbers) or down (negative numbers).

Tip:
Adding an offset
between tiles

To add more space between tiles in a tiled fill, follow these steps (see Figure 2-126).

1. Draw a square around the original tile. Apply a fill and line of None to the square.

2. Select the square and the original tile and press Command-C/Ctrl-C to copy the objects.

3. Display the Fill Inspector by pressing Command-Option-F/Ctrl-Alt-F.

4. Choose Tiled from the Fill Type pop-up menu (if the tiled fill options aren't already visible in the Fill Inspector).

5. Click Paste In.

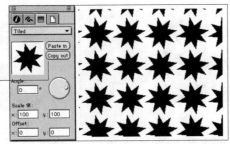

FIGURE 2-126
Increasing the
distance between tiles

*Click the Copy Out
button to copy the
original tile to the
Clipboard.*

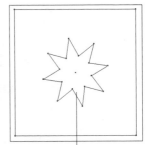

*Paste the object into a publication and draw a box around it.
Apply a fill and stroke of "None" to the box (shown here in
keyline view). Copy the new tile to the Clipboard...*

*...select the original
path, and click the Paste
In button. FreeHand
updates the tiled fill.*

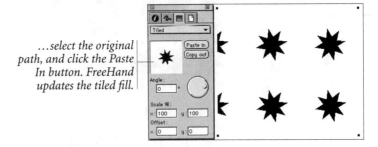

The objects you copied appear in the Fill Inspector. The square you drew adds a margin around the object you're tiling, but doesn't print or obscure objects behind the tiled fill. Make the square larger or smaller to change the distance between tiles.

Tip:
Moving Paths
Without Moving
Tiles

Using the X and Y Offset fields to move a fill inside a path can be frustrating. Can't you just drag the path over the part of the tiled fill you want to see? Sure—here's how you do it (see Figure 2-127).

1. Press Command-M/Ctrl-M to display the Transform palette, if it's not already visible.

2. Click the Move button in the Transform palette.

3. Uncheck the Fills checkbox.

4. Drag the path to a new location.

FreeHand moves the path, but doesn't change the starting point of the tiled fill. You can also accomplish this task using the Transform palette (see Chapter 5, "Transforming," for more on moving a path without changing the appearance of its fills or contents).

FIGURE 2-127
Moving paths
without moving fills

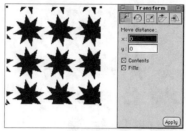

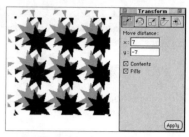

*When you move a path with the
Fills option checked…*

*…the fill moves along with the path
(original tiles shown in gray).*

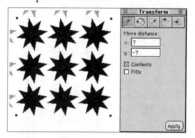

*If you want the fill to stay where it is
while the path moves, uncheck Fills
(original path position shown in gray).*

Textured Fills

Choose Textured from the Fill menu to use one of FreeHand's textured fills, such as Denim, Burlap, or Coquille (see Figure 2-128). The textured fills are actually small bitmap images that FreeHand tiles inside a path—in older versions of FreeHand, you could see an obvious pattern in paths filled with the textured fills. These days, the pattern is a little less apparent, because FreeHand randomly rotates and flips the bitmaps as it creates the tiles.

Textured fills print with an opaque background—as if you'd drawn a shape behind the fill and colored it white. If you want textured fills to print with a transparent background, take a look at "Making Textured Fills Transparent," in Chapter 8, "PostScript."

Tip:
Scaling
Textured
Fills

When you change the size of a path containing a Textured fill, FreeHand doesn't scale the contents of the fill. To make this happen, group the object, then turn on the Object Transforms as Unit option in the Object Inspector, and then scale the group—you won't see the change until you print.

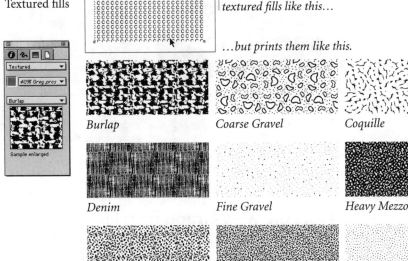

FIGURE 2-128
Textured fills

*FreeHand displays
textured fills like this...*

...but prints them like this.

Burlap   *Coarse Gravel*   *Coquille*

Denim   *Fine Gravel*   *Heavy Mezzo*

Light Mezzo   *Medium Mezzo*   *Sand*

Editing Fills

Once you've applied a fill to a path, you can change the fill using any of the following methods.

◆ Press Command-Option-F/Ctrl-Alt-F to display the Fill Inspector, then make changes to the path's appearance in the Inspector.

◆ Use the Colors palette to apply a color to the path (see Chapter 6, "Color").

◆ Drag and drop a color swatch (from the Colors palette, the Color Mixer, the Tint palette, or the Inspector) inside the path (see Chapter 6, "Color").

◆ Click a style name in the Styles palette.

Removing Fills

To quickly remove a fill from a path, click None in the Colors palette when the Fill selector at the top of the Colors palette is selected, or drag a color swatch from None in the Colors palette and drop it on the Fill selector (Figure 2-129).

FIGURE 2-129
Removing a fill

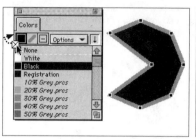 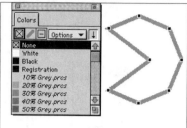

Drag a swatch from "None" into the Fill icon and drop it.

The fill is gone. The thrill may still be around, but the fill is gone.

Working with Graphic Styles

Styles are named collections of formatting attributes. What do I mean when I say "collections of formatting attributes?" I mean that the style includes all the formatting you can apply to an object. If you're using a two-point line that's colored 60 percent gray, you can create a style with those attributes (you can even name it "2-point 60% gray line") and apply it to every path you want to have those attributes, rather than going to the Fill Inspector, the Stroke Inspector, or the Colors palette every time you want to use that formatting.

In FreeHand, you can work with both graphic styles and text styles. Graphic styles apply strokes and fills; text styles apply character and paragraph formatting. Because graphic styles and text styles work about the same way, I'll refer to either as "styles," and only call them "graphic styles" or "text styles" if there's some distinction I need to make.

When you format a path using the Fill or Stroke Inspectors, or by dragging and dropping color swatches, you're formatting the path locally. I call this "local" formatting because the formatting applies to the selected path only, and is not explicitly shared with any other paths in your publication.

Style formatting, on the other hand, is global. When you apply a style to a path, FreeHand makes an association between that path and all the other paths formatted with that style. This means that you can change the style and have the changes you make applied to all the paths formatted with that style. This doesn't mean you lose flexibility—you can always apply local formatting to override the style formatting for styled paths.

Thinking About Styles

While styles are one of the most useful features of FreeHand, in my experience, as soon as you mention the word "styles," people start to panic.

There's no need to be scared—you're already thinking of the elements in your FreeHand publications as having styles. You think of each path as having a particular set of formatting attributes, and you think of groups of paths as having the same set of attributes ("These are all 12-point gray strokes"). FreeHand's graphic styles give you the ability to work with FreeHand the way you already think about your publications.

Use styles. Any time you find yourself choosing the same formatting attributes over and over again, you can create a style and dramatically speed up the process of creating your publication. With styles, you can use more of your brain for doing your creative work, rather than trying to remember that this sort of path has this sort of a stroke, this sort of a fill, this color, this line width, and this halftone screen. Forget that! Set up a style and let FreeHand do that kind of thinking for you.

While styles encourage you to think ahead, they're also flexible; you can change all the paths tagged with a particular style at any time by simply editing the style's definition.

The Styles palette (see Figure 2-130) is the key to working with and applying styles. If the Styles palette is not visible on your screen, press Command-3/Ctrl-3 to display it. If the Styles palette is visible and you want to put it away, press Command-3/Ctrl-3.

FIGURE 2-130
Styles palette

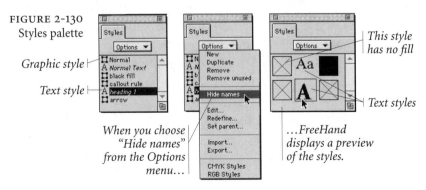

Graphic style

Text style

When you choose "Hide names" from the Options menu...

...FreeHand displays a preview of the styles.

This style has no fill

Text styles

FreeHand displays an icon next to each style name in the Styles palette, using different icons for text styles and graphic styles.

When you choose Hide Names from the Styles palette's Options menu, FreeHand displays a preview of each style's formatting in the Styles palette. I don't like working this way—it's too easy to confuse one style with another. Strokes, in particular, are hard to tell apart.

Creating Styles by Example

In FreeHand, the easiest way to create styles is by example. Once you've applied a set of attributes to a path using local formatting, you can turn that formatting into a style, which you can then apply to any other paths (see Figure 2-131).

1. Select the path with the attributes you want.

2. Choose New from the pop-up menu at the top of the Styles palette (if the Styles palette isn't currently visible, press Command-3/Ctrl-3 to display it). FreeHand adds a new style name to the Styles palette.

3. To give the style another name (FreeHand's default names—"Style 1," "Style 2," etc.—aren't very descriptive), double-click the style name in the Styles palette and type a new name. When you're through, press Return.

That's all there is to it. You've just created a style with the fill, line, color, and halftone attributes of the path you selected.

Tip: Stroke-Only and Fill-Only Styles

To make the style apply only to the stroke of a path, or only to the fill of a path, select the style name in the Styles palette and then choose "Edit Style" from the Styles palette's pop-up menu. Free-Hand displays the Edit Style dialog box. Choose "Fill Attributes" from the Style Affects pop-up menu to create a fill-only style, or choose "Stroke Attributes" to create a stroke-only style (see Figure 2-132).

Tip: Select One Example

When you're creating a style based on an example, make sure you select a single path before you define the style. If you select more than one path, there's a good chance the paths in your selection will have different formatting attributes. What happens then? Free-

FIGURE 2-131
Defining a new style

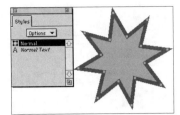

Select a path that has the
formatting attributes you want.

Choose New from the Styles
palette's pop-up menu.

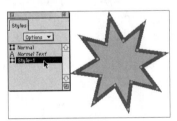

FreeHand creates a new style,
applying the style to the selected
path as it does so.

*What's in a style? All of the settings for
all of the controls in the Halftone
palette, the Stroke Inspector, and the Fill
Inspector are stored under one name in
the Styles palette.*

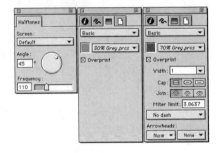

*FreeHand's default style names aren't
very descriptive, so you might want to
change them.*

*Double-click the style
name in the Styles
palette.*

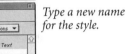

*Type a new name
for the style.*

*Press Return. FreeHand
changes the name of the
style in the Styles palette.*

Hand doesn't save the formatting for the attributes that differ (that
is, if the selected paths have differing fills, FreeHand won't save the
Fill attributes in the style you've created).

Tip:
Halftone-Only
Styles

You can use the above FreeHand behavior to your advantage to
create "halftone-only" styles. Create two paths, applying different
fill and stroke attributes to each path. Apply the same halftone
settings to both paths. Select the two paths and choose "New" from
the Styles palette's pop-up menu. FreeHand creates a style that applies
only the halftone formatting. You can then use these halftone-only

FIGURE 2-132
Fill-only and
stroke-only styles

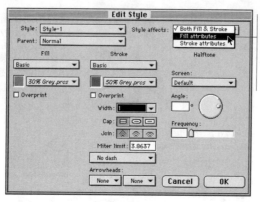

*Choose "Fill attributes"
to affect only the fill of
paths you apply this style
to, or choose "Stroke
attributes" to affect only
the stroke.*

styles to apply specialized line screens to imported TIFF images
(the halftone setting is the only part of a style definition that gets
applied to TIFFs).

Creating Styles by Specifying Attributes

If you prefer creating styles by specifying formatting in a dialog
box (instead of creating a style from an example path), FreeHand
gives you a way to do that (see Figure 2-133).

1. Deselect everything (press Tab or click on an uninhabited
    area of the page).

2. Choose "New" from the Styles palette's pop-up menu.
    FreeHand creates a new style and adds it to the list of styles
    in the palette.

3. Without deselecting the style, choose "Edit style" from the
    Styles palette's pop-up menu. FreeHand displays the Edit
    Style dialog box.

4. If you want to base the style on some other style (other than
    the default style "Normal"), choose that style from the
    Parent pop-up menu. Note that choosing this option does
    not apply the parent style's attributes to the current style
    (see "Basing One Style on Another," later in this chapter).

5. If you want the style to apply only to the stroke or fill of
    paths, choose "Stroke Attributes" or "Fill Attributes" from
    the Style Affects pop-up menu. If you want the style to
    apply to both attributes, choose "Both Fill & Stroke."

FIGURE 2-133
Defining a style by
specifying attributes

Choose New from
the pop-up menu.

FreeHand creates
a new style.

Choose Edit from
the pop-up menu.

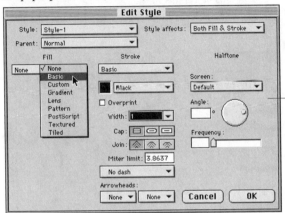

FreeHand displays
the Edit Style
dialog box. Set up
the halftone, fill,
and stroke for your
style using the
controls in the Edit
Style dialog box.
Press Return (or
click the OK
button) when
you're done, and
FreeHand applies
the formatting to
the new style.

6. Set the fill, stroke, and halftone of the style using the corresponding sections of the dialog box (they work just like the Fill and Stroke Inspectors and the Halftone palette). When the style has the attributes you want, press Return or click the OK button to close the Edit Style dialog box.

7. If you want to change the name of the style, double-click the style name in the Styles palette, type a new name, and press Return.

Applying Styles

To apply a style, select the path you want to tag with the style, and then click the style in the Styles palette. The path takes on all the formatting attributes of the style (see Figure 2-134). The path is now "tagged" with the style.

Alternatively, you can apply the style using the "drag and drop" method: drag the icon next to the style name out of the Styles palette, and drop it on a path. FreeHand tags the path with the style. Change the style, and you change the formatting of the path.

FIGURE 2-134
Applying styles

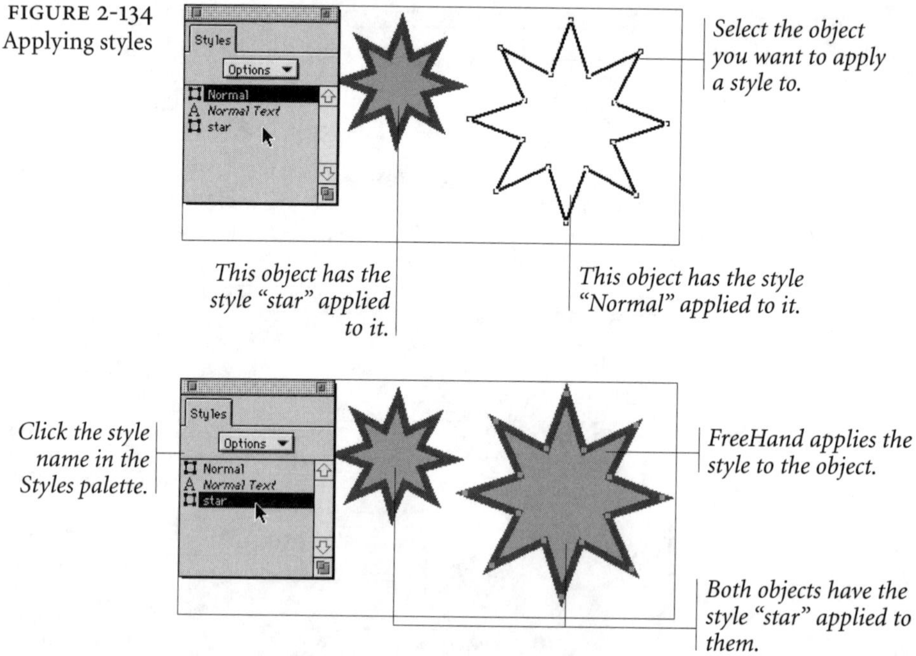

Select the object
you want to apply
a style to.

This object has the
style "star" applied
to it.

This object has the style
"Normal" applied to it.

Click the style
name in the
Styles palette.

FreeHand applies the
style to the object.

Both objects have the
style "star" applied to
them.

Redefining Styles

To redefine a style, create or select a path with the style applied to it. Make local changes using the Fill and Stroke Inspectors and the Halftone palette. When the path looks the way you want it to, choose Redefine from the pop-up menu on the Styles palette. All of the paths formatted using that style change to reflect the changes you've just made (see Figure 2-135).

Basing One Style on Another

Styles can inherit attributes from other styles. You can create a style that's just like an existing style except for some small difference, or create a style that's linked to any changes you make to an original style (color is a good example).

I call the original style the "parent" style and the inheriting styles "child" styles. When you change the properties of the parent style, the changes you make ripple through the child styles. Child styles inherit changes only in the properties they share with their parent style. The attributes which differ between the parent and child styles remain the same.

People often have difficulty understanding the use and worth of parent and child styles—even to the point of calling attribute inheritance a bug. It's not a bug, it's a feature.

FIGURE 2-135
Editing styles

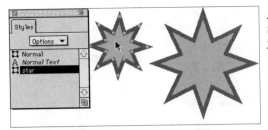

Select a path that's tagged with the style you want to redefine.

When you apply "local" formatting (that is, formatting independent of styles) to an object, FreeHand displays a "+" to the left of the style's name in the Styles palette.

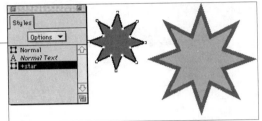

Change the path's formatting (using any of the formatting techniques discussed earlier in this chapter).

Choose Redefine from the Styles palette's pop-up menu.

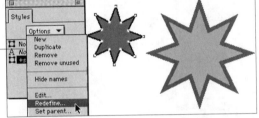

FreeHand displays the Redefine Style dialog box. Select the style you want to redefine (usually, it's the one applied to the current path) and press Return.

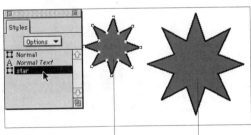

The formatting changes ripple through all of the paths tagged with the style you just redefined—even if they're not selected.

To create a new style that's based on the existing style, follow these steps (see Figure 2-136).

1. Select a path tagged with the style you want to base the new style on.

2. Make a change to the path's formatting.

FIGURE 2-136
Basing one style
on another

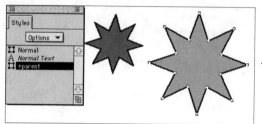

Select a path that's
tagged with parent
style and change its
formatting.

Choose New from the
Styles palette's pop-up
menu to create a new
style.

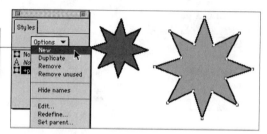

Choose Set Parent
from the Styles palette's
pop-up menu.

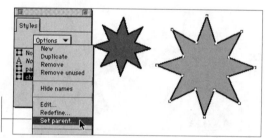

FreeHand displays the
Set Parent dialog box.
Select the style you want
to base your new style
on and press Return.

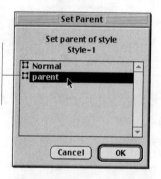

Once you've established a
link between styles, changes
to the parent style apply to
any identical formatting
attributes of the child style.

In this example, the
strokes of the styles are
the same, so FreeHand
applies changes to the
stroke of the parent to
any paths tagged with
the child style.

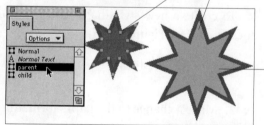

The child style's fill
differs, and is
unaffected by changes
to the fill of the parent
style.

3. Choose New from the Styles palette's pop-up menu. Free-Hand adds a new style name to the Styles palette.

4. Double-click the default style name in the Styles palette and type a new name for the style, if you want. When you're done, press Return.

5. Choose Set Parent from the pop-up menu in the Styles palette. FreeHand displays the Set Parent dialog box.

6. Choose the parent style in the Set Parent dialog box and press Return to close the dialog box.

If you know what you're doing, you can use attribute inheritance to experiment—to try out new ideas quickly and easily. What would happen if all those red lines (of whatever line width and pattern) were blue? What would happen if all the paths you've filled with this tiled fill were filled with that graduated fill? The ripple-through effect of attribute inheritance from parent to child styles lets me ask "what if" questions that improve my designs.

Attribute inheritance also makes it easier for me to make last-minute production changes almost painlessly (there are no totally painless last-minute production changes).

Duplicating Styles

If you want to base one style on another, select the style you want to copy and choose Duplicate from the Styles palette pop-up menu. FreeHand creates a new style with the same formatting attributes as the style you selected. At this point, you can edit or redefine the style to make it different from its parent.

Styles and Local Formatting

Styles don't prevent you from applying local formatting. You can always override the formatting for a styled path by selecting the path and making changes locally using Fill and Stroke Inspectors, or the Colors palette. When you've changed a styled path locally, the style name in the Styles palette appears with a "+" before it when you have the path selected. The "+" indicates that the path's style has been overridden by some sort of local formatting.

Attribute inheritance for paths that are both styled and have local formatting works like this: child styles still inherit changes in the properties they *share* with their parent style; the attributes that *differ* between the parent and child styles (including local formatting) stay the same when you change the parent style.

If you've overridden the formatting of a styled path with local formatting, and you want to reassert the path's original style, select the path and click the style name in the Styles palette. The style overrides (wipes out) the local formatting, and the "+" disappears from the style name in the Styles palette (see Figure 2-137).

FIGURE 2-137
Overriding local
formatting

Select an object you've
formatted using local
formatting. A "+"
appears next to
the style's name
to indicate that the
style's formatting has
been overridden.

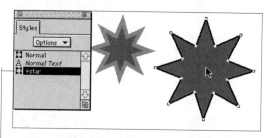

Click the style's name in
the Styles palette.

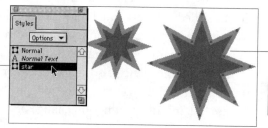

FreeHand applies the
style's formatting to the
path, overriding any
local formatting
attributes defined in the
style (if they aren't
defined in the style, they
won't be affected).

You can select more than one path with more than one sort of local formatting override and reassert the original style—select the paths and click the style name in the Styles palette.

If you've locally formatted several paths with the same local formatting attributes and want to clear the formatting for each of the paths without having to select each one, try this.

1. Select one of the locally formatted paths and choose Redefine from the pop-up menu in the Styles palette. This incorporates the local formatting into the style's definition.

2. Use local formatting to change the selected path to match the original style's definition. As you change the path's formatting, a "+" appears next to the style's name in the Styles palette.

3. Choose Redefine from the Styles palette's pop-up menu.

After you choose Redefine, all the paths—even those that had local overrides before you started this process—change back to the formatting specified by the style.

Note that you may have to go through this process several times if you have paths with different local formatting overrides.

Merging Styles

When you copy objects from one publication to another, the styles in the publication you're pasting the objects into override the styles in the objects you're pasting (when the style names in the pasted objects match style names in the publication). The home team always wins. We can use this rule to merge two styles into one style. Why would you want to merge two styles? Most of the time, it's because someone you're working with made a mistake.

To combine two styles into a single style, follow these steps.

1. Select a path that's tagged with the style ("style 1") you want to end up with and copy it into another publication.

2. Change the name of the style to the name of the style you want to merge it with ("style 2").

3. Return to the original publication. Press Command-Shift-A/Ctrl-Shift-A to select everything in the publication.

4. Press Command-C/Ctrl-C to copy everything.

5. Go to the second publication and press Command-V/Ctrl-V. FreeHand pastes all the objects you copied into the current publication, changing the definition of "style 2" as it does so.

Removing Styles

To remove a style from a publication, select the style name in the Styles palette and choose Remove from the Styles palette's options menu. FreeHand removes the style from the list of styles in your publication. The formatting of the objects tagged with the style does not change—it simply becomes local formatting.

If your Styles palette is full of styles you're not using, choose Remove Unused from the Styles palette's Options menu. If Free-Hand can't find an object tagged with a particular style in the publication, it removes the style.

Importing Styles   Choose Import from the Styles palette's Options menu to import styles from other FreeHand publications. FreeHand displays the styles defined in the publication in the Import Styles dialog box. Select the styles you want to import (hold down Shift to select a range of styles, or Command/Ctrl to select individual styles from the list). Click OK, and FreeHand imports the styles into the current publication (see Figure 2-138). If the name of an incoming style matches the name of a style that's already in the publication, FreeHand leaves the definition of the existing style unchanged (the "home team" wins).

The CMYK Styles and RGB Styles items on the Styles palette's Options menu are shortcuts to the styles defined in the files "CMYK Styles" and "RGB Styles," which you'll find in the Styles folder in your FreeHand folder (on the Macintosh) or in the English folder in your FreeHand folder (Windows).

FIGURE 2-138
Importing Styles

Choose Import from
the Styles palette's
Options menu...

...or choose one of the
shortcuts. These are file
names, and correspond
to style libraries saved
in the Styles folder
(inside your FreeHand
folder on the Macin-
tosh; inside the English
folder in your FreeHand
folder in Windows).

FreeHand opens the
publication and
displays the styles in
that publication in the
Import Styles dialog
box.

Preview

Style name

Locate and select the
FreeHand publication
containing the styles.

If you chose one of the shortcuts,
you won't see this dialog box.

Hold down Command/Ctrl
as you click to select more
than one
style.

Click the
Import
button, and
FreeHand
imports the
styles.

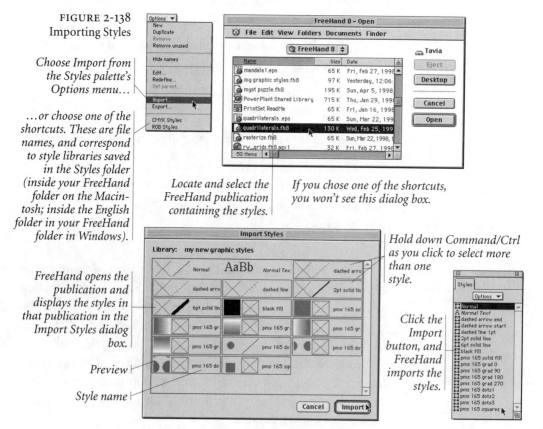

Exporting Styles   While you can always import styles from any FreeHand document, you might also want to save your styles in a "style library" file—a FreeHand publication containing *nothing but* the styles. To do this, choose Export Styles from the Styles palette's Options menu. Free-Hand displays the Export Styles dialog box. Select the styles you want to export (hold down Shift to select a contiguous range of styles, or hold down Command/Ctrl to select noncontiguous styles), then click the Export button (see Figure 2-139).

   If you want to add a shortcut to a styles "library" file to the Styles palette's Options menu (like the default "CMYK Styles" or "RGB Styles" files), save the file in the Styles folder in your Free-Hand folder (on the Macintosh) or in the Styles directory inside the English directory in your FreeHand directory (Windows). Free-Hand will add the publication's name to the Options menu.

FIGURE 2-139
Exporting Styles

Choose Export from the Styles palette's Options menu...

...and FreeHand displays the Export Styles dialog box.

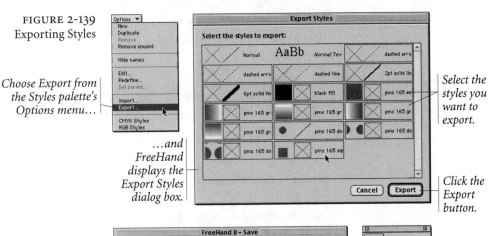

Select the styles you want to export.

Click the Export button.

Enter a name for the styles library (a FreeHand publication containing only the styles you export), then click the Save button to save the file.

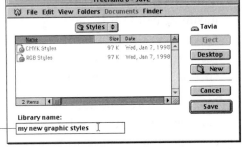

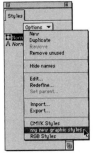

If you save the file in the Styles folder (it's inside your FreeHand folder on the Macintosh—you'll find it in the English folder inside your FreeHand folder in Windows)...

...FreeHand adds a shortcut to the new style library to the Styles palette's Options menu.

Adding Styles to Your Defaults File

You can add styles to your FreeHand defaults template by opening the template, copying in elements having the styles you want, and then saving the file as a template. This way, the styles you've added appear in every new publication you create. See "Setting Document Defaults" in Chapter 1, "FreeHand Basics."

Creating Charts and Graphs

With the Chart tool Xtra, you can create six different types of charts (Grouped Column, Stacked Column, Line, Pie, Area, and Scatter charts) by entering values in FreeHand or by importing data from a spreadsheet.

To create a chart, follow these steps (see Figure 2-140).

1. Press Command-Option-X/Ctrl-Shift-X to display the Xtra Tools palette, if it's not already visible.

2. Select the Chart tool.

3. Drag the Chart tool on your page. This creates a "dummy" chart you'll edit. After you stop dragging, FreeHand displays the Chart dialog box.

4. Enter numbers in the cells of the chart, just as you would in any spreadsheet (in other words, click the cell, then enter numbers in the Cell Edit field), or paste data from your favorite spreadsheet, database, or word processor (when you paste, the cell you've selected sets the starting point for the incoming data).

   When you want to enter a number as a label (see the years running across the X axis of the example chart), enclose the number in straight quotes.

6. Click the Chart Type button. FreeHand displays another panel of the Chart dialog box. When you click the button corresponding to the chart type you want to use, FreeHand displays options for that chart type.

7. Once you've entered the numbers you want to use to create the chart have set up the chart and formatting options, click

FIGURE 2-140
Creating charts

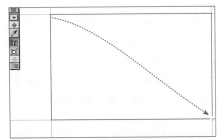

Drag the Chart tool to define the area taken up by the chart. Note that this area defines the X and Y axis of the chart—labels will appear outside the area.

FreeHand displays the Chart dialog box. Enter numbers in the Chart cells as you would in any spreadsheet.

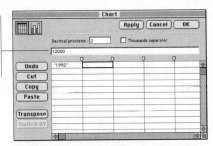

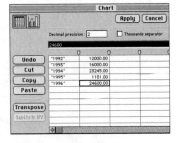

Click the Chart Type button to define the appearance of the chart.

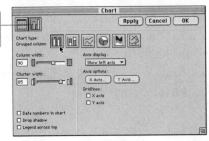

When you've entered all the data and set up the appearance of your chart, click the Apply button (to create the chart and keep the Chart dialog box open), or click the OK button (to close the dialog box and create the chart).

FreeHand creates the chart, based on the data you entered and the options you selected.

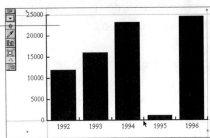

The chart is a collection of FreeHand objects, grouped together. To edit the chart, select it and double-click the Chart tool in the Xtra Tools palette, or choose Edit from the Chart submenu of the Xtras menu. FreeHand takes you back to the Chart dialog box.

Hold down Option/Alt to select any of the objects in the chart (as you would to select any object in a group).

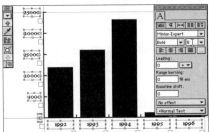

Once you've selected items, you can format them as you would any other object in FreeHand. In this example, I've formatted the text blocks in the chart.

the Apply button. FreeHand updates the chart. If you've got room on your screen, you can even drag the Chart dialog box off to one side so that you can see your chart. When everything looks the way you want it to, click the OK button to close the Chart dialog box.

What are all these chart types? Why would you use one chart type over another? It all depends on how you want to look at the data you've used to construct the chart.

 Grouped Column Charts. These charts are good for displaying raw amounts (dollars, metric tons, concerned citizens, and other basic units of measurement). Each column of data is represented by a single bar.

 Stacked Column Charts. Stacked Column charts break larger bodies of data into smaller parts, plotting those parts inside the area covered by the total. In Stacked Column charts, each bar represents a row of data from the Chart dialog box; each area inside the bar represents a cell in that row.

 Line Charts. Use a Line chart when you want to see a change in data over time. Each line in a Line chart represents a column of data in the Chart dialog box.

 Pie Charts. Use the Pie chart type when you want to see how the values you're plotting make up a whole (what percentage of our income came from widget sales?). Each wedge in a Pie chart corresponds to a field in the Chart dialog box. If you've entered more than one row of data, you'll see more than one Pie chart.

 Area Charts. Like Line charts, Area charts show the progress of data over time. Each area in an Area chart represents a column of data you entered in the Chart dialog box.

 Scatter Charts. Scatter charts show how data points relate to each other. Like Area charts and Line charts, Scatter charts are good at showing the change in data over time. The next time you have to plot the change in two political candidates' "approval" ratings, use a Scatter chart. Each point in a Scatter chart corresponds to two cells in the Chart dialog box. The first cell in a column sets the X, or horizontal, position of the point, the second cell in the column sets the Y, or vertical, position.

Tip:
Charting with
Pictographs

You've seen charts constructed of pictographs: little coffee cups, pianos, and tropical fruit. How can you get this effect in FreeHand? Follow these steps (see Figure 2-141).

FIGURE 2-141
Using Pictographs

Select the object you want to use as a pictograph and press Command-C/Ctrl-C to copy it.

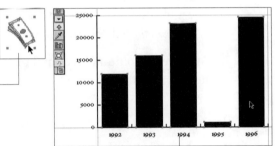 

Hold down Option/Alt and click on the objects in the chart you want to convert to pictographs.

Choose Pictograph from the Chart submenu of the Xtras menu.

Turn on the Repeating Option, and FreeHand repeats the pictograph to represent the data.

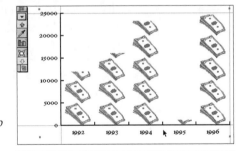

Turn off the Repeating Option, and FreeHand stretches the pictograph to represent the data.

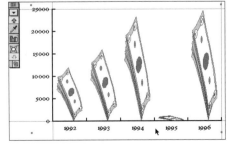

1. Select the object you want to use as a pictograph.

2. Copy the object.

3. Hold down Option/Alt and select a column (or series of columns) in a chart.

4. Choose Pictograph from the Chart submenu of the Xtras menu. FreeHand displays the Pictograph dialog box.

5. Click the Paste In button. The object you copied appears in the Pictograph dialog box.

6. Turn on the Repeating option if you want the object to repeat to show a value in the chart, or turn it off to have the object *stretch* to display a value.

7. Click the OK button. FreeHand fills the selected column of the chart with the object.

Using the Graphic Hose

FreeHand's new Graphic Hose tool gives you the ability to "spray" objects into a publication. It's a lot of fun, but it's also extremely useful. Need to quickly create a textured background? Reach for the Graphic Hose tool. The following steps show you how it works (see Figure 2-142).

1. Double-click the Graphic Hose tool in the Xtra Tools palette (if the palette's not already visible, press Command-Option-X/Ctrl-Alt-X). FreeHand displays the Graphic Hose palette.

2. Choose a hose from the Hose pop-up menu. FreeHand comes with a variety of predefined graphic hoses.

3. Click the Options button. FreeHand displays the Options panel. Use this panel to define the behavior of the Graphic Hose tool. See Table 2-1 for an explanation of the options.

4. Click or drag the Graphic Hose tool. As you click or drag, FreeHand places objects from the hose.

FIGURE 2-142
Graphic Hose Tool

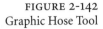

Choose the hose you want to use. | *Buy FreeHand and you get the very groovy "Flowers" hose free!*

Double-click the Graphic Hose tool in the Xtra Tools palette.

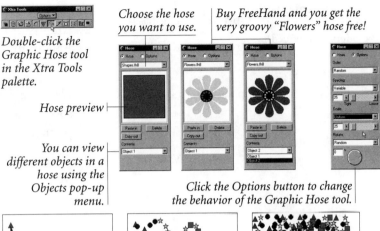

Hose preview

You can view different objects in a hose using the Objects pop-up menu.

Click the Options button to change the behavior of the Graphic Hose tool.

Go wild. As far as I know, this sort of thing is still legal in most areas.

As you drag the Graphic Hose tool...

...FreeHand adds objects from the hose to the page...

...spacing, rotating, and scaling the objects according to your settings.

Hoses are FreeHand files—they're stored in the Graphic Hose folder in the Xtras folder (that's FreeHand 8:Xtras on the Macintosh, Program Files\Macromedia\FreeHand 8\English\Xtras in Windows). To remove a hose, move the corresponding file (the file names are the same as the hose names) out of that folder or delete it.

TABLE 2-1
Graphic Hose Tool
Options

Option	Choice	What it does
Order	Loop	Places the objects from the selected hose in order, from first to last, and then starts again with the first object.
	Back and Forth	Places the objects from the selected hose in order, from first to last, and then places the objects in reverse order (from last to first). FreeHand continues stepping through the objects in this manner until you stop dragging.

Option	Choice	What it does
Order	Random	Randomly places objects from the selected hose.
Spacing	Grid	Places objects on a grid. You specify the size of the grid (in points) using the attached field.
	Variable	Places objects a specific distance from each other as you drag the Graphic Hose tool. You set the distance (as a percentage of the size of the object) using the attached field/slider. Regardless of the setting you enter here, Free-Hand spaces objects at varying distances when you drag the tool quickly. To get exactly the spacing you specify here, drag the tool slowly (very slowly if your hose contains complex graphics).
	Random	Randomly spaces objects as you drag the Graphic Hose tool. You can specify the range from which this random distance will be chosen using the field/slider (as a percentage of the object's size).
Scale	Uniform	Scales objects at a fixed percentage (of the object's size).
	Random	Randomly scales objects as you place them. The value you enter sets the range of random values FreeHand chooses from (as a percentage change from the object's original size—zero percent means no variation in size).

TABLE 2-1
Graphic Hose Tool Options (continued)

Option	Choice	What it does
Rotate	Uniform	Rotates objects as you drag the Graphic Hose tool. Every object will be rotated by the same angle relative to its original angle.
	Incremental	Rotates objects by an increasing or decreasing angle as you place them. If the angle you specify is 20 degrees, for example, the first object will be rotated by 20 degrees, the next by 40 degrees, and so on.
	Random	Randomly rotates objects as you place them. The angle you enter sets the range from which a random angle will be chosen.

Creating Your Own Hoses

The Graphic Hose feature wouldn't be nearly as much fun if you couldn't create your own hoses (though it can take some time to get tired of the groovy "Flowers" hose). A hose can contain anything—paths, text, or imported graphics. To create your own hose, follow these steps (see Figure 2-143).

1. Choose New from the Graphic Hose pop-up menu. FreeHand displays the Hose dialog box.
2. Enter a name for your new hose and click the Save button. FreeHand displays a new, empty hose in the Graphic Hose palette.
3. Select an object or group you want to add to the hose and copy it.
4. Click the Paste In button. FreeHand adds the object to the hose. Now you can start using the hose, or add more objects to the hose.

FIGURE 2-143
Creating a New Hose

Choose New from the Hose pop-up menu.

Type a name for your new hose and click the Save button.

Select an object to add to the hose and copy it.

Click the Paste In button. FreeHand adds to the object you copied to the hose. Now you can create your own patterns and backgrounds.

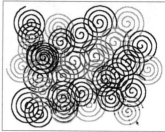

Tip:
Hose Library

You can use the Graphic Hose tool as a "library" for commonly-used objects (map symbols, your logo, your address, and so on). Remember, anything can be added to a hose, provided you group it first (see Figure 2-144)

FIGURE 2-144
Using a Hose as a
Graphic Library

In this example, I've added a company logo to a hose, and then set up the Graphic Hose Options to retain the original size and rotation of the logo.

The next time I want a copy of my logo, I point the Graphic Hose tool at the page...

...and click. FreeHand inserts the logo. This is similar to the "graphic library" feature found in other programs.

Creating Drop Shadows

They're everywhere I look. Every object, in every catalog, appears to be floating in space above the page. Every object casts a shadow, as if illuminated by a light source located somewhere off of the page. Everything, everywhere, has a shadow.

It only makes sense, therefore, that FreeHand should honor this fundamental shift in reality by providing an automated way to add these "drop" shadows to paths in your FreeHand publications. Like the Smudge tool, the Shadow tool automates the creation of a blend. To create a drop shadow (they're now required by law), follow these steps (see Figure 2-145).

FIGURE 2-145
Shadow Xtra

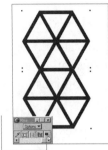

Experiment with the options, pressing Apply every now and then to see a preview of the effect.

Press the OK button to apply the Shadow effect. Click Cancel, to leave the publication unchanged.

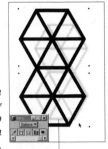

Double-click the Shadow tool in the Xtra Tools palette.

Soft edge

Once you've set up the Shadow tool's options, you can drag the Shadow tool to specify the X and Y offset of the shadow effect.

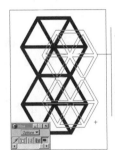

As you drag, FreeHand displays a keyline preview of the shadow's position.

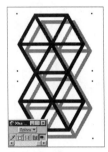

Hard edge   Zoom

1. Display the Xtra Tools palette, if it's not already visible (press Command-Option-X/Ctrl-Alt-X).

2. Double-click the Shadow tool. FreeHand displays the Shadow dialog box (see Table 2-2 for an explanation of the Shadow tool options).

3. Using the controls in the Shadow dialog box, specify the appearance of the shadow. Click the OK button when you're done. FreeHand applies the shadow effect.

The next time you use the Shadow tool (that is, once you've set up the options the way you want them), you can select a path, then drag the Shadow tool. As you drag, FreeHand displays a keyline of the position of the shadow. When the shadow falls where you want it to, stop dragging. FreeHand creates a blend where you dropped the shadow.

To apply a shadow to text, you'll have to convert the text to paths (select the text and press Command-Shift-P/Ctrl-Shift-P) before you apply the Shadow effect.

TABLE 2-2
Shadow Tool Options

Option	Variant	What it does
Type	Hard Edge	Duplicates the original path and changes its color or tint according to the other options (does not create a blend).
	Soft Edge	Creates a blend that "softens" the edges of the shadow.
	Zoom	Creates a blend that fades to a soft edge (at one end) and a hard edge (at the other end).
Fill	Tint	Sets the color of the shadow to a tint of the color of the original path.
	Shade	Sets the color of the shadow to the color of the original object plus a percentage of black.
	Color	Creates a blend between the color of the original path and the color in the associated color well (drop a color swatch into the color well to change the color).
Scale		Sets the size of the shadow (as a percentage of the size of the original path.
Offset		Sets the X (horizontal) and Y (vertical) offset of the shadow, relative to the position of the original path (in the publication's current measurement units). If you want to use the Shadow Xtra as a tool, you don't need to worry about these fields.

The blends created by the Shadow Xtra use process colors. If you want to create a drop shadow using a spot color, you'll have to do it yourself (or rely on some of the spot-to-process tricks described in Chapter 6, "Color").

Embossing Paths

When you want to create the illusion that a path has been embossed (raised or lowered, relative to the plane of the page), reach for the Emboss Xtra (see Figure 2-146). The Emboss Xtra automates the creation of a pair of blends (which I'll refer to as the "highlight" blend and the "shadow" blend) which give you the effect you want.

1. Display the Operations palette, if it's not already visible (press Command-Option-O/Ctrl-Alt-O).

2. Click the Emboss button. FreeHand displays the Emboss dialog box.

3. Experiment with the options in the dialog box (see Table 2-3), clicking the Apply button every now and then to see a preview of the effect. When you see what you like, click the OK button. If you want to leave the dialog box without making any change to your publication, press Cancel.

The blends created by the Emboss Xtra use process colors. If you want to create an "embossed" object using a spot color or hi-fi color, you'll have to do it manually (or rely on the workarounds described in Chapter 6, "Color").

FIGURE 2-146
Embossing Paths

To apply the Emboss settings you've most recently used, select a path, then hold down Command/Ctrl and click the Emboss button in the Operations palette. FreeHand applies the Emboss effect without displaying the Emboss dialog box.

Display the Operations palette and click the Emboss button.

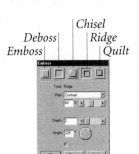

Deboss | *Chisel*
Emboss | *Ridge*
           | *Quilt*

Experiment with the options in the Emboss dialog box, pressing Apply to see a preview of the effect.

Click the OK button to apply the effect, or click the Cancel button to close the dialog box and leave your publication unchanged.

TABLE 2-3 Emboss Xtra Options	Option	What it does
	Type	The five buttons at the top of the Emboss dialog box control the way FreeHand creates the highlight and shadow blends. From right to left, these buttons are Emboss, Deboss, Chisel, Ridge, and Quilt (as you click a button, FreeHand displays the effect type in the Type field).
	Vary	When you choose Contrast from the Vary pop-up menu, FreeHand uses tints of the color you applied to the original path to create the highlight blend and uses tints of that color plus tints of black to create the shadow blend. When you choose Colors from the Vary pop-up menu, FreeHand uses tints of the color swatches you drag into the Highlight and Shadow fields to create the blends.
	Depth	Sets the distance (in current measurement units) of the outside edge of the blends from the edges of the original path.
	Angle	Sets the angle of the virtual light source (and, therefore, the angle of the blends).
	Soft Edge	Adds more blend steps to the outside of the blends generated by the Emboss Xtra, creating a smoother transition around the edges of the blends. This option is only available for the Emboss and Deboss options.

Path Transformation Xtras

FreeHand has a number of tools and commands for transforming paths. You'll find them in the Xtra Tools palette (press Command-Shift-K/Ctrl-Shift-X to display the palette, or choose Xtra Tools from the Xtras submenu of the Window menu) or in the Operations palette (press Command-Shift-I/Ctrl-Shift-O).

Add Points Xtra   The Add Points Xtra, as you'd expect, adds points to a path. To use this Xtra, select a path and then click the Add Points Xtra in the Xtra Tools palette (or choose Add Points from the Distort submenu of the Xtras menu). FreeHand adds a point exactly half way between each pair of points on the path (see Figure 2-147). Adding points to a path using this Xtra doesn't usually change the appearance of the path.

FIGURE 2-147
Adding Points

Select the path you
want to add points to.

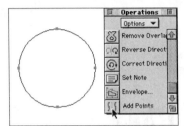 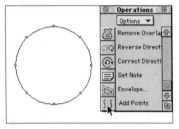

Click the Add Points button in the Operations palette, or choose Add Points from the Distort submenu of the Xtras menu.

FreeHand adds a point between each pair of points on the path.

To add more points, press Command-+/ Ctrl-Alt-Shift-X, or click the Add Points button again.

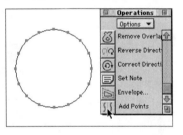

Envelope Xtra   No—this Xtra doesn't print envelopes. "Envelope," in this case, refers to the underlying two-dimensional geometry of a path. The Envelope Xtra gives you a way of distorting that geometry—which changes the shape of a path. To distort a path using the Envelope Xtra, follow these steps (see Figure 2-148).

1. Select the path.

2. Click the Envelope Xtra button in the Operations palette (or choose Envelope from the Distort submenu of the Xtras menu). FreeHand displays the Envelope dialog box. The path you see displayed in red (if you have a color monitor) in the preview window inside the Envelope dialog represents the envelope.

FIGURE 2-148
Applying an
envelope to a path

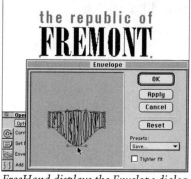

Select the path you want to distort,
then click the Envelope button in the
Operations palette.

FreeHand displays the Envelope dialog
box. Adjust the outline in the preview
window and click the OK button...

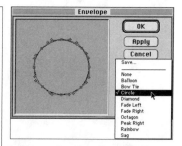

...and FreeHand applies the envelope
to the selected path.

You can also choose a predefined
envelope from the Presets pop-up
menu, or save the envelope you've
created (choose Save from the Presets
pop-up menu).

3. Reshape this path—by moving control handles or points—
    and you're distorting the path. You can also choose among
    a variety of predefined envelopes from the pop-up menu
    at the bottom of the dialog box.

4. If you want to save the envelope shape you've created,
    choose Save from the Presets pop-up menu. Enter a name
    for the envelope in the dialog box FreeHand displays, then
    click the OK button. FreeHand saves the envelope you've
    created into a text file. The new envelope appears on the
    Presets pop-up menu.

5. Click the OK button to apply the envelope to the selected
    path and close the Envelope dialog box, or click apply to
    apply the envelope and keep the Envelope dialog box open.

Roughen Tool

Sometimes, the perfect smoothness of FreeHand's paths isn't what you want. You want something that looks rougher, something that looks more like a line drawn by a shaky human hand. That's where the Roughen tool (an Xtra) comes in. Select a path, then select the Roughen tool from the Xtra Tools palette. Drag the Roughen tool, and FreeHand adds points to the selected path, moving each point a random distance away from the center of the path. The result? A "rougher" path (see Figure 2-149).

You can control the amount of "roughness" the Roughen tool applies. To do this, double-click the Roughen tool in the Xtra Tools palette. FreeHand displays the Roughen dialog box, where you can change the default settings for the tool. The Amount field controls the number of points per inch added to the path. Turn on the

FIGURE 2-149
"Roughening" a path

Select the path you want to distort.

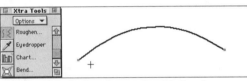
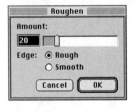

Double-click the Roughen tool to display the Roughen dialog box. Set up the options you want...

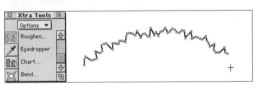

...then click OK to close the dialog box. Drag the Roughen tool...

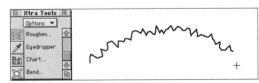

...and FreeHand adds points to the path, randomly positioning them away from the path's center.

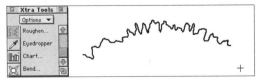

When you turn on the Rough option in the Roughen dialog box, FreeHand adds corner points.

When you turn on the Smooth option, FreeHand adds curve points.

Smooth option to make FreeHand add curve points to the path (this means that all of the line segments created by the Xtra are curved); turn on the Rough option to make FreeHand add the points as corner points with no control handles extended from them (this means that the line segments will be straight).

Fractalize Xtra

Want to introduce arbitrary complexity into your FreeHand publication? Try the Fractalize Xtra. Select a path and choose "Fractalize" from the Distort submenu of the Xtras menu. FreeHand adds points to your path (see Figure 2-150). The Fractalize Xtra doesn't change your path much the first time you run it. Press Command-Shift-+/Ctrl-Alt-Shift-X to run the Xtra again—your path gets more complex each time you run it (until it gets too complex, and FreeHand gives up).

FIGURE 2-150
Fractalizing paths

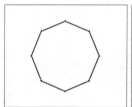

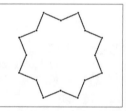

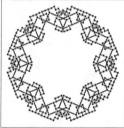

Select the path you want to "fractalize."

Choose "Fractalize" from the Distort submenu of the Xtras menu, and FreeHand changes the shape of the path.

Keep pressing Command-+/Ctrl-Alt-Shift-X until the path looks the way you want it to.

Fisheye Lens Tool

The Fisheye Lens tool distorts paths, changing the path so that it looks like you're viewing the path through (you guessed it) a fisheye, or "wide angle," lens. The Fisheye Lens tool has no effect on imported graphics.

To use the Fisheye Lens tool, select a path (or paths), select the tool from the Xtra Tools palette, and drag the tool over the paths. As you drag, FreeHand extends an ellipse (hold down Shift as you drag to make it a circle) behind the tool. This ellipse sets the area the Fisheye Lens tool affects. When you stop dragging, FreeHand applies the effect (see Figure 2-151).

FIGURE 2-151
Using the Fisheye
Lens tool

*If the Xtra Tools palette
isn't already visible,
display it by pressing
Command-Option-X/
Ctrl-Alt-X.*

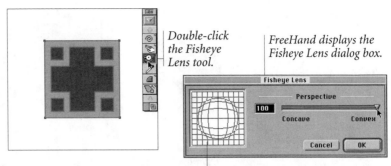

*Double-click
the Fisheye
Lens tool.*

*FreeHand displays the
Fisheye Lens dialog box.*

*As you make changes in this dialog box,
FreeHand displays a preview of the
effect in this window.*

*Change the Fisheye Lens effect by
dragging the slider or entering a
new value in the field.*

*Drag the Fisheye Lens
tool over the objects you
want to distort. As you
drag, FreeHand extends
an ellipse from the point
at which you started
dragging—this
indicates the area the
effect will apply to.*

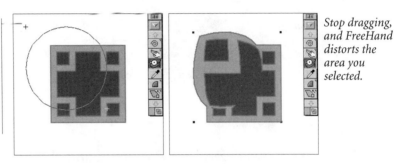

*Stop dragging,
and FreeHand
distorts the
area you
selected.*

To set options for the Fisheye Lens tool, double-click the tool in the Xtra Tools palette. FreeHand displays the Fisheye Lens dialog box. Change the effect of the Fisheye Lens tool by dragging the Perspective slider (or entering a number in the field). FreeHand shows you a preview of the effect.

3D Rotation Tool

The 3D Rotation tool applies several transformations at once—mostly scaling, skewing, and rotation—to make paths look as if they've been rotated away from the plane of the page. The 3D Rotation tool has no effect on imported graphics (TIFFs or EPSes).

To use the 3D Rotation tool, select a path (or paths), select the tool from the Xtra Tools palette, and drag the tool. As you drag, FreeHand extends a line from the point at which you started dragging (or the point you specified in the 3D Rotation dialog box). In addition, FreeHand displays a preview of the transformed state of the path. Stop dragging, and FreeHand applies the effect to the path (see Figure 2-152).

FIGURE 2-152
Using the 3D
Rotation tool

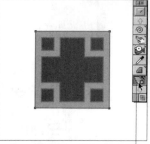
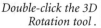
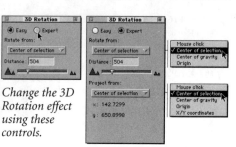

*If the Xtra Tools palette
isn't already visible,
display it by pressing
Command-Option-X/
Ctrl-Alt-X*

*Change the 3D
Rotation effect
using these
controls.*

*Double-click the 3D
Rotation tool .*

*If you click the Expert button,
you'll see more preferences.*

*As you drag the 3D
Rotation tool, FreeHand
displays a preview of
the effect.*

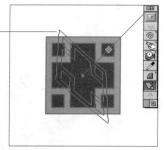

*Stop
dragging,
and Free-
Hand applies
the effect to
the selected
paths.*

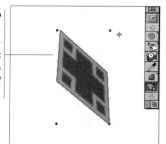

Bend Tool

What gets bent when you distort a path using FreeHand's Bend tool? Everything. The Bend tool extends control handles from each point on a path, then moves the control handles toward, or away from, the center of the path. Select a path, then drag the Bend tool down to move all of the control handles toward the geometric center of the path; drag the Bend tool up to drag the control handles away from the center (see Figure 2-153).

FIGURE 2-153
Bending Paths

*Double-click the Bend
tool to display the Bend
dialog box.*

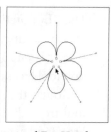

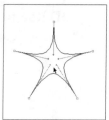

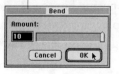

Drag down...

*...and FreeHand
pulls control handles
away from the center
of the path (or the
point at which you
started dragging).*

*Drag up, and
FreeHand pushes
control handles
toward the center of
the path.*

Perspective Drawing

When we draw, we use a variety of tricks to turn the three-dimensional objects we see into lines on two-dimensional paper (or pixels on our two-dimensional computer screens). This process is called "projection," because it involves *projecting* the image of a three-dimensional object onto a plane. There are two types of projection: *perspective* and *parallel* (see Figure 2-154).

FIGURE 2-154
Projection

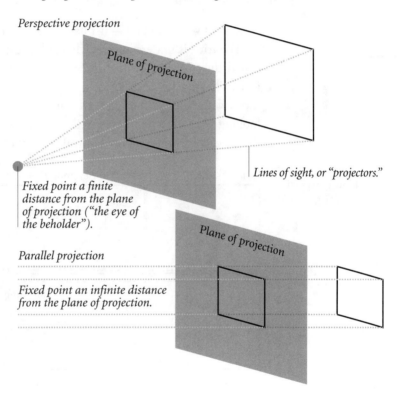

Perspective projection

Plane of projection

Lines of sight, or "projectors."

Fixed point a finite distance from the plane of projection ("the eye of the beholder").

Parallel projection

Plane of projection

Fixed point an infinite distance from the plane of projection.

Perspective

Perspective rendering is a drawing technology dedicated to rendering an image in space much the same way as our eyes see things. The use of perspective came into vogue during the renaissance, and we haven't yet found a better way of representing our three-dimensional world on two-dimensional media. There are three major types of perspective drawing: single-point, two-point, and multi-point. The number of "points" refers to the number of different vanishing points used to create the drawing.

Perspective rendering relies on models of the physical positions of these items.

◆ The eye of the observer

◆ The object or objects being viewed

◆ The plane of projection

◆ The vanishing point or vanishing points

Scared yet? Don't be—just have a look at Figure 2-155.

The trick is understanding where objects fall inside a frame (also called the plane of projection) that lies between you and the objects. The objects exist between the plane of projection and one or more vanishing points. When you look at a photograph, you're looking at an exercise in perspective rendering, frozen in time, where the piece of film is roughly equivalent to the plane of projection.

FIGURE 2-155
How perspective
rendering works

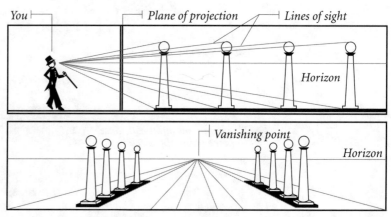

When did this book become a drafting class? About the time I discovered I couldn't explain how to do this stuff in FreeHand without defining some terms.

Single-View Perspective

Single-view perspective relies on a single vanishing point. You rarely see single-view perspective in the real world, because there's almost always more than one natural vanishing point in your field of vision. The classic example of single-view perspective is that of a highway stretching into the distance on a perfectly flat plain.

To create guidelines for a single-view perspective in FreeHand, follow these steps (see Figure 2-156).

1. Draw a horizon line and place the vanishing point at its center.

2. Use the Line tool to draw a vertical line from the vanishing point to a point well below the area you'll be drawing in.

3. Press Command-=/Ctrl-Shift-C to clone the line.

4. Select the bottom point on the vertical line, then select the Scale tool. Position the Scale tool over one end of the horizon line and drag down.

5. Press Command-D/Ctrl-D to repeat the clone-and-scale operation you've just performed. Continue pressing Command-D/Ctrl-D until you've created as many guidelines as you want.

6. Clone the lines, then use the Reflect tool to flip them over the vertical line.

7. Add vertical guides by cloning the horizon line and aligning each cloned line with the bottoms of the guidelines.

8. Select all the lines and send them to the Guides layer. Now you can use them as drawing guides.

To use this technique to create a grid for two-point perspective, use the two end points of the horizon as vanishing points, and draw a vertical line below each of them.

Multi-point Perspective

Multi-point perspective is much more like the way we see the world, because it uses more than one vanishing point. You can use the single-view perspective grid building techniques in multi-point perspective—you just use more than one grid (see Figure 2-157).

Scaling and Perspective

You can use scaling to assist you in your perspective drawing—especially when you're drawing an object whose cross-section is the same at either end. The trick is to scale around a vanishing point, as shown in Figure 2-158.

FIGURE 2-156
Creating a
single-point
perspective grid

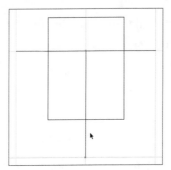

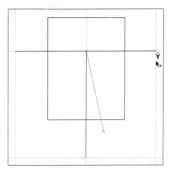

Draw a horizon line and place the vanishing point its center, then draw a vertical line from the vanishing point to a point below the drawing area.

Press Command-=/Ctrl-Shift-C to clone the line, then select the bottom point on the vertical line. Position the Scale tool over one end of the horizon line and drag down.

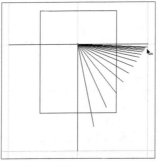

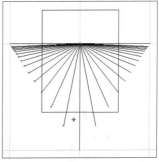

Press Command-D/Ctrl-D until you've created as many guidelines as you want.

Clone the lines, then use the Reflect tool to flip them over the vertical line.

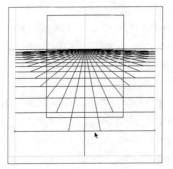

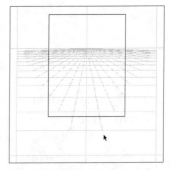

Add vertical guides by cloning the horizon line and aligning each cloned line with the bottoms of the guidelines.

Select all the lines and send them to the Guides layer.

FIGURE 2-157
Multi-point
perspective

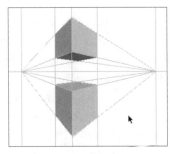

Multi-point perspective depends on the use of more than one vanishing point.

In this example, I've moved the Guides layer to the front to better show the perspective guides.

FIGURE 2-158
Scaling and
perspective drawing

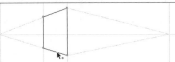
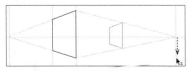

Draw one end of the object, clone it...

...and then position the Scale tool over one of the vanishing points and drag down. FreeHand scales the object around the vanishing point.

Orthographic Projection

In orthographic projection, you create an independent drawing of each primary face (top, bottom, left, right, front, and back) of an object (see Figure 2-159). When you look at the floorplan of a house, for example, you're looking at one of the views of a orthographic projection (the top view). Orthographic projection is a type of parallel projection—the projection lines radiating away from the object are perpendicular to both the face of the object being rendered and to the plane of projection.

FIGURE 2-159
Orthographic
projection

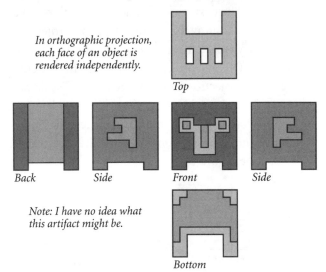

In orthographic projection, each face of an object is rendered independently.

Top

Back *Side* *Front* *Side*

Note: I have no idea what this artifact might be.

Bottom

Oblique Projection

Unlike perspective projection, oblique projection is nothing like the way we see objects. It's an abstraction that's good for keeping measurements intact for manufacturing drawings, and it's also a good way to render a 3-D shape quickly.

In oblique projection, one face of an object is *against* the plane of projection. This side of the object is rendered exactly as it appears in multiview projection. The horizontal lines on the other sides of the object are drawn at the same angle, rather than at angles that converge on a vanishing point. 45 degrees, 30 degrees, and 60 degrees are commonly used angles (see Figure 2-160).

FIGURE 2-160
Oblique Projection

Orthographic projection

Oblique projection

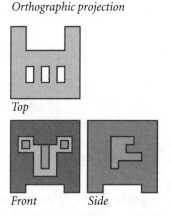

Top

Front   *Side*

The front face of the object is the same as the Front view in the orthographic projection, but the side and top are skewed and projected at an angle.

The next trick of oblique projection is that the scale of the objects drawn away from the plane of projection isn't foreshortened as they recede from the viewer; they are drawn to a single, fixed scale.

Oblique projections in which measurements away from the plane of projection are rendered at full scale are called *cavalier* projections, because they were often used for drawing fortifications in renaissance and medieval times. Half-scale renderings are called *cabinet* projections because they were used by furniture builders (see Figure 2-161).

FIGURE 2-161
Full- and Half-scale
Oblique projection

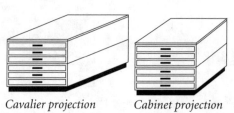

Cavalier projection   *Cabinet projection*

If you've been around the computer-graphics community for long, you've seen lots of oblique projection—because 45-degree lines offered the least jagged line you could get out of early painting programs. Early Macintosh artists created a style that's stuck with us—even now that we can draw smooth lines at any angle.

Axonometric Projection

Objects drawn using perspective projection look "natural," because they're rendered the way our eyes see them. But, in some cases, simply being "natural" isn't enough. As objects get farther away from the plane of projection, they become smaller and smaller. This makes it difficult to see details in a drawing. In addition, there's no practical way to measure distances in perspective drawings. In technical illustration, we need to be able to see all of the detail in a drawing, and we almost always need to be able to measure things.

To solve these problems, we use axonometric projection. Instead of having our projection lines converge at a vanishing point (or vanishing points), we draw them all at the same angle, and parallel to each other. This means that objects in the drawing don't get smaller as they get farther away from the plane of projection, so we retain detail. Next, we can choose the best set of axonometric scales and angles with which to draw and measure the object's faces. You might have to use up to three different scales to measure objects in an axonometric drawing, but you'll be able to do it. The ability to trust the measurements gives axonometric drawings a unique combination of advantages: they're almost as accurate as orthographic drawings, and they're almost as "natural looking" as perspective drawings.

There are three types of axonometric projection: isometric, dimetric, and trimetric (see Figure 2-162).

FIGURE 2-162
Axonometric
projection

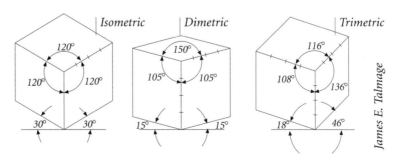

James E. Talmage

You can use FreeHand's Transformation tools to create axonometric projection drawings from multiview projections. See Chapter 5, "Transforming."

Isometric projection In isometric projection, the object you're drawing has all three of its faces rotated away from the plane of projection by the same angle (see Figure 2-163). This means that the same scale can be used to measure any of the three axes.

FIGURE 2-163
Isometric projection

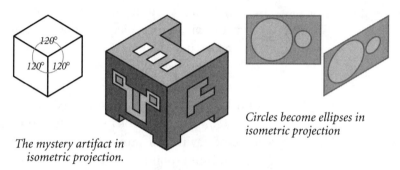

The mystery artifact in
isometric projection.

Circles become ellipses in
isometric projection

You can create grids for isometric projection using the techniques shown in Figure 2-164.

I often want to create a grid of points, rather than a grid of lines, because "Snap To Point" is often the "snap" I want to use—it feels more accurate and powerful than "Snap to Guides." But I can't, because "Snap to Point" doesn't work for objects on the Guides layer. To get a similar effect, I create "snap guides," as shown in Figure 2-165.

FIGURE 2-164
Creating Grids for
Isometric Projection

Enter the angle you want to
use in the Angle field of the
Constrain dialog box.

Draw a series of lines,
hold down Shift to
constrain them to the
angle you set above...

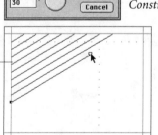

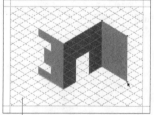

Turn on
"Snap to
Guides" and
draw objects.

...then send the lines to
the Guides layer.

FIGURE 2-165
Creating a grid
of "snap guides"

Create a "snap point" by drawing four lines. The lines should touch at the center of the point, but shouldn't be joined together.

Clone and move the points to create a grid.

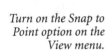

Rotate the grid to whatever angle you want to work with. In this example, I've tinted the objects making up grid to make it easier to see what I'm doing.

Turn on the Snap to Point option on the View menu.

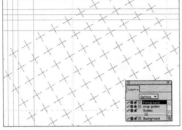

Send the grid to a layer, then lock the layer.

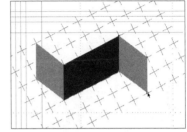

When you draw, points will snap to the "snap points" in the grid.

Dimetric projection. In dimetric projection, two of the axes of the object use one scale; the other axis uses another scale. In dimetric projection, one face of the object is rotated away from the plane of projection by one angle, the other two faces are rotated by another angle (see Figure 2-166).

FIGURE 2-166
Dimetric projection

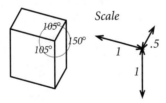

The head of a robot? A new toaster design?

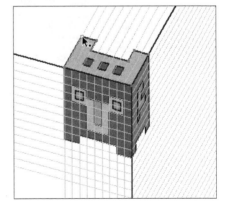

When you're creating drawings using dimetric projection, you might want to create a grid for each face of the object. The heavy lines in this example show the primary axes of the object—at 15, 60, and 90 degrees.

Trimetric projection. You guessed it, in trimetric projection, the axes of the object you're drawing are rotated at three different angles from the plane of projection (and, therefore, use three different scales for measurement). Once again, you can create a grid that has one angle going from left to right, and another, different angle going from right to left (see Figure 2-167).

FIGURE 2-167
Trimetric projection

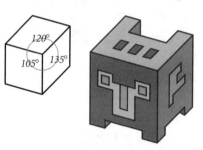

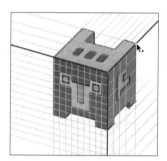

Grids in trimetric projection.

Drawing Conclusions

Earlier in this chapter, I noted that I was confused by FreeHand's approach to drawing when I first encountered it. As I worked with the tools, however, I found that the parts of my brain that were used to using rapidographs (an obsolete type of pen used by the ancient Greeks), triangles, curves, and rulers quickly adapted to the new drawing environment. Eventually, I realized that this was the easier way to draw.

Then, after reading a related article in a tabloid at the supermarket, it dawned on me that the archaic methods I'd learned were nothing less than an extraterrestrial plot, forced on us in classical antiquity by evil space gods, to some cosmic purpose which I cannot—as yet—reveal.

Just keep at it.

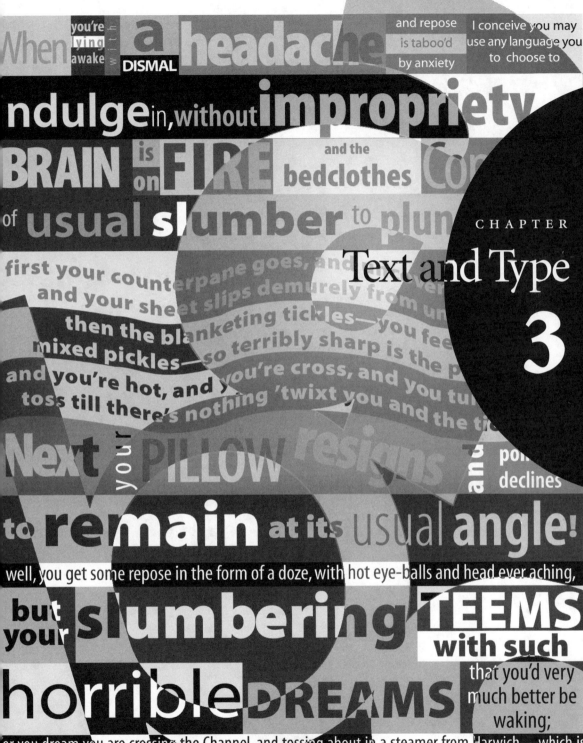

When you're lying awake with a DISMAL headache and repose is taboo'd by anxiety, I conceive you may use any language you to choose to ndulge in, without impropriety Con BRAIN is on FIRE and the bedclothes Con of usual slumber to plun

CHAPTER

Text and Type

3

first your counterpane goes, and ver and your sheet slips demurely from un then the blanketing tickles—you fee mixed pickles—so terribly sharp is the p and you're hot, and you're cross, and you tu toss till there's nothing 'twixt you and the ti

Next your PILLOW resigns po declines

to remain at its usual angle!

well, you get some repose in the form of a doze, with hot eye-balls and head ever aching,

but your slumbering TEEMS with such that you'd very much better be waking;

horrible DREAMS

or you dream you are crossing the Channel, and tossing about in a steamer from Harwich—which is omething between a large bathing machine and a very small second-class carriage—and you're giving treat (penny ice and cold meat) to a party of friends and relations—they're a ravenous horde—and hey all came on board at Sloane Square and South Kensington Stations.

Words.

Somehow, we can never quite get away from them. In academic circles, debate continues on whether we're born with the ability to understand language, or whether it's something we're taught. I don't know the answer, and, most of the time, I don't even know which side of the debate I'm on. What I do know is that language is the most important technology we humans have yet developed.

As I mentioned at the start of the last chapter, FreeHand serves the language of drawing very well. Does FreeHand neglect text in favor of points and paths, strokes, and fills? Not anymore—FreeHand gives you almost all the text-formatting tools you could ever ask for (though I'm still asking for character-based styles and an XPress Tags import filter). If you consider Convert to Paths a character format, FreeHand provides more character-formatting flexibility than any page-layout program.

This chapter is all about working with text and type in FreeHand. Why do I say "text and type?" What's the difference? To me, "text" means content—the stream of words in a publication, how they're organized, and how they behave. "Type," on the other hand, means how the characters of text look—their font, size, color, and paragraph formatting.

There are areas of overlap between these definitions—entering a column-break character (which is really text editing), for example, forces text to the top of the next available column—which does change the appearance of the text. It gets confusing. I've tried to cover things in order: first create some text, then arrange it on the page, and then format it. In the last part of the chapter, I'll talk about commands and procedures that change text into something that's not quite text anymore: text that's bound to a path, or text that's been converted into paths.

Entering and Editing Text

Before we can work with text, we've got to create some. Select the Text tool from the toolbox (or press A), click or drag the tool in the publication window, and type (see Figure 3-1). FreeHand creates a text block and enters the characters you type in the text block. For FreeHand 3 users, this should be a thrill—no more trips to the Text dialog box to enter and edit text. (If you missed the Text Editor—as the dialog box is now named—in FreeHand 4, you'll be happy to know that it came back with FreeHand 5.)

If the New Text Containers Auto-Expand option in the Text Preferences dialog box is turned off, clicking to create a text block creates a text block that's a fixed size (18 picas wide by 12 picas tall). If you've set your text containers to auto-expand, the text block increases in width as you add text. Instead of clicking to create a text block, drag the Text tool—when you do this, Free-Hand creates a text block that's the width and height you specified by dragging (see Figure 3-2).

The text in a FreeHand publication exists inside text blocks, on paths, or inside paths (see Figure 3-3). You can even think of text blocks as a special kind of rectangle, or you can think of paths as

FIGURE 3-1
Entering text

To enter text, click or drag the text tool in the Publication window...

Text Ruler

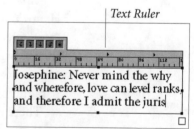

...and type. The Text Ruler and tab icons appear at the top of the text block you've created.

FIGURE 3-2
Drag-creating
a text block

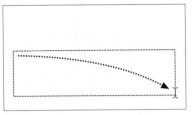

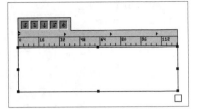

Drag the text tool on the page…

…and FreeHand creates a text block that's the width and height you specified by dragging.

FIGURE 3-3
Text blocks

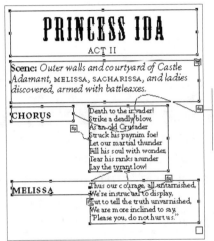

Link boxes attached to each text block show you if the text block is linked to any other text blocks. The goofy lines show you which text block it's linked to.

text blocks with certain weird properties. It's up to you. A text block can contain any number of different character formats, type effects, paragraph specifications, inline graphics, or colors.

Text blocks can contain up to 100 columns or rows (see Figure 3-4). When you flow text inside a path, on the other hand, you're limited to a single column and row. Columns break a text block into evenly-spaced horizontal sections. Rows break the text block up vertically. I call the area of intersection between a row and a column a "cell." You can think of each cell in a text block as a miniature text block, complete with margins.

Text blocks can be resized, reshaped, and manipulated in a variety of other ways, and we'll talk more about them in "Working with Text Blocks," later in this chapter.

When you create or select a text block, FreeHand displays three things around the text block: the Text Ruler, the text box's selection handles, and the Link box (see Figure 3-5).

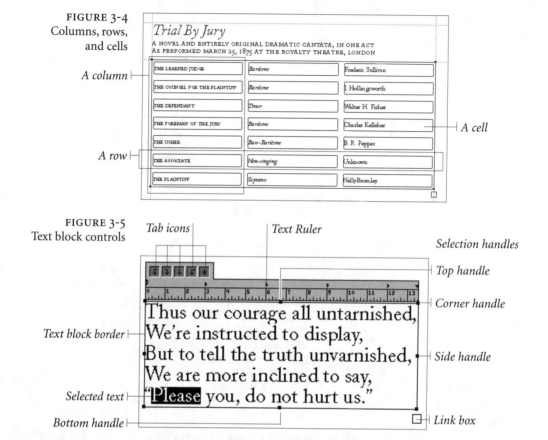

FIGURE 3-4
Columns, rows,
and cells

A column

A row

A cell

FIGURE 3-5
Text block controls

Tab icons   *Text Ruler*

Selection handles

Top handle

Corner handle

Text block border

Side handle

Selected text

Bottom handle

Link box

The Text Ruler. You use FreeHand's Text Ruler to set indents and tabs (see "Setting Indents and Tabs," later in this chapter).

Tip:
Turning Off the
Text Ruler

If you don't like looking at the Text Ruler and the selection handles as you edit text, you can turn them off by pressing Command-\/ Ctrl-Alt-Shift-T (or by choosing Text Rulers from the View menu). Now, when you select text with the Text tool, you won't see the Text Ruler or the boundaries of the text block (see Figure 3-6).

If you want to see the boundary of the text block, but don't want to see the Text Ruler, turn on the Show Text Handles When Text Ruler is Off option in the Text Preferences dialog box.

Selection Handles. You can use the text block's selection handles to resize the text block, to change the formatting of the text inside the

FIGURE 3-6
Turning Off
the Text Ruler

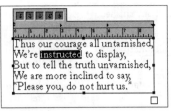

Text Ruler on.

*Press Command-\/Ctrl-Alt-Shift-T,
and the Text Ruler disappears. Press
the shortcut again to bring it back.*

text block, and to turn auto-expansion on and off for the text block
(see "Working with Text Blocks," later in this chapter).

When a text block is set to auto-expand horizontally, the selection handles on the sides of the text block display as hollow squares
(see Figure 3-7). When you've set a text block to auto-expand vertically, the bottom handle displays as a hollow square.

FIGURE 3-7
Selection handles
and auto-expanding
text blocks

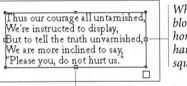

*When you've set a text
block to auto-expand
horizontally, both side
handles display as hollow
squares.*

*When you've set a text block to auto-
expand vertically, the bottom handle
displays as a hollow square.*

The Link box. The Link box, which appears below the lower-right
corner of the text block, gives you the ability to link the text block
to, or unlink the text block from, other text blocks or paths (see
"Linking Text Blocks," later in this chapter).

If a text block contains more text than is currently displayed,
you'll see a filled circle inside the text block's Link box. When a text
block is linked to any other text blocks or paths, you'll see a link
symbol in the text block's Link box (see Figure 3-8).

You can link text blocks to other text blocks, and to open or
closed paths. In this book, I'll refer to all the text in a series of
linked text blocks (including text that isn't in any text block), as a
story. Text that doesn't fit within a series of linked boxes I call
"overset," or "unplaced" text.

You don't have to add text to the text blocks you create—you
can leave empty text blocks on your page until you have text to add

FIGURE 3-8
Link box icons

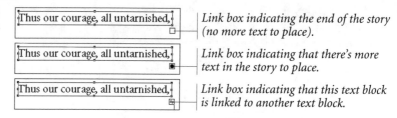

Link box indicating the end of the story (no more text to place).

Link box indicating that there's more text in the story to place.

Link box indicating that this text block is linked to another text block.

to them (provided, of course, that these aren't auto-expanding text blocks, which disappear if you don't enter any text in them). This way, you can work on your publication's layout—including setting up links between text blocks—without necessarily having the publication's copy on hand.

Tip:
Deleting Empty
Text Blocks

If you've created more text blocks than you've used, you can get rid of all the empty text blocks in your publication by choosing "Delete Empty Text Blocks" from the Delete submenu of the Xtras menu.

If you don't see this menu choice, you haven't installed the Delete Empty Text Blocks Xtra. Locate this file on your original FreeHand installation disks (or CD-ROM), uncompress it using the Installer, and place it in the Xtras folder in your FreeHand folder.

If you see text blocks you thought were empty hanging around after this Xtra does its work, they're probably not really empty. FreeHand won't delete text blocks that have spaces, tabs, or other invisible characters in them, so you'll have to delete these yourself.

Tip:
Applying
Formatting to
Text Blocks

When you want to apply the same formatting—character or paragraph—to all the text inside a text block, select the text block using the Pointer tool and then apply formatting using the Text Inspector (or the Text toolbar, or the submenus of the Text menu). You don't have to select text with the Text tool to apply formatting.

Tip:
Finding Empty
Text Blocks

If you've lost track of an empty text block, switch to keyline view; FreeHand always displays the boundaries of all text blocks when you're in keyline view.

Auto-expanding
Text Blocks

One of the biggest new features in FreeHand 5 was auto-expanding text blocks—text blocks that expand horizontally or vertically as you add text to them (see Figure 3-9). FreeHand 5.5 added a

FIGURE 3-9
Auto-expanding
text blocks

Note: In FreeHand 5,
horizontally auto-
expanding text blocks
were always left aligned.
In FreeHand 8, auto-
expanding text blocks
use the alignment of
the paragraphs they
contain.

Click the Text tool to create an auto-expanding
text block.

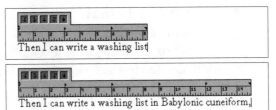

As you type, FreeHand enlarges the text block.

If you've set the text
block to auto-expand
vertically...

...FreeHand increases the height of the
text block as you type.

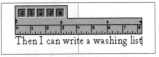

The paragraph alignment you've
selected affects the way that the text
block expands. In this example, the
paragraph is centered...

...which means that the text
block expands equally to the left
and to the right.

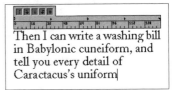

Drag the text tool horizontally...

...and FreeHand creates a text
block that auto-expands vertically.

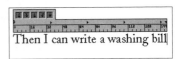

Drag vertically...

...and you get horizontal
auto-expansion.

number of improvements to this feature. You can turn auto-expansion on and off for any text block, at any time. Here are a few things you should keep in mind when you're working with auto-expanding text blocks.

◆ You can't drag the text block's selection handles to change the width of text blocks you've set to auto-expand horizontally. When you do this, the text block snaps back to the width defined by the text in the text block.

◆ You can't change the height of vertically auto-expanding text blocks by dragging the text block's selection handles. Again, the height of an auto-expanding text block is determined by the text in the text block.

◆ In FreeHand 5, text in text blocks you set to auto-expand horizontally would always expand to the right, regardless of the alignment you specify in the Alignment Inspector. These days, text blocks auto-expand according to the alignment of the paragraphs they contain.

If you turn on the New Text Containers Auto-Expand option in the Text Preferences dialog box, any text block you create by clicking the Text tool will be set up to auto-expand horizontally and vertically (see "Text Preferences" in Chapter 1, "FreeHand Basics").

To turn on auto-expansion for a text block, follow these steps (see Figure 3-10).

1. Select a text block with the Pointer tool.

2. Display the Object Inspector for the text block by pressing Command-I/Ctrl-I. In the Object Inspector, you'll see two small icons to the right of the W(idth) and H(eight) fields.

3. Click the icon next to the W(idth) field to make the text block auto-expand horizontally; click the one next to the H(eight) field for vertical auto-expansion. As you click these icons, you'll see the text block expand in the direction you specified. Click the button once to turn auto-expansion on; click it again to turn auto-expansion off.

FIGURE 3-10
Turning on
auto-expansion

FIGURE 3-10
Turning on
auto-expansion

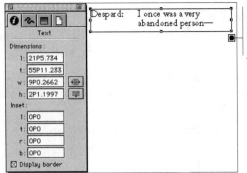

The Link box shows us that there's more text in this text block than we can see on the page.

Click the vertical auto-expansion button in the Object Inspector for the text block...

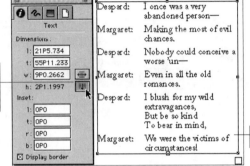

...and FreeHand expands the text block vertically.

Tip:
Auto-expansion
Shortcuts

Double-click one of the side handles of a text block with the Pointer tool to turn horizontal auto-expansion on or off for the text block. Double-click the bottom handle of a text block to turn vertical auto-expansion on or off (see Figure 3-11). If you're editing text and find that you want to change the expansion properties of a text block, hold down Command/Ctrl to switch to the Pointer tool, then double-click one of the text block's handles.

FIGURE 3-11
Auto-expansion
shortcuts

Double-click the bottom handle to make the text block auto-expand vertically, or either of the side handles to make the text block auto-expand horizontally.

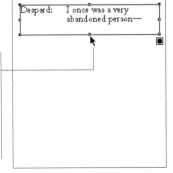

FreeHand expands the text block.

Double-click the handle again to turn off auto-expansion.

Entering and Editing Text with the Text Editor

If you'd rather enter or edit text using FreeHand's Text Editor, you can turn on the Always Use Text Editor option in the Text Preferences dialog box (see "Text Preferences" in Chapter 1, "FreeHand Basics"). When you do this, clicking (or dragging) the Text tool on the page displays the Text Editor—a moveable dialog box that's something like a little word processor inside FreeHand (see Figure 3-12). Cartographers, in particular, begged for the return of this feature after it was dropped in FreeHand 4.

FIGURE 3-12
Text Editor

Click the OK button (or, on the Macintosh, press Enter) to close the Text Editor and save your changes.

Click this button to display the contents of the Text Editor in 12 point black text (this makes tiny text easier to edit)

Turn on Show Invisibles to display tabs, carriage returns, spaces, and other invisible characters in the Text Editor.

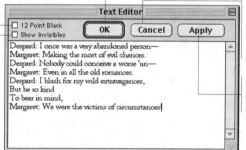

Click the Cancel button (or press Escape) to close the Text Editor without saving your changes.

Click the Apply button to apply your changes without closing the Text Editor.

Symbol	What it is
·	Space
→	Tab
⌣	Nonbreaking space
☐	Em space
◻	En space
|	Thin space
¬	Discretionary hyphen
↵	Line break
¶	Carriage return
↴	Column break

In the Text Editor, you can view your text and its formatting (though the line breaks will probably differ from those you'll see on the page), or you can choose to view all the text in black at 12 point. Give your eyes a break and click the 12 Point Black option in the Text Editor when you're working with very small type, with pale-colored or white type, or other hard-to-see text.

To see carriage returns, tabs, and other invisible characters, turn on the Show Invisibles option. If text isn't behaving the way it should, look at it with this option turned on—chances are good you'll see extra tabs, spaces, or other characters (see table at left).

If you want to see what the text you're entering or editing looks like without leaving the Text Editor, drag the Text Editor so that it's not obscuring the type you want to see, then click the Apply button. FreeHand applies any changes to the text or formatting you've made in the Text Editor.

When the Text Editor is open, you can apply formatting to both selected text and the current text block using any of FreeHand's type formatting tools.

Tip: Using the Text Editor to Create Text Blocks	Hold down Option/Alt as you click or drag the Text tool, and Free-Hand creates a text block and opens the Text Editor. This is a little quicker than creating the text block and then pressing Command-Shift-E/Ctrl-Shift-E to open the Text Editor.
Tip: The Quick Way to Open the Text Editor	Hold down Option/Alt as you double-click a text block with the Pointer tool, and FreeHand will open the text in the text block in the Text Editor. This is quicker than selecting the text block and pressing Command-Shift-E/Ctrl-Shift-E.
Tip: Closing the Text Editor	On the Macintosh, pressing Enter closes the Text Editor. In earlier versions of FreeHand (excepting FreeHand 4, which had no Text Editor), I kept pressing Return, hoping it would close the dialog box. It doesn't—it simply enters carriage returns. In Windows, you've got to click the OK button—sorry.

Moving the Cursor

When you're typing text into a text block, you shouldn't have to take your hands off the keyboard to move the cursor. While Free-Hand's cursor movement shortcuts aren't perfect (it'd be great to have cursor movement keyboard shortcuts like those found in Page-Maker or Word), they can come in handy (see Table 3-1). Hold down Shift as you press any of these shortcuts, and FreeHand selects text as you move the cursor.

TABLE 3-1
Cursor movement shortcuts

Press	To move to
Right Arrow	Next character
Left Arrow	Previous character
Up Arrow	Previous line
Down Arrow	Next line
Command-Right Arrow/Ctrl-Right Arrow	Next word
Command-Left Arrow/Ctrl-Left Arrow	Previous word
Command-Up Arrow/Ctrl-Up Arrow	Previous line
Command-Down Arrow/Ctrl-Down Arrow	Next line
Home	Beginning of story
End	End of text block

Tip:
Switch to the
Text Tool by
Clicking

Double-click a text block with the Pointer tool to position a text cursor at the end of the text block. This is the same as switching to the Text tool and clicking an insertion point at the end of the text, but it's quicker.

Selecting Text

As in most word processing programs, holding down Shift as you press cursor movement keys selects text (Command-Shift-Right arrow/Ctrl-Shift-Right arrow, for example, selects the next word in the story). Also, as you'd expect, dragging a text cursor through text selects the text you drag over. In addition, you can use any or all of the following shortcuts.

◆ Double-click a word with the Text tool to select the word.

◆ Triple-click in a text block with the Text tool to select all the text in a paragraph (the one you clicked on).

◆ Triple-click a text block with the Pointer tool to select a paragraph (same as triple-clicking with the Text tool).

◆ Press Command-A/Ctrl-A when you have a text insertion point active in a story to select all the text in the story.

Entering Special Characters

What makes a special character special? Is it innate, or is it the character's upbringing? In FreeHand, it's hard to tell—some of the characters listed on the Special Characters submenu of the Text menu are active—they "tell" FreeHand to break a line or a column at a specific place. Some of the characters on the list, on the other hand, enter a character that's really no different from any other text character you can type, except that it doesn't appear printed on your keyboard. Table 3-2 tells you what special characters do when you enter them in your text.

While you can use the Special Characters submenu of the Text menu to enter special characters in your text, I prefer typing the characters from the keyboard (after all, that's where my hands are when I'm working with text). Table 3-3 shows keyboard shortcuts for FreeHand's special characters.

Character:	What it does:
End of column	Tells FreeHand to break the text following that character, and start the next line of text at the start of the next available column in the story. If no column is available, FreeHand stores the text as overset text and displays a solid circle in the text block's Link box.
End of line	Breaks the line at the point you entered it (like a carriage return); but, unlike a carriage return, an end-of-line character doesn't start a new paragraph. End-of-line characters are great when you're working with tables.
Nonbreaking space	Keeps the words on either side of the character together, on the same line. If you don't want FreeHand to break a line between "H.M.S." and "Pinafore," for example, enter a nonbreaking space between the two words. This space expands or contracts based on the kerning, letterspacing, and wordspacing applied to the line it appears in.
Em space	A fixed (non-breaking) space (that is, it doesn't change size depending on the surrounding kerning, letterspacing, and wordspacing) equal in width to the point size applied to the character. An em space set to a size of 12 points is 12 points wide.
En space	A fixed space equal to half an em space. A 12 point en space is 6 points wide.
Thin space	A thin space is equal to one tenth of an em space. A 12-point thin space is 1.2 points wide.
Em dash	A dash equal to the width of an em space.
En dash	A dash equal to the width of an en space.

	Character:	What it does:
TABLE 3-2 Special characters and what they do (continued)	Discretionary hyphen	Or "dishy"—tells FreeHand that it can hyphenate the word at the point you enter the special character, if necessary. If FreeHand doesn't break the word, it doesn't display the hyphen. Whenever possible (that is, any time the character following the hyphenation point is anything other than a return or end of line character), use discretionary hyphens rather than entering a hyphen in your text.

	Special character:	What you press:
TABLE 3-3 Typing special characters	End of column	Command-Shift-Enter/Ctrl-Shift-Enter
	End of line	Shift-Enter
	Nonbreaking space	Option-spacebar/Ctrl-Shift-H
	Em space	Command-Shift-M/Ctrl-Shift-M
	En space	Command-Shift-N/Ctrl-Shift-N
	Thin space	Command-Shift-T/Ctrl-Shift-T
	Em dash	Option-Shift--(hyphen)/Alt-1,5,1 (keypad)
	En dash	Option--(hyphen)/Alt-1,5,0 (keypad)
	Discretionary hyphen	Command--(hyphen)/Ctrl-Shift-_

Changing Case

I don't know about you, but I find that at least half of the text I receive for page layout is typed incorrectly. One of the most common problems is that WRITERS want you to KNOW that a certain paragraph is a HEADLINE, SO THEY TYPE IT IN ALL CAPS. Unfortunately, this is not what your suave, hip, retro, happening design calls for. So you have a choice. You can retype every headline, or you can use FreeHand's Convert Case feature to do the work for you.

Convert case can change the case of a text selection to lowercase, uppercase, small caps, title caps, or sentence caps. For the most part, these aren't formatting changes—FreeHand actually retypes the text for you (the exception is small caps, where FreeHand also changes the size of the text).

To change the case of a text selection or text block, select the text, then choose the conversion option you want from the Convert Case submenu of the Text menu (see Figure 3-13).

FIGURE 3-13
Converting Case

Here's a headline a helpful writer has typed in ALL CAPS.

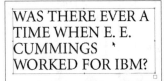
WAS THERE EVER A TIME WHEN E. E. CUMMINGS WORKED FOR IBM?

Note that this headline has some problems—"A," "For," and (possibly) "E. E. Cummings" should be lower case, and "Ibm" should remain "IBM." If this matters to you, read on for solutions.

Choose a case conversion option from the Convert Case submenu of the Text menu.

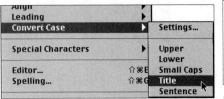

Was There Ever A Time When E. E. Cummings Worked For Ibm?

FreeHand converts the case of the text.

You can tell FreeHand to leave some words unchanged when you change case. You do this by adding "exceptions" to FreeHand's Exceptions list (see Figure 3-14).

1. Choose Settings from the Convert Case submenu of the Text menu. FreeHand displays the Convert Case dialog box.

2. Click the Add button. FreeHand adds a field to the list of exceptions.

3. Type the word or words you want FreeHand to leave unchanged when you convert case. The case of the word you type doesn't matter.

4. You can choose to have some case conversion types ignore the contents of the exceptions list. To do this, turn off the corresponding option in the Use Exceptions For section of the dialog box. If, for example, you want the Lower Case conversion type to ignore the exceptions, turn off the Lower Case option.

What's wrong with this approach? In titles (such as headlines), you want the articles (a, an, the) and prepositions (of, to, for, in, etc.) to be in lower case. If you're converting from all caps to title caps, have entered these words in the exceptions list, and have turned on the Title Case option, these words will be left unconverted—all caps. You'll have to convert to lower case (and ignore exceptions), then convert to title case to get the effect you want.

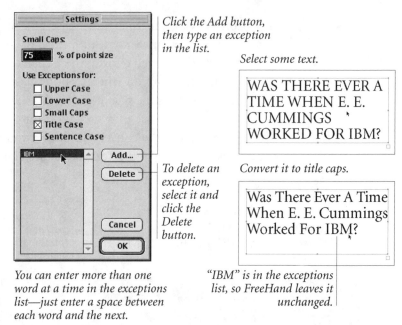

Click the Add button, then type an exception in the list.

Select some text.

WAS THERE EVER A TIME WHEN E. E. CUMMINGS WORKED FOR IBM?

To delete an exception, select it and click the Delete button.

Convert it to title caps.

Was There Ever A Time When E. E. Cummings Worked For IBM?

You can enter more than one word at a time in the exceptions list—just enter a space between each word and the next.

"IBM" is in the exceptions list, so FreeHand leaves it unchanged.

In some cases—such as the headlines mentioned earlier—you'll have to use multiple case conversions to get the effect you want. Or you'll have to do some typing.

If you have VectorCaps (part of the VectorTools plug-in set from Extensis), use it instead of FreeHand's Case Conversion. It's better (see Figure 3-15). VectorCaps' exceptions list works differently from FreeHand's—VectorCaps uses the capitalization of a word in the Exceptions list whenever it encounters the word, which means it's more likely you'll get the conversion you want the first time.

Debra Kosky and I wrote VectorCaps for Extensis. As far as I know, we were the first to use an exceptions list for this purpose and ought to patent the idea (a small idea, but my own). I admit it—I'm proud of the case conversion engine in VectorCaps.

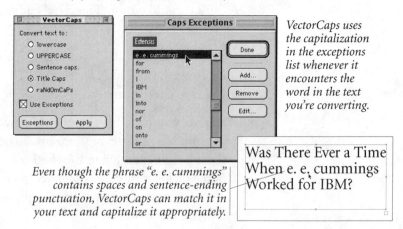

VectorCaps uses the capitalization in the exceptions list whenever it encounters the word in the text you're converting.

Was There Ever a Time When e. e. cummings Worked for IBM?

Even though the phrase "e. e. cummings" contains spaces and sentence-ending punctuation, VectorCaps can match it in your text and capitalize it appropriately.

Tip:
Small Caps and
True Small Caps

When you use FreeHand's Small Caps case conversion option, Free-Hand enters capital letters for the selected text and reduces the size of the type. It does not change the font. This, unfortunately, doesn't give you true small caps, which are entirely different characters from capital letters (see Figure 3-16). True small caps characters are designed for their role, and are usually found in expert fonts (which typically include oldstyle figures, ligatures, ornaments, and other special characters). You can see both true small caps and oldstyle figures (in Adobe Minion Expert Regular, an expert font that matches Adobe Minion, the font you're reading right now) in the page headers of this book.

Ideally, FreeHand would look for an expert font corresponding to the selected font and, on finding one, switch to that font and enter the appropriate characters. It doesn't, so you'll have to do it yourself. If you decide to make do with FreeHand's Small Caps case conversion, make sure you use Range Kerning to add space around the converted characters—small caps are hard to read without a little extra space.

FIGURE 3-16
True Small Caps

Regular capital letters (14 point) from Adobe Minion

ABCDEFGHIJKLMNOPQRSTUVWXYZ

*Scaled capital letters (10.5 point)
from Adobe Minion*
ABCDEFGHIJKLMNOPQRSTUVWXYZ

*True small caps (14 point)
from Adobe Minion Expert Regular*
ABCDEFGHIJKLMNOPQRSTUVWXYZ

*Capital
(56 point)*

*Small cap
(80 point)*

Checking Spelling

When I'm close to the end of a project, every word in the project looks misspelled. Is "dog" *really* spelled "d-o-g"? At that point in a project, I can't take anything for granted. While years of psychotherapy haven't gotten me past this last-minute panic, FreeHand's ability to check the spelling of the text in publications helps. (It doesn't help with my seeming inability to type any zip code other than "98103," on the other hand—the code of the area I've lived in for the last twenty years.)

To check the spelling of the text in all or part of your publication, press Command-Shift-G/Ctrl-Alt-S (or choose Spelling from the Text menu). FreeHand displays the Spelling palette (see Figure 3-17). You can control what and which text gets checked.

◆ To check the spelling of all the text in your publication, deselect everything (press Command-Tab/Tab or Alt-E,S,N, if the cursor is inside a text block), display the Spelling palette (if it's not already visible), and click the Start button.

◆ To check an entire story, select one of the text blocks in the story with the Pointer tool, display the Spelling palette, then click the Start button.

◆ To check the spelling in a range of text, select the text with the Text tool, display the Spelling palette (if it's not already visible), and click the Start button.

FIGURE 3-17
Checking spelling

If you've turned on the Show Selection option, FreeHand scrolls to display any suspect words it finds while checking spelling.

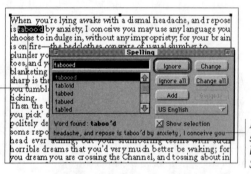

FreeHand always shows the suspect word here, regardless of the state of the Show Selection option.

As FreeHand processes the text, it selects words it thinks are misspelled (and displays the word, in context, at the bottom of the Spelling palette), along with a list of alternative spellings (if it can think of any). At the same time, it copies the most-likely alternative spelling (if any) into the Suggestion field.

If you've turned on the Show Selection checkbox in the Spelling palette, FreeHand displays suspect words as it selects them, scrolling your view of the document to make them visible, if necessary. If this option is turned off, you'll have to figure out where the word is, based on the text displayed at the bottom of the Spelling palette. What's the point of this option? Scrolling to display the suspect word is slower.

You can direct FreeHand to scan your text for repeated words ("the the") or for capitalization errors (a sentence starting with a lowercase character), using the Spelling Preferences dialog box (see "Spelling Preferences" in Chapter 1, "FreeHand Basics").

How does FreeHand know a word is misspelled? It doesn't. From FreeHand's point of view, words not found in the spelling dictionary or the user dictionary are misspelled. FreeHand, however, leaves the final decision up to you. Once FreeHand's encountered a misspelled word, the Spelling palette gives you a series of choices.

◆ Click the Ignore button to direct FreeHand to skip the selected word without changing it.

◆ If you see the word you're looking for in the list of suggestions, select it. FreeHand changes the text in the Suggestion list to match the word you selected.

◆ Click the Change button to change the selected word into the text displayed in the Suggestion list in the Spelling palette. If you've directed FreeHand to check for duplicate words, and FreeHand's found a duplicate word, this button becomes the Delete button: click it to remove one of the duplicate words.

◆ Click the Ignore All button to tell FreeHand to ignore other occurrences of the selected word for the rest of this FreeHand session (that is, until you quit FreeHand).

◆ Click the Change All button to change every occurrence of the selected word to whatever you've entered in the Suggestion list of the Spelling palette.

◆ Click the Add button to add the selected word to FreeHand's user dictionary (that's the word that's selected, not the alternative spelling displayed in the Suggestion list in the Spelling palette). How the word is entered in the user dictionary depends on the settings in the Spelling Preferences dialog box (see "Spelling Preferences" in Chapter 1, "FreeHand Basics").

Tip:
Add Names to
Your User
Dictionary

Okay, I mention this because I'm tired of FreeHand suggesting "Olive Cavern" whenever it encounters my name, but the truth is that very few names appear in FreeHand's dictionary. Save yourself a lot of mouse clicks ("Ignore," "Ignore," "Ignore!") in the Spelling palette by adding your name—and any other names you type often—to your user dictionary.

Finding and Changing Text

One of the most important and useful features in a word processor, text editor, or page layout application is the ability to find a particular string of text (a "string" being a series of characters) and change it to another string of text. Why is this so important? First, it helps you clean up text that's been typed by someone else (all those straight quotes and double dashes); second, it gives you a way to make last-minute text changes—which we all run into at one point or another—quickly and easily.

Setting the Range

How much, or how little, of the text in your publication do you want to search? To search all the text in a publication, deselect everything (press Command-Tab/Tab or Alt-E,S,N, if the cursor is inside a text block) before you start searching. To search an entire story, select one of the text blocks in the story with the Pointer tool before you search. To search a smaller amount of text, select the text with the text tool, then start searching.

Finding Text

First of all, I often need to find a word or phrase in a publication—I don't need to change it into another word or phrase, I just need to find it. That's where FreeHand's "Find" command comes in. To search for a string of text, follow these steps (see Figure 3-18).

1. Display the Find Text palette, if it's not already visible, by pressing Command-Shift-F/Ctrl-Alt-Z.

2. Enter the text you want to find in the Find field. If you need to enter a special character (such as a tab, a carriage return, or an em space), choose the character from the Special pop-up menu next to the field.

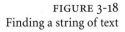

FIGURE 3-18
Finding a string of text

*Type the text you want
to find in the Find field
of the Find Text palette.*

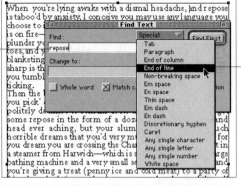

*Enter any special characters
you want to find using the
Special pop-up menu.*

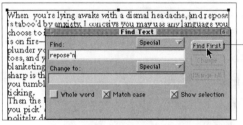

*Click the Find First button
to find the text you've
entered in the Find field.*

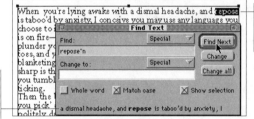

*FreeHand displays the
text you've found, in
context, at the bottom
of the palette.*

*If you've checked the Show
Selection option, FreeHand
scrolls to display the text
you've found.*

*Click the Find Next button
to find the next occurrence
of the text.*

If you want FreeHand to pay attention to the case of the characters you've entered (that is, you're looking for "Free-hand," not "FreeHand"), turn on the Match Case option. If you want FreeHand to only consider entire words that match the text you've entered (that is, you want "Free," but not "FreeHand"), turn on the Whole Word option.

3. Click the Find First button. FreeHand searches through your text until it finds the word (or pattern of characters) you entered.

   If you've turned on the Show Selection option in the Find palette, FreeHand changes your view of the publication to display the text. If you're simply searching for a text string, leave this option on.

4. Once FreeHand finds the first occurrence of the text, the Find First button changes, becoming the Find Next button. To find the string of text again, click the Find Next button.

In the procedure above, I mentioned choosing special characters from the Special pop-up menu. If you'd rather type the special character yourself (I would), you can—by entering the character shown in Table 3-4. As you look at the table, note that capitalization counts—"^t," for example, finds a different character than "^T" would.

TABLE 3-4
Find and Change
metacharacters

When you want to find/change:	Enter:
Tab	^t
Carriage return	^p
End of column	^d
End of line	^n
Non-breaking space	^S
Em space	^M
En space	^N
Thin space	^T
Discretionary hyphen	^-
Caret	^^
Any single character	^@
Any single letter	^*
Any single number	^#
White space	^w*

* "White space" is any space character following selected punctuation (:.!?), or any string of more than two space characters or tabs.

Changing Text   Most of the time, you're looking for text so that you can change it. While FreeHand doesn't—yet—give you the ability to change the formatting of the text you find, you can change any string of text into any other string of text. To change text you find, follow these steps (see Figure 3-19).

FIGURE 3-19
Changing text

Enter the text you want to find in the Find field. In the Change To field, Enter the string you want to use to replace the text you find.

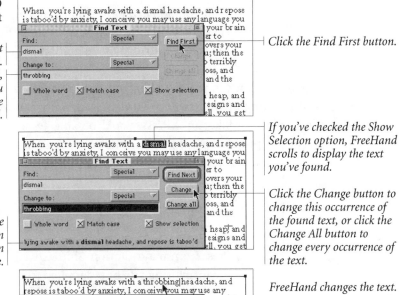

Click the Find First button.

If you've checked the Show Selection option, FreeHand scrolls to display the text you've found.

Click the Change button to change this occurrence of the found text, or click the Change All button to change every occurrence of the text.

FreeHand displays the text you've found, in context, at the bottom of the palette.

FreeHand changes the text.

Click the Find First button again to find the next occurrence of the string you entered in the Find field.

1. Display the Find Text palette and enter the string you want to search for in the Find field (for a more complete description, see "Finding Text," earlier in this chapter).

2. Enter the string you want to have replace the string you entered in Step 1 in the Change field. If you need to enter a special character, type it, or choose it from the Special pop-up menu next to the field.

3. If you want to view the text FreeHand finds (before you change it), turn on the Show Selection option and click the Find First button. FreeHand finds the string you entered. Click the Change button to change the text to the string you entered in the Change field. After you click the Change button, FreeHand finds the next occurrence of the string.

   If you want to change every occurrence, click the Change All button. FreeHand changes all the strings it finds.

If you don't want to change this occurrence of the string, click the Find Next button. FreeHand finds the next occurrence of the string you entered in the Find field.

What can you do when you need to apply a specific set of formatting attributes to a word in your publication? If you were using PageMaker or XPress, you'd be able to search for the word and apply formatting to it. While you can't do that in FreeHand, you can use FreeHand's ability to copy and paste formatting to do something very similar (see Figure 3-20).

1. Select some text that's formatted with the attributes you want.

2. Press Command-Option-Shift-C/Ctrl-Alt-Shift-C to copy the formatting attributes applied to the selected text.

FIGURE 3-20
Changing formatting
with the Find
Text palette

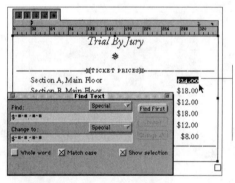

In this example, I've used wild card characters to search for all dollar amounts between $10.00 and $99.00.

Once FreeHand finds the first occurrence of the text, format the text the way you want it (in this case, I've changed the font from Adobe Caslon Regular to Adobe Caslon Expert Regular).

Press Command-Option-Shift-C/Ctrl-Alt-Shift-C to copy the formatting attributes.

Click the Find Next button to find the next occurrence of the text.

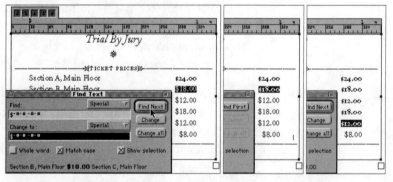

Work your way through the prices in the publication, pressing Command-Option-Shift-V/Ctrl-Alt-Shift-V ("Paste Attributes") to format each price as you find it, then clicking the Find Next button to move to the next price.

3. Press Command-Shift-F/Ctrl-Shift-S to display the Find Text palette (if it's not already visible). Type the text you want to find in the Find field. Turn on the Show Selected option so that you can see what you're doing.

4. Click the Find First button. FreeHand finds and selects the first occurrence of the string.

5. Press Command-Option-Shift-V/Ctrl-Alt-Shift-V to paste the formatting attributes you copied.

6. Work your way through the publication, clicking the Find Next button to find the string and applying the formatting you copied as you go.

Finding and Changing Fonts

Strangely enough, FreeHand's controls for finding and replacing (or finding and selecting) text formatting aren't in the Find Text dialog box. You can, however, find text that's been formatted with a specific font, type style, or size, and can change its formatting. The trick is that you use the Find and Replace Graphics dialog box, to do this, not the Find Text dialog box (see Figure 3-21).

1. Press Command-Shift-Option-E/Ctrl-Alt-E to display the Find and Change Graphics dialog box, if it isn't already visible. If the Select tab is visible, click the Find and Replace tab to display that section of the dialog box.

2. Choose Font from the Attribute pop-up menu.

3. Set the attributes you want to find (in the From section of the dialog box) and the attributes you want to replace them with (in the To section). You can search for any combination of font, type style, or type size. You can set a minimum and a maximum type size you want to search for.

4. Choose an option from the Change In pop-up menu to set the range in which you want to make changes (selection, page, or entire publication).

5. Click the Change button. FreeHand changes the formatting of any text it finds that matches the specified attributes.

FIGURE 3-21
Finding and
changing formatting

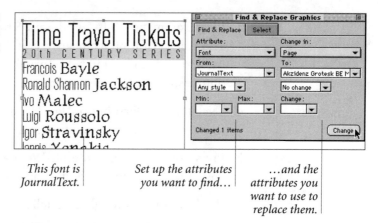

*This font is
JournalText.*

*Set up the attributes
you want to find...*

*...and the
attributes you
want to use to
replace them.*

*Click the Change
button, and FreeHand
replaces every occur-
rence of the font
or formatting in the
range you specified.
In this example, I found
all of the text formatted
using JournalText...*

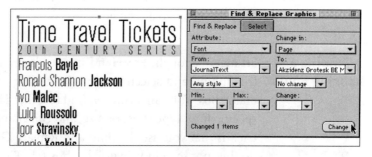

*...and formatted it using
Berthold Akzidenz Grotesk.*

You can also find and select text blocks by their formatting, just as you can find and select graphics by their attributes. The trick here is that if the text block contains any characters formatted with the attribute (or attributes) you're searching for, FreeHand will select the entire text block (see Figure 3-22).

Working with Text Blocks

Once you've created a text block, you can work with it just as you would with anything else on the FreeHand page and pasteboard. You can rotate text blocks, scale them, reflect them, skew them, group and ungroup them, and apply colors to them. You cannot, however, paste objects inside the characters of a text block without first converting the text to paths (see "Converting Characters into Paths," later in this chapter).

FIGURE 3-22
Finding and
selecting formatting

Click the Select tab, then choose the attributes you want to find.

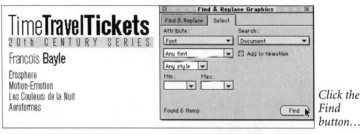

Click the Find button…

…and FreeHand selects all of the text blocks in the range you specified that have at least one character formatted with the attributes you selected.

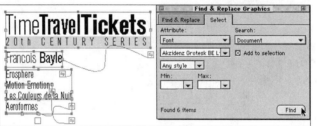

Copying and Pasting Text

If you want to copy some text from an existing text block into a new text block, select the text using the Text tool, and then press Command-C/Ctrl-C to copy the text. Press Command-Tab/Alt-E,S,R to deselect the current text block and press Command-V/Ctrl-V. FreeHand creates a new text block and pastes the text you copied into it (see Figure 3-23).

If you want to copy the contents of a text block into another text block, select the first text block with the Pointer tool and press Command-C/Ctrl-C to copy (or Command-X/Ctrl-X to cut) the text block to the Clipboard. Press A to select the Text tool, and click an insertion in the second text block at the location at which you want to paste the text, then press Command-V/Ctrl-V to paste. FreeHand pastes the contents of the first text block into the second text block (see Figure 3-24).

FIGURE 3-23
Creating a new
text block from
existing text

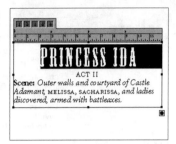

Select the text you want to turn
into an independent text block.

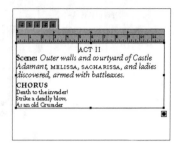

Cut or copy the text.

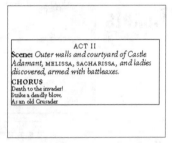

Press Command-Tab/Alt-E,S,R
to deselect the text block.

Paste the new text block into
your publication.

FIGURE 3-24
Inserting text blocks

Select a text block using the Pointer
tool. Cut or copy the text block.

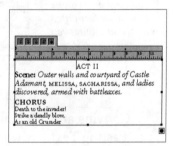

Click the Text tool where you
want to insert the text.

Paste the text into the text block.

Resizing text blocks. You can use the selection handles on a text block to resize the text block itself, resize the text inside the text block, change the kerning of the text, adjust the word spacing used inside the text block, and change the leading of all the lines inside the text block, as shown in Table 3-5 and Figure 3-25.

Changing the shape of a text block by dragging a corner handle recomposes the lines of text inside the text block. You don't have to enter carriage returns, end-of-line characters, or (don't even think about it!) tabs to break lines, unless you really want a line break at that specific point in your text, and want it there regardless of any changes you might make.

You can also use a text block's selection handles as a method of moving the text block. Why would you want to do this? It can sometimes be difficult to drag a text block into a precise position. It always seems to snap to the wrong grid mark or ruler guide (or the wrong side of the text block snaps to the grid). You can get around this by simply dragging one of the corner handles to the point you want to move the text block, then adjusting the other handles (see Figure 3-26).

	To do this	Do this
TABLE 3-5 Working with text block handles	Resize the text block	Drag a corner handle
	Resize the text block proportionally	Drag a corner handle while holding down Shift
	Resize the text while resizing the text block	Drag a corner handle while holding down Option/Alt
	Proportionally resize the text and the text block	Hold down Option-Shift/Alt-Shift and drag a corner handle
	Change the leading of text inside a text block	Drag the top or bottom handle of the text block*
	Change the kerning of text inside a text block	Drag a side handle*
	Adjust the wordspacing of text inside a text block	Hold down Option/Alt and drag a side handle*

*Only applies to a single-column text block.

FIGURE 3-25
Working with text
block selection handles

PATIENCE
I cannot tell what this love may be
That cometh to all, but not to me.
It cannot be kind, as they'd imply,
Or why do these ladies sigh?

To change the size of the text block…

PATIENCE
I cannot tell what this love may be
That cometh to all, but not to me.
It cannot be kind, as they'd imply,
Or why do these ladies sigh?

…drag a corner handle.

PATIENCE
I cannot tell what
this love may be
That cometh to
all, but not to me.
It cannot be kind,
as they'd imply,

FreeHand resizes the text block, reflowing the text inside the text block to fit the new shape.

PATIENCE
I cannot tell what this love may be
That cometh to all, but not to me.
It cannot be kind, as they'd imply,
Or why do these ladies sigh?

To change the size of the text inside a text block…

PATIENCE
I cannot tell what this love may be
That cometh to all, but not to me.
It cannot be kind, as they'd imply,
Or why do these ladies sigh?

…hold down Option/Alt and drag a corner handle (hold down Shift and Option/Alt as you drag to resize the text proportionally).

PATIENCE
I cannot tell what this love may be
That cometh to all, but not to me.
It cannot be kind, as they'd imply,
Or why do these ladies sigh?

FreeHand resizes the text and the text block.

FIGURE 3-25
Working with text
block selection handles
(continued)

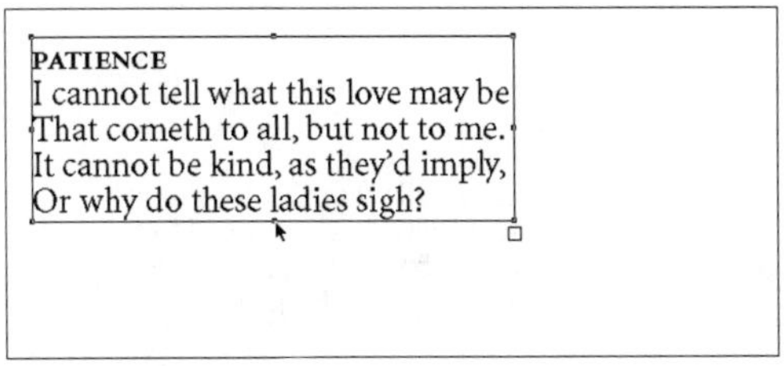

> PATIENCE
> I cannot tell what this love may be
> That cometh to all, but not to me.
> It cannot be kind, as they'd imply,
> Or why do these ladies sigh?

To change the leading of the text in a text block...

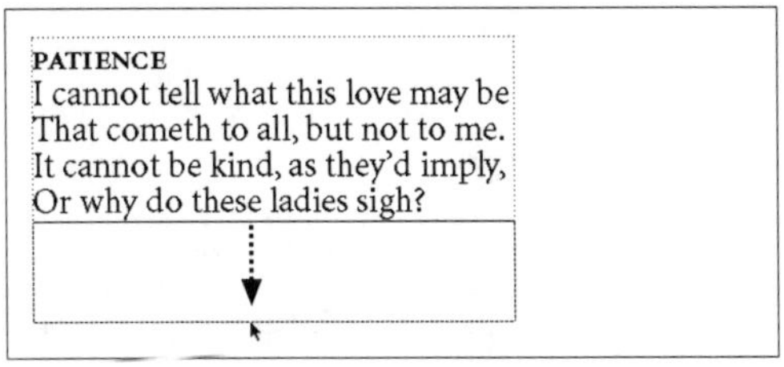

> PATIENCE
> I cannot tell what this love may be
> That cometh to all, but not to me.
> It cannot be kind, as they'd imply,
> Or why do these ladies sigh?

...drag a bottom or top handle.

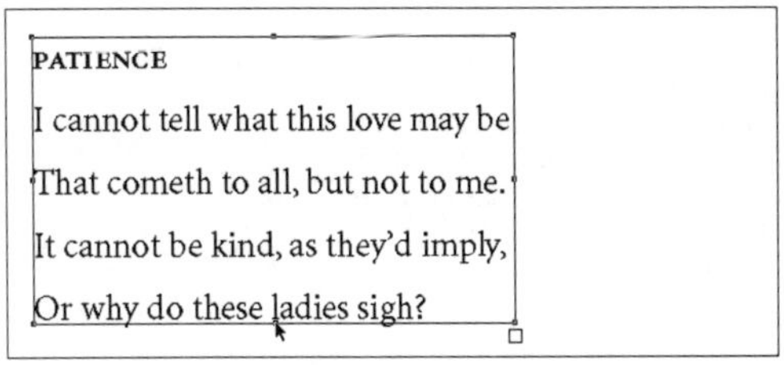

> PATIENCE
>
> I cannot tell what this love may be
>
> That cometh to all, but not to me.
>
> It cannot be kind, as they'd imply,
>
> Or why do these ladies sigh?

FreeHand changes the leading of the text in the text block.

> PATIENCE
> I cannot tell what this love may be
> That cometh to all, but not to me.
> It cannot be kind, as they'd imply,
> Or why do these ladies sigh?

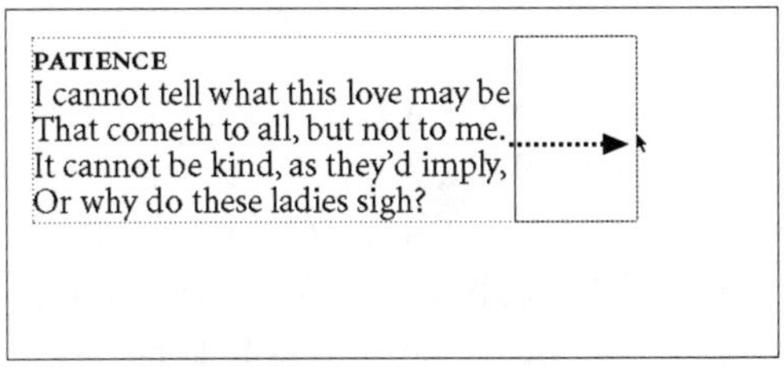

To change the range kerning of text in a text block, drag a side handle.

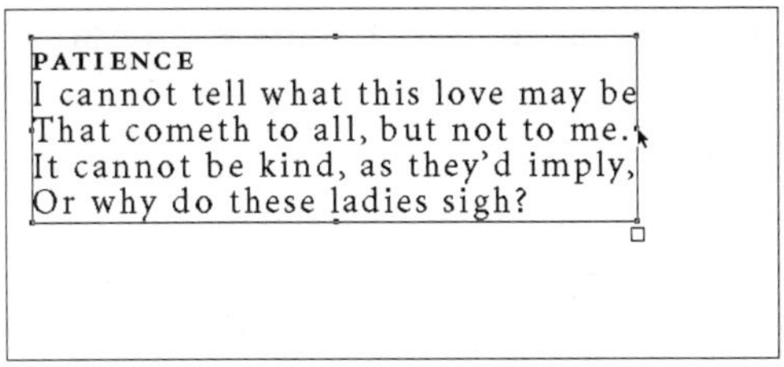

> PATIENCE
> I cannot tell what this love may be
> That cometh to all, but not to me.
> It cannot be kind, as they'd imply,
> Or why do these ladies sigh?

FreeHand increases or decreases the range kerning of the text inside the text block.

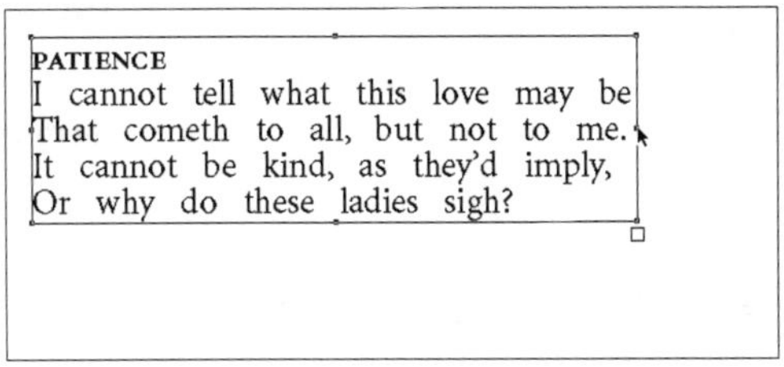

> PATIENCE
> I cannot tell what this love may be
> That cometh to all, but not to me.
> It cannot be kind, as they'd imply,
> Or why do these ladies sigh?

Hold down Option/Alt as you drag a side handle, and FreeHand changes the wordspacing of the text in the text block.

FIGURE 3-26
Moving text blocks by
dragging handles

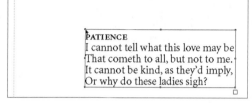

*If you're having trouble
moving a text block to a
new location...*

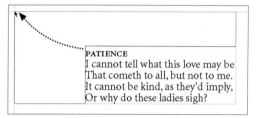

...drag a corner handle...

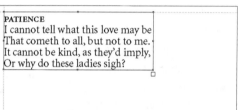

*...and adjust the shape of
the text block once you've
got one corner where you
want it.*

Tip:
Resizing Text
Blocks Using the
Inspector

If you want to make a text block a specific size, use the Inspector. Select the text block, then display the Object Inspector by pressing Command-I/Ctrl-I. In the Object Inspector for the text block, enter the width and height you want for the text block in the W(idth) and H(eight) fields, and press Return to apply your changes. FreeHand sizes the text block to the dimensions you specified.

Tip:
Deselecting
Text Blocks

When you're editing text, you can't press Tab to deselect the text block; pressing Tab just enters tab characters in the text block. Press Command-Tab/Alt-E,S,R, and FreeHand deselects the text block. These shortcuts deselect everything, regardless of the tool you're using. I've gotten in the habit of using them to deselect all objects. This way, I only have to remember one shortcut (though I do wish the Windows shortcut were as easy to remember—and use—as the shortcut for the Macintosh).

Linking
Text Blocks

FreeHand's text blocks, like those found in PageMaker or XPress, can be linked together so that text can flow from one text block to another. By linking text blocks, you can create articles that flow over several magazine pages, for example. Linking and unlinking text blocks, like many other activities in FreeHand, is a drag-and-drop process (see Figure 3-27).

1. Select a text block.

2. Position the cursor over the Link box and drag a line to the interior of another text block.

3. Release the mouse button to drop the link. You've just linked the two text blocks.

4. To see the effect of the link between the text blocks, size the first text block so that it's too small to contain all the text you entered. The text appears in the second text block.

FIGURE 3-27
Linking text blocks

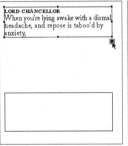
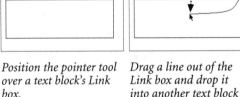

Position the pointer tool over a text block's Link box.

Drag a line out of the Link box and drop it into another text block (example shown in keyline for clarity).

FreeHand links the two text blocks, flowing any overset text from the first text block into the second text block.

Unlinking text blocks is just as easy—select the text block you want to unlink, and then drag a line from the Link box to an empty area on your page or pasteboard. Linked text, if any, flows back into the other text blocks in the selected story (see Figure 3-28).

Alternatively, you can break a link between text blocks by deleting one of the text blocks. If the text block you deleted isn't the last text block in the story, FreeHand flows the text from the text block into the next text block in the story. If the text block you deleted is at the end of the story, FreeHand stores the text in the last text block in the story (as overset text).

FIGURE 3-28
Unlinking text blocks

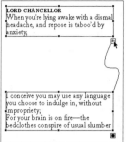 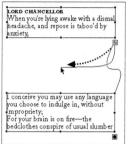 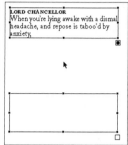

Position the pointer tool over a text block's Link box (examples shown in keyline view).

Drag a line out of the Link box and drop it on an empty area in the publication window.

FreeHand unlinks the text blocks, storing any overset text in the first text block.

Multicolumn and Multirow Text Blocks

A FreeHand text block can contain up to 100 rows and 100 columns. Any time you look at a FreeHand text block, you'll see at least one column and one row—you can't have fewer.

Multicolumn text blocks are pretty similar to those found in a variety of other programs, but multirow text blocks may take some getting used to. In essence, they let you set up any text block as a big table. You can think of each cell inside a text block as a smaller text block, with its own margins and border. All of the cells inside a text block have the same margin and border properties, and have whatever background fill you've applied to the entire text block.

How do you add rows and columns to FreeHand's text blocks? Use the Column Inspector (see Figure 3-29).

1. Select a text block using the Pointer tool.

2. Press Command-Option-R/Ctrl-Alt-R to display the Column Inspector (if it's not already visible).

3. In the Column Inspector, enter the specifications you want for your rows and columns. Columns divide the text block evenly—you can't have columns of unequal width in FreeHand 5 (unless you use wrapping tabs, as shown in "Setting Tabs," later in this chapter).

The height of the rows in a text block depends on the amount of text inside each row. You can make rows taller by adding end-of-line characters in the text if you want. You can make rows taller by entering a number in the Column Height field that's larger than the height of the tallest cell in the text block (see Figure 3-30).

FIGURE 3-29
Multicolumn
text blocks

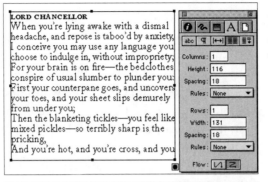

*Press Command-
Option-R/Ctrl-Alt-R to
display the Column
Inspector.*

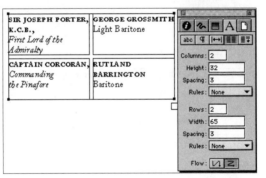

*Use the Column field to
specify the number of
columns you want.*

*Use the Spacing field to
set the distance between
columns.*

FIGURE 3-30
Controlling row height

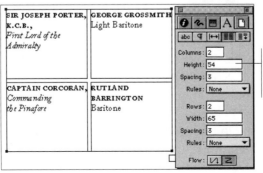

*Enter a new value in
the Column Height
field to make a text
block's rows taller.*

Column width, along with font choice, type size, and leading, is one of the most important typesetting parameters affecting the appearance of a block of type. Many typesetters (including this author) want to define the width of a column early in the process of setting a story. You can set the width of columns in FreeHand's text blocks using the Column Inspector. It's a little confusing, at first: the Column section of the Inspector doesn't include a setting for width. Instead, it includes a setting for the height of the columns in the text block. You enter the column width in the Width field in the Row section of the Inspector (see Figure 3-31). This makes a little more sense when you're working with a multirow text block, such as one containing a table.

FIGURE 3-31
Specfiying
column widths

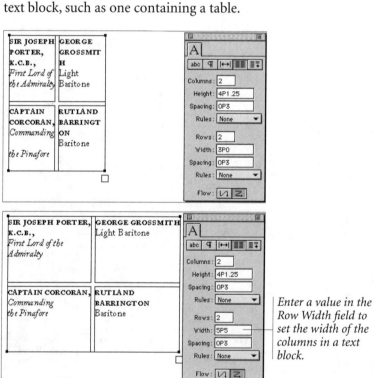

Enter a value in the Row Width field to set the width of the columns in a text block.

Note that, as you'd expect, changing the column widths (or row heights) of a text block also changes the width (or height) of the text block.

You can control the order in which FreeHand flows text inside the columns and rows in a text block using the buttons at the bottom of the Column Inspector (see Figure 3-32).

FIGURE 3-32
Text flow order

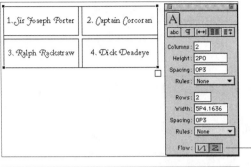

Click these icons to change the order in which FreeHand fills a text block's columns and rows.

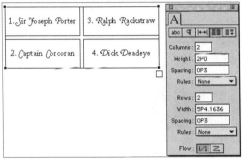

Borders and Fills for Text Blocks

Here's how to add a border and/or a background fill to a text block (see Figure 3-33).

1. Select a text block using the Pointer tool.

2. Press Command-I/Ctrl-I to display the Object Inspector.

3. Check the Display border option.

4. Format the border and the background fill of the text block using the Fill Inspector (press Command-Option-F/Ctrl-Alt-F) and the Stroke Inspector (press Command-Option-L/Ctrl-Alt-L).

You can also set the background fill of a text block by selecting the text block with the Pointer tool and then dropping a color swatch on it. For more on applying fills using drag-and-drop, see Chapter 6, "Color."

Adding Borders to Rows, Columns, or Cells

You use the pop-up menus in the Column Inspector to add rules around cells (the text areas created by the intersection of rows and columns) at either the column's full height (or the row's width) or

FIGURE 3-33
Adding borders
to text blocks

*To add a border
to a text block...*

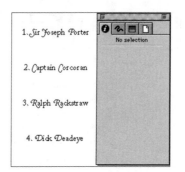
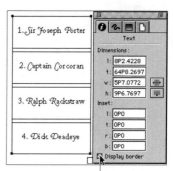

*...select the text block and click Display
Border in the Object Inspector.*

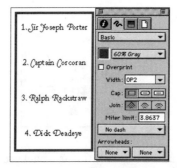

*Format the text block's
border using the
Fill Inspector and the
Stroke Inspector.*

*FreeHand displays the
border (or borders, if
you're working with a
multicolumn or
multirow text block).*

at the inset you've specified (the inset distances are the same as you specified for the entire text block). Confused? Don't be. Take a look at Figure 3-34.

A few things about column rules:

♦ Column rules don't convert to paths when you convert the text block containing them (they disappear).

♦ In the Column section, choose Full Height if you want your column rules to extend to the top and bottom edges of the text block. Choose Inset if you want the column rules to stop inside the cell (the Inset distances—from each edge of the cell—are the same as the text block's margins).

♦ In the Row section of the Column Inspector, choose Full Width from the pop-up menu to make the rules attached to the rows of the text block extend to the right and left edges of your text block. Choose Inset if you want the rules to stop, in each cell, at the cell's margin.

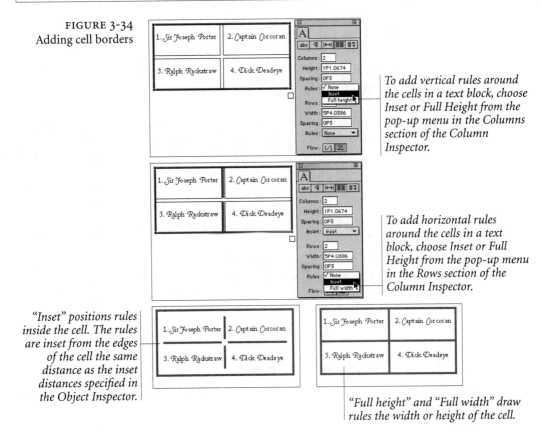

FIGURE 3-34
Adding cell borders

To add vertical rules around the cells in a text block, choose Inset or Full Height from the pop-up menu in the Columns section of the Column Inspector.

To add horizontal rules around the cells in a text block, choose Inset or Full Height from the pop-up menu in the Rows section of the Column Inspector.

"Inset" positions rules inside the cell. The rules are inset from the edges of the cell the same distance as the inset distances specified in the Object Inspector.

"Full height" and "Full width" draw rules the width or height of the cell.

To add borders to the rows and/or columns in a text block, follow these steps.

1. Select a multicolumn text block.

2. If the Column Inspector's not already open, display it by pressing Command-Option-R/Ctrl-Alt-R.

3. Use the two Rules pop-up menus to choose the type of rules you want.

4. Press Return to apply your changes.

Tip:
If You Can't See the Border of a Text Block

If you've applied a stroke to a text block and still can't see the border, make sure you've checked Display Border in the Object Inspector for the text block. If you've turned on the Display Border option, and *still* can't see the border when you select the text block, it's probably because the border you've applied is smaller than one point wide. In this case, you won't see the border when you have the text box selected—it's smaller than the text block boundary FreeHand displays when you select a text block (see Figure 3-35).

When you've applied formatting to a text block but it doesn't seem to be having any effect...

...you need to turn on the Display Border option in the Object Inspector. Note that turning this option on can make a text block's selection handles difficult to see or select.

Tip:
Balancing
Columns

When you want to distribute your text evenly among a number of columns, so that each column contains the same number of lines of text, try this—check the Balance Columns field in the Copyfit Inspector (press Command-Option-C/Ctrl-Alt-C to display the Copyfit Inspector if it's not visible). FreeHand will try to put an equal amount of text in each column in the current text block (or story, if the text block's linked to other text blocks), while keeping in mind the other settings for the text in the text block (see Figure 3-36, on the next page). The number you enter in *N* Lines Together in the Paragraph Inspector affects FreeHand's ability to balance columns.

Character Formatting

Character formatting is all about controlling the way the individual letters, symbols, or punctuation of your text look. Font, type style, type size, color, leading, and text effect are all aspects of character formatting.

FIGURE 3-36
Balancing columns

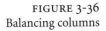

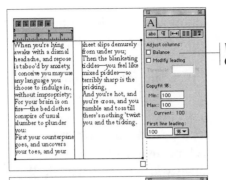

When you check Balance Columns…

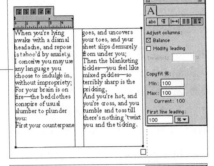

…FreeHand distributes the text in the story among the available columns.

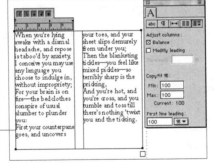

If you've set the N Lines Together value for this paragraph to "2" (in the Paragraph Inspector), FreeHand takes that value into account when balancing the columns—in this case, it means the columns won't balance as well.

I refer to all formatting that can be applied to a selected range of text as "character" formatting, and refer to formatting that Free-Hand applies at the paragraph level as "paragraph" formatting. Tab settings, indents, paragraph rules, space above, and space after are examples of paragraph formatting. There are areas of overlap in these definitions. Leading, for example, is really a property that applies to an entire line of text (FreeHand uses only one leading value for a line of text), but I'll call it "character" formatting, none-theless, because you can apply it to individual characters.

In addition to these distinctions, FreeHand's paragraph styles can include character formatting, but apply to entire paragraphs. See "Working with Text Styles," later in this chapter.

While there are loads of commands on the submenus of the Text menu, I usually set or change type specifications using the Character Inspector or the Text toolbar (see Figure 3-37). Why? Try selecting a font, type style, and size using the Font, Size, and Leading submenus a few times.

As soon as you're tired of that, display the Character Inspector (press Command-T/Ctrl-T if it isn't already visible) and try the following steps (see Figure 3-38).

1. Move to the Font field. On the Macintosh, you can press Command-` until the field becomes active; in Windows, press Ctrl-Tab until the Character Inspector becomes the active window, then press Tab until the Font field becomes active (if you've been there recently, you'll jump right to it).

2. Type the first few letters of the font name you want (stop typing when FreeHand matches the font name).

3. Press Tab to move to the Type Style field.

4. Type "i" for Italic, "b" for bold, "p" for plain, or "boldi" for bold italic.

5. Press Tab to move to the Type Size field.

6. Type a number for the size of your type and press Enter to apply your changes. FreeHand formats the text as you've specified.

FIGURE 3-37
Character
formatting controls

Type Style field

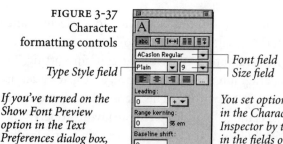

If you've turned on the Show Font Preview option in the Text Preferences dialog box, see a preview of the selected font appears next to the font field.

Font field
Size field

You set options in the Character Inspector by typing in the fields or by making choices from the pop-up menus.

Alternatively, you could use the character formatting controls on the Text toolbar. Either method is easier than using the submenus of the Text menu.

Size field

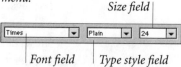

Font field   Type style field

I use the Character Inspector, because I can find all of the type formatting controls I need there. The Text toolbar offers fewer (even with customization).

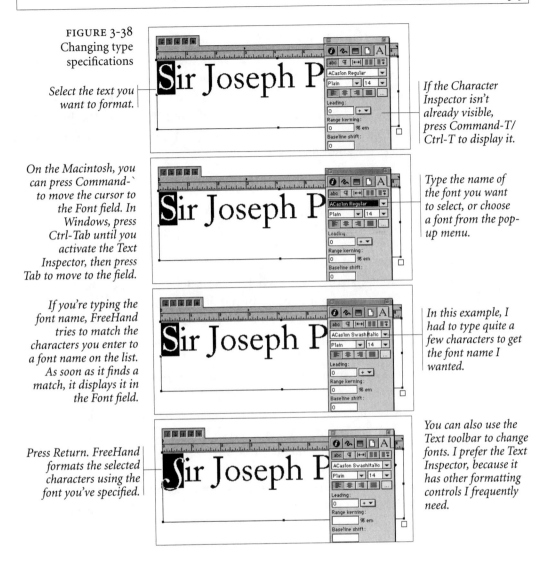

FIGURE 3-38
Changing type
specifications

Select the text you want to format.

If the Character Inspector isn't already visible, press Command-T/Ctrl-T to display it.

On the Macintosh, you can press Command-`to move the cursor to the Font field. In Windows, press Ctrl-Tab until you activate the Text Inspector, then press Tab to move to the field.

Type the name of the font you want to select, or choose a font from the pop-up menu.

If you're typing the font name, FreeHand tries to match the characters you enter to a font name on the list. As soon as it finds a match, it displays it in the Font field.

In this example, I had to type quite a few characters to get the font name I wanted.

Press Return. FreeHand formats the selected characters using the font you've specified.

You can also use the Text toolbar to change fonts. I prefer the Text Inspector, because it has other formatting controls I frequently need.

Even though the steps, when written down, sound like they'd take longer, they're much quicker—and your hands stay on the keyboard, ready to enter or select more text. Best of all, you don't have to follow those little arrows off the side of the menu and then track down the number or name you want on the submenu that pops out.

I could, of course, have used the Text toolbar to apply the example formatting I've shown above. Why didn't I? As I've gotten older, I've found that I'm better off when I have fewer things to remember. In FreeHand, I use the panels of the Text Inspector to do my text formatting because it's the *only* place in FreeHand that has controls for *every* text attribute. If you have a younger or more supple mind, you might prefer to use the Type toolbar to choose fonts and set point sizes, the Alignment submenu of the Text menu to specify paragraph alignment, and the Character Inspector to set leading amounts. It's up to you.

Font   To apply a particular font to text you've selected, type the name of the font you want in the Font field in the Character Inspector (or Text toolbar), or use the attached pop-up list of font names (or, if you prefer, choose the font name from the Font submenu of the Text menu). As you type, FreeHand displays the names of fonts in your system that match the characters you type. Once the font name you want appears in the field, you can stop typing. At that point, you can press Tab to move to the next field in the Character Inspector, or press Return to apply your font change.

Font substitution. When you open a FreeHand publication containing fonts that aren't currently loaded, FreeHand displays the Missing Fonts dialog box (see Figure 3-39), which tells you which fonts you're missing, and also lets you substitute fonts you have installed for the missing fonts. Or you can press Return to substitute Courier for all missing fonts.

FreeHand temporarily applies a different font to the characters formatted with the missing font. By "temporarily," I mean that the publication retains the information about what font was originally applied to the text. What's the use of that? Let me use an example.

Suppose you create a publication on a machine at your office, save it, and take it home for the evening. At home, you open the publication—and FreeHand warns you that you're missing "Oz Handicraft," a font you have on the machine you have at your office. You substitute Courier for Oz Handicraft, and make a few changes to an illustration in your publication. You then—without applying any font changes to the text—save your publication.

FreeHand does not apply the spacing of the original font to the substituted font (as PageMaker, for example, does). This means that all the text you formatted using the font changes position,

FIGURE 3-39
Missing fonts
dialog box

*FreeHand lists the
missing fonts here.*

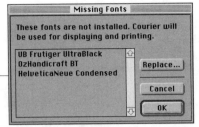

*Press Return to use Courier, or press
the Replace button...*

*...and FreeHand displays the
Replace Font dialog box, where
you can replace missing fonts
with specific fonts you have
installed on your system.*

usually to the point that the line breaks in your publication change. When this happens, I avoid making any formatting changes to the text. I may enter new copy, or edit the existing copy, but it's pointless to do any kerning or text-block adjustment when you're working with substituted fonts.

The next day, you open the publication on the computer at your office. Because you haven't applied any permanent font changes to your text, FreeHand formats and displays the text in its original font, Oz Handicraft.

If you don't want to work with substituted fonts, you need to load the required fonts. If you're working with Suitcase, Master-Juggler (on the Macintosh), or Adobe Type Manager 4.0 Deluxe (on either platform), load the fonts, without closing the publication. If you're loading and unloading fonts by moving them to and from the Fonts folder (on the Macintosh), or using the Fonts control panel (in Windows), you'll need to quit FreeHand, move the fonts, then restart FreeHand.

Obviously, loading the font is better than working with substitute fonts. If you hadn't wanted that font, you wouldn't have used it in the first place.

Tip:
Use an Ugly Font

When I have to use FreeHand's font substitution, I substitute Zapf Chancery for the missing font—I'd never use it for anything else, and it stands out from all the other text in the publication (which makes it very easy to find).

Tip:
Spotting Mixed
Specifications

When the selected text contains multiple type specifications, Free-Hand leaves the fields representing the mixed attributes blank (see Figure 3-40).

FIGURE 3-40
Mixed type
specifications

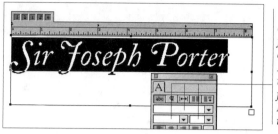

The selected text contains differing fonts, type styles, and type sizes, so FreeHand leaves the corresponding fields in the Character Inspector (or Text toolbar) blank.

Type Style

To apply a type style to text, type "p" for plain, "i" for italic, "b" for bold, or "boldi" for bold italic in the Type Style field in the Character Inspector (or Text toolbar), or choose a type style from the attached pop-up list (or choose a type style from the Style submenu of the Text menu). If a font doesn't have an alternate type style (bold, italic, or bold italic), FreeHand grays the name of the type style in the menus (see Figure 3-41).

When you try to type the name of a type style that's not available in the Type Style field, FreeHand beeps.

After you've chosen the type style you want, press Tab to move to the Size field, or press Return to apply your changes.

FIGURE 3-41
Grayed-out type styles

This font doesn't have these typestyles, so FreeHand grays them out.

Size

Type the point size you want in the Size field of the Character Inspector, or choose a size from the attached pop-up menu. If you're directly entering the size, you can specify it in .0001-point increments. You can also change the size of the type in a text block by stretching the text block (see "Working with Text Blocks," earlier in this chapter).

After you've entered the size you want, press Return to apply your changes.

Tip:
Bumping Text
Up or Down
in Size

You can make selected text larger or smaller, in one-point increments, using the keyboard. To make selected text larger by one point, press Command-Shift->/Ctrl-Shift->. To make it smaller by one point, press Command-Shift-</Ctrl-Shift-<.

Tip:
Greeking

Remember that greeking—whether the type is displayed or drawn as a gray bar—is set in the Preferences dialog box. If you make the type smaller (at the current magnification) than the threshold you set in the Display Preferences dialog box, it'll appear as a gray bar (see "Preferences" in Chapter 1, "FreeHand Basics.")

Leading

Text characters—usually—sit on an imaginary line, which we call the baseline. Leading (pronounced "ledding") is the vertical distance from the baseline of one line of text to the next text baseline. In FreeHand, leading is measured from the baseline of the current line of text to the baseline of the line of text above (see Figure 3-42). When you increase the leading in a line of text, you push that line farther from the line above it, and farther down from the top of the text block.

FreeHand's Character Inspector offers three different leading methods: Extra, Fixed, and Percentage.

Extra leading method. When you choose Extra from the Leading Type pop-up menu, FreeHand adds the point size of the largest character of text in the selection to the value you enter in the Leading field. If, for example, you wanted to add four points of leading between each line of type and the next, you'd choose "+" (Extra) and enter "4" in the Leading field. When you change the size of the characters, the distance between the baselines changes, even though the leading value you've entered remains the same.

Fixed leading method. When you use Fixed leading, FreeHand sets the leading of the selected lines of text to the value you enter in the Leading field. Fixed is the most precise leading method, because you'll always get the leading value you enter, regardless of the size of the selected text. You can enter a leading value in .0001-point increments.

Percentage leading method. When you choose Percentage ("%") from the Leading Type pop-up menu, FreeHand uses a leading value that's a percentage of the size of the selected text, based on the largest point size in the selection. Again, your leading will change if you change the size of the text. This may, or may not be, what you want.

FIGURE 3-42
Leading

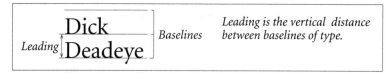

Leading is the vertical distance between baselines of type.

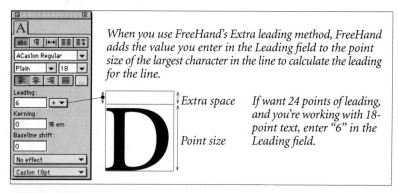

When you use FreeHand's Extra leading method, FreeHand adds the value you enter in the Leading field to the point size of the largest character in the line to calculate the leading for the line.

If want 24 points of leading, and you're working with 18-point text, enter "6" in the Leading field.

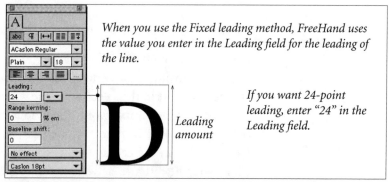

When you use the Fixed leading method, FreeHand uses the value you enter in the Leading field for the leading of the line.

If you want 24-point leading, enter "24" in the Leading field.

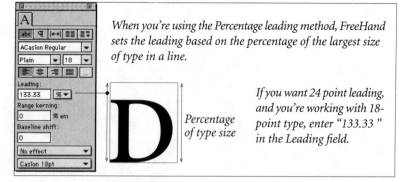

When you're using the Percentage leading method, FreeHand sets the leading based on the percentage of the largest size of type in a line.

If you want 24 point leading, and you're working with 18-point type, enter "133.33 " in the Leading field.

You can set any leading amount using any one of the three leading methods. That said, however, I admit that I only use the Fixed leading method. I like knowing the distances between the baselines of the text in my text blocks, without having to do any multiplication or addition. I also believe that leading shouldn't—necessarily—have anything to do with the size of the characters in the line. Fixed is the only leading method that doesn't change as I change type sizes.

Regardless of the leading method you're using (Fixed, Percentage, or Extra), the largest leading in the line predominates to the next line break. If the character with the larger leading flows to a new line, the leading moves with it (see Figure 3-43).

FIGURE 3-43
The largest leading in a
line predominates

This character has a larger leading value than the other characters in the line.

When the character with the larger leading moves to another line (if, for example, the width of the text block changes, as in this example), the larger leading is applied to that line.

Baseline Shift

Sometimes, you need to raise the baseline of a character or characters above the baseline of the surrounding text. You can't do this by changing the leading setting of the characters (remember, the largest leading in the line predominates). Instead, you use the Baseline Shift field in the Character Inspector (see Figure 3-44).

Enter an amount in the Baseline shift field to shift the baseline of the selected text by that amount. As you'd guess, positive values move the selected text up from the baseline; negative values move the selected text down from the baseline.

Tip:
Baseline Shift
Keyboard
Shortcut

You can apply baseline shift using your keyboard. To do this, select some text and press Option-Up Arrow/Ctrl-Alt-Up Arrow to move the baseline of the text up, or Option-Down Arrow/Ctrl-Alt-Down Arrow to shift the baseline down. Each key press moves the text up or down one point.

FIGURE 3-44
Baseline shift

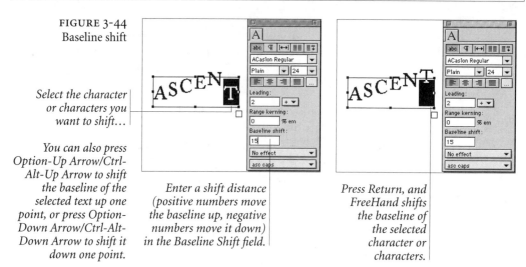

Select the character
or characters you
want to shift...

You can also press
Option-Up Arrow/Ctrl-
Alt-Up Arrow to shift
the baseline of the
selected text up one
point, or press Option-
Down Arrow/Ctrl-Alt-
Down Arrow to shift it
down one point.

Enter a shift distance
(positive numbers move
the baseline up, negative
numbers move it down)
in the Baseline Shift field.

Press Return, and
FreeHand shifts
the baseline of
the selected
character or
characters.

First line leading

Because I like to position and align text blocks by snapping their tops to ruler guides or the grid, it's very important to me to know where the first baseline in a text block falls, relative to the top of the text block.

To set the distance from the top of the text block to the first baseline, display the Copyfit Inspector (press Command-Option-C/Ctrl-Alt-C). At the bottom of the Copyfit Inspector, you'll see the First Line Leading field and the Leading Type pop-up menu. The choices on the pop-up menu correspond to FreeHand's leading methods.

♦ Percent uses a percentage of the height of the text in the first line of the text block.

♦ Extra adds an amount equal to the height of the first line in the text block plus some measurement you enter.

♦ Fixed uses the leading value that you enter, regardless of the size of the characters in the line.

I only use Fixed—I can enter a precise leading value, and not worry about the leading changing because I've added a drop cap or other enlarged character. If I want the baseline of the first line of text in a text block to fall twelve points from the top of the text block, I enter 12 (see Figure 3-45).

FIGURE 3-45
Setting the first
baseline

The trouble with
the "Extra" and
"Percentage" first line
leading methods.

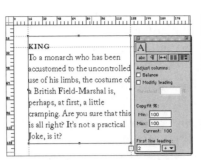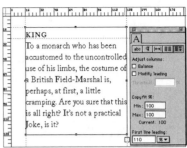

"Extra" first line leading method.
Where does the baseline fall (get out
your calculator)?

"Percentage" first line leading method.
Where does the baseline fall?

Use the "Fixed"
first line leading
method—it's easy to
get the baseline right
where you want it.

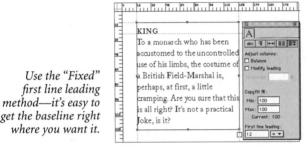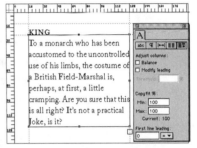

"Fixed" first line leading method. The
baseline falls precisely where you want
it (in this example, 12 points from the
top of the text block).

If you choose "Fixed" and enter zero,
the first baseline falls exactly at the
top of the text block. Don't tell any
software engineers you know how to
do this.

If you enter zero using the Fixed first baseline method, Free-Hand does just what it should: it hangs the characters of the first line of text out of the top of the text block, and positions the zero point of that line of text at the top of the text block. This way, you'll be able to snap the baseline of the first line of text in a text block to a ruler guide. Since the baseline is at the top of the text block, the characters in the first line hang out of the top. This is sometimes just what you need, even though it's the eventuality the other leading methods were designed to prevent (for some reason, software engineers *hate* it when text hangs out of text blocks).

Tip:
If Your Leading
Looks Funky

If your leading looks odd inside a text block that should have only one leading setting, select the text block and press Command-T/Ctrl-T to display the Character Inspector (if it's not already visible). If the Leading field is blank, you've somehow gotten another

leading setting inside the text block. Either re-enter the proper leading value, or move your cursor through the text block until you
find which character is carrying the rogue leading value (you'll see
it in the Character Inspector).

**Applying
Colors to Text**

Characters in FreeHand's text blocks can be filled or stroked with
any color. While text blocks can be filled or stroked with any of
FreeHand's fills (see "Borders and Fills for Text Blocks," earlier in
this chapter), you can apply only Basic fills and strokes to text (if
you convert the characters to paths, of course, you can format them
as you would any FreeHand path).

The Color List Shows Container Color and Color List Shows
Text Color options in the Colors Preferences dialog box specify
which part of a text block—the block itself, or the text it contains,
respectively—sets the colors displayed in the Colors palette, the
Fill Inspector, and the Stroke Inspector. These options also control
which part of the text block is affected when you apply a color to it.
Turn on the Color List Shows Text Color option, and FreeHand
applies any color changes you make to the text in the text block.

FreeHand offers several ways of applying color to text and to
text blocks—try them and see which methods work best for you.

Filling text. To apply a fill to selected text inside a text block, follow
these steps (see Figure 3-46).

1. Select the text you want to color using the Text tool.

2. Click a color name in the Colors palette. FreeHand applies
   a basic fill of the color you clicked to the text.

If you want the color you've applied to the text to overprint,
select the text and press Command-Option-F/Ctrl-Alt-F to display
the Fill Inspector, then turn on the Overprint option (for more on
overprinting, see "Trapping," in Chapter 6, "Color").

You can also use the Fill Inspector to apply a color fill to text.

1. Use the Text tool to select the text you want to fill.

2. Press Command-Option-F/Ctrl-Alt-F to display the Fill
   Inspector, if it's not already visible.

FIGURE 3-46
Applying color to text

Select some text.

Click a color name in the Colors palette.

FreeHand applies the
color to the selected text.

3. Choose Basic from the Fill Type pop-up menu in the Fill
   Inspector (the other fill types have no effect on text).
   FreeHand applies a basic fill to the text you selected.

4. Choose a color from the pop-up menu next to the color
   well in the Fill Inspector (or click a color in the Colors
   palette). Check Overprint in the Fill Inspector if you want
   the fill to overprint objects behind it.

To apply a color to text using the drag-and-drop method, follow these steps (see Figure 3-47).

1. Select the text you want to color using the Text tool. You
   don't *have* to do this, but I strongly recommend it.

2. Drag a color swatch from a color well (ideally, from the
   Colors palette) and drop it on the text.

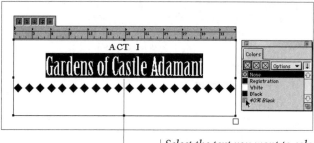

Select the text you want to color.

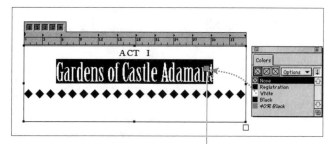

*Drag a color swatch from one of the
color wells in the Colors palette and
drop it on the selected text.*

*FreeHand applies the
color to the fill of the
selected text.*

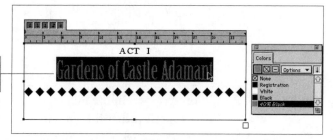

To apply a color to all of the text in a text block, turn on the Color List Shows Text Color option in the Colors Preferences dialog box, then select a text block using the Pointer tool and click on a color in the Colors palette. FreeHand applies the color to all of the text in the text block.

Alternatively, you can use the drag-and-drop method to color all the text in a text block—select all the text, drag a color swatch from a color well, and drop it on the selection. FreeHand applies the color to all the text in the text block (see Figure 3-48).

Stroking text. I keep running into people who think that you have to convert text characters to paths before you can apply a stroke to

FIGURE 3-48
Another way to apply a
color using the drag-
and-drop method

*Drag a color swatch from one of
the color wells in the Colors palette...*

...and drop it onto a character.   *FreeHand applies the color to all
of the text in the text block.*

them. You don't—as far as basic strokes and fills go, FreeHand treats
text characters as if they are paths.

To apply a stroke to text using the Stroke Inspector, follow these
steps (see Figure 3-49).

1. Select the text you want to stroke.

2. Press Command-Option-L/Ctrl-Alt-L to display the Stroke
   Inspector, if it's not already visible.

3. Choose Basic from the Stroke Type pop-up menu in the
   Stroke Inspector (the other stroke types have no effect).

4. Click a color in the Colors palette. Check Overprint in the
   Stroke Inspector if you want the stroke to overprint objects
   behind it (including the character's fill, if any).

FIGURE 3-49
Applying a
stroke to text

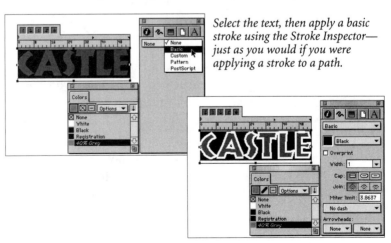

*Select the text, then apply a basic
stroke using the Stroke Inspector—
just as you would if you were
applying a stroke to a path.*

To apply a stroke to text using the drag-and-drop method, follow these steps (see Figure 3-50).

1. Select some text using the Text tool.

2. Drag a color swatch from a color well (ideally, from the Colors palette) and drop it on the Stroke selector at the top of the Colors palette.

FreeHand applies a basic stroke of the color you dropped to the selected text. Use the Stroke Inspector to set the width of the stroke, if necessary.

FIGURE 3-50
Applying a color
stroke to text using
drag-and-drop

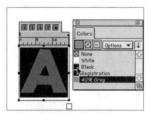

Select the text you want to
apply a stroke to.

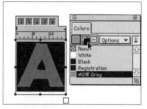

Drag a color swatch from the
Colors palette…

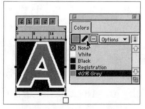

…and drop it on the Stroke
button in the Colors palette.

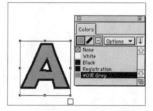

FreeHand applies the stroke to the selected
text, using the default stroke width.

Tip:
Graphic Styles
and Text Blocks

Given that you can apply strokes and fills to text using the Fill and Stroke Inspectors, you'd think you could apply graphic styles to text, as well. Unfortunately, FreeHand doesn't work that way. When you select text with the Text tool and apply a graphic style, FreeHand applies the fill, stroke, and halftone properties of the style to the text block itself—not to the text contained in the text block. FreeHand does this regardless of the setting of the Color List Shows Text Color option in the Colors Preferences dialog box.

You can, however, specify text color as an attribute of a text style. See "Working with Text Styles," later in this chapter.

Tip:
Avoid Fuzzy
Type

Even the most skilled color separators will tell you to avoid apply-ing a process-color tint build to fine hairlines and text smaller than about 14 points (12 points for bold). It's difficult, even on the very best presses (or even the best-maintained imagesetters and film processors) to keep small type and fine lines in register, so it ends up looking fuzzy in your printed publication. Use spot colors for fine lines and type. If you're stuck, try to find a process color that gives you 80 percent of cyan, magenta, or black, and try to apply it to a sans serif face; it's less likely to look fuzzy.

**Stretching
Characters
Horizontally**

Enter a value in the Horizontal Scale field in the Spacing Inspector to create expanded (wider) or condensed (narrower) versions of your type (see Figure 3-51). Before I became too old and tired, I used to argue that these aren't true expanded or condensed fonts, which involve custom-designed, hand-tuned character shapes and spacings, but never mind.

FIGURE 3-51
Scaling characters
horizontally

40% 60% 80% 100% 120% 140% 160%

You can also change the horizontal scaling of type by dragging the selection handles of text blocks (see "Working with Text Blocks," later in this chapter).

Text Effects

Text effects are just that—special effects for type. They're generally for creating eye-catching display type. To apply one of FreeHand's text effects, select some text and choose an effect from the Text Effects pop-up menu at the bottom of the Character Inspector. Press Enter, and FreeHand applies the text effect to the text you've selected. If you can't see the text effect, make sure that Display Text Effects is checked in the Display Preferences dialog box. If Display Text Effects is checked and you still can't see the text effect, are you sure you're not in keyline view? (Text effects don't display in key-line view.)

The rules drawn by the Highlight, Underline, and Strikethrough text effects interact with FreeHand's paragraph rules. See "Para-graph Rules and Text Effects," later in this chapter.

Highlight. When I designed Guy Kawasaki's book *Database 101* for Peachpit Press, I wanted a text effect that would look like someone had gone through the book highlighting words and phrases with a thick felt marker. I didn't want to have to draw a box behind every piece of text needing this effect, so I hacked my copy of PageMaker so text formatted with the "Strikethru" type style would print with a solid gray bar behind the text. What's this got to do with Free-Hand? One of the text effects does the same thing—and you don't even have to write any custom PostScript code.

When you want to place a rule (of any thickness) behind your text, select the text, then choose "Highlight" from the Text Effects pop-up menu. FreeHand applies the Highlight text effect (see Figure 3-52). By default, the Highlight effect adds a light gray rule with a thickness of the height of the selected text (based on the largest character in the selection). The rule is vertically centered around a position one-fourth of the height of the text from the baseline of the text (based on the largest leading value in the selection).

To adjust the width of the rule, or its position, color, overprinting setting, and dash pattern (yes, you heard that right), select the text and choose Edit from the Text Effects pop-up menu. Free-Hand displays the Highlight dialog box.

◆ The Position field in the Highlight dialog box sets the vertical center of the rule FreeHand draws behind your text, measured from the baseline of the text. You can enter positive or negative numbers in the Position field.

FIGURE 3-52
Highlight text effect

When you apply the Highlight effect to text, FreeHand draws a rule behind the text, simulating the effect of a "highlighter" pen.

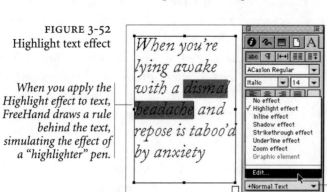

Choose Edit from the Text Effects pop-up menu, and FreeHand displays the Highlight Effect dialog box, where you can edit the effect.

- The Dash pop-up menu sets the dash pattern for the rule. As in the Stroke Inspector, you can create and edit your own dash patterns if you don't see the pattern you want—hold down Option and choose one of the patterns on the menu.

- The value you enter in the width field sets the width of the rule.

- The color well sets the color of the rule, and works just like any other color well in FreeHand (don't let the dialog box fool you—you can drag color swatches into this color well as you would any other).

- The Overprint checkbox gives you the ability to set the rule to overprint.

Inline. FreeHand's Inline draws outlines around solid characters. To set the number and thickness of the outlines, click the Edit button at the bottom of the Character Inspector. FreeHand displays the Inline Effect dialog box (see Figure 3-53).

FIGURE 3-53
Inline text effect

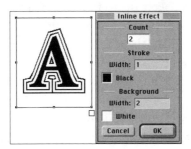 

Shadow. Use Shadow to apply a drop shadow to the selected text. This drop shadow is offset to the right and below the text it's applied to (see Figure 3-54). The distance that the drop shadow is offset is based on the size of the characters. The drop shadow is set to 50 percent of the color of the selected text.

Strikethrough. The Strikethrough text effect is identical to the Highlight text effect, except the default position, width, and color of the rule it creates differ. Strikethrough adds a rule behind your text with a position setting of 6, a line weight of 1, and the color Black (see Figure 3-55).

FIGURE 3-54
Shadow text effect

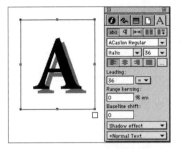

FIGURE 3-55
Strikethrough effect

When you apply the Strikethrough effect to text, FreeHand draws a rule through the text.

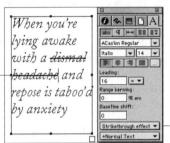

Choose Edit from the Text Effects pop-up menu, and Free-Hand displays the Strikethrough Effect dialog box, where you can edit the effect.

After you've applied the Strikethrough text effect, you can change the appearance of the effect by clicking the Edit button at the bottom of the Character Inspector. See the discussion of the Highlight text effect, earlier in this chapter, for more on the options in the Strikethrough dialog box.

Underline. The Underline text effect is (you guessed it) the same as Highlight and Strikethrough, but has different default settings for position, width, and rule color. For the Underline text effect, these are set to -2, 1, and Black, respectively (see Figure 3-56).

After you've applied the Underline text effect, you can change the way the underline looks. To do this, select the text and choose Edit from the Text Effects pop-up menu. See the discussion of the Highlight text effect, earlier in this chapter, for more on the options in the Underline dialog box.

Zoom text. Zoom text creates a string of characters that appear to recede toward a vanishing point. You see zoom text all the time in television commercials, usually for furniture and carpet dealers' goin' out of business/liquidation/oncoming recession sales.

Use this one with caution, though, and it can be a useful tool (see Figure 3-57). To control the distance, offset, and color range

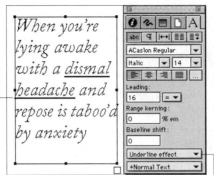
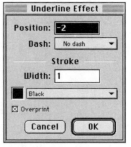

When you apply the Underline effect to text, FreeHand draws a rule beneath the text.

Choose Edit from the Effect pop-up menu, and FreeHand displays the Underline Effect dialog box, where you can edit the effect.

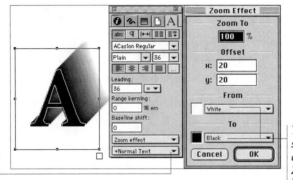

Printed example

Click the Edit button to display the Zoom Effect dialog box.

You can drop color swatches into the color wells in the Zoom Effect dialog box.

of the Zoom Effect, choose Edit from the Text Effects pop-up menu. FreeHand displays the Zoom Effect dialog box, where you can specify the size of the most distant character in the zoom, the offset of that character, and the change in color from one end of the zoom to the other. If you're using process colors, or are zooming from one spot color to white or a tint of the same spot color, you can even zoom from one color to another.

Tip:
Bounding Boxes
and Zoom Text

If you're exporting text which has the Zoom text effect applied to it, make sure that the bounding box of the EPS is large enough to accommodate the full extent of the zoomed text. These days, Free-Hand handles this pretty well, but, if you're having problems with your text effect getting clipped off in your EPSes, you'll have to fix it yourself. The easiest way to do this is to draw a no-line, no-fill box around the text that extends to the edge of the effect.

Tip:
In Search of the
Elusive Macron

The Macintosh and Windows character sets include many interesting and useful diacritical marks, but don't include the one you need if you're working with clients in Korea (and other Pacific-Rim countries): the macron. If you've looked in a dictionary, you've seen this mark everywhere—it's used to denote a long vowel sound (like the "O" in "Olav").

In FreeHand, you can create a "fake" macron by using the Highlight, Underline, or Strikethrough text effects. All you need to do is set the rule these effects create to something that matches the size of the character you're attaching it to, then set the position of the rule so that it falls above the character (see Figure 3-58).

FIGURE 3-58
Creating a macron

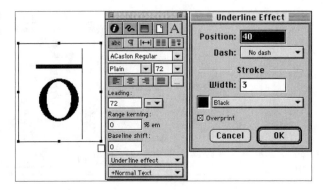

Tip:
Text on a Path
and Text Effects

When you apply the Highlight, Strikethrough, or Underline text effect, the effect applies to any space characters in the selected text. If you then bind the text to a path, however, the effect doesn't apply to the spaces (see Figure 3-59).

FIGURE 3-59
Text effects and
text on a path

Normal paces create a gap in the text effect.

You can enter non-breaking spaces—FreeHand always applies text effects to them.

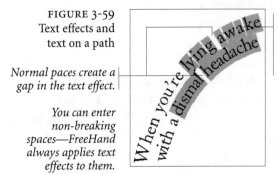

Regardless of the type of space you enter, however, the text effects break up when you join text to a path.

Kerning   Kerning brings characters closer together horizontally, or (these days) moves them farther apart (once, kerning meant *decreasing* the space between characters) by fine increments (see Figure 3-60). FreeHand kerns in percentages of an em, and can kern in increments as fine as .0001, or .01 percent, of an em. Just as a reminder: an em is equal to the size of the type in the line. An em space in 24-point type is 24 points wide. You can use kerning to add up to 10 ems (1000%) or subtract two ems (-200%) of space.

FIGURE 3-60
Kerning

Unkerned text   Kerned text

Most current typesetting systems (desktop and otherwise), kern in units relative to the size of the type. This is good, because it means that you can make the type larger or smaller and retain the same relative amount of kerning.

You can kern any amount of text in FreeHand—from an individual character pair to all the character pairs in all the text blocks in a publication.

To kern a pair of characters, position the text cursor between the two characters and either press keyboard shortcuts (see Table 3-6) or enter a kerning value in the Kerning field of the Character Inspector (see Figure 3-61). Enter positive values in the Kerning field to move the characters farther apart; enter negative numbers to move them closer together.

FIGURE 3-61
Kerning a pair of
characters

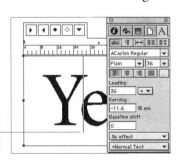

Position the cursor
between the characters
you want to kern.

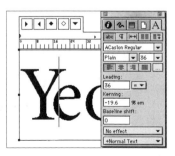

The Kerning field shows you any kerning that's already in effect between the characters.

Press keyboard shortcuts to kern the characters. As you kern, the Kerning field shows you the kerning amount.

To kern	Press
.1 em (10 percent) closer	Command-Option-Shift-Left Arrow
.01 em (one percent) closer	Command-Option-Left Arrow
.1 em (10 percent) apart	Command-Option-Shift-Right Arrow
.01 em (one percent) apart	Command-Option-Left Arrow

To kern a range of text, select some text—select text with the Text tool, or select a text block (or blocks) using the Pointer tool—and then press keyboard shortcuts or enter a value in the Kerning field (Figure 3-62).

Range kerning is often referred to as "tracking," but tracking is actually something very different. Range kerning adjusts intercharacter spacing by a set amount (.5 percent of an em, for example), regardless of the size of the type. Tracking, on the other hand, adjusts intercharacter spacing by different amounts for different type sizes. For example, 12-point text in a particular font might be adjusted by one-half of a percent of an em, while 48-point type of the same face might be adjusted by -2 percent of an em. FreeHand doesn't offer a tracking feature (yet).

FIGURE 3-62
Kerning a range of
characters

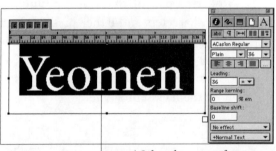

Select the range of text you want to kern.

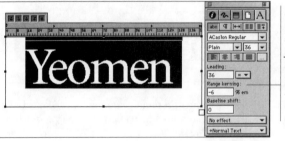

Enter a kerning amount in the Range Kerning field and press Return, or press keyboard shortcuts. FreeHand kerns the selected range of text.

Paragraph Formatting

What's a paragraph? FreeHand's definition is simple—a paragraph is any string of characters that ends with carriage return or an end-of-column character (see "Entering Special Characters," earlier in this chapter, for an explanation of end-of-column characters).

When you apply paragraph formatting, the formatting applies to all the characters in the paragraph. Paragraph alignment, indents, tabs, spacing, and hyphenation settings are all examples of paragraph formatting.

You don't have to select all the text in a paragraph to apply paragraph formatting. To select a paragraph, all you have to do is click an insertion point in the paragraph. To select more than one paragraph for formatting, drag the cursor through the paragraphs you want to format—the selection doesn't have to include all the text in the paragraphs, it only has to *touch* each paragraph.

If you want to select all the paragraphs in a text block for formatting, select the text block with the Pointer tool. If you want to select all of the paragraphs in a story, triple-click one of the text blocks in the story with the Pointer tool (or click the Text tool on one of the text blocks in the story) and then press Command-A/Ctrl-A (for Select All).

Alignment

Click the paragraph alignment buttons in the Character Inspector (press Command-T/Ctrl-T to display the Inspector if it's not already visible) to set the alignment of the selected paragraphs. You can align paragraphs in the usual ways—Right (also known as "rag left"), Left (also known as "rag right"), Center, and Justify (see Figure 3-63). FreeHand 4 dropped FreeHand 3's kooky Vertical alignment feature, probably because no one was using it.

Tip:
Forced
Justification

Sometimes, you want to justify a single line of text—when you want to spread a heading across the width of a column, for example. When you select the text and click the Justify button in the Character Inspector, nothing happens. When you justify a paragraph, FreeHand sets the last line of the paragraph flush left. This is good, because (most of the time) you don't want the last line of the paragraph stretching all the way across the column.

FIGURE 3-63
Aligning paragraphs

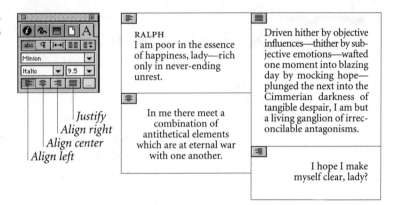

Justify
Align right
Align center
Align left

RALPH
I am poor in the essence of happiness, lady—rich only in never-ending unrest.

In me there meet a combination of antithetical elements which are at eternal war with one another.

Driven hither by objective influences—thither by subjective emotions—wafted one moment into blazing day by mocking hope—plunged the next into the Cimmerian darkness of tangible despair, I am but a living ganglion of irreconcilable antagonisms.

I hope I make myself clear, lady?

How can you get your text to stretch across the column? Use the Flush Zone setting (see Figure 3-64).

1. Select the paragraph.

2. Display the Character Inspector, if it's not already visible, by pressing Command-T/Ctrl-T.

3. Click the "…" button (to the right of the paragraph alignment buttons). FreeHand displays the Edit Alignment dialog box.

4. Enter "0" in the Flush Zone field, then press Return.

At this point, your text should be stretched out across the column. If it isn't, you probably forgot to click the Justify button in the Character Inspector.

Tip:
Unjustified
Justification

You may know people who call align right "right justify," or align left "left justify." Feign ignorance until they correct themselves. As you know, "justify" means "to spread a line from one margin to the other," so there can't be anything called "right justify" or "left justify."

Spacing

Now that FreeHand has paragraph formatting features, you're faced with a dilemma you didn't have to face in the first version of the program. I call it the text composition balancing act. Word- and letterspacing, hyphenation, alignment, and the values you enter for Ragged Width and Flush Zone (in the Edit Alignment dialog box) *all* interact, with FreeHand using each setting to compose the best-looking text it can.

FIGURE 3-64
Forced justification

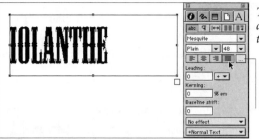

This text is justified, but doesn't spread out to fill the column. Why?

Click the "…" button. FreeHand displays the Edit Alignment dialog box.

…where you can see that the text isn't justified because the width of the line is less than the percentage of the column width set in the Flush Zone field.

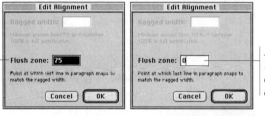

Enter 0 (zero) in the Flush Zone field and click the OK button to close the dialog box.

FreeHand spreads the text across the column.

What do I mean by "the best-looking text"? It's more than a little subjective. In general, I think that the right edges of your left-aligned type shouldn't be too ragged (that is, there shouldn't be extreme variation in the widths of the lines in a paragraph), and the word- and letterspacing inside lines of justified text shouldn't be noticeably tight or loose, or vary too much from line to line.

I do know three entirely objective things about spacing text in FreeHand.

♦ What constitutes "good spacing" varies from font to font and line width to line width. There is no "perfect" spacing setting that will work every time.

♦ FreeHand's default settings will not produce good text spacing and hyphenation for all fonts and all column widths.

◆ It's up to you to space your text the way you like it. The best thing you can do for the appearance of the type in your FreeHand publications is to experiment until you see what you like.

When FreeHand composes a line of text, it has to make decisions—decisions about where to hyphenate words, and about how much type to fit on a line. FreeHand needs your help in these tasks; it can't figure out what sort of spacing is appropriate for your text. You use the Spacing Inspector (and the Edit Alignment dialog box) to give FreeHand spacing guidelines.

To display the Spacing Inspector, press Command-Option-K/Ctrl-Alt-K (see Figure 3-65). The values you enter in the Spacing Inspector apply to all selected paragraphs.

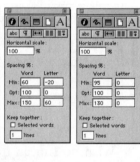

FIGURE 3-65
Spacing Inspector

ROBIN
For a week I have fulfilled my accursed doom! I have duly committed a crime a day! Not a great crime, I trust, but still, in the eyes of one as strictly regulated as I used to be, a crime. But will my ghostly ancestors be satisfied with what I've done, or will they regard it as an unworthy subterfuge?

These spacing settings allow FreeHand to letterspace the text (sometimes too much, as you can see from the last line).

ROBIN
For a week I have fulfilled my accursed doom! I have duly committed a crime a day! Not a great crime, I trust, but still, in the eyes of one as strictly regulated as I used to be, a crime. But will my ghostly ancestors be satisfied with what I've done, or will they regard it as an unworthy subterfuge?

These spacing settings tell FreeHand to increase or decrease wordspacing, and leave letterspacing alone.

What are the percentages in the Spacing Inspector based on? What does 100 percent mean? FreeHand bases word- and letterspacing percentages on values specified in the font itself, by the font designer. These values represent the designer's vision of the ideal spacing for the font, and they're different for every font. You aren't required to agree with these values—both word spacing and letter spacing for the font Utopia Regular, for example, seem extremely wide to me—you just need to know that they're where FreeHand gets its ideas about how to space the font.

The percentages you see in the Spacing Inspector work differently for word spacing and letterspacing. For word spacing, the percentages you see in the Minimum, Optimum, and Maximum fields are *percentages* of the font's default word spacing value. For letterspacing, the percentages you see in the fields represent the *amount of variation* from the font's letterspacing value you'll allow.

All of this means that there aren't any "perfect" spacing values that work for all fonts, line widths, and alignments. What can you do? There's nothing for it—you have to work with each font (and, frequently, each publication) until you come up with spacing settings that look good to you. After a while, you'll develop a "feeling" for certain fonts, and you'll be able to space them well without even thinking about it.

What spacing values should you start with? For non-justified type, set all letterspacing values to zero percent to start with, and then work from there. For justified type, start experimenting with word spacing percentages of 95, 100, 120 (that's Minimum, Optimum, and Maximum, respectively), and letterspacing percentages of 0, 0, 0. I prefer letting FreeHand word space up to 180 percent before I even think about using letterspacing.

Ragged Width. When FreeHand varies word- and letterspacing in non-justified type, it's just trying to make your text match the value you entered in the Ragged Width field (in the Edit Alignment dialog box—click the "..." button to the right of the paragraph alignment buttons in the Character Inspector). The percentage you enter in the Ragged Width field sets the minimum width for lines in non-justified paragraphs (see Figure 3-66). Smaller values produce paragraphs with more ragged edges (the right edge, in left-aligned text; the left edge in right-aligned text); larger values produce text with more uniform edges.

If you're setting non-justified text, and want FreeHand to leave your word and letter spacing alone (that is, to use only the percentages you entered in the Optimum fields in the Spacing Inspector), enter zero for Ragged Width—any other setting gives FreeHand the go-ahead to adjust spacing according to the Minimum and Maximum settings in the Spacing Inspector.

FIGURE 3-66
Ragged width
and spacing

Why does spacing sometimes vary when you're working with nonjustified copy? Shouldn't FreeHand space the text according to the percentages you've entered in the Optimum fields in the Spacing Inspector? That depends on what you've entered in the Ragged Width field in the Edit Alignment dialog box.

ROBIN
For a week I have fulfilled my accursed doom! I have duly committed a crime a day! Not a great crime, I trust, but still, in the eyes of one as strictly regulated as I used to be, a crime. But will my ghostly ancestors be satisfied with what I've done, or will they regard it as an unworthy subterfuge?

What's the difference between these two examples? Take a look at the second and third lines in each. In the example above, FreeHand has increased the letterspacing to make the shorter lines fill the line; in the example below, we've encouraged FreeHand to leave the letterspacing of those lines alone.

ROBIN
For a week I have fulfilled my accursed doom! I have duly committed a crime a day! Not a great crime, I trust, but still, in the eyes of one as strictly regulated as I used to be, a crime. But will my ghostly ancestors be satisfied with what I've done, or will they regard it as an unworthy subterfuge?

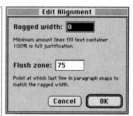

To keep FreeHand from using spacing values other than those you've entered in the Optimum fields, enter zero in the Ragged Width field.

FreeHand is—as far as I know—alone among page-layout programs in that its minimum and maximum settings for word spacing and letterspacing can apply to paragraphs of any alignment. This only happens when you've entered a value larger than zero in the Ragged Width field.

Flush Zone. The percentage you enter in the Flush Zone in the Edit Alignment dialog box field controls the spacing of the last line of a justified paragraph. The question FreeHand's asking is: "If the last line in your paragraph gets within a certain distance of the right side of the column, should I justify it?" When you enter anything less than "100%" in the Flush Zone field, you're specifying the line width—expressed as a percentage of the width of the column—at which you want FreeHand to start justifying text (see Figure 3-67).

In my opinion, you should set Flush Zone to either "100", to leave the last lines of justified paragraphs alone (that is, flush left, ragged right), or "0", to force-justify a single line of text (see "Forced Justification," earlier in this chapter).

FIGURE 3-67
Flush Zone

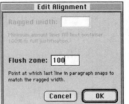

Enter a percentage in the Flush Zone field (in the Edit Alignment dialog box) to tell FreeHand how to justify the last line of a justified paragraph. Most of the time, you can leave it set to 100.

Hyphenation

Another key factor in the spacing of your text is hyphenation—when and where FreeHand can break words in order to compose lines of text (see Figure 3-68). Like spacing, hyphenation settings are very subjective, and what "looks good" varies from person to person and publication to publication.

FreeHand's hyphenation controls are very simple.

♦ Use the language pop-up menu to choose the dictionary you want to use.

♦ Check Automatic to use the hyphenation points defined in the hyphenation dictionary. Automatic has no bearing on any discretionary hyphens you've entered.

FIGURE 3-68
Hyphenation

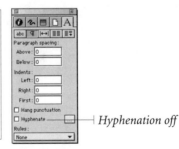

Hyphenation off

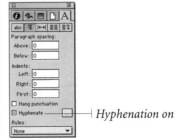

Hyphenation on

♦ Check Skip Capitalized to tell FreeHand not to break words typed with initial capital letters, such as names (where would you break "Kvern"?) or acronyms ("SPECTRE").

♦ Enter a number in the Consecutive field to set the number of consecutive hyphens you'll allow in a paragraph. The larger the number you enter here, the less difficult it'll be for FreeHand to obey your spacing settings. I usually enter "1", unless I'm working in an extremely narrow column, because I hate seeing "ladders" of hyphens at the right edge of a column of type (though they're sometimes unavoidable).

Paragraph Indents

FreeHand's paragraphs can be indented from the left and right sides of the column using the Left and Right fields in the Paragraph Inspector. You can enter positive or negative numbers in either field. Enter positive numbers to push the edges of the paragraph in from the edges of the column it occupies; enter negative numbers to push the edges of the paragraph beyond the column's edges (see Figure 3-69).

In addition, there's a special indent, First, that applies to the first line of the paragraph alone. The value you enter in First sets

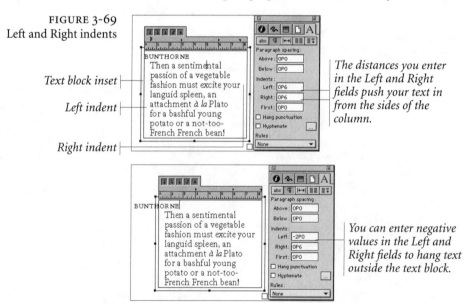

FIGURE 3-69
Left and Right indents

Text block inset

Left indent

Right indent

The distances you enter in the Left and Right fields push your text in from the sides of the column.

You can enter negative values in the Left and Right fields to hang text outside the text block.

the distance between the first-line indent and the left indent, and can be positive or negative. You can even enter a first-line indent that causes text to hang outside the text block (see Figure 3-70).

FIGURE 3-70
First line indent

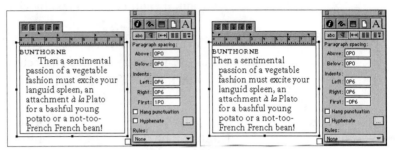

Positive first line indent   Negative first line indent

Hanging Punctuation

Because we don't "see" punctuation when we're reading, a line beginning (or, in some cases ending) with punctuation (especially quotation marks) doesn't look like it aligns with other lines in the surrounding text. It's a kind of typographic optical illusion. To compensate, typographers since Gutenberg have "hung" punctuation—moving the punctuation slightly beyond the edge of the text column. (Gutenberg also changed the spelling of words to fit his justification scheme—just as we do today when we're in a hurry or just desperate to make a line fit!)

You can think of FreeHand's hanging punctuation as something like a special, negative indent for a specific line. In fact, you can hang punctuation manually using FreeHand's right and left paragraph indents—just enter the distance you want the punctuation to extend beyond the edge of the text box. When text reflows, however, you have start again from scratch.

FreeHand gives you an easy way to apply hanging punctuation that automatically adjusts as text reflows (see Figure 3-71). Hanging punctuation applies to ' ' " " . , ; : ` -

1. Type some text that begins with a quotation mark.

2. If the Paragraph Inspector isn't already visible, display it by pressing Command-Option-P/Ctrl-Alt-P.

3. Without deselecting the text block you created, check the Hanging Punctuation checkbox. Watch as FreeHand hangs

the quotation mark outside the text margins of the text block, which produces a better visual alignment. FreeHand does this any time one of the special characters appears at the left or right edge of a text block or column.

You can't set the distance the special characters hang outside the text block, and you can't add characters to the list of characters hanging punctuation affects.

FIGURE 3-71
Hanging punctuation

"Oh, a private
buffoon is a light-
hearted loon, if you
listen to popular
rumor."

Normal punctuation

"Oh, a private
buffoon is a light-
hearted loon, if you
listen to popular
rumor."

Hanging punctuation

Tabs

Tabs (which we knew as "tab stops" when we used typewriters— that is, sometime before we came down from the trees) define what FreeHand does when it encounters a tab character in your text, and you use tabs to control the horizontal position of text in your text blocks. FreeHand's Text Ruler features left, right, center, decimal, and wrapping tabs (see Figure 3-72).

FIGURE 3-72
FreeHand's tab icons
and the Text Ruler

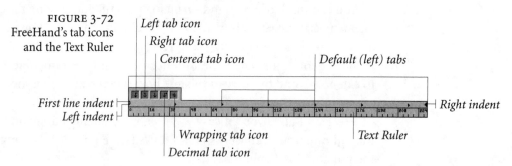

Left tab icon

Right tab icon

Centered tab icon

Default (left) tabs

First line indent

Left indent

Right indent

Wrapping tab icon

Decimal tab icon

Text Ruler

You can also use FreeHand's Text Ruler to set indents—this is handy, because indents and tabs often work together.

A few things about tabs:

◆ Use tab characters and tabs, not spaces, to add horizontal space in your lines of text.

◆ Tabs apply to entire paragraphs—you can't have different tab settings inside a single paragraph.

◆ Don't force line breaks using tab characters—use return, end-of-column, or end-of-line characters when you want a line to break in a specific place.

◆ Use tabs and indents to create hanging indents—not carriage returns and tab characters (or, worse, spaces).

Left, Right, and Center tabs. FreeHand's left, right, and center tabs are the same as the basic tabs you'll find in any word processor (see Figure 3-73).

◆ Left tabs push text following a tab character to a specific horizontal location in a column, and then align the text to the left of the tab.

◆ Right tabs push text to a location and then align the text to the right of a tab character.

◆ Center tabs center a line of text at the point at which you've set a tab character.

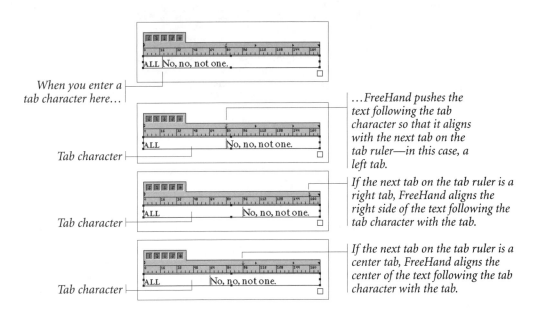

When you enter a tab character here...

Tab character

...FreeHand pushes the text following the tab character so that it aligns with the next tab on the tab ruler—in this case, a left tab.

Tab character

If the next tab on the tab ruler is a right tab, FreeHand aligns the right side of the text following the tab character with the tab.

Tab character

If the next tab on the tab ruler is a center tab, FreeHand aligns the center of the text following the tab character with the tab.

Decimal tabs. Decimal tabs push text following a tab character so that any decimal point you've entered in the text aligns with the point at which you set the tab (see Figure 3-74). If there's no decimal in the text, FreeHand treats the decimal tab as a right tab.

FIGURE 3-74
Decimal tabs

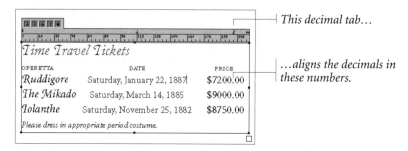

This decimal tab…

…aligns the decimals in these numbers.

Wrapping tabs. Wrapping tabs create a column inside a column of your text block (see Figure 3-75). No other page layout or illustration program has anything like them. Wrapping tabs are great for creating columns within columns, or for creating columns of unequal widths inside a text block (columns set using the Column Inspector always divide a text block evenly).

FIGURE 3-75
Wrapping tabs

Wrapping tabs create a column inside a column of text.

When you position a single wrapping tab at the left or right margin, FreeHand creates a column. It's as if the margin is another wrapping tab.

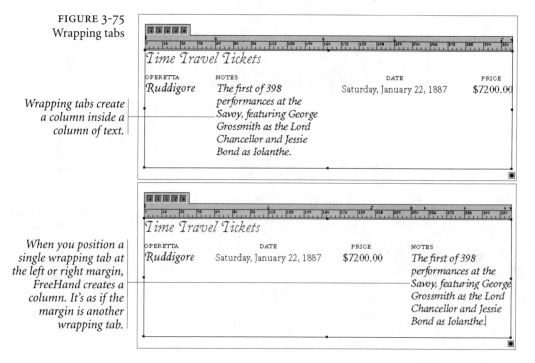

Setting tabs. To set a tab, follow these steps (see Figure 3-76).

1. Select the text you want to format.

2. If you haven't already entered tab characters in the text, enter them.

3. Drag a tab icon for the type of tab you want to set onto the Text Ruler. As you drag, the Info Bar shows you the position of the tab icon.

4. When the tab icon reaches the position at which you want to set the tab, drop it onto the ruler.

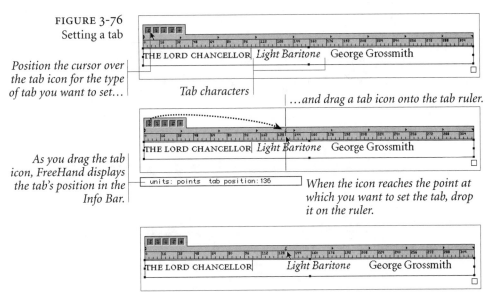

FIGURE 3-76
Setting a tab

Position the cursor over
the tab icon for the type
of tab you want to set...

Tab characters

...and drag a tab icon onto the tab ruler.

As you drag the tab
icon, FreeHand displays
the tab's position in the
Info Bar.

units: points   tab position: 136

When the icon reaches the point at
which you want to set the tab, drop
it on the ruler.

To change a tab's position, drag the tab on the Text Ruler (see Figure 3-77).

To change a tab's alignment, drag a tab of the alignment you want onto the tab's position (see Figure 3-78). You've got to drop the new tab icon precisely on the old one, or you'll end up with two tabs on your Text Ruler right next to each other.

To remove a tab, drag the tab icon off the Text Ruler and drop it on your page or pasteboard (see Figure 3-79). Note that this doesn't remove any tab characters you've typed in your text, though it does make them behave differently.

FIGURE 3-77
Changing a tab

Select the tab you want to move...

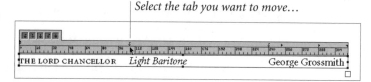

...and drag it to a new position.

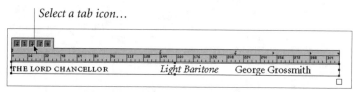

FIGURE 3-78
Changing
tab alignment

Select a tab icon...

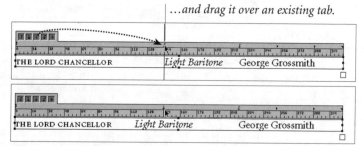

...and drag it over an existing tab.

FreeHand changes the tab's alignment.

FIGURE 3-79
Removing a tab

Drag a tab off the tab ruler...

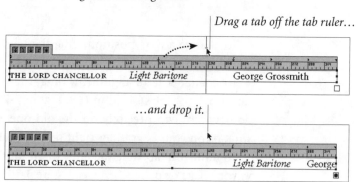

...and drop it.

FreeHand removes the tab and reformats the text.

Creating a hanging indent. As in both Word and PageMaker, you create a hanging indent by dragging the left margin icon to the right of the first-line indent icon, then setting a left tab at the same position as the left margin icon (see Figure 3-80).

FIGURE 3-80
Creating a
hanging indent

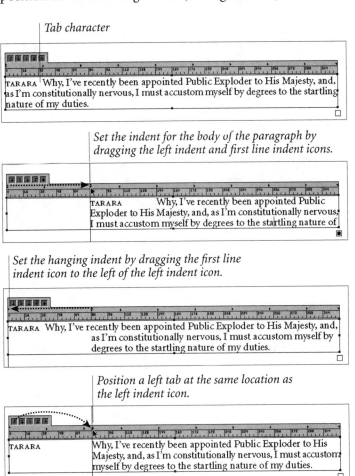

Tab character

TARARA Why, I've recently been appointed Public Exploder to His Majesty, and, as I'm constitutionally nervous, I must accustom myself by degrees to the startling nature of my duties.

Set the indent for the body of the paragraph by dragging the left indent and first line indent icons.

TARARA Why, I've recently been appointed Public Exploder to His Majesty, and, as I'm constitutionally nervous, I must accustom myself by degrees to the startling nature of

Set the hanging indent by dragging the first line indent icon to the left of the left indent icon.

TARARA Why, I've recently been appointed Public Exploder to His Majesty, and, as I'm constitutionally nervous, I must accustom myself by degrees to the startling nature of my duties.

Position a left tab at the same location as the left indent icon.

TARARA Why, I've recently been appointed Public Exploder to His Majesty, and, as I'm constitutionally nervous, I must accustom myself by degrees to the startling nature of my duties.

Tip:
Hanging
Side Heads

Headings that appear in a column next to text (such as the heading for this tip) are difficult to create in most publishing or word processing software (only Corel Ventura Publisher features an automated method for creating hanging side heads). Using FreeHand's wrapping tabs, it's easy, as shown in Figure 3-81.

FIGURE 3-81
Creating hanging
side heads

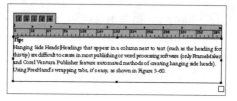

Position two wrapping tabs.

Enter two tab characters between the side head and the paragraph it accompanies.

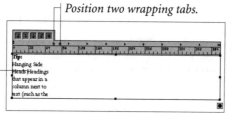

The space between the wrapping tabs defines the "gutter" between the side head and the body text.

This tab makes text wrap between it and the left margin.

This tab makes text wrap between it and the right margin.

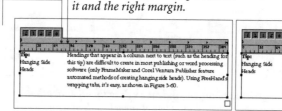

If you enter only one tab character, text wraps inside the two wrapping tabs, creating a very narrow column.

Setting Tabs with the Edit Tab Dialog Box

Another way to set tabs is to use the Edit Tabs dialog box. It's also the only way to specify tab leaders—repeating characters that fill the space taken up by a tab. To set a tab using the Edit Tabs dialog box, follow these steps (see Figure 3-82).

1. Click the Text tool in a text block. Display the Text Ruler, if it's not visible, by pressing Command-/\Ctrl-Alt-Shift-T.

2. Double-click the area immediately above the Text Ruler (the place where you see tabs you've set and any of FreeHand's remaining default tabs). FreeHand displays the Edit Tabs dialog box.

3. Type a tab position in the Position field.

4. Choose a tab alignment from the Alignment pop-up menu.

5. If you want to use a tab leader, type the character you want to use for your leader in the Leader field, or choose one from the pop-up menu attached to the field. Note that you

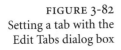

FIGURE 3-82
Setting a tab with the
Edit Tabs dialog box

Select the paragraphs
you want to format.

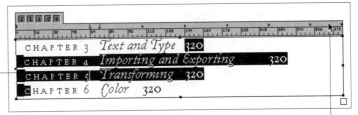

Double-click the Text Ruler.

FreeHand displays the Edit Tab dialog box.

In this example, I'm
setting a right tab at the
right edge of the text
block (which I know is
280 points wide).

Choose an alignment, position, and
tab leader (if you want one) for the tab.

Press Return to add
your new tab to the
Text Ruler.

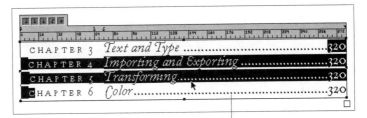

Tab leader characters

can enter more than one character in the Leader field, but
FreeHand uses only the first character you type.

6. Press Return (or click the OK button) to set the tab.

To edit a tab, double-click a tab marker in the Text Ruler. Free-
Hand displays the Edit Tab dialog box. Edit the tab's position, leader,
or alignment as you would if you were creating the tab.

Tip:
Make These Tabs
Like Those

When you want to make a series of selected paragraphs have the
same tab settings as the first paragraph in the selection, hold down
Option/Alt and click above the ruler in the Text Ruler. FreeHand
applies the tab settings of the first line to the rest of the selection
(see Figure 3-83).

FIGURE 3-83
Applying the same tab
settings to a series of
paragraphs

Select the paragraphs
you want to format,
making sure that the
start of the selection
touches some part of the
paragraph containing
the tab settings you
want to use.

Hold down Option/Alt and double-
click the area above the ruler in the
Text Ruler…

…and FreeHand applies the tab
settings of the first paragraph in the
selection to all of the other paragraphs.

Spacing Before and After Paragraphs

To increase or decrease the amount of space above or below a paragraph, enter a value (distance) in the Above or Below field in the Paragraph Inspector (press Command-Option-P/Ctrl-Alt-P to display the Paragraph Inspector, if it's not already visible) and press Return. FreeHand adds the space above or below the paragraph, as you specified (see Figure 3-84).

You can enter positive or negative numbers in the Paragraph Spacing fields. Enter a negative number in the Above field, and FreeHand moves the paragraph up—even to the point where the paragraph hangs out of the top of the text block or collides with the paragraph above. Enter a negative number in the Below field, and FreeHand moves the following paragraph up in the text block. I haven't found any limit to the numbers you can enter in these fields—either positive or negative.

Controlling Widows and Orphans

Everyone has a different definition for the meaning of the typographic terms "widow" and "orphan." To me, a "widow" is a single line of a paragraph at the top or bottom of a page or column, and

FIGURE 3-84
Vertical spacing
around paragraphs

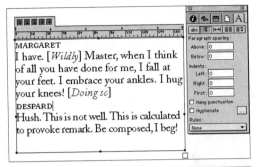

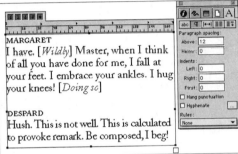

*Enter a value in the
Above field to add
space before a
paragraph.*

an "orphan" is when a paragraph ends with a single, short word on a line by itself. To FreeHand, a "widow" is a single line of a paragraph at the top of a text block or column. I don't know what it thinks an "orphan" is.

The *N* Lines Together field in the Paragraph Inspector controls the way FreeHand breaks a paragraph between columns or linked text blocks. When you enter "1" here (the default), you're telling FreeHand that it's free to break paragraphs however it sees fit. When you enter "2," or a larger number, FreeHand always breaks paragraphs so that two (or more) lines of the paragraph appear at the top of the next text block (see Figure 3-85).

Paragraph Rules   In the old days, we had to add rules between paragraphs manually, dragging the rules around every time the text changed. Many of today's page layout applications feature rules you can attach to a paragraph, which then move with the paragraph as the text reflows. FreeHand features a limited version of this feature (compared, at least, to PageMaker and Quark XPress).

To attach a rule to a paragraph, position the text cursor inside the paragraph, press Command-Option-P/Ctrl-Alt-P to display the

FIGURE 3-85
Keeping lines together

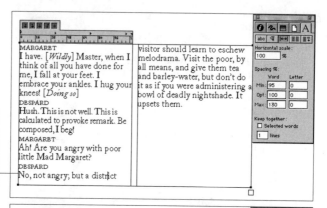

With "1" entered in the
N Lines Together field,
FreeHand leaves the
first line of this
paragraph at the
bottom of the column.

If you enter "2" in the
N Lines Together
field...

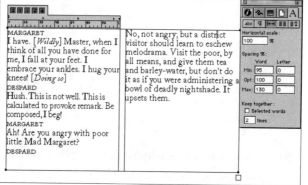

...FreeHand
pulls the first
line of the
paragraph to
the top of the
next column.

Paragraph Inspector, choose a rule type (Centered or Paragraph) from the pop-up menu at the bottom of the Inspector, and press Return. Centered rules are centered in the column or text block; Paragraph rules have the same alignment as the paragraph they're attached to (see Figure 3-86).

A few notes about paragraph rules:

◆ You can't select paragraph rules by clicking on them with the Pointer tool.

◆ When you convert text to paths, any paragraph rules selected with the text are not converted—they disappear.

◆ FreeHand vertically centers paragraph rules in the space between their paragraph (the paragraph where you specified the rule) and the following paragraph, taking leading, paragraph space before, and paragraph space after into account.

FIGURE 3-86
Paragraph rules

Move the cursor to the paragraph you want to attach a paragraph rule to.

"Centered" rules are centered on the paragraph or the column. "Paragraph" rules use the alignment of the paragraph they're attached to.

Choose a paragraph rule option from the Rules pop-up menu.

FreeHand attaches a rule to the paragraph.

If you don't see a rule, you haven't applied a stroke to the text block. Use the Stroke Inspector to apply a stroke to the text block.

FreeHand vertically centers paragraph rules between the bottom of the last line of the current paragraph and the top of the first line of the following paragraph.

Click the Edit button, and the Paragraph Rule Width dialog box appears.

Paragraph rule spanning the column.

Choose whether you want the paragraph rule to span the width of the text (that is, the last line of the paragraph it's attached to) or the width of the column.

◆ FreeHand strokes the paragraph rules with the stroke that's applied to the text block. You can't apply different strokes to a text block's border and to the paragraph rules within that text block (you can, however, uncheck Display Border in the Object Inspector and draw a path around the text block— it's easier than drawing paragraph rules, most of the time).

Tip:
Paragraph Rules
and Text Effects

The rules drawn by the Highlight, Strikethrough, and Underline text effects print *over* any paragraph rules (see Figure 3-87). You can think of a text block as having (at least) three internal layers, with paragraph rules at the back, text at the front, and rules drawn by text effects in between.

FIGURE 3-87
Paragraph rules
and text effects

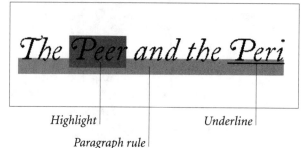

The rules in
Freehand's text
effects print over
FreeHand's
paragraph rules.

Highlight

Paragraph rule

Underline

Working with Text Styles

When you think about the text in your publication, chances are good you're thinking of each paragraph as being a representative of a particular *kind* of text. You're thinking, "That's a headline, that's a subhead, and that's a photo caption." Chances are also good that you're thinking of those paragraphs as having certain formatting attributes: font, size, color, and leading.

That's what text styles do—they bundle all those attributes together and make it possible for you to apply them to text with a single click. But there's more—if you then change your mind about the formatting, you can edit the style, and all the text with that style applied to it (that is, "tagged" with the style) is reformatted automatically.

Text styles work about the same way as graphic styles do—see "Working with Graphic Styles" in Chapter 2, "Drawing"—but they can save you even more time. What makes me say this? Think about it—FreeHand has far more controls for text formatting than it does for formatting paths. Once you've created a text style for a specific kind of text, you'll never have to go through the Character Inspector, Paragraph Inspector, Spacing Inspector, or Alignment Inspector again to format that text—unless, of course, you want to apply a local formatting override to your styled text, which you're always free to do.

**Global versus
Local Formatting**

I just mentioned "local" formatting. What am I talking about? The key to understanding text styles is understanding the difference between style-based formatting and local formatting.

Local formatting is what you get when you select text and apply formatting directly, using the Type Specifications palette and the different sections of the Type Inspector. When you apply formatting using text styles from the Styles palette, on the other hand, you're applying "global" formatting (that is, formatting specified by the selected style).

You can tell if there's local formatting applied to a styled paragraph by looking at the Styles palette. Click the text tool in a styled paragraph, and you'll see a "+" before the style name if the paragraph contains local formatting (see Figure 3-88).

FIGURE 3-88
Global and local
formatting

The "+" next to the style name in the Styles palette shows that the selected character doesn't conform to the style's formatting—it's formatted "locally."

Note: FreeHand marks
text styles by putting a
paragraph symbol (A)
next to the style name
in the Styles palette.

This selection, on the other hand, gets its formatting from the selected style. All of the other text tagged with this style shares the same "global" formatting attributes.

Styles Are More than Formatting

When you apply a style to a paragraph (which I call "tagging" a paragraph with a style), you're doing more than just applying the formatting defined by the style. You're telling FreeHand *what the paragraph is*—not just what it looks like, but what role it has to play in your publication. Is the paragraph important? Is it an insignificant legal notice in type that's intentionally too small to read? The style says it all.

The most important thing to remember when you're creating and applying styles is that tagging a paragraph with a style creates a link between the paragraph and all other paragraphs tagged with that style, and between the paragraph and the definition of the style. Change the style's definition, and watch the formatting and behavior of the paragraphs tagged with that style change to match.

What's Not Included in a Style

Some attributes don't make it into a paragraph style (this list keeps getting shorter): ragged width, flush zone, hyphenation, "no break," and stroke (the fill color is included in the paragraph style).

Creating a
Text Style

The easiest way (in my opinion) to create a text style is to use local formatting to format a paragraph, then create a new style based on that paragraph (see Figure 3-89).

1. Select a formatted paragraph.

2. Display the Styles palette (press Command-3/Ctrl-3).

3. Choose "New" from the Styles palette's pop-up menu. FreeHand adds a new text style to the list of available styles in the Styles palette. This style includes all the formatting applied to the selected paragraph (with the exception of the attributes not supported by paragraph styles, see above).

4. If you want to change the name of the style, double-click the style's name in the Styles palette, type the name you want, and press Return.

That's all there is to it—you've created a text style, and Free-Hand has applied the style to the selected paragraph (text styles pay no attention to the status of the New Graphic Styles Auto-Apply to Selection option in the Object Preferences dialog box—see "Object Preferences" in Chapter 1, "FreeHand Basics"). If you had more than one paragraph selected, FreeHand either takes the formatting of the first paragraph in the selection or takes the for-matting common to all the paragraphs in the selection, depending on your settings of the Build Paragraph Styles Based On option of the Text Preferences dialog box (see the corresponding section in Chapter 1, "FreeHand Basics").

If you've selected more than one paragraph, and you've turned on the Build Paragraph Styles Based On Shared Attributes option in the Text Preferences dialog box, any of the formatting attributes that aren't shared between the selected paragraphs are omitted from the style's definition.

If you prefer, you can create a text style by entering text format-ting for the style in a dialog box that's similar to the text format-ting controls (see Figure 3-90).

1. Choose "New" from the pop-up menu in the Styles palette. FreeHand creates a new text style and adds it to the list of styles in the palette.

FIGURE 3-89
Creating a style
by example

Use local formatting to format a paragraph.

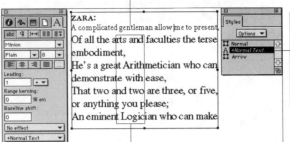

*The "+" next
to FreeHand's
"Normal" style
shows that you've
overridden the
style's default
formatting.*

*These paragraphs are formatted with FreeHand's
default style, "Normal."*

*Click the Text tool
inside the example
paragraph and choose
New from the Options
pop-up menu on the
Styles palette.*

*FreeHand adds a new
style to the Styles palette.
This style contains all of
the formatting of the
example paragraph.*

*Click the style name in
the Styles palette to
apply the style to the
example paragraph.*

*When you create a style, FreeHand
assigns a default name to the style.
To change the name, double-click
the style name, type a new name,
and press Return or Enter.*

*To apply the new style
to other paragraphs,
select the paragraphs...*

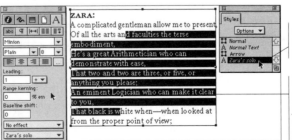

*...and click the
style name in the
Styles palette.*

*FreeHand
applies the style's
formatting to all
of the selected
paragraphs.*

FIGURE 3-90
Creating a style by
specifying attributes

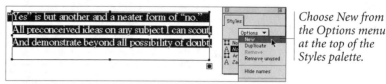

*Choose New from
the Options menu
at the top of the
Styles palette.*

*FreeHand creates a new
style and adds it to the
Styles palette. At this
point, the style's
formatting is identical
to that of "Normal."*

*Select the new style name and choose Edit Style
from the Styles palette's Options menu (or hold
down Option and click the style name in the
Styles palette).*

*FreeHand displays the
Edit Style dialog box.*

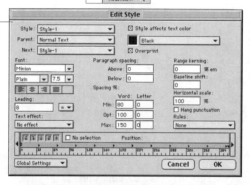

*Set the formatting attributes
you want for the style, using
the controls in the Edit Style
dialog box. When you're
done, click the OK button.*

*FreeHand applies the
formatting to any
paragraphs tagged
with the style.*

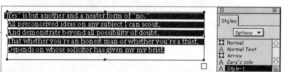

To change the style name, double-click the name in the Styles palette, type a new name, and press Return.

2. Hold down Option/Alt and click the style name in the Styles palette. FreeHand displays the Edit Style dialog box. In this dialog box, you'll see most (but not all) of FreeHand's text formatting controls.

3. Work your way through the Edit Style dialog box, setting the options as you want them for your new style. When everything looks the way you want it to, press Return to close the dialog box.

Creating a style this way is a little bit more awkward than simply basing a style on an example paragraph, but it does offer a couple of advantages.

- You can set the parent style of a style as you create the style. For more on creating hierarchies of styles, see "Basing One Style on Another" in Chapter 2, "Drawing"—everything I said there about graphic styles also applies to text styles.

- You can direct FreeHand to apply—or not apply—a color as part of the style, using the Style Affects Color checkbox.

- You can specify the "next" style (that is, the style you get when you enter a carriage return at the end of a paragraph while you're entering text).

- You can set tabs on the Text Ruler at the bottom of the Edit Style dialog box. This may or may not be an advantage; I only mention it because I've met at least one person who likes setting tabs "without all that pesky text in the way."

Applying a Text Style

Once you've created a style, you'll probably want to apply it to a paragraph. To apply a text style to a paragraph, select the paragraph with the Text tool (all you have to do to select the paragraph is click the Text tool in it; you don't have to drag the cursor through the text to select all the text in the paragraph), then click the style name in the Styles palette. FreeHand applies the style to the text (see Figure 3-91).

If you want to apply a text style to all the paragraphs inside a text block, select the text block with the pointer tool and click the style in the Styles palette. As you'd expect, this also applies the style

FIGURE 3-91
Applying a style to text

Click the Text tool in the paragraph you want to apply a style to (or drag through a series of paragraphs—you don't have to select the entire paragraph).

Click the style name in the Styles palette. FreeHand applies the style to the selection.

to any paragraphs in other, linked, text blocks that start or end in the selected text block.

You can also apply styles using the same sort of "drag-and-drop" technique as you use to apply colors to objects—position your cursor over the icon (A) to the left of the style name in the Styles list, then drag. As you drag, FreeHand displays an icon representing the text style (does this make it a "style swatch"? I don't know!). Drop the icon on the text you want to tag with the style (see Figure 3-92).

FIGURE 3-92
Applying styles with
drag-and-drop

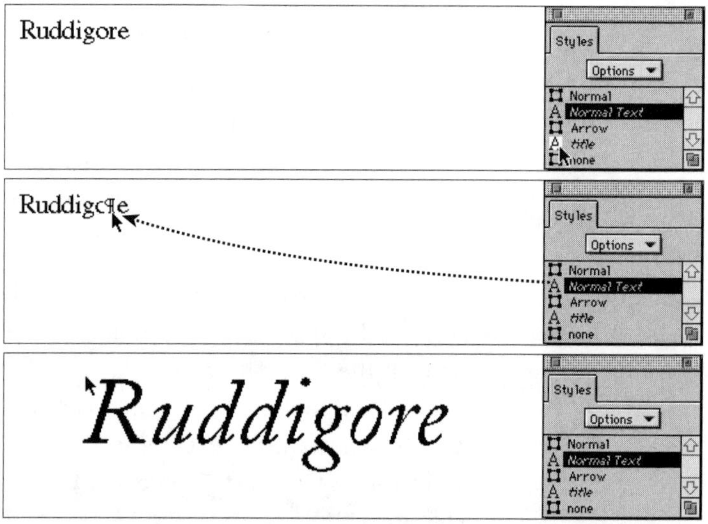

Drag the paragraph
icon (A) from the Styles
palette and drop it on
top of the paragraph
you want to format.

FreeHand applies the
style to the paragraph
you dropped the
paragraph icon on.

If you're using the drag-and-drop technique, the extent of the text you're applying the style to depends on settings in the Text dialog box. If you've turned on the Dragging a Paragraph Style Changes a Single Paragraph option, only the paragraph under the icon is affected when you release the mouse button. If you've turned on the Dragging a Paragraph Style Changes Entire Text Container (I've got to talk the FreeHand engineers into shorter titles for their controls), on the other hand, the style affects the text block you dropped it on (and the beginnings or ends of any paragraphs beginning or ending inside the text block).

Editing Styles

After you've created a style, you can edit the style's formatting and behavior—its *definition*. To edit a style by example, follow these steps (see Figure 3-93).

FIGURE 3-93
Editing a style

This paragraph is tagged with the style "title."

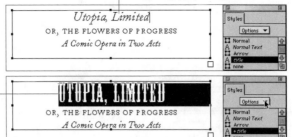

Format the paragraph using local formatting (in this example, I've changed the font, type style, range kerning, and size).

Choose Redefine from the Style palette's Options menu.

FreeHand displays the Redefine Style dialog box. Most of the time, the selected style is the one you want to redefine, so you can simply press Return.

FreeHand changes the formatting of all of the paragraphs tagged with the redefined style.

1. Select a paragraph tagged with the style, then format it the way you want.

2. Choose "Redefine" from the pop-up menu at the top of the Styles palette. FreeHand displays the Redefine Style dialog box. Select the style you want to redefine from the list—usually, the style you want to redefine (the one you selected and edited) is selected. Press Return.

3. FreeHand updates the style based on the paragraph attributes you've selected, changing any other paragraphs tagged with the style as it does so.

If you'd rather change a style by entering specifications, follow these steps (see Figure 3-94).

1. Hold down Option/Alt and click the style name you want to edit in the Styles palette. FreeHand displays the Edit Style dialog box.

FIGURE 3-94
Editing a style using
the Edit Styles method

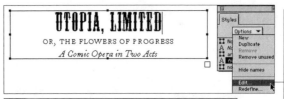

Select the style you want to edit and choose Edit from the Styles palette's Options menu (or hold down Option/ Alt and click the style name in the Styles palette).

FreeHand displays the Edit Style dialog box. Make any formatting changes you want (if you can—not all formatting attributes are supported by the Edit Style dialog box), then click the OK button.

FreeHand changes all of the paragraphs tagged with the style you edited.

2. Make changes to the controls in the Edit Style dialog box. When you're done, press Return to close the dialog box and apply your changes to the style. FreeHand updates all the paragraphs tagged with the style.

Tip:
Creating a Text
Style Mask

What if you want to leave some formatting attributes alone when you apply a paragraph style? It's easy—use the Edit Style dialog box to disable the attributes you *don't* want to apply when you apply the style to a paragraph. Every control in the Edit Style dialog box has a "disabled" state: for fields, move the cursor to the field and press Delete (this leaves the field blank); for pop-up menus, choose No Selection from the menu; for paragraph alignment, click the blank button to the right of the Justify button; click the Hang Punctuation option until you see a "-".

When you apply the style, FreeHand leaves the formatting attributes corresponding to the disabled controls unchanged. The style still applies to the entire paragraph—for true "character styles" we'll just have to wait.

**Importing and
Exporting Styles**

The procedures for importing or exporting paragraph styles are identical to the procedures for importing or exporting graphic styles—see the description in Chapter 2, "Drawing."

Automatic Copyfitting

When you've got to make your text fit into a particular space, there are several things you can do. I've arranged your options, from best to worst (in my opinion), in the following list.

◆ Edit the text.

◆ Range kern the text.

◆ Reduce or increase the size, leading, and interparagraph spacing of the text.

◆ Use FreeHand's automatic copyfitting features (essentially an automated method of performing the previous step).

What if you can't edit the text, and there's too much text to range-kern into the space you have available? At that point, you're stuck, and the only thing you can do is to add or remove space and/or increase or decrease type size until your copy fits in your publication. The best way to do this is to try different combinations of type size, leading, and interparagraph spacing. The disadvantage is that this "hit and miss" method takes time—and sometimes time is that last thing you have. Sometimes, FreeHand's automatic copyfitting might be just what you need.

To use FreeHand's automatic copyfitting, follow these steps (see Figure 3-95).

1. Select a text block.

2. Press Command-Option-C/Ctrl-Alt-C to display the Copyfit Inspector.

3. Check the Modify Leading checkbox if you want FreeHand to change the leading as it tries to fit your text.

FIGURE 3-95
Automatic copyfitting

There's too much text in this story to fit in this text block. For whatever reason, the text has to fit in the text block, and we can't edit it. What can we do?

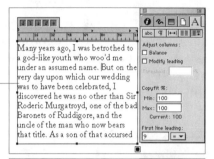

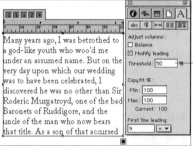

Check the Modify Leading checkbox to tell FreeHand to try to fit the text by changing the leading. In this case, FreeHand changes the leading, but still can't make all of the text fit. In my experience, "Modify Leading" works best when you're trying to fill a text block.

Direct FreeHand to make the text fit by changing its size using the Min and Max fields. In this example, I told FreeHand it could make the text as small as 80% of its original size.

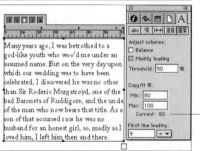

FreeHand reduces the size of the text in the story to make it fit in the text block.

This (non-editable) field displays the current text reduction (or enlargement).

4. In the Ignore Columns Less Than *N* % field, enter a number. Entering "0" tells FreeHand to fit all the columns in the story equally, which is probably what you want. If not, experiment with values until you get what you want (sorry, you're on your own with this one).

5. Enter minimum and maximum percentages in the Max and Min fields. The value you enter in the Min field specifies how small you'll let FreeHand make the type (as a percentage of the type's current size); Max specifies how large FreeHand can make the type to fit it in the text block.

6. Press Return to apply your changes.

FreeHand changes the type size and leading of the lines in the selected story so that the text vertically fills all the text blocks in the story. The following are a few points about copyfitting:

♦ When you select a text block for copyfitting, FreeHand applies copyfitting changes to any text blocks linked to that text block. That is, copyfitting applies to entire stories, not just to individual text blocks.

♦ When you check Modify Leading in the Copyfit Inspector, you're telling FreeHand that it can decrease or increase the leading in the selected story. When FreeHand changes the leading in a story, it changes all the leading by the same percentage.

♦ The Min and Max fields in the Copyfit Inspector set the minimum and maximum percent change in type size FreeHand can use to try to fit the story in the space you have available. Like Modify Leading, this control changes all the type in your text block by a fixed amount. To leave the size of your text alone, enter "100%" in both fields.

♦ The Current percentage (displayed below the Max field) shows you the current scaling of the text in the story, if any. What's the use of this? If FreeHand's been unable to copyfit a story, it's probably because the percentage you entered in the Min field is too large. If you see that the Current percentage is the same as the minimum or maximum percentage, and the text still doesn't fit in the space available, you know that you have to lower the percentage in the Min field or increase the percentage in the Max field.

Joining Text to a Path

One of FreeHand's signature features is the ability to place text along paths of any shape or length. To join text to a path, select some text, press Shift and select a path, and then press Command-Shift-Y/Ctrl-Shift-Y (or choose Bind to Path from the Text menu). FreeHand joins your text to the path (see Figure 3-96).

FIGURE 3-96
Joining text to a path

*Select some text,
select a path, and press
Command-Shift-Y/
Ctrl-Shift-Y...*

*...and FreeHand binds the
text to the path.*

*To edit text that's been
bound to a path, drag the
text tool through it, just as
you'd do to select any other
text on your page (FreeHand
3 users note—no more trips
to the Text dialog box).*

Once you've joined text to a path, you select the text and the
path as you'd select any other text—select the Text tool and drag it
through the characters you want to select, double-click to select a
word, or triple-click to select all the text on the path. Selecting the
path itself can be a little more difficult, but switching to Keyline
view can make it easier to see and select the path.

If you want to unjoin, or split, the text from the path, select the
path and choose Remove From Path from the Text menu. The text
and the path become separate objects again.

Joining text to a path is a great—if somewhat overused—feature. It's often confusing, though. People have a hard time understanding why the text they've just joined to a path falls where it
does on the path. There are a few simple rules to keep in mind
when you're joining text to a path.

◆ Text joins the path according to the alignment of the text
   block; left-aligned text starts at the first point in the path,
   right-aligned text starts at the last point on the path,
   centered text is centered between the first and last points,
   and force-justified text is spread over the length of the path.

- If the path is shorter than the first line of text, the excess text gets shoved off the end of the path.

- The first line (that is, text in a text block up to the first carriage return) of text in the text block you join to the path gets joined to the top of the path; the second line of text gets joined to the bottom of the path.

- Justified text will bunch up when joined to a path that's shorter than the text.

If you're confused, I understand. Take a look at Figure 3-97.

FIGURE 3-97
Joining text and
text alignment

Align left

Align right

First point in the path ⊢

Note: You can always adjust the position of type on a path by dragging the position triangle—the little triangle that appears at the text's alignment point (at the left edge of the text for left-aligned text, at the center for centered text, etc.). As you drag the triangle, FreeHand changes the position of text on the path.

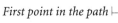

Align center

Justify

FreeHand composes as much text on a path as it can (according to the settings in the Spacing Inspector), then stores the rest as overset text.

The first paragraph of text in a text block joins to the top of the path; the second paragraph joins to the bottom of the path. If you join more than two paragraphs to a path, the other paragraphs are stored as overset text.

In the Object Inspector, you can set the way that the text you've joined to a path follows that path. The Top and Bottom pop-up menus in the Object Inspector control the way that the baseline of your text aligns to the path (see Figure 3-98), and the Orientation pop-up menu controls the way that your text follows the path (see Figure 3-99).

FIGURE 3-98
Baseline alignment
options for text
on a path

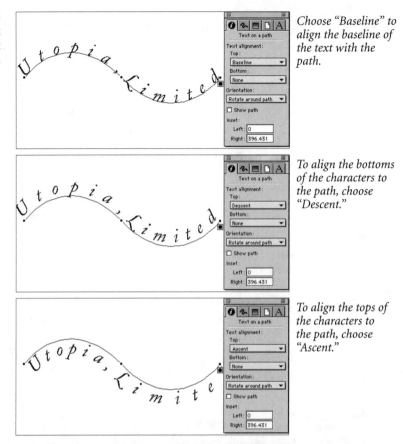

Choose "Baseline" to align the baseline of the text with the path.

To align the bottoms of the characters to the path, choose "Descent."

To align the tops of the characters to the path, choose "Ascent."

This system (the Top and Bottom pop-up menus) takes some getting used to—especially if you're a FreeHand 3 user. The weirdest thing is that if you choose None from both the Top and the Bottom pop-up menus, FreeHand doesn't display any text at all. If the text you've bound to the path is linked to any other text, FreeHand flows the text into the next text block in the story. This is all perfectly logical, but it still took me months to understand it.

Beyond these options, the Show Path option makes the path a visible and printing path. You can alter the stroke and color of the path as you would any other path.

Tip:
Creating an
Ornamental
Border

Here's a tip that's so obvious that many people miss it. When you put together a character (or series of characters) from a symbol font (such as Zapf Dingbats), a path, and FreeHand's ability to attach text to a path, you can create an almost infinite variety of

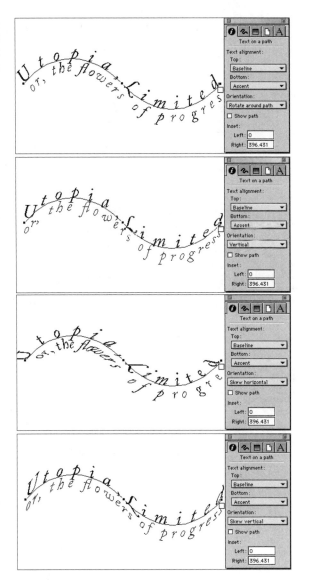

FIGURE 3-99
Controlling the
orientation of text
on a path

ornamental rules and borders (see Figure 3-100). The only catch? Getting the characters to fill the path the way you want them to can take some experimentation.

Tip:
Autoskewing
Text

The Skewing tool (see "Skewing" in Chapter 5, "Transforming") is lots of fun, but this trick is even more fun. When you need to make some text appear as if it's on a plane that's rotated away from the plane of the page, follow these steps (see Figure 3-101).

FIGURE 3-100
Creating ornamental
rules and borders with
a symbol font

*Enter a bunch of
characters in the
symbol font of your
choice (these are "f"
from Zapf Dingbats).*

*Join the characters to a
path, or (as in this
example) a series of
paths.*

*I find that justified
text does the best job
of filling paths from
end to end.*

*Getting the spacing
and alignment of
the characters on
the path just right
can take some work.
Usually, it's easier
to use multiple
paths to create a
border like this one
than it is to work
with kerning and
spacing the text.*

FIGURE 3-101
Autoskewing text

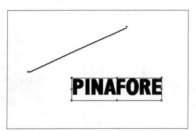

Select the text and the line.

*Press Command-Shift-Y/Ctrl-Shift-Y
to join the text to the line. Press
Command-I/Ctrl-I to display the
Object Inspector.*

*Choose Skew Vertical from
the Orientation pop-up
menu and press Return.*

*Why you (might) want
to do stuff like this.*

1. Draw a path using the Line tool.

2. Type some text.

3. Select the text and the path.

4. Press Command-Shift-Y/Ctrl-Shift-Y to join the text to the path.

5. Press Command-I/Ctrl-I to display the Object Inspector.

6. Choose Ascent from the Top pop-up menu, and choose Skew Vertical from the Orientation pop-up menu. Press Return to apply your changes.

7. Now you can skew the text by dragging either end of the path anywhere you want.

Flowing Text Inside Paths

When you need a text block that's not rectangular, you can flow text inside a closed path of any shape. To flow text inside a path, follow these steps (see Figure 3-102).

1. Select the text block containing the text you want to flow inside the path.

2. Shift-select the path you want to flow the text inside (this only works with closed paths).

3. Select Flow Inside Path from the Text menu (or press Command-U/Ctrl-U). FreeHand flows the text in the text block inside the path.

If you flow a multicolumn text block inside a path, FreeHand converts it to a single column.

When you flow text inside a path, you won't be able to scale the text, or change its leading, kerning, or word spacing, by dragging the corner handles of the text block. In fact, you won't see the selection handles of the text block at all—only those of the path. When you drag the corner handles of the path, FreeHand reflows the text inside the path as if you'd dragged a corner handle (that is, line breaks change, but the type formatting remains the same).

To remove text from the inside of a path, choose Remove From Path from the Text menu. FreeHand separates the path and the text block, and places them on your page as individual objects.

FIGURE 3-102
Flowing text
inside a path

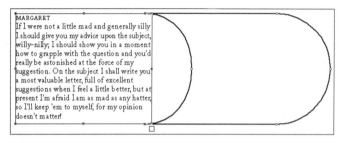

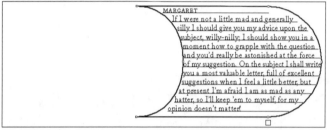

Tip:
The Quick Way
to Flow Text
Inside a Path

If you want to flow text inside a path, and you haven't already created the text block, here's a quick way to get text inside a path. Select the path, press Command-Shift-U/Ctrl-Shift-U (or choose Flow Inside Path from the Text menu), and start typing text (see Figure 3-103). FreeHand flows the text you type inside the path.

FIGURE 3-103
Typing text into a path

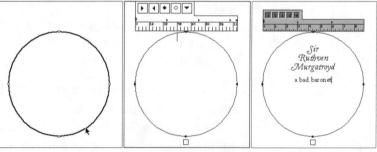

Select a path.   *Press Command-Shift-U/Ctrl-Shift-U. A text cursor appears inside the path.*   *Enter and format text.*

Wrapping Text around Objects

Wrapping text around an object is something like the opposite of flowing text inside a path. In the former, you want text to stay inside a path; in the latter, you want to keep it out. To wrap text around a path, follow these steps (see Figure 3-104).

1. Place a basic shape or path on top of a text block that contains a few paragraphs of text. If the text block's in front of the object, the text won't wrap around the object.

2. Select both the text block and the path.

3. Press Command-Option-W/Ctrl-Alt-W (or choose Run Around Selection from the Text menu). FreeHand displays the Run Around Selection dialog box.

4. Click the Wrap button (the one on the right) and press Return (or click the OK button) to close the dialog box. FreeHand wraps the text in the text block around the path.

FIGURE 3-104
Wrapping text around
an object

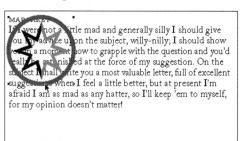

Select the path you want to wrap text around and bring it to the front (in this example, I've selected the circle). Press Command-Option-W/Ctrl-Alt-W.

FreeHand displays the
Run Around Selection
dialog box. Click the
Wrap button.

Enter the standoff
distances you want for
your text wrap and
press Return.

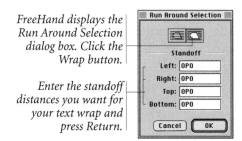

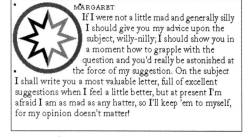

FreeHand wraps text around the path.

You can apply a text wrap to any single object in FreeHand, including other text blocks. If you want to apply a text wrap to all the objects in a group, subselect (hold down Option/Alt to subselect objects inside groups) the objects in the group and apply a text wrap to them.

Converting Characters into Paths

When you work in graphic design, you frequently need to alter characters of type for logos or packaging designs. For years, we dreamed about the ability to turn type into paths we could edit. Finally, applications such as FreeHand and Illustrator added the feature.

You can convert characters from just about any font (TrueType, PostScript Type 1 and Fontographer PostScript Type 3 fonts) for which you have the printer (outline) font into freeform paths.

Once you've converted the characters into paths, you lose all text editing capabilities, but you gain the ability to paste things inside the character outline, to apply lines and fills that you can't apply to normal text (including tiled, graduated, radial, or Post-Script fills), and to change the shape of the characters themselves.

To convert characters into paths, select the text block or text blocks you want to convert, and then press Command-Shift-P/Ctrl-Shift-P (or choose Convert to Paths from the Text menu). Free-Hand converts the characters into paths (see Figure 3-105).

When you first convert characters into paths, all the converted characters are grouped together. To work with an individual character, press Command-U/Ctrl-U to ungroup the paths. If FreeHand runs out of memory while converting the characters to paths, try selecting fewer characters and trying again.

When you convert characters containing interior space (such as "P," or "O") into paths, FreeHand turns them into composite paths (see "Composite Paths" in Chapter 2, "Drawing"). This is handy. Not only are multiple-part characters (such as i, é, and ü) treated as single paths, but characters with interior paths (such as O, P, A, and D) are transparent where they should be, and fill properly (see Figure 3-106).

FIGURE 3-105
Converting text
to paths

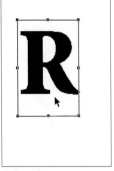 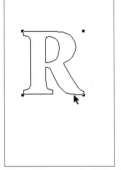 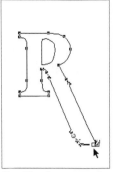

Select the text you want to convert to paths.

Press Command-Shift-P/ Ctrl-Shift-P (or Choose Convert to Paths from the Text menu).

FreeHand converts the characters to paths.

FIGURE 3-106
Text converted into
composite paths

When you convert characters to paths, FreeHand groups the converted characters.

To work with individual characters, choose Ungroup from the Arrange menu.

Characters with internal spaces are converted to composite paths.

To work with paths inside a composite character, hold down Option as you click on points inside the path (to subselect the points), or choose Split Element from the Arrange menu to convert the composite path to a series of normal paths.

You can always make the characters into normal (that is, not composite) paths. To do this, select the character and choose Split Element from the Element menu.

Tip:
If Your
Characters
Won't Convert

If you weren't able to convert the text into paths, make sure that you have the outline (printer) fonts and that they're somewhere FreeHand can find them. If you don't have the outline fonts, FreeHand won't be able to convert your text into paths.

Tip:
How to Avoid
Worrying About
Downloadable
Fonts

If you've exported FreeHand files containing lots of downloadable fonts as EPS, then imported them into other page-layout applications, you've probably had trouble getting the EPS to print with the proper fonts. For whatever reason, EPS graphics and downloadable fonts don't mix very well.

So why bother with fonts at all? Instead, you can convert all your text to paths (though this might not work for zoom text and other text effects) before you export your publication as an EPS (clearly, this isn't going to work if your publication contains lots of text). This way, the application that's printing your EPS doesn't have to worry about getting the downloadable fonts right. Your EPSes will print faster, too.

Tip:
Justifying
Character
Outlines

Here's something that happens to me all the time: I convert a force-justified line of characters into paths, and then I find that I need to make them fill a different horizontal distance. Instead of creating a new text block, formatting and force-justifying it, and then converting the characters to paths again, you can follow these steps (see Figure 3-107).

1. Drag the first character of the line to the left edge of the space you want to spread the text across.

2. Drag the last character of the line to the right edge of the of the space you want to fill.

3. Select all the characters in the line.

4. Press Command-Option-A/Ctrl-Alt-A to display the Alignment palette, if it's not already visible.

5. Choose Distribute Widths from the Horizontal pop-up menu in the Alignment palette.

FreeHand distributes the characters you selected across the width defined by the first and last character in the line. If the text contains more than one word, you'll have to adjust the word spacing manually, and then use the Alignment palette again to distribute the characters in each word—but it's still quicker than the alternative methods.

FIGURE 3-107
Justifying character
outlines

*You've converted some
characters to paths,
and, later, realize
you want them to
fill a wider (or
narrower) column.
What can you do?*

*Select the converted characters and ungroup the paths,
then drag one character to the width you want to fill.*

*Select all the characters and press
Command-Option-A/Ctrl-Alt-A to
display the Alignment palette (if it's
not already visible).*

*Choose Distribute Widths from the
Horizontal pop-up menu and click
Apply to distribute the characters.*

FreeHand spreads the characters to fill the line.

*If there are spaces in the text, you'll have to adjust the positions of
the characters, then redistribute the characters inside each word.*

Tip:
Making Type
Glow

When you want to add a glowing outline to your type, follow these
steps (see Figure 3-108).

1. Convert the text to paths.

2. Press Command-=/Ctrl-Shift-C to clone the paths.

3. Apply a stroke to the cloned paths. This stroke width should
   be two times the width of the glow, and should be the color
   you want for the outside of the glow effect.

4. Press Command-B/Ctrl-B to send the cloned paths behind
   the original paths.

FIGURE 3-108
Creating glowing type

Select the text.

Convert the text to paths.

Ungroup the converted paths, clone them, and then apply a thick, colored stroke to the cloned paths.

Printed example

Send the cloned paths to the back. Apply a thin stroke to the original characters.

Select corresponding points on the original characters and clones (sometimes, it'll be hard to see what's selected)...

...and press Command-Shift-B/Ctrl-Shift-B to blend the paths.

5. Apply a stroke to the original paths. This stroke should be the color you want for the inside of the glow effect.

6. Character by character, blend the original paths with their corresponding background paths. For characters with internal spaces (such as "O"), you'll have to split the paths and then blend the interior spaces separately.

Inline Graphics

One of my favorite features in FreeHand is the ability to paste any path or imported graphic inside a text block. Once inserted into a text block, the object behaves (more or less) like a character of text. I call these embedded objects "inline graphics."

What's so great about inline graphics? They come in handy when you want to keep a corporate logo next to the corporation's address, regardless of where that address flows as the text before the address expands or contracts during editing. Or you want to put a box around a paragraph and have the box travel with the paragraph. Inline graphics also give you a way around some of the limitations of FreeHand's paragraph rules.

Creating an Inline Graphic

Creating an inline graphic is simple. Cut or copy the object you want to convert to an inline graphic to the Clipboard, then click the Text tool inside a text block and paste. FreeHand pastes the object from the Clipboard into the text block (see Figure 3-109).

FIGURE 3-109
Creating an inline graphic

Select the object you want to paste into a text block and cut or copy it.

Click the text tool in a text block.

Paste the object into the text block. You've just created an inline graphic.

Working with Inline Graphics

Inline graphics can take some getting used to. For starters, here are a few things you should keep in mind as you're working with inline graphics.

◆ When you paste an object into a text block, it behaves just as if it were a character of text. Inline graphics respond to changes in size, leading, kerning, and horizontal scaling.

◆ When you select multiple objects and paste them into a text block, FreeHand groups the objects together (that is, they don't become separate inline graphics).

◆ Inline graphics transform (skew, scale, rotate, and flip) when you transform the text block.

◆ Inline graphics appear as black dots in the Text Editor (see Figure 3-110).

FIGURE 3-110
Inline Graphics
in the Text Editor

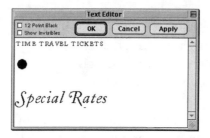

Removing inline graphics. To remove an inline graphic from a text block, select the graphic with the text tool and press Delete.

Extracting inline graphics. To turn an inline graphic back into an independent object, convert the text block containing the inline graphic to paths. You might want to copy the inline graphic to its own text block before you do this.

Adjusting the text wrap of inline graphics. When you create an inline graphic, FreeHand applies a default text wrap to the graphic. You can't turn the text wrap of an inline graphic off (you can, however, set the text wrap so that text overlaps the inline graphic). To edit the text wrap, follow these steps (see Figure 3-111).

1. Select the inline graphic with the Text tool.

2. Click the Edit button at the bottom of the Character Inspector (press Command-T/Ctrl-T to display the Inspector if it's not already visible). FreeHand displays the Text Wrap dialog box.

3. Adjust the text wrap by entering new values in the Standoff Distances fields.

Inline graphics and leading. When you think about adjusting the position of a character in a text block, what do you think of first? Shifting the baseline. That's just what you should be thinking of when you think about positioning inline graphics.

When you first paste an inline graphic into a text block, Free-Hand assigns a leading value to the graphic. This value differs from object to object, but its intent is always the same—to get the bottom of the graphic to sit on the baseline of the line you've pasted it into. Change this value and you move the graphic up and down inside the text block.

FIGURE 3-111
Adjusting the
Text Wrap of
Inline Graphics

When you paste an
object into a text block
as an inline graphic,
FreeHand assigns a
leading value that puts
the bottom of the
graphic on the baseline
of the text.

This inline graphic is in a
paragraph by itself.

In this example, I'll show you how
to drop the inline graphic behind
this text—once that's done, we'll
have a background image that
follows the text it surrounds.

When you adjust the leading and
baseline shift amount, the selection
sometimes looks strange (in this
case, it doesn't even look like the
inline graphic is still selected).
Don't worry about it.

Assign a fixed leading
value to the inline
graphic.

Set a baseline shift for
the graphic. In this case,
I've chosen a baseline
shift equal to the height
of the graphic.

How did I know the height of the
graphic? I can see it in the Size field
of the Character Inspector.

Select the inline graphic
with the Text tool and
choose Edit from the
Effect pop-up menu at
the bottom of the
Character Inspector.

FreeHand displays the Text Wrap
dialog box. Enter a negative value
in the Bottom field (in this
example, I've entered the height of
the graphic).

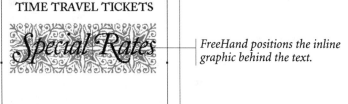

FreeHand positions the inline
graphic behind the text.

Exporting inline graphics. The only export formats that support inline graphics are the EPS formats (Macintosh, Generic, and MS-DOS) and PDF. If you want to export FreeHand publications containing inline graphics to any other format, convert the text blocks containing the graphics to paths before you export the file. Neither text export format (RTF and text-only) supports inline graphics. See "Exporting," in Chapter 4, "Importing and Exporting."

Tip:
Using Inline
Graphics to
Create Rules
and Borders

If you can't find the ornamental border line you need in FreeHand's built-in Custom strokes (display the Stroke Inspector, then choose Custom from the Stroke Type pop-up menu to see FreeHand's Custom strokes), don't despair—you can always create your own "custom" border line using inline graphics. There's no real "trick" to it—all you need to do is paste a graphic into a text block (several times), then attach the text block to a path. FreeHand spaces the inline graphics along the path (see Figure 3-112).

FIGURE 3-112
Creating an
ornamental border
with inline graphics

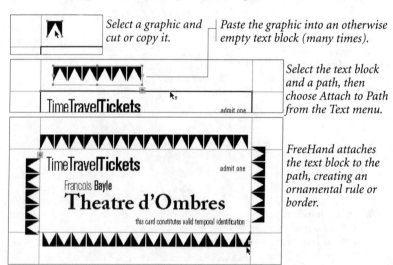

Select a graphic and cut or copy it.

Paste the graphic into an otherwise empty text block (many times).

Select the text block and a path, then choose Attach to Path from the Text menu.

FreeHand attaches the text block to the path, creating an ornamental rule or border.

After Words

A picture may be worth a thousand words, but 3,000 bytes of text are worth about 1,000,000 bytes of image data. There are lots of words you'd have a hard time getting across with a thousand pictures. Take "mellifluous," for example. Please.

CHAPTER

Importing and Exporting

4

Someday, you'll need to do something that's beyond the drawing and typesetting capabilities of FreeHand. You'll need to edit TIFF images, or do serious 3-D rendering, or create Web pages. Other applications do these things better than FreeHand does. But you can add the files you create in other applications to your FreeHand publication. And you can export Free-Hand graphics for use in other page-layout and drawing programs.

You can scan an image, edit it with an image-editing program, then import it into FreeHand and use it in your FreeHand publication. You can color-separate imported images when you print—or before you print, if you prefer. You can open graphics created in almost any drawing program—FreeHand can import Adobe Illustrator formats (1.1, 88, 3.0, 5.0, 5.5, 6.0, and 7.0) and CorelDRAW files (CDR), among others. When you open or import files from other drawing programs, you can convert the objects inside the files into editable FreeHand objects—paths, text blocks, and imported graphics.

You can use a word processor, text editor, or page-layout programs to enter and format text and then import the formatted text into FreeHand as RTF (Rich Text Format—a Microsoft text-only format capable of describing anything that can appear in a Microsoft Word document). Using RTF has its advantages and disadvantages, as you'll see in "Importing RTF," later in this chapter. You can import text-only (ASCII) files from text editors and databases.

FreeHand can also open Adobe Acrobat Portable Document Format (PDF) files—which means you can take a PDF created by almost any application, open it in FreeHand, and edit it. As you'll see, this makes PDF a great format for getting pages out of other page layout programs (such as PageMaker or Quark XPress)—or just about anything else—and into FreeHand.

FreeHand's no slouch at exporting graphics for use in other applications—FreeHand's EPS formats can be imported into every major page-layout or illustration program and combined with text and graphics created in those programs. If exporting as an EPS doesn't work, you can export object-PICT graphics on the Macintosh, or Windows Metafiles (WMF) in Windows. Why would you want to do this? Even in this day and age, not all applications support the EPS format. Shocking, but true.

Want to put your FreeHand publication on-line, or send it to a client for an approval? Even without the Acrobat Distiller, it's easy to make a FreeHand PostScript file into a PDF. Or you might want to create a GIF (bitmap), JPEG (bitmap), Flash, or Shockwave file for use in an HTML or PDF document. I'll cover some of the process of creating files for on-line use in this chapter, but I'll devote more space to it in Chapter 9, "FreeHand and the Web").

Last, but not least, you can export text from a FreeHand publication as either RTF or text-only files.

Getting Files into FreeHand

FreeHand offers five ways to bring files from other applications into your FreeHand publications. Here are your options, in my preferred order:

- Import the file. Importing a file inserts the file into the current publication. What, exactly, happens to the content of the file depends on the file's type.

- Open the file. Any file FreeHand can import, it can open. When you open most graphics or text files, FreeHand positions the content of the file at the lower-left corner of the first page of a new, untitled publication.

- Copy and paste. The most obvious, simplest, and least reliable method of getting information from another application is to copy it out of the application and paste it into FreeHand. While this technique works well for small amounts of text, it can spell disaster for graphics and images created in other programs. I don't mean to imply that you should *never* use copy and paste, just that you should approach it with caution.

- Drag and drop. As I mentioned in Chapter 1, "FreeHand basics," you can drag objects out of one FreeHand publication and drop them into another. You can drag files from your desktop (the Macintosh Finder or the Explorer in Windows 95) and drop them into your FreeHand publication window. This works the same as importing the files using the import command. You can drag objects from other programs and drop them into FreeHand. This, in general, works the same as copying and pasting, and comes with the same cautions.

- Publish and subscribe (Macintosh only). FreeHand can subscribe to (import) Macintosh data that other applications have published (exported) as PICT or EPS graphics. Either way, FreeHand doesn't convert the contents of the graphic—to edit the file, you'll have to return to the application you used to create it.

- OLE (Object Linking and Embedding) linking (Windows only). FreeHand can act as an OLE server application, which means you can use FreeHand graphics in OLE client applications (such as Microsoft Word for Windows).

When you import a TIFF image or an EPS graphic (and have turned off the Convert Editable EPS When Imported option in the Import Preferences dialog box), FreeHand doesn't store the file inside your FreeHand publication. Instead, FreeHand creates a "link" to the file you imported, and stores only a low-resolution, "preview" image in the publication. When you print, FreeHand gets the information it needs to print the graphic from the file on your disk. You can change this behavior, if you want—and make Free-Hand store the file inside your publication—see "Linking and Embedding," later in this chapter.

When you import a graphic file that *isn't* an EPS, a TIFF, a PNG, or an LRG, FreeHand converts contents of the file into Free-Hand objects (vector formats) or to a TIFF image (bitmap formats), and stores the converted file inside your FreeHand publication (see Table 4-1).

TABLE 4-1
File conversion
on import

File type	Converted to
Adobe Illustrator, Corel Draw, DXF, FreeHand 2-7, PLT (HPGL), PICT*, WMF, EPS†	FreeHand objects (paths, text blocks, and images)
Adobe Photoshop, GIF, JPEG, PICT*, BMP, TGA	TIFF (embedded in the FreeHand file)
TIFF, LRG, PNG	Unchanged

* If a PICT contains only an image, it's converted to a TIFF and embedded in the FreeHand file; if it contains only vector objects, the objects are converted to FreeHand paths.

† If you've turned on the Convert Editable EPS when Imported option in the Import/Export Preferences dialog box, FreeHand makes an attempt to convert the contents of the EPS into FreeHand objects. If FreeHand can't convert the contents of the EPS, or if you've turned the Convert Editable EPS When Placed option off, FreeHand imports the EPS without converting it (and creates a link to the EPS file on your disk).

Importing Anything

It doesn't matter what kind of file you're importing; the process of getting it into FreeHand always works the same way (see Figure 4-1). If all you want to know is how to get a file into your publication, read the next procedure and skip the rest of the chapter. If you really want to know all the tricks to working with the different file types, read on!

FIGURE 4-1
Importing any file

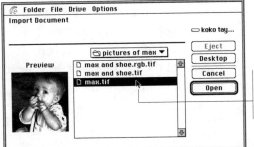

Press Command-R/ Ctrl-R. FreeHand displays the Import Document dialog box.

Double-click a file name in the list, or select a file name and press Return...

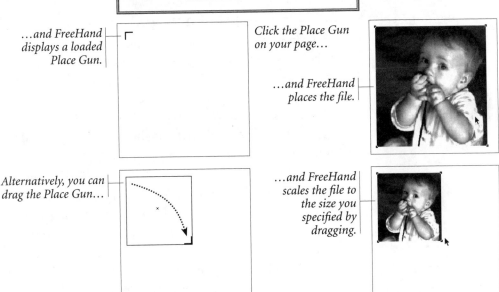

...and FreeHand displays a loaded Place Gun.

Click the Place Gun on your page...

...and FreeHand places the file.

Alternatively, you can drag the Place Gun...

...and FreeHand scales the file to the size you specified by dragging.

1. Press Command-R/Ctrl-R (or choose Import from the File menu). The Import Document dialog box appears.

2. Choose a file and click the OK button (or press Return). The cursor changes into an icon (I call the icon a "Place Gun"—a usage left over from the days when FreeHand's import command was named "Place").

3. Click the Place Gun on your page (or on the pasteboard), and FreeHand imports the file you selected (positioning the upper-right corner of the file where you clicked the Place Gun). If you're placing a graphic file, FreeHand imports the file at its original size.

    Instead of clicking, you can *drag* the Place Gun to scale the file as you import it. If the incoming file is a graphic,

FreeHand proportionally scales the graphic as you drag—stop dragging when the graphic is the size you want. When you're importing a text file, you can set the width and height of the text block by dragging the Place gun (just as you can by dragging the Text tool).

About Graphic File Formats

FreeHand can import a wide range of graphic file formats, including Adobe Illustrator formats, DXF vector graphics from CAD programs (such as AutoCAD), TIFF images, EPS files, and PICT or WMF-type graphics. From FreeHand's point of view, there are certain limitations and advantages to each of these file formats.

Just to refresh everybody's memory, here are a few quick definitions, rules, and exceptions regarding graphic file formats.

There are three fundamental types of graphics file formats:

◆ Bitmap files store pictures as matrices (rows and columns) of squares known as pixels, with each pixel having a particular gray or color value (also known as a gray depth, color depth, or bit depth). Bitmap files are typically created by image editing programs such as Adobe Photoshop, or by the software you use to run your scanner. TIFF, BMP, MacPaint, and GIF are all bitmap graphic file formats.

◆ Vector files contain sets of instructions for drawing graphic objects—typically geometric shapes, such as lines, ellipses, polygons, rectangles, and arcs. The drawing instructions say, "Start this line at this point and draw to that point over there"; or, "This is a polygon made up of these line segments." Vector files are typically created by CAD programs, such as AutoCAD. DXF files are an example of a vector format graphics file. PostScript paths, such those as you'd find in an EPS, are another example of a vector format, but they're usually contained in a metafile (see below).

◆ Metafiles can contain both vector and bitmap graphics. Macintosh PICT, Adobe Illustrator, EPS, CGM, and WMF (Windows metafile) formats are all examples of metafiles.

Metafiles don't have to contain *both* vector and bitmap objects. Sometimes you'll find metafiles that contain only an image.

There are a lot of different ways to talk about the files saved in these three format types. I usually refer to bitmap files as "images," vector files as "drawings."

Note that these formats are all "interchange" formats—they're for moving information from one application to another. All programs support their own, "native," file format, but many can read or write files in other formats. Some programs can open or import files saved in the native formats of other programs. FreeHand, for example, can import files saved in Photoshop's native format. Whenever you move data between programs, or save files in formats other than an application's native format, a process of translation occurs. And, as in the translation of a text from one language to another, the translation will differ from the original. Sometimes, the differences are subtle; sometimes they're more obvious—but there are always differences.

The key to the accuracy of the translation lies in the differences between the native format and the nonnative format. How accurate is the object positioning information in the file format you're exporting to? For example, many vector PICT or WMF export filters round object coordinates to some fundamental unit of accuracy (points for PICT; *twips*—twentieths of a point—for WMF). When you export to a vector PICT or WMF file from a program capable of greater accuracy (FreeHand, for example), you'll get rounding errors. Objects will shift on the page.

The way that the format deals with system-specific information is also important. How does the format store fonts, or colors? If the file relies on the settings of the system it's created on, look out—you'll see color changes and font substitutions when you take the file to another system (or when you change your system's setup).

Some programs are real "Swiss Army knives," and can open and save files in lots of different formats. Photoshop, for example, can open and save files in a dozen different bitmap formats. Photoshop is a great program to have around even if you use it for nothing more than file conversions.

There are several different file-conversion programs that can make it easier to convert an unreadable image file into a file type that FreeHand can read, but the best by far is DeBabelizer, available for both the Macintosh and Windows. DeBabelizer is available from Equilibrium (www.equilibrium.com).

A Philosophical Note

There's always a temptation, as an explaining parent or as a computer book author, to simply say, "Because I say so." I feel that you deserve better. At the same time, a basic explanation of the problems inherent in, say, the Macintosh PICT vector format would consume all of the pages of this chapter. And then there's WMF, PICT's Windows counterpart, to think about.

There's just not room, so I'll try to be brief.

The biggest problem is that many graphics file formats, in spite of their being designed as "interchange" formats, make too many assumptions about the system they'll be viewed on or printed from. We say such formats are "device specific," because they're tied to some feature of a particular video display system or printer (the "device"). Most of these formats assume that files stay on the computer system they're created on—not a reasonable assumption to make for anyone doing any kind of publishing. PostScript files (including EPS files) are practically the definition of a device-*independent* file format.

In many cases, it's not the specification of the file format itself that's the problem—it's the way the import and export filters that read and write the files have been written. There's no reason (any more) to convert curves into a series of straight line segments when you export a vector file as a Windows Metafile—yet many export filters do just that.

Many bitmap formats incorrectly assume that the color palette of the system they're on will remain the same (this is particularly true of bitmap-only PICT files. This means that colors can shift as you move the file from computer to computer—which means that the colors change when you print. This can mean that you lose colors or levels of gray when you print.

Most metafile and vector formats—except EPS—assume that the font list of the system they're created on will remain the same, and refer to fonts by their *number* (as they appear in the list of fonts at the time the file was created) rather than by their *name*. This can cause problems when you move to another system, or even when you install a new font.

It all comes down to using the formats for what they were intended for. BMP files were intended to be viewed onscreen, in Windows—not printed. PICT and WMF files were intended for printing on (different types of) non-PostScript printers. DXF and CGM files were intended for printing on pen plotters. EPS and TIFF were designed to work well on high resolution PostScript printers; GIF and JPEG were designed to carry a great deal of image information in the smallest possible package—which makes them ideal for on-line publishing. In addition, EPS, TIFF, JPEG, and GIF were designed for interchange between different computing environments and platforms—something you can't say of PICT (Macintosh-only) and WMF (Windows-only).

WMF is a file format for saving commands written in the Windows Graphic Device Interface (or GDI)—the language Windows uses to draw objects onscreen (or print to non-PostScript printers). PICT is based on QuickDraw, the native drawing language of the Macintosh. When you send files in these formats to a PostScript printer, they have to be translated into PostScript commands. This process isn't perfect, which means that what you see on your screen may not be what you get from your printer.

About File Types and Platforms

You've probably noticed that I refer to PICT and WMF as if they were the same format. They're not—but they do occupy approximately similar ecological niches in the graphics environments of their respective operating systems. Table 4-1 shows other, roughly corresponding file types.

The Windows and Macintosh versions of FreeHand cannot open the same set of file formats (see Table 4-2). Macintosh FreeHand, for example, can't import WMF files; Windows FreeHand can't

TABLE 4-2
Corresponding
file types

File type	Macintosh	Windows
Vector	PICT, EPS	WMF, CGM, HPGL, DXF
Bitmap	TIFF, LRG	TIF, BMP, WMF, GIF, JPG
Bitmap Metafile[1]	PICT, EPS	EPS, WMF, DRW
Vector Metafile[2]	PICT, EPS	EPS, WMF, DRW
Metafile	PICT, EPS	EPS, WMF

[1] A metafile containing only a single bitmap image.
[2] A metafile containing only vector artwork.

TABLE 4-3
Platforms
and File Import

Macintosh only	Windows only	Both platforms
PICT, PICT2	CGM, CorelDRAW version 3, 5, 6, PLT (HGML), DRW, WMF, EMF	Adobe Illustrator version 1.1-7, Adobe Photoshop version 3-4, CorelDRAW version 4 and 7, EPS, FreeHand 3-7, GIF, JPEG, PNG, TIFF, TGA, LRG, BMP, DXF

import PICT files. When in doubt, use file formats supported by both platforms: Adobe Illustrator (all versions), TIFF, EPS, GIF, JPEG, PNG, and LRG. FreeHand, on either platform, can always import text files saved as text-only (ASCII) or RTF.

Images embedded in FreeHand publications can always be transferred between the Windows and Macintosh versions of the program—as you'll recall, embedded images are always stored inside the publication as TIFF data. Want to move a BMP-format graphic to your Macintosh? Open the file in FreeHand (which converts the objects in the BMP file into a TIFF), then copy the FreeHand file to your Macintosh.

On either platform, you'll probably have to deal with "legacy" graphics in formats that have passed out of general use (MacDraw vector PICTs on the Macintosh; ancient CGM clip-art files in Windows). You may even have a stock of FreeHand 3 EPS files lying around. While there's a temptation to leave these graphics in their original formats (you can, after all, still import and print them from, for example, PageMaker and Word), I urge you to convert them to FreeHand 8 and clean them up as soon as you get the chance. Every time I put off converting "legacy" graphics, they cause me last-minute production headaches. Better to fix them *before* you commit them to expensive imagesetter film.

Importing Object Graphics

FreeHand can import PICT or WMF graphics created by charting programs (such as Adobe Persuasion or Microsoft Excel), PICT graphics created by drawing programs (MacDraw), and PICT tables created by Microsoft Word or Aldus Table Editor. Don't I mean the *Adobe* Table Editor? Nope—I mean the Aldus Table Editor included with PageMaker 4.2 (and still at large). *Adobe* PageMaker has the *Adobe* Table Editor, which can write EPS files (and is therefore covered by "Importing EPS Graphics," later in this chapter).

As you open or import these files, each of the elements in the original illustration is converted to a FreeHand element. Often, it'll seem like you've got two or three times as many elements as you need. This is just because PICT and WMF have weird ideas about how to draw things (see Figure 4-2).

FIGURE 4-2
"Extra" elements in
converted PICT or
WMF graphics

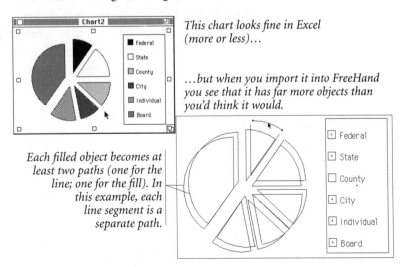

This chart looks fine in Excel (more or less)...

...but when you import it into FreeHand you see that it has far more objects than you'd think it would.

Each filled object becomes at least two paths (one for the line; one for the fill). In this example, each line segment is a separate path.

Tip:
Before you
import that
PICT…
(Macintosh Only)

Before you import or open an object-PICT file, make sure you've turned on the Convert PICT Patterns to Grays option in the Import/Export Preferences dialog box. This way, the nasty patterns that PICT drawing applications use to represent shades of gray will get converted into what they should be—shades of gray—as you import them.

Tip:
Importing Charts
from Microsoft
Excel

You can bring Excel's charts into FreeHand with a minimum of fuss (before you do, you might want to take a look at FreeHand's new charting features in Chapter 2, "Drawing"). Excel can't export its charts as PICTs on the Macintosh, so you'll have to copy them to the Clipboard, and then paste them into FreeHand. When you paste the chart into FreeHand, the objects in the chart are converted into editable FreeHand elements. In Windows, export the Excel chart as a WMF file, then import the file into FreeHand

Importing WMF (Windows Only)

When you import or open a Windows Metafile (or WMF) containing only vector objects, FreeHand converts the objects in the file into FreeHand paths composed of straight line segments (see Figure 4-3). If the file contains only an image, FreeHand converts the image to a TIFF and embeds it inside the publication. If the file contains a mix of vector objects and image information, FreeHand converts the vector objects into FreeHand paths, and converts the images to TIFF. In theory. In practice, I have never seen an image included in a WMF file convert properly. How well this process works seems to depend entirely on the export filter that wrote the WMF file to disk in the first place.

Importing Drawings from CAD Programs

Most CAD programs are capable of saving their drawings in the vector PICT format (on the Macintosh) or DXF format (in Windows), so it's easy to bring engineering or architectural drawings into FreeHand. Why would you want to take the drawings out of their native CAD program? CAD programs are great at rendering precise views of an object or building, but they're just not that good at making a drawing "sexy" or handling type in a professional manner. Often, versions of the drawings for created for publication in marketing materials or documentation need the PostScript drawing features found in FreeHand.

FIGURE 4-3
Imported
WMF clip art

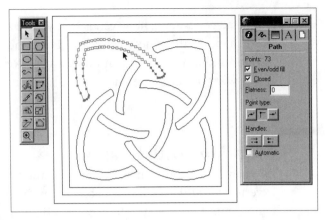

To get objects out of your CAD program and into FreeHand, export or save your drawing as a vector PICT file (on the Macintosh) or as a DXF file (in Windows), then open and interpret the file with FreeHand. I haven't had good luck opening DXF files in the Macintosh version of FreeHand (they *do* open, but the results aren't pretty), so I'd stick with vector PICT on that platform, if possible. Here are a few things about converted CAD drawings you need to keep in mind (see Figure 4-4).

◆ In many cases, FreeHand will convert each line segment into a closed path.

◆ Arcs and ellipses are often converted into sets of closed paths made up of single straight line segments.

◆ Line joins will often miss, particularly where lines meet arcs.

FIGURE 4-4
Imported CAD
drawing

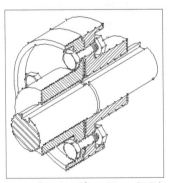

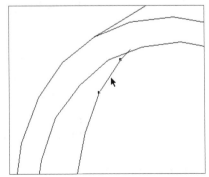

CAD drawing (from VersaCAD) imported into FreeHand.

When you zoom in on the imported drawing, you'll see that all of the curves in the drawing are rendered as straight, closed paths.

The good news, however, is that you've still got the fundamental shape of the object you want. Once the objects are in a FreeHand publication, you can do as much—or as little—clean up as you want or have time for.

Working with Images

When I talk about images, I'm referring to files saved as or converted to TIFF. It's just a habit. From FreeHand's point of view, PNG and LRG files are the same as TIFF images. I've never tried to print a FreeHand file containing LRG or PNG images on an imagesetter, so I'm not ready to tell you it's safe. This section, therefore, is primarily about working with TIFF images.

If you remember the difficulty of printing images from FreeHand 2, you should know that image printing has improved dramatically since then. If you're one of those people, you can relax, and start using TIFFs in your publications.

If you prefer separating your color images before final production, or if you prefer another program's separations, you can pre-separate your color images, then save them as CMYK TIFFs or EPS files and import them in FreeHand.

Halftones   Commercial printing equipment can only print one color per printing plate at one time. We can get additional "tints" of that color by filling areas with small dots; at a distance (anything over a foot or so), these dots look like another color. The pattern of dots is called a halftone (for more on digital halftoning and commercial printing, see Chapter 6, "Color").

We use halftones to print the different shades inside photographs. The eye, silly and arbitrary thing that it is, tells our brain that the printed photograph is made up of shades of gray (or color)—not different patterns of large and small dots.

TIFFs, Halftone Screen Frequency, and Resolution   Let me introduce you to the TIFF balancing act. It goes like this: for any printer resolution (in dots per inch, or dpi) there's an ideal halftone screen frequency (in lines per inch, or lpi)—a frequency that gives you the largest number of grays available at that printer resolution. If you go above this screen frequency, you start losing gray levels. To find the line screen that'll give you the largest number of grays for your printer's resolution, use this equation.

number of grays = (printer resolution in dpi/screen ruling in lpi)^2+1

If the number of grays is greater than 256, the number of grays equals 256. Most PostScript printers (any printer not equipped with PostScript 3) have a limit of 256 gray shades at any resolution.

So if you want 256 grays, and your printer resolution is 1270 dpi, the optimum screen ruling would be around 80 lpi.

What if you want to use a higher screen frequency? Something's got to give—and, usually, what gives is resolution. When you print at higher imagesetter resolutions, you can use much higher line screens before you start losing grays.

The next factor in the balancing act is the resolution of your images. It's natural to assume that by scanning at the highest resolution available from your scanner will give you the sharpest images. This bit of common knowledge, however, doesn't hold true for grayscale or color images; for these, scan at no more than twice the screen frequency you intend to use. Higher scanning resolutions do not add any greater sharpness (believe me, I've spent a lot of money printing test files to make *sure* that this is true), but the size of your image files increases dramatically. To determine the size of an image file, use this equation.

file size in kilobytes = (dpi^2 ¥ bit depth ¥ width ¥ height)   8192 (bits in a kilobyte)

Bit depth is eight for an eight-bit image, 24 for an RGB color image, and 32 for a CMYK image.

There's one guy I know who always complains about the size of his TIFF files. He told me the other day about a color magazine cover that took up 60 MB on his hard drive. I think he's overscanning. Here's why—if the size of his image is 8.5 x 11 inches, he's using a 150 lpi screen, and he's working with an RGB image, his file should be 21.4 MB, because 300^2 ¥ 24 ¥ 8.5 ¥ 11   8192 = 24653.3 (divide the result by 1024 to get megabytes). If he's working with a CMYK TIFF, his file size should be 300^2 ¥ 32 ¥ 8.5 ¥ 11   8192 = 32871.1   1024, or 32.1 megabytes—still nowhere near the file size he's griping about.

Ideally, you should scan at the same size as you intend to print the image. Resolution changes when you change the size of the image, so if your scanner won't create an image at the size you want, you can compensate for the effect of scaling the image in FreeHand using this equation.

(original size/printed size) ¥ original (scanning) resolution = resolution

If you'd scanned a three-by-three-inch image at 300 dpi and reduced it to 2.25 inches square (a reduction of 75 percent), the resolution of the image is 400 dpi.

Tip: Scanning Line Art

If you're scanning line art, save the files as bi-level TIFFs rather than as grayscale. You'll save lots of disk space, and your line art TIFFs will be just as sharp as if you saved them as grayscale TIFFs. Also, scan your line art at the highest resolution you can get out of your scanner. Line art, unlike grayscale and color images, benefits from increased resolution, because you're not creating halftones.

Tip: Increasing Line Art Resolution

Sometimes, your scanner can't scan at a high enough resolution to give you a good scan of line art. This is especially true when you're scanning those great, copyright-free engravings from Dover's clip art books. In this case, try this trick, which I stole (with permission) from *Real World Scanning and Halftones* by Steve Roth, Glenn Fleishman and David Blatner (Peachpit Press). This process produces a bi-level image at twice the resolution of your scanner.

1. Scan the image as grayscale at the highest optical resolution your scanner offers.

2. Resample the image to twice its original resolution using Photoshop (or other image editing program).

3. Sharpen the image.

4. Select Threshold from the Adjust submenu of the Image menu. Drag the arrow back and forth to adjust the break point for black and white. Click OK.

5. Convert the image to a bilevel TIFF and save it.

TIFF Controls   When you select an image, FreeHand adds six controls to the Object Inspector: the Edit and Links buttons, Scaling percentage fields, the Image Source pop-up menu, and the Transparent checkbox (see Figure 4-5). Which of these controls are active or inactive depends on the type of image you've selected.

FIGURE 4-5
TIFF controls

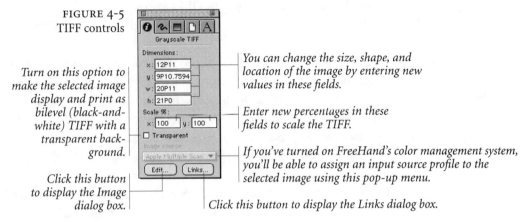

Turn on this option to make the selected image display and print as bilevel (black-and-white) TIFF with a transparent background.

Click this button to display the Image dialog box.

You can change the size, shape, and location of the image by entering new values in these fields.

Enter new percentages in these fields to scale the TIFF.

If you've turned on FreeHand's color management system, you'll be able to assign an input source profile to the selected image using this pop-up menu.

Click this button to display the Links dialog box.

FIGURE 4-6
Making the background of a TIFF transparent

Gray rectangle behind bilevel image.

Paint-type graphics set to Black and White have an opaque background.

Click Transparent, and you'll be able to see through the background.

Scaling percentage fields. To change the width or height of an imported image, enter new scaling percentages in the X (horizontal scaling) or Y (vertical scaling) fields.

Transparent. When you turn on the Transparent option in the Object Inspector, the white areas of a TIFF become transparent (see Figure 4-6). If you choose this option when you've got a grayscale TIFF selected, FreeHand temporarily converts the TIFF to a bilevel

TIFF. Turn the Transparent option off, and all your grayscale information will reappear.

Ordinarily, FreeHand treats the background of a grayscale or bilevel TIFF as an opaque white box the size of the TIFF's selection rectangle. This differs from PageMaker, where bilevel TIFFs are transparent by default, and grayscale TIFFs are opaque by default.

When you select a color TIFF, FreeHand disables this button.

Tip: For Faster Printing, Set Bilevel Images to "Transparent"	Bilevel TIFFs (and paint files) set to Transparent print four times faster than the same images set to Black and White. Why? To make a long story short, it has to do with conformance to the OPI specifications (and isn't really necessary, as I understand it). If you need an opaque background, why not draw a box with an opaque fill behind the transparent image?

Links. Click the Links button to display the Links dialog box, which you use to update or change the link to an imported graphic, or to extract an embedded graphic (see "Linking and Embedding," later in this chapter).

Working with the Image Dialog Box

When you click the Edit Image button in the Object Inspector, FreeHand displays the Image dialog box (see Figure 4-7), where you can change the brightness, contrast, and (in a very rudimentary way) the gray map for the image. When you have a color image selected, FreeHand disables this button.

Lightness and Contrast. The Lightness slider controls the brightness of the entire image. Increase the brightness of the image by clicking the up arrow; decrease the brightness of the image by clicking the down arrow. Note that clicking on the arrow changes the position of the gray slider bars (see Figure 4-8).

If you want to increase the contrast of the image, click the up arrow above Contrast. If you want to decrease the contrast of the image, click the down arrow. As you click on the arrow, the slider bars in the window to the left of Contrast move (see Figure 4-9).

Gray level sliders. Each slider inside the Image dialog box applies to $\frac{1}{16}$ of the gray levels in the image, so each slider in four-bit TIFF

FIGURE 4-7
Image dialog box

The Image dialog box isn't modal; you can drag it out of your way if you need to see an image behind it.

Gray level presets

Click to increase contrast

Click to increase brightness

Click to decrease brightness

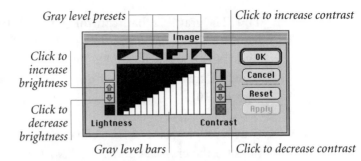

Gray level bars

Click to decrease contrast

The dialog box above is for a grayscale TIFF. If you select a bilevel TIFF or a paint-type graphic, the gray level bars show that there are only two gray levels in the image.

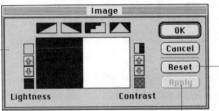

Click the Reset button to reset the image's gray levels to the default gray map (it's the same as clicking the first gray level preset).

If you change the gray level bars, the Apply button becomes active. Click it to apply your changes to the image. By clicking the Apply button, you can see your changes without closing the Image dialog box.

FIGURE 4-8
Changing lightness

Default lightness

Image darkened by pressing on the down arrow in the Lightness control

FIGURE 4-9
Changing contrast

Default contrast

Increased contrast

equals one gray level (there are 16 possible gray levels in a four-bit TIFF); each slider in an eight-bit TIFF represents 16 adjacent gray levels, because there are 256 possible gray levels in an eight-bit

TIFF. The gray level bars control gray levels from the darkest to the lightest in your image as they go from left to right. Slide a gray level bar up to increase the lightness of all the pixels with that group of gray levels; slide it down to decrease their lightness (see Figure 4-10).

Gray level presets. The Image dialog box contains four default settings for the grayscale slider bars: Normal, Negative, Posterize, and Solarize (see Figure 4-11). Clicking the Normal icon returns the image control settings for the TIFF to the position they were in when the TIFF was first imported. Clicking the Negative icon inverts all the grayscale slider bar settings from their Normal setting. Posterize maps all the gray levels in the TIFF to four gray levels. Solarize maps all the gray levels to a kind of bell curve. This produces an effect similar to the photographic effect "solarization," which is produced by exposing photographic film to light before developing the film.

FIGURE 4-10
Working with
gray level bars

Default gray levels   *You can adjust individual gray bars until you've achieved the effect you want.*

FIGURE 4-11
Gray level presets

Normal   *Negative*   *Posterize*   *Solarize*

Reset. Click the Reset button to undo any changes you've made in the Image dialog. Clicking Reset returns the gray bars to their default position—the "normal" ramp.

Apply. Click the Apply button to see what the changes you've made in the Image dialog box look like without having to close the Image dialog box (remember, you can drag the dialog box around to get a better look at the TIFF).

Resizing Images to Your Printer's Resolution

Paint-type images and bilevel TIFFs often use regular patterns of pixels to represent gray areas. You can see these patterns of black and white pixels in the scroll bars in many applications. You'll also see them if you're scanning and saving images as "halftones" from most popular scanner software (see Figure 4-12).

When you print graphics containing these patterns, you'll often get moiré patterns in the patterned areas (see Figure 4-13).

FIGURE 4-12
Pixel patterns
representing grays

Paint-type graphics and bilevel TIFFs often use patterns of black and white pixels to represent grays.

FIGURE 4-13
Moiré patterns

Moiré patterns

This pattern, ugly though it is, is what you're hoping to see.

Not resized to printer resolution

Resized to match printer resolution

Purists will argue that these aren't true moiré patterns, and state that moiré patterns are created by the mismatch of two (or more) overlapping screens. While it's true we have only one overlay, we nevertheless have two overlapping, mismatching screens—the resolution of the image and the resolution of the printer. Both are matrices of pixels.

When the resolution of the image you're trying to print and the resolution of the printer don't have an integral relationship (that is, when the printer resolution divided by the image resolution equals something other than a whole number), some rounding is going to have to occur, because your printer can't render fractional dots. When this happens, parts of pixels get cut off or added to make up the difference (see Figure 4-14).

FIGURE 4-14
Integral and non-
integral resolutions

Your printer can't print fractional dots—they're either on or off.

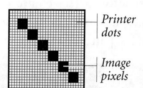

— Printer dots

— Image pixels

When image pixels and printer dots have an integral relationship (4:1 in this example), everything's fine.

When image pixels don't match the printer's resolution, it has to guess which printer dots it should turn on or off...

...which distorts the image.

Instead of figuring out the scaling percentages for each bilevel image you're working with, take advantage of FreeHand's "magic stretch" feature, which resizes images to match the resolution of your target printer.

Hold down Option/Alt as you resize an image and the image snaps to sizes that have an integral relationship with the selected printer resolution. Hold down Shift and Option/Alt as you size the graphic both to size the graphic proportionally and to match the printer's resolution (see Figure 4-15).

Where do you set the printer's resolution? Enter a value in the Printer Resolution field in the Document Inspector that matches the resolution of the printer you'll be use for the *final* printing of the publication (not the resolution of your proof printer).

The value you enter in the Printer Resolution field does not affect the actual resolution of your printer; it's just there to give

FreeHand a value to use when calculating magic stretch sizes (and the default number of steps to use in blends).

Magic stretching doesn't improve the printing of grayscale or color TIFFs—even though they'll snap to the same sizes—and it doesn't have any effect on object-PICT or EPS graphics.

FIGURE 4-15
Magic-stretching
an image

 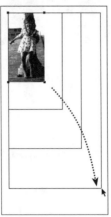 

Point at a corner of an image, hold down Option-Shift/Alt-Shift…   *…and drag. The image snaps to possible sizes as you drag.*   *When you've reached the size you want, stop dragging.*

Cropping TIFF Images

If you're used to PageMaker's Cropping tool, and are looking for a similar tool in FreeHand, you're out of luck—there isn't one. Instead, however, you can use FreeHand's Paste Inside feature to crop your image. It's better than the Cropping tool anyway. When you want to use just part of a TIFF image in your FreeHand publication, try this (see Figure 4-16).

1. Size the TIFF to the size you want.

2. Draw a path around the part of the TIFF you want to use.

3. Select the TIFF and press Command-X/Ctrl-X.

4. Select the path and press Command-Shift-V/Ctrl-Shift-V (or choose Paste Inside from the Edit menu). FreeHand pastes the TIFF inside the path.

While I'm on the topic of cropping images, I should mention that it's better to create your images in your scanning or image-editing software so that you don't have to crop. When you crop an

FIGURE 4-16
Cropping a TIFF

Draw a path around the area you want to crop.

Cut the TIFF image to the Clipboard, then select the path and paste the image inside the path.

image, the parts of the TIFF you can't see don't just go away; Free-Hand still has to keep track of the entire TIFF, which means slower screen redraw and printing.

Tip:
Adjusting
Cropping

If you just need to make a minor adjustment to the way you've cropped a TIFF, try this (see Figure 4-17).

1. Select the cropped TIFF.

2. Press Command-M/Ctrl-M to display the Transform palette, if it's not already visible. If the Move panel of the Transform palette isn't already visible, click the Move icon to display it.

3. Uncheck Contents, then drag the path (or move the path using the X and Y fields in the Transform palette). Free-Hand moves the clipping path without changing the position of the TIFF inside the clipping path.

Creating an Outline Mask for a TIFF Image

Something that people often miss when they think about cropping images in FreeHand is that the path you're using to crop the image can be any size or shape. You can paste TIFFs inside ellipses, characters, or totally freeform paths. This comes in handy when you've got to pull a particular object out of an imported TIFF file. Trace the part of the TIFF you want, cut the TIFF to the Clipboard, and paste it inside the shape you've just drawn (see Figure 4-18).

If you're working with an image that's surrounded by a large white area, use the Trace tool (see Figure 4-19).

FIGURE 4-17
Adjusting cropping

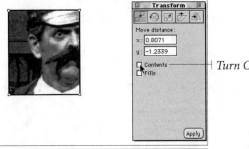

Turn Contents off.

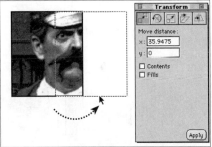

Drag the path to a new location.

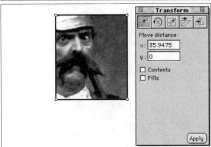

FreeHand moves the path, but leaves the path's contents in their original position. To move the path back to its original position, turn Contents on again, so that the TIFF moves with the path.

FIGURE 4-18
Creating an outline mask

In this example, I've sent the image on the left to the background. FreeHand lightens the image, making it easier to trace. The image on the right has been moved back to a foreground layer.

Draw a path around parts of the image.

Paste the image into the path. You can adjust the points on the path to change the cropping of the image.

FIGURE 4-19
Another way to create
an outline mask

*To remove the white
background of this
imported image...*

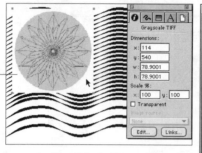
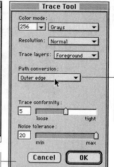

*Choose Outer
Edge from the
Path conversion
pop-up menu.*

*...double-click the Trace tool in the
Toolbox. FreeHand displays the Trace
Tool dialog box.*

*Drag the Trace tool
around the image (in
this example, I've
hidden the layer
containing the back-
ground objects).*

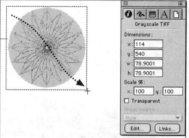
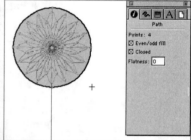

*FreeHand creates a path that (usually)
follows the outline of the shape.*

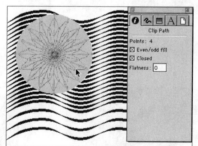

*At this point, you can paste
the image into the path you've
created (in the example, I've
made the background objects
visible again).*

1. Double-click the Trace tool to display the Trace Tool
   dialog box.

2. Set the Color Mode to approximate the range of colors
   in the image.

3. Set the Path Conversion method to "Outer Edge."

4. Click OK to close the Trace Tool dialog box.

5. Drag the Trace tool around the image.

Voilà! Instant outline mask. Note that you can adjust the cropping by dragging individual points on the clipping path to get it just right, and that you can stroke the path to trap the image if you need to (for more on trapping images, see Chapter 6, "Color").

Preseparating Color Images

If you prefer, you can use another program—Adobe Photoshop comes to mind—to create color separations of images. Save the separated image as either an EPS or as a CMYK TIFF, and you'll be able to import it into FreeHand. When you print your publication, FreeHand sends the color separations of the image to the printer. In a way, FreeHand isn't really creating color separations of the image—it's just passing along the separations stored in the file.

As you can see from Color Figure 10, you shouldn't assume that a color separation created by another program will always be superior to the separations created by FreeHand. As long as you have FreeHand's color management system turned on (and turned on for the image, as well), and have set up your color management profiles to match your input and output devices, you can get good results. In previous versions of FreeHand, this wasn't the case. See Chapter 6, "Color," for more on color management.

EPS files created by Photoshop (or other applications) contain all the information needed to print color separations of an image. DCS is a variation of the EPS format, and exists in (at least) two versions. DCS1 files store the color-separated image as five separate files (one for each color, plus a "header" file that's the part you work with). DCS2 files generally contain all of the separations in a single file (although they, too, can be split into multiple files). When you choose any of the DCS options in Photoshop's EPS Format dialog box, Photoshop creates five files.

CMYK TIFFs contain the separated image data, but don't contain any halftoning information from the application that created the separations. In most cases, in my opinion, that's fine.

Here's how you'd separate an image using Adobe Photoshop.

1. In Photoshop, make sure that your separation settings are the way you want them. Switch to CMYK mode, and Photoshop separates the image according to the settings in the Separation Setup dialog box.

2. Choose Save As. In the Save As dialog box, choose "EPS" or "TIFF" from the Format pop-up menu. Click the Save button. If you selected "EPS," the EPS Format dialog box appears. If you chose "TIFF," the TIFF Options dialog box appears.

3. In the EPS Format dialog box (see Figure 4-20), choose a screen preview from the Preview pop-up menu.

   Choose either "ASCII" or "Binary" from the Encoding pop-up menu (binary files are smaller, but Windows users should choose ASCII if they plan to print through a serial cable, rather than over a network). Don't choose any of the JPEG options—FreeHand can't print separations of JPEG images stored inside an EPS.

   Turn on the Include Halftone Screens option if you want to include Photoshop's screening in the EPS. In my opinion, you should turn off the Include Transfer Functions option—transfer functions differ from printer to printer, so it's better to use a transfer function calibrated to an individual printer.

FIGURE 4-20
Photoshop
EPS options

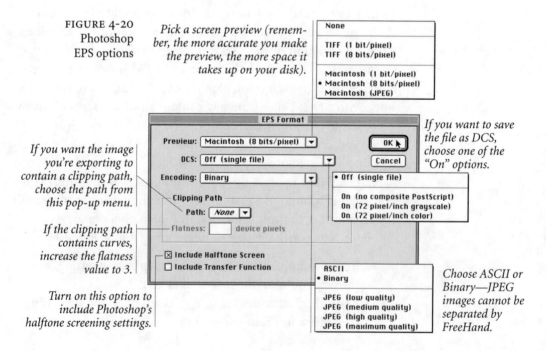

Pick a screen preview (remember, the more accurate you make the preview, the more space it takes up on your disk).

None

TIFF (1 bit/pixel)
TIFF (8 bits/pixel)

Macintosh (1 bit/pixel)
• Macintosh (8 bits/pixel)
Macintosh (JPEG)

If you want the image you're exporting to contain a clipping path, choose the path from this pop-up menu.

If the clipping path contains curves, increase the flatness value to 3.

Turn on this option to include Photoshop's halftone screening settings.

EPS Format

Preview: Macintosh (8 bits/pixel) ▼
DCS: Off (single file) ▼
Encoding: Binary ▼

Clipping Path
Path: None ▼

Flatness: ___ device pixels

☒ Include Halftone Screen
☐ Include Transfer Function

OK
Cancel

If you want to save the file as DCS, choose one of the "On" options.

• Off (single file)

On (no composite PostScript)
On (72 pixel/inch grayscale)
On (72 pixel/inch color)

ASCII
• Binary

JPEG (low quality)
JPEG (medium quality)
JPEG (high quality)
JPEG (maximum quality)

Choose ASCII or Binary—JPEG images cannot be separated by FreeHand.

Choose one of the Desktop Color Separation options from the DCS menu (other than "Off," of course) if you want to use the DCS method of storing the image. The options on the DCS pop-up menu have to do with the preview image saved in the "master" file. Choose "On (no composite PostScript)" to omit the preview, "On (72 pixel/inch grayscale)" for a grayscale preview, or "On (72 pixel/inch color)" to save a color preview image.

If you've used a clipping path in the image, choose the path's name from the Path pop-up menu. If the clipping path contains curves, increase value in the Flatness field to make the image print faster (see "Thinking Like a Line," in Chapter 2, "Drawing"). You don't need to enter a large number—I usually enter "3."

If you're saving your file as a TIFF, you've got fewer options to worry about (see Figure 4-21). Choose the Macintosh or MS-DOS option for the TIFF's image data (choose the option that matches the platform on which you'll be using the image). Check the LZW Compression option if you want to compress the TIFF as you save it. (FreeHand has no trouble with LZW-compressed TIFFs from Photoshop.)

4. Press Return to save the image.

FIGURE 4-21
Photoshop
TIFF options

Running Photoshop Plug-Ins

You can apply Photoshop plug-ins (also known as filters) to images in your publication. FreeHand can't run *all* Photoshop filters— the Unsharp Mask filter, for example, isn't supported (which is a pity, because it's the most important one), but most of the special effects filters, such as the wildly popular Page Curl plug-in from Kai's Power Tools, work well.

How do you use the Photoshop plug-ins? First, you've got to set them up. On the Macintosh, move or copy the plug-in, or (better yet), an alias of the plug-in from your Photoshop Plug-Ins folder to the Xtras folder inside the Macromedia folder in your System folder. In Windows, copy the plug-in to ~/Program Files/Common Files/Macromedia/Xtras. Restart FreeHand, and you'll see Photoshop plug-ins on the submenus of the Xtra menu. When a filter is intended for use on bitmap images, FreeHand adds "[TIFF]" to the plug-in's name on the menu.

To apply a Photoshop filter to an image, follow these steps (see Figure 4-22).

1. Select the image.

2 Choose one of the plug-ins from the Xtras submenus.

    Some plug-ins simply run, some display a dialog box. If the plug-in you've chosen does display a dialog box, adjust the dialog box controls, then click the OK (or whatever—it varies from plug-in to plug-in) button to apply the effect.

Running Photoshop plug-ins on images in FreeHand requires lots of RAM. On the Macintosh, you can make more RAM available by increasing FreeHand's RAM allocation (quit FreeHand; then, in the Finder, select the FreeHand application icon and press Command-I, then enter a larger value in the Preferred Size field), then restart FreeHand and try again. In Windows, you can free system resources by closing other applications and windows, or increase the amount of space you're using as virtual memory.

After you've run a Photoshop plug-in, you can repeat the effect on any other image you select by pressing Command-Shift-+/Ctrl-Alt-Shift-X (or by choosing Repeat *plug-in name* from the top of the Xtras menu).

When you run a Photoshop filter on an image that's linked to an external file (rather than embedded in the FreeHand publication, FreeHand creates a copy of the image, embeds it in the publication, and applies the filter to the copy of the image. If you want to store the image externally, you can extract the image, then link to the new file (see "Extracting Embedded Images," later in this Chapter).

FIGURE 4-22
Applying a Photoshop
Filter to an Image

Select an image.

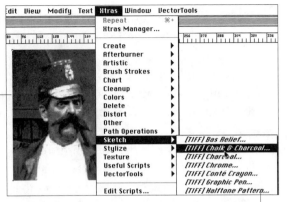

Choose a Photoshop filter from the Xtras menu.
Note FreeHand adds "[TIFF]" before the names of
filters that work on images.

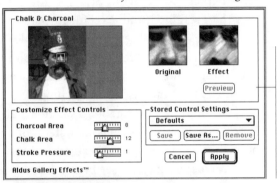

Make any changes
you want in the
filter's dialog box (if
it has one). In this
example, I've used a
plug-in from the
Adobe (my package
still says "Aldus")
Gallery Effects
package.

FreeHand applies
the effect to the
selected image.

Note: When you run a
Photoshop filter on an image
that's linked to your publication, FreeHand embeds an
altered copy of the image in
the publication. This increases
the size of the publication. If
you want to store the image
externally, use FreeHand's
"Extract" feature.

Tip:
Why Don't I See
All My Plug-Ins?

Some of Photoshop's plug-ins don't work in FreeHand—some, in
fact, make FreeHand crash. To see a list of incompatible plug-ins
on the Macintosh, take a look at the file named Disabled Plug-Ins
in the Xtras folder inside the Macromedia folder in your Preferences
folder (which is inside your System folder). In Windows, you'll find
the file in ~/Program Files/Common/Macromedia/Xtras—it's named
"dsbl_plg."

If you see a plug-in on this list that you've just *got* to use, and have installed the plug-in (or its alias) in your Xtras folder, you can try running it (don't say you weren't warned). Delete the plug-in's name from the list, then save the file (make sure you save the file as text-only). When you restart FreeHand, you'll see the plug-in on the Xtras menu. Select an image and give it a try.

Launching External Editors

FreeHand can't edit the content of images you've imported, but it does make it easier to open the images in a program capable of editing them. First, however, you've got to let FreeHand know which program you want to use. To do this, use the External Editors section of the Object Preferences dialog box (see "Object Preferences," in Chapter 1, "FreeHand Basics"). You can define external editors for the TIFF, LRG, and PNG file formats.

If you want to keep from accidentally launching external editors (a problem in FreeHand 7), turn on the Warn Before Launch and Edit option in the Object Preferences dialog box. When you do this, FreeHand displays a warning before switching to an external editor. It's annoying, but it's better than having FreeHand start another program or scan your system for appropriate editors.

Once you've defined an external editor (or editors) for images, you can use a shortcut (see Figure 4-23). Select the image you want to edit and choose External Editor from the Edit menu, or hold down Option/Alt and double-click the image. If you have enough RAM available to do so, FreeHand starts the application you defined as the editor for the selected type of image, then opens the image in that application. FreeHand then displays the Editing in Progress dialog box. Make any changes you want in the image editing application, then save the image. Return to FreeHand, and click the Done button in the Editing in Progress dialog box. FreeHand updates the image in your publication.

Importing EPS Graphics

If you work with other programs that can export files as EPS, or if you write your own PostScript programs, you can import those files into FreeHand and combine them with text and graphics you've

FIGURE 4-23
Using an
External Editor

*After you've defined an
external image editor
(for TIFF or LRG
images) using the
External Editors control
in the Object Editing
Preferences dialog box,
you can use an image
editing shortcut.*

*Hold down Option/Alt and
double-click an image…*

*…FreeHand opens the image in the external
editor you defined (Photoshop, in this example).*

Edit the image.

*In this example, I'm
applying a Photoshop
filter to the image
(imagine that I tried to
run the filter in
FreeHand, but ran out
of RAM).*

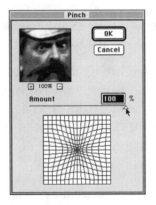

*Save the Edited version of the image,
then return to FreeHand.*

*If you've double-clicked
a graphic you've
embedded in the
publication, FreeHand
makes the Cancel
button active. If you
click the Cancel button,
FreeHand leaves the
original image in your
publication.*

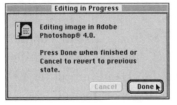

*Click the Done button to update
the image. If you've selected an
embedded image, FreeHand
embeds the edited version of the
image in your publication. If not,
FreeHand links to the new file on
disk.*

Edited image, back in FreeHand.

created in FreeHand. You have the choice of placing EPS files as imported graphics or—with some EPS formats—converting the graphic into FreeHand objects.

What happens when you import an EPS? That depends on the EPS, and on the Convert Editable EPS When Imported option in the Import/Export Preferences dialog box (see "Import Preferences" in Chapter 1, "FreeHand Basics").

◆ If the EPS is a format that FreeHand can convert (FreeHand or Illustrator), *and* the Convert Editable EPS When Imported option is turned on, FreeHand converts the objects in the imported EPS into editable FreeHand elements.

◆ If FreeHand can't convert the EPS format, or if the Convert Editable EPS When Imported option is turned off, FreeHand imports the EPS as a graphic. In this case, you won't be able to edit the content of the EPS.

Another preference setting, the Embed Images and EPS upon Import option in the Expert Import/Export Preferences dialog box, controls whether FreeHand links to external EPS files, or whether those EPS files are embedded in the FreeHand publication. See "Linking and Embedding," later in this chapter. Here are a couple things to keep in mind, however.

◆ If both the Embed Images and EPS upon Import option and the Convert Editable EPS When Imported option are turned on, FreeHand converts the objects in an editable EPS to FreeHand objects when you import the file.

◆ If the Embed Images and EPS upon Import option is turned on and the Convert Editable EPS When Imported option is turned off, FreeHand embeds the EPS in your publication file when you import the file.

If You See an "X" Instead of a Graphic

When you import an EPS graphic (and you're not in Keyline mode), if you see a box with an "X" through it instead of a screen preview, you've imported a file that doesn't have a screen preview attached. The file contains the dimensions of the graphic, and it'll probably print correctly, but there's nothing for you to look at as you lay out your page. This happens in these scenarios.

♦ There's not enough memory to display the preview. On the Macintosh, you can increase the amount of memory you've allocated to FreeHand, or close some publications. In Windows, try quitting other programs or closing windows to free some of your system resources.

♦ There was too little memory available to create the screen preview when FreeHand (or other application) created the EPS file. If you're placing a FreeHand EPS, think again: wouldn't it be better to paste that graphic into the current publication instead of placing it?

♦ The graphic has no screen preview attached. This happens if the file is a PostScript program written by an application that doesn't support preview images, or if the file was created using a word processor, or if the person creating the EPS saved it without a screen preview. This also happens if you've edited a normal EPS with a word processor and have not reattached the screen preview PICT. See "Converting FreeHand 3 EPS Files to Illustrator 1.1 EPS Format" below on editing old EPS graphics with a word processor.

♦ The graphic is an EPS, hasn't been converted to FreeHand objects, and you've transformed (scaled, skewed, or rotated) it. In this case, FreeHand can't create a new screen preview image for the graphic.

If you can't get by without a screen preview, see the section "Working with PDF," later in this chapter.

Importing FreeHand EPS

If you've turned off the Convert Editable EPS When Imported option in the Import/Export Preferences dialog box, placing a Free-Hand EPS in a FreeHand publication is a silly thing to do. Think about it—why do you want to import FreeHand objects in a state that you can't edit? Instead, either turn on the Convert Editable EPS When Imported option and imports the EPS, or, better yet, paste the FreeHand elements from another FreeHand publication.

There's more to it than editing—a FreeHand EPS includes the PostScript code needed to print the EPS correctly *outside* of FreeHand. This EPS information makes the file take longer to print when you're printing from *inside* FreeHand (see Figure 4-24).

To make sure this doesn't happen to you, turn on the Convert Editable EPS When Imported option in the Import Preferences dialog box (see "Import Preferences" in Chapter 1, "FreeHand Basics").

If you're placing the EPS because you want to deal with the elements as a single object, why not group them?

FIGURE 4-24
Importing FreeHand
EPS versus pasting
FreeHand objects

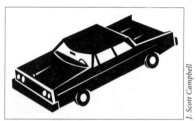

J. Scott Campbell

FreeHand EPS imported into a FreeHand publication without conversion. Processing time: 34 seconds.

FreeHand elements pasted from one publication to another. Processing time: two seconds.

Importing Illustrator EPS

If I had to choose between FreeHand and Illustrator, I'd pick FreeHand. In fact, I don't use Illustrator much these days, though it's an excellent program. But I do know lots of people who swear by Illustrator, and I know even more people who strongly prefer using both. Luckily, the path from Illustrator to FreeHand is clear. FreeHand can open or import EPS files created by Illustrator (all versions through 7.0, at the time of this writing).

When you open an Illustrator EPS, FreeHand converts the paths and type into FreeHand elements. If you import an Illustrator EPS without converting it, FreeHand displays the screen-preview image (if there is one) and treats the file as an imported graphic—you can transform it, but you can't edit its contents.

When you open an Illustrator EPS, some of Illustrator's features are converted; some aren't.

Paths. FreeHand imports paths in Illustrator EPSes just as they were drawn in Illustrator. FreeHand converts Illustrator points into curve points whenever possible, though points defining sharp angles or sudden changes of curve direction are converted into corner points. As points are converted, FreeHand adds handles to each converted point so that the path matches the path you drew in Illustrator.

Text. FreeHand converts Illustrator text into FreeHand text blocks. Typically, the Illustrator text is converted one line at a time, though any changes in type style or font will create new text blocks, as will any kerning (including automatic kerning pairs). If the EPS was saved in the Illustrator 1.1 format, each line of text will be an individual text block.

Color. Process colors you've defined in Illustrator are imported as you defined them, but the color names don't appear in your Colors palette. To add colors from a converted Illustrator file to your Colors palette, follow the steps described in "Adding Colors from Illustrator" in Chapter 6, "Color."

Blends. Illustrator blends are often made up of separate objects, so you can't change the blend once you've imported it except by deleting the intermediate blend steps and blending again.

Complex Paths. Compound paths created in Illustrator using the Make Compound command are converted to FreeHand's composite paths. ("Composite path" and "compound path" are just two ways of saying the same thing.)

Creating Your Own EPS Graphics

You can create EPS graphics using a word processor or text editor, but you've got to remember two things.

◆ Test the file before you import it. If it doesn't print when you download it to your printer, it won't print after you've imported it into FreeHand. Always test every change you make in your word processor by downloading the text file to the printer and seeing what you get before you bring the file into FreeHand, or at least before you take the FreeHand file to a service bureau.

◆ If you use a word processor to edit an EPS graphic you created using a drawing program on the Macintosh, you (usually) break the link between the PostScript text part of the EPS and the screen preview PICT resource (so you'll lose the preview).

Why would you want to create your own EPS graphics? There are lots of things you can do with PostScript that FreeHand doesn't do (yet). And it's fun. See Chapter 8, "PostScript," for more on the topic (and some examples).

Creating Invisible EPS Graphics (Macintosh Only)

I often want to use full-page EPS backgrounds but I can't stand waiting for the background's screen preview to redraw every time I do something. In FreeHand, of course, the easiest thing to do is to set the layer the background's on to be invisible. But if you're creating a FreeHand EPS background to place in some (other) page-layout program, you need this trick (see Figure 4-25).

FIGURE 4-25
Creating an invisible
EPS graphic

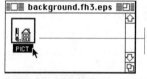

Locate and open the EPS file using ResEdit.

Once the file's open, double-click on the PICT resource class icon.

ResEdit displays the EPS file's screen-preview image. Select the image and press Delete.

Press Command-K to create a new PICT resource.

Press Command-I to display the Info dialog box. Type "256" in the ID field.

Press Command-S to save your work, and quit ResEdit.

When you place the EPS file, you won't see the screen preview, but it'll print just as it did before.

1. Open the EPS file with ResEdit or Resourcerer.

2. Open the PICT resource class and select the single resource you'll find inside.

3. Choose Clear from the Edit menu.

4. Press Command-K to create a new PICT resource.

5. Make sure that the new PICT has a resource ID of 256 by pressing Command-I and typing 256 in the ID field in the Info window that appears.

6. Press Command-S to save the file, and quit ResEdit.

Now, when you place the edited EPS file, you'll get a transparent bounding box that's the size of the graphic, but no screen preview will appear—so it won't take any time to display the preview image (because there isn't one). When you print, you'll see the graphic.

Linking and Embedding

In FreeHand, you can choose to embed (that is, store) imported graphics in your FreeHand publication, or you can choose to store them externally and link to them. When you link to a graphic, FreeHand creates a low resolution screen preview of the graphic, and uses that preview to draw the image on your page.

When you print, FreeHand includes data from linked graphics in the stream of PostScript it's sending to your printer or to disk. This means that you need to take any linked graphics with you when you want to print your publication at an imagesetting service bureau.

If you've turned on the High Resolution TIFF Display option in the Redraw Preferences dialog box, FreeHand refers to the external TIFF files when you change your view of the imported graphic, using image data in the file to give you a better view of the image.

Which method should you use? It's up to you. When you embed graphics, your publication size increases, but you don't have to keep track of the original files. When you link to externally-stored graphics, your publications will be smaller, but you'll have to keep track of more than one file.

In some cases, FreeHand automatically embeds graphics in your publications.

◆ If you turn on the Embed Images and EPS upon Import option in the Import/Export Preferences dialog box, FreeHand always embeds TIFF and EPS graphics you place. If you've turned on the Convert Editable EPS When Imported option in the Import/Export Preferences dialog box, editable EPSes are converted to FreeHand objects when you place them—EPSes in formats that can't be edited are embedded.

◆ If you apply a Photoshop filter to a linked image, FreeHand embeds an altered copy of the image in your publication.

◆ If you import an image file saved in any format other than TIFF, LRG, or PNG, FreeHand converts the image to a TIFF and embeds it in your FreeHand publication.

◆ If you open a Photoshop file, FreeHand converts the image to a TIFF and embeds the TIFF in your publication.

When you select an imported graphic and display the Object Inspector, you'll see the Links button at the bottom of the Inspector. Click the Links button, and FreeHand checks the status of each file in the publication (is the file stored internally or externally? is the file still around? has it been modified recently?). After checking on the status of the imported files, FreeHand displays the Links dialog box (see Figure 4-26). To export an embedded graphic, click the Extract button. FreeHand exports the graphic to a disk file (you'll be prompted to enter a file name after you click the button). To embed a file you've linked to, select the graphic in the list and click the Embed button. Click the Change button to display the Set Link dialog box to update or change the link (see Figure 4-27).

To replace an imported graphic with another file, follow these steps (see Figure 4-28).

1. Select the graphic.

2. Display the Object Inspector (press Command-I/Ctrl-I).

FIGURE 4-26
Links dialog box

FreeHand displays information about the linked and embedded imported files in this list.

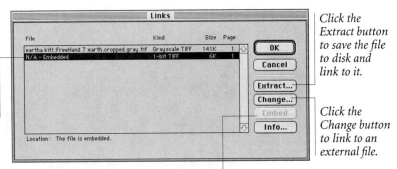

Click the Extract button to save the file to disk and link to it.

Click the Change button to link to an external file.

If you've selected a linked graphic, FreeHand makes the Embed button active—click it to embed the graphic in your publication.

FIGURE 4-27
Set Link dialog box

When you click the Change button in the Links dialog box, FreeHand displays the Set Link dialog box.

Select a file to change the link, or select the same file, then click the Open button to update the link.

3. Click the Links button at the bottom of the Object Inspector. FreeHand displays the Links dialog box.

4. Click the Change button. FreeHand displays the Set Link dialog box (well—that's what I call it—it beats saying "Select a File to Change the Link dialog box").

5. Select the file you want to link to and press Return (or click the OK button). FreeHand replaces the selected graphic with the file you selected. Adjust the size and position of the graphic so that it matches the original, if necessary.

To embed a linked graphic, follow these steps (see Figure 4-29).

1. Select the graphic.

2. Display the Object Inspector (press Command-I/Ctrl-I).

FIGURE 4-28
Replacing a graphic

Select the graphic you want to replace.

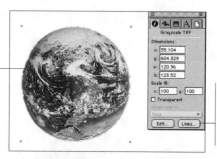

Click the Links button in the Object Inspector (if the Object Inspector isn't currently visible, press Command-I/Ctrl-I to display it).

FreeHand displays the Links dialog box, and selects the name of the graphic you selected in the list of imported files.

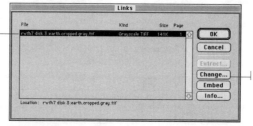

Click the Change button.

FreeHand displays the Set Link dialog box.

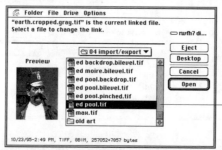

Select the file you want to use to replace the original graphic, then click the Open button.

FreeHand imports the file you selected. The new file's name replaces the name of the file you originally selected in the list of imported files.

Click the OK button.

FreeHand replaces the graphic.

FIGURE 4-29
Embedding a graphic

*Select the graphic you
want to embed.*

*Display the Object Inspector,
if it isn't already visible, by
pressing Command-I/Ctrl-I.*

Click the Links button.

*FreeHand displays a file
name here to let you
know that this graphic
is stored outside the
publication (it's
"linked").*

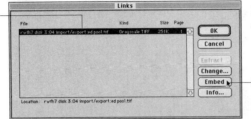

*FreeHand displays the
Links dialog box.*

Click the Embed button.

*FreeHand embeds the
graphic in the publica-
tion. The graphic won't
look any different, but
it's now stored inside
the publication.*

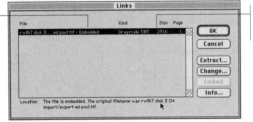

*The size of the publication
(on disk) has just increased
by this amount.*

3. Click the Links button at the bottom of the Object Inspector. FreeHand displays the Links dialog box.

4 Click the Embed button. FreeHand embeds the file.

Because FreeHand can embed graphics in its publications, you
also need to have a way to get them *out* again. In FreeHand, you
can export, or "extract" graphics embedded in FreeHand publications. This is a good thing because, as you'll recall, FreeHand often
embeds graphics without asking (see "Linking and Embedding,"
earlier in this chapter).

To extract an embedded graphics file, follow these steps (see
Figure 4-30).

1. Select the embedded graphic.

2. Display the Object Inspector (press Command-I/Ctrl-I) and
   click the Links button at the bottom of the Inspector.
   FreeHand displays the Links dialog box.

FIGURE 4-30
Extracting an
embedded graphic

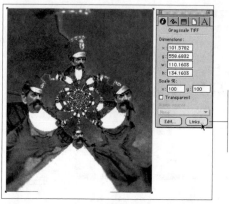

*If you've applied a
Photoshop filter (in
this example, the KPT
Vortex Tiling plug-in)
to a TIFF, FreeHand
embeds a copy of the
image in your
publication, then runs
the filter on the copy.*

*To extract the
image, select it,
display the Object
Inspector, and click
the Links button.*

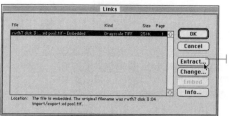

*FreeHand displays the
Links dialog box.*

Click the Extract button.

*FreeHand displays the
Extract dialog box.*

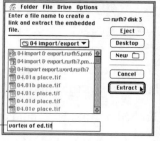

*Select a volume and
folder, then type a
filename for your
extracted file.*

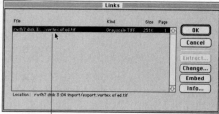

*The image is now stored outside
the publication.*

3. Click the Extract button. FreeHand displays the Extract dialog box (this is what I call it—its given name is "Enter a File Name to Create a Link and Extract the Embedded Graphic").

4. Enter a name for your file, then click the OK button to extract the embedded graphic. FreeHand exports the graphic, then links to the graphic file on disk.

Managing Linked Files

When you link to a TIFF or EPS file, FreeHand doesn't include the file in your publication, but establishes a link between the publication and the imported file. Linking means you don't have to store two copies of the original file—one on disk, and one in your Free-Hand publication—thereby saving disk space.

When you move a linked file, or change its name (including any changes you might make to the name of the folder you've stored it in—or the volume you've stored it on), you break the link between the file and any FreeHand publication you've placed it in. You can also break the link when you move the publication file to another volume.

When you do this, FreeHand displays a box where the linked graphic would appear in your publication (see Figure 4-31). Don't worry—FreeHand maintains the link information. This means you can still link the file, once you find it.

Losing links

When you move, delete, or rename a linked file, FreeHand displays a box where the file appeared in your publication.

 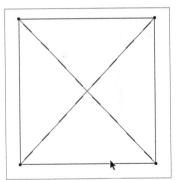

If FreeHand can't find a linked file when you're opening a publication, it looks in the folder containing the illustration for the linked file. If FreeHand can't find the linked file there, it displays the Locate File dialog box (see Figure 4-32). Use the Locate File dialog box to locate and link to the file.

If you can't find the original file, you can close the Locate File dialog box without linking to a file. Locate the original file, and put it inside the same folder as the publication, and FreeHand updates the link (unless you're in keyline mode, you'll see the image replace the placeholder in the publication window).

FIGURE 4-32
Locate File dialog box

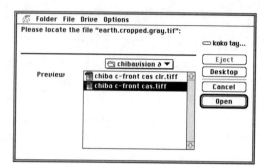

| Folder | File | Drive | Options |

Please locate the file "earth.cropped.gray.tif":

koko tay...

chibavision ∂ ▼

Preview

chiba c-front cas clr.tiff
chiba c-front cas.tiff

Eject
Desktop
Cancel
Open

Tip:
Losing Links
on Purpose

I work on my FreeHand documents at my office and at home. When I need to work on a FreeHand publication at home, I often leave linked TIFF images behind, and take home only the FreeHand file. This means that I can still work on any text or paths in the file, but don't have to carry the TIFF files around (also, working with TIFFs on my slow home machine is pretty painful). I can even change the position and size of the TIFF placeholders. When I open the file back at my office, FreeHand re-links to the TIFFs.

Importing Text

After I'd finished producing the documentation for FreeHand 2 at Aldus, FreeHand's product manager asked me what one feature I'd like to see in FreeHand 3. "Give me a Text Place Gun," I said. In FreeHand 4, I finally got my wish (though I doubt it had much to do with my request). These days, in FreeHand, you can import, format, and edit both formatted (RTF) and unformatted (text-only) text files.

Importing
Text-Only Files

Word-processing programs, databases, spreadsheets, and almost all other applications speak one common language—they can all save their documents as text-only, or ASCII files. Text-only files don't include any formatting information—no font, size, leading, or paragraph spacing—they're just characters.

Sometimes you want to save files as text-only to strip out any formatting that's been applied to them (usually because the person who entered the text applied formatting you don't want). Sometimes text-only is the only kind of file an application can write.

Either way, you can import the text files into FreeHand and format them there.

The only real trick to working with text files has do with where they came from. Often, text files generated by applications on platforms other than your own (MS-DOS machines, Sun Workstations, and NeXT machines), or from on-line services, are full of weird characters, or, most often, have carriage returns at the end of every line in a paragraph. Sometimes, you need to run these text files through a conversion utility—or a word processor—before you import them into FreeHand.

Tip:
Inserting Text
into an Existing
Text Block

When you're placing a text file in FreeHand, you can't choose to insert the text into an existing text block (unlike PageMaker, where you have the option of either inserting the incoming text in existing text, or of replacing the existing text with the incoming text). So you have to place the text, then copy text out of the new text block and paste it into the original text block. The following steps show you the least-painful method I've come up with for doing this (see Figure 4-33).

FIGURE 4-33
Inserting text in an
existing text block

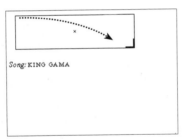

Drag-place the text.

Cut the text to the Clipboard.

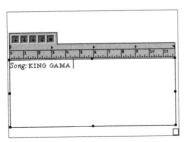

Click the text tool where you want to insert the text.

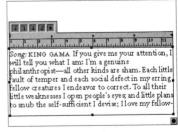

Paste the text into the story.

1. Drag-place the text file in your FreeHand publication (drag-placing means you can keep the text block small). After you place the file, FreeHand selects the new text block.

2. Press Command-X/Ctrl-X to cut the text.

3. Click the Text tool where you want to insert the text, or, if you want to replace all the text in a story, triple-click one of the text blocks in that story with the Pointer tool.

4. Press Command-V/Ctrl-V to paste the text you copied. FreeHand inserts the text in the text block (or text blocks).

Using this technique, you can set up your text blocks *before* you have any text to place in them. It gives you something to do while you're waiting for someone else to finish writing or editing the text—a handy thing, especially if you're laying out a magazine or newspaper in Freehand.

Importing RTF

Being able to import text-only files is wonderful, but what if you need to import formatted text from your word processor or page layout application? That's where Microsoft's Rich Text Format (RTF) comes in. Technically, RTF isn't a file format—RTF files are saved in the text-only format—it's a method of organizing (or "marking up") text inside a file. RTF files contain text codes and values capable of describing anything and everything that can appear in a Microsoft Word document. The best way to understand how RTF works is to look at a sample RTF file, created by FreeHand (see Figure 4-34). This example file shows almost all the text formatting FreeHand can import or export from an RTF file.

One of the peculiarities of RTF is that it repeats local formatting for each paragraph, even if the formatting hasn't changed between paragraphs, as you can see in the example below. This is just how RTF, as defined by Microsoft, works. If you leave out the repetition for a paragraph, FreeHand formats the text using the default text formatting when you import the file.

If you look at a Microsoft Word RTF file, you'll see a lot more information at the start of the file than you see in Figure 4-34—most of it, from FreeHand's point of view, useless. Word, when it writes an RTF file, includes every font that's currently installed in

FIGURE 4-34
FreeHand RTF file

```
{\rtf1\mac{\fonttbl{\f3\fnil Times;}{\f4\fnil Bembo;}}
{\colortbl\red0\green0\blue0;\red0\green0\blue0;\red158\green48\blue0;}
\deftab720\pard \li0 \ri0 \fi0 \sb0 \sa0 \fs48 \f4 \cf1 \ql \sl-200 RTF Test Document\par
\pard \li0 \ri0 \fi0 \sb0 \sa0 \fs20 \f4 \cf1 \ql \sl-200 {\b bold}\par
\pard \li0 \ri0 \fi0 \sb0 \sa0 \fs20 \f4 \cf1 \ql \sl-200 {\i italic}\par
\pard \li0 \ri0 \fi0 \sb0 \sa0 \fs20 \f4 \cf1 \ql \sl-200 {\b \i bold italic}\par
\pard \li0 \ri0 \fi0 \sb0 \sa0 \fs20 \f4 \cf1 \ql \sl-200 {\up6 baseline shift up}\par
\pard \li0 \ri0 \fi0 \sb0 \sa0 \fs20 \f4 \cf1 \ql \sl-200 {\dn6 baseline shift do}{\dn6 wn}\par
\pard \li0 \ri0 \fi0 \sb0 \sa0 \tqr\tx2162 \fs20 \f4 \cf1 \ql \sl-200 \tab right tab\par
\pard \li0 \ri0 \fi0 \sb0 \sa0 \tqr\tx727 \fs20 \f4 \cf1 \ql \sl-200 \tab left tab\par
\pard \li0 \ri0 \fi0 \sb0 \sa0 \tqc\tx1322 \fs20 \f4 \cf1 \ql \sl-200 \tab center tab\par
\pard \li0 \ri0 \fi0 \sb0 \sa0 \tqdec\tx2162 \fs20 \f4 \cf1 \ql \sl-200 \tab decimal tab.\par
\pard \li0 \ri0 \fi0 \sb0 \sa0 \fs20 \f4 \cf1 \ql \sl-200 align left text\par
\pard \li0 \ri0 \fi0 \sb0 \sa0 \fs20 \f4 \cf1 \qr \sl-200 align right text\par
\pard \li0 \ri0 \fi0 \sb0 \sa0 \fs20 \f4 \cf1 \qc \sl-200 centered text\par
\pard \li0 \ri0 \fi0 \sb0 \sa0 \fs20 \f4 \cf1 \qj \sl-200 justified text\par
\pard \li0 \ri0 \fi0 \sb120 \sa0 \fs20 \f4 \cf1 \ql \sl-200 {\expnd20 range k}{\expnd20
er}{\expnd20 ned text}\par
\pard \li0 \ri0 \fi0 \sb120 \sa0 \fs20 \f4 \cf1 \ql \sl-200 space above\par
\pard \li0 \ri0 \fi0 \sb0 \sa1440 \fs20 \f4 \cf1 \ql \sl-200 space below\par
\pard \li720 \ri0 \fi0 \sb0 \sa0 \fs20 \f4 \cf1 \ql \sl-200 left indent\par
\pard \li720 \ri0 \fi0 \sb0 \sa0 \fs20 \f4 \cf1 \ql \sl-200 right indent\par
\pard \li0 \ri0 \fi240 \sb0 \sa0 \fs20 \f4 \cf1 \ql \sl-200 first line indent\par
\pard \li0 \ri0 \fi0 \sb0 \sa0 \fs20 \f4 \cf1 \ql \sl-200 end of \line line character \par
\pard \li0 \ri0 \fi0 \sb0 \sa0 \fs20 \f4 \cf1 \ql \sl-200 dis\-chy\par
\pard \li0 \ri0 \fi0 \sb0 \sa0 \fs20 \f4 \cf2 \ql \sl-200 color\par
\pard \li0 \ri5330 \fi0 \sb0 \sa0 \fs48 \f4 \cf1 \ql \sl-480 {\shad shadow}\par
\pard \li0 \ri5330 \fi0 \sb0 \sa0 \fs48 \f4 \cf1 \ql \sl-480 {\outl outline}\par
\pard \li0 \ri5330 \fi0 \sb0 \sa0 \fs48 \par }
```

your system in the font table (the section in the RTF file beginning with "\fonttbl"), whether that font is used in the document or not (FreeHand includes only the fonts you've actually *used*, which makes more sense to me).

Following the font table, most RTF files will include a color table ("\colortbl"), and sometimes a table containing the styles defined in the document ("\stylesheet"). Table 4-4 shows the RTF codes you'll see and use most often.

A few notes about RTF files:

◆ Most measurements in an RTF file are in *twips*, or twentieths of a point (.05 point). Type size is measured in half-point increments. If you export FreeHand text containing measurements finer than a twip (a leading value of 10.12, for example), or type sizes finer than half a point (10.7, for example), FreeHand rounds to the nearest twip, or half point, respectively.

◆ Type styles and baseline shift are typically enclosed in braces (for example: "{\b \i bold italic}")—the braces mark the beginning and end of the formatting.

TABLE 4-4
Frequently used
RTF codes

Code	What it means
\s*n*	Style number. This won't make any difference to FreeHand, but you may see it in RTF files generated by other applications. In addition, RTF files generated by applications which support paragraph styles, such as PageMaker, QuarkXPress, and Microsoft Word, will have a table (like the RTF font table or color table) at the start of the document listing the styles and style names used in the document.
\f*n*	Font number. The number of the font in the font table at the start of the RTF document.
\fs*n*	Font size in half points
\b	Bold
\i	Italic
\sl-*n*	Leading. For some reason, both FreeHand and Word put a "-" in front of the leading amount.
\li*n*	Left indent
\ri*n*	Right indent
\fi*n*	First line indent
\tx*n*	Tab position
\cf*n*	Text color. The number of the color determined by the color's position in the color table at the start of the RTF document.
\par	Carriage return
\ql	Left alignment
\qr	Right alignment
\qj	Justified alignment
\qc	Centered alignment
\tqr	Right-aligned tab
\tql	Left-aligned tab
\tqc	Center tab

	Code	What it means
TABLE 4-4 Frequently used RTF codes (continued)	\pard	Start of a new paragraph (you can think of "\par" and "\pard" as a carriage return/line feed combination—it's what they might be if you transfer this RTF file to a DOS/Windows PC. On the Macintosh, of course, all you really need is "\par," but FreeHand adds "\pard" because that's how the RTF specification says it's done).
	\tqdec	Decimal tab
	\tx$n$	Tab position (always follows "\tqr," "\tql," "\tqc," or "\tqdec")
	\'n	Special character expressed as a hexadecimal number
	\up$n$	Baseline shift up (sometimes superscript)
	\dn$n$	Baseline shift down (sometimes subscript)
	\-	Discretionary hyphen
	\tab	Tab character
	\deftab	Distance between default tabs
	\line	End-of-line character
	\~	Nonbreaking space
	\shad	Shadow text effect
	\outl	Stroked text
	\expnd$n$	Range-kerning amount
	\sb$n$	Space above.
	\sa$n$	Space below.
	\fnil, \froman	Alternate fonts—RTF includes its own font substitution scheme. "\froman" and "\fswiss" tell Word on DOS/Windows PCs to use Times (or even "TmsRmn") or Helvetica instead of the original font, if the original font's not found. FreeHand always uses "\fnil,"—no substitution.

◆ Wrapping tabs are not supported by RTF.

◆ Column breaks are not supported by RTF.

◆ Horizontal scaling of text is not supported by RTF.

◆ Text colors are imported as unnamed, process colors (they're represented as RGB colors in the RTF file, but they're converted to CMYK as FreeHand imports the file).

◆ FreeHand doesn't support case changes you can specify in a word processor or page layout application. When FreeHand imports an RTF file containing "\caps" (all capitals) or "\scaps" (small capitals), it ignores the codes and draws the text as it was typed (small caps will appear in lowercase).

◆ FreeHand doesn't support the type styles Strikethrough and Underline. FreeHand imports text coded with the RTF codes "\strike" (strikethrough), or "\ul" (underline) without the formatting.

◆ FreeHand doesn't import style definitions in RTF files, and doesn't export style definitions when you export files as RTF.

◆ Hidden text ("\v"), table of contents markers ("\tc'), and index entries ("\xe" and "\:") are stripped out of RTF files on import into FreeHand.

◆ FreeHand doesn't support graphics (PICT, EPS, or TIFF) embedded in RTF files.

◆ FreeHand's text effects aren't supported by RTF, so they're not exported when you create an RTF file.

◆ RTF codes specifying page layout information, such as page headers and footers, explicitly specified paragraph positions, or page margins, are stripped out of the RTF file on import.

Tip:
Learning more
about RTF

If you want to learn more about RTF, you can view or download a copy of the RTF specification (the specification is updated every few months). You can find the specification by searching Microsoft's Web site at http://www.microsoft.com. A separate file containing additions and changes to the specification for Word 97 is also available at the site.

Importing Text Tagged with XPress Tags

Part of the "Real World" tradition of this book is the idea that you might, someday, have to convert files from one format to another using nothing but a text editor. For example, let's say you're stranded in the middle of the Sahara, you have a file that's been exported from Quark XPress as an XPress Tags (Quark's text-only equivalent to RTF) file you need to import into FreeHand, and you don't have a copy of Quark XPress (if you did, you could export the text as RTF, a format FreeHand understands). Do you wait until a passing caravan offers you the use of their copy of XPress, or do you roll up your sleeves and convert the file yourself?

Now that your forearms are bare, take a look at Table 4-5, which shows the RTF equivalents for commonly-used XPress Tags.

There's Always a Way

At some point, you'll run into a file type FreeHand can't open or edit. It might be an old FreeHand 3 EPS, or a page from Microsoft Publisher or Word, or a page from Quark XPress. Sure—you can import anything you can save as an EPS—but what if you need to edit the contents of the EPS once you reach FreeHand? What if all you have is a PostScript file?

That's all you need, these days—a PostScript file. Once you've got that, and have the Acrobat Distiller (or other software PostScript interpreter, see below), you can convert the file to a PDF, then open the file in FreeHand. It doesn't matter where the file came from—once you open the PDF, you'll be able to edit the objects in the file.

Follow these general steps.

1. If you're not already working with an EPS or PostScript file, create one (save the page as an EPS if the application can do that; print the file to disk as PostScript if it can't). PostScript printer drivers for both the Macintosh and Windows make it fairly easy to print a file to disk.

2. Run the file through the Acrobat Distiller to create a PDF (turn off all image compression and font inclusion options in the Distiller's Job Options dialog box).

TABLE 4-5
Converting XPress
Tags to RTF

Attribute	XPress Tag	RTF equivalent
Plain	<P>	\plain
Bold	<B>	\b
Italic	<I>	\i
Outline	<O>	\outl
Shadow	<S>	\shad
Baseline shift up/superscript	<+> (or <bn>)	\up
Baseline shift down/subscript	<-> (or <b-n>)	\dn
Font	<f"name">	\f$n$ (Where *name* is the name of the font in your system and n is the number of the font in your font table.)
Type size	<zn>	\fs$n$ (multiply the XPress Tag specified font size by 20 to convert it to twips.)
Color	<c"name">	\cf$n$ (Where *name* is the name of the color in your XPress publication and n is the number of the color in your RTF color table.)
Left align	<*L>	\ql
Right align	<*R>	\qr
Center	<*C>	\qc
Justify	<*J>	\qj
Return	<\n>	\par
End-of-line character	<\d>	\line

TABLE 4-5
Converting XPress
Tags to RTF
(continued)

Attribute	XPress Tag	RTF equivalent
Dischy	<h>	\-
Paragraph format	<*p($n, n, n,$ $n, n,$ G or g)>	The values in the tag specify left indent, first-line indent, right indent, leading, space before, and space after, respectively (so you'd convert them to twips by multiplying them by 20, and then use \li n, fi n, ri n, \sl-n, \sb n, and \sa n to render them in RTF syntax. "G or g" specifies whether the paragraph is locked to XPress' baseline grid, and has no RTF counterpart.
Tabs	<*t($n, n,$ "character")>	The first value in the tag is the tab's position, the second value is the tab's alignment (where 1=center, 2=right, 3=decimal, and 4=left), followed by the tab's leader *character*. In RTF, you'd set the tab's alignment first using \tqr, \tql, \tqc, or \tqdec, and then set the position (again, convert the value in the XPress Tag file to twips by multiplying by 20) using \tx n.
Kerning or range kerning	<kn> or <tn>	Convert the values in the tags to twips by multiplying them by .0005 (each increment is $1/200$ of an em), then multiplying them by the

TABLE 4-5
Converting XPress
Tags to RTF
(continued)

Attribute	XPress Tag	RTF equivalent
Kerning or range kerning (continued)		current type size, and then dividing by 20. An XPress Tag value of 4000, in 24-point text, therefore, is equal to an RTF value of two, because 4000 ¥ .0005 ¥ 24 20 = 2.4 (which we round down, because you can't have fractional twips).

3. Open the PDF with FreeHand. FreeHand converts the text and graphics in the PDF into editable FreeHand objects.

If you don't have the Acrobat Distiller, try GhostScript—it's a free PostScript "clone" RIP. GhostScript can convert a PostScript file into an image, or to an Adobe Illustrator file (with an image embedded in it), or into a PDF. You can download GhostScript from the GhostScript Home Page at http://www.cs.wisc.edu/~ghost/. GhostScript is available for the Macintosh, Windows (NT, 95, 98, and 3.1), DOS, and various Unix flavors—and others. I haven't yet found a version for CP/M, but I haven't been looking very hard.

GhostScript can also help you print PostScript special effects (like FreeHand's Custom Fills and Strokes) on non-PostScript printers. If you've been wanting to see your PostScript code in color on your Epson color printer, GhostScript is the cheapest way to go.

You can also use PS EditLink (Macintosh only), a PostScript RIP masquerading as a FreeHand Xtra or any of the Transverter software PostScript RIPs (Macintosh and Windows) from Tech-Pool (www.techpool.com). These, however, are not free.

In previous editions of this book, I showed how to convert an old (unopenable) FreeHand 3 EPS to the Illustrator 1.1 format using a text editor. I'm still proud of that section (and still recall the hours of agony it took to figure it all out), but it's obsolete. Now if I could just reclaim the part of my memory devoted to remembering it, I'd be fine.

Exporting

All of the tricks shown earlier in this chapter for importing data from other applications make it clear that FreeHand's good at importing. But what about exporting? FreeHand supports seven EPS export formats (Generic, MS-DOS, Macintosh, Photoshop 3 EPS, Photoshop 4 RGB EPS, QuarkXPress EPS, and a new one, Editable EPS, which is hiding in the Save As dialog box) and all current Adobe Illustrator formats. On the Macintosh, you can copy Free-Hand elements out of FreeHand, creating a PICT with attached PostScript that can be pasted into just about anything. You can also export as PICT or WMF (don't), PICT2 or DXF (don't, unless you have to), or export the text in your publication as text-only (without formatting) or as RTF (with formatting).

Something you should understand about exporting: unless you choose to include your original FreeHand file in one of the EPS formats (check Include FreeHand document in EPS when you're exporting the file), *the file is going to change.* I don't mean that objects in the EPS are going to move around, or change color, or anything like that. Layers, styles, and other attributes of a typical FreeHand document are going to be lost. The file might *look* the same, but the *structure* of the file will be different.

That's not—necessarily—a bad thing. I mention it here because I don't want you to be surprised the night before a deadline.

When you export a FreeHand page in any format other than a FreeHand 8 file, template, or EPS, its appearance will change significantly (objects will *move*—PICT and WMF are less accurate formats than EPS, and rounding errors occur when you use these formats). If you save the file in any of the Adobe Illustrator formats, you'll lose features specific to FreeHand, such as graphic styles and wrapping tabs.

In all the cases mentioned, you'll be able to open and edit the file again. If you export the file in an EPS and don't include the FreeHand page inside the EPS, you may not even be able to open the EPS (though you'll probably be able to).

You can convert FreeHand objects to TIFF images by rasterizing them on the page, or you can render objects in your FreeHand publication to an image file (usually TIFF or xRes LRG).

The first half of this chapter covered how to get from there to here. Here's the dope on how to get from here to there. Exporting works the same way for any type of file, as shown in the following steps (see Figure 4-35).

1. Choose Export from the File menu (or press Command-Shift-R/Ctrl-Shift-R). FreeHand displays the Export Document dialog box.

2. Choose a format from the Format/Save As Type pop-up menu.

   If you choose any of the Adobe Illustrator formats, EPS formats, or PICT formats, FreeHand displays page export options at the bottom of the dialog box. You can export any or all of the pages in your publication as EPS. If you select a range of pages, FreeHand creates one EPS file for each page you export.

   If you choose any of the EPS formats, you can include the FreeHand page in the EPS file by checking Include FreeHand Document in EPS. The FreeHand file that's included in the EPS is exactly the same file as FreeHand creates when you save the file, so all your layers and styles are available when you open the EPS. (Note that you can't include the FreeHand document in any of the Adobe Illustrator formats.)

   When you choose any of the image formats (BMP, GIF, JPEG, TIFF, Targa, or LRG), FreeHand activates the Options/Setup button. Click the button to set options for the bitmap image you're creating (see "Exporting Images," later in this chapter).

   When you export text (as ASCII text or RTF), FreeHand includes *all* of the text in the publication in the exported file.

3. Type a name for your file and direct it to the folder and volume you want.

4. Press Return to export the file.

That's all there is to the process of exporting a file. Now, on to the fun stuff—the details.

FIGURE 4-35
Exporting a file

Select the objects you want to export (if you don't want to export an entire page or publication), then press Command-Shift-R/Ctrl-Shift-R (or choose Export from the File menu) to display the Export Document dialog box.

Type a name for the file you're exporting.

Choose a file type from this pop-up menu.

Turn this option on to export only the selected objects.

Set the range of pages you want to export here. When you export more than one page at a time, FreeHand creates separate files and numbers them sequentially "filename1.eps", "filename2.eps", etc.).

In Windows, you'll have to click the Setup button to see most of the above options (if available). FreeHand displays a dialog box with options for the file type you're exporting.

When you select an image file type, You can click the Options/Setup button to display options for exporting images.

Click the More button, and FreeHand displays export options specific to the file type you've chosen.

Turn on this option to make it possible for FreeHand to open the EPS in the future.

Format:
Adobe Illustrator 1.1™
Adobe Illustrator 88™
Adobe Illustrator® 3
Adobe Illustrator™ 5.5
Adobe Illustrator™ 7.x
ASCII text
BMP
DCS2 EPS
Flash 2 SWF
FreeHand 3.1
FreeHand 3.1 text editable
FreeHand 4.x/5.x document
FreeHand 7 document
Generic EPS
GIF
JPEG
✓ Macintosh EPS
MS-DOS EPS
PDF
Photoshop™ 3 EPS
Photoshop™ 4 RGB EPS
PICT
PICT (paths)
PICT2 (paths)
PNG
QuarkXPress™ EPS
RTF text
Targa
TIFF
xRes (paths)
xRes LRG

ASCII Text [*.txt]
Adobe Illustrator 1.1 [*.ai]
Adobe Illustrator 3.0/4.0 [*.ai]
Adobe Illustrator 5.x [*.ai]
Adobe Illustrator 88 [*.ai]
BMP [*.bmp]
EPS with TIFF Preview [*.eps]
Encapsulated PostScript [*.eps]
FreeHand 3.1 Document [*.fh3]
FreeHand 3.1 text editable [*.fh3]
FreeHand 4.x/5.x files [*.fh4/*.fh5]
GIF [*.gif]
JPEG [*.jpg]
PDF [*.pdf]
PNG [*.png]
Photoshop EPS [*.ai]
RTF Text [*.rtf]
TIFF [*.tif]
Targa [*.tga]
Windows Metafile [*.wmf]
xRes LRG [*.lrg]
xRes paths [*.pth]

The Macintosh and Windows versions of FreeHand offer different export options.

If export options are available for the file type you've chosen, FreeHand makes the Options/Setup button active. Click the button to display the options (this example shows the PDF export options).

Creating EPS Graphics

Actually, exporting EPS graphics is what most people think of when they think of using FreeHand with other applications. It's only because of the twisted orientation of this book (that FreeHand is your main publishing program for short, complex documents) that exporting FreeHand elements appears in this chapter as a kind of afterthought.

EPS Output Options. Before you export a file as EPS, choose Output Options from the File menu. FreeHand displays the Output Options dialog box (see Figure 4-36). These options affect both printing and EPS export.

- ♦ Check Include Invisible Layers when you want to print all the foreground layers in the publication.

- ♦ Check Split Complex Paths to make paths containing graduated, radial, and tiled fills—or paths you've pasted other objects inside—easier to print. Don't check this option if you're exporting an EPS containing a large TIFF you've pasted inside a path—it can cause the TIFF to download over and over again, increasing your printing time dramatically.

- ♦ The first two choices on the Images pop-up menu—ASCII and Binary—determine how FreeHand sends imported TIFF images to your printer (or to an EPS). Unless you're directly connected to your printer via serial cable, you should choose Binary —this makes the images more compact and (therefore) quicker to transmit to your printer. In practice, this means that Macintosh users should generally use Binary; Windows users should use ASCII.

FIGURE 4-36
Output Options
dialog box

If you're taking your EPS to an OPI (Open Prepress Interface) system, such as Kodak's Prophecy, choose "None". Since you'll be linking to another version of the image, your FreeHand file need only contain the location and size of the image, and doesn't need to contain the image data.

♦ If you plan to print the EPS from an application that can't separate RGB TIFFs, or if you prefer FreeHand's color separations, check Convert RGB TIFF to Process. PageMaker and Quark XPress can both separate RGB TIFFs, so you should leave this option off if you're going to those applications.

♦ If you're printing to a color prepress system, or a continuous-tone film recorder, enter 256 in the Maximum Color Steps field. This limits the number of shades of color FreeHand uses to render blends and graduated and radial fills. These devices can only print so many colors at once.

♦ For faster printing, enter a value above zero in the Flatness field (for more on flatness, see "Thinking Like a Line" in Chapter 2, "Drawing"). You can safely enter up to "3" with no noticeable change in your publication's printed quality on most printers and imagesetters.

The Output Options dialog box is one of the most important features in FreeHand. In versions of FreeHand before version 5.0, you could set global flatness for a publication only when you were printing from FreeHand—you couldn't set the flatness for all the paths in an EPS without editing the EPS using a word processor. Similarly, the Split Complex Paths feature affected only FreeHand printing, not EPS files exported from FreeHand.

Exporting selected objects. If you want, you can choose to export only the object you have selected. I love this feature. Just turn on the Selected Objects Only option in the Export Document dialog box, and only the objects you've selected will end up in the EPS you export. Unfortunately, you can't use the Include FreeHand Document in EPS option when this option is turned on.

Setting a page range. FreeHand, by default, exports all of the pages in your publication when you export using the EPS format. Each exported page becomes a single EPS file (FreeHand appends numbers to the filenames of the EPS files that correspond to the page numbers of the pages in the publication). To set the range of pages, click the From button and set a page range using the attached field.

Embedding FreeHand files in EPS graphics. When you check Include FreeHand Document in EPS in the Export Document dialog box (in Windows, you'll have to click the Setup button to display the EPS Export dialog box), FreeHand embeds the publication in the EPS file.

What good is this? In versions of FreeHand prior to version 4, you had to keep two versions of a FreeHand file on your disk—the EPS, which you could import into other programs, and the original FreeHand file, which you could open and edit in FreeHand. These days, you can choose to save only one file.

When you use a word processor to edit an EPS file that's been exported with Include FreeHand document in EPS checked, you'll see the line "%%BeginAGDEmbeddedDoc: version 1.0," lots of gibberish, and the line "%%EndAGDEmbeddedDoc." What is that stuff? It's your FreeHand page, saved as text.

Tip:
Breaking a
Multi-Page
Publication into
Single Pages

When you want to create a new publication from a single page of a multipage publication, export the page as an EPS, checking Include FreeHand Document in EPS as you do so. You can then open the EPS file and save the page as a separate FreeHand document, complete with the styles, layers, and colors of the original publication.

Convert Colors to. Choose the color model you want to use in the EPS file. In general, you should choose CMYK and RGB—this leaves the colors in the EPS alone, and means you'll have a choice when you import the EPS into another application.

Generic EPS. When you need to create an EPS file containing the PostScript required to print the FreeHand publication you've created, but don't want the file to have a screen preview attached, choose Generic EPS from the Format/Save As Type pop-up menu.

If you place a Generic EPS file in FreeHand, you'll see a box with an "X" through it.

Use Generic EPS when you're exporting a FreeHand graphic for use in a non-Macintosh, non-MS-DOS system (if you're preparing a graphic that'll be placed in a FrameMaker publication on a Sun workstation, for example), or if you just don't want to bother with a screen image. The Generic EPS file is a straight text file.

Macintosh EPS. A Macintosh EPS file is a PostScript text file with a PICT resource attached to it. When you place the EPS file in Free-Hand or any other Macintosh program that can import EPS, the PICT is what you see on your screen.

MS-DOS EPS. Because MS-DOS files are structurally different from Macintosh files in that they're data files only (there's no concept of different forks for data and resources in the MS-DOS or Windows world) MS-DOS EPS files have a TIFF image of the graphic embedded in the file as hexadecimal data.

If you're exporting a FreeHand file as MS-DOS EPS, don't forget to use a file name your MS-DOS system can understand (eight characters or fewer), and add the extension ".eps" to the file name. Most MS-DOS applications have no way of knowing what type a file is without the extension.

Photoshop EPS. In FreeHand 5.0, the best way to rasterize a Free-Hand file (that is, convert it to a bitmap) was to export the file using one of the Adobe Illustrator export formats. The whole trick is getting Photoshop to recognize the EPS—Photoshop couldn't see or recognize FreeHand EPSes. That's what the Photoshop EPS format does—it makes an EPS Photoshop can recognize.

Use the Photoshop 3 EPS format only if you're using Photoshop 3. Photoshop 4 (and, I imagine, 5) can't rasterize Photoshop 3 EPS format files from FreeHand. Use the Photoshop 4 RGB EPS format if you want Photoshop to rasterize the EPS using the RGB color model (if you're creating artwork for screen display, this is probably the export option you want to use). Most of the time, when you want to rasterize FreeHand elements in Photoshop, you should use one of the other EPS (or Illustrator) formats.

QuarkXPress EPS. Choose this format when you want to import your FreeHand graphics into an XPress picture box. It's something like an MS-DOS EPS in that it includes a TIFF preview, so you can see the same preview in the Windows and Macintosh versions of XPress.

Editable EPS. You can also *save* single-page publications in an EPS format—Editable EPS. To do this, press Command-Shift-S/Ctrl-Shift-S to display the Save As dialog box, then choose Editable EPS from the Format/Save As Type pop-up menu. Enter a name for the file and click the OK button to save the file. Why use Editable EPS to save a file, rather than embedding using the Include FreeHand Document in EPS option in the Export Document dialog box? The "FreeHand document" included in the EPS doesn't include page positioning information, guide positions, or styles and colors that aren't used in the publication. When you use the Editable EPS format, the entire FreeHand document is included in the EPS.

Tip:
Creating
Color Previews
(Windows Only)

If you want to export EPS graphics with color preview images, make sure you've turned on the Export EPS with Color Previews option in the Import/Export Preferences dialog box. This option is on by default. Why not use color preview images? They make your file size larger—even if the objects in the EPS don't use color (that is, their fills and strokes use only black, white, or shades of gray). If your graphics don't use color, you can turn this option off.

EPS Files and
Downloadable
Fonts

You've probably heard that EPS graphics include any download-able fonts used in the file. It's not necessarily true—sometimes EPS files contain the fonts; sometimes they only *list* the fonts.

When your page-layout program's printing, it creates the image of the page in your printer's memory by starting with the objects on the page that are the farthest to the back (actually, I'm only certain of this for PageMaker and Quark XPress). When the application starts to print an EPS graphic, it reads the fonts listed in the EPS and downloads any needed fonts to your printer.

This does not guarantee that the fonts will still be in the printer's memory when they're called for inside the EPS, because a lot can happen between the start of the EPS file (when your page layout program downloads the font) and whenever the font is needed.

Your page-layout application cannot manage the printer's memory once you're inside the EPS—only before and after your printer processes the EPS. By contrast, when you're printing objects you've created using your page-layout program's tools, your page-layout application manages font downloading and printer memory on an object-by-object level—it can always download another copy of the font if necessary.

If you've got an older printer with one megabyte of RAM, like a LaserWriter or LaserWriter Plus, it's much more likely that this will be a problem, because it's much more likely that your page-layout program will have to flush the downloadable font from the printer's RAM to make room to print something else. It's also something you'll sometimes run into when you're printing to an imagesetter, because the higher resolution of imagesetters also means that these printers will run short of RAM.

If you have enough RAM in your printer, or if your printer has a hard disk, manually download the fonts to your printer. This guarantees they'll print, and your file will print faster, too.

Tip:
Including Fonts
in EPS Files
(Windows only)

In Windows FreeHand, you can embed fonts in an EPS as you export it. This increases the size of the EPS by the size of the font, but it's worth it to know that you'll get the fonts you've used when you print the EPS from another program, system, or platform. To embed fonts in an EPS, select an EPS format, then click the Setup button in the Export Document dialog box. FreeHand displays the EPS Export dialog box. Turn on the Include Fonts in EPS option, and FreeHand adds the fonts to the EPS (see Figure 4-37).

FIGURE 4-37
Including Fonts

Choose an EPS format.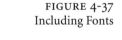

Turn on the Include Fonts in EPS option, then export the EPS.

Click the Setup button.

FreeHand displays the EPS Export dialog box.

Placing FreeHand Graphics in Page-Layout Programs

If you need to produce documents longer than a few dozen pages, you're going to have to look to a page layout program. Luckily, you can take your FreeHand illustrations with you. There are a few tricks and twists to this process.

Bounding boxes. You'll note that FreeHand's bounding boxes are sometimes just a little bit larger than the edges of the graphic, or that the graphic is not positioned inside the bounding box the way you'd like it.

What's going on? According to Adobe's EPS specification, EPS bounding box measurements should be expressed in integers (such as 100, 612, or 792). In FreeHand 3, Altsys engineers, with their usual mania for accuracy, used EPS bounding boxes accurate to $\frac{1}{10000}$ of a PostScript point (which meant you'd see numbers such as 100.0125, 612.0005, or 792.9999 in FreeHand 3 EPS files). Most applications don't observe the fractional part of the EPS bounding box when they create a box to put the graphic in, so you could lose up to half a point (more or less) around the boundary of your graphic.

All of this changed with FreeHand 4, whose EPS bounding boxes are expressed in integers. I actually believe that the more accurate way is the better way, but this is, after all, the "real world," and we've got to get along with other applications.

If you've been using FreeHand 5.0 and the edges of your exported EPS graphics seem to be getting clipped off when you place them in other applications, you've run into a new bounding box bug that's unrelated to the above discussion. This problem was fixed in FreeHand 5.5, and should still be fixed in FreeHand 8.

If you're having this problem, and don't have time to update your copy of FreeHand before your next deadline, draw a box around the graphics you're exporting, making the box a little larger than the objects it encloses. Set the line and fill of the box to None, and export the EPS.

FreeHand, TIFFs, and PageMaker

A funny thing happened after FreeHand broke up with Aldus and started dating Macromedia: PageMaker stopped printing TIFFs in FreeHand EPS files. I believe that this problem has been patched up with PageMaker 6.5.

Here's the deal. When FreeHand writes coordinates into an EPS, it bases the coordinate system used in the EPS on the FreeHand pasteboard, rather than on the coordinate system of the individual page. Every time you've printed spreads, or printed objects off your page, you benefit from this behavior. FreeHand includes the PostScript operator "translate," along with the appropriate location of the lower-left corner of the current page. This resets the coordinate system of the page—and it's an entirely legitimate PostScript programming practice, regardless of the misleading and incorrect note in the PageMaker 6.0 ReadMe file.

Trouble is, PageMaker's OPI reader doesn't know about it, and assumes that all EPSes have a coordinate system starting at the lower-left hand corner of the page. This wouldn't be bad—except the option activating the OPI reader for EPS graphics is buried in a hidden dialog box, and it's *on* by default.

What happens? When you place a FreeHand EPS containing TIFFs in PageMaker, PageMaker won't print the TIFFs (unless the FreeHand page was positioned at the lower-left corner of the FreeHand pasteboard). The EPS prints, but the TIFFs disappear.

How you fix this problem depends on whether you're using an OPI system or not. If you're not, and simply want to print the TIFFs in your FreeHand EPSes to an imagesetter, follow these steps (see Figure 4-38).

1. When you're ready to place the EPS in PageMaker, hold down Shift as you click the OK button in the Place Document dialog box. PageMaker displays the EPS Import Filter dialog box. In PageMaker 6.5, turn on the Show Filter Preferences option, then click the OK button.

2. Uncheck the Read Embedded OPI Image Links option and press Return to place the EPS.

    If you're working with an EPS that's already been placed in a PageMaker publication, replace the EPS with the original EPS file, making the change in the EPS Import Filter dialog box as you replace the file.

If you *are* using an OPI system, and want to link to high-resolution images, drag the FreeHand page containing the FPO (or low

FIGURE 4-38
PageMaker's EPS
Import Options

In PageMaker 6.0x

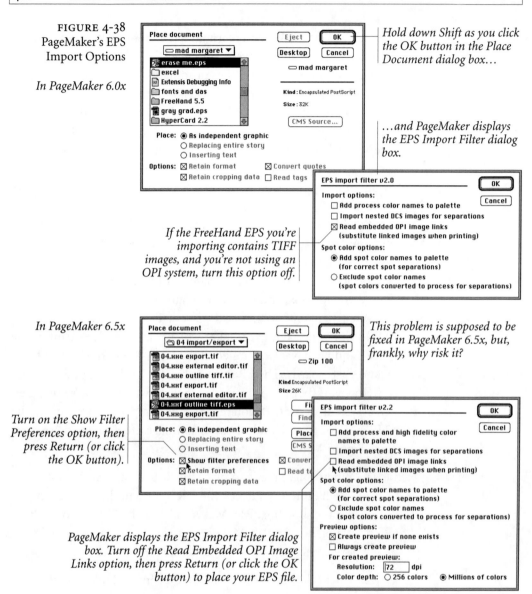

Hold down Shift as you click the OK button in the Place Document dialog box…

…and PageMaker displays the EPS Import Filter dialog box.

If the FreeHand EPS you're importing contains TIFF images, and you're not using an OPI system, turn this option off.

In PageMaker 6.5x

This problem is supposed to be fixed in PageMaker 6.5x, but, frankly, why risk it?

Turn on the Show Filter Preferences option, then press Return (or click the OK button).

PageMaker displays the EPS Import Filter dialog box. Turn off the Read Embedded OPI Image Links option, then press Return (or click the OK button) to place your EPS file.

resolution) images to the lower-left corner of the FreeHand paste-board, then export the page as EPS. This way, the coordinate system in the EPS will match PageMaker's expectations, and you'll be able to use the positioning information in the EPS. In this case, you can turn on the Read Embedded OPI Image Links option in the EPS Import Filter dialog box.

PageMaker, FreeHand, TIFFs, and Clipping Paths

But wait, it gets worse. If a FreeHand EPS you've placed in Page-Maker includes a clipping path which contains an image and a FreeHand path (or several paths), *PageMaker will not print the paths.* It will print the image, and the clipping path, but all of the paths pasted inside the clipping path disappear (see Figure 4-39).

You can work around this by creating two copies of the clipping path. Paste the image into one of the paths, then paste the other objects into the other, change the stacking order of the clipping paths as needed, then export the EPS and place it in PageMaker.

FIGURE 4-39
A PageMaker Bug

These paths...

...and this image...

...are both pasted inside a clipping path.

If you export this clipping path as an EPS, place it in PageMaker, and print, you'll see the clipping path and the image, but the white lettering will disappear.

To combat this PageMaker problem, duplicate the clipping path. Delete the lettering from one copy of the path. Delete the image the image from the other copy of the path, then export the EPS. Place the EPS in your PageMaker publication, and you'll see the lettering when you print.

Importing Named Process Colors into QuarkXPress

When you import a FreeHand EPS into a QuarkXPress picture box (in version 3.3), XPress adds the spot colors used in the EPS to its list of colors, but doesn't add any named process colors you might have used in the graphic. You can add them yourself, or follow these steps.

1. Select the process color in the Colors palette and choose Duplicate from the Colors palette's pop-up menu. Free-Hand adds a duplicate of the color to the Colors palette.

2. Select the duplicate color and choose Make Spot from the pop-up menu.

3. Apply the new spot color to an object on your page.

4. Export the page as an EPS.

5. Import the EPS into XPress. XPress adds the spot color to its color list.

6. Delete the EPS.

7. Convert the spot color to a process color. Now you can apply the named process color to other elements in your XPress publication.

In a review of a previous version of this book, the reviewer commented that this method might result in shifts in the color's definition. While that's true for spot colors defined in FreeHand using the RGB or HLS color models, the above technique works with named process colors (which I assume you've defined using the CMYK model). So you should be OK.

I haven't seen any changes in color definitions when I use this method, but the reviewer is right—you've got to watch out when you're converting from process to spot colors, or when you're moving colors from one application to another.

Exporting Publications in Adobe Illustrator Format

When you export your FreeHand file in the Adobe Illustrator 7, 6, 5.5, or 5 file formats, several things happen.

◆ You lose all style information (Illustrator doesn't have styles). The objects on your page are all formatted using local formatting instead (their appearance doesn't change).

◆ Illustrator 5.0 and 5.5 don't support the import of TIFF images, so any TIFF images in your FreeHand publication are omitted from the files when you export to these formats.

◆ Multicolumn and multirow text blocks are converted to linked, single-column text blocks.

◆ Any Custom or PostScript line or fill effects you've used in your FreeHand publication are omitted from the exported Illustrator file. You just get the paths.

In addition to the above problems, several other things happen when you export files in the Adobe Illustrator 3 file format.

◆ You lose all layer information. The appearance of your page won't change (that is, objects will still be stacked up in the same order), they just won't be assigned to layers.

◆ Graduated and radial fills get rendered as Illustrator blends—versions of Illustrator prior to Illustrator 5 didn't feature graduated and radial fills.

When you export to Adobe Illustrator 88 or Adobe Illustrator 1.1 format, a few other things happen (in addition to the changes described for the Adobe Illustrator 3 format).

◆ Composite paths are converted to individual paths.

◆ The text blocks in your FreeHand publication are converted to single-line text blocks in the exported Illustrator 88 file.

Tip:
Breaking Text
Blocks into
Single Lines

A friend of mine needed to break all of the text in a text block into separate text blocks, each text block containing a single line of text. He didn't want to copy and paste the text (it was a large text block, containing captions he wanted to position on a map). He asked me if I had any idea how he could do this.

I told him to export the text block in the Illustrator 88 format, then open the file he'd exported in FreeHand. Sure enough, his text block had been broken into many smaller text blocks, each one containing a single line of his text.

Copying: Another
Way to Export
(Macintosh Only)

There's another way to get objects out of FreeHand, and this one doesn't involve the Export dialog box—copying. There's not much to it: select the objects copy them, then switch to the other application and paste. Use this technique when you want to use a Free-Hand graphic in an application that can't import EPS files, but can handle PICTs. FreeHand attaches PostScript code to the PICT, so the graphic will print correctly on a PostScript printer.

The following are some points about copying.

◆ The screen image that results when you copy a graphic to another application is not as good as the image FreeHand adds to an EPS file when you're exporting a file as EPS.

◆ Graphics that you copy to another application do not include any downloadable fonts, and it's often difficult to get the fonts to download from whatever application you've pasted the graphics into; so be prepared to manually download fonts if you're using these graphics. Or you can convert type to paths before copying.

◆ When you copy objects out of FreeHand, FreeHand copies the objects as PICT (with attached PostScript), RTF, AGD1 (native FreeHand format), and ASCII (or text-only). When you paste the Clipboard's contents into another application, that application pastes the data in the format it likes best. See "Expert Import/Export Preferences" in Chapter 1, "FreeHand Basics."

Converting FreeHand Objects to Bitmaps

When you want to turn something you've drawn in FreeHand into a bitmap (a process known to the jargon-enabled as "rasterizing"), you have a variety of options open to you, each with advantages and disadvantages. Here they are, in my order of preference:

◆ You can rasterize the file in place, on your page, by choosing Rasterize from the Modify menu.

◆ You can save the file in the Photoshop EPS format, then open the file using Photoshop. If you want to move Free-Hand paths to Photoshop as Photoshop paths, and are using a Macintosh, you can do that, too.

◆ If you want to use your FreeHand artwork in xRes, you can export the objects in the xRes LRG format. This works well, unless your artwork contains Custom, Textured, or Post-Script fills or strokes. If your publication contains any of these fills or strokes, you can save the file in any of the EPS formats and open the file using xRes. Finally, if you want to use FreeHand paths in xRes as paths, you can export the paths using the xRes (Paths) file format.

♦ You can export the objects using one of the bitmap formats (GIF, JPEG, or TIFF, for example) you see on the Format/ Save As Type pop-up menu.

♦ On the Macintosh, you can use the Create PICT Image Xtra to convert selected objects into a PICT file. You can then import this file into FreeHand (which, in turn, converts the file into a TIFF and embeds it in your publication).

Why would you want to turn a FreeHand object into a bitmap? Because, if you do, you'll be able to take it into a painting program (such as Photoshop or xRes) for editing. Finally, there's the Macromedia angle—you might want to use them in a Director presentation, or use the image as a texture in an Extreme 3D scene.

Rasterizing FreeHand Elements in Place

In previous versions of FreeHand, converting objects to bitmap images was somewhat cumbersome. Typically, you'd export the objects using an Illustrator format, then open and rasterize the exported file using Photoshop. To get the graphics back into your publication, you had to import them. To get them into the same position you had to drag them there or enter coordinates in the Object Inspector. In FreeHand 8, it's easier (see Figure 4-40).

1. Select the objects you want to convert to an image.

2. Choose Rasterize from the Modify menu (or press Command-Option-Shift-Z/Ctrl-Alt-shift-Z). FreeHand displays the Rasterize dialog box.

3. Set the resolution at which you want to rasterize the objects (bearing in mind, as you do so, what you learned in the TIFF Balancing Act, earlier in this chapter), choose an anti-aliasing setting (bearing in mind that higher anti-aliasing settings mean longer rasterization times), and click the OK button. FreeHand creates an embedded TIFF image (the TIFF uses the RGB color model) of the selected objects and deletes the original FreeHand objects.

At this point, you can work with the image as you would any other. You can extract the image to create a TIFF file, or apply Photoshop filters to it.

FIGURE 4-40
Rasterizing
FreeHand Objects

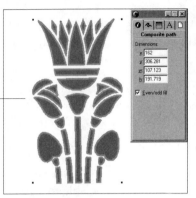

Select the object (or objects) you want to convert to an image…

…and choose Rasterize from the Modify menu (or press Command-Option-Shift-Z/ Ctrl-Alt-Shift-Z).

FreeHand displays the Rasterize dialog box.

Enter a Resolution that's twice the screen frequency you intend to use to print the publication, choose an anti-aliasing level, and click the OK button.

FreeHand converts the object (or objects) to a bitmap image (a TIFF file embedded in your publication).

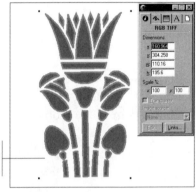

If FreeHand can't rasterize the selected objects at the resolution (and anti-aliasing) setting you requested, you have several options. You can reduce the resolution and/or the anti-aliasing setting, you can try exporting the objects using one of the image export formats, or you can save the objects in one of the Illustrator formats and then rasterize them using Photoshop. Or you can buy more RAM (on the Macintosh, you might try increasing the amount of memory allocated to Freehand).

Now, if you're like me, you're probably wondering how objects rasterized "in place" on the page differ from objects exported using the TIFF format. As far as I can tell, and assuming identical resolution and anti-aliasing settings, there's no difference. There's also no difference between objects rasterized in place, then extracted using the Links dialog box, and exported images (again, assuming identical rasterization and anti-aliasing settings). If you export using the JPEG or GIF format, on the other hand, you can expect some changes.

From FreeHand to Photoshop

If you own Photoshop, you can use it to rasterize FreeHand objects (see Figure 4-41). If you're running out of RAM while rasterizing (or exporting) objects in FreeHand, try this.

1. Export the file you want to rasterize using the Photoshop EPS format.

2. Start Photoshop, if it's not already running, and open the EPS file you created. Photoshop displays the Rasterize Generic EPS Format (the title of this dialog box varies slightly from version to version).

4. Choose the options you want in the Rasterize Generic EPS Format and press Return. Photoshop rasterizes the objects in the file.

Once you've converted the file to a bitmap image, you can set it up for color separation, if necessary, or apply effects to it with Photoshop's plug-ins.

FIGURE 4-41
Opening FreeHand
Files in Photoshop

When you're ready to export the FreeHand objects you want to rasterize, choose Photoshop EPS as your export format.

When you open an EPS, Photoshop displays the Rasterize Adobe Illustrator Format dialog box.

Note: Photoshop 4 will rasterize images you've placed in your FreeHand publication (earlier versions didn't).

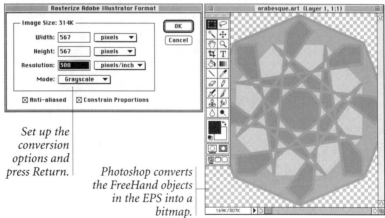

Set up the conversion options and press Return.

Photoshop converts the FreeHand objects in the EPS into a bitmap.

Exporting FreeHand Paths to Photoshop (Macintosh Only)

Sometimes, you don't want Photoshop to turn your FreeHand paths into an image. Sometimes, you want Photoshop to import the paths *as paths* (so that you can use them as clipping paths or selections in Photoshop). To do this, follow these steps (see Figure 4-42).

1. In FreeHand, select a path and cut or copy it.

2. Switch to Photoshop and paste. Photoshop displays the Paste dialog box.

3. Turn on the Paste As Paths option, then click the OK button. Photoshop imports your FreeHand path as a Photoshop path. Like any other Photoshop path, the imported path has no formatting.

If this technique doesn't work, or if you don't see the Paste dialog box when you paste into Photoshop, it's because you've turned off the Adobe Illustrator option in the Export Preferences dialog box. Turn the option on, and you'll be able to paste FreeHand paths into Photoshop.

FIGURE 4-42
Moving FreeHand
paths to Photoshop

In FreeHand, select the path you want to take to Photoshop and copy it.

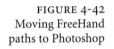

Switch to Photoshop, and paste. Photoshop displays the Paste dialog box. Choose the Paste as Paths option.

Photoshop creates a path. At this point, you can use the path as you'd use any other path in Photoshop. In this example, I'm using the path to apply special effects. When I'm finished doing that, I'll use it as a clipping path.

Photoshop adds the path to the Paths palette.

Here's the clipped image, back in FreeHand.

From FreeHand to xRes

If you want to take objects from FreeHand and use them in xRes, you can use any of the following techniques:

- Copy the objects from FreeHand and paste them into an xRes window.

- Drag the objects out of FreeHand and drop them into an xRes window (Macintosh only).

- Export the objects, then open the file using xRes (xRes can open LRG, EPS, and all of the image formats FreeHand can export). See "Exporting Images," later in this chapter.

- Export paths as xRes paths using the xRes (Paths) format.

Copying and pasting to xRes. First, you'll need to set your xRes document to "Direct" mode—you can't paste FreeHand objects into xRes documents when they're in "xRes" mode. Once that's done, pasting FreeHand objects into xRes displays the PostScript Options dialog box (see Figure 4-43). If you turn on the Rasterize EPS option, xRes creates an image from the PostScript FreeHand copied to the system clipboard. Turn on the Bitmap option, and xRes pastes the bitmap FreeHand copied to the clipboard (the quality of this bitmap is set by the previous settings in the Bitmap Export Defaults dialog box—which appears when you click the Options/Setup button in FreeHand's Export Document dialog box).

FIGURE 4-43
xRes PostScript
Options

Choose the Rasterize EPS option to rasterize the FreeHand objects using xRes' build-in PostScript (clone) RIP. This produces a better image.

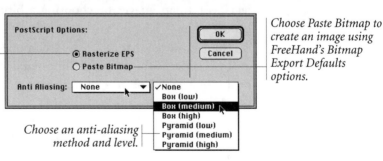

Choose Paste Bitmap to create an image using FreeHand's Bitmap Export Defaults options.

Choose an anti-aliasing method and level.

Dragging and dropping to xRes. Just as you can drag objects from one FreeHand window to another, you can drag FreeHand objects out of FreeHand and drop them into an xRes window. When you do this, xRes pastes an image of the objects you're dragging into the xRes document. How does xRes know what image conversion options to use? It doesn't—FreeHand takes care of it for you. The previous settings of the Bitmap Export Defaults dialog box determine the quality of the bitmap image.

Exporting FreeHand objects to LRG files. See "Exporting Images, "later in this chapter.

Exporting paths to xRes. Want to use your FreeHand paths as paths (rather than converting them to bitmap images) in xRes? Export the paths using the xRes (Paths) format (also known as PTH, the file's extension). Press Command-Shift-R/Ctrl-Shift-R to display the Export Document dialog box. Choose xRes (Paths) from the Format/Save As Type pop-up menu. FreeHand exports all of the paths in the publication to the xRes PTH file—you can't use the Selected Objects Only option or set the page range. This means you may want to copy the path you want to export to a new, single-page FreeHand publication before you export.

When you export paths to the xRes LRG (Paths) format, you sometimes end up with one point too many—usually at the point where the path closes.

Exporting Images

While you can rasterize FreeHand objects "in place" on your pages using the Rasterize command, you can also export FreeHand objects as bitmap images by choosing a bitmap image type as you export a file.

Note, however, that this is the technique you use to create JPEG and GIF images for use in on-line publications and the Web. To export FreeHand objects to a bitmap format, follow these steps (see Figure 4-44).

1. Select the objects you want to export, if necessary.

2. Press Command-Shift-R/Ctrl-Shift-R to display the Export Document dialog box.

3. Choose the bitmap format you want to use from the Format/Save File As pop-up menu. After you choose a format, FreeHand activates the Options/Setup button.

FIGURE 4-44
Exporting images

Select the object you want to export, if necessary, then press Command-Shift-R/ Ctrl-Shift-R.

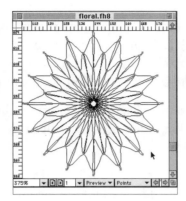

FreeHand displays the Export Document dialog box. Choose an image type from the Format/Save As Type pop-up menu, then click the Options/Setup button.

Set up the resolution, anti-aliasing, and alpha channel options you want to use for the image you're exporting.

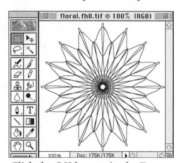

Click the More button to display options for the image format you've chosen (see Figure 4-37, on page 425 for more examples).

Click the OK button in the Export Document dialog box to export the image. Here's the example graphic, open in Photoshop.

4. Click the Options/Setup button. FreeHand displays the Bitmap Export Defaults dialog box. This dialog box does not vary from one file type to another; to see format-specific options, click the More button. When you click the More button, FreeHand displays a dialog box containing the export options available for the format you've selected.

5. Set up the options you want in the format-specific dialog box (for more on setting up GIF and JPEG export options, see Chapter 9, "FreeHand and the Web").

   Most of the options in the format-specific dialog boxes (the TIFF dialog box, for example) concern the color depth you want to use in the exported file. Which color depth you choose depends on the format you've chosen, the intended use of the bitmap image you're creating (on-line or on paper?), and how much RAM you have available. Once you've made the series of agonizing decisions required, click the OK button to close the dialog box.

6. In the Bitmap Export Defaults dialog box, choose the resolution, anti-aliasing, and alpha channel settings you want.

Alpha channel. The two items in the Default Bitmap Options dialog box I haven't discussed yet are the mysterious Alpha Channel twins—Include Alpha Channel and Alpha Includes Background. An alpha channel, in FreeHand's view, is a part of a bitmap image where there's no content (other than the background color). It's where the image isn't. You can include alpha channels in files exported in the LRG, TIFF, TGA (Targa), PNG, and BMP formats (in other bitmap formats, turning on the alpha channel options in the Default Bitmap Options dialog box has no effect). When you turn on Alpha Includes Background, the background layers become the alpha channel for the exported image (see Figure 4-45).

You use alpha channels when you get to an image editing program—they make a masking operations easier to accomplish.

FIGURE 4-45
Alpha channel

Create the alpha channel by drawing objects on the background layer.

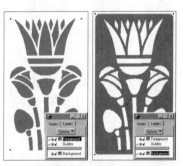

Foreground layer   Background layer

When you open the file in a program that supports alpha channels, you'll be able to use the channel for selection and editing.

Choose Export from the File menu. FreeHand displays the Export Document dialog box.

Click the Setup button.

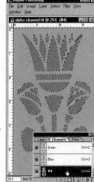

Turn on the alpha channel options and export the file.

Using the Create PICT Image Xtra (Macintosh Only)

You can convert objects in your publication into a PICT image using the Create PICT Image Xtra.

When you use the Create Pict Image Xtra, FreeHand converts the color values in the objects you've selected to RGB values in the bitmap it generates. This can cause color shifts in the objects (relative to original objects, and to other objects in the publication). If you've turned on FreeHand 8's color management system, the colors in the image will be a great deal closer to the original colors.

To turn FreeHand objects into a bitmap PICT, follow these steps (see Figure 4-46).

1. Select the objects you want to rasterize.

2. Choose PICT Image from the Create submenu of the Xtras menu (or click the corresponding button in the Operations palette). The Create PICT Image dialog box appears.

   This is the place where you have to make some tough decisions. Choosing to use a larger number of colors, or a higher resolution, makes your image look better, but also makes the conversion process take longer—*and* makes it more likely you'll run out of RAM.

   As you choose a resolution value, consider your intended use of the image. Will you be printing the final version of the publication using a laser printer? An imagesetter? The same rules that I outlined earlier in the chapter (see "TIFFs, Halftone Screen Frequency, and Resolution," above) apply here—use a resolution (in dots per inch) that's not greater than twice the halftone screen frequency (in lines per inch) you'll use to print the image. If you're planning to use the image in an electronic publication, you can probably get away with using a resolution of 72 dots per inch.

   When you turn the Dither option on, FreeHand applies a random "dither" pattern to colors outside the range of colors available (which you've defined using the Colors pop-up menu). If you're using Thousands or Millions of colors, the Dither option becomes unavailable.

   Turn the Antialiasing option on if you want FreeHand to smooth the edges of the paths in the bitmap image. Larger

FIGURE 4-46
Rasterizing Objects
with the Create PICT
Image Xtra

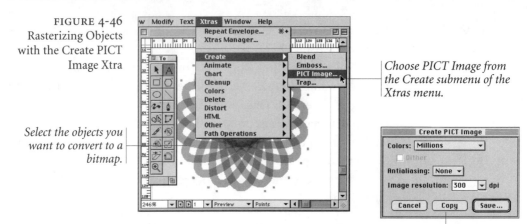

Choose PICT Image from
the Create submenu of the
Xtras menu.

Select the objects you
want to convert to a
bitmap.

FreeHand displays the Create Pict Image dialog box. Adjust the
controls in the dialog box, then click Copy (to copy the image to
the Clipboard) or Save (to save the image to disk).

Rasterizing FreeHand
objects uses up lots of
memory, so don't be
surprised if you see this
alert. You'll have to
export the selected
objects as a Photoshop
EPS, then rasterize the
EPS using Photoshop.

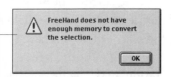

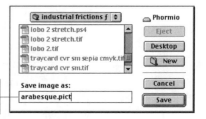

If you've chosen to save your image to
disk (rather than copying), type a
name for the file and press Return.

numbers mean more antialiasing, and a longer wait; smaller
numbers mean more "jaggies."

3. When you've set up the conversion options you want, click
the Copy button to copy the PICT image to the Clipboard,
or click the Save button to save the PICT image to a disk
file. If you click the Save button, FreeHand displays a
standard file dialog box. Enter a name for the PICT image
file, navigate to the folder you want to save the image in,
and click the OK button. FreeHand saves the PICT image.

Tip:
Bypassing the
Create PICT
Image dialog box

If you know that the last settings in the Create PICT Image dialog
box are the same settings you want to use, you can skip the Create
PICT Image dialog box by holding down Shift as you choose PICT
Image from the Create submenu of the Xtras menu. When you do
this, FreeHand creates a PICT image of the selected objects and
copies the image to the Clipboard.

Publishing and Subscribing (Macintosh Only)

One of the features that appeared in System 7 is Publish and Subscribe—a way of linking data between applications. With Publish and Subscribe, you can import a chart from Excel into a Word document in such a way that the graphic in the Word document updates when you change the chart in Excel. It's an alternative to the usual export-and-then-import process, and features the ability to open the originating application (Excel, in the above example) from the subscribing application (Word).

I don't use Publish and Subscribe, myself—I find the process of saving files and importing them using Place easier to work with. I have been told that Publish and Subscribe is most useful when you need to update FreeHand graphics placed in multiple documents, or when you want to be able to launch FreeHand from an application containing a FreeHand EPS (though you can do this without using Publish and Subscribe; see "Linking to PageMaker," later in this chapter).

When you make a file available to Publish and Subscribe, you're "publishing" an "edition," and the application the file came from is called the "publisher." When you import the edition file, the application you're using is called the "subscriber." Just to make things a bit confusing, the edition file, once placed in your subscribing application, is also called the "subscriber."

FreeHand can act as both a publisher and a subscriber. To subscribe to an edition file, follow these steps (see Figure 4-47).

1. Publish the file (precisely how you do this differs from application to application, but it's usually the Create Publisher menu item under the Edit menu).

2. Switch to FreeHand and choose Subscribe To from the Editions submenu of the Edit menu.

3. In the Subscribe To dialog box, select the edition file you want to subscribe to and click OK. FreeHand changes the cursor into the Place Gun.

4. Click (or drag) the Place Gun in the publication window to position the edition file you're subscribing to.

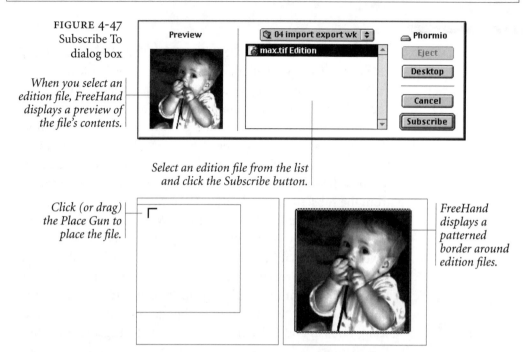

FIGURE 4-47
Subscribe To
dialog box

*When you select an
edition file, FreeHand
displays a preview of
the file's contents.*

Preview

04 import export wk

max.tif Edition

Phormio

Eject

Desktop

Cancel

Subscribe

*Select an edition file from the list
and click the Subscribe button.*

*Click (or drag)
the Place Gun to
place the file.*

*FreeHand
displays a
patterned
border around
edition files.*

When you're subscribed to an edition, you can set the update options for that edition—do you want it to update (change) when and if the edition file changes? Do you want to update the edition now? Do you want to stop your subscription to the edition? To do any or all of these tasks, choose Subscriber Options from the Editions submenu of the Edit menu. FreeHand displays the Subscriber Options dialog box (see Figure 4-48).

To publish an edition, follow these steps (see Figure 4-49).

1. In FreeHand, turn to the page you want to publish as an edition file. FreeHand publishes whole pages only—you can't publish selected items.

2. Choose Create Publisher from the Editions submenu of the Edit menu. The Create Publisher dialog box appears.

3. In the Create Publisher dialog box, you can choose to publish your edition as either an EPS or a PICT file. Unless the application in which you're planning to place the edition file can't accept EPS graphics, use EPS, rather than PICT.

FIGURE 4-48
Subscriber Options
dialog box

*Click Automatically if
you want the edition file
you've placed in
FreeHand to update
whenever the original
edition file changes.*

*Select an edition file from
this pop-up menu.*

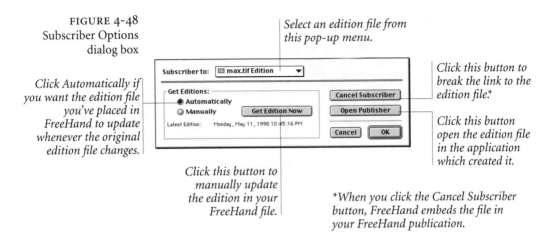

*Click this button to
break the link to the
edition file.**

*Click this button
open the edition file
in the application
which created it.*

*Click this button to
manually update
the edition in your
FreeHand file.*

**When you click the Cancel Subscriber
button, FreeHand embeds the file in
your FreeHand publication.*

4. Enter a name for your edition file and press Return. Free-Hand publishes the file, making it available to any application that supports Publish and Subscribe.

You can choose to update an edition you published with Free-Hand (and, potentially, the way that edition appears in all subscribing documents), or cancel an edition, from FreeHand. To do this, choose Publisher Options from the Editions submenu of the Edit menu. FreeHand displays the Publisher Options dialog box.

If you're in FreeHand and you want to edit an edition file in its originating application, choose Edit Original from the Editions submenu of the Edit menu. Your Macintosh switches to the application (if it's running) or locates and launches the application (if it's not), and then opens the edition file in that application.

Keep the following things in mind when you're working with Publish and Subscribe.

◆ When you subscribe to an edition that's been published as a PICT or as an EPS, FreeHand doesn't convert the file to FreeHand elements (as it would if you placed the file).

◆ You can't apply text wrap to a subscriber.

◆ Instead of the usual selection handles, edition files display a dotted border when you select them in your FreeHand publication. When you cancel a subscription to a particular edition, the file displays normal selection handles.

FIGURE 4-49
Publishing an edition

*Create the objects you
want to publish.*

*Choose Create Publisher from
the Editions submenu of the
Edit menu.*

*FreeHand displays the
Create Publisher
dialog box.*

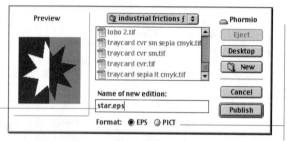

*Type a name for your
edition file here.*

*Choose an edition
file format (choose
EPS, unless you'll be
printing to a non-
PostScript printer,
or know that the
subscribing applica-
tion can't subscribe
to EPS).*

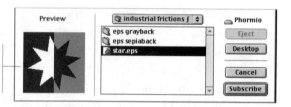

*Here's your edition
file, as seen from
PageMaker's Subscribe
To dialog box.*

When you want to delete an edition file published by FreeHand,
thereby breaking the link between the edition and all subscribing
documents, choose Subscriber Options or Publisher Options from
the Editions submenu of the Edit menu. In either dialog box,
click the Cancel Publisher button. FreeHand deletes the edition
file. When you do this, the appearance of your subscribing publications doesn't change—they'll still contain the edition file, just as
if you'd placed it.

Tip:
Linking to
PageMaker
(Macintosh
Only)

Hold down Option and double-click a selected FreeHand EPS in a
PageMaker publication, and PageMaker switches to FreeHand
(if it's running), or launches FreeHand (if it's not running), and
opens the original file (or the EPS file, if the EPS file contains the
FreeHand file). When you save the file from FreeHand, PageMaker
updates the EPS in your PageMaker publication.

Object Linking and Embedding (Windows Only)

The Windows counterpart to the Macintosh Publish and Subscribe feature is Object Linking and Embedding, or OLE (usually pronounced as though you were cheering a matador). The idea behind either "technology" is to make it easier to combine elements from disparate applications into a container—a document—without having to go through an "interchange" file format (such as EPS or TIFF). Like Publish and Subscribe, OLE also gives you a way of starting an application from a document being edited by a different application.

Unlike its Macintosh cousin, however, OLE is implemented by Windows applications in a bewildering variety of different ways. Some applications can act as an OLE client (that is, a receiver of information), some as an OLE server (a distributor of information), and some can act as both client and server. FreeHand can act as an OLE server, but not as an OLE client.

Here's how you'd add FreeHand elements to a Word document using OLE (see Figure 4-50). The process of linking FreeHand documents to documents created by other applications is similar—though I have yet to successfully create a link between FreeHand and PageMaker (versions 6.0x through 6.51) or between FreeHand and Quark XPress (version 4.0).

1. In Word, choose Insert from the Object menu. Word displays the Object dialog box.

2. Click the Create New tab (if it's not already active).

3. Choose "Macromedia FreeHand 8 Doc" from the list of object types, and then click the OK button. Word starts FreeHand and opens an untitled publication.

4. Create some FreeHand objects.

5. When you've created the objects you want to insert into the Word file, press Ctrl-S (note that the "Save" command on the File menu changes to "Update" when you're editing an OLE object).

FIGURE 4-50
Object Linking and
Embedding (OLE)

In Microsoft Word
(Word 97 shown),
choose "Object" from
the Insert menu.

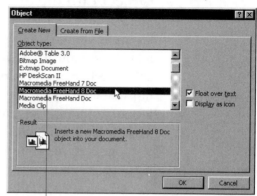

*Word displays the Object dialog box. Click the
Create New tab (if it's not already active).*

*Choose a FreeHand object
type and click the OK button.*

*Word starts FreeHand and
opens a new document. Create
some objects, choose Update
from the File menu, then
switch back to Word...*

*...and you'll see the
contents of the
FreeHand document,
embedded in a Word
file. To edit the
FreeHand objects,
double-click the
graphic.*

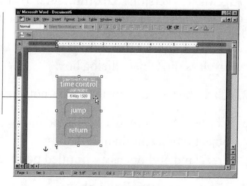

6. Switch back to Word, and you'll see the FreeHand objects
    inside a graphic frame.

To update a FreeHand graphic you've embedded in a Word file,
double-click the graphic. Word will start FreeHand and open the
graphic for editing.

Working with PDF

FreeHand can open and export Adobe Acrobat Portable Document Format files (or PDF), turning the contents of the files into editable FreeHand objects as it does so. Many of you have gotten the idea that PDF is great for putting publications on the World Wide Web, or for creating other sorts of on-line publications. Many of you, on thinking this, have to stifle a yawn whenever the topic comes up. Sure, it's a great format for that pie-in-the-sky "paperless office" stuff, but what's it got to do with the world of ink-on-paper where most of us spend our time?

I'll tell you. PDF isn't just for on-line publications. It makes a great format for moving laid-out pages from one publishing application to another—what's usually called an "interchange format" (RTF is another example of an interchange format). Having FreeHand read PDF files makes it easy to take a page you laid out in PageMaker, or XPress, and open it in FreeHand. The conversion won't always be perfect, but it's usually close enough to save you hours of time.

At the time of this writing, FreeHand can open and export PDF files in the Acrobat 1.0, 2.1, and 3.0 formats. The Acrobat 3.0 Distiller (the creator of most PDFs) is set to create Acrobat 2.1 format PDF files by default, so there's a good chance most of the PDF files you'll encounter will be in this format. If you encounter a PDF in a newer format, you should be able to use the Acrobat Distiller or Exchange to open and save the file in an earlier format. Watch Macromedia's Web site at http://www. macromedia.com for updated PDF import and export filters for FreeHand.

Opening PDFs For the most part, in applications other than FreeHand (which can save files directly to PDF—with certain exceptions, see "Exporting PDFs," later in this chapter) creating a PDF file is a two-step process. First, you print a publication to disk as PostScript, then you run the PostScript file through the Acrobat Distiller (which is a limited PostScript interpreter—see Chapter 8, "PostScript"). The Distiller saves the rendered PostScript file as a PDF.

You can also use the Acrobat PDFWriter on the Macintosh, or the Acrobat Distiller Assistant in Windows—both masquerade as printer drivers and take system-specific drawing commands (Quick-Draw on the Macintosh; GDI in Windows) and convert them to PostScript drawing commands in a PDF. It's a lot simpler than running the files through the Distiller—you print to the "driver" software just as if you were printing to a printer, and it creates a PDF file. This method, unfortunately, doesn't convert any EPS graphics in the source document. If the documents you want to convert to PDF don't contain EPS graphics, feel free to give it a try.

There's no trick to opening a PDF—you open it as you would any FreeHand publication. Multiple-page PDF documents open as multipage FreeHand publications. Once you've opened a PDF, however, there are a few things you should look for.

◆ Bookmarks, annotations, and thumbnails in PDF files are not converted when you open the PDF.

◆ If some or all of the fonts used in a PDF file aren't available, you'll have to substitute fonts (just as you would if you'd opened a FreeHand publication containing fonts FreeHand can't find on your system)

◆ Text will sometimes be broken into short "runs" of text—creating a new text block for every change in formatting. You can combine these text blocks as you would any Free-Hand text blocks.

◆ If each page of a converted PDF file appears as a single object, the elements on the page have probably been enclosed by a clipping path. Select each page and press Command-Shift-X/Ctrl-Shift-X to remove the elements from the clipping path.

Exporting PDFs FreeHand can *save* files as PDF—virtually every other application has to go through the Acrobat Distiller, first. Even PageMaker, the best application for creating PDF files available, uses the Distiller (though PageMaker automates and hides the process). If your publication uses Custom, Textured, or PostScript fills, Custom or

PostScript strokes, imported EPS graphics, or any of FreeHand's text effects, you'll need to do what every other application does—create a PostScript file (an EPS will work just fine), then run the PostScript file through the Acrobat Distiller to create a PDF.

To export a file as a PDF, follow these steps (see Figure 4-51).

1. Press Command-Shift-R/Ctrl-Shift-R. FreeHand displays the Export Document dialog box.

2. Turn on the Selected Objects Only option, if necessary, then choose PDF from the Format/Save As Type pop-up menu.

FIGURE 4-51
Exporting PDF

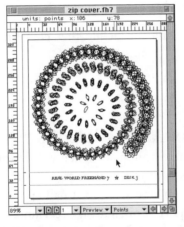

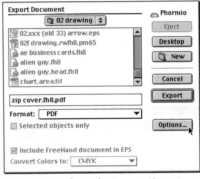

To export objects from a FreeHand publication, press Command-Shift-R/Ctrl-Shift-R.

FreeHand displays the Export Document dialog box.

Choose PDF from the Format/Save As Type pop-up menu, then click the Options button.

FreeHand displays the PDF Export dialog box.

Set the page range you want to export to the PDF.

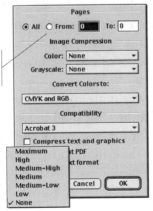

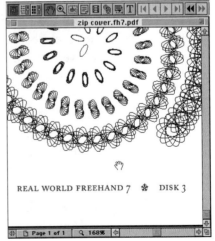

If you plan to use the PDF to produce printed materials, leave the Image Compression options set to "None."

If you'll be publishing the PDF online, experiment with the PDF compression options.

Here's the PDF, open in Acrobat Exchange (I've zoomed in a little).

3. Click the Options/Setup button. FreeHand displays the PDF Export dialog box. If you want to compress any images in the file you're exporting, choose a compression level from the Color and/or Grayscale pop-up menus.

   I compress images in PDF files I don't intend printing, but turn compression off (choose "None") if I think there's a chance I might print the PDF—or if I plan to open and edit it in another application. FreeHand's PDF export filter uses JPEG compression, which means that you *will lose image data* in the compressed images stored in the PDF.

   Set the range of pages you want to export, then click the OK button to close the dialog box.

4. Enter a name for the file, then click the OK button to export the file.

The Best of All Possible Worlds

Can you get there from here? When you're working with FreeHand, you can almost always export or save files in a form you can use in another program, and you can usually produce files in other programs you import or open using FreeHand.

There are definitely bumps in the road—PageMaker's confused EPS Import filter, for example. Sometimes, you've got to go through an intermediate program—such as the amazing DeBabelizer—to convert files from one format to another (particularly if the files came from another type of computer).

Someday, we'll have a more complete, universal, and sophisticated file format for exchanging publications. I'd like to think that Adobe's PDF is that format, and it's certainly making steps in the right direction. When the great day arrives (and it's getting closer), we'll be able to take page layouts from FreeHand to PageMaker to Photoshop—using each program for what it's best at—without losing any formatting.

And the streets will be paved with gold, mounted beggars will spend the day ducking winged pigs, and the Seattle Mariners will win the World Series.

Transforming

In the previous chapters, I've covered the process of creating FreeHand elements. This chapter talks about what you can do with those elements once you've drawn, typed, or imported them. The process of rotating, reflecting, skewing, scaling, cloning, or moving objects is called *transformation.*

Many of the topics in this chapter have been touched on in the preceding chapters—mainly because everything you can do in Free-Hand is interconnected. In the old days, software was entirely linear or modal: one had to proceed from this screen to that screen following a particular sequence of steps. These days, software is extremely nonlinear and nonmodal (that is, you can do things many different ways in many different orders), and, therefore much harder to write about. Your purchase of this book will make my time at Looney Farm that much more pleasant. Thank you.

Transformations are the key to using FreeHand efficiently. I don't know how many times I've seen people laboriously drawing and redrawing shapes when they could have been using the Clone, Rotate, and Reflect commands to accomplish the same ends faster and with far less trouble. Any time you can see a similarity between the shapes on one side of an object and another, you should be thinking about reflection. Any time you see an object that's made up of the same shape rotated around a center point, you should be thinking about rotation. Start looking at the paths you draw as patterns of clones and transformations, and you'll be a long way toward becoming a FreeHand wizard.

Like the Inspector, the Transform palette has several different subpanels (for moving, rotating, scaling, skewing, and reflecting objects). I refer to each panel as a separate palette: the Move, Rotate, Scale, Skew, and Reflect palettes. This beats saying "the Rotate panel of the Transformation palette."

In addition to the operations corresponding to the transformation tools, I think of several other FreeHand features as "transformations." Specifically, I include clipping paths (using Paste Inside), locking objects, and alignment and distribution. You'll find these topics at the end of the chapter.

There are three ways to transform an object on a FreeHand page.

♦ Select an object, select a transformation tool from the Toolbox, and then drag transformation tool (see Figure 5-1)

♦ Double-click an object. FreeHand displays transformation handles around the object (unless you've turned off the Show Transform Handles option in the Object Preferences dialog box). Drag one of the transformation handles to transform the object (see Figure 5-2).

♦ Select an object, display the Transform palette, and then enter numeric values in the panel of the palette corresponding to the transformation you want (see Figure 5-3).

There's no "right" or "best" way to do transformations—you can experiment with the different methods and see which you like best. I change methods depending on the situation (and my mood).

If that's all there is to transforming, then what's in the rest of this chapter? Homespun philosophical insights guaranteed to make this book a checkout counter bestseller? Nope. As you might expect, there's more to transforming objects than meets the eye. The rest of the chapter covers the down-and-dirty details.

Grouping and Transformation

When you transform a group, FreeHand transforms all the lines and fills inside the group proportionally, unless you've checked the Transform As Unit option (which you'll find in the Object Inspector for the group). Check this option if you want to transform the line weights and fills inside the group nonproportionally, resulting in an effect that resembles perspective drawing (see Figure 5-4).

FIGURE 5-1
Transforming using the transformation tools

Rotation tool

Axis of transformation

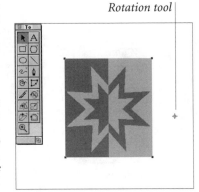

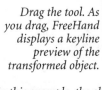

Select the object you want to transform, then select the transformation tool you want to use. In this example, I've selected the Rotation tool.

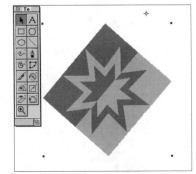

When the object looks the way you want it to, stop dragging. FreeHand transforms the object.

Drag the tool. As you drag, FreeHand displays a keyline preview of the transformed object.

In this example, the object is a group. When you transform a group or a compound path, you'll see only a box representing the object.

FIGURE 5-2
Transforming using the transformation handles

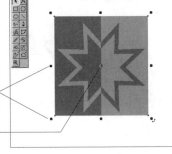

Double-click an object, and FreeHand displays the transformation handles.

Center point

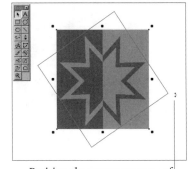

Position the cursor over one of the transformation handles and drag. As you drag, FreeHand transforms the object around the center point.

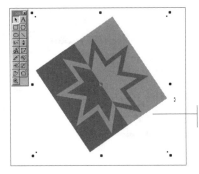

When the object looks the way you want it to, stop dragging.

Cursor	Drag to
	Scale width and height
↔	Scale width.
↕	Scale height
↻	Rotate
✛	Move
▶	Move the center point

FIGURE 5-3
Transforming
using the Transform
palette

*You can also use
keyboard shortcuts to
display the panels of the
Transform palette.*

Panel	Command/Ctrl-
Scale	F10
Move	E
Rotate	F2
Reflect	F9
Skew	F11

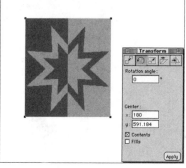

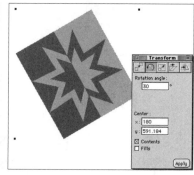

Select the object you want to rotate and double-click the tool for the transformation you want to apply. FreeHand displays the Transform palette, open to the corresponding panel. In this example, I'm using the Rotate palette.

Enter the values you want in the Transform palette (in this example, the Rotate palette), check any appropriate checkboxes (they vary from palette to palette), and click the Apply button (or press Return).

FIGURE 5-4
Transforming groups

With Transform As
Unit turned off...

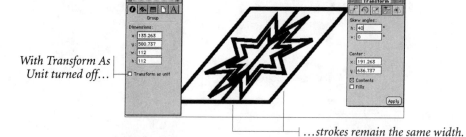

...strokes remain the same width.

With Transform As
Unit turned on...

...stroke widths change.

When you ungroup objects you've transformed with Transform As Unit turned on, any lines and fills applied to those objects revert to their undistorted appearance.

Transformation Shortcuts

As you think about transforming objects, keep in mind two of Free-Hand's most important keyboard shortcuts: Command-, (comma)/Ctrl-Shift-G and Command-D/Ctrl-D.

To repeat the most recent transformation, press Command-,/Ctrl-Shift-G (see Figure 5-5). You don't even have to have the same object selected as the one you originally transformed—you can transform an object, select an entirely different object, and then transform that object using the same settings.

FIGURE 5-5
Transform again

Transform an object (in this example, I'm skewing the object using the Skewing tool).

Press Command-,/Ctrl-Shift-G, to transform the object again.

Command-,/Ctrl-Shift-G is great for experimentation—by pressing the keyboard shortcut you can ask, What if I moved it a little bit more? or What if I skewed it a little bit more? If you don't like what you see, press Command-Z/Ctrl-Z to undo it.

If you haven't transformed anything lately, pressing Command-D/Ctrl-D does what the menu item (Duplicate) suggests—it duplicates the object, placing the duplicate at a slight offset from the original object. If you've recently cloned, then transformed the object, however, Command-D/Ctrl-D means, "Clone and transform it again," and repeats the most recent transformation (or series of transformations) while cloning the object. You can use Command-D/Ctrl-D to do all kinds of things (see Figure 5-6).

FreeHand remembers the last transformation (whatever it was). If you rotate something, drag out some ruler guides, then select an object and press Command-D/Ctrl-D, FreeHand rotates the object—*even if it's not the object you originally transformed.*

FIGURE 5-6
Clone and
transform again

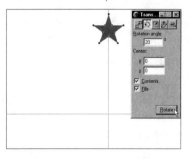

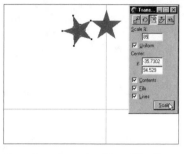

Create an object, clone it, and then transform it (in this example, I'm about to rotate the clone of the object using the Rotate palette).

Transform it again, if you like (in this example, I'm about to scale the object using the Scale palette).

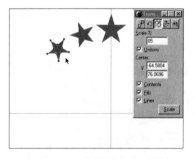

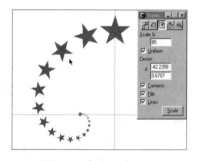

Press Command-D/Ctrl-D, to clone the object and apply the last transformation (or, in this example, series of transformations) to it.

Press Command-D/Ctrl-D again (as many times as you like) to repeat the clone-and-transform process.

Transformation Handle Shortcuts

FreeHand's new transformation handles come with their own set of tips and tricks.

◆ To hide the transform handles once you've displayed them, double-click again.

◆ The center point sets the center of rotation. By default, the center point appears at the geometric center of the selected object (or objects). You can drag the center point to a new location, if you want to rotate around that point (see Figure 5-7). As you drag the center point, you can see the X and Y location of the point in the X and Y fields of the Rotate palette.

◆ To move an object *without* moving the center point, press Command/Ctrl as you drag (see Figure 5-8).

FIGURE 5-7
Moving the
center point

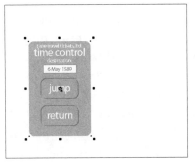

Point at the center point.

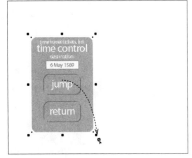

Drag the center point.

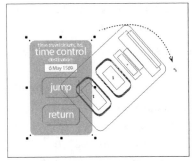

When you drag to rotate the object...

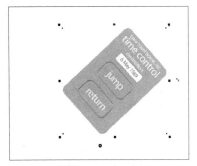

*...FreeHand rotates the object
around the center point.*

FIGURE 5-8
Leaving the center
point behind

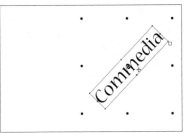

*Ordinarily, when you
move an object...*

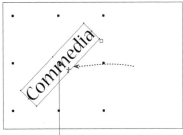

*...the center point moves
with the object.*

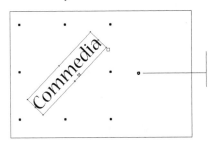

*If you hold down Command/Ctrl
as you drag the object, however,
the center point stays put.*

♦ You can use the transformation handles to rotate, move, or scale points without transforming the entire path containing the points. To do this, select the points, then double-click one of the selected points to display the transformation handles. When you drag one of the transformation handles, only the selected points are affected.

♦ If you double-click an object to display its transformation handles, then copy it, and then paste, FreeHand displays transformation handles around the copy of the object, but leaves the center point in the location it was in when you copied the original object.

♦ If you subselect an object (an object in a group or a subpath of a composite path), then double-click that object, FreeHand displays transformation handles around the subselected object, *not* around the group or composite path. If you then press accent grave (`), FreeHand displays the transformation handles around the group or composite path, *but leaves the center point at the center of the object you initially subselected.* This might come in handy if you want to transform a group around the center of one of the objects in the group.

♦ To reset the center point to the geometric center of the object, double-click the object (to hide the transformation handles, then double-click again to display them).

Moving

Moving an object from one place to another is probably the task you do most often in FreeHand. There are (at least) four ways to move objects in FreeHand—try any of the following.

♦ Drag the objects with the Pointer tool.

♦ Enter values in the Move palette.

♦ Change coordinates in the Object Inspector.

♦ Press the arrow, or "nudge" keys.

Moving Path Contents and Fills

Check the Contents box when you want objects that you've pasted inside a path to move with that path (see Figure 5-9). Check Fills to move the fill you've applied to the path (see Figure 5-10)—though it only makes a difference when you're moving paths filled with tiled fills. If you don't want the paths' contents or fill to move, uncheck the appropriate checkbox (or checkboxes).

Note that these checkboxes affect movement whether you're using the Move palette to move objects or not.

These checkboxes have no effect on objects other than paths.

FIGURE 5-9
Moving contents

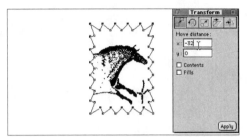

In this example, I'll use the Move palette to move the selected path to the left.

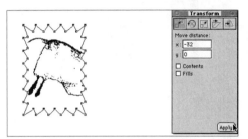

With Contents off, objects you've pasted inside a path don't move when you move the path.

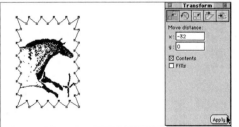

With Contents turned on, objects you've pasted inside a path move with the path.

Tip:
Moving Points

When you drag some, but not all, of the points on a path, Free-Hand doesn't move objects you've pasted inside the path, regardless of the state of the Contents checkbox in the Move palette. This comes in handy when you need to adjust a path you've used to crop a TIFF image (see Figure 5-11).

FIGURE 5-10
Moving fills

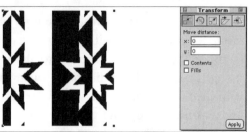

In this example, I'll use the Move palette to move the selected path to the right.

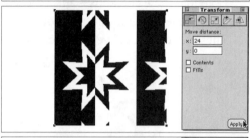

With Fills off, the path's tiled fill doesn't move with the path.

With Fills turned on, the tiled fill moves as you move the path.

FIGURE 5-11
Moving selected points

Regardless of the setting of the Contents check-box in the Move palette, moving points does not move the contents of the path (unless, that is, you select all of the points in the path).

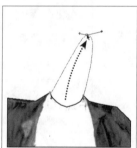

This is a good thing, because it makes it easy to edit paths you've used to crop TIFFs.

Moving by Dragging

FreeHand's just like any other program—if you want to move something, select the object with the Pointer tool and drag.

Tip:
Dragging Things Quickly Versus Dragging Things Slowly

If you select something and immediately start dragging, you'll see only a box the shape of the object's selection rectangle. If, on the other hand, you hold down the mouse button for a second before dragging, you'll see the object as you drag it (whether this works for multiple selected objects or not depends on the setting you've entered in the Preview Drag field in the Editing Preferences dialog box; see "Setting Preferences" in Chapter 1, "FreeHand Basics").

Dragging quickly is great for snapping objects into position by their outlines; waiting a second before dragging is best for seeing things inside a selection as you position them on the page (see Figure 5-12).

FIGURE 5-12
Seeing objects as you drag them

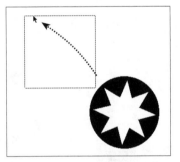

Drag quickly, and you'll see only an outline of the objects.

Pause a second before you drag, and you'll see the objects.

Tip:
Seeing What You Drag

To make FreeHand show you a screen display of the object you're dragging—regardless of the number of objects you've selected and no matter what the setting of the Preview Drag preference—tap the Option/Alt key before you start dragging (that is, after you've pressed the mouse button down, but before you move the mouse). Wait for FreeHand to draw the objects you've selected, and then drag the objects. As you drag, FreeHand displays the objects.

Moving "By the Numbers"

When I need precision, I always move objects by entering numbers in the Move palette (see Figure 5-13). And it's not just because I'm a closet rocket scientist; it's because I don't trust a 72-dpi screen, even at 800 percent magnification (at 256k percent magnification,

I'm still skeptical). You shouldn't either, when it comes to fine adjustments in your FreeHand publication.

1. Select the object you want to move.

2. Display the Transform palette, if it's not already visible (you can double-click any of the transformation tools in the toolbox to display the palette, or press Command-M/ Ctrl-M). Click the Move icon button at the top of the Transform palette to display the Move palette, if necessary.

3. Enter values in the fields. Type positive numbers to move objects up (toward the top of the screen) or to the right; type negative numbers to move them down or to the left).

4. Set the Contents and Fills checkboxes the way you want them (see "Moving Contents and Fills," earlier in this chapter).

5. Press Return (or click the Apply button). FreeHand moves the selected object.

FIGURE 5-13
Moving with
the Move palette

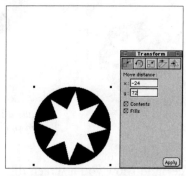

Select the object you want to move and type distances in the Move palette.

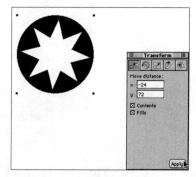

Click the Apply button, and FreeHand moves the object the distance and direction you specified.

Moving Objects with the Inspector

The X and Y fields in the Object Inspector aren't only there to show you where the object is; you can use them to move the object to a specific location on your page. To move the object to a new location, type coordinates in the X and Y fields (remember, coordinates are measured from the current position of the zero point, and specify the location of the lower-left corner of the selected object), and press Return (see Figure 5-14).

FIGURE 5-14
Moving with
the Object Inspector

When you move an object using the Object Inspector, FreeHand doesn't move the object's contents (if any)—regardless of the state of the Contents checkbox in the Move palette. Group the object first, and the contents will move with the object. This is almost certainly a bug.

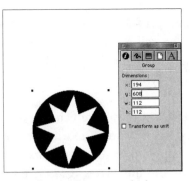

Enter the coordinates at which you want to position the lower-left corner of the object in the X and Y fields of the Object Inspector and press Return.

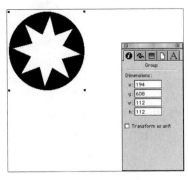

FreeHand moves the object to the new coordinates.

If you're looking at the Object Inspector, and you don't see the X and Y fields, you're looking at an ungrouped path. Group the path, and the fields appear in the Object Inspector. You can always ungroup the path after you've moved it.

Moving by Pressing Arrow Keys

As if dragging by eye and specifying coordinates weren't enough (in terms of movement options), FreeHand also sports "nudge" keys. Select an element and press one of the arrow keys, and the element moves in that direction in the increments you set in the Cursor Key Distance field in the Editing Preferences dialog box (see "Setting Preferences" in Chapter 1, "FreeHand Basics").

Scaling

In FreeHand, you can change the size of objects using any of the following techniques.

- Drag the Scaling tool.
- Drag transformation handles.
- Enter values in the Scale palette.
- Drag a selection handle with the Pointer tool.
- Change values in the Object Inspector.

In addition, you can change the size of text boxes by changing the sizes of the column heights and row widths in the Column Inspector (see "Multicolumn and Multirow Text Blocks" in Chapter 3, "Text and Type").

Scaling Contents, Fills, and Lines

When you scale a path, you can choose to scale the path's contents (that is, whatever you've pasted inside the path), or the fill and stroke you've applied to the path. To scale these items, check the Contents, Fills, or Lines boxes, respectively, in the Scale palette (see Figure 5-15). To keep the paths' attributes from scaling as you scale the path, uncheck the appropriate box or boxes.

FIGURE 5-15
Scaling path attributes

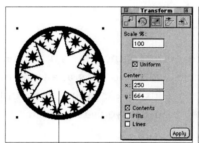
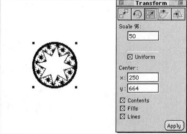

Original object before scaling

When you turn on the Fills and Lines options, FreeHand scales those path attributes as it scales paths.

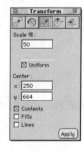

When you turn the Fills and Lines options off, FreeHand does not scale strokes or fills as it scales paths.

Using the Scaling Tool

When you want to scale an object until it "looks right," use the Scaling tool (see Figure 5-16).

1. Select the object you want to scale.

2. Select the Scaling tool from the toolbox.

FIGURE 5-16
Using the Scaling tool

 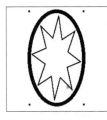

To scale an object vertically, select the object and drag the Scaling tool up (to make the object larger) or down (to make the object smaller).

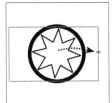 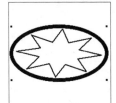

To scale an object horizontally, select the object and drag the Scaling tool to the left (to make the object smaller) or to the right (to make the object larger).

Macintosh only: To scale from an object's center, hold down Control as you drag the Scaling tool.

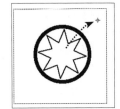 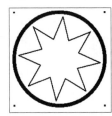

To proportionally scale an object, select the object and hold down Shift as you drag the Scaling tool.

3. Position the Scaling tool at the point around which you want to scale. If you're using a Macintosh, you can hold down Control to scale an object around its center.

4. Drag the Scaling tool horizontally to scale the object's width, or drag vertically to scale the object's height. Dragging diagonally sizes the object's width and height. Hold down Shift as you drag to scale the object proportionally.

   If the object you're scaling is a paint-type graphic or a bi-level TIFF, you can hold down Option/Alt and Shift to scale the object both proportionally and to the printer's resolution (which you set in the Target Printer Resolution field in the Document Inspector; see "Using the Document Inspector" in Chapter 1, "FreeHand Basics").

5. When the object's the size you want it, stop dragging.

Using the Scale Palette

When you know you want to make an object larger or smaller by an exact percentage, use the Scale palette (see Figure 5-17).

FIGURE 5-17
Using the Scale palette

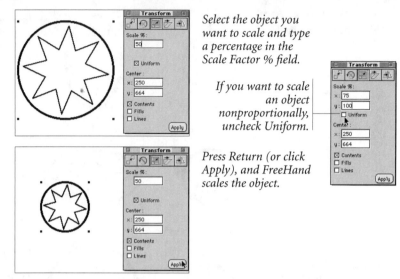

Select the object you want to scale and type a percentage in the Scale Factor % field.

If you want to scale an object nonproportionally, uncheck Uniform.

Press Return (or click Apply), and FreeHand scales the object.

1. Select the object you want to scale.

2. Display the Scale palette (if it's not already visible, double-click the Scaling tool in the toolbox).

3. Uncheck Uniform if you want to scale the object's width and height by different percentages (leave Uniform checked to scale both dimensions by the same percentage).

4. Set the Contents, Fills, and Lines checkboxes the way you want them (see "Scaling Contents, Fills, and Lines," earlier in this chapter).

5. Enter percentages in the Scale Factor field (or, if you're scaling width and height separately, enter percentages in the X and Y fields).

6. Press Return to scale the object.

Tip:
Resetting the
Center of Scaling

If you want to use the Scale palette to resize an object around its center point, and see that the coordinates in the X and Y fields in the Scale palette aren't at the center of the object (it's easy to accidentally set them to other coordinates—all it takes is clicking the scaling tool on the page), you can reset them to the object's center.

Click the object with the Pointer tool (hold down Command/ Ctrl to turn the current tool into the Pointer tool, if necessary), and FreeHand enters the coordinates of the object's geometric center in the X and Y fields.

Tip:
Picking a Point
to Scale Around

Suppose you want to enlarge or reduce an object, but you want the lower-left corner of the object to stay in its original location (that is, you want the object to grow up, and to the right). If you know the location of the point you want to scale around, you can enter that point in the Scale palette—but I rarely go to all that trouble— I simply click the Scaling tool on that point (being careful, as I do so, that I don't drag the tool). FreeHand enters the coordinates of the point I click on in the X and Y fields in the Scale palette.

Tip:
Positioning
Objects by
Setting the Zero
Point

One of the easiest ways to set the center of transformation is to position the zero point where you want the center of the object to fall, and then enter "0" in the Horizontal and Vertical fields in the Center options section of the Scale dialog box. It's easier than entering "23.0476" and "47.135" (for example).

Scaling with the Pointer Tool

As in almost any other drawing or page-layout application, you can change the size of objects by dragging their corner handles with the Pointer tool (see Figure 5-18). As you drag, the object you're dragging gets larger or smaller. Hold down Shift as you drag to resize the object proportionally.

I confess: I use this method far more often than I use the Scaling tool (mainly because I can switch to the Pointer tool from any tool by holding down Command, while there's no keyboard shortcut for the Scaling tool).

When you resize a rectangle, ellipse, or grouped path by dragging a selection handle, FreeHand doesn't resize anything you've pasted inside the object, regardless of whether Contents is checked in the Scale palette.

Tip:
Resizing from an
Object's Center

Hold down Option/Alt as you drag a selection handle to resize an imported graphic, group, rectangle, or ellipse from its center point. This trick doesn't work for ungrouped paths.

FIGURE 5-18
Scaling objects by
dragging selection
handles

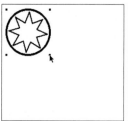 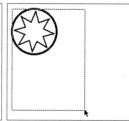 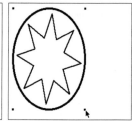

With the Pointer tool, position the cursor over a corner handle... *...and drag to scale the object.* *When the object is the size and shape you want, stop dragging.*

 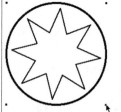 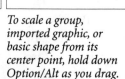

To scale an object proportionally, hold down Shift as you drag a corner handle.

To scale a group, imported graphic, or basic shape from its center point, hold down Option/Alt as you drag.

Scaling with the Transformation Handles

To scale an object using the transformation handles, double-click the object. FreeHand displays the transformation handles around the object. Position the cursor directly over one of the handles, then drag. As you drag, FreeHand scales the object (see Figure 5-19). If you hold down Shift as you drag, FreeHand scales the object proportionally.

Scaling with the Object Inspector

When you select any object other than an ungrouped path, that object's width and height appear in the W and H fields in the Object Inspector (to see the width and height of a path, first select the path and press Command-G/Ctrl-G to group it). To change the object's width or height, enter new values in these fields, and press Return. FreeHand changes the size of the object.

I find this feature particularly useful when I'm working with rectangles I've drawn with the Rectangle tool. I use rectangles a lot when I'm laying out a page, and I usually know what size they need to be, so I use the Object Inspector to set their width and height. Doing that is often easier than drawing them to precisely the right size.

FIGURE 5-19
Using the
transformation
handles to scale
an object

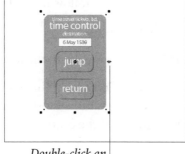

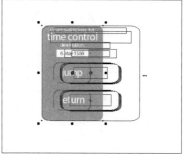

You can drag a side handle to scale the object's width, or drag the top or bottom handle to scale the object's height, or drag any of the corner handles to scale the object's height and width. To scale the object proportionally, hold down Shift as you drag the transformation handle.

Double-click an object to display the transformation handles, then move the cursor over one of the handles.

Drag the transformation handle. As you drag, FreeHand scales the object.

When the object looks the way you want it to, stop dragging.

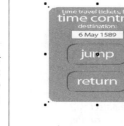

Rotating

Some applications (such as PageMaker) store the original orientation and angle of objects on their pages. To these applications, rotation is an *absolute* measurement—the current angle of an object always refers to that object's original rotation angle (usually zero degrees). In FreeHand, rotation is a *relative*—the object's current angle of rotation is always considered to be zero degrees, regardless of any previous rotation.

This approach has advantages and disadvantages. You can't rotate an object back to its original state by giving it a rotation angle of zero, as you can in PageMaker (in FreeHand, a rotation angle of zero means the object doesn't rotate at all). In FreeHand, however, you can always rotate the object another 12.5 degrees, without adding that value to the object's existing rotation angle to derive the angle you enter (as you would in PageMaker).

You can rotate an object back to its original angle, provided you keep track of how far you've rotated it away from that angle.

Using the Rotation Tool

To rotate an object "by eye," follow these steps (see Figure 5-20).

1. Select the object you want to rotate.

2. Select the Rotation tool from the toolbox.

3. Position the Rotation tool at the point where you want to put the center of rotation. On the Macintosh, you can hold down Control to set the center of rotation at the center of the object.

4. Drag the Rotation tool. As you drag, FreeHand displays the angle of rotation in the Info Bar.

5. When the object looks the way you want, stop dragging.

FIGURE 5-20
Rotating an object
using the Rotation tool

*Select the object you
want to rotate.*

*Position the Rotation
tool at the point you
want to rotate around.*

*Drag the Rotation tool.
As you drag, FreeHand
displays a keyline
preview of the rotated
object.*

*When the object looks
the way you want it
to, stop dragging.
FreeHand rotates
the object.*

*As you drag the Rotation tool,
FreeHand displays the angle of
rotation in the Info Toolbar.*

Using the Rotate Palette

To rotate an object using FreeHand's Rotate palette, follow these steps (see Figure 5-21).

1. Select the object you want to rotate.

2. Display the Rotate palette (if it's not already visible, double-click the Rotation tool in the toolbox).

3. If you're rotating a path, make sure that the Contents and Fills checkboxes are set the way you want them (see "Rotating Contents and Fills," later in this chapter).

4. Enter values in the Rotation angle field.

FIGURE 5-21
Rotating an object
"by the numbers"

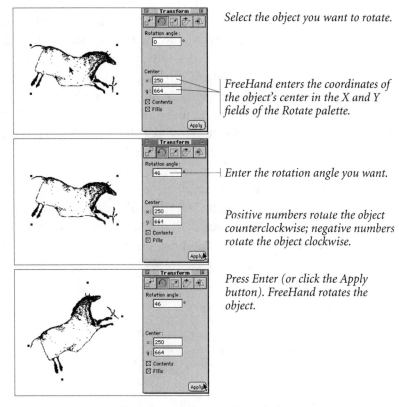

Select the object you want to rotate.

FreeHand enters the coordinates of the object's center in the X and Y fields of the Rotate palette.

Enter the rotation angle you want.

Positive numbers rotate the object counterclockwise; negative numbers rotate the object clockwise.

Press Enter (or click the Apply button). FreeHand rotates the object.

FreeHand's Rotate palette isn't picky. You can enter positive numbers (such as "45"), negative numbers (such as "-270"), and absurd numbers (such as "478") in the Rotation Angle field. Positive rotation angles rotate the selected object counterclockwise; negative values rotate the object clockwise. You enter rotation angles in .1 degree increments.

5. Press Return (or click the Apply button in the Rotate palette) to rotate the object.

Tip:
Rotating Around
a Specific Point

When you're rotating an object using the Rotate palette, it's easy to get it to rotate around its center. What if, instead, you want to rotate the object around some other point?

You can always enter the coordinates of the location you want to rotate around in the X and Y fields in the Rotate palette, but wouldn't it be nice to click on a spot on the page, as you can when you're rotating using the Rotation tool?

You can: just click the Rotation tool on the page before you enter anything in the Rotate palette. Don't drag the Rotation tool, and don't click too quickly—I find it takes a second for the palette to update. When the X and Y fields in the palette change to match the current location of the cursor, release the mouse button and move your cursor to the Rotation Angle field. Enter an angle and press Return to rotate the object. FreeHand rotates the object around the point you specified by clicking.

Rotating Objects Using the Transformation Handles

To rotate an object using the transformation handles, double-click an object. FreeHand displays the transformation handles around the object. Position the cursor just outside one of the handles, then drag. As you drag, FreeHand rotates the object around the center point (see Figure 5-22).

FIGURE 5-22
Rotating an
object using the
transformation
handles

Double-click an object. FreeHand displays the transformation handles.

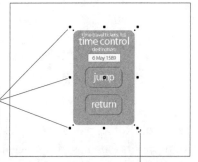

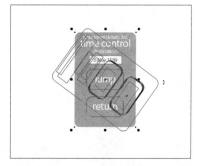

Position the cursor just outside one of the transformation handles...

...and drag. As you drag, FreeHand rotates the object around the center point.

When the object looks the way you want it to, stop dragging.

Rotating Multiple Selected Objects

When you rotate more than one object (in this sense, I'm counting groups as single objects), the objects rotate around a single point (see Figure 5-23). This point can be their joint geometric center,

FIGURE 5-23
Rotating multiple
objects

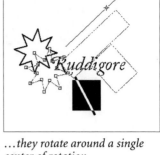

When you rotate multiple objects in FreeHand...

...they rotate around a single center of rotation.

Like this: Objects rotated around a single point.

Not like this: Objects rotated around their individual centers.

or around any other point you've specified. They don't all rotate around their individual center points.

Rotating Contents and Fills

You can choose to have a path's contents (objects you've pasted inside the path) or fills rotate with the path as you rotate the path (see Figure 5-24). To rotate the path's contents, check the Contents checkbox in the Rotate palette before you rotate the path. To rotate the path's fill, check Fills.

Rotating a fill doesn't change the screen angle of any halftone screen you've applied to the fill (you control screen angles using the Halftone palette).

Rotating Points

You don't have to select all the points in a path to apply rotation to that path; you can rotate some or all of the points. What possible use is this? Look at Figure 5-25.

Rotation and Path Direction

While you're rotating things, remember that the direction, or winding, of rotated paths does not change (for more on PostScript path

FIGURE 5-24
Rotating contents
and fills

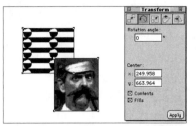

In this example, I'll use the Rotate palette to rotate two paths. One path is filled with a tiled fill; the other has a scanned image pasted inside it.

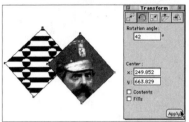

With Contents unchecked, objects you've pasted inside a path don't rotate when you rotate the path. Turn Fills off, and tiled fills won't rotate when you rotate the path.

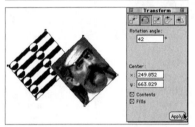

Turn on Contents, and objects inside paths rotate with the paths. When you want tiled fills to rotate with the path, turn on Fills.

FIGURE 5-25
Rotating selected
points

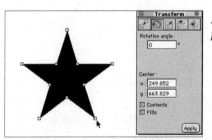

Select some, but not all, of the points on a path.

The selected points rotate...

...the unselected points stay in their original positions.

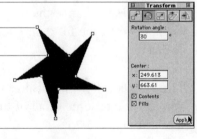

Rotate the selected points.

direction, see "Thinking Like a Line" in Chapter 2, "Drawing")—it still starts from the same point as it did before you rotated it (see Figure 5-26).

FIGURE 5-26
Rotation doesn't
change the direction
of a path

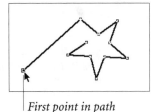 

First point in path
*Even though you've rotated
this path 180 degrees...*

First point in path
*...the first point in the
path remains the same.*

Reflecting

Reflection flips a selected object or objects across a specified axis. When we're drawing, we very often work with paths which are mirror images of each other around an axis. FreeHand's reflection tool makes it possible for us to work the way we think.

You can reflect selected objects by dragging the Reflection tool, or by entering values in the Reflect palette, or by using the Mirror tool, which creates multiple reflections at once.

**Using the
Reflection Tool**

To reflect an object "by eye," follow these steps (see Figure 5-27).

1. Select the object you want to reflect.

2. Select the Reflection tool from the toolbox.

3. Move the cursor to the point where you want to place the axis of reflection.

4. Drag the object across the axis of reflection (as you drag, FreeHand displays a dotted line showing the axis of reflection). On the Macintosh, you can hold down Control as you drag to locate the center of reflection at the center of the object. Hold down Shift as you drag to constrain the reflection angle to 45-degree angles.

5. When you're through reflecting the object, stop dragging. FreeHand reflects the object as you've specified.

FIGURE 5-27
Reflecting
objects using the
Reflection tool

*Select the object you
want to reflect.*

*Drag the Reflection tool in the publication window.
The point where you start dragging determines the
axis around which FreeHand reflects the object.*

*As you drag, FreeHand
displays a preview of
the reflected object.*

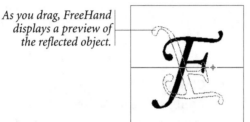 

*Hold down Shift and drag toward the top or bottom
of the publication window to reflect the object
across its vertical axis. Hold down Shift and drag
left or right to reflect the object horizontally.*

Using the Reflect Palette

Most of the time, I know precisely how I want to reflect an object, so I use the Reflect palette (see Figure 5-28). Come to think of it, I don't think I ever use reflection to do anything other than flip objects across their vertical or horizontal axes.

To reflect an object using the Reflect palette, follow these steps.

1. Select the object you want to reflect.

2. If the Reflect palette isn't already visible, display it by double-clicking the reflection tool in the toolbox.

3. Set the Fills and Contents checkboxes the way you want them (see "Reflecting Contents and Fills," later in this chapter).

4. Type the values you want in the Reflect Axis field (enter "90" to reflect the object across its vertical axis, "180" to reflect the object across its horizontal axis). Positive values reflect the selected object counterclockwise; enter negative values to reflect the object clockwise.

FIGURE 5-28
Reflecting an object
using the Reflect
palette

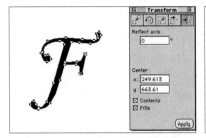 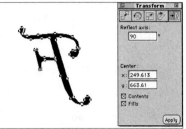

Select the object you want to reflect, type an angle in the Reflect Axis field of the Reflect palette…

…and press Return (or click the Apply button). FreeHand reflects the selected object across the axis you entered.

5. Press Return. FreeHand reflects the object as you specified.

Reflecting Contents and Fills

When you're reflecting a path, you can choose to reflect the path's contents (what's pasted inside the path) or fills as you reflect the path (see Figure 5-29). To reflect path contents, check Contents. To reflect the path's fill, check the Fills box.

FIGURE 5-29
Reflecting contents
and fills

In this example, I'll use the Reflect palette to reflect a path containing both a tiled fill and an image.

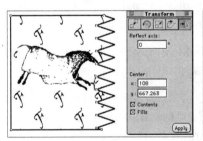 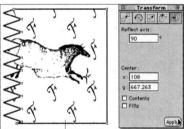

With the Contents and Fills checkboxes off, FreeHand reflects the path, but doesn't reflect the object pasted inside the path or the path's tiled fill.

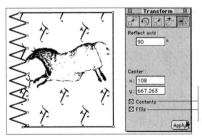

With the Contents and Fills checkboxes turned on, FreeHand reflects the image and the tiled fill.

Reflection and Path Direction

Reflection changes the winding, or direction, of reflected paths (for more on PostScript path direction, see "Thinking Like a Line" in Chapter 2, "Drawing"). The path still starts from the same point as it did before you reflected it, but the path's direction now goes the opposite direction (see Figure 5-30).

FIGURE 5-30
Reflection and
path direction

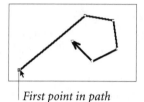
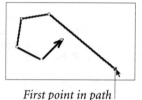

First point in path

First point in path

*Before reflection, this
path winds clockwise.*

*After reflection, the path
winds counterclockwise.*

Reflecting Objects Using the Mirror Tool

One of my favorite new FreeHand features is the Mirror tool, which can clone and reflect a path a specified number of times. It's great for creating geometric patterns or textures. It's an Xtra, so you'll find it in the Xtra Tools palette (press Command-Option-X/Ctrl-Alt-X to display the palette, if it's not already visible). To see how the Mirror tool works, follow these steps (see Figure 5-31).

1. Double-click the Mirror tool to display the Mirror dialog box.

2. Choose the reflection axes you want to use: Vertical, Horizontal, Horizontal and Vertical, or Multiple. If you choose Multiple, FreeHand displays additional controls. If you turn on the Close Paths option, FreeHand will join and close any open paths whose endpoints fall within the distance, in screen pixels, set in the Snap Distance field of the General Preferences dialog box (see Figure 5-32). Click the OK button to close the dialog box.

3. Hold down Command/Control to temporarily switch to the Pointer tool. Select the object or objects you want to reflect. You can select any type of FreeHand object.

3. Drag the Mirror tool. As you drag, FreeHand displays a preview of the effect of the dragging.

FIGURE 5-31
Mirror tool

Display the Xtra Tools palette.

*Double-click the
Mirror tool.*

*FreeHand displays
the Mirror dialog box.*

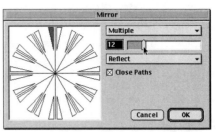

Mirror tool options

Horizontal Vertical Horizontal Multiple Reflect Rotate
and Vertical

*Set up options for the
Mirror tool, then hold
down Command/Ctrl
to switch to the Pointer
tool and select the object
you want to reflect.*

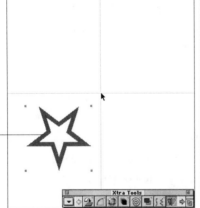
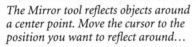

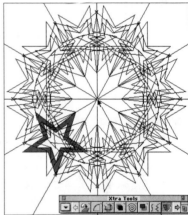

The Mirror tool reflects objects around
a center point. Move the cursor to the
position you want to reflect around...

...and drag the Mirror tool. As you
drag, FreeHand displays a keyline
preview of the objects you're reflecting.

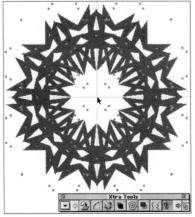

When you see a pattern you like, stop
dragging. FreeHand creates duplicates
of the objects you selected, rotating and
reflecting them around the point at
which you started dragging.

FIGURE 5-32
The Mirror tool's
Close Paths option

*When you turn on the
Close Paths option,
FreeHand joins and
close any open paths
whose endpoints fall
within the distance you
set in the Snap Distance
field of the General
Preferences dialog box.*

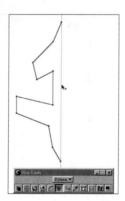

Before reflection.

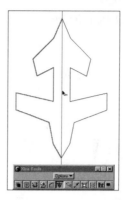

Close Paths option off.

Close paths option on.

4. When the preview looks the way you want it to look, stop dragging. FreeHand reflects and rotates the duplicated objects.

Skewing

Skewing an object makes it appear that the plane the object's resting on has been rotated. It's good for creating perspective effects.

Skewing is hard to get used to at first, because vertical skewing seems to affect the horizontal lines in an object, while horizontal skewing affects the vertical lines in an object. It's just something you'll have to get used to (see Figure 5-33).

Using the Skewing Tool

Follow these steps to skew an object by eye (see Figure 5-34).

1. Select the object you want to skew.

2. Choose the Skewing tool from the toolbox.

3. Position the cursor where you want the skew to start.

4. Drag the Skewing tool to skew the object. As you drag the cursor, the skewing angles display on the status bar.

5. When the object looks the way you want it to look, stop dragging.

FIGURE 5-33
Horizontal and
vertical skewing

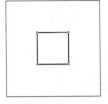

Original object

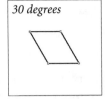

30 degrees

-30 degrees

Horizontal skewing

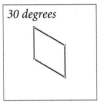

30 degrees

-30 degrees

Vertical skewing

FIGURE 5-34
Skewing an
object by eye

*Select the object you
want to skew.*

*Position the cursor to
define the center point
you're skewing around
and drag the cursor in
the publication window.*

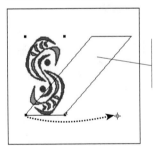

*FreeHand displays a preview of
the skewed object as you drag. If you're
skewing a group or a composite path,
you'll see a rectangle.*

*Hold down Shift as you
drag to constrain the
skewing to either
vertical or horizontal.*

*When you stop
dragging, FreeHand
skews the object.*

Using the Skew Palette

To skew an object using the Skew palette, follow these steps (see Figure 5-35).

1. Select the object you want to skew.

2. Display the Skew palette by double-clicking the Skewing tool in the toolbox, if necessary.

3. Set the Contents and Fills checkboxes (see "Skewing Contents and Fills," later in this chapter).

4. Enter skewing angles in the H (horizontal) and V (vertical) fields in the Skew palette.

5. Press Return (or click the Apply button in the Skew palette) to skew the selected object.

FIGURE 5-35
Skewing with
the Skew palette

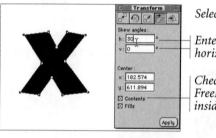

Select the object you want to skew.

Enter skewing angles in the H (for horizontal) and V (for vertical) fields.

Check the Contents box if you want FreeHand to skew any objects pasted inside the path when it skews the path.

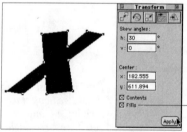

Press Return (or click the Apply button), and FreeHand skews the selected object.

Check the Fills box if you want FreeHand to skew the path's fill.

Skewing Contents and Fills

If you want to skew a path's contents (objects you've pasted inside the path) as you skew the path, check the Contents box. To skew the path's fill, check Fills.

Transformation and Projective Drawing

If you survived the parts of Chapter 2, "Drawing," covering perspective, oblique, and axonometric projections, here's your reward: skewing, scaling, and rotation, in combination, give you a great way to create oblique and axonometric (isometric, mainly) projection drawings.

Which brings us to a geometric puzzle—one that can be of use to us. When you *rotate* an object, its dimensions remain the same. But when you *skew* an object—which is what we need to do—the object's dimensions change (see Figure 5-36).

When you know how the dimensions will change for a given skew angle, you can scale the object *before you skew it* so that you end up with the dimensions you want *after skewing*. To find the scaling percentage for a given length and skew angle, use the following equation (you'll need a calculator or spreadsheet capable of resolving the trigonometric function cosine), or refer to Table 5-1.

(length   (length   cosine(skewing angle))) ¥ scale = **scaling percentage**

FIGURE 5-36
Width, height,
and skewing

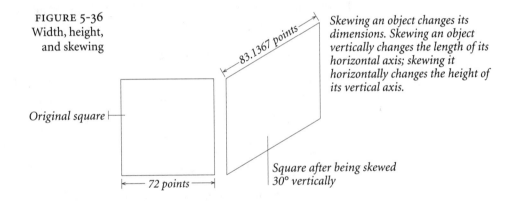

Skewing an object changes its dimensions. Skewing an object vertically changes the length of its horizontal axis; skewing it horizontally changes the height of its vertical axis.

Where *length* is the length of the longest part of the side of the object we want to skew (in the above example, it's 72 points) and *scale* is the measurement scale we want to use to measure that side. If we wanted to create a full-scale rendering of the above object, the equation would look like this:

(72   (72   (cosine(30)))) ¥ 1 = **86.6**

TABLE 5-1
Scaling percentages for
common projection
angles

Angle	Percentage	Angle	Percentage
15	96.6	30	86.6
45	70.7	60	50

How do you make use of these numbers? The following steps show you how to create an oblique projection of an object (see Figure 5-37).

1. Draw the orthographic views (top, side, and front) of an object.

2. Select the side view of the object.

3. Display the Scale palette (if the palette's not visible, double-click the Scale tool in the toolbox). Enter 70.7 in the W(idth) field (if you see only one field, turn off the Uniform option and you'll see separate fields for scaling the object's width and height). Click the Apply button. FreeHand scales the width of the object.

4. Display the Skew palette. Type "45" in the V field and press Return. FreeHand skews the side view of the object.

5. Select the top view of the object.

6. Display the Scale palette. Enter 70.7 in the H(eight) field and click the Apply button. FreeHand scales the height of the object.

7. Type "-45" in the Horizontal field and click the Apply button. FreeHand skews the top view.

8. Snap all the objects together, and, *voilà*, you've got an oblique projection (a "cabinet" projection, as you'll recall from Chapter 2, "Drawing").

The following steps show you how to create an isometric drawing (using 30 degree angles) of the same object (see Figure 5-38).

1. Draw the orthographic views of an object.

2. Select the side view of the object.

3. Display the Scale palette. Enter 86.6 in the W(idth) field. Click the Apply button. FreeHand scales the width of the object.

FIGURE 5-37
Using transformation
to create an oblique
projection

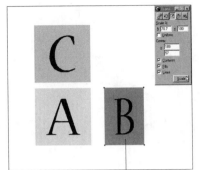

*Select the side view and
scale it to 70.7 percent
of its width.*

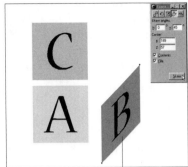

*Skew the side view 45
degrees vertically.*

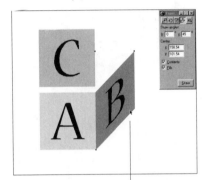

*Snap the side into
position next to the
front of the object.*

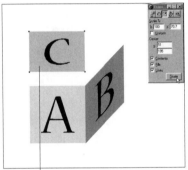

*Select the top view and scale
it to 70.7 percent of its height.*

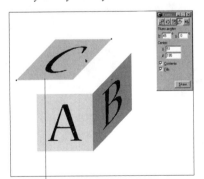

*Skew the top view -45 degrees
horizontally.*

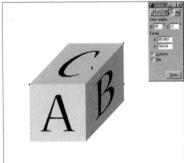

*Move the top view into position above
the front and side views. In this
example, each side can be measured
using the same scale (even though it
appears that the angled sides are
longer).*

FIGURE 5-38
Using transformation
to create an isometric
projection

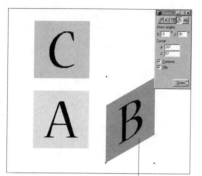

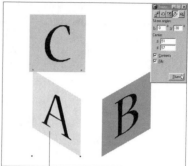

*Select the side view. Use
the Scale palette to scale it
to 86.6 percent of its
width, then use the Skew
palette to skew it 30
degrees vertically.*

*Select the front view. Use
the Scale palette to scale it
to 86.6 percent of its width,
then use the Skew palette
to skew it -30 degrees
vertically.*

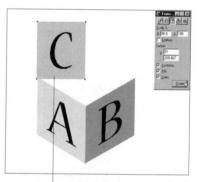

*Snap the front and side
views together.*

*Select the top view. Scale it
to 86.6 percent of its width.*

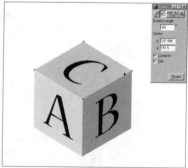

*Use the Skew palette to skew
the top view horizontally 30
degrees, then use the Rotate
palette to rotate it -60 degrees.*

*Snap the three faces together, and
you've created an isometric view.*

4. Display the Skew palette. Type "30" in the V field and press Return. FreeHand skews the side view of the object.

5. Select the front view of the object. Display the Scale palette and scale the width of the front view as you did the side (unless you've entered a new percentage in the W field, you can click the Apply button to apply the same scaling).

6. Display the Skew palette. Enter "-30" in the V(ertical) field and click the Apply button. FreeHand skews the front view.

7. Select the top view. Use the Scale palette to scale the width to 86.6 percent, then use the Skew palette to skew the object's horizontal axis by -60 degrees.

8. Snap the objects together, and you've got an isometric drawing.

Creating Clipping Paths

Another of FreeHand's basic transformations is Paste Inside—the ability to use any path as a clipping path for any object or objects. Paste Inside has already gotten some coverage in Chapter 2, "Drawing," but here's more. Clipping paths are the key to three other FreeHand techniques.

◆ Cropping imported graphics (this technique is covered in Chapter 4, "Importing and Exporting").

◆ Trapping objects that cross color boundaries (this technique is covered in depth in Chapter 6, "Color").

◆ Creating transparency and translucency effects (you'll probably want to use Lens fills for this, but I'll show you how to do it manually, just in case).

Clipping paths are also just plain fun. Be aware, however, that clipping paths increase the complexity of your publication by an order of magnitude as far as the PostScript interpreters in printers and imagesetters are concerned. This doesn't mean that you shouldn't ever use clipping paths! Just remember that publications containing clipping paths will take longer to print, and may produce overtime charges at your imagesetting service bureau. In other words, make sure that the effect you hope to achieve by using clipping paths is worth the added time and expense.

Use the following steps to create a clipping path (see Figure 5-39).

1. Draw, type, or import an object.

2. Draw a path on top of the initial object.

3. Select the original object and press Command-X/Ctrl-X.

4. Select the first object and press Command-Shift-V/Ctrl-Shift-V (or choose Paste Inside from the Edit menu). FreeHand pastes the object inside the path.

FIGURE 5-39
Creating a
clipping path

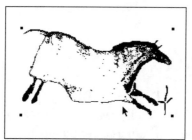

Draw, type, or import something...

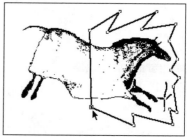

...and draw a path on top of it. Select the original object and press Command-X/Ctrl-X to cut it.

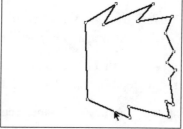

Select the path...

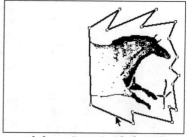

...and choose Paste Inside from the Edit menu. FreeHand pastes the object inside the path.

What happens when you use Paste Inside more than once for the same clipping path? Each Paste Inside places the contents of the Clipboard on top of any objects already inside the clipping path.

You'll still be able to see any objects not obscured by opaque lines or fills (see Figure 5-40).

If you need to edit the objects you've pasted inside a path, or if you want to remove them, select the object that contains them and choose Cut Contents from the Edit menu (or press Command-Shift-X/Ctrl-Shift-X). The objects that had been pasted inside the path you selected are pasted on top of the path you cut them from (see Figure 5-41). The objects retain the stacking order they had inside the path (the last object pasted inside it on top).

FIGURE 5-40
Multiple Paste Insides

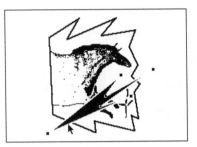 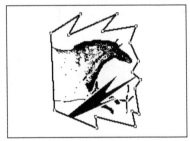

When you paste a new object inside a clipping path that contains other objects...

...FreeHand pastes the new object on top of the other objects already inside the path.

FIGURE 5-41
Removing objects from inside a clipping path

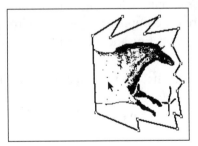 

Select the clipping path...

...and choose Cut Contents from the Edit menu. FreeHand pastes the path's contents on top of the path.

Editing Path Contents

To edit an object you've pasted inside a path, hold down Option/Alt and click on the object inside the path. FreeHand selects the object you clicked (it's just like subselecting an object inside a group). At this point, you're free to edit and format the object (see Figure 5-42).

FIGURE 5-42
Editing objects inside
a clipping path

To select an object inside a clipping path, hold down Option/Alt and click the object (in Windows, click the right mouse button). In this example, I've selected an image that's quite a bit larger than the clipping path it's been pasted inside.

Once the object is selected, you can edit, transform, and format it (just as if it weren't inside a clipping path).

In this example, I'm moving the image inside the clipping path.

When I stop dragging, FreeHand repositions the object inside the clipping path.

Using Paste Inside to Crop Imported Images

FreeHand lacks a tool analogous to PageMaker's Cropping tool, but you can simulate the behavior of the Cropping tool using Free-Hand's Paste Inside feature. Actually, the ability to create clipping paths of any shape in FreeHand is more powerful and flexible than PageMaker's Cropping tool (which crops only in rectangles).

For more on cropping images, see "Cropping TIFF Images" in Chapter 4, "Importing and Exporting."

Creating a Color Change Where an Object Crosses a Color Boundary

Here's an effect that we used to sweat over in the dark days when everything was done with a copy camera, hot wax, cold beer, and a knife. Suppose you have some text that crosses from a background of one color onto a background of another color (let's call the two colors "Color 1" and "Color 2"). How can you get the text to appear to change color as it crosses the boundary between the two background colors? With FreeHand, it's so easy that a number of power users I know have missed it (see Figure 5-43).

1. Create the text block and the two background objects.

2. Apply one of the colors ("Color 1") to the text, then cut the text block.

FIGURE 5-43
Changing colors as you
cross a color boundary

*Create two paths. Fill
one path with one color;
fill the other with a
different color...*

*...then create a text block that
crosses both paths.*

*Color the text block with one
of the background colors,
then paste it into the path of
the other color.*

*Clone the text block
(you can hold down
Option/Alt to select the
text block you pasted
inside the background
path), then apply the
second background
color to the path.*

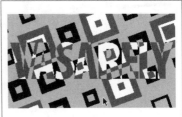

*Cut the text block to the
Clipboard, then paste it
inside the background path.*

*It's easy to get carried away with this
effect, but I urge you to resist the
temptation.*

3. Select the background path colored with "Color 2." Press Command-Shift-V/Ctrl-Shift-V to paste the text block into the path.

4. Hold down Option/Alt and click the text block you've just pasted inside the path, then press Command-=/Ctrl-Shift-C to clone it. A clone of the text block appears on top of the background paths. Apply the color "Color 2" to the text, then press Command-X/Ctrl-X to cut the text block.

6. Select the background path colored with "Color 1" and press Command-Shift-V/Ctrl-Shift-V to paste the text block inside the path.

Creating the Illusion of Transparency

Most of the time, you'll probably want to use FreeHand's Lens fills when you want to create translucent objects. But, as usual, I think you should know how to do it yourself. For more on FreeHand's Lens fill type, see Chapter 2, "Drawing."

When PostScript fills an object, it assumes that the fill is opaque. FreeHand, being a child of PostScript, adheres to this assumption, but also gives you a number of ways to fool PostScript into rendering objects that look transparent.

When an object passes behind some transparent or translucent plane, it changes color—sometimes very subtly. To simulate this effect in FreeHand, clone the partially obscured object and change the colors of the cloned objects from their original colors. Then paste those objects inside the transparent or translucent object (see Figure 5-44).

FIGURE 5-44
Creating transparent
objects

This object is colored 20-percent gray, and has lightened copies of the background objects pasted inside it.

You can use this optical illusion to simulate the effect of viewing an object through a number of simple transparent/translucent planar surfaces. The main difficulty of rendering transparency and translucency in two-dimensional work is that you walk a fine line. If the color shift is too great, it'll look like you've created another object; if the color shift is too slight, it won't look like an object's transparent. Transparency is harder to simulate than translucency.

Locking Objects

In a previous edition of this book, I mentioned locking objects only once, in the section on alignment and distribution. It's the way I was brought up—out in the mountains in Idaho we never locked anything (our car keys spent the night, undisturbed, in the ignition switches of our cars). I view the difficulties of urban living as the result of a large-scale conspiracy of keys and locks.

In FreeHand, locking an object means that you can't transform it or change its appearance. You can still select the object, and you can copy it or clone it, but you can't do anything to it.

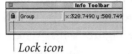

Lock icon

To lock an object, select the object and press Command-L/Ctrl-L (or choose Lock from the Arrange menu). When you select a locked object, you'll see a lock icon in the Info toolbar.

To unlock an object, press Command-Shift-L/Ctrl-Shift-L (or choose Unlock from the Arrange menu).

Aligning and Distributing

For many of us, MacDraw ushered in the era of object alignment. You could align the left, right, top, bottom, or center of selected objects. It was the greatest. I spent whole afternoons just aligning things. You couldn't do that in MacPaint.

FreeHand, which counts MacDraw as one of its forebears, also features object alignment. FreeHand aligns objects based on the rectangular area each object takes up, which I'll call the object's bounding box. The selection handles of the object show you the object's bounding box (to see the bounding box of a path, group the path). Note that imported EPS graphics and TIFF files can have bounding boxes that have nothing to do with the actual content of the graphic (see Figure 5-45).

FreeHand's object alignment capabilities include both Align, which does exactly what you'd expect; and Distribute, which means, "Evenly arrange the selected objects inside the selection rectangle formed by the objects." Align and Distribute can be used at the same time; you can, for example, vertically align objects while horizontally distributing them.

FIGURE 5-45
Object bounding boxes

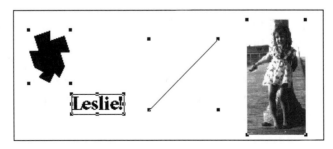

Aligning Objects   When you've selected the objects you want to align, press Command-Option-A/Ctrl-Alt-A to display the Align palette. At this point, you can pick an alignment using the palette's pop-up menus, or by clicking in the preview window (in the middle of the Align palette). FreeHand updates the preview window to show you the effect of the alignment options you've chosen (see Figure 5-46). When the preview looks the way you want it to, click the Apply button in the palette. FreeHand aligns the selected objects as you've specified (see Figure 5-47).

FIGURE 5-46
Align Palette

Turn on the Align to Page option to align objects relative to the edges or center of the page they're on.

 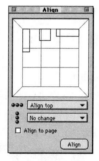  

To set an alignment, choose the alignment you want from the Align palette's pop-up menus...

...or click an area in the palette's preview window. FreeHand updates the preview to show you the effect of the alignment you've chosen.

To align objects to the page, turn on the Align to Page option. Choose an alignment and click the Apply button, and FreeHand aligns the objects to the top, center, bottom, left, or right of the page as you've specified.

Tip:
Alignment
Shortcut

To quickly apply an alignment, double-click an area in the Align palette's preview window.

Tip:
Aligning Points

In versions of FreeHand before 7.0, you couldn't align points using the Align palette. These days, you can (see Figure 5-48). While this is a great feature, it means you've got to be more careful about the way you select objects. If you have *points* selected, and want to make sure that you're aligning *paths*, press ` (accent grave) before you align the objects.

FIGURE 5-47
Aligning objects

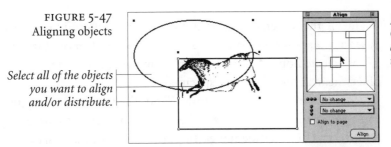

*Select all of the objects
you want to align
and/or distribute.*

*Press Command-
Option-A/Ctrl-Alt-A to
display the Align palette,
if it's not already visible.*

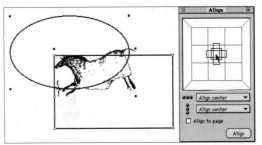

*Pick an alignment from
the Horizontal and
Vertical pop-up menus,
or click on an area in the
preview window.*

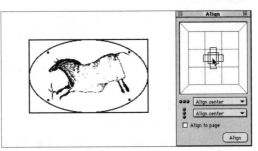

*To apply the alignment,
double-click the area in
the preview window, or
click the Apply button.
FreeHand aligns (and/or
distributes) the objects.*

FIGURE 5-48
Aligning Points

*Select the points you want
to align, then double-click
the area in the Align
palette's preview area
corresponding to the
alignment you want.*

*FreeHand aligns the
points you selected.*

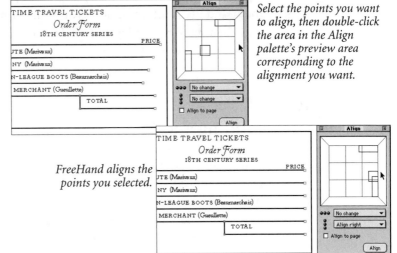

Tip:
Locking as an
Adjunct to
Alignment

If any of the selected objects is locked, FreeHand aligns objects based on that object's position (see Figure 5-49). If more than one of the selected objects is locked, FreeHand bases alignment on the object nearest the alignment specified.

I use this technique all the time—and it's virtually the only reason I lock individual objects. When I want to protect part of my publication from accidental editing, I usually put that part of the publication on a layer and lock that layer. Unlocking a layer is easier than tracking down individual, locked objects.

FIGURE 5-49
Locking and alignment

This object is locked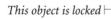

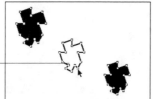 

Align the tops of these objects, and they'll align to the top of the locked object—even if it's not the topmost object selected.

Distributing Objects

Have you ever wanted to space a bunch of objects at even distances from each other (from each other's centers, at any rate) across a particular horizontal measurement? If you have, FreeHand's Distribute feature should make your day.

To distribute objects, select the objects, press Command-Option-A/Ctrl-Alt-A to display the Align palette, select the alignment and distribution options you want from the pop-up menus, and then click the Apply button in the palette. FreeHand aligns and distributes the objects as you've specified (see Figure 5-50).

Finding and Replacing Graphics

One of FreeHand's greatest features is the ability to find and replace graphics in your publication. You can also search for a particular kind of object and have FreeHand select it for you. To find a graphic and change something about it, follow these steps (see Figure 5-51).

FIGURE 5-50
Distributing objects

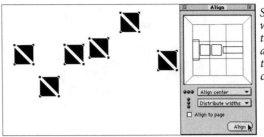

Select the objects you want to distribute, set up the distribution and alignment you want in the Align palette, and click the Apply button.

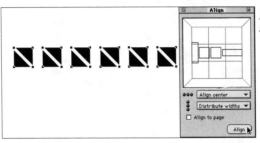

FreeHand distributes the selected objects.

1. Choose Graphics from the Find and Change submenu of the Edit menu (or press Command-Option-E/Ctrl-Alt-E). FreeHand displays the Find and Replace dialog box.

2. Choose the attribute you want to find from the Attributes pop-up menu. Take a good look at the options on this menu—they're the key to using the Find and Replace Graphics feature effectively. If, for example, you want to find all of the paths with a particular color applied to them, choose Color from the Attributes menu.

3. Set the range you want this operation to affect using the Change In pop-up menu. You can choose to affect only the selected objects, only objects found on this page, or objects found anywhere in the current publication

4. Click the Change button. FreeHand changes all of the objects matching the attributes you specified in the range you selected.

Finding and selecting graphics finds graphics, but doesn't change them. Instead, it selects them. To find and select graphics, follow these steps (see Figure 5-52).

FIGURE 5-51
Finding and
Replacing Graphics

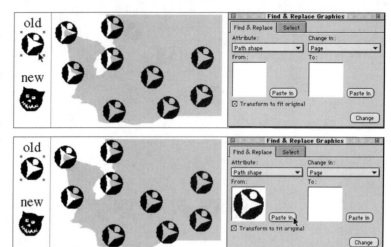

You've got to replace the instances of the old logo with the new one. Here's what to do. Display the Find and Replace Graphic dialog box. Choose Path Shape from the attribute pop-up menu. Select an example of the old logo and copy it, then click the Paste In button in the From section of the dialog box.

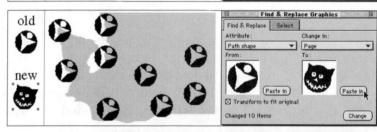

Select an example of the new logo (note that both logos are composite paths) and copy it. Click the Paste In button in the To section of the dialog box.

Click the Change button. FreeHand changes all of the instances of the old logo into the new logo.

FIGURE 5-52
Finding and
Selecting Objects

Use "find and select" when you can't find objects—or change them into what you want—using Find and Replace. Once Free-Hand selects the objects, you can format them, or send them to a layer, or export them.

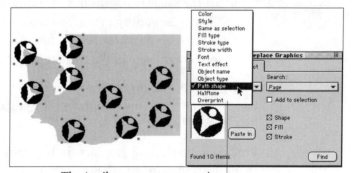

The Attributes pop-up menu gives you more choices when you're finding and selecting objects.

1. Choose Graphics from the Find and Change submenu of the Edit menu (or press Command-Option-E/Ctrl-Alt-E). FreeHand displays the Find and Replace dialog box. Click the Select tab.

2. Choose the attribute you want to find from the Attributes pop-up menu (note that this pop-up menu has more options than the Attributes pop-up menu in the Find and Replace dialog box). If you want to find all of the objects you've named "Erase me" using the Set Note Xtra, you can use the Find and Select dialog box—the Find and Replace Attributes pop-up menu doesn't include object names.

3. Set the range you want this operation to affect using the Change In pop-up menu. If you choose the Page or Document from the Change In pop-up menu, and have an object selected, you can turn on the Add to Selection option to add any objects you find to the current selection. If you choose Selection as your range, you can turn on the Remove from Selection option to have FreeHand deselect any objects it finds.

4. Click the Find button. FreeHand finds and selects all of the objects matching the attributes you specified in the range you selected (unless it can't find any matching objects, or you've turned on the Remove from Selection option).

My Life Was Transformed

All around you, every day, things are changing from one thing to another. Fuzzy caterpillars turn into moths. Clark Kent jumps into a phone booth and emerges as Superman. Democrats turn into Republicans (I understand it's part of their mating cycle). Werewolves stalk the moors under the full moon. The bat on page 179 is, by day, a harmless graphic designer with prominent canines. These transformations are all everyday, natural phenomena.

I didn't understand this when I first approached FreeHand's transformation tools. The tools seemed alien, awkward; and I didn't use them very much. Then, one day, I saw them as extensions of the way I already thought about drawing. Now, I use them more than I use the drawing tools.

Make FreeHand's transformation tools an integral part of how you work with the program, and you'll have their powerful, almost magical forces on your side. And that means you'll have more time for other things. Like howling at the moon.

CHAPTER

Color

6

Remember

drawing things when you were a kid? Making black marks on paper with a pen or pencil was fun, but *coloring*—using crayons, watercolors, or finger-paints—was better. Much better. Even as a child, you could see that color added something special to your artwork.

Color communicates, telling us things about the object bearing the color. Without color cues, we'd have a hard time guessing the ripeness of a fruit or distinguishing a poisonous mushroom from an edible one. And many animals would have a hard time figuring out when to mate, or with whom.

We associate colors with human emotions: we are green with envy; we've got the blues; we see red. Colors affect our emotions, as well. Various studies suggest that we think best in a room of one color, or relax best in a room of another color.

What does all this mean? Color's important. A rule of thumb in advertising is that a color advertisement gets something like ten times the response of a black-and-white ad. Designers of mail-order catalogs tell me that color is often cited as the reason for buying a product—and it's usually the reason a product is returned.

FreeHand features a formidable array of features dedicated to creating, editing, applying, and printing colors. In addition, FreeHand's color management, can make what you see on your screen much closer to what you'll get when you print. Before I go any further, however, I have to talk about color printing.

Color Printing

It's impossible to discuss creating and using colors in FreeHand without talking a little about printing. If you already know about color printing, feel free to skip ahead, though you'll miss all the jokes if you do. Everyone else should note that this is a very simple explanation of a very bizarre and complex process.

The Printing Process

After you've printed your FreeHand publication on film and delivered it to your commercial printer (I like to walk in through the loading dock), the printer takes the film and uses it to expose (or "burn") a photosensitive printing plate. The surface of the plate has been chemically treated to repel ink. When the printing plate is exposed, the image areas from your film become able to accept ink. Once the plate's been exposed, the printer attaches the printing plate to the cylinder of a printing press.

As the cylinder holding the plate turns, the parts of it bearing the image become coated with ink, which is transferred (via another, rubber covered cylinder—the offset cylinder) to the paper. This transfer is where we get the term "offset," as in "offset printing," because the plate itself does not touch your paper.

Printing presses put ink on paper one ink color at a time. Some presses have more than one printing cylinder (also called a printing "head" or "tower") and can print several colors of ink on a sheet of paper in one pass through the press, but each printing cylinder carries only one color of ink. We can make it look like we've gotten more than one color of ink on a printing plate by using screens—patterns of dots that, from a distance, fool the eye into thinking it sees a separate color (see Figure 6-1).

Spot and Process Inks

Spot-color printing is simple: your commercial printer uses inks that exactly match the color you want (or mixes inks to get the same result), then loads the press with that ink. Sometimes, we use "tint builds"—screens of inks printed on top of each other—to create a new color without using another ink. In process-color printing, tint builds are where it's at; we use overlapping screens of four inks (cyan, magenta, yellow, and black) to simulate a large part of the spectrum of visible color. If everything's gone well, the

FIGURE 6-1
Black and…gray?

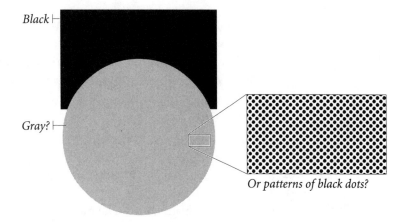

Black

Gray?

Or patterns of black dots?

dots of the different colored inks are placed near each other in a pattern called a rosette (see Color Figure 6 on the color pages for an example of a rosette).

Process-color printing can't simulate all the colors our eyes can see (notably metallic and fluorescent colors), but it can print color photographic images. Spot colors can print any color you can make with pigments, but aren't generally used to reproduce color photographic images (that's what process color printing was designed to be good at).

New Screening Technologies

Stochastic, or Frequency Modulation (FM), screening avoids half-toning altogether. Stochastic screening converts grayscale and color information into high-resolution dithered bitmaps (shades of Mac-Paint!). When you apply colors (that is, cyan, magenta, yellow, and black) to these bitmaps and then print them on top of each other, the eye sees more colors—just as it does when you print rosettes.

As I'm writing this (in June 1998), imagesetter manufacturers offer stochastic screening hardware and software for their RIPs under various tradenames (Agfa's, for example, is called Crystal Raster). In addition, various software manufacturers have developed software that does the same thing while running on your desktop computer.

You don't have to print to a specially-equipped imagesetter to experiment with stochastic screening—you can do it (or something like it) yourself, using Photoshop and FreeHand. See "Do-It-Yourself Stochastic Screening," later in this chapter, for more infor-

mation on separating color images using stochastic screening—
we'll use Photoshop's diffusion dither.

Or you can purchase a stochastic screening application, such as
Icefields, from Isis Imaging, and screen your images yourself. For
more on Icefields, see "Stochastic Screening Without an Imagesetter," later in this chapter.

New Color Printing Technologies

You'll often hear stochastic screening mentioned in the same breath
as a new process-color printing method, high-fidelity color (usually called "hi-fi" color). The most popular current hi-fi color scheme
is Pantone's Hexachrome system, which uses six inks (cyan, magenta, yellow, black, orange, and green). Other systems use seven
inks—cyan, magenta, yellow, orange, green, violet, and black—and
some even use eight inks. Each system can simulate more of the
visible spectrum of light (color) than can be simulated using four-
color process printing. The idea's still the same as in conventional
process color printing—put dots close together, and people see more
colors than you've printed. In any case, you don't have to use hi-fi
color to use stochastic screening.

The samples of hi-fi color I've seen have been very impressive—
the technique makes it possible to print fluorescent, metallic, and
intense colors that would be impossible to print using conventional
four-color process printing.

As I write this book, few commercial printers are set up to do
hi-fi color (in fact, you can probably count on your fingers the
number of printers in North America equipped to print seven colors in a single pass through the press). The numbers have grown
significantly since the last edition of this book (two years ago).
Pantone's Hexachrome system, in particular, seems to be gathering
momentum (which is good, from a FreeHand user's point of view—
Hexachrome is the hi-fi color system FreeHand supports).

Color Management

FreeHand comes with the Kodak Digital Science Color Management System, and, on the Macintosh, supports Apple's ColorSync.

What's that mean? What's a color management system?

When I think of color management, I keep thinking of target shooting. When you aim at a target—and it doesn't matter whether you're aiming a rifle, a bow, a laser, or a camera—you have to make adjustments. You've got consider the atmospheric conditions, the distance to the target, the characteristics of the target itself. Once you know what the variables are, and understand how they affect what you're trying to do, you've got a better chance of hitting the target.

The same thing is true in color management. You need to understand the tools you have to work with, how they work together (or don't), and how they combine to produce the colors you see in the printed version of your publication.

It would be nice if we could make what we see on our screen exactly match what we'll get when we print. But we can't, for a variety of practical and physiological reasons (not to mention simple lack of time and money). That said, I must also add that we can get very close—and we can also make the relationship between the display and the printed piece more consistent, reliable, and predictable.

The "device" (a printer, scanner, monitor, or printing press) is the key. Every device renders colors in a slightly different way. To adjust color in one environment so that it matches the color as seen in another environment, color management systems refer to a file containing information on the color characteristics of a device (how it displays or prints color). This file is called a "device profile." Device profiles are usually created by the manufacturers who make the hardware, though quite a few come with FreeHand. The process of creating a device profile is called "characterizing" a device.

Once a device profile has been created for a device, you've got to maintain (or "calibrate") the device so that it doesn't vary from the profile. Imagesetter operators and commercial printers calibrate their equipment regularly (or should) to match industry standards.

FreeHand's color management system uses device profiles approved by the International Color Consortium (ICC). If you're on the Macintosh, you can also use device profiles provided by Apple with the system-level ColorSync color management system (these profiles are also approved by the ICC).

For more on choosing device profiles, see "FreeHand's Color Management Controls," later in this chapter.

Controlling Your Color-Viewing Environment

If it's important to you that what you see on your screen looks as much like the printed version of your publication as possible, there are a few rules you need to follow.

- Use a monitor and video system capable of displaying at least 24-bit color.

- Calibrate your monitor. Radius and Tektronix, for example, make color monitor calibration systems (hardware and software). If color is of critical importance to you and your publications, find a system that works with your monitor, or buy a monitor that works with the calibration system you prefer.

- Control the lighting around your monitor and keep it consistent when you're working. Just about everyone agrees that the fluorescent lighting used in most of our office buildings is the worst possible lighting for viewing colors. Turn it off, if you can, and rely on incandescent lighting (desk lamps with one sort of bulb or another) to light your work area. If you can't turn it off, try getting some "full spectrum" (or "amber") fluorescent tubes to install above your monitor. These also reduce eye strain.

- Control the lighting of the area where you'll be viewing your color proofs. Ideally, you'd have a room or small booth equipped with "daylight" (or 5,000-degree Kelvin) lamps— but few of us can afford the money or space required.

Why is lighting important? Basically, the temperature of the light affects what a color "objectively" looks like. You can't assume ideal-viewing conditions, but you have to work in them to be able to do consistent work.

These rules have been passed on to me by people who are serious about color, and whose opinions I respect. But, this being a "Real World" book, I have to point out that these conditions are difficult to achieve. My monitors have never been anywhere near a calibration system. The lights above my desk are fluorescent tubes—and white ones, at that. And as for having a special booth or room for viewing color proofs—hah!

To compensate, I base my design decisions on printed examples of spot and process colors and pay little attention to what's on the screen except to remind me of what colors I've put where. When I get a color proof, I look at it in several different lighting environments: outdoors, indoors under typical fluorescent lighting, and indoors under typical incandescent lighting. These are, after all, the conditions under which people will be viewing it.

At the same time, I have to admit that I'm not doing work where color matching is crucially important—as it would be if I were producing clothing catalogs or coffee-table art books.

Is What You See Anything Like What You'll Get?

Any time you're working with ink, refer to printed samples, rather than looking at the colors on your screen. Remember that, unlike the paper you'll be printing on, your screen is backlit, so it displays colors very differently from what they'll look like when printed. In addition, screens flicker—something I've never been able to get paper to do.

If you're using uncoated paper, look at samples of the ink (spot color) or ink mix (process color) printed on uncoated stock. If you're using coated paper, look at examples printed on coated paper. If you're using a colored paper, try to find an example of the ink printed on a colored paper—though these examples are much harder to find.

If you're working with Pantone colors, Pantone makes a line of swatch books showing their libraries of spot and process colors (including process color equivalents of the spot colors); they're printed on both coated and uncoated stocks, and although they're kind of expensive, they're not as expensive as pulling a job off of a press because you didn't like the press check. They're downright cheap if you consider what it must cost to print them.

Don't use Pantone spot colors (the ones you find in the Pantone library) to specify a process color. The Pantone Matching System is a spot-color specifying system, and the colors don't convert to process colors particularly well because you can't make any given hue just using process colors (see the discussion earlier in this chapter).

Still, Pantone has included the process color conversions for these colors (as seen in their *Process Color Imaging Guide*) in the definitions of these spot colors. The colors in the Pantone "ProSim" library are process-color simulations of Pantone spot inks.

Don't trust color PostScript printers to give you an accurate simulation of what the colors in your publication are going to look like when they're printed by your commercial printer. They simply lack the resolution and color range to produce good process colors (and bear in mind that, because most color PostScript printers print using something akin to the process-color method, your spot colors will be converted to process colors during printing).

When you need to create a color proof of your publication, but aren't yet ready to have your commercial printer set up their press to print a sample for you, use one of the color proofing processes (such as Chromalin or Press Match) to create your proofs from the film you've gotten out of your imagesetter. Imagesetting service bureaus frequently offer color proofing as part of their business. Some of these proofing processes can give you a proof on the paper you're intending to use, or can give you transparent overlays that you can place on top of your selected paper to get an idea of what your publication will look like when printed.

FreeHand's Color Management Controls

You can reach FreeHand's color management controls using either or both of the following methods (see Figure 6-2):

◆ Choose Preferences from the File menu (or press Command-Shift-D/Ctrl-Shift-D). FreeHand displays the Preferences dialog box. If the Colors Preferences dialog box isn't visible, click "Colors" from the Category list to display it. At the bottom of this dialog box, you'll see the color management controls.

◆ Click the Color Management button in the Print dialog box, and FreeHand displays the Color Management Preferences dialog box. This dialog box contains the same controls as the Colors Preferences dialog box. Any changes you make here are reflected in the Colors Preferences dialog box.

Why put this dialog box here? If you're anything like me, you probably bring up the Print dialog box to print a

FIGURE 6-2
Color management
controls

You can reach
FreeHand's color
management controls
through the Colors
Preferences dialog box
(press Command-Shift-
D/Ctrl-Shift D, then
click the Colors tab—
on the Macintosh,
click Colors in the list
in the Preferences
dialog box)...

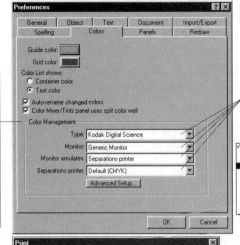

The pop-up menus give
you a way to set the device
profiles for the hardware
you'll use to proof and
print your publication.

...or in through the
Print dialog box. Click
the Color Management
button in the Print
dialog box...

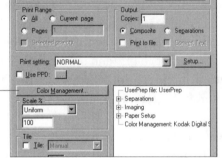

...and FreeHand displays the
Color Management Preferences
dialog box.

publication, and *then* remember that you want to separate
some RGB images in the publication. Rather than closing
the Print dialog box and returning to the Colors Preferences
dialog box to turn on the color management system, you
can click the Color Management button and turn color
management on or off without having to close the Print
dialog box.

Color Management. As you'd expect, this option turns color management on or off. FreeHand's color management system is either
on, or off, for all open publications. General color management
settings are not stored in individual publications (though device
profiles assigned to individual RGB images *are*—I'll have more to
say on this topic later).

Monitor. If you've chosen "None" from the Monitor Simulates pop-up menu (see below), FreeHand adjusts the colors you see on your screen according to the device profile you choose from this pop-up menu. Pick a profile that best matches the make, model, and calibration of your monitor.

Monitor Simulates. When you choose "None" from this pop-up menu, FreeHand adjusts your on-screen colors according to the device profile you've chosen from the Monitor pop-up menu (see above). When you choose either of the other options ("Composite Printer" or "Separations Printer"), FreeHand uses the device profile you've selected from the corresponding pop-up menu (see below). If you're creating publications or artwork that will be printed using process inks, choose "Separations Printer." Choose "Composite Printer" when you're using a color printer for your final output. If you're creating artwork for electronic distribution (GIFs, JPEGs, and Shockwave files for web publishing, for example), or if you're working with spot colors (and only with spot colors), choose "None" and pick a monitor profile from the Monitor pop-up menu. Or turn color management off altogether.

Composite Printer. Choose a color profile that matches your color printer. If you're using a color printer to produce the final copies of a publication or artwork, you may want to choose "Composite Printer" from the Monitor Simulates pop-up menu.

Separations Printer. Choose a color profile corresponding to the way you plan to print your final copy of the publication. If you're printing using commercial offset printing, choose a CMYK printer profile (do this even if you're printing using spot inks).

Composite Simulates Separations. Turn this option on to make the composite images printed on a color printer more closely match the colors you'll see when you print separations. In most cases, turning on this control limits (or attempts to limit) the composite's color range to that of process printing. If you want more intense, saturated colors in your color proofs (here I'm assuming that your proof printer can print colors outside the process color range—most can), leave this option turned off.

RGB Image Default. If you turn on color management for an RGB image, you'll be able to print better color separations of the image (see Color Figure 10). Once you've turned on color management, you can apply device profiles to any or all of the RGB images you've imported into your publication. This pop-up menu gives you a way to set the default device profile. Even though it looks as if this option is related to the option above it (Composite Simulates Separations), it's not.

Applying Device Profiles to RGB Images

When you select an RGB image in a FreeHand publication, you can use the Image Source pop-up menu in the Object Inspector to assign a device profile (a monitor or scanner profile) to the image (see Figure 6-3). Why do this? When you use FreeHand's color management system on an RGB image, you'll get better color separations (see Color Figure 10).

When you assign a device profile to an RGB image, FreeHand saves the setting in the publication file. To specify a default device profile for RGB images, choose the profile from the RGB Image Default pop-up menu in the Colors Preferences dialog box.

FIGURE 6-3
Applying color management to individual images

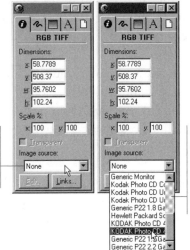

If this pop-up menu isn't available, you've probably turned off FreeHand's color management system.

Select a device profile from the Image Source pop-up menu. When you do this, FreeHand manages the colors inside the RGB image according to the profile—which means you get a more accurate screen display, and better color separations.

Color in FreeHand

Now that you know all about color printing and color management, it's time to get down to the process of specifying colors in your FreeHand publication.

The colors you work with in your publication correspond to the inks you'll use to print your publication. When you create, edit, or import a color in FreeHand, you're working with a single ink, or a tint of that ink, or a set of inks (a "tint build") which, when printed, optically blend together to produce the color.

When it comes time to print, the ink list (in the Print Setup dialog box) displays the inks needed to print the colors you have defined in your publication. If you've defined process colors, you'll see the process inks (cyan, magenta, yellow, and black) in the ink list. If you've defined spot colors, you'll see the spot inks associated with those colors in the ink list. If you want, you can print simulations of spot colors using process inks by turning on the Print Spot Colors as Process option. This converts the colors as you print—the color definition is not changed in your publication.

Spot Color or Process Color or Both?

Whether you use spot colors, process colors, or both depends on the needs of your specific publication—which has to do with your printing budget, your communications goals, and, most importantly, your mood. If you plan to use color photographs in your publication, you're going to have to use at least the four process inks. If you're printing on a tight budget, you'll probably want to use one or two inks.

When you're creating a color, you're offered a variety of choices: is the color a spot color, a process color, or a tint? You can change the definition later, if you want (but don't wait until you've trapped the publication). It's much easier to go from spot to process than the other way around.

Color Models

FreeHand lets you define colors using any of five color models—CMYK, RGB, HLS, Tint, and system. Which one should you use? That depends on how you plan to produce your publication.

Spot colors. If you're working with spot colors, it doesn't matter what color model you choose, and it really doesn't matter what the color looks like on the screen, as long as you let your commercial printer know what color of ink they need to use to print your publication. How do you know what ink to use? If you use Pantone colors (the most likely scenario), you can tell them the PMS color number. If you don't, it's trickier, but your printer can help you match the color you want to an ink they can mix.

Process colors. If you're working with process colors, *specify your color using the CMYK color model or a CMYK color-matching system,* or be ready for some nasty surprises when your publication gets printed. Once again, look at a printed sample of the process color, and enter the values given in the sample book for the color. It might seem too obvious to state, but don't enter other CMYK values unless you want a different color!

Tints. In addition, if you're trying to create a tint of an existing color (process or spot), use the Tints palette—don't try to approximate the right shade by mixing colors. You can base your tint on a spot color, a process color, or another tint. Don't base your tints on other tints unless you want to lose your mind. What's a 20-percent tint of a 67-percent tint of a 45-percent tint of PMS 327?

On-screen colors. If you're creating a publication for online distribution (on a CD-ROM or on the web), use the RGB color model or the System color model. If you're creating a publication for distribution on the web, you'll also want to stick with "browser safe" colors—colors that appear (more or less) the same on platforms supported by Microsoft Internet Explorer or Netscape Navigator. For more on picking browser-safe colors, see Chapter 9, "FreeHand and the Web."

FreeHand's Color Libraries

FreeHand supports the most frequently used color-matching systems in the graphic arts industry. There's nothing magical about these color libraries—they're just sets of agreed-upon industry standards. You can create these colors yourself, and name them however you like (and for process-color work, that's what we do—

choosing colors and entering tint percentages from a process-color swatch book). And using canned spot colors means you don't have to figure out what color specifications will simulate the spot ink on your screen and your color printer.

- ◆ DIC. A spot-color specifying system corresponding to inks manufactured by Dainippon Ink and Chemicals, Inc. It's something like a Japanese version of Pantone—and not seen frequently in North America or Europe—except in printing subsidiaries of Japanese printers. Still, it's a nice set of colors, which you might want to use if you can get a printer to match them.

- ◆ Focoltone. A process-color specification system (mostly used in Europe). Colors in the Focoltone library are organized in sets of colors with common percentages of at least one process color. The idea is to create a library of colors that, when applied to objects, are easy to trap, or don't need trapping at all.

- ◆ Munsell. RGB colors based on a 3D color model capable of describing every color we can perceive. Some nice colors, but I can't think how I'd use them. They're not CMYK, so I wouldn't use them for a process color job. They're not spot inks, so I wouldn't use them for a spot color job.

- ◆ Pantone (including Metallics and Pastels, with special library versions for coated and uncoated paper). A set of spot-color inks manufactured by Pantone, Inc. These inks are the industry standard for spot color in the North American printing business (as always, ask your commercial printer).

- ◆ Pantone Process. A set of Pantone process-color tint builds. These colors have no relation to the Pantone spot colors.

- ◆ Pantone ProSim. A set of Pantone process-colors designed to simulate Pantone's spot colors.

- ◆ Pantone Hexachrome. Hexachrome, as I've previously mentioned, is a six-color Hi-Fi color printing system.

FreeHand includes color libraries that correspond to the *Pantone Hexachrome Color Selector* (for both coated and uncoated paper stocks).

◆ Toyo. A spot-color library for matching inks from the Toyo Ink Manufacturing Company, Ltd., and corresponding to their Toyo 88 Color Guide ink sample book. Like DIC, Toyo is primarily used in Asian countries, and isn't seen much in Europe or North America.

◆ TruMatch. A process-color specifying system featuring small percentage changes from one process color to another. Their swatch book is often preferred by designers over any of the others for specifying process color.

◆ Web Safe Color Library. You can't count on everyone viewing your Web page to have the same video system you have. To compensate for the differences, most web browsers (Netscape Navigator and Microsoft Internet Explorer, for example) include a standard palette of colors. Use colors from this palette, and you can be assured that the colors in the files you export from FreeHand will appear (more or less) as you intended. See Chapter 9, "FreeHand and the Web," for more on this topic.

You can create your own color libraries by exporting colors from FreeHand, or you can create them yourself using a word-processing program (or a spreadsheet, or a database—anything that can write text-only—or ASCII—files). See "Creating Color Libraries," later in this chapter.

FreeHand's Color Controls

You create and add colors using three palettes—the Colors palette, the Color Mixer, and the Tints palette. FreeHand's color wells and color swatches are the key to using either palette. What's a color swatch? What's a color well? Take a look at Figure 6-4. Many color-related procedures in FreeHand involve dragging a color swatch

FIGURE 6-4
Color wells and
color swatches

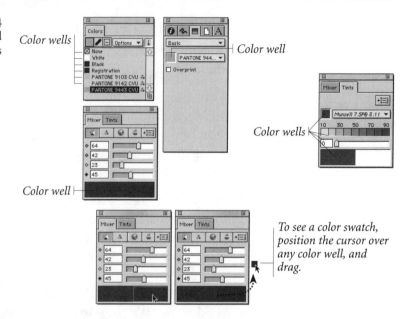

Color wells

Color well

Color wells

Color well

*To see a color swatch,
position the cursor over
any color well, and
drag.*

from one color well to another (though the pop-up menus next to
many of the color wells should cut down on dragging and provide
a way to rest your aching wrist).

Colors Palette

The most important of the color-related controls the Colors palette (see Figure 6-5). You use the Colors palette to import colors
from color libraries, export colors to color libraries, name colors,
apply colors, duplicate colors, and convert colors from spot to process (or from process to spot).

Fill and Stroke selectors. At the top of the Colors palette, below
the palette's title bar, you'll see the Fill selector, the Stroke selector,
and the Both selector. These aren't labelled in any way, but the Fill
selector is the one on the left (here's proof that FreeHand's user
interface, while easy to use, is hard to write about). When you want
to work with an object's fill, click the Fill selector; to work with an
object's stroke, press the Stroke selector; to work with both the fill
and the stroke, click the Both selector. FreeHand shows you which
selector is active by displaying a black border around the selector.

The Colors palette's pop-up menu. The Colors palette's pop-up
(or "Options") menu is what you use to duplicate colors, delete

FIGURE 6-5
FreeHand's
Colors palette

Fill and Stroke selector | Zoom box
Stroke selector |
Close box |

Fill selector ⊢   ⊣ Add arrow

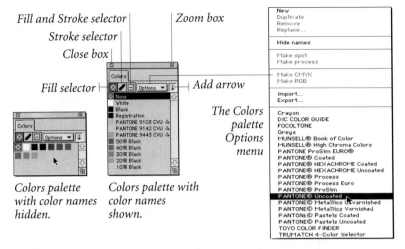

The Colors
palette
Options
menu

*Colors palette
with color names
hidden.*

*Colors palette with
color names
shown.*

*To change the
position of a color
in the Color List:*

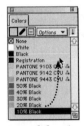

Select the color...   *...and drag it up or
down in the Color List.*   *When the color's where you
want it, stop dragging.*

colors, choose color libraries, and convert colors from one color type (spot or process) to another.

The Add arrow. The Add arrow is another unnamed feature of the Colors palette. It's to the right of the pop-up menu—a little box with an arrow in it. Ordinarily, you add colors to the Colors palette by dropping color swatches into the open area at the bottom of the list. If you can't see an open area, drop the swatch on the Add arrow. FreeHand adds the color to the end of the list.

For more on adding new colors to the Colors palette, see "Creating New Colors," later in this chapter.

Changing the order of the colors in the Colors palette. To change the order in which colors appear in the Colors palette, point at a color name and then drag the color name up or down in the Colors palette. Once you've got the color where you want, drop it. This can be handy when you've got a long list of colors and want to position frequently-used colors near the top of the palette.

If you can't see the Colors palette, double-click any color well (in the Inspector, or in the Color Mixer, for example). FreeHand displays the Colors palette. This also displays the Color Mixer, if it wasn't already visible. This shortcut is a toggle—if the palette is already visible, double-clicking a color well closes the palette.

Hiding and showing color names. If you want, you can hide the color names displayed in the Colors palette. To do this, choose Hide Names from the Colors palette's pop-up menu. When you do this, FreeHand displays only color wells in the Colors palette. To display the color names, choose Show Names from the pop-up menu.

Without seeing the color names, it's too easy to pick the wrong color. You can't even (easily) see whether a color is a spot color or a process color. When you pick the wrong color, you might get more, or fewer, color separations than you expect. In other words, hiding the color names in the Colors palette is likely to cost you money, make you miss deadlines, and generally mess up your life. It is, of course, your decision—but don't say I didn't warn you.

In the Windows version of FreeHand, FreeHand displays the color name when you position your cursor over a color swatch. I grudgingly admit that this makes hiding the color names a more reasonable thing to do, but that doesn't mean I have to like it.

The Color Mixer

You use the Color Mixer to create and edit the colors in your publications. The Color Mixer gives you five different color models to choose from: CMYK, RGB, HLS, or System (on the Macintosh, you'll see the Apple Color Picker, in Windows you'll see the current Windows system colors). To display the controls for a color model, click the corresponding button (see Figure 6-6). To create a tint of a color, use the Tints palette.

If the Color Mixer isn't visible, you can display it by double-clicking any color well. FreeHand displays the Color Mixer, and loads it with the color definition of the color you clicked. This won't work in Windows FreeHand if you've combined the palettes.

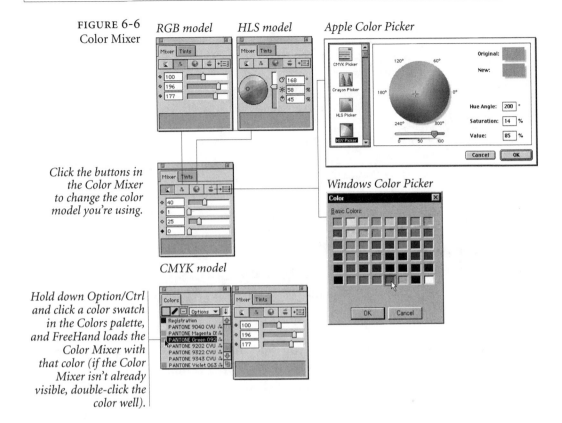

FIGURE 6-6
Color Mixer

RGB model   *HLS model*   *Apple Color Picker*

*Click the buttons in
the Color Mixer
to change the color
model you're using.*

Windows Color Picker

CMYK model

*Hold down Option/Ctrl
and click a color swatch
in the Colors palette,
and FreeHand loads the
Color Mixer with
that color (if the Color
Mixer isn't already
visible, double-click the
color well).*

Tip:
The Quick Way
to Load the
Color Mixer

When you want to edit a color, but your wrist is too tired to drag a color swatch from a color well (in the Colors palette, Fill Inspector, or elsewhere) into the Color Mixer, hold down Option/Ctrl and click any color well filled with the color you want to edit. Free-Hand loads the Color Mixer with the color you clicked.

The Tints Palette

I wish they could make up their minds. FreeHand 5 had a separate Tints palette, which FreeHand 7 installed as a color model in the Color Mixer. In FreeHand 8, it's a palette again.

Regardless of where they put it, the Tints palette (or panel) is where you create tints of an existing color (see Figure 6-7).

Tip:
The Quick Way
to Load the
Tints Palette

Hold down Option/Ctrl and click any color well filled with the color you want to edit. FreeHand loads the Color Mixer with the color you clicked. If you've clicked a tint of an existing color, Free-Hand loads the Tints palette with the base color, not the tint.

FIGURE 6-7
Tints palette

Drag a color swatch into this color well...

Don't drag the color swatch into this color well. If you do, FreeHand gets confused.

...and FreeHand generates tints of the color, in 10-percent increments.

To create a custom tint, enter a percentage in the field, or drag the slider.

Creating and Adding Colors

Now that you know what the tools are, you're probably wondering how they work.

Adding Colors from a Color Library

Most of the time, you'll be adding colors from FreeHand's color libraries. Why do this? Because your commercial printer wants you to (when they talk in their sleep, they call out Pantone numbers), and because it's the quickest way to add a named color to your publication. To choose a color from a color library, follow these steps (see Figure 6-8).

1. Display the Colors palette (if it's not already visible, press Command-9/Ctrl-9).

2. Choose a color library from the Colors palette's pop-up menu. FreeHand displays the Library dialog box.

3. Pick a color by clicking one of the color swatches in the Library dialog box. To select more than one color, hold down Shift as you click on the color swatches (if you want, you can Shift-drag through the entire library to select all the colors in the library).

4. Press Return (or click the OK button). FreeHand closes the Library dialog box and adds the selected color or colors to the Colors palette.

FIGURE 6-8
Adding a color from
a color library

Type the name or number of the color you want here, and FreeHand selects the color. This saves you the trouble of scrolling through the list of colors.

Choose a color library from the Colors palette's Option menu.

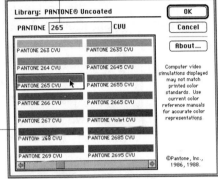

Hold down Shift as you click colors to select more than one color at a time from the list.

After you click OK to close the Library dialog box, FreeHand adds any color (or colors) you've selected to the Colors palette.

Tip:
Leave the Color
Name Alone

If you're working with Pantone spot colors, don't rename the color unless you're working with one of the applications that names PMS colors differently from FreeHand (see "Keep Your Color Names Straight," below). Just stick with the color name that's entered in the Name field when you select the PMS color. This way, when you print, you can turn on the Separation Names option in the Print Setup dialog box and the color name will print on the correct color overlay. Your commercial printer has a pretty good idea what "PMS 327 CV" means, but might go mad trying to guess what you meant by naming a color "angry spam."

Then again, if you know you're going to be using a Pantone ink but don't know which one, you can always name the color "Spot Color" or some such, and tell the printer which ink to use when you hand over the job.

Tip:
Why Import
Colors?

What's the difference between importing colors using the Import command and choosing a listed library? The libraries shown on the menu are the ones FreeHand found in the Color folder in your FreeHand folder. If you've stored a library somewhere else, you can retrieve colors from it using Import. You may want to store your color libraries somewhere else to keep the pop-up list shorter.

Tip:
Keep Your Color
Names Straight

If you're using FreeHand to create EPS graphics containing spot colors that will be imported into a publication created by another application, and you want color separations, make sure that your spot color names match between FreeHand and the other application. Color separation programs are as literal-minded as every other piece of software, so when you're separating a publication containing the spot colors "OceanBlue" and "Ocean_Blue" you can expect to get two overlays. Since you want all of the objects colored with this spot-color to print on one overlay, keep color names consistent between documents. Make sure they're identical—right down to capitalization and punctuation.

This is especially true when you're working with Pantone colors, because different applications use different names for the same Pantone colors.

Note that all of this makes no difference whatever if you're converting these colors to process colors as you separate the file.

Creating a Color

To create a new color, follow these steps (see Figure 6-9).

1. Display the Colors palette (press Command-9/Ctrl-9).

2. Double-click a color swatch in the Colors palette to display the Color Mixer, if it's not already visible.

3. Pick a color model by clicking the buttons at the top of the Color Mixer. If you're working on a publication that you'll be printing using process colors, use the CMYK color model. If you're creating a custom spot color (have you talked with your commercial printer about this?), it really doesn't matter which color model you use. If you're creating a tint of an existing color, use the Tints palette.

4. If you're using the CMYK or RGB color model, specify your color by entering numbers in the fields or sliding the sliders. If you're using the System color model, click a color in the dialog box that your system displays. If you're using the Tints palette, click on one of the color wells for the tint

FIGURE 6-9
Creating a new color

*Create a new color
using the Color Mixer
or the Tints palette.*

 *Add arrow*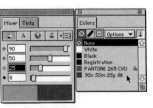

*Drag a color swatch from the Color
Mixer (or Tints palette) and drop it
into an empty area in the Colors palette
(or on the Add arrow).*

*FreeHand adds the new color
to the Colors palette, and assigns
the color a default name.*

Or...  | *Click the Add to
Color List button.*

*FreeHand displays the Add to Color
List dialog box. Type a new name,
or change the color model, if
necessary. Click the Add button...*

*...and FreeHand adds
the color to the Colors
palette.*

percentage you want, or enter a percentage in the Tint
Percentage field.

5. At this point, add the color to the Colors palette using either
of the following techniques.

   u Click the Add to Color List button (it appears in both
   the Color Mixer and the Tints palette). FreeHand
   displays the Add to Color List dialog box. At this point,
   you can either accept the default name suggested by
   FreeHand, or enter a name for the color. You can also
   change the color model.

   u Drag a color swatch into the empty area at the bottom of
   the Colors palette. If you can't see an empty area in the
   palette, drop the color swatch on the Add arrow at the
   top of the palette. FreeHand adds the color to the Colors
   palette, assigning it a default color name as it does so.

   If you want to change the color's name, double-click the color
name in the Colors palette, type the new name for your color, and
press Enter (see Figure 6-10).

FIGURE 6-10
Renaming a color

*To change a color
name...*

...double-click the
name in the Colors
palette...

...type a new
name for the
color...

...and press Enter.
FreeHand renames
the color.

**Tip:
Keep Your Color
Definitions
Straight**

If you're using FreeHand to create EPS graphics for use in another page layout application, make sure that your color specifications match between FreeHand and the other application. PageMaker imports named process colors, so you're safe there—but Quark XPress doesn't import named process colors from an EPS (XPress does import named spot colors).

Once again, you can't rely on your screen display, because different applications display colors differently. Make the CMYK settings for your named process colors identical from one application to another, and you can count on their printing identically when you separate the publication.

Creating Color Libraries

FreeHand can read two different types of color libraries—binary files, which are stored in a proprietary format, and text files, which are saved as text-only. Binary files generally have the file extension .BCF, and text-only files have the extension .ACF. If you create your own color libraries, you can use any file name you want, but I'd advise you to stick with FreeHand's file extensions.

Exporting color libraries. You create binary color libraries when you export colors from FreeHand. To do that, follow these steps (see Figure 6-11).

1. Choose Export from the Colors palette's pop-up menu. FreeHand displays the Export Colors dialog box.

2. Select the colors you want to export from the list in the Export Colors dialog box and press Return. FreeHand exports the colors you've selected.

Creating color libraries using a word processor. You can edit an existing color library (such as "CrayonLibrary.acf") to create a new

FIGURE 6-11
Exporting a binary
color library

Choose Export from the Colors palette's Options menu, and FreeHand displays the Export Colors dialog box.

Type the name you want to see on the Colors palette's pop-up menu here.

Type the filename here.

Select the colors you want to export and press Return (or click the OK button).

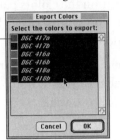

FreeHand displays this text when you click the About button in the Library dialog box.

Enter the number of rows and columns you want to see in the Library dialog box here.

Choose the library's name from the pop-up menu, and FreeHand displays the Library dialog box.

The next time you display the Color List pop-up menu, you'll see your new color library.

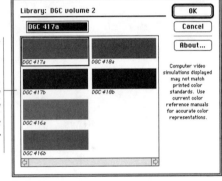

color library using any word processor that can save files as text-only (ASCII). If you're working from a process-color swatch book, here's your chance to enter lots of colors at once.

Color library files begin with the following text (items you enter are shown in italic). Table 6-1 shows what the different lines and keywords mean.

```
ACF 1.0
library name
LibraryVersion: number
Copyright: © your name here
AboutMessage: your message here
Names: Partial or Full
Rows: number of rows
Columns: number of columns
Entries: number of entries
Prefix: prefix you want for the colors in the library
Suffix: suffix you want for the colors in the library
```

TABLE 6-1
Color Library
Keywords

Keyword	What it means
Library name	The name of the library as you want it to appear on the Colors palette's pop-up menu. Your library's name can be up to 31 characters long.
LibraryVersion	Enter a number here to represent the version number of your library. You can leave this line blank if you want.
AboutMessage	The message you want to see when you click the About button in the Library dialog box.
Names	Enter "Full" to display names with their suffixes and prefixes attached (see "Suffix" and "Prefix," later in this table), or "Partial" to display only the names of the colors. If you're insane, you can even enter "None", which means you won't see any color names in the Colors palette.
Rows	The number of vertical color swatches FreeHand displays in the Library palette. Larger numbers mean smaller swatches; smaller numbers mean bigger swatches. Enter a "1" to produce the tallest possible color swatch.
Columns	The number of horizontal swatches FreeHand displays in the Library palette. Enter a "1" to produce the widest possible color swatch.
Entries	The total number of colors in the library.
Prefix	Any text you want to appear before your color names in the Colors palette.
Suffix	Any text you want to appear after your color names in the Colors palette.
Type	The type of colors contained in the library. You can enter "Process", "Spot", or "Mixed".
Models	A list of the color models used in the library. You can enter "CMYK" and "RGB".

	Keyword	What it means
TABLE 6-1 Color Library Keywords (continued)	PreferredModel	Enter "CMYK" or "RGB" here—it doesn't seem to make any difference to FreeHand. If you're creating a color library to use with PageMaker, on the other hand, the value you enter here determines which color model PageMaker's Edit Color dialog box displays when you edit the color.

```
Type: Process, Spot, or Mixed
Models: color models
PreferredModel: preferred color model
Data:
```

After you create the library header, enter your color definitions as shown below, where *colorname* is the name you give the color and *cyan*, *magenta*, etc. are the color percentages for the color model being used (where 1.0 = 100 percent).

```
percentageC percentageM percentageY or percentageK
process or spot
colorname
```

For example

```
0 0 0 .1
Process
10% Gray
```

If you want to define a color using the RGB color model, enter the RGB values as shown below. Enter each of the component colors ("Red", "Green", and "Blue") using a scale where "65535" equals 100 percent of that color and "0" equals zero percent.

```
Red Green Blue
Spot
colorname
```

For example

```
65535 65535 0
Spot
10% Gray
```

When you're through adding colors to your color library, save the file as text-only (ASCII), giving the file the extension .ACF. An example of a very short color library is shown in Figure 6-12.

FIGURE 6-12
A very short
color library

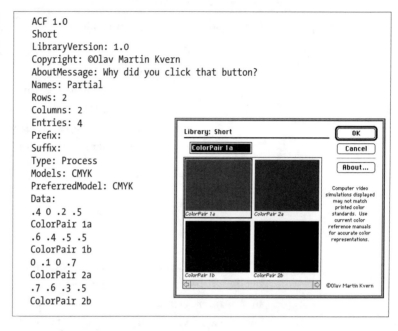

```
ACF 1.0
Short
LibraryVersion: 1.0
Copyright: ©Olav Martin Kvern
AboutMessage: Why did you click that button?
Names: Partial
Rows: 2
Columns: 2
Entries: 4
Prefix:
Suffix:
Type: Process
Models: CMYK
PreferredModel: CMYK
Data:
.4 0 .2 .5
ColorPair 1a
.6 .4 .5 .5
ColorPair 1b
0 .1 0 .7
ColorPair 2a
.7 .6 .3 .5
ColorPair 2b
```

Importing Colors from PageMaker

Because it's so important to have your spot-color names—or your process-color specifications—match, it's great to be able to import objects from PageMaker into FreeHand and add the color names and specifications used in PageMaker to your Colors palette.

Most of the time, it's easiest to pick the colors you want from a color library—FreeHand and PageMaker can use the same color libraries. If you're working with lots of custom spot colors (i.e., colors that didn't come from a color library), follow these steps to bring those spot colors into FreeHand.

1. Create spot colors in PageMaker.

2. Save one page containing objects with the colors you want to bring into FreeHand to disk as an EPS file.

3. In FreeHand, press Command-R/Ctrl-R (or choose "Import" from the File menu).

4. Locate and select the EPS file you just printed to disk and press Return. FreeHand displays an Import icon. Click the icon to place the PageMaker EPS. As FreeHand places the EPS file, it adds the colors defined in the PageMaker EPS to the Colors palette.

You can take color names and definitions created in FreeHand back to PageMaker—when you import a FreeHand EPS file, Page-Maker updates the Colors palette with any named colors in the placed EPS.

When you import an EPS from PageMaker or QuarkXPress, FreeHand doesn't import the named process colors in the EPS. Process-colored objects in the EPS separate correctly when you print, but the name of the color doesn't get added to the Colors palette. If you want to use these colors in your FreeHand publication, you'll have to either re-create them in FreeHand, or follow these steps.

1. Convert the named process colors you want to import into FreeHand to spot colors in PageMaker or XPress.

2. Export an EPS containing examples of the colors.

3. Import the EPS into FreeHand. The spot color names appear in the Colors palette. You can delete the placed EPS, if you want.

4. Convert the imported spot colors to process colors (select each color and choose Convert to Process from the Colors palette pop-up menu).

Adding Colors from Illustrator

When you open an Illustrator file, any named colors in the file are added to FreeHand's Colors palette. When you import an Illustrator EPS file, any named colors in the EPS are also added to the Colors palette. The trouble is that Illustrator users don't often name the process colors they use in their drawings (and early versions of Illustrator *wouldn't let you* name colors you defined using the process color model). What can you do when you want to add the colors used in an Illustrator file to your FreeHand Colors palette when the colors haven't been named?

1. Open or import the EPS (if you're importing the file, make sure you've turned on the Convert Editable EPS When Imported option in the Import/Export Preferences dialog box).

2. Select an object in the converted graphic that's filled with the color you want to add to your Colors palette.

3. Press Command-Option-F/Ctrl-Alt-F to display the Fill Inspector.

4. Click the Add to Colors List button. FreeHand displays the Add to Color List dialog box. Enter a name for the color (if you want—FreeHand will have suggested a name), then choose "Process" or "Spot," and then click the OK button. Alternatively, you can drag a color swatch from the Fill Inspector's color well to an empty area in the Colors palette (or drop it on the Add arrow at the top of the palette).

Importing Colors from Other Applications

In general, you can import spot-color definitions from any other application that supports named colors. To do this, create an EPS file containing the spot colors you want, and then import the EPS into FreeHand. Named colors in the EPS file *should* appear in the Colors palette. At that point, you can delete the EPS, if you want.

If you edit the properties of a color you've imported with an EPS graphic, don't expect the changes you've made to affect the color definitions inside the EPS—they won't. The colors inside the EPS are, in effect, locked.

If you imported the EPS only to get the color definitions and have deleted the EPS, there's no problem. If you've imported an EPS, edited the colors that are imported with the EPS, and applied the edited colors to FreeHand objects, you can expect the colors inside the EPS and the colors of the FreeHand objects to separate differently. If they're spot colors, you'll end up with (at least) an extra overlay. If they're process colors, colors that should look the same will look different.

Editing Colors

To edit a color, follow these steps (see Figure 6-13).

1. If the Color Mixer isn't already visible, double-click the color well in the Colors palette for the color you want to

FIGURE 6-13
Editing a color

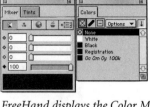

Double-click the color you want
to edit in the Colors palette.

FreeHand displays the Color Mixer.

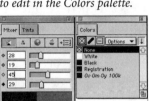
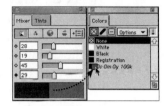

Use the fields or sliders in the
Color Mixer to adjust the color.

Drag a color swatch from the Color Mixer
to the color well of the color you're editing
in the Colors palette.

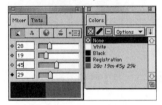

FreeHand updates the color.

edit. If the Color Mixer is already visible, hold down
Option/Ctrl and click the color you want to edit. The Color
Mixer fills in with the specifications of the color you clicked.

2. Drag the color sliders or type numbers in the fields (if
    you're using the CMYK or RGB color models). If you're
    using the Windows or Macintosh System color models,
    pick a color in the dialog box.

3. When the color has the specifications (or appearance) you
    want, drag a color swatch from the color well in the Color
    Mixer to the color well in the Colors palette.

Converting Spot Colors to Process Colors

Sometimes you need to change a color you've specified as a spot
color into a process color. Your budget's expanded, you've got a
sweetheart deal from your commercial printer, your client/boss/
whatever just *has* to have a color photograph—something happens

so that you find you have to change your publication's color printing method from spot color to process color. Select the color in the Colors palette, then choose Make Process from the Colors palette's pop-up menu (see Figure 6-14).

FreeHand converts your spot color to a process color. The process colors will rarely match the spot color—this is partly because the conversion process isn't perfect, but it's mostly because process color can't simulate the range of colors you can print with spot color inks (especially, as I've noted elsewhere, Pantone inks). Edit the definition of the new process color until it looks the way you want, or until it matches your process color swatch book.

When you convert a Pantone spot color into a process color, FreeHand uses the CMYK percentages listed in Pantone's *Process Color Imaging Guide*.

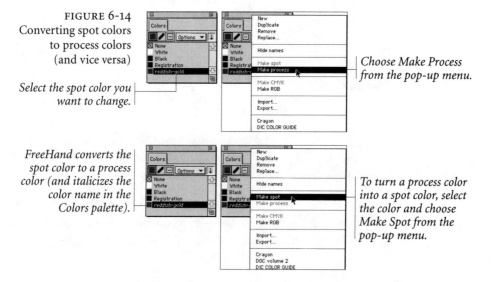

FIGURE 6-14
Converting spot colors
to process colors
(and vice versa)

Select the spot color you
want to change.

*Choose Make Process
from the pop-up menu.*

*FreeHand converts the
spot color to a process
color (and italicizes the
color name in the
Colors palette).*

*To turn a process color
into a spot color, select
the color and choose
Make Spot from the
pop-up menu.*

Tip:
Changing from
one library color
to another

You've just changed your mind—you want all the "PANTONE 192 CVU" in your publication to change to "PANTONE 274 CVU." You can change the name and color specifications of "PANTONE 192 CVU" to match "PANTONE 274 CVU"—though it's easy to make an error typing the name. Or (in this case) you could tell your commercial printer that the film overlay labelled "PANTONE 192 CVU" should be printed as "PANTONE 274". But what if you're compulsive (I know you're out there), and really want to change the one color to another, precisely as it's listed in the color library? Follow these steps (see Figure 6-15).

1. In the Colors palette, select the color you want to replace.

2. Choose "Replace" from the Colors palette's pop-up menu. FreeHand displays the Replace Color dialog box.

3. If you want to replace the color with a color from a color library, turn on the Color Library option and choose the library from the associated pop-up menu. If you want to replace the color with another color from the Colors palette, turn on the Color List option and choose the color from the associated pop-up menu.

4. Click the OK button. If you chose a color from the Colors palette, FreeHand replaces the color. If you choose a color library, FreeHand displays the Library dialog box. Pick the color you want to use to replace the original color, then click the OK button, and FreeHand replaces the color. Any objects colored with the original color will now have the replacement color applied to them.

FIGURE 6-15
Changing from
one library color
to another

Select the library color you want to change.

Choose "Replace" from the Colors palette's Options menu. FreeHand Displays the Replace Color dialog box.

Note: When you replace a color, FreeHand applies the replacing color to any objects filled or stroked with the original color. You could do this using Graphic Find and Replace, but it's sometimes easier this way.

Choose the color (from either a color library or from a color currently in the Colors palette) you want to use to replace the selected color. Click the OK button.

FreeHand replaces the color.

Applying Colors

Once you've selected an object, you can use any of the following techniques to apply a color to the object (see Figure 6-16).

◆ Click one of the selectors (Fill, Stroke, or Both) at the top of the Colors palette, then click a color in the Colors palette (click the color name, not the color swatch). FreeHand applies the color to the object's fill and/or stroke.

◆ Drag a color swatch from the Colors palette to one of the three selectors (Fill, Stroke, and Both) at the top of the Colors palette.

◆ Drag a color swatch from any color well and drop it on an object. If you drop the swatch inside a closed path, FreeHand applies the color to a path's fill. If you drop the swatch on the path, FreeHand applies the color to the object's stroke.

◆ Drag a color swatch from any color well into the color well in the Fill or Stroke Inspector and press Return. FreeHand applies the color to the fill or stroke of the object.

◆ Choose a color from a pop-up menu associated with a color well in the Fill Inspector or the Stroke Inspector.

Applying Colors to Text

You can apply a fill or stroke to the characters of text in your publication. To apply a color to text, select the text with the Text tool and apply a color using any of the techniques described in the previous section. What happens when you select the text block with the Pointer tool and apply a color depends on the setting of the Colors palette Shows option in the Colors Preferences dialog box (see "Colors," in Chapter 1, "FreeHand Basics").

Applying Colors to Groups

You can apply a color to a group, changing the stroke and fill of all the objects inside the group. There are some odd wrinkles to this.

◆ Objects inside the group with any basic fill or a fill of None will be filled with a basic fill of the color you apply.

FIGURE 6-16
Applying colors

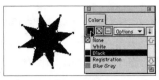

Select an object. Click the
Stroke or Fill selector...

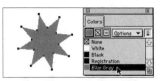

...and click a color name. FreeHand
applies the color to the selected object.

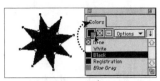

Select an object. Drag a color
swatch from a color well...

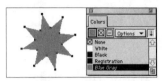

...and drop it on the Fill or Stroke
selector. FreeHand applies the color.

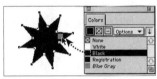

Drag a color swatch
from a color well...

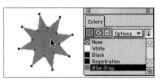

...and drop it on an object
(the object need not be selected).

Select an object. Drag a color
swatch from the Colors palette
(or the Color Mixer) to the color
well in the Fill (or Stroke)
Inspector.

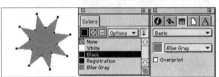

FreeHand applies the color.

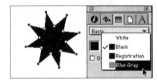

Choose a color from the Color
pop-up menus in the Fill or
Stroke Inspector.

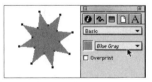

FreeHand applies the color.

◆ Patterned fills are colored with the color you apply, but
remain patterned fills (you shouldn't be using these anyway,
as explained in "Fills" in Chapter 2, "Drawing").

◆ Graduated and radial fills change so that the color you've applied to the group is their starting color.

◆ Tiled and PostScript fills are unaffected.

You can still subselect objects inside the group and change their color and fill specifications, regardless of any color you've applied to the group.

Applying Colors to Imported Graphics

FreeHand separates imported EPS graphics according to the color definitions inside the EPS, so applying a color to an EPS image has no effect.

You can apply colors to paint-type graphics, bi-level TIFFs, and grayscale TIFFs. To apply a color to an imported image, use any of the following techniques.

◆ Drop a color swatch on the image.

◆ Click the Fill selector at the top of the Colors palette, then click the color you want to apply.

◆ Drag a color swatch into the Fill selector in the Colors palette.

◆ Select the image, display the Fill Inspector, and either drop a color swatch into the Fill Inspector's color well or choose a color from the pop-up menu next to the color well.

When you print, FreeHand separates the image (or prints it as tints of a spot color, if you've applied a spot color to it). Applying a color to a color TIFF has no effect on the way that TIFF is separated by FreeHand.

Creating Duotones

Contrary to what you may have heard elsewhere, a single grayscale TIFF with two process inks applied to it does not a duotone make. It doesn't even make a "fake" duotone—which you create by printing a grayscale image on top of a tint of an ink.

The trouble is, I haven't found two people who agree on how to create a duotone. Some people change the screen frequency of the image for one color. Some people enhance the highlights in the image that prints on the overlay for the more dominant color and enhance the shadows in the image that prints on the overlay for the subordinate color. Some people do both. And so on.

Inside this book, I'm the absolute dictator, and I say that a duotone is created by printing two slightly different TIFFs on top of each other. The TIFF for the more dominant color in the color scheme has had its shadows enhanced; the TIFF for the subordinate color has had its highlights enhanced. By "enhanced," I mean that the darkest five percent (or so) of the pixels in the image become black and that the lightest five percent become white. The darkest—or lightest—areas in the image seem to spread out slightly. The screen frequencies and screen angles are the same for the two TIFFs.

If you have Photoshop, of course, you can use it to create your duotones. But if you don't, read on.

To create duotones using only FreeHand, follow these steps (see Figure 6-17 and Color Figure 8).

1. Import the grayscale TIFF you want to print as a duotone.

FIGURE 6-17
Creating duotones

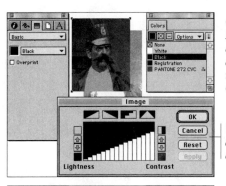

Create two copies of the image. Place the two images on top of each other in FreeHand (in this example, I've offset the images so that you can see what's going on). Color the images different colors.

Use the Image dialog box to decrease the lightness and contrast of the darker image.

Use the Image dialog box to increase the lightness and contrast of the lighter image.

Turn on the Overprint option (it's in the Fill Inspector) for the top image.

2. Enhance the shadows in the image. To do this, display the Image dialog box (select the TIFF and click Edit in the Object Inspector), then decrease the contrast and lightness of the image.

3. Clone the image, then enhance the highlights in the image. To do this, use the Image dialog box to increase the contrast slightly, then increase the lightness of the image.

4. Apply the dominant color you intend to use to create the duotone to the image you edited in Step 2. Apply with the duotone's subordinate color to the image you edited in Step 3.

5. Select the image on top, then display the Fill Inspector. Turn on the Overprint option.

When plates are made from the two overlays, the TIFFs overprint each other, producing a real duotone. I won't say this produces *great* duotones, but it does work.

Removing Colors To remove a color, select the color name in the Colors palette and choose Remove from the pop-up menu attached to the Colors palette. If there are other colors in the publication based on the selected color (tints, mostly), or if there are objects with that color applied to them, or if the color is used in a style's definition, FreeHand will complain that the color is in use somewhere in the publication.

FreeHand gives you a choice (see Figure 6-18) of courses of action. You can remove the color, which removes the color from the Colors palette and applies an unnamed process color to any objects originally colored with the color you've removed. Or you can choose to keep the color, after all.

FIGURE 6-18
Always give
the user a choice

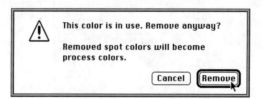

If FreeHand tells you a color is in use that you're pretty sure you aren't using, it's probably used as the base color for a tint you are using, or it's used in a style.

Copying Colors

If you need to copy a color or set of colors from another FreeHand publication, open the source publication, select some objects with those colors applied to them, copy them out of the publication and paste them into the current publication. Remember FreeHand's "home team wins" rule—any colors in the current publication with names the same as those of the incoming colors override the incoming color definitions.

Color Xtras

FreeHand comes with several Xtras dedicated to working with color in your publication—you'll see them on the Colors submenu of the Xtras menu. In addition, you'll find the Unused Named Colors Xtra on the Delete submenu of the Xtras menu and the Eyedropper tool on the Xtra Tools palette.

Many of these Xtras (Color Control, Darken Colors, Desaturate Colors, Lighten Colors, Randomize Named Colors, and Saturate Colors, to be exact) create new process colors when you use them. So you can't expect to use them in your spot-color publications (instead, use the Tints palette to create lighter or darker tints of spot colors). Note, too, that these Xtras don't change the color definitions in the Colors palette, and don't add the new colors they create to the Colors palette. To add the colors to the Colors palette, use the Name All Colors Xtra (see "Name All Colors," later in this chapter).

Color Control

Do you ever need to add a percentage of some color to a series of objects? I've seen it happen: the client looks at the color proofs, then in an authoritative voice says, "Add 15 percent yellow to this character's face." You know that the character's face is made up of several dozen blended objects and graduated fills, and start to panic at the thought of changing the colors of so many objects (and this always happens close to a deadline). You can stop sweating—the

Color Control Xtra gives you a way to change the colors applied to any number of selected objects (see Figure 6-19).

1. Select the objects whose colors you want to change.

2. Choose "Color Control" from the Colors submenu of the Xtras menu. FreeHand displays the Color Control dialog box.

3. Click the button corresponding to the color model you're working with, then make changes to the slider settings (drag the sliders or enter new percentages in the attached fields). If you've turned on the Preview option, you'll see the result of your changes on the selected objects.

4. When the colors look the way you want them to, press Return (or click the OK button) to apply your changes.

FIGURE 6-19
Color Control Xtra

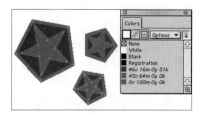

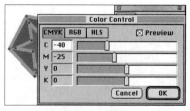

If you want to change the color definitions for an object or objects...

...choose Color Control from the Color submenu of the Xtras menu. Choose a color model and adjust color values.

If you've turned on the Preview option, FreeHand shows you the effect of your changes.

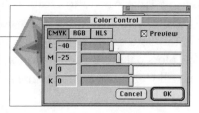

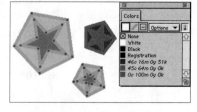

When the objects look the way you want them to...

...press Return to close the Color Control dialog box. Note that FreeHand does not add the edited colors to your Color List.

Darken Colors   When you choose "Darken Colors" from the Colors submenu of the Xtras menu, FreeHand makes the colors applied to the selected objects a little darker. What's that mean? Well, if you're using the

CMYK color model, FreeHand adds three percent to the values of cyan, magenta, and yellow applied to the selection, and adds two percent to the color's black percentage. If you're using the RGB model, FreeHand subtracts five percent from each base color's setting. If you're using the HLS model, FreeHand subtracts five from the Lightness value of the color.

What about tints? You'd think FreeHand would increase the percentage of the base color when you apply this Xtra, but it doesn't. Instead, the Xtra changes the color components of the tint, effectively creating a new, unnamed color. Which means you should use the Tints panel of the Color Mixer when you want to make tints lighter or darker, rather than using this Xtra.

Desaturate Colors

According to my dictionary, "saturation" of a color is its "vividness of hue." If I were someone other than who I am, I'd probably leave it at that, or simply tell you to run the Xtra and see what happens to your color definitions. Maybe we'd both be better off.

As I understand it, saturation is a measurement of the amount of the primary colors (red, blue, and green, the colors we *see*, not the various color models we use to *simulate* them on a computer monitor or printing press) in a color. Saturated colors have a lot of one or two primary colors in them. When we desaturate a color in FreeHand, we're simulating the removal of some amount of the third primary color from the color we've defined.

In practical terms, that means that FreeHand changes the percentages of cyan, magenta, yellow, and black in the colors applied to the selected objects. The percentages changed, however, vary for each component color, and depending on the color's definition.

The percentage of cyan changed in a color defined as 80C 40M 0Y 30K, for example, differs from the percentage changed in a color defined as 80C 0M 100Y 10K—even though the original percentage of cyan in the two colors is the same. In general, desaturating colors *removes* percentages from each component color, but that's not always the case. (In our example colors, for instance, eight percent would be *added* to the percentage of magenta in the second color.) Run the Desaturate Colors Xtra enough times, however, and you'll reach zero percent for all component colors.

Lighten Colors   The Lighten Colors Xtra works just like the Darken Colors Xtra in reverse. If you're using the CMYK model, the Lighten Colors Xtra decreases the percentages of cyan, yellow, magenta, and black applied to the selected objects. If you're using the RGB, HLS, and System models, FreeHand decreases the base color components used in the colors applied to the selection.

Import RGB Color Table   Choose Import RGB Color Table when you want to import the colors from an RGB image into your Colors palette. This can make it easier to match colors in an RGB image (it's a bit more reliable than using the Eyedropper tool for the same purpose).

Name All Colors   Have you applied colors to objects from the Color Mixer (rather than applying them using the Colors palette)? If so, the Name All Colors Xtra can save you when your client decides to change their corporate colors as you're getting ready to imageset their new brochure. Choose "Name All Colors" from the Colors submenu of the Xtras menu, and FreeHand adds all the colors you've used in your publication to the Colors palette—including any colors generated by blending (that is, the colors applied to the intermediate object in a blend). Each color shows up in the list only once (see Figure 6-18). FreeHand creates a names based on the CMYK definition of the color.

FIGURE 6-20
Naming unnamed
colors

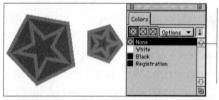

What's wrong with this picture? There are paths on the page, and they've obviously had colors applied to them, but no colors (apart from the default colors) appear in the Color List.

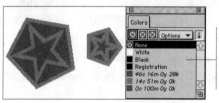

Choose Name All Colors from the Colors submenu of the Xtras menu, and FreeHand adds every color used in the publication to the Color List.

Randomize Named Colors   You guessed it—the Randomize Named Colors Xtra randomly changes the color values in all named colors in a publication. Of what possible use is this? I don't know about you, but I need shaking up from time to time. When my creative process gets stuck in a rut, I find that introducing some random element sometimes gives me the inspiration I need. Choose "Randomize Named Colors" from the Colors submenu of the Xtras menu, and watch FreeHand redefine your colors. The results are generally hideous, but may give you the creative jolt you need.

This Xtra also makes for a good practical joke to pull on your fellow FreeHand users while they're away from their machines for a minute or two, but don't tell anyone I said so (it can, of course, be undone).

Saturate Colors

When you run the Saturate Colors Xtra, you increase the saturation of the colors in the objects you've selected. What's saturation? I'm glad you asked—take a look at "Desaturate Colors," earlier in this chapter.

Sort Colors Palette by Name

Having trouble finding a color you know you named "Aardvark" or "Zymurgy" because there are so many colors in your Colors palette? Choose "Sort Colors palette by Name" from the Colors submenu of the Xtras menu, and FreeHand alphabetizes the color names in your Colors palette (see Figure 6-21).

FIGURE 6-21
Alphabetizing
color names

If you're having trouble locating a color in your Colors palette...

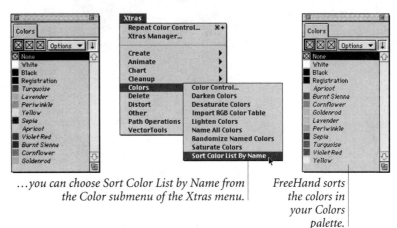

...you can choose Sort Color List by Name from the Color submenu of the Xtras menu.

FreeHand sorts the colors in your Colors palette.

Delete Unused Named Colors

Is your Colors palette longer than it should be? Filled with dozens of named colors you were "trying out" but then decided against? To shorten your Colors palette, choose "Unused Named Colors" from the Delete submenu of the Xtras menu, and FreeHand will remove all the colors it finds in the Colors palette that aren't applied to an object or used in a style definition.

Eyedropper Tool

In my career as a graphic artist, I've matched colors to shoes, shirts, horses, grapes, jewelry, lawnmowers, and a host of other items (not to mention things I can't mention in a family publication). I used to do this by comparing printed swatches of ink to photographs or to the item itself. These days, I'd use the Eyedropper tool to pull a color out of a scanned image of the photograph.

The Eyedropper tool is an Xtra, and appears on the Xtra Tools palette (press Command-Option-K/Ctrl-Alt-Shift-X to display the Xtra Tools palette, if it's not already visible). Select the Eyedropper tool, then point at an object on your page or pasteboard with the tip of the tool. Hold down the mouse button, and a swatch of the color of the pixel immediately beneath the tip of the Eyedropper tool appears, stuck to your cursor. Drag the color swatch to an empty area in the Colors palette (or to the Add arrow at the top of the Colors palette), then drop it. FreeHand adds a new color to your Colors palette, basing the color on the color value of the pixel you clicked on (see Figure 6-22).

FIGURE 6-22
Eyedropper tool

Select the Eyedropper tool from the Xtra Tools palette.

Position the end of the Eyedropper tool over the color you want to acquire (in this case, I've pointed at a pixel in an image, but you can point the Eyedropper tool at any object on a FreeHand page). Drag the Eyedropper tool, and a color swatch appears.

Drop the color swatch into the Colors List, or into any color well, or onto a path or object.

Obviously, you'll get better results if you turn on the High Resolution Image Display option in the Redraw Preferences dialog box (see "Redraw Preferences" in Chapter 1, "FreeHand Basics"). Also, if the image is RGB instead of CMYK, you get FreeHand's idea of what the resulting CMYK values will be after separation; this won't be accurate unless FreeHand does the separations.

The current bit depth setting of your monitor has no effect on the Eyedropper tool—it gets the color definition from the object's color definition.

You can also drag the color swatch to any color well, or drop it on objects to apply the color to them. If you're loading the Eyedropper tool with a color from a path, or from an object (such as a grayscale TIFF) that you've applied a named color to, FreeHand loads the Eyedropper tool with the named color (which you can then apply to other objects).

Creating Spot-Color Tint Builds

When you're working with spot-color publications, you often want to create tint builds (also known as stacked screens) of the colors you're working with to broaden the range of colors in your publication. Since you can't create a color containing percentages of two or more spot colors (20-percent black and 60-percent PMS 327, for example), it'd seem, at first glance, that you're stuck. You're not, though, as the following exercise demonstrates.

1. Open a new publication and add a spot color (create your own, or use one from the Pantone spot-color library). If one doesn't already exist, create a 20-percent tint of black.

2. Draw a rectangle.

3. Without deselecting the rectangle, fill it with the spot color you created in step 1. Set the rectangle's stroke to None.

4. Clone the rectangle by pressing Command-=/Ctrl-Shift-C.

5. Fill the clone with the 20-percent tint of black.

6. Press Command-Option-F/Ctrl-Alt-F to display the Fill Inspector. Turn on the Overprint option to make the rectangle overprint.

That's all there is to it. When you print, the gray rectangle over-prints the spot-color rectangle, creating a combination of the two spot colors. Unfortunately, you can't see the tint build onscreen or on color printouts; you only see the color of the frontmost object. The next section shows another means to the same end.

Using Blending to Create Process-Color Tint Builds

Here's a trick I use to create a palette of tint builds for my publications (see Figure 6-23).

1. Draw a rectangle, fill it with 100-percent cyan, magenta, or yellow, and set the rectangle's stroke to None.

2. Clone the rectangle, move it away from the original rectangle, and fill it with 100-percent black.

3. Select both rectangles, press Command-U/Ctrl-U to ungroup them, and select a blend reference point on each rectangle. Press Command-Shift-B/Ctrl-Shift-B (or choose Blend from the Combine submenu of the Modify menu). FreeHand blends the rectangles.
   Display the Object Inspector by pressing Command-I/ Ctrl-I. Type the number of tint builds you'd like to create in the Number of Steps field and press Return to change the blend. The intermediate objects in the blend are colored with tints. These new colors do not appear in your Colors palette.

4. Ungroup the blended objects.

5. Select an object filled with one of the colors you want and press Command-Option-F/Ctrl-Alt-F to display the Fill Inspector. The color well in the Fill Inspector displays the color of the path you selected.

6. Choose Add to Color List from the pop-up menu next to the color well. FreeHand adds the color to your list of colors (you can change the name of the color, if you want).

COLOR FIGURE 1
Overprinting
and knockouts

Objects colored with spot color 1 set to knock out (Overprint box unchecked).

Spot color 1 plate

Spot color 2 plate

Color 1 knocks out color 2

Objects colored with spot color 1 set to overprint (Overprint box checked).

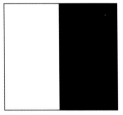

Spot color 1 plate

Spot color 2 plate

Color 1 prints over color 2

COLOR FIGURE 2
Trapping an
open path

This cyan path needs to be trapped.

To create a spread, clone the path, and then increase the width of the cloned path. Set the cloned path to overprint.

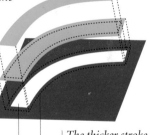

The thinner stroke knocks out objects behind it.

The thicker stroke overprints objects behind it.

To create a choke, clone the path and then decrease the stroke width of the cloned path. Set the original path to overprint.

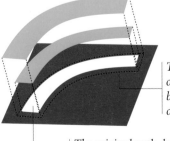

The cloned path overprints the background objects.

The original path knocks out objects behind it.

Trapped path

COLOR FIGURE 3
Trapping closed
paths and text

Unless I've been very lucky, you'll see the paper showing through around the cyan circle in this example. To prevent the paper from showing, you need to trap the object.

Select the object you want to trap and press Command-Option-L/Ctrl-Alt-L to display the Stroke Inspector. There, add a stroke to the object by choosing Basic from the Stroke Type popup menu.

Enter a value in the Width field that's twice the width of the spread you want, and turn on the Overprint option.

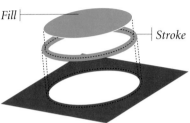

When you print, the the stroke of the ellipse overprints the background rectangle, while the fill knocks out. This creates a spread.

To create a choke, apply an overprinting stroke the color of the background rectangle to the ellipse.

Here's the trapped version of the example.

Fill ⊢

Stroke

When you print, the stroke decreases the size of the knockout created by the fill of the ellipse.

Not trapped

Again, unless I've been lucky, you'll see the paper showing through around these characters. That means that this text needs to be trapped.

Trapped using a spread

This stroke overprints the background objects, creating a spread. Unless I've been very unlucky, you won't see the paper showing around the edges of these characters.

Trapped using a choke

The stroke decreases the size of the knockout behind the text, creating a choke.

COLOR FIGURE 4
Overprinting and
process colors

*Background rectangle is
80C20M80Y10K*

●★ *0C80M0Y40K*
■⬠ *20C80M20Y40K*

Overprint off

Overprint on

*Where the overprinting object's percentage of a
process color is zero, the background color will show
through.*

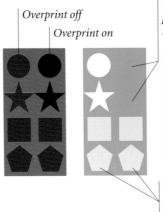
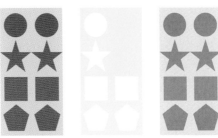

*These objects contain percentages of each process
color, so overprinting and non-overprinting objects
print identically on each plate.*

COLOR FIGURE 5
TrapWise trapping

You shouldn't even think of trapping this manually.

*TrapWise displays a
preview of the spreads
and chokes it uses to
trap the file. This screen
shot is from the Windows
version of TrapWise
1.0—the one I have.
The actual example was
trapped using TrapWise
2.0 on the Macintosh.
Newer versions of
TrapWise look different,
and dr job, but I think
you the idea.*

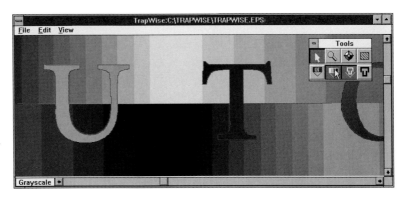

Example EPS trapped by TrapWise.

COLOR FIGURE 6
Rosettes

Rosettes for an area of flat color: 10C 10M 10Y 10K (ugly, but good for demonstration purposes).

COLOR FIGURE 7
Creating tint builds

You can quickly create palettes of tints using FreeHand's Blend command.

To see the color definition for a tint, drag a color swatch from the Fill Inspector's color well into the Color Mixer's color well (or Option/ Ctrl-click the color well).

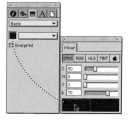

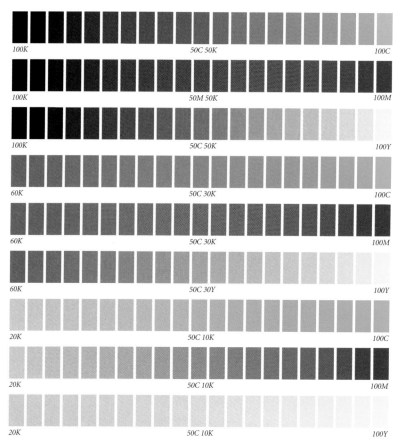

100K   50C 50K   100C

100K   50M 50K   100M

100K   50C 50K   100Y

60K   50C 30K   100C

60K   50C 30K   100M

60K   50C 30Y   100Y

20K   50C 10K   100C

20K   50C 10K   100M

20K   50C 10K   100Y

COLOR FIGURE 8
Duotones

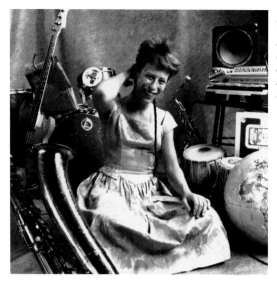

*FreeHand duotone.
Two overlapping TIFFs
colored with different
colors (cyan and black)
and with different
settings in FreeHand's
Image dialog box.*

Photoshop duotone.

Photographs of Amy Denio by Roger Schreiber

*Two "fake"
duotones*

100 percent cyan background *50 percent cyan background*

COLOR FIGURE 9
Color Examples

FreeHand's Neon custom stroke effect is great—but you can't see it on your screen. Here's a way to create glowing lines you can see on your screen.

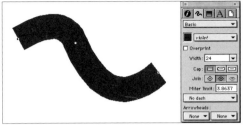

Draw a path.

Assign a thick stroke weight to the path that's the color of the outside of the "glow"you want to create.

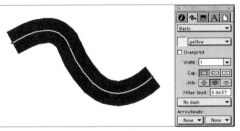

Clone the path.

Assign a thin stroke weight to the cloned path. This stroke should be the color you want for the inside of the "glow" effect.

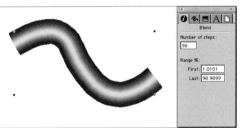

Blend the two selected paths.

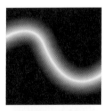 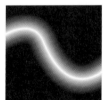

For an effect that looks more like a neon lighting tube, blend from white to the glow color, then blend from the glow color to the background color.

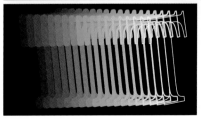

Each "neon" character above is composed of two blends. One blend goes from white to a color; the other goes from that color to black.

COLOR FIGURE 10
Separating color images

Example RGB TIFF separated by FreeHand (using color management).

Example color TIFF separated by Photoshop, saved as an EPS, and printed from FreeHand (you could also save the file as DCS from Photoshop).

COLOR FIGURE 11
Printing color
images using random
dither patterns

*If you look closely at these
images, you won't see
rosettes—you'll see
overlapping, random
dither patterns (in this
example, I've used a
600 dpi diffusion dither
from Photoshop.*

*This technique is also called "stochastic" screening, and my version of it is still at
an extremely experimental stage (it looked pretty good in the last edition, but I
have no idea what it will look like this time).*

COLOR FIGURE 12
Stochastic screening

*Real stochastic screening (as opposed to the "fake" stochastic screening
shown above) created by Icefields from Isis Imaging (at 800 dpi).*

FIGURE 6-23
Creating a palette
of tint builds

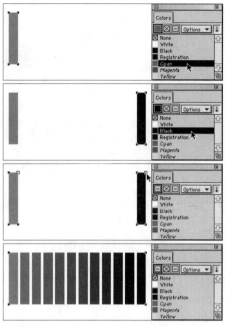

*Draw a rectangle and fill it
with 100-percent cyan,
magenta, or yellow.*

*Clone the rectangle and drag
the clone away from the
original rectangle. Color the
clone 100-percent black.*

*Press Command-U/Ctrl-U to
convert the rectangles to paths.
Select each path press Com-
mand-Shift-B/Ctrl-Shift-B to
blend the rectangles.*

*Adjust the number of blend
steps using the Object Inspector.
Ungroup the blend (press
Command-U/Ctrl-U twice)
and select a rectangle that's
filled with a color you like.*

Display the Fill Inspector.

*Choose Add to Color
List from the pop-up
menu next to the color
well.*

*FreeHand adds
the color to the
Colors palette.*

*FreeHand displays the Add to Color
List dialog box. Click the Add button.*

7. Repeat steps 5 and 6 until you've defined all the colors
    you want.

Trapping

A "trap" is a method of overlapping abutting colored objects to
compensate for the imperfect registration of printing presses. Because registration, even on good presses with good operators, can
be off by a quarter point or more, abutting elements in your publication may not end up abutting perfectly when the publication is
printed by your commercial printer. What happens then? The paper shows through where you don't want it to (see Figure 6-24).

FIGURE 6-24
Why you need to trap

Color 1
Color 2

When you don't trap, you can end up with paper showing through where it shouldn't.

When you trap, you enlarge (or shrink) the objects so that they'll overlap a little bit when they print—regardless of the paper stretching or shifting on the press.

Do I need to tell you what happens if you take your work to a less skilled printer? Or to a press that's badly out of register or run by turkeys? Disaster. Also, some printing processes, notably silkscreening, require larger traps than others. In any case, talk with your commercial printer regarding the tolerances of their presses and/or operators.

Before I start describing trapping techniques in FreeHand, you ought to know that the best technique is one you find outside FreeHand—use Luminous (formerly Adobe) TrapWise. TrapWise can trap your publications better than you can, and if you use TrapWise, you won't even have to think about trapping. I'll provide descriptions of what you can do to trap your files, but I'll say at the outset—find a service bureau that'll trap your files with TrapWise, and save yourself time and trouble.

If you can't, or don't want to, use TrapWise, you don't have to trap every potential registration problem yourself—you can use FreeHand's Trap Xtra. It does a good job of trapping objects formatted using basic fills or strokes. I'm still going to describe how to do the trapping yourself, then I'll talk about the Trap Xtra. I do this because I believe that you should know how to add and subtract, multiply and divide before you ever use a calculator.

Object-Level Overprinting

The key to trapping, in FreeHand and elsewhere, is in controlling which objects—or which parts of objects—print on top of other objects as the printing press prints your publication. While choosing to overprint entire inks can be handy (especially overprinting black), you really need to control the overprinting characteristics of individual objects to make trapping work (see Color Figure 1).

Luckily, you can. Any FreeHand path can be specified as an over-printing object (that is, it won't knock a hole in any objects behind it when you print), regardless of the object's color. The controls for object-level overprinting are found in the Fill Inspector and the Stroke Inspector (see Figure 6-25).

FIGURE 6-25
Overprinting controls

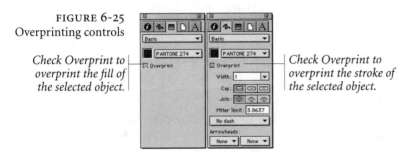

Check Overprint to overprint the fill of the selected object.

Check Overprint to overprint the stroke of the selected object.

Ink-Level Overprinting

In the Separations tab in FreeHand's Print Setup dialog box, you can choose to knock out or overprint an ink (see Figure 6-26). To do this, click the "O" (for "overprint") column to the left of the ink's name. FreeHand displays the Overprint Ink dialog box. You can turn overprinting on or off for the ink, or you can set a threshold at which the ink will overprint (enter a percentage in the Threshold field, and FreeHand overprints the ink when the ink density in an object is greater than that percentage). I find I usually

FIGURE 6-26
Ink-level overprinting

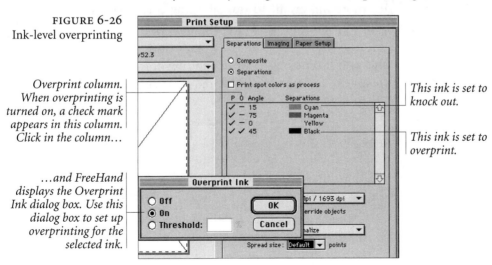

Overprint column. When overprinting is turned on, a check mark appears in this column. Click in the column...

...and FreeHand displays the Overprint Ink dialog box. Use this dialog box to set up overprinting for the selected ink.

This ink is set to knock out.

This ink is set to overprint.

leave ink-level overprinting turned off, and overprint selected paths using the Overprint options in the Fill and Stroke Inspectors.

Object-level overprinting settings override ink-level overprinting settings for individual objects.

Manual Trapping

The keys to trapping in FreeHand are the Overprint checkboxes in the Fill Inspector and the Stroke Inspector. These controls, used in combination with FreeHand's Paste Inside command, provide incredible manual trapping flexibility.

When you're working with FreeHand's trapping features, you'll be creating *spreads* (outlines of objects, in the same color as the object, that are slightly larger than the object itself) and *chokes* (outlines of the object that are the same color as the underlying object's color). Spreads make the object larger so that the edges of the object print over the underlying object; chokes make the area knocked out of the underlying object smaller than the outline of the foreground object.

Use chokes when the foreground object is a darker color than the background object; use spreads when the foreground object is lighter. In other words, trap from light colors into darker colors. Sound subjective? It is. I use chokes when I'm trapping type—text characters often look distorted when you use spreads (the eye is very critical when it comes to text).

Spot-Color Trapping

It's more important to trap abutting color fields in publications you're printing using spot colors than it is in process color publications. When you're working with process colors, you'll almost always see some ink between abutting objects, so you're less likely to see the tell-tale paper-colored lines showing a poor trap (see Figure 6-27).

The easiest way to demonstrate how spot-color trapping works is to show you some examples. As you work through these examples, you'll trap an ellipse into a rectangle by manipulating the color, width, and overprinting specifications of the path that surrounds the ellipse. First, draw the colored objects.

1. Create a rectangle. Fill the rectangle with a spot color ("Color 1"). Set the rectangle's stroke to None.

FIGURE 6-27
Spot-color trapping
and process-color
trapping

When you're trapping process colors, there's almost always some color value—dots—on one of the other plates...

...while in spot-color trapping, there's usually not.

2. Draw an ellipse on top of the rectangle. Make sure that the ellipse is entirely inside the rectangle. Fill the ellipse with a different color from that of the rectangle ("Color 2"). Set the stroke of the ellipse to None.

3. Save the file.

Creating a spread. The ellipse needs to be trapped, or you'll run the risk of having paper-colored lines appear up around the ellipse when you print the publication. You can either spread or choke the ellipse, or both.

To spread the ellipse, follow these steps (see Color Figure 3).

1. Select the ellipse.

2. Press Command-Option-L/Ctrl-Alt-L to display the Stroke Inspector.

3. In the Stroke Inspector, choose Basic from the Stroke Type pop-up menu, set the line color to "Color 2" (the color of the ellipse), type a line width for your trap in the Width field. Finally, turn on the Overprint option.

The line width you enter in the Width field should be equal to twice the trap amount—if you enter "2", you'll get a stroke of one point on either side of the path, because PostScript lines grow out from the line's center. If your commercial printer has asked for a trap of .5 points, enter "1" in the Width field.

When you print, the ellipse is larger than the hole that's been knocked out of the background rectangle, which means that the outside of the ellipse slightly overprints the background rectangle. You've just created a spread.

After you're through looking at the objects, or printing, choose Revert from the File menu and revert to the version of the file you saved earlier. This way, you're ready for the next procedure.

Creating a choke. To choke the ellipse, follow these steps (see Color Figure 3).

1. Select the ellipse.

2. Press Command-Option-L/Ctrl-Alt-L to display the Stroke Inspector.

3. In the Stroke Inspector, choose Basic from the Stroke Type pop-up menu, set the line color to "Color 1" (the color of the background rectangle), type a line width for your trap in the Width field. Finally, turn on the Overprint option.

When you print, the hole that's knocked out of the background rectangle is slightly smaller than the ellipse. This way, the outside of the ellipse slightly overprints the background rectangle. You've just created a choke.

Choose Revert from the File menu to get the file ready for the next procedure.

Trapping across color boundaries. The techniques described above work well as long as objects don't cross color boundaries. If the objects do cross color boundaries (especially going from a color background to a white background), it's too obvious that you've changed the shapes of the objects. What do you do?

1. Drag the ellipse so that it's partially outside of the rectangle.

2. Clone the ellipse by pressing Command-=/Ctrl-Shift-C.

3. Without deselecting the cloned ellipse, press Command-Option-L/Ctrl-Alt-L to display the Stroke Inspector.

4. In the Stroke Inspector, choose Basic from the Stroke Type pop-up menu, set the stroke color to "Color 1" (the color of the background rectangle), enter a stroke width for your

trap in the Width field. Finally, turn on the Overprint option and press Return to apply your changes.

5. Press Command-X/Ctrl-X to cut the ellipse.

6. Select the background rectangle and choose Paste Inside from the Edit menu.

7. Select the original ellipse and press Command-B/Ctrl-B to send it to the back.

At this point, the ellipse you pasted inside the rectangle spreads slightly, while the part of the ellipse outside of the rectangle remains the same size and shape (see Color Figure 3). Choose Revert from the File menu to get ready for the next trapping example.

What happens when the object you need to trap overlaps more than one other, differently colored object? In this case, you can run into trouble. The trap you use for one background color might not be the trap you want to use for the other. You might want to spread one and choke the other, depending on the colors you're using.

In these cases, you use the same basic techniques described above for all of the overlapping objects. Try it (see Color Figure 3).

1. Draw another new rectangle (I'll call it Rectangle 2) so that it partially overlaps the original rectangle (which I'll call Rectangle 1). Create a third spot color ("Color 3") and apply it to the rectangle's fill. Set the rectangle's stroke to None. Drag the ellipse so that it partially overlaps both rectangles.

2. Select Rectangle 2 and press Command-=/Ctrl-Shift-C to clone it. Without deselecting the clone, press Command-Option-L/Ctrl-Alt-L to display the Stroke Inspector.

3. In the Stroke Inspector, choose Basic from the Stroke Type pop-up menu, set the line color to "Color 1" (the color of the background rectangle), enter a line weight for your stroke in the Width field, and turn on the Overprint option. Press Return to apply the stroke.

4. Select the ellipse and repeat step 3. Make sure that the clone of the ellipse is in front of the clone of the rectangle, then

select both of the clones you've created and press Command-X/Ctrl-X to cut them to the Clipboard.

5. Select Rectangle 1 and choose Paste Inside from the Edit menu. You've just created chokes for the ellipse and Rectangle 2 at the points they overlap Rectangle 1.

6. Select the Ellipse and press Command-=/Ctrl-Shift-C to clone it. Change the stroke of the cloned ellipse as directed in step 3. Press Command-X/Ctrl-X to cut the new clone. Select Rectangle 2 and choose Paste Inside from the Edit menu. The ellipse is now choked where it overlaps Rectangle 2.

Trapping Lines

The trapping techniques above work well for filled paths, but what about lines? After all, you can't apply two different line properties to a single line. Instead, you clone the line and make the width of the cloned line larger or smaller to achieve the spread or choke you want. One of the lines overprints; the other line knocks out.

Follow these steps to spread a line (see Color Figure 2).

1. Draw a rectangle. Create a spot color and fill the rectangle with it.

2. Draw a line inside the rectangle. Create another spot color and apply it to the line. Do not set this line to overprint.

3. Select the line and press Command-=/Ctrl-Shift-C to clone the line.

4. Press Command-Option-L/Ctrl-Alt-L to display the Stroke Inspector. Increase the width of the line by twice the amount of spread you need (remember, PostScript lines grow out from their centers) and check the Overprint box to make the stroke overprint.

That's all there is to it. The original line knocks a hole in the background rectangle, and the clone of the line spreads to just a little bit beyond the edges of the knockout.

To choke the line, follow these steps (see Color Figure 2).

1. Draw a rectangle. Create a spot color and fill the rectangle with it.

2. Draw a line inside the rectangle. Create another spot color and apply it to the line. Set this line to overprint.

3. Select the line and press Command-=/Ctrl-Shift-C to clone the line.

4. Display the Stroke Inspector. Decrease the width of the line by twice the amount of choke you need, and leave the Overprint box unchecked.

5. Hold down Control and select the original line. Press Command-F/Ctrl-F to bring it to the front.

This time, the cloned line is narrower than the original line, and knocks out an area that's slightly smaller than the original line, creating a choke.

If the line you need to trap crosses a color boundary, follow the same steps described above for trapping paths: clone the line, edit the line, cut the line, select the background object, choose Paste Inside, and send the original line to the back.

Trapping Text   Text is usually the element in a publication that needs trapping the most. For whatever reason, it's easier to notice poor trapping around text than around other elements. At the same time, traps that are too large distort the shapes of the characters you're trapping. It's especially a problem with small type, especially serif type.

Here's how to create a spread for text (see Color Figure 3).

1. Draw a rectangle, create a spot color ("Color 1"), and apply it to the rectangle.

2. Type a text block. Position the text block on top of the rectangle so that it's entirely within the area occupied by the rectangle.

3. Create a second spot color ("Color 2") and apply it to the text in the text block.

4. While the text is still selected, press Command-Option-L/ Ctrl-Alt-L to display the Stroke Inspector. Enter the width

you want (remember, it's two times the amount of trap you want) in the Width field. Turn on the Overprint option and press Return.

The next example shows how you can choke text by making the shape the characters knock out of the background a bit smaller than the characters themselves.

1. Draw a rectangle, create a spot color ("Color 1"), and apply it to the rectangle.

2. Create a text block. Position the text block on top of the rectangle so that it's entirely within the rectangle.

3. Create a second spot color ("Color 2"). Select all the text in the text block and click "Color 2" in the Colors palette. FreeHand applies a fill of "Color 2" to the text.

4. Without deselecting the text, press Command-Option-L/ Ctrl-Alt-L to display the Stroke Inspector. Enter the width you want for the trap in the Width field. Turn on the Overprint option and press Return.

If text crosses color boundaries, use the techniques described earlier for trapping overlapping paths.

Tip:
Type and
Black Ink

Type that's specified as 100-percent black always overprints, regardless of the settings you've made in the Fill and Stroke dialog boxes or in the ink list in the Print Setup dialog box. You probably want 100-percent black text to overprint most of the time, but what if you don't? Create a color that's specified as 99-percent black and apply it to the text you want to knock out of whatever is behind it. 99-percent black works just like every other color. It can be set to knock out or overprint as you want, and it'll look just like 100-percent black.

Advanced Spot
Color Trapping

All of the trapping techniques demonstrated above assume that you're working with solid (that is, 100 percent) spot colors. What happens when you're working with tints of spot colors, and what happens when you're working with graduated or radial fills?

When you're working with tints, you use the above procedures, substituting the tints for the colors specified for the overprinting strokes you're using to create traps. When you're trapping graduated and radial fills, on the other hand, things get complicated.

Trapping Spot Color Graduated Fills

When graduated fills abut in your spot color publications, you need to provide for some sort of trapping between the two fills, or you'll end up with your paper color showing through between the fills. Apart from using Luminous (formerly Aldus, formerly Adobe) TrapWise (see "Trapping with TrapWise," later in this chapter), the simplest thing to do is to set one or both spot colors to overprint, and then overlap the graduated fills by some small amount (something less than one point).

Trapping Spot-Color Radial Fills

After all the trouble we had to go through to create a trap for adjacent spot-color graduated fills, you'd think radial fills using spot colors would be more difficult. Luckily, that's not the case all the time. When you create a radial fill inside an object, you can simply add an overprinting stroke to the object containing the radial fill that's the color of the background object, thereby creating a choke. Alternatively, you can set the radial fill to overprint using the Overprint option in the Fill Inspector.

Process-Color Trapping

Process-color trapping is a bit simpler than spot-color trapping, because it's usually less critical that process-colored elements have traps (as simulated in Figure 6-25, earlier in this chapter), but it can be far harder to figure out exactly what color to make the stroke for a process-colored object. And when you're talking about trapping two process-colored graduated fills, watch out!

The main thing to keep in mind, however, is that, for each of the process inks, the ink percentage used in the topmost object in any stack of objects always wins—they knock out all percentages of that ink behind them, regardless of any overprinting settings.

Unless, that is, the ink percentage is zero. If, for example, the percentage of cyan used in the fill color of the topmost object in a stack of objects is zero, turning Overprint off makes the path knock out any other cyan in the area covered by the path. Overprinting the fill, in this case, means that the area taken up by the fill disappears from the cyan plates—the percentage of cyan in the next object in the stack shows through the area where the objects overlap (see Figure 6-28).

Another way to think of this is to think of each ink in a process color as behaving like a separate spot ink.

Simple Process-Color Trapping

In process-color trapping, you've got to make your overprinting strokes different colors from either the background or foreground objects. Why? Because process colors have a way of creating new colors when you print them over each other. It's what they do best.

As in the spot-color trapping section above, I'll demonstrate process-color trapping techniques by example. First, create a couple of objects.

1. Create a rectangle that's filled with "Color 1", which is specified as 20C 100M 0Y 10K.

FIGURE 6-28
Overprinting and
process inks

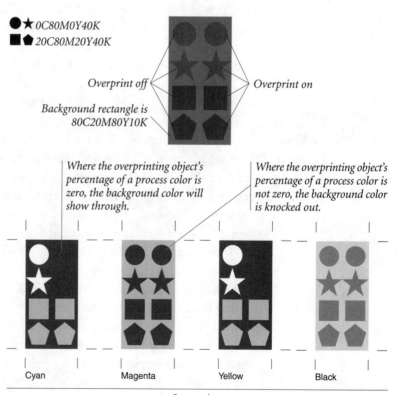

2. On top of this rectangle, draw an ellipse and fill it with "Color 2", which is specified as 0C 100M 50Y 0K.

3. Select both objects and set their stroke to None.

4. Save the file.

The ellipse needs to be trapped, or you run the risk of having cyan-colored lines showing up around the ellipse when the publication is printed—which could happen if the cyan and yellow plates aren't in good register, or if your paper stretches. Whether you spread or choke the ellipse depends on its color. If the ellipse is darker than the background rectangle, choke the ellipse. If the ellipse is a lighter color than the background rectangle, spread the ellipse. In this case, the ellipse is a lighter color, so you'll use a spread. To spread the ellipse, follow these steps.

1. Create a new process color containing only those colors in "Color 2" having higher values than "Color 1". Quick quiz: what component colors in "Color 2" have higher values than their counterparts in "Color 1"? If you said 50Y, you're the lucky winner. Specify a new color: 0C 0M 50Y 0K.

2. Select the ellipse.

3. Press Command-Option-L/Ctrl-Alt-L to display the Stroke Inspector.

4. In the Stroke Inspector, choose Basic from the Stroke Type pop-up menu.

5. Drag a swatch of "Color 3" into the color well in the Stroke Inspector.

6. Enter the width you want for your stroke in the Width field. It should be twice the width of your desired trap.

When you print, all the areas around the ellipse have some dot value inside them, and the new colors created where the objects abut won't be too obvious. Choose Revert from the File menu to get ready for the next example.

What if the ellipse were the darker color? If it were, we'd have to choke it. To choke the ellipse, follow these steps.

1. Select the ellipse and fill it with "Color 1". Select the rectangle and fill it with "Color 2".

2. Create a new color ("Color 3") that contains only the largest color component in "Color 1". That's 100M, so "Color 3" should be specified as 0C 100M 0Y 0K.

3. In the Stroke Inspector, choose Basic from the Stroke Type pop-up menu, set the line color to "Color 3", type the width of the trap you want in the Width field. Finally, turn on the Overprint option.

When you print, the stroke you applied to the ellipse guarantees that there's no gap around the ellipse, even if you run into registration problems when you print the publication.

Complex Process-Color Trapping

What if the ellipse in the examples given above was not completely contained by the underlying rectangle? What if, in fact, only half of the ellipse passed into the rectangle?

You don't want to make the entire ellipse larger, so limit the spread and choke of the ellipse to the area inside the underlying rectangle by using the Paste Inside techniques shown in the section on spot color trapping earlier in this chapter.

Trapping Imported Images

Because you can place color TIFF images in FreeHand, you can run into some truly hairy trapping situations. What happens when you need to cut out part of a color TIFF and place it on a process-color background? This isn't actually as scary as it sounds. Follow the instructions in the section "Cropping TIFF Images" in Chapter 4, "Importing and Exporting," to construct a clipping path for the TIFF, and then stroke the path with an overprinting line that's the same color as the background colors.

In this case, if the object passes over several color boundaries, avoid pasting both the TIFF and the path containing it into the underlying objects—it'll never print. Instead, clone the path, choose Cut Contents from the Edit menu and delete the extra TIFF. Fill the new object with white, stroke it with the overprinting path (the choke), and paste it inside the underlying object. Then place the original clipped TIFF above the area you've just choked.

If you've gotten this far, call me the next time you're in Seattle and I'll buy you a beer at the brew pub of your choice (it's amazing to me how few readers have taken me up on this). You've mastered the basic trapping techniques for spot and process colors, and for creating keylines around images.

Using the Trapping Xtra

If you need to trap a path that you've formatted using a basic stroke or fill, you can use FreeHand's Trap Xtra. You're still going to need to know a lot of the manual techniques I outlined earlier—mostly for text you don't want to convert to paths—but the Trap Xtra can take care of many (maybe even most) misregistration problems you're likely to encounter in a FreeHand publication.

To use the Trap Xtra to add traps between overlapping or abutting paths, select the paths and choose "Trap" from the Create submenu of the Xtras menu. FreeHand displays the Trap dialog box (see Figure 6-29). Fill in the dialog box and press Return, and FreeHand creates traps for the objects you've selected.

FIGURE 6-29
Trap Xtra

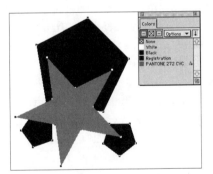

Select the objects you want to trap and select Trap from the Create submenu of the Xtras menu.

FreeHand displays the Trap dialog box. Set up your trapping by adjusting the controls here.

Note: I've used an absurdly large trap to make the process a little clearer.

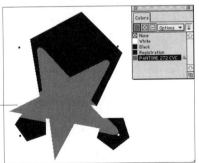

FreeHand traps the objects.

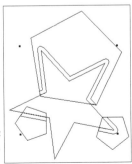

In Keyline view, you can see the trapping paths.

Trap Width. Enter the amount you want to trap the overlapping objects in this field (or move the slider until the value you want appears in the field). As I've been saying, this amount should be the amount your commercial printer says they need for their presses. In this case, you don't have to double the trapping amount—the Xtra takes care of that for you as it creates the traps.

Reverse Traps. When you check the Reverse Traps checkbox, you force FreeHand to spread traps it would normally choke, and choke traps it would normally spread. Use this option when you want to force a "darker" object to spread into a "lighter" object (ordinarily, FreeHand would choke behind the darker object). Why would you want to do this? Because the color definitions we use for objects— which is where FreeHand gets its ideas about the relative lightness and darkness of colors—might not match the properties of the inks we're using to print a publication. If the background ink is a fluorescent or metallic spot color, you probably want other inks to spread into the spot color (metallic and fluorescent spot inks are both more opaque and brighter than other inks). Alternatively, if you're working with a varnish, you'll probably want to spread the varnish into all other inks.

Trap Color Method. When FreeHand creates a new color to use for a process color trap, you can choose to trap using a color that's the sum of the difference between the abutting colors (turn on the Use Maximum Value option), or you can choose to decrease the ink percentages of that color (turn on the Use Tint Reduction option and enter a value in the Tint Reduction *n*% field). Most of the time, you should check the Use Tint Reduction option—traps created with lighter colors are less obvious.

Separating Color Images

FreeHand can separate color TIFFs (both CMYK and RGB) you've placed, and can also separate DCS and EPS (preseparated) images. In my opinion, the fastest and best method is to use a color-separation program (such as Photoshop) to create a CMYK TIFF, an

EPS file, a DCS 2.0 file, or a set of DCS 1.0 files, and place the separated image in FreeHand.

Why not just place an RGB TIFF in FreeHand? The color-separation programs have controls for correcting and improving color images. FreeHand really has very few tools for working with the content of color images. Like none, now that I think of it.

Still, FreeHand's separations of RGB images aren't bad (as long as you've done a decent job of correcting them and sharpening them in advance, and have turned on FreeHand's color management system)—take a look at Figure 10 in the color pages to see an example.

Preseparating Color Images

If you want to separate your color images using Photoshop (or any other program capable of creating color separations), and then place the preseparated image in FreeHand, you can save the file as an EPS file or as a CMYK TIFF.

If you save the image as a single EPS, DCS 2.0, or CMYK TIFF file, you can import the entire file into FreeHand. If you save the image in the DCS 1.0 format, place the DCS header file (it's the one without a C, M, Y, or K extension on its file name). In any case, when you separate the image with FreeHand, the separations will be the same as if you'd printed the separations directly from Photoshop. You might like FreeHand's separations better, though. Take a look at the side-by-side FreeHand, Photoshop, and PrePrint separations in the color section of this book (see Color Figure 10).

Which preseparation file format should you use? Saving the file as an EPS (including DCS) or CMYK TIFF makes a single large file, but saving as DCS 1.0 creates five files you've got to look after. The four DCS 1.0 separation files (the ones with C, M, Y, or K in their file names) have to be in the same folder as the DCS 1.0 header file, or FreeHand won't be able to find them to print. It's your call. I use CMYK TIFF, unless I need to include a clipping path (in which case I use EPS).

FreeHand and OPI

Open Prepress Interface (OPI) is a standard for links between desktop systems and dedicated color prepress systems, such as those manufactured by Kodak, Scitex, Hell, and Crosfield. OPI concerns imported images (TIFFs and paint-type graphics) only.

When you export an EPS from FreeHand, the EPS contains OPI information (a set of PostScript comments) that these systems need to be able to work with the file. OPI comments are most important if you're going to do something like drop a Scitex-separated color image into a FreeHand publication.

To be entirely frank, I'm not sure it's worth it. For my purposes, separations created using FreeHand and Photoshop can produce excellent quality in the 150-lpi-and-under range, which is where I do most of my work. If you want better than 150 lpi, OPI might be better for you.

Additionally, if you're working with very large images, or if you're working with a large number of images, you may want to have your prepress or imagesetting service bureau store and manage the files for you (while you take lower-resolution "For Position Only" images to work with on your system). Then, when you take your files to the service bureau to produce film, use OPI to link to the stored images.

Do-It-Yourself "Stochastic" Screening

Warning! This section is still under construction! Use the techniques described here with extreme caution (and, I might add, at your own risk). I've only just started figuring this out myself, but had to share it with you.

You can separate your own color images using the "stochastic" screening I described at the start of the chapter, using Photoshop (or any other image-editing program capable of creating a CMYK TIFF). You don't need to print on an imagesetter equipped with a special (and expensive) RIP, and you don't need to find a press capable of printing incredibly small dots. You can print on garden-variety imagesetters, at low resolutions, and then print on whatever presses you normally use.

Here's the deal—you can split the channels of a CMYK TIFF, save each channel as a separate diffusion dither (that is, as a bi-level bitmap), and stack the dithered images up in FreeHand, applying colors to them as you do.

What are the advantages? There aren't any regular patterns in the dithered images, so you don't have to worry about moiré patterns. Images look sharper, because halftone cells actually blur the focus of an image slightly. You can print at lower resolutions (to get a fine linescreen for a halftoned image, you've got to print at resolutions of 2,400 dpi or higher—but you can print dithered images at 1,200 dpi). The dithered images print faster (they're just bi-level bitmaps), and they don't take any time for FreeHand to separate (as an RGB TIFF would).

What are the disadvantages? Dither patterns are more obvious in areas of flat color than halftone screens. Skin tones, in particular, can look blotchy. It's still a somewhat experimental technique, and your commercial printers might look askance at it.

To separate a CMYK TIFF using "stochastic" screening, follow these steps (see Figure 6-30). I've shown the process using an earlier version of Photoshop, but it's about the same in Photoshop 4.0 and in other programs.

1. Open the TIFF with Photoshop. Set up your separation options as you normally would using the various setup dialog boxes in the Preferences submenu.

2. Select CMYK from the Mode menu.

3. Choose Split Channels from the Mode menu. Photoshop creates a separate grayscale TIFF for each channel (that is, each channel now shows what would be printed on each separation).

4. Choose Bitmap from the Mode menu. Photoshop displays the Grayscale to Bitmap dialog box. Click the Diffusion Dither button, and enter a resolution for the dithered bitmap you want to create.

   Most presses (and papers) have no problem printing the dots in bitmaps in the range of 400 dpi to 600 dpi (I like 600 dpi best, but you've got to experiment). Why not make a bitmap at imagesetter resolution—say, 2,400 dpi? Because your press won't be able to print the dots making up the image (ask your printer if their press can hold a one-percent spot in a 300-lpi screen, and you'll get the idea—the dots are just too small).

5. Save each of the bitmaps.

FIGURE 6-30
Do-it-yourself
stochastic screening

*Open the TIFF you
want to separate.
If you haven't
already converted it to
CMYK, or done any
color correction or
sharpening, do it now.*

*Display the Channels
palette (choose
Channels from the
Windows menu).
Choose Split Channels
from the Channels
palette's pop-up menu
(the commands are a
little different in
Photoshop 4—this is
in Photoshop 2.5).*

*Photoshop displays the four,
separate channels.*

*For each channel,
choose Bitmap from the
Mode menu. Photoshop
displays the Bitmap
dialog box.*

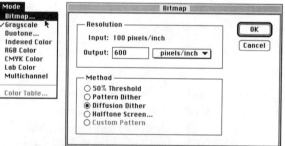

*Enter a resolution
for the dithered
image (the range
from 400–600 dpi
seems most
promising). Press
Return (or click
OK)…*

*…and Photoshop
converts the grayscale
image (this channel) to
a bi-level bitmap. Save
the bitmap. Repeat this
process for the other
three channels.*

*Stack the four bitmaps
on top of each other in
FreeHand. Set the
bitmaps to Transparent
using the Object Inspec-
tor. Apply the appropriate
process color to each
image, and print.*

6. Place the four bitmaps on top of each other in FreeHand, coloring each one the appropriate process color. As you import and color each bitmap, check the Transparent box in the Object Inspector. Make sure that the bitmaps are all the same size and in the same position.

When you print separations of your publication, FreeHand prints the dithered bitmaps on separate pages (or pieces of film). When you make a color proof, or print your publication on a press, you'll see the image.

I've only started using this technique—there are about a million details that I still need to work out (for example, separation settings that work well for conventional halftoning don't really work for this technique).

Most people working with stochastic screening see it as a high-end printing method—they're working with presses that can hold 300 lpi halftone screens. I don't see it that way at all. I think this technique would be best for people working at 150 lpi and under, on cheaper papers (like newsprint).

For an example of a color image separated using this technique, see Color Figure 11 in the color pages.

Stochastic Screening Without an Imagesetter

If you're like me, you looked at early examples of FM screening from Agfa's Crystal Raster system and got excited. Here, at last, were clarity, improved color depth, and a lack of moiré patterns. On further reflection, however, I realized that the dots produced by Crystal Raster were far too small to be printed on anything but the highest-quality, best-maintained, and most expensive printing presses around.

Here's the deal. The dots produced by the initial version of Agfa's Crystal Raster are, at their *largest*, around 20 microns (a micron is *one millionth* of a meter, or around $\frac{1}{25000}$ of an inch) in diameter. In terms of a conventional halftone, that's only a little bit bigger than a *one-percent* halftone dot at 150 lines per inch. Ask your average commercial printer if their presses can consistently reproduce (or "hold") a dot that small. Once they stop laughing, they'll tell you they can't. If they're honest.

So the key to making FM screening useful to most of us is controlling minimum dot size—and this need is apparently being addressed by Agfa and Linotype-Hell in new revisions of their systems. However, in my opinion there's another flaw in these systems: they're "RIP-based"—they're circuit boards (containing hardware and software) that attach to an imagesetter's RIP (or "raster image processor"—the part of the imagesetter that turns the PostScript commands sent by your page layout or illustration program into the bitmap that the imagesetter prints).

This approach has several disadvantages. The add-on boards are expensive, which means you'll pay more for imagesetting time (as imagesetting service bureaus attempt to recoup the expense of the equipment). The RIP-based FM screening systems also tend to be an "all-or-nothing" approach—it's difficult (if not impossible) to mix FM and conventional halftone screening methods on a single page (again, I expect future revisions of the products will remedy this).

RIP-based FM screening systems also usually require that the imagesetter they're attached to be calibrated for the fine dots these systems produce, rather than for conventional halftones. This means, in practical terms, that imagesetting service bureaus who want to move to a RIP-based FM screening system have to dedicate an entire imagesetter to the output of FM-screened jobs.

A better approach—so much better that many manufacturers are now adopting it—is to do the processing using commercially available software on a general-purpose computer. This approach has several advantages:

◆ You can produce FM versions of your separated images yourself, on your own computer.

◆ You can apply FM screening to photographic images (where you want it) while leaving any EPS graphics or text on your page for conventional halftoning.

◆ You're not using expensive imagesetter RIP time to process images.

◆ FM screening software tends to be less expensive than imagesetter RIP hardware upgrades.

◆ You can build the calibration needed for your FM screens into your separations, rather than having to calibrate the imagesetter for FM screening.

◆ You can match the size of the dots you're printing to the characteristics of the press you're printing on.

I've been experimenting with an FM-screening program called Icefields, from Isis Imaging. Icefields is a software package that runs on a Macintosh or Power Macintosh, and it's so easy to use it's almost frightening. All you need to do is choose an imagesetter resolution, pick a screening resolution, set the grayscale compensation for the imagesetter you're using (this is a particularly nice feature), and open an image (one you've scanned, color corrected, and saved as a grayscale or CMYK TIFF). Icefields then creates a file (or set of files, for a color image—Icefields saves in the DCS format) containing an FM-screened version of the image. To print the file, place it in your page layout or illustration program and print as you normally would. Color Figure 12 shows an image separated using Icefields. IceFields and FreeHand, however, have a disagreement about how to write and read DCS files—so you'll probably have to do what I did—stack up the cyan, magenta, yellow, and black files on a FreeHand page.

Here are a few things to keep in mind when you're working with FM screening:

◆ Film you've created using FM methods must be the film you use to make your printing plates. In other words, you can't expect your printer to make another copy of your film, for whatever reason, as they prepare your job for printing.

◆ You can't enlarge or reduce the image once you've created the final version of it. Enlarging or reducing the FM dots either makes them too big (so they're obtrusive) or too small (which means they won't print).

◆ Some imagesetter-based screening systems will try to apply a halftone screen to the FM-screened image. You don't want this, so turn off the screening system when you print.

◆ The usual techniques for getting a sharper image from a digital halftone don't apply. Ordinarily, you want to slightly oversharpen a scanned image (using the Unsharp Mask filter in Adobe Photoshop, for example); when you use FM screening, this sharpening looks unnatural. Remember, you're sharpening to overcome the fuzziness imposed by the halftone screen; you don't need to worry about that when you're working with FM screening.

◆ Because halftones tend to desaturate (or reduce the color intensity) of a color image, people have taken to increasing the color saturation of their images before creating separations. FM screening produces more saturated colors than halftoning, so you don't need to adjust color saturation. If anything, you may want to *reduce* the color saturation of your images when you're using FM.

Color Me Gone

When you're working with color, use restraint. Experimenting with color printing (like doing your color separations using dithered bitmaps from Photoshop) can cost lots of money. Every now and then, however, you'll find a commercial printer who wants to learn about this crazy desktop stuff—and who will run your experiments on unused parts of other jobs.

As you work with commercial printing, always remember that you're at the mercy of a series of photochemical and mechanical processes—from your imagesetter through the printing press—that, in many ways, haven't changed since the turn of the century (if that recently). Temperature, humidity, and ambient static electricity play large roles in the process, and the people who operate these systems are at least skilled craftspeople; at best, artists. Ask them as many questions as they'll answer, set your job up the way they want it, and then sit back and watch your job come off the press.

are rooted in the dim and primordial past (giant ground sloths, woolly mammoths, and Linotronic L100s roamed the earth), and some, while true today, might not apply when this book reaches your hands. That's the thing about computer software—as soon as you really know something, it's obsolete.

The Publication Window

When you open or create a FreeHand publication, you view and work on the publication in the publication window (see Figure 1-1). ...cation window gives you a view on FreeHand's ...place everything happens in FreeHand.

Title bar   Feed area   Page   Horizontal ruler   Zoom box

FreeHand ...

Scrollbar
...menu

Start

FreeHand, and you enter another world—a software model of a graphic artist's studio. Most programs are based on some real-world model: PageMaker works like a layout board, Excel works like an accountant's worksheet, and Word works like a great electric typewriter. ...

CHAPTER

FreeHand Basics
1

CHAPTER

Printing
7

What you se...
and Windows v...
the title (the na...
close the window...
tion window the...
publication wind...
the title, control m...
them to close, shrin...

Info Bar   Immediately below the ...
formation about the ...
position of the curso...
don't see the Info Bar, ...
hide the Info Bar by p...
you can't move it, as yo...

FIGURE 1-2
FreeHand's Info Bar

Info Bar showing that you've ...
is off the page. "h" shows the lo...
shows the vertical position of th...
coordinates from the Publicatio...

When you rotate an object, the I...
horizontal center of the object; "C...
shows you the angle of rotation.

...and slowest way to change
...way to click
Scroll Bars   The most obvious, least con...
your view of your publication is to use a scroll bar (that is, to click
in a scroll bar, drag a scroll handle, or click the arrows at either end
of a scroll bar). For more on better ways to get around, see "Moving Around in Your Publication," later in this chapter.

Page Icons   Now that FreeHand publications can contain multiple pages, you
and the Page   need a way to move from one page to another. One way is to click
Pop-up menu   the left page icon to move to the previous page in your publication, and click the right page icon to move to the next page. If
you know which page you want to go to, you can choose the page
number from the Page pop-up menu, or enter the page number in
the field associated with the pop-up.

page 1 chapter 1 title page

Preview mode   Keyline mode (note that FreeHand
displays the TIFF as a box)

Each viewing mode has advantages and disadvantages. In Pre...
view mode, you'll see something resembling your printed publica...
tion, but you'll also wait longer for it to display; Keyline m...
redraws quickly but doesn't usually resemble the printed pub...
tion. It's easier to select points in Keyline mode, and it's ea...
select objects in Preview mode. You'll find yourself sw...
between Preview and Keyline often.

You can also set specific layers to display in either K...
Preview mode using the Layers palette. For more on...
this, see "Working with Layers," later in this chapter.

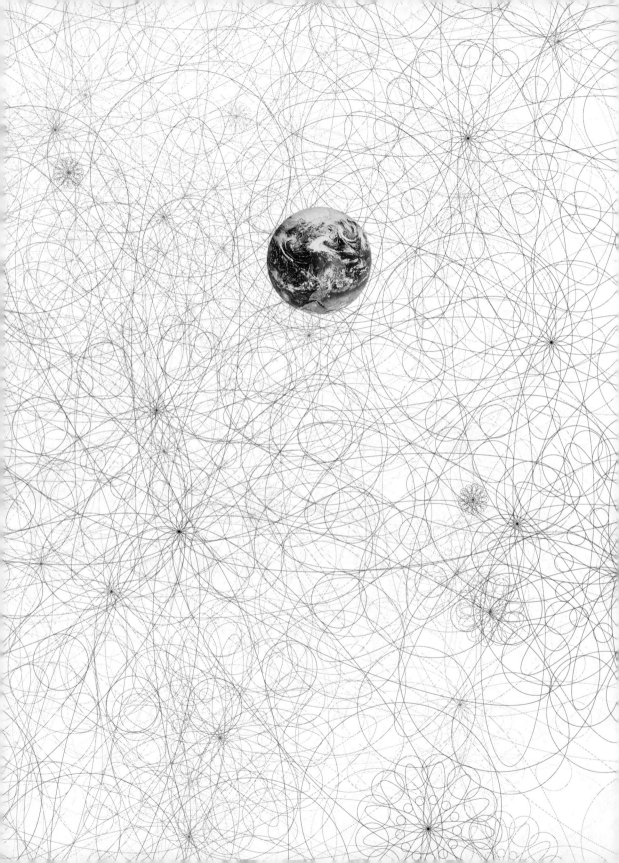

Roll a carved cylinder over a sheet of wet clay, and the carvings on the cylinder are transferred to the surface of the clay. Once the clay hardens, the marks are there to stay.

The ancient Mesopotamians noticed this. They figured that by carving characters on the cylinders in reverse they could transfer them to the clay tablets. Roll the cylinders over several tablets, and you've made several copies of the symbols on the cylinders. They were a bureaucratic bunch, and covered their tablets with bills of lading, legal contracts, nondisclosure agreements, and other rules and regulations.

They invented printing.

We've improved on this process a little bit since then.

We found that, by smearing ink over the surface of the cylinder (or over the tablets, for that matter), we could transfer the images from the clay cylinder to that new stuff—the white sheets of beaten, bleached papyrus reeds the Egyptians made. It was easier to carry than the tablets.

Later, somebody came up with moveable type, and scribes the world over lamented the decline in the quality of written materials. The romance novel followed closely on the heels of this technological advance. Printing—the ability to make dozens, hundreds, thousands, millions of copies of an image—flourished.

FreeHand is a good program for creating graphics for use on the web (and other electronic media), but—don't tell the web folks (who'll skip this chapter anyway)—this program was created to help you put ink on paper. And it's darn good at it.

The FreeHand Print Dialog Box

When you press Command-P/Ctrl-P, FreeHand displays the Print dialog box (see Figure 7-1). Never mind that it says "Printer *'printer-name'*" on the Macintosh instead of "Print." It's the Print dialog box and everybody knows it (or the Windows version of FreeHand does, anyway).

FIGURE 7-1
Print dialog box

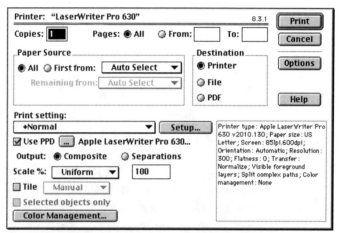

Macintosh

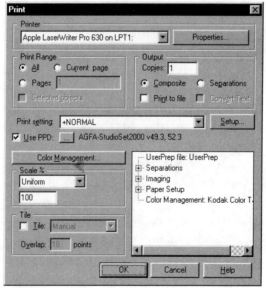

Windows

Tip:
Your Print
Dialog Box May
Differ (Do Not
Panic)

Does your Print dialog box look like the one shown in Figure 7-1? If not, don't panic—differing printer drivers (the system software that makes it possible to send information to printer) will display differing options depending on their capabilities. In some cases, add-on software will also change the options in the Print dialog box. My Macintosh Print dialog box, for example, displays "PDF" in the Destination area, because I've installed the Acrobat PDF Writer.

Most of the options in the Print dialog box, however, are put there by FreeHand, and don't change when you change printer drivers. These are the options I'll focus on in this chapter.

If your Print dialog box looks different because you're not using a PostScript printer driver, see "Printing to Non-PostScript Printers," later in this chapter.

Tip:
Use the
LaserWriter 8
(or Higher)
Printer Driver
(Macintosh only)

If you're still using a version of the LaserWriter driver prior to version 8 because you were scared by the bugs in LaserWriter 8.0, you might reconsider—most of the problems were fixed in Laser-Writer version 8.1.1 (and newer versions). The biggest problem remaining, in my opinion, is that most applications (including Free-Hand) spool *their entire print job* to disk *before sending anything to the printer.* As I write this, PageMaker is the only application I know of that's been updated to behave sensibly with LaserWriter 8.

In spite of this fact, which means you'll have to have enough free space on your hard drive to hold your spooled file, I urge you to use the newer driver. FreeHand was designed with it in mind (as was your Macintosh System, if you use System 7.5x or higher).

Tip:
Use the Adobe
PostScript
Printer Driver
4.1 or Higher
(Windows only)

The Adobe PostScript printer driver version 4.1 (ADOBEPS4.DRV) was the first *good* PostScript printer driver for the Windows 95/ Windows NT platform. If you own any Adobe software, you'll probably find the Adobe printer driver on your installation CD—if you don't, or if you have a previous version of this printer driver, you can download the driver from Adobe's web site (www.adobe.com). As I write this, version 5.0 is the current version

Tip:
Use Adobe
Type Manager

If you're not already using Adobe Type Manager (ATM) to smooth the outlines of PostScript Type 1 fonts on your screen, get it. If you own any Adobe products, you'll probably find ATM on one or all of the installation CD—if not, you can download it from Adobe's web site (see Appendix B, "Resources").

If you've been using ATM 3.x, you've probably noticed (it'd be hard to miss) that Type 1 PostScript fonts have been printing in Courier (or whatever your printer's default font is). Upgrading to ATM 4 or higher will fix this problem.

In addition, you might want to spend a few extra dollars on the "Deluxe" version of ATM. When you do this, you get an excellent font management program—easily, in my opinion, the best yet seen on the Windows platform (on the Macintosh, I prefer Master-Juggler). With ATM 4's font management features, you can load and unload fonts without having to quit FreeHand or close your publication. And, best of all, without any trips to a ".INI" file.

Copies

Enter the number of copies of the page you want to print here. You can print up to 999 copies of your publication.

Tip: Printing More Than 999 Copies

Honest, I get asked about this, so here it is. If you need to print more than 999 copies of your publication, print your publication to disk as PostScript (see "Printing PostScript to Disk," later in this chapter), entering "999" in the Copies field of the Print dialog box. Open the PostScript file you've just created with a text editor, and search for "/copies 999 def." Once you've found this string, just replace "999" with the number of copies you want and save the file as text-only. Then download the PostScript file to your (long-suffering) printer.

Pages

Enter the range of pages you want to print from your publication. Remember, pages in FreeHand are numbered relative to their position on the pasteboard—if you've moved pages around, your pages may be numbered differently from the last time you printed.

Paper Source

Where's the paper coming from? Some printers have multiple paper bins. You choose the one you want here.

Destination/Print to File

Most of the time, you'll probably send your pages to a printer. To do this on the Macintosh, turn on the Printer option; in Windows, make sure that the Print to File option is turned off. For more on printing PostScript to disk, see "Printing PostScript to Disk," later in this chapter.

Selecting a PPD   Click the "..." button next to the Use PPD option to display the Select PPD dialog box and choose a PostScript Printer Description file (PPD). If no PPD matches your printer's make and model, choose "General" or "Color General" (if you're printing to a color PostScript printer).

Separations/   Turn on the Separations option when you want to print color sep-
Composite   arations of your publication (which inks print depends on the specifications you've entered in the Print Setup dialog box), and turn on the Composite option when you want to print all your colors as black and shades of gray, or when you want to print a color proof of your work on a color PostScript printer.

Scale   Choose a scaling option from the pop-up menu (see Figure 7-2).

- ◆ Choose Uniform to scale both dimensions of the pages you're printing. You can enter scaling percentages from 10 percent to 1,000 percent of the publication's original size (in one-percent increments).

- ◆ Choose Variable to apply different scaling percentages to the width and height of the pages you're printing. If you're using the flexographic printing process (often used for printing on food packaging), you can compensate for stretching on the press.

- ◆ Choose Fit On Paper option scales the page automatically to the largest size that'll fit on the selected paper size.

FIGURE 7-2
Scaling options

Choose Uniform to scale the width and height of the pages you print by the same percentage.

Choose Variable to scale the width and height by different percentages.

You can use nonproportional scaling to compensate for printing process that distrort images as you print them (i.e., flexography).

Tile   Use Tile when your pages are larger than the maximum page size of your printer. Auto Tile splits the pages in your publication into as many parts as FreeHand thinks are necessary; Manual Tile lets you tell FreeHand what size the individual tiles should be.

Auto Tile. When you choose automatic tiling, FreeHand bases the tile on the current printer's page size, and starts tiling from the lower-left corner of the page. Note that this is different from Page-Maker, which measures down and to the right from the zero point when tiling.

The measurement you enter in the Overlap N Points field is the amount of the image that's duplicated between adjacent tiles. This comes in handy when you're printing using a printer that won't print to the edge of the paper (like most laser printers).

Manual Tile. When you choose Manual Tile, FreeHand prints a tile—a page the size of the current paper size—based on the location of the zero point on the current page.

Manual Tile is generally better than Auto Tile, because Free-Hand's automatic tiling has no idea what's in your illustration, and can't, therefore, make decisions about where the seams between the tiles should fall. When you tile manually, you can make sure that the edges of the tiles don't fall across any fills (especially graduated and radial fills). When the edge of a tile falls across anything with a halftone screen, it's difficult—if not impossible—to piece the two tiles together. It's much easier to join lines and solid fills, and you should do your manual tiling with that in mind. Even if you have to make more tiles, it's better to tile across simple lines and solid fills.

Tip:
Printing Spreads
with Manual
Tiling

When you want to print more than one FreeHand page on a single sheet of paper (or piece of imagesetter film), follow these steps (see Figure 7-3).

1. Position the pages next to each other on the pasteboard. The pages don't have to touch, but the dimensions of the *area* of the pages, including any bleeds or gaps between pages, can't exceed that of the paper size you'll be printing

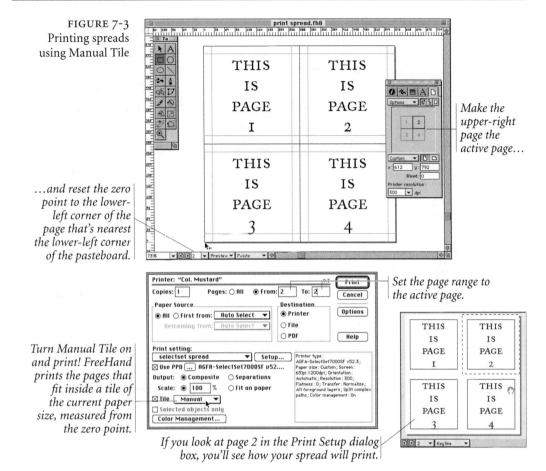

FIGURE 7-3
Printing spreads
using Manual Tile

Make the upper-right page the active page...

...and reset the zero point to the lower-left corner of the page that's nearest the lower-left corner of the pasteboard.

Set the page range to the active page.

Turn Manual Tile on and print! FreeHand prints the pages that fit inside a tile of the current paper size, measured from the zero point.

If you look at page 2 in the Print Setup dialog box, you'll see how your spread will print.

on. The pages can be side-by-side, or on top of each other, or arranged in whatever anarchic fashion you see fit.

2. Choose Fit All from the magnification submenu of the View menu. FreeHand fits all the pages in your publication in the publication window.

3. Make the page that's closest to the upper-right corner of the pasteboard the active page by clicking on the thumbnail of the page in the Document Inspector.

4. Reset the zero point so that it's at the lower-left corner of the lower-left page in the group of pages you want to print (or the lower-left corner of its bleed area, if any).

5. Press Command-P/Ctrl-P to display the Print dialog box. Use the Print Setup dialog box to specify the way you want the publication printed (it's especially important to set the page size you want in the Print Setup dialog box). Finally, in the Print dialog box, enter the page number of the active page (see Step 3) in the From and To fields, and turn on the Manual tiling option.

6. Print your publication. FreeHand prints one tile, starting at the point you set in Step 4. If your paper size is large enough, FreeHand prints the spread.

Selected Objects Only/Selected Objects

Turn this option on, and only the objects you had selected before you brought up the Print dialog box will print. I love this feature—especially when I'm troubleshooting printing problems, or only need to print a small part of my publication.

Color Management

Click the Color Management button, and FreeHand displays the Color Management Preferences dialog box (see Figure 7-4). This dialog box is essentially the same as the color management controls in the Colors Preferences dialog box, and changes you make in this dialog box are reflected there. See "Color Management," in Chapter 6, "Color." By putting this dialog box here, FreeHand's designers have saved me many a trip back to the Colors Preferences dialog box.

FIGURE 7-4
Color Management
Preferences dialog box

Click the Color Management button in the Print dialog box to display the Color Management Preferences dialog box.

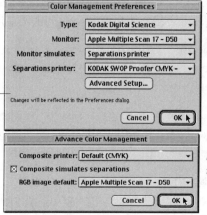

Any changes you make in the Color Management Preferences dialog box are echoed in the Colors Preferences dialog box.

When you click the Advanced Setup button, FreeHand displays a few more color management controls.

Tip:
Printing
Hexachrome
separations

To print Hexachrome (six-color) separations of your FreeHand publications (assuming that the publication contains RGB images and colors specified using either the RGB color model or colors from the Hexachrome color libraries), choose a Hexachrome printer profile from the Separations Printer pop-up menu (in the Colors Preferences dialog box or the Color Management Preferences dialog box), turn on the Separations option in the Print dialog box, and print. FreeHand produces six-color separations.

Print Setup

FreeHand's Print Setup dialog box is where you control what paper size you're printing to, whether you're printing invisible layers or not, which (if any) printer marks you want, and which inks you want to print, among other things (see Figure 7-5).

Print Preview   When you open the Print Setup dialog box, FreeHand displays a preview of the page (or pages) in your publication, including any printer's marks (crop marks, registration marks, and color bars), on the paper size you're printing on.

To reposition the page on the paper, drag the preview (when you move the cursor into the print preview window, the cursor changes to a "grabber" hand). FreeHand will print only the part of the page that appears inside the paper shown in the preview window. To reset the page to the center of the paper, click in the area surrounding the page in the preview window (see Figure 7-6).

Tip:
For a Faster Print
Setup Dialog Box

You've probably noticed that the Print Setup dialog box can take a long time to appear. Why? Because FreeHand has to generate the image shown in the print preview window. If you don't need to see a detailed preview (and most of us don't, most of the time), choose Keyline from the View Mode pop-up menu below the print preview window. If you don't want or need to see a preview image at all, choose X-Box from this pop-up menu—when you do this, FreeHand doesn't bother drawing the preview page at all, and the Print Setup dialog box will appear very quickly.

FIGURE 7-5
Print Setup dialog box

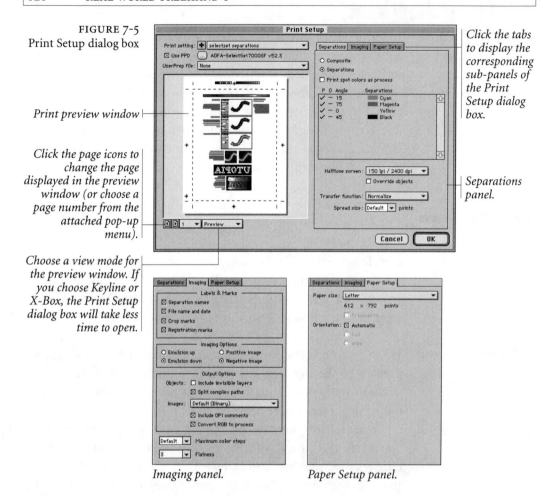

Click the tabs to display the corresponding sub-panels of the Print Setup dialog box.

Print preview window

Separations panel.

Click the page icons to change the page displayed in the preview window (or choose a page number from the attached pop-up menu).

Choose a view mode for the preview window. If you choose Keyline or X-Box, the Print Setup dialog box will take less time to open.

Imaging panel.

Paper Setup panel.

Print Settings

When I create a FreeHand publication, I print it (at least) three different ways. I print a proof copy on my laser printer, a color proof on a color printer, and then I print my final copies on an imagesetter. In the first two instances, I print composites—when I print to an imagesetter, I typically print color separations. Until FreeHand 7, changing my printer type, meant that I'd have to wade through FreeHand's multitudinous printer settings (found in the various tabbed panels of the Print Setup dialog box), checking to make sure that everything is set up correctly for the printer. The next time I print to a different printer, I'll have to walk through the options once again.

FIGURE 7-6
Moving the page
on the paper

*When you move the
cursor into the preview
window, it'll turn into a
"grabber" hand.*

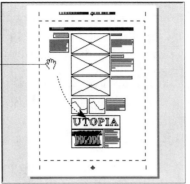

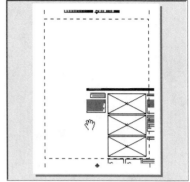

*Drag the hand in the preview
window...*

*...and FreeHand repositions the page
on the paper. Areas that fall off the
paper won't print.*

*When you move the
cursor off the page in
the preview window,
FreeHand display the
"reset" arrow.*

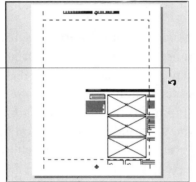

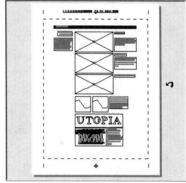

*To reposition the page in the center of
the paper, click in the gray area
surrounding the preview.*

*FreeHand centers the page on the
paper.*

With the arrival of FreeHand 7's "Print Settings" feature, my life got easier. Now I can create a printer settings file for each *type* of printing I do (black-and-white proof, color proof, and image-setter output), then apply the settings, as needed, when I print. If you find yourself spending too much time in the Print Setup dialog box, you can create printer settings for commonly-used printer settings. Here's what you do:

1. Choose Print from the File menu to display the Print dialog box.

2. Click the Setup button. FreeHand displays the Print Setup dialog box.

3. Work your way through the three panels (Separations, Imaging, and Paper Setup) of the Printer Setup dialog box, setting printing options as you normally would.

4. When the options are set up the way you want them (including your choice of PPD and UserPrep file, if necessary), click the "+" button next to the Printer Setup pop-up menu. FreeHand displays a standard "Save as" dialog box.

5. Enter a name for the printer setup you've just created, then save the printer setup file in the PrintSet folder in your FreeHand folder (yes, it's the same on both platforms). FreeHand adds the name of the printer style to the Printer Setup pop-up menu.

The next time you want to print a publication using these settings, all you need to do is choose this printer settings file from the Print Setting pop-up menu in the Print dialog box. Printer settings are like styles for printing—like styles, one action (a choice from a pop-up menu, in this case) applies a large number of attributes. This saves you time, and it also saves you the embarrassment and expense of printing with the wrong settings (I don't know how many times I've forgotten to turn on the Separations option).

What's not saved in a printer setting? Custom screen angles. If you want to add a set of custom screen angles to a printer style, you'll need to add them to the PPD you're using (FreeHand remembers the screen angles you've chosen from a PPD, but doesn't remember screen angles you've edited using the Ink List). See "Rewriting PPDs, later in this chapter.

UserPrep File

The UserPrep File pop-up menu displays the files stored in your UserPrep folder/directory (it's in your FreeHand folder). These files adjust FreeHand's printing by changing the PostScript FreeHand sends to your printer (or to a file). The UserPrep files that come with FreeHand optimize FreeHand's printing for specific printing methods or devices (see the UserPrep ReadMe in your FreeHand folder/directory). You can create your own UserPrep file to add PostScript effects, if you want—see Chapter 8, "PostScript."

Separations Click the Separations tab to display the Separations panel (refer back to Figure 7-5).

Composite/Separations. Turn on the Separations option when you want to print color separations; and turn on the Composite option when you want to print all your colors as black and shades of gray, or when you want to print a color proof of your work on a color printer.

Print Spot Colors as Process. If you've used spot colors in your publication, and want to convert them to process colors, turn this option on. For more on the difference between spot and process colors, see Chapter 6, "Color."

Ink List. I call the list that appears in the Separations section of the Print Setup dialog box the "Ink List." The Ink List is where you determine how the inks in your publication are printed; only color definitions and object-level overprinting instructions are more important (see Figure 7-7). All of the inks used in your publication are included in the Ink List. If you've used any spot colors, they appear; and cyan, magenta, yellow, and black appear if you've specified any process colors in the document.

FIGURE 7-7
Ink List

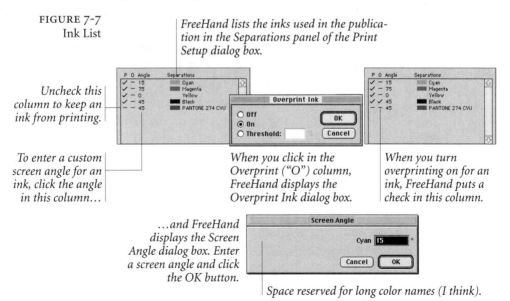

FreeHand lists the inks used in the publication in the Separations panel of the Print Setup dialog box.

Uncheck this column to keep an ink from printing.

To enter a custom screen angle for an ink, click the angle in this column...

When you click in the Overprint ("O") column, FreeHand displays the Overprint Ink dialog box.

When you turn overprinting on for an ink, FreeHand puts a check in this column.

...and FreeHand displays the Screen Angle dialog box. Enter a screen angle and click the OK button.

Space reserved for long color names (I think).

Using the Ink List, you can control whether an ink prints at all, whether an ink overprints, and the screen angle of the halftone screens used when you print the ink.

Printing or not? To keep an ink from printing, click the checkmark to the left of the ink's name (in the column headed with a "P"). To make an ink print, click the "–" in the column.

What happens when you have objects containing percentages of process inks and turn off one of the inks? Simple enough—you don't get any of that ink. Turning an ink off doesn't affect any of the other inks in the object.

Turning an ink off doesn't affect that ink's knockout/overprinting settings. If the ink was set to knock out other inks, it'll still knock them out—whether you print it or not.

Overprinting. To make an ink overprint, click in the "O" column. FreeHand displays the Overprint Ink dialog box. Turn on the Overprint option, or set a threshold at which the ink should overprint (if the ink percentage in a particular object exceeds the percentage you've entered, the ink in the object will overprint), then click the OK button. A check appears in the column, indicating that the ink is set to overprint. To make the ink knock out, click the checkmark—it'll turn back into a dash, indicating that the ink will knock out.

The Overprint ink option makes any objects with the selected ink applied to them overprint anything that's behind them. Any object-level overprinting instructions override this setting (unless you've turned on the Override Objects option).

Process colors bring up some interesting questions. If you've got an object that's colored 60C 30M 0Y 10K on top of an object that's colored 10C 40M 10Y 0K, what ink percentages do you get in the areas where the objects overlap? It's simple—the process inks on top win. Even if you set cyan to overprint, you'll still get 10-percent cyan in the areas where the top object overprints the bottom object. If there's none of a process ink in a color, however, turning Overprint on *does* make a difference. In the above example, you'd get a white object (a knockout) on the yellow plate if you set the ink to knock out; nothing if you set the ink to overprint.

To see what overprinting looks like, refer to the color pages in Chapter 6, "Color."

Screen angles. The screen angle that's shown in the Ink List comes from the PPD file you've selected. These are the imagesetter manufacturers' optimized screen angles, which help prevent moirés from occurring, so you shouldn't alter these unless you have a really good reason to do so. Still, if you want to change the angle, click the angle in the Ink List, then type a new angle in the Screen Angle dialog box FreeHand displays.

If you've applied a halftone to an individual object using the Halftone palette, that setting overrides the settings in the Print Setup dialog box (unless you've turned on the Override Objects option).

Overprinting an ink. It seems so simple—to set a halftone screen for your publication, choose a halftone screen from the Halftone Screen pop-up menu. But there's more to it than that. Higher screen frequencies produce smoother-looking tints, but increasing screen ruling can also result in a loss of grays—depending on the resolution of the printer. There's a limit to how fine a screen frequency you can print with various printing methods and paper stocks. If your printer can't print enough gray levels (at the line screen you specify), you'll see banding and posterization. Lower screen frequencies can provide more gray levels, but look coarser. What to do? Try using the following equation to determine the number of grays you'll get from the screen ruling and printer resolution you've chosen.

number of grays = (printer resolution in dpi/screen frequency in lpi)2+1

The key to this equation is that "number of grays" in the equation can't be greater than 256—that's the maximum number of grays a PostScript printer can print (some Level 2 PostScript printers can print more, by cheating, but don't count on it).

You can work the equation another way; maybe this one's more useful.

screen frequency = square root of(16*printer resolution)

Other people like to use this equation.

required resolution = screen frequency * 16

If you come up with a line screen that's too coarse for your taste, think about it—is your publication one where you can sacrifice a few grays for a finer screen?

Most of the time, and especially if you're printing color separations, you should use one of the "canned" halftone screen settings on the Halftone Screen pop-up menu. If you don't see the screen frequency you need, however, you can choose "Other"—FreeHand displays the Custom Screen dialog box, where you can enter the screen ruling you want.

Tip:
What, No
Halftone
Screens?

If the Halftone Screen pop-up menu is disabled, it's because you haven't selected a PPD. FreeHand gets its information about the screens a printer is capable of printing from the printer's PPD. Select a PPD, and you'll be able to choose a halftone screen.

Override Objects. Ordinarily, halftone screens applied to individual objects in your publication (using the Halftone palette) override the setting in the Halftone Screen pop-up menu (see above). When you turn on the Override Objects option, FreeHand applies the halftone screen specified in the Print Setup dialog box to the entire publication, regardless of the settings of objects.

Transfer Function. The choices on this pop-up menu tell FreeHand how a printer's tint densities correspond to the tint densities you specify. Why do we need this? Because gray levels printed on 300-dpi printers look very different from the same tints printed on 2540-dpi printers (in general, lower percentages of gray, especially 10 percent, look darker at lower resolutions). If you choose Unadjusted, FreeHand prints exactly the density you've specified, without reading any of the gray level adjustment information from the selected PPD.

Ordinarily, Unadjusted is the best choice. If you want to compensate for the differences between printers with different resolutions (to get a more accurate proof), use Normalize, which reads gray-level compensation information from the PPD.

Posterize creates special effects by converting the available gray levels into just four gray levels. Posterize works about the same way as the Posterize image preset (see "Working with the Image Dialog Box" in Chapter 4, "Importing and Exporting," for more on posterization). I can't think of any reason to use this, but that doesn't mean you're similarly impaired.

Spread Size. "Hurt me." That's what you're saying when you enter a value other than zero in the Spread Size field. When you enter a value greater than zero, FreeHand increases the width of *all of the basic strokes in your publication* by that amount, and sets the strokes to overprint. It's what an uninformed salesperson might refer to as "automatic trapping." Can you really use this option to guarantee that your publication prints without trapping errors?

Sure—enter a large enough value here, and you'll *never* see paper where you should see ink. Trouble is, you'll also see lots of really ugly traps. And the truth is that ugly traps are just as bad as no traps at all. In addition, if your publication contains bar codes of any sort (zip bars, universal product codes, and so forth), increasing the stroke size often makes these codes unreadable.

If you want to create traps to compensate for misregistration on a printing press, use FreeHand's Create Trap Xtra, or use manual trapping techniques, or have your publication processed by Trap-Wise (or other trapping system) before printing (see "Trapping" in Chapter 6, "Color").

Imaging   Click the Imaging tab to display the Imaging panel of the Print Setup dialog box (refer back to Figure 7-5).

Separation Names. Turn on the Separation Names option, and Free-Hand prints the name of each ink color for each separation or overlay on each printed sheet. This way, you'll have an easier time telling the magenta overlay from the cyan overlay. If you're printing a composite, FreeHand prints the word Composite.

File Name and Date. Turn on the File Name and Date option to print the file name and date of your publication on each page. This makes it easy to tell which of several printed versions is the most current. It can also make it easier for your commercial printer to tell which pieces of film in a stack of separations go together (it's easy for you to tell, but put yourself in their shoes for a minute). If the paper size is smaller than the page size, FreeHand won't print the file name and date.

Crop Marks. Turn on the Crop Marks option to print lines outside the area of your page that define the area of the page. If your paper size is not larger than your page size, FreeHand won't print your crop marks.

Registration Marks. When you turn on the Registration Marks option, FreeHand prints little targets around the edge of your page for your commercial printer to use when they're lining up, or registering, your color separations for printing. If your paper size is smaller than your page size, FreeHand won't print the registration marks.

Imaging Options. Use the controls in the Imaging Options section of the Imaging panel to set the polarity (positive or negative) of the printed publication, and to choose whether your publication prints emulsion up or emulsion down.

In North America, most printers prefer getting their film negative, emulsion down, unless they've got stripping to do, in which case they prefer it emulsion up. Many non-North American printers—those in Japan, Hong Kong, Singapore, Italy, Switzerland, and elsewhere—like their film positive, emulsion down. Everything looks the same in the end; it's just a different standard. The best way to find out which way you should print your publication is to ask your commercial printer how they'd like to receive the film.

Tip:
Image Polarity
and Calibration

Lots of people (including me) have said that the polarity of your image (whether it's positive or negative) should be controlled at the imagesetter. We said this because we'd had problems with old versions of PostScript ROMs not inverting images. At this point, PostScript ROMs and software developers' image polarity controls are in sync, and calibration routines for several color separation programs require you to use the application's image polarity controls. Use the image controls in your printing application, instead of setting the polarity at your imagesetter, unless you're working with PostScript ROMs 47.1 or earlier.

Output Options

It was frustrating—in FreeHand 3, you could set the flatness of all the paths in your document when you printed, but you couldn't do the same when you created an EPS of the same paths. Other printing controls, such as the ability to suppress printing of invisible layers, didn't apply to EPS files you created.

FreeHand puts many of the controls that used to be in FreeHand 3's Print Options dialog box in the Output Options dialog box (choose Output Options from the File menu)—and in the Output Options section of the Print Setup dialog box (see Figure 7-8). The settings in the Output Options dialog box apply to both files you print and files you save as EPS. The settings in the Output Options section of the Print Setup dialog box are reflected in the Output Options dialog box, and vice versa, so you can use whichever dialog box you find more convenient.

The choices on the Images pop-up menu determine how—and whether—TIFF images you've placed in your FreeHand publication get sent to your printer, or to an EPS or PostScript file you save to disk.

FIGURE 7-8
Output options

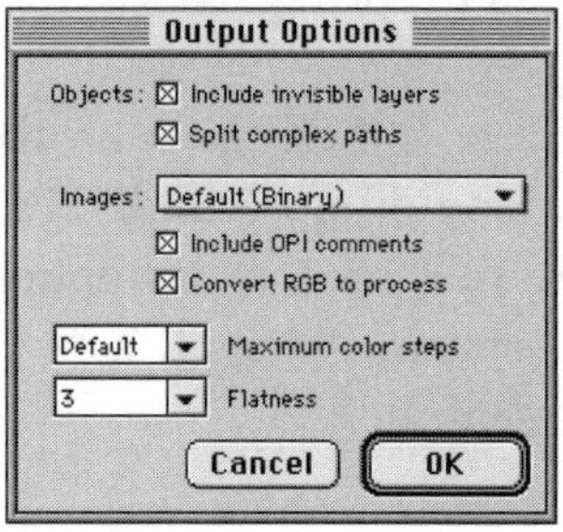

The Output Options dialog box and the Output Options section of the Imaging panel contain identical controls—the idea is to keep you from having to return to the Output Options dialog box once you've opened the Print Setup dialog box.

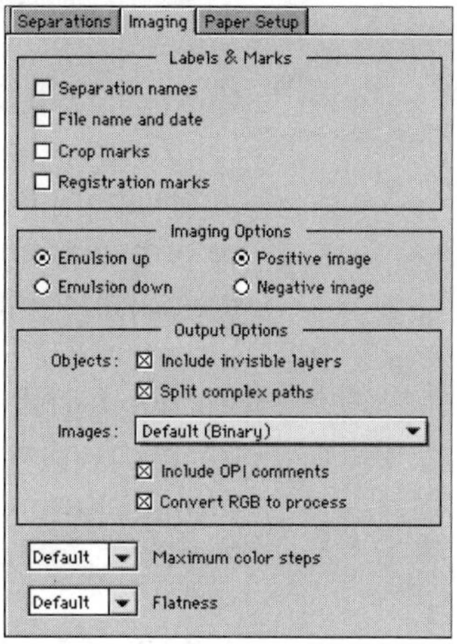

ASCII Encoding. Choose ASCII Encoding when you're creating a file you intend to transfer to a computer other than a Macintosh, or when you're connected to your printer through a serial cable.

Binary Data. Choose Binary Data to send images in a more compact form than ASCII Encoding (note that this also means a smaller file size, if you're saving the file). This option is mainly for Macintosh users, or for Windows users who know they'll be printing their files from a Macintosh. Binary image data doesn't work with most direct (i.e., serial or parallel) printer connections, nor does it work with most Windows-oriented networks. If you're using Free-Hand in Windows, and want to make your PostScript files smaller, you might give this option a try—but be aware that your chances of success are slim.

None. Choose "None" when you'll be linking to a high-resolution version of the image using an OPI system, such as Kodak's Prophecy. When you turn this option on, FreeHand includes cropping and scaling information for any TIFFs you've placed in your publication, but doesn't include the TIFFs themselves.

PageMaker 6 has trouble printing TIFFs in FreeHand EPS files when you import. This has to do with the OPI image data in your FreeHand EPS. See "FreeHand, TIFFs, and PageMaker 6" in Chapter 4, "Importing and Exporting."

Convert RGB TIFF to CMYK. Turn on this option to include a color-separated version of any RGB TIFFs you've placed in your publication. Before you turn on this option, turn on FreeHand's color management system and apply a device profile to each RGB image you want to separate.

Include Invisible Layers. If you've turned off the display of layers to speed up your publication's display on screen, you can print them by turning on the Include Invisible Layers option. If you don't want to print invisible layers, leave this option turned off.

Split Complex Paths. Turn off the Split Complex Paths option when your publication contains TIFFs you've pasted into complex paths (anything with more curves than a rectangle). Why? Each time Free-Hand fails to print a path, it simplifies the path (that is, cuts the path up into smaller, more manageable segments) and sends it to the printer again. If the path contains a TIFF, this means you'll spend extra time waiting for FreeHand to download the TIFF each time it sends the path (or portions of the path). Otherwise, leave this option turned on.

Maximum Color Steps. When you're printing to a slide recorder, or when you're creating an EPS you plan to convert using a color prepress system (such as those made by Crosfield or Scitex), enter 256 in this field. If you still have trouble printing or converting the file, enter a lower number. You need to do this because some of these devices can handle only a limited number of colors at a time.

Otherwise, leave this field blank.

Flatness. As discussed in Chapter 2, "Drawing," flatness is a property of PostScript paths that specifies how many tiny straight line segments a PostScript RIP has to draw as it renders a curve. The higher the value you enter for flatness, the fewer line segments your printer's RIP will have to draw—which means faster printing times. Even on a 300-dpi printer, the resolution of most laser printers, you won't see a difference between flatness setting of three and a flatness setting of zero, but the former will print much faster. In fact, some paths won't print at all, on any printer, unless you set their flatness to something greater than zero.

Enter a value in this field to set a flatness value for all the paths in your publication. Any flatness settings you've applied to individual paths using the Object Inspector override any value you enter here.

Paper Setup Click the Paper Setup tab in the Print Setup dialog box to display the Paper Setup panel (refer back to Figure 7-5).

Paper Size. When you choose a PPD, the available paper sizes for your printer appear in the Paper pop-up menu, including any custom paper sizes you've added to this PPD (see "Adding Custom Page Sizes to PPDs" later in this chapter).

Always choose a paper size that's at least the size of your publication's pages. If you're printing a publication that needs crop and registration marks (collectively known as printer's marks; see "Crop Marks" and "Registration Marks," later in this chapter) printed off the page, or if parts of your publication bleed (extend beyond the edge of the publication page), you'll need to choose a paper size that's larger than your publication's page size to accommodate the printer's marks and/or the bleed.

If you've chosen an imagesetter PPD, another option, Custom, appears on the pop-up menu. When you choose Custom, FreeHand displays the Paper size dialog box, in which you can type whatever paper size you want. Remember, however, that the values you enter here need to take the width of the imagesetter's paper roll into account. Enter a width value greater than the width of the imagesetter's paper roll and you'll get a "limitcheck" error when you try to print.

For more on page sizes, paper sizes, and PPDs, see "Printing and Page Setup," later in this chapter.

Tip:
Update to
FreeHand 5.0.1
or Higher

Because I expect that at least one FreeHand 5 user will read this book, I have to include this tip. If you haven't yet updated to Free-Hand 5.0.1, 5.02, 5.5, 7, or 8, do so before you try printing to a custom paper size with a wide orientation on an imagesetter. Free-Hand 5.0 would sometimes (depending on your printer and the method you used to specify your page size) crop off parts of your pages. To get a copy of the FreeHand 5.0.1 updater, look for it in the Macromedia web site (www.macromedia.com).

Printing and Page Setup

Because you're creating a publication that'll be printed on an existing PostScript printer, you've got to pay attention to the page sizes that are available. It might be too obvious to state, but if you can't print it, it's of no use to you.

You could tile your publication, but tiling only works in a few cases. Can you imagine grafting a bunch of halftoned images together? Or graduated fills? On negative film? You get the idea: it's impossible. Don't even try tiling unless you can set it up so that the edges of the tiles don't bisect anything containing a halftone screen. That brings us back to paper sizes.

Page Size and Paper Size

When I talk about page size, I'm talking about the page size you've defined for your publication using the Document Inspector. This page size should be the same as the page size of the printed piece you intend to produce. "Paper size" means the size of the paper as it comes out of your printer or imagesetter. There can be a big difference between these two sizes. Try to print your publication on a paper size that is no larger than the publication's page size, unless you need printer's marks (crop marks and registration marks). For more on page size and paper size, see "Paper Size," later in this chapter.

Tip: Paper Size and Printer's Marks

If you need printer's marks (crop marks or registration marks), print your publication on a paper size that is larger than your publication's page by about 60 points in either dimension.

Page Orientation and Paper Orientation

You set the orientation of your *page* in the Document Inspector by clicking either the Tall or Wide radio button (or, if you're working with a custom page size, by entering values in the X and Y fields). You set the orientation of the *paper* you're printing to by clicking either the Tall or Wide button in the Print Setup dialog box. What do these two orientation settings have to do with each other?

If you create a tall page and print it to a normal orientation, wide paper size, expect the top and bottom of your publication to get clipped off. Ditto for a wide page size printed to a normal orientation, tall paper size.

Always print tall pages to tall paper sizes, and wide pages to wide paper sizes—even when you're printing to a transverse page size (see Figure 7-9).

♦ If you need to print a wide publication down the length of an imagesetter's paper roll (because it's too wide for the width of the roll), use a wide, transverse orientation paper size.

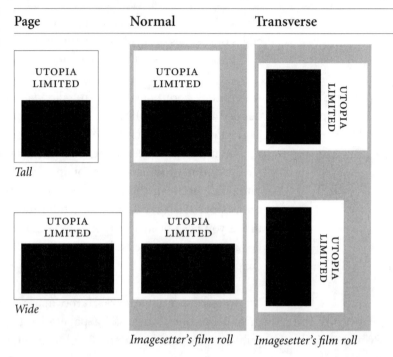

Page	Normal	Transverse

Tall

Wide

Imagesetter's film roll   *Imagesetter's film roll*

◆ If you want to save paper on the imagesetter's roll and speed up printing time, print tall page sizes to transverse paper sizes (provided that the page size isn't taller than the width of the imagesetter's paper roll). As always, ask your imagesetting service bureau what they want you to do.

Printing Signatures

FreeHand's 222-by-222-inch pasteboard is large enough that you can arrange whole press sheets for many common presses, laying out and printing multiple pages in a single FreeHand publication (see Figure 7-10). To see how to print multiple pages on a single sheet of paper, see the tip "Printing Spreads with Manual Tiling," earlier in this chapter.

Signatures can be a real brain-twister. The object of creating a signature is to get pages onto a press sheet in such a way that your commercial printer can fold and cut the sheet so that it starts on

FIGURE 7-10
Press sheet

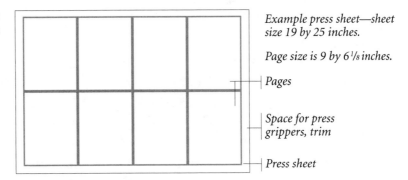

Example press sheet—sheet size 19 by 25 inches.

Page size is 9 by 6 1/8 inches.

Pages

Space for press grippers, trim

Press sheet

the first page of the signature and ends on the last page. This means you have to position the correct pages in the right places and in the right orientations on both the front and back of the signature. Figure 7-11 shows how it works for a very simple signature.

You should try to leave ¼ inch for trim on each end of the signature and ½ inch on each side of the signature for color bars and for the press' grippers. Also, if your pages have bleeds, make sure you add ⅛ inch to all four sides of the page to accommodate the bleeds.

You'll still have to find some way of printing your signatures— very few imagesetters can handle paper sizes as large as you'll want for signatures (the largest image area I know of right now is a 30-by-40-inch single sheet). Table 7-1 shows some typical press sheet sizes and typical page sizes you can get out of them. Talk to your commercial printer about the sheet sizes their presses are capable of handling.

FIGURE 7-11
Setting up a
simple signature

After you print, fold, and cut this press sheet, you've got an eight-page signature, with the pages in the correct order.

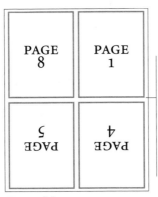

Allow some space for press grippers, color bars, folding, cutting, etc. (ask your commercial printer how much).

Front of sheet

Back of sheet

TABLE 7-1
Common press sheet
sizes and signatures

Sheet size	19 x 25	23 x 29	23 x 35	25 x 38	26 x 40
Image area	18 x 24½	22 x 28½	22 x 34½	24 x 37½	25 x 39½
3	18 x 8⅛	22 x 9½	22 x 11½	24 x 12½	25 x 13⅛
4	18 x 6½	22 x 7⅛	22 x 8⅝	24 x 9⅜	25 x 9⅞
4	9 x 12¼	11 x 14¼	11 x 17¼	12 x 18¾	12 ½ x 19¾
6	9 x 8⅛	11 x 9½	11 x 11½	12 x 12½	12½ x 13⅛
8	9 x 4⅞	11 x 7⅛	11 x 8⅝	12 x 9⅜	12½ x 9⅞
10	9 x 6⅛	11 x 5¹¹⁄₁₆	11 x 6⅞	12 x 7 ½	12½ x 7⅞
15	3⁹⁄₁₆ x 8⅛	4⅜ x 11	4 ⅜ x 11	4¾ x 12½	5 x 13⅛
16	4½ x 6⅛	5½ x 7⅛	5½ x 8⅝	6 x 9⅜	6¼ x 9⅞

Pages per sheet (row label for the page-count rows)

All dimensions in inches

Don't despair if no imagesetters in your area can handle these sheet sizes. The most important thing about understanding how many of what size pages make up a press sheet is that you set up your publication to match sizes that don't waste too much paper. This isn't a comment about saving the environment—I've found it's cheaper by far to design for certain press sheet sizes.

In addition, commercial printers do lots of their printing on smaller sheet sizes. Table 7-2 shows some typical paper sizes you can use on smaller presses. You can fit signatures on these paper sizes, as well.

TABLE 7-2
Typical sheet sizes
for smaller presses

Text weights	Cover weights	Bond
19 x 25	20 x 26	8½ x 11
23 x 29	23 x 35	17 x 22
23 x 35	26 x 40	22 x 34
25 x 38		24 x 38

All dimensions in inches

You need to be absolutely certain you want to do this and that you know what you're doing before you try it. Make folded dummies of the signatures you want to use, and make sure that all the pages, front and back, fall where you want them to. When in doubt, leave it to the pros at your commercial printer or service bureau.

FreeHand and PPDs

PostScript Printer Description files (PPDs) describe your printer to FreeHand and to your printer driver. PPDs are not, and should not be confused with, printer drivers. Printer drivers are pieces of software that direct information from your system and applications to a hardware port—usually, your Macintosh's printer port. For some applications, the printer driver does the work of translating the application's documents into PostScript; this isn't the case for FreeHand, which generates its own PostScript.

PPDs work in conjunction with printer drivers to give applications information about the printer (what paper sizes are available? what's the resolution of the printer? what do the printer error messages mean?) and to customize the printer's operation for the application (what PostScript routine does the application use to render halftones?).

FreeHand uses the printer driver on your system, and uses PPDs to optimize printing for a specific printer.

PPDs—
Who's on First?
(Macintosh Only)

Because of a territorial dispute—between your applications (FreeHand in particular) and your printer driver—you can get caught in a loop. You create a file, choose a PPD, and save the file. When you open the file, a different PPD is selected in the Print Options dialog box. In fact, every time you open the file, the same—incorrect—PPD appears, no matter what PPD you chose earlier.

This isn't a feature.

What's going on? Both FreeHand and your printer driver want to be the entity responsible for your PPD choice. If you've chosen a PPD using the options in the Chooser, the PPD appears in all your FreeHand documents. Follow these steps to make the PPD choice you make in FreeHand's Print or Print Setup dialog boxes stick.

1. Select Chooser from the Apple Menu.

2. Click the LaserWriter 8 driver icon. Make sure that the correct printer shows up in the printer list to the right. If not, select it by clicking on the name.

3. Click the Setup button that appears below the list of available printers. The Chooser displays the Current Printer Description File dialog box.

4. Click the Select PPD button. The Select PostScript Printer Description File dialog box appears.

5. Click the Use Generic button.

6. Press Return (or click the OK button) to close the dialog box and apply your change.

Note: This trick only works with the LaserWriter 8 printer driver (or newer versions). Earlier versions of the LaserWriter driver don't let you set a PPD for the printer.

Rewriting PPDs

You can edit your PPDs to add custom page sizes, to add new sets of screen angles, to download PostScript routines automatically, and to do a variety of other things.

What's in a PPD? Table 7-3 (on the following pages) is a listing of some of the keywords you'll see when you open a PPD file. I haven't tried to cover every keyword and entry you'll find in a PPD, mainly because Free-Hand doesn't use all of them. I've included keywords you might want to change, as well as keywords you shouldn't change.

FreeHand uses PPDs conforming to version 4.0 of the Adobe PPD specification. If you can't see your PPD in the list of available PPDs, you've probably got an old PPD. You can probably find a new one online (for the locations of Adobe and Macromedia-related sites, see Appendix B, "Resources").

TABLE 7-3   Keywords in PPDs

Keyword	Example	What is it?
*PSVersion	*PSVersion: "(52.3) 320"	Version of PostScript in the printer's ROMs. Change this value if your printer has a different PostScript version than that listed in the PPD.
*Include:	*Include "MyPageSizes.txt"	Includes a file at this point in the PPD. You can have any number of "*Include" keywords in a PPD.
*DefaultResolution	*DefaultResolution: 2400x2400dpi	Default resolution of the printer. If you usually run your printer in a different resolution than the one you see here, change the resolution here.
*Resolution	*Resolution 1200x1200dpi: " 1200 statusdict /setresolution get exec "	Sets the resolution of the printer, for those printers capable of switching resolutions via software commands (imagesetters, mostly). If you don't know the routine to change the setting on an imagesetter (they're all different), leave this value alone and change the resolution from the image-setter's control panel.
*ColorDevice	*ColorDevice: False	Tells FreeHand whether the selected printer is a PostScript color printer or not.
*FreeVM	*FreeVM: "992346"	Amount of the printer's virtual memory (VM) FreeHand can work with before having to flush fonts, etc. If you know your printer has more—or less—memory available, increase or decrease this value. Usually, a printer's startup page shows you how much VM the printer has available. If yours doesn't—or if you've turned off the

TABLE 7-3   Keywords in PPDs (continued)

Keyword	Example	What is it?

*FreeVM (continued)		printer's startup page and don't feel like turning it on again—download the following code (your printer will print a page with the memory amount on it):
		
		`%%show FreeVM`
		`/Helvetica findfont`
		`12 scalefont setfont`
		`72 72 moveto`
		`/memString 256 string def`
		`vmstatus exch sub memString cvs`
		`show`
		`showpage`

*Password	*Password: "0"	Provides a password for the printer. Do not change this, or if you do, make sure you remember the password. If you don't know the password, you might have to replace chips on your motherboard to be able to use your printer again. I can't think why Adobe put this keyword into their interpreter. In fact, I'm vaguely upset by the notion you'd want to prohibit someone on your network from printing on your printer (why not simply *ask* them?). **Note:** The editor and previous copy editor of this book have both supplied arguments for keeping people off some printers. Luckily, it's my book, and I see no reason to repeat their totalitarian ravings here.
*FileSystem	*FileSystem True	Lets FreeHand know if the selected printer has a hard disk attached to it. If this value is "True", FreeHand checks the printer's hard disk for downloadable fonts before looking

TABLE 7-3   Keywords in PPDs (continued)

Keyword	Example	What is it?
*FileSystem (continued)		for them on the current system. If you have a hard disk attached to your printer, set this keyword to "True"; otherwise, leave it at "False". If you have a printer that can be attached to a hard disk, FreeHand queries the printer to see if it has a hard disk attached. If you change this setting to "True", FreeHand doesn't have to ask.
*DeviceAdjustMatrix	*DeviceAdjustMatrix: "[1 0 0 1 0 0]"	Don't change this unless your printer chronically distorts the pages you're printing. If your printer does distort images, you'll have to calculate the percentage of distortion vertically and horizontally and enter it in the matrix. If you found that your printer was always stretching an image by five percent vertically, you'd change the matrix to [.95 0 0 1 0 0]. If your imagesetter is doing this, you probably ought to call a service technician. Don't even think about changing this for 300-dpi printers—they're not accurate enough for it to make a difference. See the PostScript Language Reference Manual for more (lots more) information on adjusting matrices. El Greco was just Rembrandt with a matrix adjustment.
*ScreenAngle	*ScreenAngle: "45"	Sets the screen angle the printer uses to print halftones. Change this value if you want a different default screen angle for your printer. Any setting you make in the Halftone screen dialog box overrides this value.

TABLE 7-3   Keywords in PPDs (continued)

Keyword	Example	What is it?
*DefaultScreenProc	*DefaultScreenProc: Dot	Sets the default halftone screen drawing procedure for the printer. This procedure is defined in the "*ScreenProc" keyword listing.
*ScreenProc	*ScreenProc Dot: "{abs exch abs 2 copy add 1 gt {1 sub dup mul exch 1 sub dup mul add 1 sub }{dup mul exch dup mul add 1 exch sub }ifelse }" *End	Halftone screen drawing procedures for the printer. You could enter "*ScreenProc Line: "{ pop }"" or "*ScreenProc Ellipse: "{ dup 5 mul 8 div mul exch dup mul exch add sqrt 1 exch sub }"" instead, but you've got to remember to call them from the "*DefaultScreen-Proc" keyword to get them to work.
*ScreenFreq	*ScreenFreq: "120"	Sets the screen frequency the printer uses to print halftones. If you don't like it, change it. Any setting you make in the Halftone Screen dialog box overrides this value.
*DefaultTransfer	*DefaultTransfer Normalized	Sets the default transfer function for the printer.
*DefaultPageSize	*DefaultPageSize: Letter	Sets the default paper size for your printer. The keyword for the paper size corresponds to the name of a defined paper size existing either in the printer's ROMs or in the PPD file. For more on creating custom paper sizes, see the section "Adding Custom Page Sizes to PPDs," earlier in this chapter.
*PageSize	*PageSize Letter: "letter"	Sets up a paper size. If your printer has variable page sizes (image-setters usually do; laser printers usually don't), this entry could be: "*PageSize Letter.Extra: "statusdict begin 684 864 0 1 setpageparams end""

TABLE 7-3   Keywords in PPDs (continued)

Keyword	Example	What is it?
*DefaultPaperTray	*DefaultPaperTray: None	If you have a printer with more than one paper tray, change this to the tray you want as your default. The tray selection for your printer is defined in the "*PaperTray" section of the PPD.
*PaperTray	*PaperTray Letter: "statusdict begin lettertray end"	Defines available paper trays for your printer.
*DefaultImageableArea	*DefaultImageableArea: Letter	Sets the default imageable area (the area inside a paper size that the printer can actually make marks on) for the printer. The available imageable areas for your printer are set up using the "ImageableArea" keyword.
*ImageableArea	*ImageableArea Letter.Extra: "0 1 684 864"	Sets up the imageable area for a defined page size (in the example, a page size named "Letter.Extra").
*DefaultPaper-Dimension	*DefaultPaperDimension: Letter	Sets the default paper dimension for the printer. You set up paper dimensions using the "*PaperDimension" keyword.
*PaperDimension	*PaperDimension Letter.Extra: "684 864"	Sets up the paper dimension for a specific page size (in the example, a page size named "Letter.Extra"). Enter the width and height of the paper, in points. For a wide orientation page, the entry would read "*PaperDimension Letter.Extra.Wide: "864 684"".
*VariablePaperSize	*VariablePaperSize: True	Tells FreeHand whether your printer can accept variable paper sizes. Most imagesetters can; most laser printers can't. If your printer can accept variable paper sizes, the Paper pop-up menu in *(continued on next page)*

TABLE 7-3   Keywords in PPDs (continued)

Keyword	Example	What is it?
*VariablePaperSize (continued)		FreeHand's Print Options dialog box will include Other. If you choose Other, you'll be able to enter a custom paper size in the Page Size dialog box and print to whatever size of paper you want (within the imagesetter's capabilities). You can also add your own custom page sizes to PPDs of printers capable of accepting variable page sizes. Changing this value from "False" to "True" does not give your printer the ability to accept variable page sizes.
*DefaultInputSlot	*DefaultInputSlot: Lower	Sets the default paper feed for your printer, if your printer has more than one input slot (an NEC LC 890 Silentwriter is an example of a printer with two input slots). The available input slots are set up by the entries in the "*InputSlot" keyword.
*InputSlot	*InputSlot Lower: "statusdict begin 1 setpapertray end"	Defines the available input slots for your printer.
*DefaultManualFeed	*DefaultManualFeed: False	Makes manual feed the printer's default paper feed. Don't change this unless you habitually use your printer's manual feed.
*ManualFeed	*ManualFeed True: "statusdict begin /manualfeed true store end"	Sets up the printer's manual feed mechanism, if it has one.
*Font	*Font Times-Bold: Standard "(001.002)"	Lets FreeHand know that a font is resident in the printer. Add fonts to this list if you're sure they're going to be on your printer's hard disk or memory. FreeHand will ask your printer if it has a certain downloadable font installed, unless it finds the font in this list. If you *(continued on next page)*

TABLE 7-3   Keywords in PPDs (continued)

Keyword	Example	What is it?
*Font (continued)		enter the font in this list, FreeHand doesn't have to ask, and prints faster. To add a font, type:
		`*Font: PostScriptFontName:` `Standard "(001.001)"`
		The PostScript name of the font can be a bit tricky to figure out. The best way to do it is to create a text block containing the font in FreeHand and print the file to disk as PostScript or create an EPS. Then open the file with a text editor and look at the way FreeHand names the fonts near the start of the file.
		The numbers following the font name are the font type and the font version. Most fonts, these days, are Type 1 (or "001"). Unless you know the font version, just enter "001" for the version.
*DefaultFont	*DefaultFont: Courier	Defines the default font for your printer. This is the default font that gets used if FreeHand can't find the font used for text in your publication. If you're tired of Courier, you can change it to any other printer-resident font you want.

Editing PPDs

When I say "editing PPDs," I don't actually mean opening and changing the content of a PPD. You can do that, if you want, but if you make a mistake, you'll have to either locate the original copy of the PPD, or beg a copy of the PPD from your friends, who'll laugh at you. Instead of exposing yourself to this potential humiliation, you can create a new PPD that *includes* the content of the PPD for your printer, then overrides parts of that content with your custom information or adds new features to the PPD. When you print, you choose the new PPD.

The following code is a minimal PPD customization file. You can enter it using a word processor or text editor.

```
*PPD-Adobe: "4.1"
*FormatVersion: "4.1"
*FileVersion: "1.0"
*%Enter the name of your PPD in the line below (between the quotes):
*Include: "AGFA SelectSet7000SF v52.3"
*%----------start of custom section----------
*% your custom code goes here
*%----------end of custom section-----------
*% end of PPD customization file
```

Save the file, making sure as you do so that you save it as a text-only file. When you want to customize a PPD, open this file, enter the PPD name in the line beginning with "*Include", enter your custom code (I'll show you how to add custom page sizes and screen angles later in this chapter), and then save the file in your PPDs folder. Give the new file the ".ppd" file extension.

When you want to use the new PPD, open the Print Setup dialog box and choose the PPD you just saved. If it doesn't work, check the filename you've entered in the "*Include" line—it has to *exactly* match the filename of a PPD on your system (I just copy the file name from the Finder/Explorer and paste it into the file—that way, there's less of a chance of a typo). Make sure that you've saved the file as text-only, and have saved it in the same folder as your other PPDs.

If you make changes to your custom PPD after you've chosen it in the Print Setup dialog box, you'll have to switch to another PPD and back again to get FreeHand to update the information in the Print Setup dialog box to reflect changes you've made to the PPD.

Adding Custom Paper Sizes to PPDs

The main reason to edit PPDs is to add custom paper sizes. If you find yourself entering the same numbers in the Page Size dialog box over and over again, it's a job for custom page sizes. Once you've added a custom page size to a PPD file, the size appears on the Paper size pop-up menu when the PPD file is selected.

If you're creating your publications on page sizes other than the paper size of the printed piece, stop (unless you're creating signatures, or have some other good excuse). Remember that paper size equals printer RAM. Your jobs will print faster if you use a paper size that's no larger than your publication's page size plus crop marks (which adds about 60 points in each dimension).

You can add custom paper sizes to PPDs for any printer that can accept variable page sizes. Usually, imagesetters can accept variable page sizes and laser printers can't.

To add a custom paper size to a PPD file, follow these steps.

1. Open the PPD customization template file you created earlier (see "Editing PPDs," earlier in this chapter).

2. Enter the name of the PPD in the line beginning with "*Include".

3. In the section of the template file reserved for custom code, enter three lines defining your new page size. The lines are shown below. Variables you enter are shown in italics.

```
*PageSize PageSizeName: "statusdict begin x y offset orientation end"
*ImageableArea PageSizeName: "0 0 x y"
*PaperDimension PageSizeName: "x y"
```

PageSizeName is the name you want to use for your custom page size. This name should not have spaces in it.

x is the width of the custom page size, in points (if you're an inch monger, just multiply the inch measurement by 72 to get the distance in points).

y is the height of the custom page size, in points.

Offset is a value used to offset the paper size from the edge of the imagesetter's paper (or film) roll. This value should almost always be "0".

Orientation is either "1" or "0". "0" means normal orientation (with the height of the paper being measured along the length of the imagesetter's paper roll, and type in normal orientation printing across the roll); "1" means transverse (where the width of the paper is measured along the length of the imagesetter's paper roll). Here's a custom page size for a 576-by-1,152-point (eight-by-16-inch) paper size with a normal orientation.

```
*PageSize PageSizeName: "statusdict begin 576 1152 0 0 end"
*ImageableArea PageSizeName: "0 0 576 1152"
*PaperDimension PageSizeName: "576 1152"
```

4. Save the file as a text-only file, adding the ".ppd" file extension. On the Macintosh, put the file in ~:System Folder:Extensions:Printer Descriptions; in Windows put it in ~:\Program Files\Macromedia\FH8\English\PPDs. Name the file something like "my_new_page_size.ppd."

5. Open FreeHand.

6. Press Command-P/Ctrl-P to display the Print dialog box. Click the "…" button to select a PPD. Select the PPD customization file you just saved, then click the OK button.

Click the Print Setup button to display the Print Setup dialog box. The new paper sizes should appear in the Paper Size pop-up menu in the Paper Setup panel.

Adding Custom Screen Angles

Here's how to add a new set of screen angles to a PPD. When you do this, they'll appear in the Halftone pop-up menu in the Print Setup dialog box, and can be saved as part of a printer style.

1. Open the PPD customization template file you created earlier (see "Editing PPDs," earlier in this chapter).

2. Enter the name of the PPD in the line beginning with "*Include".

3. In the section of the template file reserved for custom code, enter the following lines to define your new screen angles (variables you enter are shown in italics).

```
*ColorSepScreenAngle ProcessBlack.alpi.bdpi/a lpi / b dpi:"angle"
*ColorSepScreenAngle CustomColor.alpi.bdpi/a lpi / b dpi:"angle"
*ColorSepScreenAngle ProcessCyan.alpi.bdpi/a lpi / b dpi:"angle"
*ColorSepScreenAngle ProcessMagenta.alpi.bdpi/a lpi / b dpi:"angle"
*ColorSepScreenAngle ProcessYellow.alpi.bdpi/a lpi / b dpi:"angle"
```

Where a is the screen frequency, b is the printer resolution, and $angle$ is the screen angle for the ink. For example:

```
*ColorSepScreenAngle ProcessBlack.150lpi.2400dpi/150 lpi / 2400 dpi:"1.0"
```

4. Save the file as a text-only file, adding the ".ppd" file extension. On the Macintosh, put the file in ~:System Folder:Extensions:Printer Descriptions; in Windows put it in ~:\Program Files\Macromedia\FH8\English\PPDs. Name the file something like "my_new_screens.ppd."

5. Open FreeHand.

6. Press Command-P/Ctrl-P to display the Print dialog box. Click the "..." button to select a PPD. Select the PPD customization file you just saved, then click the OK button.

Click the Print Setup button to display the Print Setup dialog box. The new screen angles should appear on the Halftone Screen pop-up menu in the Separations panel.

Printing PostScript to Disk

If you want to print your publication (or pages from your publication) to disk as PostScript, turn on the File option in the Macintosh, or turn on the Print to File option in Windows (both options are in the Print dialog box). On the Macintosh, the Print button in the upper-right corner of the Print dialog box changes to Save. When you've set all the printing options you want, click the Save/OK button. The Create File/Print to File dialog box appears. In Windows, enter a name for the file, choose a drive and directory to save it to, and click the OK button. On the Macintosh, things are a little more complicated.

PostScript File Options (Macintosh only)

When you click the Save button in the Print dialog box, FreeHand displays a dialog box where you can set some options.

Format. Choose PostScript Job from the Format pop-up menu. Don't use the EPS options on this pop-up menu to create EPS files; use Export from the File menu instead (for more on exporting EPS files, see Chapter 4, "Importing and Exporting"). Files created using the EPS options on this pop-up menu are larger and print less reliably than EPS files created using Export.

The ASCII and Binary options are overridden by the settings in FreeHand's Output Options dialog box (or by the corresponding options in the Print Setup dialog box).

If you know that the printer you'll be sending the file to is equipped with a Level 2 PostScript RIP, choose Level 2 Only. Otherwise, choose Level 1 Compatible.

Font Inclusion. If you know that the printer you'll be sending the file to has the fonts you've used in your publication, or if you plan to send the fonts as separate files (if, for example, you're taking your file to an imagesetting service bureau and plan to give them copies of the fonts you've used in the publication), choose None from the Font Inclusion pop-up menu.

Choose All to include all the fonts you've used in the publication in the PostScript file you create. If you do this, you won't have to worry about font substitution—but your PostScript file will take up more disk space (each font adds around 40 K to the file's size).

To save all fonts except Courier, Helvetica, Symbol, and Times, choose All But Standard 13 from the Font Inclusion pop-up menu.

Preparing a FreeHand File for Imagesetting

I've listened long and carefully to the grievances of imagesetting service bureau customers and operators. I've heard about how this designer is suing that service bureau for messing up a job, and I've heard imagesetter operators talking about how stupid their clients are and how they have to make changes to the files of most of the jobs that come in. I've listened long enough, and I have one thing to say.

Cut it out! All of you! There's no reason that this relationship has to be an adversarial one. Before you throw this book across the room, let me explain. I don't mean to sound harsh. I just think that we can all cooperate, to everyone's benefit.

Designers and illustrators, you have to learn the technical chops if you want to play. That's just the way it is. The technical challenges are no greater than those you mastered when you learned how to use an airbrush, an X-Acto knife, or a rapidograph. Your responsibility to your imagesetting service bureau is to set your file up so that it has a reasonable chance of printing (the guidelines in this book should help) and to communicate to your service bureau exactly how it is you want your publication printed (or, if you're creating a PostScript file, to make sure that the settings in the publication are correct).

Service bureau folks, you've got to spell out the limits of your responsibility. If you don't think you should be fixing people's files, don't do it. If you do think it's your responsibility, tell your customer up front you'll fix the files, and tell them what you'll charge for your time. And if you get a customer who knows what they're doing, give them a discount. This will encourage everyone else.

Okay, back to the book.

If you know what you're doing, the best way to prepare your publication for printing at an imagesetting service bureau is to print a PostScript file to disk. If you've set up your printing options correctly, the file will include everything that is needed to print the publication. This way, all your service bureau has to do is download the file, instead of having to open the file, set the printing options, link to any images included in the file, and print. The only things that can go wrong are related to film handling and processing—the wrong film's used, the film's scratched, or the film's been processed incorrectly.

This means, however, that you have to be dead certain of the printing options you want before you print to disk, because it's difficult to change things after that. Look out for the following:

Links to images. Make sure any images you want to print (any that aren't on the background layer) are linked or embedded.

Tiling. If you're not tiling, make sure tiling (manual or automatic) is off. If you are, make sure you're tiling the way you want to. If you're tiling manually, you'll have to print a separate PostScript file to disk for each tile you want to print.

Scaling. It's easy to forget that you've scaled things for printing on your proof printer. Make sure that this is set to the scaling you want (generally 100 percent).

Separations/Composite. If you want to get separations from your service bureau, make sure you choose Separations in the Print dialog box. An obvious point, but I've forgotten it at least once.

Printer Type. If you don't choose the right printer type, your publication may not print, and may even crash the service bureau's imagesetter. They hate this, so pick the type of imagesetter they use from the pop-up menu. You might check with the service bureau to see if they have a custom PPD they'd like you to use.

Page Size. Pick a page size at least large enough to contain your page. If you're printing separations, pick a page size that's at least 60 points wider and taller than your page size so that printer marks (crop marks and registration marks) can be printed. Also make sure that you understand the page orientation you're working with— wide or tall; normal or transverse.

Screen Ruling. If you haven't set a screen frequency for each item in your publication using the Halftone palette, enter the screen ruling you want here. Any screen frequency you entered in the Halftone palette overrides any entry you make here.

Printer Marks. If you're printing separations, you can live without separation names and the file's name and date, but you've got to have the crop marks and registration marks if you want your printer to speak to you again. I turn them all on most of the time.

Negative/Positive Emulsion Up/Down. Are you printing negatives or positives? Emulsion up or down? Set it here.

Inks. What inks do you want to print? If you don't set them to print here, don't look askance at your service bureau when you don't get an overlay/separation for the ink. If you don't want an ink to print, make sure you turn it off or expect to pay for an additional piece of film.

Tip:
Don't Forget
Your Custom
PostScript Files

If you're using a custom UserPrep file, or if you're using FreeHand extension (AGX1—Macintosh only) files (for more on creating and using both types of files, see Chapter 8, "PostScript"), and you're giving your service bureau your FreeHand file (rather than a Post-Script file), make sure you include these files with your file. Without the files, any special effects you've used won't print. If you do send these files to your service bureau, let them know that they need to put them in the same folder as their copy of FreeHand before they print.

When you print to disk, FreeHand includes the relevant information from these files in your PostScript file, so you won't need to provide them to your service bureau.

Tip:
Learning About
FreeHand's
PostScript

The best way to learn about how FreeHand makes images using PostScript is to create simple files, print them to disk as PostScript, and then look at the PostScript file with a word processor. How does FreeHand draw a line? A box? Text? It's all easy to see in the PostScript FreeHand prints to disk. Having good PostScript books around is good, but FreeHand has its own dialect, and the best way to learn that dialect is to look at lots of examples of FreeHand's own PostScript.

How is a printed-to-disk PostScript file different from an EPS file? The former contains all the instructions needed by a Post-Script printer to render the page, including all of FreeHand's crop marks, page size information, and, specifically, the PostScript page-printing operator *showpage*.

The EPS file, on the other hand, counts on the application it's placed into for things like crop marks and page-positioning information. An EPS file doesn't include any of the options you've chosen in FreeHand's Print and Print Setup dialog boxes, while the printed-to-disk PostScript file includes all those options. In addition, the EPS file usually includes an attached PICT resource (Macintosh EPS) or TIFF (MS-DOS) for screen preview, while the printed-to-disk PostScript file doesn't.

Printing Reports

If you don't print your publication to disk as PostScript before taking it to your imagesetting service bureau (you've chosen to ignore my earlier advice out of sloth, gluttony, or because your service bureau has told you they'd rather have the publication file), you have to worry about the same things as I mentioned earlier in "Printing PostScript to Disk." You have a powerful ally, however, in FreeHand's "Report" feature (see Figure 7-12).

1. Choose "Report" from the File menu. FreeHand displays the Document Report dialog box.

2. Choose the reporting options you want. If you're preparing a report for an imagesetting service bureau, you'll want to turn on the External Files option in the Document Info category, and the Fonts Used option in the Text Info category.

3. When you've set the reporting options you want, press Return (or click the Report button). FreeHand displays the Document Report Viewer dialog box.

FIGURE 7-12
Preparing a report for
an imagesetting service
bureau

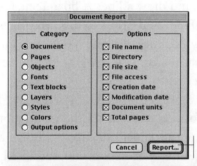

Choose Report from the File menu, and FreeHand displays the Document Report dialog box. The most important reporting categories (from your service bureau's point of view) are those concerning fonts, separations, and external files.

Click the Report button to generate your report.

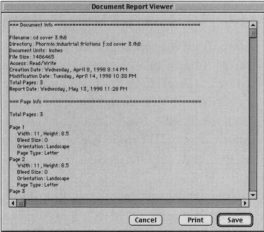

FreeHand creates and displays a report on the vital statistics of the current publication. You can print or save the report.

4. At this point, you can read the report, or save the report to a text file (click the Save button), or click the Print button to print the report. If you're taking your FreeHand publication to an imagesetting service bureau, print the report and send it with your file.

In addition to the report and all the files you've placed in a FreeHand publication, your imagesetting service bureau will also want a printed example of the publication.

Collecting Files for Output

When you use choose Collect for Output from the File menu, FreeHand gathers together copies all of the fonts and imported graphics used in the publication, and puts them in the location you specify (on a Zip disk, for example). In addition, FreeHand saves a text file containing a report on the publication, and the current printer style, PPD, and UserPrep file (if any).

This makes an excellent package to hand to your imagesetting service bureau.

The Golden Rules

These rules are mentioned elsewhere in this book, but all the service bureau operators I know think I should repeat them again here. The times I mention here are averages, based on a series of timed tests I performed.

Use Lens fills with restraint. As I mentioned in Chapter 2, "Drawing," Lens fills can make a page much more complicated from your printer's point of view.

Use blends, not graduated fills. Blends that are created to match your printer's resolution and the line screen you intend to use print more than two times faster than graduated fills covering the same area. This assumes that you're not pasting the blend inside another object, which takes longer. For more on creating blends instead of graduated and radial fills, see Chapter 2, "Drawing."

Use duplicated objects, not tiled fills. Tiled fills are a wonderful thing—as long as you're basing them on objects with basic lines and fills. As soon as you create a tiled fill containing a graduated or radial fill, watch out! My benchmarks show that tiled fills containing complex objects take more than twice as long to print as an identical series of duplicated objects.

Remember that page size equals printer RAM. The size of your page corresponds directly to the amount of printer RAM consumed when you try to print the publication. A four-by-four-inch card centered on a letter-size page takes almost twice as much time to print as the same card laid out on a four-by-four-inch page. For more on page setup and page size, see "Printing and Page Setup," earlier in this chapter.

Increase flatness whenever possible. When you're printing to high-resolution imagesetters, the difference between a flatness setting of three and a flatness setting of zero isn't noticeable, but the path with a flatness of three prints far faster. For more on flatness, see "Flatness" in Chapter 2, "Drawing."

Don't draw what you can't see. Your printer or imagesetter has to process everything on your publication's page, so why make it do extra work rendering objects that'll never be seen on the printed publication's page?

Simplify your paths. If you're working with complex paths created by autotracing images, try reducing the number of points in each path using Simplify from the Path Operations submenu of the Arrange menu (see "Simplify," in Chapter 2, "Drawing").

Avoid overscanning. When you're scanning images, it's natural to assume that you should scan them at the highest resolution available from your scanner to create the sharpest possible scans. In fact, image data scanned at a resolution greater than two times the screen frequency you intend using to print your publication does not add to the sharpness of the images—which means that the file takes up more space on disk than necessary, and takes longer to send to your printer. See "TIFFS, Line Screens, and Resolution" in Chapter 4, "Importing and Exporting."

Don't import things when you don't have to. Whenever possible, always Copy and Paste from one FreeHand publication to another, rather than exporting and importing EPS graphics. If you have a FreeHand EPS, go to the original file and copy the elements you want out of it. If you're working with an Illustrator EPS, open the file (if possible), rather than placing it. In my tests, placed EPSes took up to 16 times as long to print as the same images pasted from another FreeHand file or converted from an Illustrator EPS.

Printing Troubleshooting

It's going to happen to you. Files are going to take hours to print, and some aren't going to print at all. Or they're going to print in some way you hadn't expected. While this book can be viewed as an extended treatise on printing troubleshooting, this section deals with a few of the most common printing problems and how to fix them.

First of all, what makes a file hard to print? TIFFs, PostScript fills and lines, custom fills and lines, graduated fills, radial fills, and paths with lots of points and curves all do their part to increase the amount of time your publication spends churning around in a printer's RIP. When I say paths with lots of points, I mean paths with more than 100 points—the kind you get when you autotrace the scanned picture of Aunt Martha. Don't forget composite paths, either. At some point, one of these is going to trip you up. When that happens, you'll see a PostScript error message.

PostScript error messages can be cryptic in the extreme, and, best of all, seldom say what they really mean. Almost all of the PostScript errors that have the word "VMError" in them mean that your printer's run out of memory while processing the document. If you see error messages with the word "limitcheck" in them, something in your document is pushing your printer (or PostScript) past an internal limit. If you see these errors, you're going to have to apply some or all of the golden rules to your publication. In particular, try splitting some of the more complex paths in your publication and increasing the flatness of some or all of the paths in your publication.

Tip:
Printing to a
Local Printer
(Windows 95
only)

You've entered the Twilight Zone. You're trying to print to a Post-Script printer you've connected to LPT1 (or to a file, or to the Acrobat Distiller), but keep getting an error message that reads, "There was an error writing to LPT. There was a problem printing to the network resource. Check to make sure the printer server is working properly and try printing again." Your printer's not on a network, not talking to a printer server, and it's driving you nuts.

You've run into a bug in Windows 95 (this doesn't happen on Windows NT). Go at once to the Macromedia web site (www. macromedia.com) and download the file fh8printfix.exe. This installs a new clipdd.dll file in your FreeHand folder.

If you're wondering if the clipdd.dll file on your system needs updating, select the file and view its properties. The original Free-Hand 8 DLL is version 3.00; the new DLL is version 3.50.

Keep a copy of this file around in case you ever need to reinstall FreeHand (the Installer will install the old version of the file from your installation CD).

Tip:
Speeding
TIFF Printing
(Windows 95
only)

If you used FreeHand 7 in Windows 95, you've probably noticed that FreeHand 8 jobs take a lot longer to print—especially when there are TIFFs involved. Why this happens makes a long story, but it has to do with Macromedia deciding to use the Windows 32-bit printing system, rather than the 16-bit system left over from Windows 3.1 (and DOS).

By deciding to "do the right thing" in the long run (and I do believe that they did the right thing), Macromedia dramatically increased our printing times in the short run. Things won't get much better until you switch to Windows NT or Windows 98.

You can, however, make images print a little bit faster. To do this, open the image in Photoshop (or other image editing program) and save it as an EPS, then replace the image in your Free-Hand publication with the EPS.

Tip:
When TIFF
Images Look
Terrible

If your job prints, but your bilevel TIFF and paint-type images look terrible (that is, they look like they have moiré patterns in them), you probably need to magic-stretch them to match them to the printer's resolution. See "Resizing Images to Your Printer's Resolution" in Chapter 4, "Importing and Exporting," for more on magic-stretching.

Tip:
When TIFF
Images Don't
Print

If your job prints, but lacks a TIFF image or paint-type graphic, you probably lost your link to the image. This often happens when you take the FreeHand file to an imagesetting service bureau for printing (rather than giving them a PostScript file). Remember to take any linked TIFF or paint-type files along when you go to your service bureau, or print your file to disk as PostScript while the files are still linked; they'll be included in the PostScript file.

If you're having this problem with FreeHand EPS files you've placed in a PageMaker publication, see "FreeHand, TIFFs, and PageMaker 6" in Chapter 4, "Importing and Exporting."

Printing to Non-PostScript Printers

When you print to a non-PostScript printer, what you get depends on your printer's driver. Most of the time, FreeHand's paths print as smoothly as possible, given the printer's capabilities. If you're using Adobe Type Manager, you'll be able to print using Type 1 PostScript fonts. Your printer may, or may not do as good a job at rendering imported images as a PostScript printer. You won't be able to print Textured fills, Custom fills or strokes, or any PostScript fills or strokes you've entered.

If you want to print a FreeHand publication containing PostScript special effects (such as Custom fills or strokes), you can export each page as an EPS, then rasterize the pages using Photoshop or PageMaker, and then print from there. Alternatively, you can rasterize the file using GhostScript (a free PostScript "clone") and send the rasterized version to your printer (this works especially well with the Epson color printers). GhostScript is available for download from www.cs.wisc.edu/~ghost.

If you are printing proof pages on a non-PostScript printer, but plan to print the final version of your publication on a PostScript imagesetter, bear in mind that what you get out of the imagesetter may be very different from what you see on your proof pages.

Fortune Cookie

"Look afar, and see the end from the beginning," one fortune told me. It may have been talking about printing with FreeHand. From the time you press Command-N/Ctrl-N to create a new file, you really should be thinking, "How am I going to print this thing?"

Whenever possible, examine the processes you use to create publications in the light of the "golden rules" presented earlier in this chapter. You can almost always make something simpler from your printer's point of view without compromising the appearance of your publication.

Finally, as I always say, if something doesn't work, poke at it.

CHAPTER

PostScript

8

PostScript

is the engine that makes desktop publishing go. If you already know all there is to know about PostScript and how your printer uses it and/or just want to know how to use it in your FreeHand publications, skip the next section. I'm about to explain PostScript, laser printing, imagesetting, and the meaning of life as I understand them, in as few words as possible. Everyone else, take a deep breath.

What Is PostScript?

PostScript is a page-description language—a programming language for describing graphic objects. It's been said that page-description languages tell your printer how to make marks on paper. This isn't quite true—your printer already knows how to make marks. Page-description languages tell your printer *what marks to make, and where to make them.*

PostScript has emerged as the best of the commercially available page-description languages (other page-description languages being Hewlett-Packard's PCL, Imagen's Impress, and Xerox's Interpress)—these last two being "ancient history" by the standards of the computer world). This doesn't mean it's perfect, just that it's the highest standard we've got.

Inside your PostScript printer, there's a computer dedicated to controlling the printer. Software running on this computer interprets the PostScript sent to it and turns it into a bitmap image. The combination of printer hardware (processor and memory) and software (the version of the PostScript language in the printer's ROMs) is often called a raster image processor (RIP) because it turns a set of drawing commands into a raster image (or bitmap). You'll often hear someone talk about "ripping" a page; they mean they're running it through the RIP.

After the printer receives and processes the information for a page, the RIP transfers the bitmap from its memory to a photosensitive drum using a laser beam. The laser doesn't actually move— its beam bounces off a rotating mirror on its way to the drum. The areas where the drum is charged attract the powdered toner in the printer. When it's time to print the page, paper is pulled into the printer so that the sticky bits of toner are transferred from the drum to the paper. In an imagesetter, the laser beam directly exposes lithographic (black and white) film or paper.

What's PostScript Got to Do with FreeHand?

You can almost think of FreeHand as PostScript wearing a user interface. This isn't to say that FreeHand's internal database is PostScript (it's not), but that FreeHand approaches drawing objects the same way that PostScript does. And then there's printing. Try printing a FreeHand publication on something other than a PostScript printer, and you're in for a disappointment.

How can you use PostScript to extend FreeHand?* Here are three basic approaches.

◆ You can write your own EPS files.

◆ You can examine and modify FreeHand's PostScript.

◆ You can create your own PostScript and add it to FreeHand.

---

* All of the PostScript code shown in this chapter is available from me. See Appendix B, "About This Book," for information on how to contact me.

Writing Your Own EPS Files

If you want to write your own PostScript files and place them in FreeHand, you'll have to convert them from "raw" PostScript to EPS. Mostly, this means you need to add the following few lines to the beginning of your file (variables you change are shown in bold).

```
%!PS-Adobe-2.0 EPSF-1.2
%%BoundingBox: lowerLeftX lowerLeftY upperRightX upperRightY
%%EndComments
```

The variables following "%%BoundingBox" are the measurements of the image your PostScript code creates, in points. Usually, "lowerLeftX" and "lowerLeftY" are both zero. If you're not sure of the size of your image, print the file and measure it.

The PostScript code you use inside an EPS should not include the following PostScript operators.

banddevice	exitserver	initclip
letter	nulldevice	setsccbatch
legal	renderbands	setmatrix
stop	erasepage	grestoreall
initmatrix	copypage	note
framedevice	setpageparams	initgraphics
quit		

Figure 8-1 shows an example EPS file—and what it looks like when you print it.

When you place an EPS you've created this way in FreeHand, you'll see a box, just as if you were looking at the graphic in Keyline view. This is because the PostScript file doesn't look like anything until it's been run through a PostScript interpreter, and your system, unfortunately, doesn't have one.

Software PostScript (and PostScript clone) interpreters do exist, however. The one I'm the most familiar with is PSEditLink, a FreeHand Xtra from TechPool, which converts PostScript files to FreeHand objects (www.techpool.com). In addition, you can view raw PostScript files using Adobe Systems's Acrobat, provided you have the Acrobat Distiller application (it is, after all, most of a PostScript interpreter).

FIGURE 8-1
EPS file

```
%!PS-Adobe-2.0 EPSF-1.2
%%BoundingBox: 0 0 612 792
%%Creator:(G. Stumph & O. M. Kvern)
%%Title:(Fractal Tree)
%%CreationDate:(9-25-90)
%%EndComments
%% set up variables
/bdf
    {bind def} bind def
/depth 0 def
%% maxdepth controls how many branchings occur
%% exceeding 15 will be VERY time consuming
/maxdepth 10 def
%% after branching "cutoff" times, the branch angles increase
%% set cutoff higher than maxdepth to supress this
/cutoff 4 def
/length
    {rand 72 mod 108 add} bdf
/ang
    {rand 10 mod 10 add} bdf
/sway
    {rand 60 mod 30 sub} bdf
/NewLine
    {sway length 3 div sway length 3 div
    0 length rcurveto currentpoint
    depth 1 sub maxdepth div setgray
    stroke translate 0 0 moveto} bdf
/down
    {/depth depth 1 add def
    depth cutoff gt
        {/ang
            {rand 30 mod 20 add} bdf
        } if
    } bdf
/up
    {/depth depth 1 sub def
    depth cutoff le
        {/ang
            {rand 10 mod 10 add} bdf
        } if
    } bdf
%% FractBranch is the loop that does all the work,
%% by calling itself recursively
/FractBranch
    {.8 .8 scale
    down NewLine
    depth maxdepth lt
        {ang rotate gsave FractBranch grestore
         ang 2 mul neg rotate gsave FractBranch grestore} if
    up
    } def
gsave
```

FIGURE 8-1
EPS file
(continued)

```
306 72 translate 0 0 moveto
10 setlinewidth
1 setlinecap
currentscreen 3 -1 roll
pop 65 3 1 roll setscreen
FractBranch
grestore
%%End of file
```

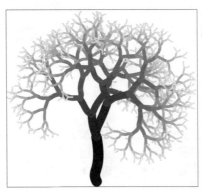

*What this EPS file looks
like when you print it.*

Looking at FreeHand's PostScript

If you're interested in creating your own PostScript code, you should take a look at FreeHand's PostScript to see if there's something there you can use. Knowing FreeHand's PostScript can keep you from "reinventing the wheel" when you write your own code.

One of the most beautiful things about PostScript is that it's just text—which means you can open it in any word processor or text editor.

While you can create PostScript files by printing to disk (as described in "Printing PostScript to Disk," in Chapter 7, "Printing"), I usually create Generic EPS files using the Export command. Files created this way are smaller and are guaranteed to contain only FreeHand code.

The first time you open a FreeHand PostScript or EPS file, what you see can be rather intimidating. What is all this stuff?

The most important code can be found between the lines

```
%%BeginResource: procset Altsys_header 4 0
```

and

```
%%EndProlog
```

Everything between these two lines is one or another of Free-Hand's PostScript dictionaries (see Figure 8-2). Specifically, you should look at the PostScript definitions following "/supdict 65 dict def" and "/ropedict 85 dict def." These are the support routines for FreeHand's Custom fills and strokes. If you can't see these dictionaries, make sure the file you've printed to disk contains at least one custom stroke or fill.

FIGURE 8-2
Finding FreeHand's
PostScript dictionaries

Everything from this line...

...to this line is one of FreeHand's PostScript dictionaries.

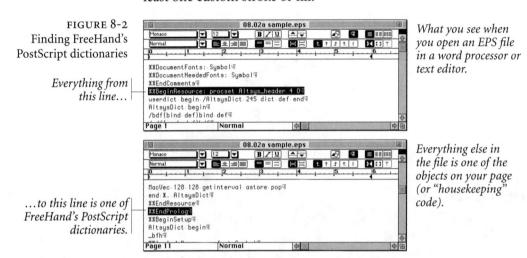

What you see when you open an EPS file in a word processor or text editor.

Everything else in the file is one of the objects on your page (or "housekeeping" code).

If you're looking for the objects you've drawn, scroll to the end of the file, then scroll up a couple of screens. When you see the line "%%BeginPageSetup," you've reached the start of a FreeHand page (while your publication may contain more than one page, I advise examining FreeHand's PostScript one page at a time—it's less confusing). Scroll down until you see a line ending with "m"—it's the start of the first path you've drawn (see Figure 8-3).

Don't be scared—you don't have to know this stuff to enter most of the new PostScript strokes and fills in this chapter. Keep an eye out for comments—they explain what the code is supposed to be doing. PostScript comments are preceded by a "%" and are ignored by PostScript interpreters.

If you're having trouble making sense of the PostScript file, remember that procedures begin with a "/" and end with a "}def" or "}bdef". Here's an example of a procedure.

```
%%procedure for picking a random integer
/randint {rand exch mod } def
```

FIGURE 8-3
Finding what
you've drawn

Here's the start of
a path drawn in
FreeHand.

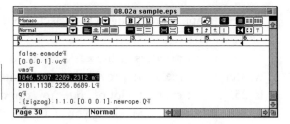

What's the rest of the
code you can see in the
example screen mean?

`false eomode`	*Turns off overprinting.*
`[0 0 0 1] vc`	*Sets the color to black.*
`vms`	*Manages printer memory.*
`1846.5307 2289.2312 m`	*Moves to the coordinates shown.*
`2181.1138 2256.8689 L`	*Draws a path to these coordinates, from the coordinates in the previous line.*

`q` *Manages printer memory ("gsave")*
`{zigzag} 1 1 0 [0 0 0 1] newrope` *Applies the custom line style "zigzag."*
`Q` *Manages printer memory ("grestore")*

Creating Your Own PostScript Effects

There are several different ways to add PostScript code to FreeHand.

◆ You can attach PostScript code to FreeHand objects by choosing PostScript in the Fill Inspector or the Stroke Inspector and entering up to 255 characters of code.

◆ You can use PostScript effects you've saved in a "UserPrep" file. To use procedures from your UserPrep file, enter the procedure names and any appropriate parameters in the PostScript Code field of the Fill and Stroke Inspectors. This gets you around the 255-character limit.

◆ If you're using a Macintosh, you can turn your PostScript effects into FreeHand external resource files. When you do this, they'll appear in the Custom section of the Fill and Stroke Inspectors.

Entering PostScript in the Fill and Stroke Inspectors

When you choose PostScript from either the Fill Type or Stroke Type popup menus in the Fill Inspector or Stroke Inspector, a large field appears at the bottom of the Inspector. You can type up to 255 characters of PostScript code in this field. Press Return, and

FreeHand applies the code to the selected object as a PostScript fill or stroke effect.

In some ways, this is the easiest way to get PostScript you've written into FreeHand, provided the code fits in the field. Trouble is, 255 characters isn't a lot of code. You can cut down the number of characters used by making your variable and procedure names shorter ("m" instead of "moveto," for example), but this only works up to a certain point.

In fact, it sometimes *looks* as if you can enter more than 255 characters in this field—FreeHand accepts the extra characters without complaint. When you press Return, however, FreeHand truncates the contents of the field, leaving only 255 characters.

The following steps show you how to apply a simple PostScript stroke to a path (see "PostScript Strokes" in Chapter 2, "Drawing").

1. Draw a path.

2. Without deselecting the path, press Command-Option-L/ Ctrl-Alt-L to display the Stroke Inspector.

3. Choose PostScript from the Stroke Type pop-up menu. The PostScript Code field appears in the Stroke Inspector.

4. Enter PostScript code in the field (you can delete the default code "stroke").

5. Press Return to apply the PostScript stroke.

The path won't look any different on the screen, but when you print to a PostScript printer, you'll see the effect.

Figure 8-4 shows a few stroke effects you can enter. As you enter this code, you'll see procedures that don't look like "normal" PostScript. That is, instead of typing "exch def" you'll type "xdf". I can do this because I know FreeHand's already defined "xdf" as "exch def"—it's a kind of shorthand. For a list of PostScript shortcuts defined by FreeHand, see Table 8-1.

PostScript fill effects work just like PostScript stroke effects (see "PostScript Strokes" in Chapter 2, "Drawing"). You can type up to 255 characters in the PostScript Code field (see Figure 8-5).

1. Draw a rectangle.

FIGURE 8-4
PostScript strokes

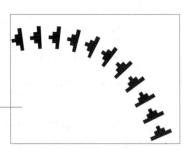

Shorthand version

```
currentlinewidth /lw
exch cvi def q [lw lw
4 mul] 0 d lw 6 mul w
S Q q [lw lw 4 mul] lw
d lw 3 mul w S Q q [lw
lw 4 mul] lw 2 mul d
lw w S Q
```

Example PostScript stroke code

```
currentlinewidth /lw exch cvi def gsave
[lw lw 4 mul] 0 setdash lw 6 mul
setlinewidth stroke grestore gsave [lw
lw 4 mul] lw setdash lw 3 mul
setlinewidth stroke grestore gsave [lw
lw 4 mul] lw 2 mul setdash lw
setlinewidth stroke grestore
```

Dimension line code

```
pathbbox /t xdf /r xdf /b xdf /l xdf /
dx r l sub def /dy t b sub def S /ts 20
string def /Helvetica-Bold findfont 9
scalefont setfont l b translate dx 2
div dy 2 div 3 sub m dx 2 exp dy 2 exp
add sqrt ts cvs stringwidth pop 2 div
neg 0 rmoveto ts show S
```

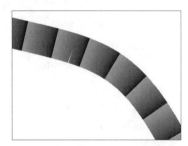

Graduated line code

```
cvc /CC xdf /ks 25 def /kp 1 1 ks div
sub def 0 1 ks { /c xdf [1 ks 1 sub] c
2 add d cvc length 4 eq {cvc {kp mul}
forall 4 array astore /cvc xdf}{cvc 0
get kp mul /nt xdf cvc 0 nt put} ifelse
cvc vc q S Q } for CC vc
```

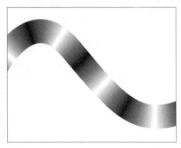

Ribbon line code

```
cvc /CC xdf /ks 25 def /kp .5 ks div
def 0 1 ks 2 mul {/c xdf [1 ks 2 mul 1
sub] c 2 add d /kz c ks le {{kp
sub}}{{kp add}} ifelse def cvc length 4
eq {cvc {kz} forall 4 array astore}{cvc
0 get kz /nt xdf cvc 0 nt put cvc}
ifelse vc q S Q} for CC vc
```

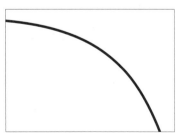

Shaky line code

```
23 srand 0 setflat /ri {cvi rand exch
mod} def flattenpath {newpath m} {2 {1
dup 2 mul ri sub add exch} repeat L}
{} {} pathforall S
```

Name	What it does
F	Fills the current path with the current color
f	Closes the current path, then fills it with the current color
S	Strokes the current path with the current line weight, color, and dash pattern
s	Closes the current path, then strokes it
q	Saves the current graphic state (more or less the same as PostScript's "gsave" operator)
Q	Restores the previously saved graphic state (like PostScript's "grestore" operator)
w	Sets the stroke width. Same as the PostScript operator "setlinewidth"
n	Same as the PostScript operator "newpath"
d	Sets the dash pattern of a path. Same as the PostScript operator "setdash"
xdf	Defines the current variable name with whatever's on top of the operand stack. Same as "exch def"
vc	Sets the current color
cvc	Current color array

2. Press Command-Option-F/Ctrl-Alt-F to display the Fill Inspector.

3. Choose PostScript from the Fill Type popup menu. The PostScript Code field appears at the bottom of the Fill Inspector.

4. Enter PostScript code in the field.

5. When you're through entering code, press Return to apply your PostScript fill. The rectangle fills with "PS."

FIGURE 8-5
PostScript fills

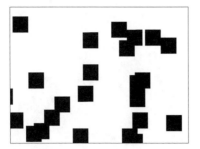

Random Squares code

```
23 srand pathbbox clipper /kt xdf /
kr xdf /kb xdf /kl xdf n /dx kr kl
sub def /dy kt kb sub def /ri {cvi
rand exch mod} def /sz 12 def kl sz
sub kb sz sub translate 0 0 m /rl
{rlineto} def 24 {dx ri dy ri m sz 0
rl 0 sz rl sz neg 0 rl f} repeat
```

Random Triangles code

```
23 srand pathbbox clipper /kt xdf /
kr xdf /kb xdf /kl xdf n /dx kr kl
sub def /dy kt kb sub def /ri {cvi
rand exch mod} def /sz 12 def kl sz
sub kb sz sub translate 0 0 m /rl
{rlineto} def 24 {dx ri dy ri m sz 0
rl sz 2 div neg sz rl f} repeat
```

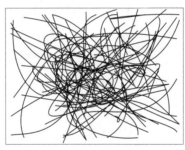

Scribble code

```
23 srand pathbbox clipper /kt xdf /
kr xdf /kb xdf /kl xdf n /dx kr kl
sub def /dy kt kb sub def /ri {cvi
rand exch mod} def /xy {dx ri dy ri}
def kl kb translate 0 0 m 60 {q xy m
xy xy xy C .5 w S Q} repeat
```

Straight Scribble code

```
23 srand pathbbox clipper /kt xdf /
kr xdf /kb xdf /kl xdf n /dx kr kl
sub def /dy kt kb sub def /ri {cvi
rand exch mod} def /xy {dx ri dy ri}
def kl kb translate 0 0 m 60 {q xy m
xy L .5 w S Q} repeat
```

Creating and Using a UserPrep File

If you've created your own PostScript stroke or fill effects, or have borrowed them from some other source (such as this book, other PostScript books, or the text files you found on someone's Corel-Draw disks) and want to use them in FreeHand, you can create a PostScript dictionary of your own (see Figure 8-6).

FIGURE 8-6
Using UserPrep

A sample UserPrep file. This file defines a single PostScript fill effect, "scribble."

```
%%UserPrep
/scribble
%%on stack: random number seed, line weight, number of lines
{/ns xdf
/lineWeight xdf
/seed xdf
seed srand lineWeight w
flattenpath pathbbox clip
/top xdf
/right xdf
/bottom xdf
/left xdf
cvc /CVC xdf
cvc length 4 eq
{/colorChange{cvc {newTint} forall 4 array astore vc} def}
{/colorChange{cvc 0 get {newTint} mul /tint xdf cvc 0 tint put vc} def
} ifelse
/randint {rand exch mod} def
/newTint {/random {100 randint .01 mul} def random mul} def
/xy
{rand right left sub cvi mod left add rand
top bottom sub cvi mod bottom add
} bdf
ns {n xy m xy xy xy C colorChange S CVC vc} repeat
} def
%%End UserPrep
```

Select the path you want to format using the PostScript fill, then choose PostScript from the Fill type pop-up menu in the Fill Inspector.

Enter the parameters your new fill effect expects in the PostScript code field. In this example, you'd type a seed for the random number generator, the line width, and the number of lines you want, followed by "scribble" (the name of the fill).

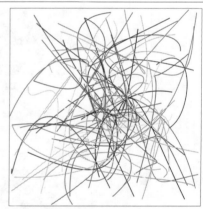

"scribble" PostScript fill effect

1. Use a word processor or text editor to create a series of procedures you want to use.

2. Save the code as a text-only file and place the file inside the UserPrep folder in your FreeHand folder (in Windows, add the file extension ".prp").

3. In FreeHand, select a path.

4. Display the Fill or Stroke Inspector.

5. Choose PostScript from the Fill Type or Stroke Type pop-up menu.

6. Enter the code required to invoke your effect (usually, this is the name of the procedure, preceded by one or more parameters).

7. Press Return to apply the effect to the path.

8. Before you print, select the UserPrep file you created from the UserPrep pop-up menu in the Print Setup dialog box.

9. Print.

If you get a PostScript error—or if nothing prints at all—you made a mistake in either the UserPrep file or the PostScript Code field. Errors containing the words "nostringval", "nocurrentpoint", and "stack underflow" are usually caused by entering a variable improperly before the procedure name in the PostScript Code field (in either the Fill or Stroke Inspector).

Creating PostScript Strokes

You can use FreeHand's built-in custom stroke drawing routines to create virtually any line pattern you can imagine. Here's how it works. FreeHand's Custom stroke routines (found in the "newrope" procedure) take instructions for an object and repeat that object on a path. The procedures scale, space, and color the objects along the path according to the values you enter in the Stroke Inspector (see Figure 8-7). We can use these procedures to create our own custom stroke patterns.

The heart of a FreeHand custom stroke effect is a kind of cell— like a tiny FreeHand page that's one unit square. The size of the unit itself doesn't matter because the scale of the cell gets determined later by the values you enter in the PostScript Code field of the Stroke Inspector. The zero point of this cell is at its center, and all of FreeHand's drawing commands (which you use to construct the line pattern) get their coordinates relative to it.

You can create an enlarged version of this cell to use in plotting the placement of line segments and paths inside the cell, as shown in Figure 8-8.

FIGURE 8-7
How FreeHand draws
custom PostScript lines

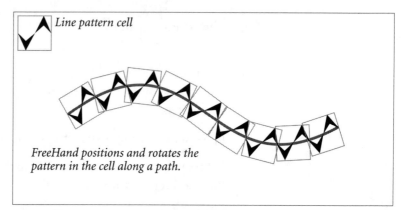

Line pattern cell

FreeHand positions and rotates the pattern in the cell along a path.

FIGURE 8-8
Creating a template
for custom lines

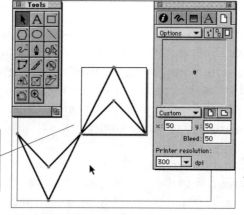

Draw whatever you want in this area, then export the graphic in one of the Adobe Illustrator formats.

Once you've done that, you can extract the pattern for your custom line using your word processor.

1. Open FreeHand and press Command-N/Ctrl-N to create a new file.

2. In the Document Inspector, select Custom from the pop-up menu. Enter "p50" (fifty points) for both the width and height of the page, and enter a bleed amount of "p50".

When you've got something you think would make a good line pattern (start with a simple shape), draw it so that it's centered around the zero point of this tiny page, then export it as an Adobe Illustrator file (any format), and then use a word processor to extract the line pattern from the EPS graphic.

Why not export the graphic as a Generic EPS file? The coordinate system used in FreeHand's EPS formats is based on the lower-left corner of the pasteboard—not on the lower-left corner of the page (see Figure 8-9). This makes no difference to applications im-

FIGURE 8-9
Which would you
rather work with?

FreeHand version	Illustrator version
1735.3014 1559 m	43.3014 -25 m
1692 1533.9998 L	0 -50.0002 L
1648.6986 1558.9998 L	-43.3014 -25.0002 L
1648.6986 1609 L	-43.3014 25 L
1692 1634.0002 L	0 50.0002 L
1735.3014 1609.0002 L	43.3014 25.0002 L
1735.3014 1559 L	43.3014 -25 L

porting or printing the EPS, but makes it more difficult to use this technique. Illustrator format keeps things simple, which is just what we want, in this case.

1. Open the file with your word processor.

2. Delete everything preceding the first line ending with an "m" ("moveto") instruction.

3. Delete everything from the end of the last line ending with an "L" or a "C" to the end of the file.

4. Delete any occurrence of "vmrs", "vmr", "vms", "u", or "U" remaining in the file.

At this point, the file contains only the commands for drawing the shape (or shapes) you drew.

Once you've got the line pattern, you can plug it into the following PostScript routine. Enter the code shown below, replacing the variables shown in bold with the names you want your routines to use and with the drawing commands you extracted from the EPS you created in the previous procedure.

```
%strokeName
ropedict begin
%Enter the name for your custom stroke here
    /strokeName
    {
    blocksetup
    .01 .01 scale
    %paste your drawing commands here
    drawingCommands
    %enter "s" instead of "f" below to stroke, rather than fill, the path
    f Q
    } def
end
%end strokeName custom stroke effect
```

Here's an example line pattern.

```
%hexagon
ropedict begin
    /hexagon {
        blocksetup
        .01 .01 scale
        43.3014 -25 m
        0 -50.0002 L
        -43.3014 -25.0002 L
        -43.3014 25 L
        0 50.0002 L
        43.3014 25.0002 L
        43.3014 -25 L
        f Q
    } def
end
%end hexagon custom stroke effect
```

To make this custom stroke work, we'll have to include the Free-Hand PostScript dictionaries ("supdict" and "ropedict") containing various support routines for custom strokes. Here's an example UserPrep file containing the "hexagon" custom stroke effect (it's at the end). Again, you don't have to type this in—send me an email message and I'll send you the file.

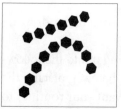

Printed example of the "hexagon" custom stroke

```
%Custom Strokes UserPrep
%filename: "custom strokes.prp"
% ------------------
% support dictionary for custom stroke effects
% from "Real World FreeHand 8"
% by Olav Martin Kvern <ole@desktopscience.com>
% FreeHand's "supdict" for custom fill and stroke effects
userdict begin /supdict 65 dict def end
supdict begin
    /str1 512 string def
    /dx 500 def
    /dy 700 def
    /cnt 0 def
    /newinside {
        {flattenpath} fp clipper pathbbox
        1 index 4 index sub round cvi /dx xdf
        0 index 3 index sub round cvi /dy xdf
        pop pop translate
        222 srand
        newpath
    } bind def
    /randint {rand exch mod} def
    /rand8 {rand -16 bitshift 255 and} def
    /rand2 {rand -16 bitshift 3 and} def
    /brandxy {dx randint dy randint} def
```

```
/x1 {angle cos abs dx mul} def
/x2 {90 angle sub cos abs dy mul} def
/y1 {angle sin abs dx mul} def
/y2 {90 angle sub sin abs dy mul} def
/backgnd {
    xstart ystart m
    xstart ystart abs L
    xstart abs ystart abs L
    xstart abs ystart L
    closepath fill
} def
/incrcnt {/cnt cnt 1 add def} def
/colorchoice {
    /found false def
    gray? {
        /CCblack [0 0 0 0] def
        color 1 exch sub
        CCblack 3 3 -1 roll put
        CCblack vc
    } {
        color length 2 eq {
            color 1 get type (text) type eq {
                0 1 spots length 1 sub {
                    /cnt xdf
                    spots cnt get 4 get color 1 get eq {
                        /found true def
                        exit
                    } if
                } for
                found {
                    color 1 cnt put
                } {
                    color 1 3 put
                } ifelse
            } if
            color vc
        } if
        color length 4 eq {
            color vc
        } if
    } ifelse
} def
/gray? {
    color type 0 type eq color type .0 type eq or
} def
end
%end supdict
%FreeHand's "ropedict" for custom stroke effects
userdict begin /ropedict 85 dict def end
ropedict begin
    /blocksetup {q translate rotate scale n} def
    /blockend {closepath fill} def
    /blockfinish {closepath fill Q} def
```

```
/movetoproc {
  dup /sby xdf
  /spy xdf
  dup /sbx xdf
  /spx xdf
  sbx sby m
} def
/1stlinetoproc {
  /esy xdf /esx xdf
  blockdata
  /totdist totdist dist add def
  /sbx esx def
  /sby esy def
  deltax 0 ne deltay 0 ne and {
    /prevtotdeltax deltax def
    /prevtotdeltay deltay def
  } if
} def
/2ndlinetoproc {
  /esy xdf /esx xdf
  bdflag false eq {
    blockdata esx spx eq esy spy eq and {
      lastsegdist
    } if
  } if
  offset ldelta add dist le {
    deltax 0 eq deltay 0 eq and {
      /ang 0 def
    } {
      /ang deltay deltax atan def
    } ifelse
    offset 0 lt {
      /prevang prevdeltax 0 eq prevdeltay 0 eq and {
        0
      } {
        prevdeltay neg prevdeltax neg atan
      } ifelse
      def
      ang prevang sub abs dup 120 le exch 240 ge or {
        /offset 0 def
        bdflag true eq {
          lastsegdist
        } if
      } if
    } if
    offset ldelta dist {
      /curdelta xdf
      /ldeltax ang cos curdelta ldelta 2 div add mul def
      /ldeltay ang sin curdelta ldelta 2 div add mul def
      bll2 blw ang sbx ldeltax add sby ldeltay add drawblock
      /offset curdelta ldelta add dist sub def
      ldelta offset abs .001 add gt {exit} if
    } for
```

```
                /prevdeltax deltax def
                /prevdeltay deltay def
                /deltax 0 def
                /deltay 0 def
                /sbx esx def
                /sby esy def
            } if
        } def
        /1stcloseproc {spx spy 1stlinetoproc} def
        /2ndcloseproc {
            sbx spx ne sby spy ne or {
                /esx spx def /esy spy def
                blockdata /bdflag true def lastsegdist
                spx spy 2ndlinetoproc
            } if
        } def
        /blockdata {
            /deltay esy sby sub def /deltax esx sbx sub def
            /dist deltay dup mul deltax dup mul add sqrt def
        } def
        /lastsegdist {
            /dist dist offset sub ldelta div round ldelta mul offset add def
        } def
    end
    /newrope {
        supdict begin
            ropedict begin
                /color xdf
                colorchoice
                /spacing xdf
                /blw xdf
                /bll xdf
                /drawblock xdf
                q {flattenpath} fp
                /totdist 0 def
                /totdeltax 0 def
                /totdeltay 0 def
                {movetoproc} {1stlinetoproc} {} {1stcloseproc} pathforall
                /nm totdist bll spacing add div def
                /nm2 nm floor def
                nm2 0 ne {
                    /fr nm nm2 sub def
                    /nm2 fr 0.5 ge {nm2 1 add} {nm2} ifelse def
                    /bll2 fr 0.5 ge {fr 1.0 sub} {fr} ifelse
                    bll spacing add mul nm2 div bll add spacing add def
                    /ldelta bll2 def
                    /bll2 bll2 bll bll spacing add div mul def
                    /offset 0 def
                    /totdeltax 0 def
                    /totdeltay 0 def
                    /cnt 0 def
                    /prevtotdeltax 0 def
                    /prevtotdeltay 0 def
```

```
                           /bdflag false def
                           {movetoproc} {2ndlinetoproc} {} {2ndcloseproc} pathforall
                        } if
                        Q n
                    end
                end
            } def
            %end "ropedict"
            %----------------------------
            %hexagon custom stroke effect
            %on stack: "{hexagon}" xscale yscale spacing "cvc newrope"
            %the following example ignores the setting in the "width" field
            %example: {hexagon} 12 12 12 cvc newrope
            %the following example uses the setting in the "width" field for
            %both xscale and yscale.
            %example2: {hexagon} currentlinewidth dup 0 cvc newrope
            ropedict begin
                /hexagon {
                    blocksetup
                    .01 .01 scale
                    43.3014 -25 m
                    0 -50.0002 L
                    -43.3014 -25.0002 L
                    -43.3014 25 L
                    0 50.0002 L
                    43.3014 25.0002 L
                    43.3014 -25 L
                    f Q
                } def
            end
            %end hexagon custom stroke effect
            %----------------------------
```

Creating PostScript Fills

Because you can create tiled fills inside FreeHand, there's not much need to create fill effects that simply repeat one pattern over and over again. If you want a fill effect that randomly resizes, scales, or skews a pattern inside a filled object or if you want to create a tiled effect where each tile rotates around its center point, however, custom fills are just the ticket.

Use the FreeHand template file we created (see "Creating Post-Script Strokes," earlier in this chapter) to draw the shape you want to use in the new PostScript fill, then export it in the Illustrator 1.1 format. Open the exported file using a text editor or word processor and extract the drawing commands. Paste the drawing commands into the following fill procedure (the variables and commands you enter are shown in bold).

```
% fillName_f
/fillName_f {
    /fillName {
        drawing commands
    } def
    {fillName} rw_tile_f
} def
```

For example:

```
% boldX
/boldX_f {
    /boldX {
        -25 -50 m
        -50 -25 L
        -25 0 L
        -50 25 L
        -25 50 L
        0 25 L
        25 50 L
        50 25 L
        25 0 L
        50 -25 L
        25 -50 L
        0 -25 L
        -25 -50 L
    } def
    {boldX} rw_tile_f
} def
```

Once again, this code depends on a larger PostScript dictionary. This time, it's not one that comes with FreeHand—not quite. I had to modify a few things to get random color changes, random rotation, and random skewing to work. Enter the text shown below in your word processor—or, better yet, send me an email message (ole@desktopscience.com)—and I'll send you the file.

```
% Real World FreeHand 8 UserPrep
% filename: "real world freehand 8.prp"
% -----------------
% support dictionary for stroke and fill effects
% from "Real World FreeHand 8"
% by Olav Martin Kvern <ole@desktopscience.com>
% start rw_supdict
userdict /rw_supdict known not {
    userdict begin
        /rw_supdict 500 dict def
    end
    rw_supdict begin
        /str1 512 string def
        /dx 500 def
```

```
/dy 700 def
/cnt 0 def
/newinside {
    {
        flattenpath
    } fp clipper
    pathbbox
    1 index 4 index sub round cvi /dx xdf
    0 index 3 index sub round cvi /dy xdf
    pop pop translate
    rw_supdict /randomSeed known not {
        /randomSeed 222 def
    } if
    randomSeed srand
    newpath
} bind def
/randint {rand exch mod} def
/rand8 {rand -16 bitshift 255 and} def
/rand2 {rand -16 bitshift 3 and} def
/brandxy {dx randint dy randint} def
/x1 {angle cos abs dx mul} def
/x2 {90 angle sub cos abs dy mul} def
/y1 {angle sin abs dx mul} def
/y2 {90 angle sub sin abs dy mul} def
/backgnd {
    xstart ystart m
    xstart ystart abs L
    xstart abs ystart abs L
    xstart abs ystart L
    closepath fill
} def
/incrcnt {/cnt cnt 1 add def} def
/colorchoice {
    /found false def
    gray? {
        /CCblack [0 0 0 0] def
        color 1 exch sub
        CCblack 3 3 -1 roll put
        CCblack vc
    } {
        color length 2 eq {
            color 1 get type (text) type eq {
                0 1 spots length 1 sub {
                    /cnt xdf
                    spots cnt get 4 get color 1 get eq {
                        found true def
                        exit
                    } if
                } for
                found {
                    color 1 cnt put
                } {
                    color 1 3 put
```

```
                    } ifelse
                } if
                color vc
            } if
            color length 4 eq {
                color vc
            } if
        } ifelse
    } def
    /gray? {color type 0 type eq color type .0 type eq or} def
    /rw_ustroke {
        [{/moveto cvx} {/lineto cvx} {/curveto cvx} {/closepath cvx}
        pathforall] cvx
        matrix currentmatrix matrix invertmatrix q
        newpath exch systemdict begin cvx exec end concat stroke Q
    } def
  end
} if
%end rw_supdict
% ---------------------
% tiled fill effect
% from Real World FreeHand 7
% by Olav Martin Kvern
rw_supdict begin
    /rw_oneTile_f {
        randomSeed srand
        ystart spacing ystart abs {
            /ycur xdf
            xstart spacing xstart abs {
                q ycur m
                currentpoint translate
                %random rotation?
                randomRotate true eq {360 randint rotate} if
                %random skewing?
                randomSkew true eq {
                    /xSkew 360 randint def
                    /ySkew 360 randint def
                    [1 xSkew sin ySkew sin neg 1 0 0] concat} if
                % random scaling?
                randomScale true eq {
                    maxSize minSize sub randint minSize add /size xdf} if
                %scale the tile
                size 100 div dup scale q
                tileType colorChange f
                %end drawing commands
                Q Q
                %restore original color
                rw_spot true eq {
                    cvc 0 originalTint put cvc vc
                } {
                    CVC vc
                } ifelse
            } for
```

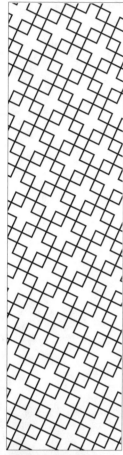

```
            } for
        } def
end
/rw_tile_f {
    rw_supdict begin q
        /tileType xdf
        cvc
        %process or spot?
        length 4 eq {
            /rw_spot false def
            cvc /CVC xdf
        } {
            /rw_spot true def
            cvc 0 get
            /originalTint xdf
        } ifelse
        /randomSkew xdf
        /randomRotate xdf
        /changeTint xdf
        /randomSeed xdf
        /angle xdf
        /spacing xdf
        /maxSize xdf
        /minSize xdf
        minSize maxSize eq {
            /randomScale false def
            minSize /size xdf
        } {
            /randomScale true def
        } ifelse
        %color change stuff follows
        changeTint true eq {
            /newTint {
                100 randint .01 mul
            } def
            rw_spot false eq {
                /colorChange {
                    cvc {
                        newTint mul
                    } forall
                    4 array astore vc
                } def
            } {
                /colorChange {
                    cvc 0 get newTint mul /tint xdf cvc 0 tint put cvc vc
                } def
            } ifelse
        } {
            /colorChange {
            } def
        } ifelse
        newinside
        /xstart x1 x2 add 2 div neg spacing sub def
```

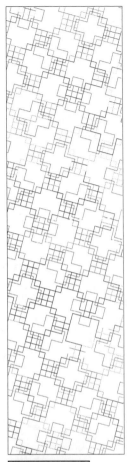

```
        /ystart y1 y2 add 2 div neg spacing sub def
        dx 2 div dy 2 div translate
        angle rotate
        rw_oneTile_f Q
    end
} def
%end of rw_tile_f
% --------------------------
%tiled fill effect
%from Real World FreeHand 7
%by Olav Martin Kvern
rw_supdict begin
    /rw_oneTile_s {
        randomSeed srand
        ystart spacing ystart abs {
            /ycur xdf
            xstart spacing xstart abs {
                q ycur m
                currentpoint translate
                %random rotation?
                randomRotate true eq {360 randint rotate} if
                %random skewing?
                randomSkew true eq {
                    /xSkew 360 randint def
                    /ySkew 360 randint def
                    [1 xSkew sin ySkew sin neg 1 0 0] concat
                } if
                % random scaling?
                randomScale true eq {
                    maxSize minSize sub randint minSize add /size xdf
                } if
                %scale the tile
                currentlinewidth 100 size div mul w
                size 100 div dup scale q
                %start drawing commands
                tileType
                colorChange
                s
                %end drawing commands
                Q Q
                % %restore original color
                rw_spot true eq {
                    cvc 0 originalTint put cvc vc
                } {
                    CVC vc
                } ifelse
            } for
        } for
    } def
end
/rw_tile_s {
    rw_supdict begin q
        /tileType xdf
```

```
cvc
%process or spot color?
length 4 eq {
    /rw_spot false def
    cvc /CVC xdf
} {
    /rw_spot true def
    cvc 0 get
    /originalTint xdf
} ifelse
/randomSkew xdf
/randomRotate xdf
/changeTint xdf
/lineWeight xdf
lineWeight w
/randomSeed xdf
/angle xdf
/spacing xdf
/maxSize xdf
/minSize xdf
minSize maxSize eq {
    /randomScale false def
    minSize /size xdf
} {
    /randomScale true def
} ifelse
%color change stuff follows
changeTint true eq {
    /newTint {
        100 randint .01 mul
    } def
    rw_spot false eq {
        /colorChange {
            cvc {
                newTint mul
            } forall
            4 array astore vc
        } def
    } {
        /colorChange {
            cvc 0 get newTint mul /tint xdf cvc 0 tint put cvc vc
        } def
    } ifelse
} {
    /colorChange {
    } def
} ifelse
newinside
/xstart x1 x2 add 2 div neg spacing sub def
/ystart y1 y2 add 2 div neg spacing sub def
```

```
        dx 2 div dy 2 div translate
        angle rotate
        rw_oneTile_s
        Q
    end
} def
%end of rw_tile_s
% --------------------------
% boldX ("boldX_f") filled tiled fill effect
% example: 24 24 24 30 1 false false false boldX_f
/boldX_f {
    /boldX {
        -25 -50 m
        -50 -25 L
        -25 0 L
        -50 25 L
        -25 50 L
        0 25 L
        25 50 L
        50 25 L
        25 0 L
        50 -25 L
        25 -50 L
        0 -25 L
        -25 -50 L
    } def
    {boldX} rw_tile_f
} def
% --------------------------
% boldX ("boldX_s") stroked tiled fill effect
% example: 24 24 24 30 1 0.5 false false false boldX_s
/boldX_s {
    /boldX {
        -25 -50 m
        -50 -25 L
        -25 0 L
        -50 25 L
        -25 50 L
        0 25 L
        25 50 L
        50 25 L
        25 0 L
        50 -25 L
        25 -50 L
        0 -25 L
        -25 -50 L
    } def
    {boldX} rw_tile_s
} def
% --------------------------
```

FreeHand's PostScript Resources (Macintosh)

The Post resources inside FreeHand contain all of FreeHand's PostScript code. If you're creating your own PostScript code, or if you're creating external resource files, you'll probably find it helpful to take a look at these resources.

To open FreeHand's Post resources using ResEdit (a free programmer's tool available from user groups and Apple's Web site), follow the steps below (see Figure 8-10).

1. Launch ResEdit.

2. Locate and open a copy of FreeHand. Always work on a copy of FreeHand so that you don't inadvertently damage the application (and you will).

FIGURE 8-10
Viewing FreeHand's
PostScript resources

When you open a copy of FreeHand with ResEdit, ResEdit displays the resources inside FreeHand.

Double-click the Post resource class.

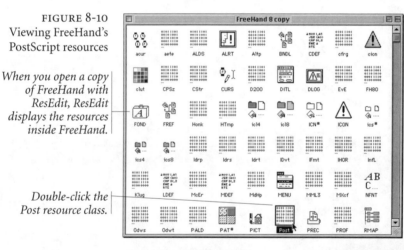

ResEdit displays a listing of the Post resources in FreeHand.

Double-click one of the Post resources...

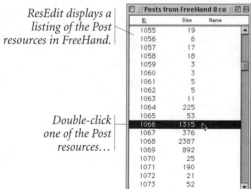

...and ResEdit displays the PostScript code inside the resource.

3. Type "post" to scroll down to the Post resource class and press Return to open the class (or double-click the icon).

4. ResEdit displays a list of the Post resources in FreeHand.

5. Double-click any one of the resources to see its contents.

6. When you're finished looking at the resources, close the file or quit ResEdit.

The resources are labelled by number, and it can take a while to locate the code you want. Since I've already gone through the resources, I can tell you where things are (see Table 8-2). When you see "\n" inside these resources, read it as a carriage return.

What's the point of all this? If you know where something is, you can change it. If you're happy with everything about the way FreeHand prints, or don't feel the urge to create your own Post-Script effects, or aren't curious, you can skip the rest of the chapter. If you want to change the way FreeHand prints crop marks, or add new PostScript line and fill effects, or really know what's going on under the hood, read on.

Variables in FreeHand's PostScript

Have you ever wondered how FreeHand tells your printer what to do? It's all quite clear, once you look at FreeHand's PostScript resources. How, for example, does FreeHand change to a new font, scale the font, and draw a string of text? If you open Post resource IDs 1228 and 1054 inside FreeHand, you'll see the resources shown in Figure 8-11.

FIGURE 8-11
Filling out the form

When you print (or export a file as an EPS), FreeHand takes the information (in this example, some text set in Sabon) in your publication and merges it with PostScript from its Post resources.

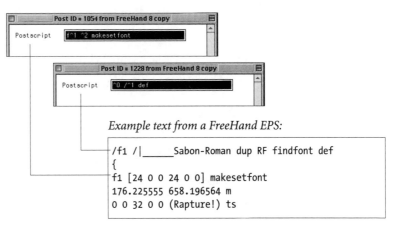

Post ID = 1054 from FreeHand 8 copy

Postscript   f^1 ^2 makesetfont

Post ID = 1228 from FreeHand 8 copy

Postscript   ^0 /^1 def

Example text from a FreeHand EPS:

```
/f1 /|_____Sabon-Roman dup RF findfont def
{
f1 [24 0 0 24 0 0] makesetfont
176.225555 658.196564 m
0 0 32 0 0 (Rapture!) ts
```

TABLE 8-2
Selected FreeHand
Post resources

Resource ID	What's in it
1066	Zoom text effect (known internally as "extrude")
1067	Inline text effect
1085	AltsysDict, FreeHand's main PostScript dictionary
1086	PostScript error handler, the code that prints PostScript error messages on your pages when something goes wrong
1127	Code for drawing crop marks
1128	Code for drawing registration marks
1147	supdict, which contains procedures used by the custom fill and custom stroke effects
1148	ropedict, the PostScript dictionary containing support routines for custom PostScript strokes
1149	texturedict, the PostScript dictionary containing code for rendering FreeHand's textured fills (Coquille, Sand, Denim, etc.)
1150	Bricks fill effect
1151	Tiger Teeth fill effect
1152	Circles fill effect
1153	Squares fill effect
1154	Hatch fill effect
1155	Random Leaves fill effect
1156	Random Grass fill effect
1157	Noise fill effect
1158	Black-and-White Noise fill effect
1160	Neon stroke effect
1161	Burlap textured fill
1162	Denim textured fill
1163	Sand textured fill
1164	Coarse Gravel textured fill
1165	Fine Gravel textured fill

Resource ID	What's in it
1166	Light Mezzo and Heavy Mezzo textured fills
1167	Medium Mezzo textured fill
1168	Coquille textured fill
1169	Arrow stroke effect
1170	Braid stroke effect
1171	Crepe stroke effect
1172	Snowflake stroke effect
1173	Teeth stroke effect
1174	Two Waves stroke effect
1175	Three Waves stroke effect
1176	Wedge stroke effect
1177	Star stroke effect
1178	Cartographer stroke effect
1179	Checker stroke effect
1180	Dot stroke effect
1181	Diamond stroke effect
1182	Right Diagonal stroke effect
1183	Left Diagonal stroke effect
1184	Rectangle stroke effect
1185	Ball stroke effect
1186	Squiggle stroke effect
1187	Swirl stroke effect
1188	Zigzag stroke effect
1189	Roman stroke effect
1190	Heart stroke effect

Compare the example with the Post resources. Do they look similar? You bet—the Post resource is a blank form for the code FreeHand sends (to your printer or to disk) when it specifies a font. The characters preceded by a caret (^) are FreeHand's internal representations of the data it'll use to fill out the form. Some of the tags are pretty easy to figure out—in this example, "^1" in Post ID 1228 equals "1" and "^0" equals "Sabon-Roman."

"^2" in Post ID 1054 is a little more complicated—it's an array containing the font's scaling. The example text is 24 points and hasn't been scaled horizontally (if it had been, you'd see a different number in the first position in the array).

Changing FreeHand's PostScript (Macintosh)

There's more to opening FreeHand's PostScript resources with Res-Edit than merely snooping around, of course. Once you have an idea of where things are, you can change them.

If you do change FreeHand's resources, however, bear in mind that you do so entirely at your own risk. These techniques are not supported by Macromedia or Peachpit Press—though I'll take a shot at helping you if you get stuck (see Appendix B, "About This Book," for contact information).

Making Textured Fills Transparent

If you want FreeHand's textured fills (Burlap, Denim, Coquille, etc.) to print with a transparent background, you can edit the Post resource that controls the way they print. This is one of the simplest, easiest, and most useful changes you can make to FreeHand's Post resources.

First, if you haven't already skipped ahead to build yourself a Post resource template, do so now. The example screens I'll show use the template, not the hexadecimal display.

To make FreeHand's textured fills transparent, follow these steps (see Figure 8-12).

1. Start ResEdit. Locate and open a copy of FreeHand.

2. Locate and select the Post resource class, and open it by pressing Return (or by double-clicking on the icon). ResEdit opens FreeHand's Post resource class and displays a list of all the Post resources inside FreeHand.

3. Select and open Post resource ID 1149.

FIGURE 8-12
Making textured
fills transparent

*Default (textured fill prints
with an opaque background).*

*Edited version (textured fill prints
with a transparent background).*

Color 1 overlay *Black overlay* *Color 1 overlay* *Black overlay*

*Use ResEdit to open a
copy of FreeHand.
Locate and open Post
resource ID 1149.*

*Scroll through the resource until
you locate these four lines of text.*

*Type "%" before
each of the four lines
and save this copy
of FreeHand.*

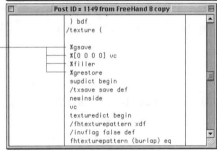

*When you use this copy of
FreeHand, textured fills will print
with transparent backgrounds.*

4. Scroll through the resource until you see the following lines.

```
gsave
[0 0 0 0] vc
filler
grestore
```

5. Type "%" in front of each of these lines.

```
%gsave
%[0 0 0 0] vc
%filler
%grestore
```

6. Press Command-S to save the edited copy of FreeHand.
   Quit ResEdit.

When you print textured fills from this copy of FreeHand, they'll print with transparent backgrounds (though they'll still be opaque on screen). What, exactly, this means depends on whether you've set the color you've applied to the textured fill to overprint or not, and whether the color is defined as a spot or process color.

If you're working with a spot color, and overprint the spot ink, the textured fill simply overprints any objects behind the textured fill—no part of the fill is knocked out of those objects. If, on the other hand, you've set the ink to knock out, FreeHand knocks out the solid areas of the textured fill from any objects behind the filled object. (Note that this is bound to produce trapping problems, as you can't trap the pattern inside the textured fill.) If you're working with a process color, the solid areas in the textured fill are knocked out of any objects behind the fill regardless of the overprinting settings of the process inks.

If you're using this technique, and want an opaque background behind one of your textured fills, you'll have to draw an opaque shape behind the object containing the fill. It's a small price to pay.

Creating External Resource Files (Macintosh)

One of FreeHand's most significant features is that you can extend the program using external resource files. How does this work? FreeHand, on startup, loads files of type AGX1 it finds in its folder. FreeHand loads the resources found in these files as if they were resources found inside your copy of FreeHand. If the resource IDs in your AGX1 files match the IDs of resources that FreeHand's already loaded, the resources in the external files override the internal resources.

Almost any preexisting resource in FreeHand can be replaced by an external resource file, and whole new resources can be added. External resource files, such as the ones shown in this chapter, aren't the same as FreeHand Xtras—you won't be able to add new drawing tools (for example) to FreeHand using external resource files.

If you're interested in learning how to write FreeHand Xtras (something that's *way* beyond the scope of this book), you'll find the FreeHand Xtras Software Development Kit on your FreeHand installation CD, or you can download the newest version of the XDK from Macromedia's web site. Install the XDK, and you'll be able to start coding your own FreeHand Xtras (in C and C++).

Still, the number of things you can do with external resource files is mind-boggling. The FreeHand extensions that I find most exciting are the ones that change the way FreeHand prints objects and the ones that add new PostScript strokes and fills. I've placed most of this book's discussion of external resource files in this chapter because these exciting modifications have to do with PostScript.

Why use external resource files to add PostScript effects instead of creating a UserPrep file? External resources make it easy to remember what variables a procedure needs, because you can add your own buttons, fields, and pop-up menus to the Fill and Stroke Inspectors. Creating external resource files is much more difficult than creating a UserPrep file, but it's worth it.

Copying resource templates. Before you can create any external resources for FreeHand, you've got to use ResEdit to copy three resource templates out of FreeHand—and then you've got to create one of your own. Don't let that deter you, though. This part is easy. You don't have to know the theory of how this stuff works—I don't. I just know what to do to get the results I want, and I'm happy to share the results of my trial-and-error experimentation with you.

We'll be using templates named GnEf, Post (PostScript; this resource type differs from ResEdit's built-in "Post" and "POST" resource templates, so don't think you can skip this one), UIrz, and Xvrs. If you developed any FreeHand 3 external resource files, you should note that the LnEf, FlEf, and Scrn resources are not used by FreeHand 4, 5, 7, and 8, and that the Post resource has a new format. "Great," I said when I first opened FreeHand 4 with ResEdit. "Everything I know is wrong."

I used ResEdit 2.1.3 to create my templates, and I strongly suggest you use this version or later. Versions 2.1 and after are light-years ahead of earlier versions in terms of their stability, capability, and ease of use. If it gets much better, they'll have to start charging money for it.

I cannot thank Apple Computer enough for this tool, which makes it (relatively) easy for Macintosh users to augment and customize their system software and applications. Nothing like ResEdit exists on any other platform (as far as I can tell—the tools in Visual C++ are getting better, but they're *not* free).

We'll start by copying the templates we need out of FreeHand, and then we'll create the missing one (see Figure 8-13).

1. Start ResEdit.

2. Open the copy of FreeHand.

3. Locate and open the TMPL ("template") resource class.

4. Select the TMPL resources named "CStr," "UIrz," "GnEf," and "Post."

5. Press Command-N to create a new resource file. ResEdit displays the Save dialog box. Enter a name for the file, and click the New button to create the file.

6. Paste the TMPL resources into the file.

7. Save the file.

FIGURE 8-13
Copying ResEdit
templates

Use ResEdit to open the copy of FreeHand.

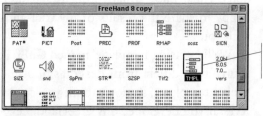

Double-click the TMPL (template) resource class.

Select these TMPL resources. This is a list, so you can hold down Shift to select "CStr," "UIrz," and "GnEf," and then hold down Command to select "Post."

Press Command-N to create a new resource file, enter a name for the file, and then paste the TMPL resources into it. Save the file.

Why are we going to all this trouble? ResEdit templates make the process of editing resources less painful than it would otherwise be, as shown in Figure 8-14.

FIGURE 8-14
What's the point
of templates?

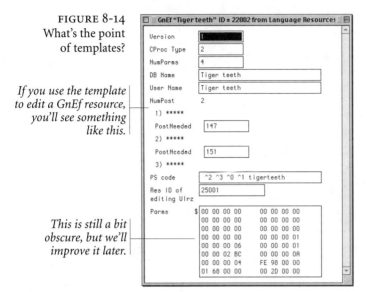

*If you use the template
to edit a GnEf resource,
you'll see something
like this.*

*This is still a bit
obscure, but we'll
improve it later.*

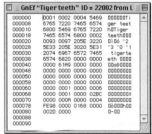

*If you don't use the GnEf
template, this is what you'll
have to work with. (Hope you
like hex!)*

What do these resources do? When you choose a custom fill or stroke from the Inspector's popup menu, FreeHand looks for a GnEf matching the menu item. The GnEf then tells FreeHand where to look for the UIrz resource, which contains the fields, buttons, and color wells that appear in the Inspector. Values in the GnEf then set the defaults for the Inspector items. The GnEf also tells FreeHand the IDs of the Post resources needed to print the effect.

The last part of the GnEf template we copied out of FreeHand isn't really finished. The section labeled "Parms" (which is programmer speak for "parameters") is hard to read. And that's bad, because the values here are the ones that set the default values for the controls we're going to be adding to the Inspector. We can fix it, though, by editing the copy we made of the TMPL resource (see Figure 8-15).

1. Open the resource file you saved earlier.

2. Open the TMPL resource class and open the GnEf template.

FIGURE 8-15
Fixing the
GnEf template

*Open the resource file
you created earlier.
Open the TMPL
resource class and
double-click the GnEf
template. Scroll to the
bottom of the template.*

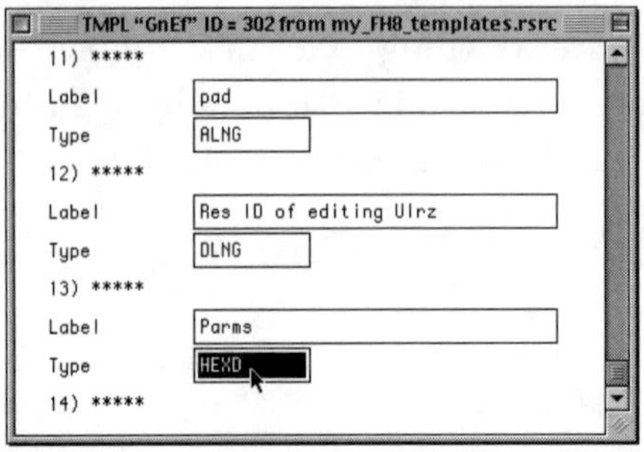

*Change item 13 as
shown, then select
item 14 and press
Command-K to add
another field.*

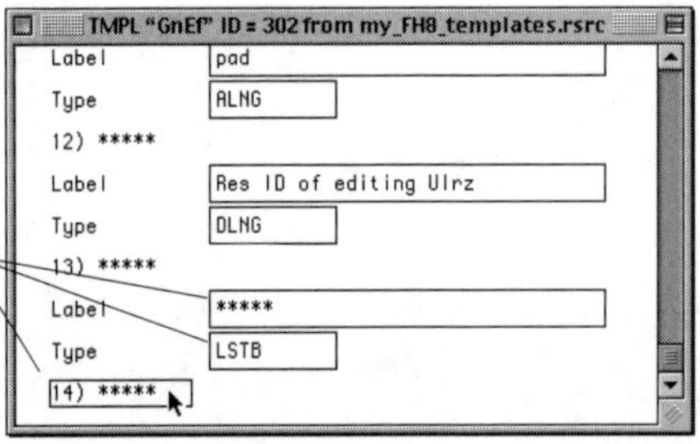

Add fields as shown.

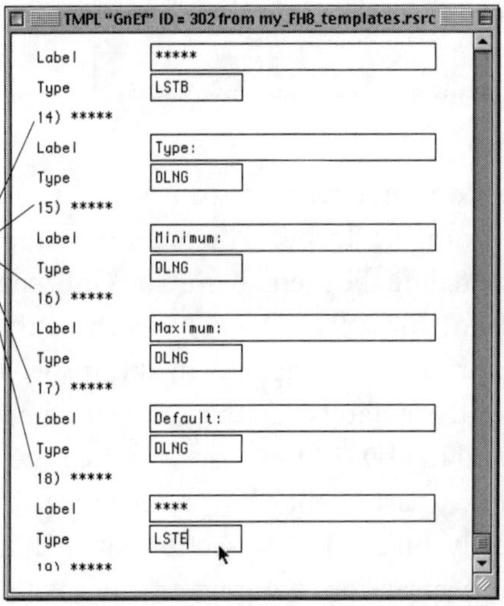

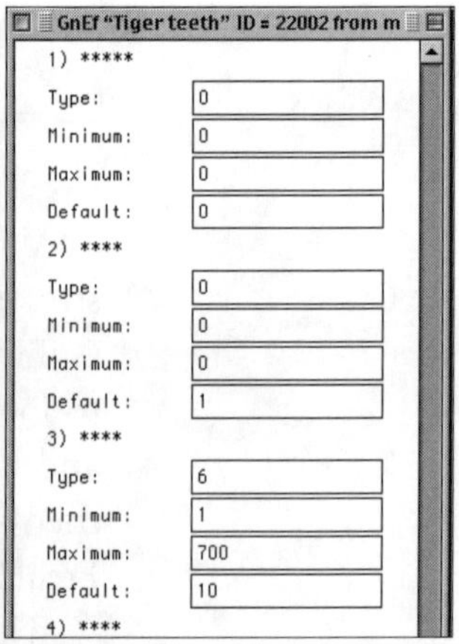

*When you open a GnEf using the
edited template, you'll see a more
readable view of the control
settings.*

3. Scroll through the template to the section with the label
"Parms." Enter "*****" in the Label field, then replace
"HEXD" with "DWRD".

4. Select the next field tag (number 14) and press Command-
K five times. ResEdit creates fields 15 through 18. Fill in the
fields as shown in Table 8-3.

TABLE 8-3
Filling in the GnEf
parameter fields

Field	Label	Type
13	*****	LSTB
14	Type	DLNG
15	Minimum	DLNG
16	Maximum	DLNG
17	Default	DLNG
18	*****	LSTE

5. Save the file.

GnEfs are the key to FreeHand's custom stroke and fill resources, as you can see in Figure 8-16 (on the next page).

Before we get to the fun part—creating our own FreeHand Post-Script extensions—there's one more resource type template to create—one for editing Xvrs resources (see Figure 8-17).

1. Open the resource file containing the resource templates.

2. Double-click the TMPL resource class to open it.

3. Press Command-K to create a new resource. ResEdit opens the resource.

4. Select the field tag "1)*****" in the template window and press Command-K to create a new field. Two new fields, Label and Type appear, along with the field tag "2)*****".

5. Type "Just type 0:" in the Label field, then type "CSTR" in the Type field.

6. Press Command-I to display the Info window for the template. Press Tab to move to the Name field. Type "Xvrs" in the Name field and press Command-W twice to close both the Info window and the TMPL window.

Your new resource template appears in the listing of templates. I'll explain the use of the Xvrs resource later.

FIGURE 8-16
The GnEf resource
keeps track of other
resource locations

*These fields point to
the Post resources
required to print the
effect (the number you
enter here is 1000
less than the actual
Post resource ID).*

*This field points to the
location of the effect's
UIrz resource.*

*These fields (from
here to the end of the
resource) tell FreeHand
how to work with the
buttons and fields
for the effect (which
are found in the
UIrz resource).*

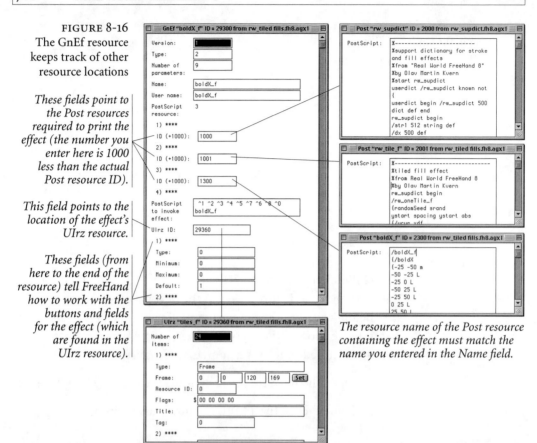

*The resource name of the Post resource
containing the effect must match the
name you entered in the Name field.*

Creating a Custom Stroke Resource

Arrows, hearts, and stars—FreeHand sure packs a lot of "border" strokes into the Stroke Inspector when you choose the Custom stroke type. But if you're a nut about fancy rules, you might want to create your own Custom strokes. And if you're *really* a nut, you might want to add them to the list of Custom strokes in the Stroke Inspector. I know I did. The following sections show you how to add the "hexagon" custom stroke to FreeHand's Stroke Inspector.

Creating a GnEf resource. First, we need to fill in a GnEf resource for our custom stroke (see Table 8-4).

1. Start ResEdit and create a new resource file. Paste the TMPL resource you created earlier into the new 5le.

2. Press Command-K and create a new GnEf resource. Fill in the fields in the GnEf resource as shown in Table 8-4.

FIGURE 8-17
Creating a template
for Xvrs resources

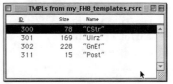

*Double-click the
TMPL resource c lass.*

*ResEdit opens the TMPL resource
class. Press Command-K.*

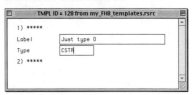

*ResEdit creates a new template.
Select the first field tag and press
Command-K.*

*ResEdit adds two fields. Fill in the
fields as shown. Press Command-I.*

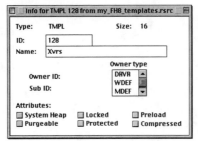

*ResEdit adds the template to the
list of available templates. Save
the file.*

*ResEdit displays the Info dialog box. Enter
"Xvrs" in the name field, then press
Command-W twice to close the Info dialog
box and the TMPL window.*

3. Press Command-I and give the GnEf resource an ID that's
   higher than that of any GnEf ID in FreeHand (above 23000
   is safe, but keep the ID number under 28000—I've gotten
   weird "out of memory" errors when using higher IDs).
   Enter the same name for the effect as you entered in the
   User name field of the GnEf.

4. Save your work.

Tip:
On Beyond Z

When you're creating new custom PostScript stroke effects, you've
got to make sure that they appear on the Stroke Inspector's popup
menu following the built-in effects. To do this, type characters in
front of the names of your effect so they'll get sorted to the end of
the list. I use "~" ("~Hexagon", for example).

TABLE 8-4
Creating a GnEf
resource for a custom
stroke effect

Field*	Example	What it means
Version	1	Version number
CProc Type	3	Type (2 = custom fill, 3 = custom line)
NumParms	4	Number of PostScript parameters—all custom fill effects have four: color, width, length, and spacing
DB Name	~Hexagon	The internal name for your custom stroke effect. This name must match the name of the last Post resource you refer to. Use a tilde (~) or other character to put your new effect at the end of the pop-up menu (see "On Beyond Z," later in this chapter, for the reason we need to do this).
User Name	~Hexagon	Name of the custom stroke effect as you want it to appear on the pop-up menu in the Stroke Inspector.
PostNeeded	147	Location of supdict (this resource ID is 1000 less than the actual Post ID—the actual Post containing the support dictionary is 1147).

* The field names shown here are the labels used by Macromedia in the templates we copied out of FreeHand. They're a little more obscure than I'd like, but they are what you'll see on your screen.

TABLE 8-4
Creating a resources
for a custom stroke
effect
(continued)

Field	Example	What it means
PostNeeded	148	Location of ropedict (again, subtract 1000— the Post ID is 1148).
PostNeeded	1200	This is the location of the PostScript you need to draw the object you're repeating along the path (again, this number is 1,000 less than the actual ID of the Post resource).
PS code	{~Hexagon} ^1 ^2 ^3 ^0 newrope	PostScript needed to draw the effect. The variables ^1, ^2, ^3, and ^0 refer to the Width field, the Length field, the Spacing field, and the color in the color well, respectively.
Res ID of editing UIrz	0	All custom PostScript stroke effects use the same UIrz.

Control	Field	Value
Control 1	Type	0 0 = color well, 2, 3 = text edit field, in points, 4 = text edit field, in degrees, 6 = text edit field, integer, 7 = boolean (a checkbox), 8 = text edit field, percentage
	Minimum	0
	Maximum	0
	Default	0

TABLE 8-4
Creating a resources
for a custom stroke
effect
(continued)

Control	Field	Value
Control 2	Type	3
	Minimum	0*
	Maximum	19660500*
	Default	1572840*
Control 3	Type	2
	Minimum	0*
	Maximum	19660500*
	Default	1572840*
Control 4	Type	3
	Minimum	0
	Maximum	19660500*
	Default	1572840*

* Multiply the measurement you want by 65,535 to come up with the value you enter here.

Creating a Post resource. Once you've gotten the drawing commands you need (see "Creating a PostScript Stroke," earlier in this chapter), it's time to create a Post resource (see Figure 8-18).

1. If you're not still in ResEdit, start ResEdit and open the external resource file you've been working on.

2. Press Command-K and add a new Post resource.

3. Open the Post resource you created and paste the code from your word processor into the resource.

4. Set the Post resource ID to the last ID you entered in the GnEF (in our earlier example, you'd use ID 2200). Give the Post resource the same name as you've entered in the User name field of the GnEf (in our example, "~Hexagon").

5. Save the resource file.

Adding an Xvrs Resource. The last thing you need to do, before you launch FreeHand and test your new custom stroke effect, is to

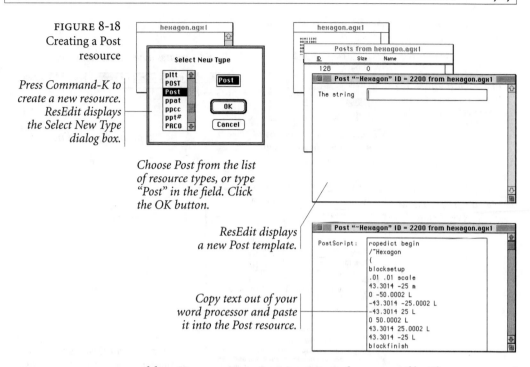

FIGURE 8-18
Creating a Post
resource

*Press Command-K to
create a new resource.
ResEdit displays
the Select New Type
dialog box.*

*Choose Post from the list
of resource types, or type
"Post" in the field. Click
the OK button.*

*ResEdit displays
a new Post template.*

*Copy text out of your
word processor and paste
it into the Post resource.*

add an Xvrs resource to your external resource file. If your external resource file contains an Xvrs resource, FreeHand won't complain about the file during startup (see Figure 8-19).

1. Open the resource file you added the GnEf and Post resources to.

2. Create a new resource of type Xvrs.

3. Enter "0" (or anything, for that matter) in the Xvrs resource.

4. Give the Xvrs resource an ID of 9999.

5. Save the file.

Tip:
Omitting Xvrs
Resources on
Purpose

In some cases, you may want to omit Xvrs resources from your external resource files because you may want to choose which external resource files FreeHand loads. To keep the resource from loading, click the Cancel button when FreeHand displays the "earlier version" message. If you do this, you won't have to move files around in the Finder to keep FreeHand from loading them.

FIGURE 8-19
Creating an
Xvrs resource

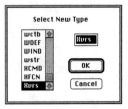

*Press Command-K to
create a new resource.
ResEdit displays the
Select New Type dialog
box.*

*Choose Xvrs from the list of
resource templates, or type
"Xvrs" in the field.*

ResEdit creates a new Xvrs resource.

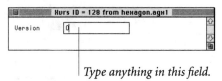

Type anything in this field.

*Press Command-I to
display the Info window
for the Xvrs Resource.*

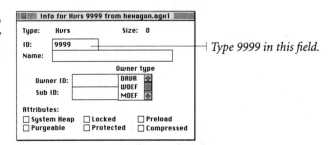

Type 9999 in this field.

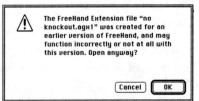

*Once you've added an Xvrs resource
to your external resource file, you
shouldn't see this error message again.*

Setting the resource file's type and creator. If an external resource
file doesn't have the correct file type and creator, FreeHand ignores
it. Here's how to add those key bits of information (see Figure 8-20).

1. Choose Get Info for *filename* (where *filename* is the name
   you gave the file when you created it) from the File menu.
   ResEdit displays the Info dialog box for the file.

2. Type "AGX1" in the Type field and type "FH80" in the
   Creator field.

3. Press Command-W to close the dialog box. ResEdit asks if
   you want to save your changes. You do, so click Yes.

4. Quit ResEdit.

Testing your new external resource file. Test your new external
resource file by opening FreeHand, drawing a path, and pressing

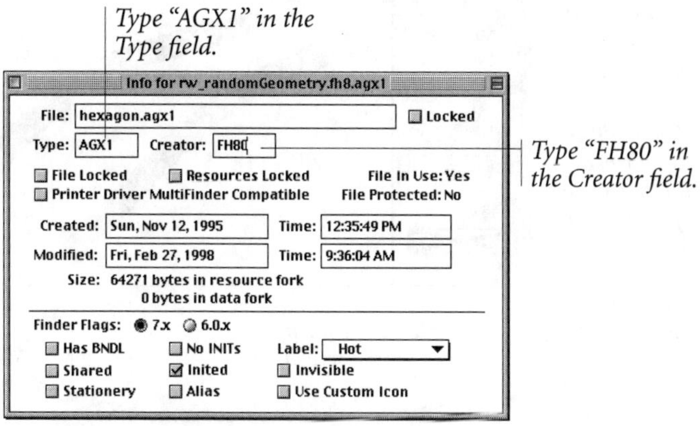

FIGURE 8-20
Setting the file
type and creator

*Type "AGX1" in the
Type field.*

Info for rw_randomGeometry.fh8.agx1

File: hexagon.agx1   ☐ Locked

Type: AGX1   Creator: FH80

☐ File Locked   ☐ Resources Locked   File In Use: Yes
☐ Printer Driver MultiFinder Compatible   File Protected: No

Created: Sun, Nov 12, 1995   Time: 12:35:49 PM

Modified: Fri, Feb 27, 1998   Time: 9:36:04 AM

Size: 64271 bytes in resource fork
0 bytes in data fork

Finder Flags: ● 7.x ○ 6.0.x
☐ Has BNDL   ☐ No INITs   Label: Hot ▾
☐ Shared   ☑ Inited   ☐ Invisible
☐ Stationery ☐ Alias   ☐ Use Custom Icon

*Type "FH80" in
the Creator field.*

Command-Option-L to display the Stroke Inspector. Choose Custom from the Stroke Type popup menu. Can you see your example stroke effect on the Effect popup menu? If so, select it. If not, run through the procedures above and try to see where you made an error (I got tired of getting errors because of mismatches between the PostScript procedure name, the "User name," and the "Internal name," so I started using the same name for all three purposes).

Apply the stroke effect to a path and try printing the file. If it prints, congratulations! You've just added a stroke effect to your copy of FreeHand (see Figure 8-21). If it doesn't print, it's most likely you've either typed something wrong or have made an incorrect entry in the Post resource containing the drawing commands (suspect this first if you get an "undefined" PostScript error).

Adding a preview of your stroke effect. As far as I know, you won't be able to add a preview image of your custom stroke effect, as FreeHand does for its built-in effects. At this point, I can get *something* to appear in the preview window, but it's never what I want. If you figure it out, please give me a call!

**Tip:
Space Out**

Make sure that you add a space or a carriage return following the last character of your PostScript code. If you don't, characters FreeHand sends following your effect might get appended to one of your procedure names, resulting in PostScript files that won't print. This is especially true for the PostScript you enter in the GnEf— FreeHand's going to put a "Q" right at the end of it. If there's no space, you're going to be in trouble.

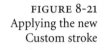

FIGURE 8-21
Applying the new
Custom stroke

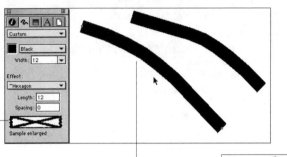

This isn't really a preview of the stroke! I haven't found a way to get my preview to appear here.

If FreeHand displays an "out of memory" error when you choose the Custom stroke, it's likely that the names and/or resource IDs in the resource file don't match.

You won't see your new stroke on the screen...

...but you'll get something like this when you print.

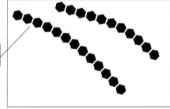

Creating Custom Fill Resources

Just as you can create resources that add a new Custom stroke type to the Stroke Inspector, you can add Custom fills to FreeHand's Fill Inspector. To do this, you create new UIrz, GnEf, Post, and Xvrs resources, then save them in a resource file. The only new item here is the UIrz resource—it defines the user interface items displayed in the Fill Inspector.

Creating a UIrz resource for a custom fill. The contents of the UIrz resources are controls: the buttons, fields, and static text you see in the Fill Inspector. Your custom fill effect can use up to ten controls.

Creating UIrz resources is a complex process, and the only way I can think of to make it easier is to show you how to create an example custom PostScript fill. I'll use the fill effect "boldX" that we used in the example UserPrep we created earlier. I'll try to explain what we're doing as we work through the process.

Start ResEdit and create a new resource file in your FreeHand folder. Set the file's type to AGX1 and its creator to FH80 (if you've forgotten how to do this, refer back to the procedure for creating external resource files, earlier in this chapter). Create a new UIrz resource and fill it in as shown in Table 8-5.

The Flags field in the UIrz resource tells FreeHand how to format and how to interpret the control. Table 8-6 shows what the different flags mean.

Item	Field	Enter	What it does
TABLE 8-5 Example UIrz Resource			
1	Widget Name	Frame	"Frame" is the area of the Inspector that the effect's controls take up. Every UIrz resource starts with a frame.
	Frame*	0 0 121 161	This rectangle takes up (more or less) all of the available space in the Inspector (that is, everything but the Inspector buttons and the Fill Type pop-up menu).
	Resource ID	0	Leave this at zero for the UIrz resources you create.
	Flags	$00000000	See Table 8-6 for a description.
	Title		If the control has a title, enter it here. Otherwise, leave this field blank.
	Tag	0	Leave this set to zero for the UIrz resources you create.
2	Widget Name	ColorWell	Creates a FreeHand color well.
	Frame	7 140 115 160	Defines a frame for the color well. Note that this frame is wide enough to display the name of any color you drop into it.
	Resource ID		0
	Flags	$000B0002	See text.
	Title		
	Tag	0	

* Enter these four values in the fields named "Low X," "Low Y," "High X," and "High Y." FreeHand's rectangles—whether they're for a Frame, a TextView, a BtnView, or a ColorWell, are measured, PostScript-style, from their lower-left corners. The lower-left corner of the Inspector, therefore, is 0,0. The measurements are in pixels.

Item	Field	Enter	What it does
3	Widget Name	TextView	Creates both static text (labels) and text edit fields.
	Frame	76 106 108 122	
	Resource ID	0	
	Flags	$00030002	
	Title		
	Tag	0	
4	Widget Name	TextView	
	Frame	42 106 74 122	
	Resource ID	0	
	Flags	$00030002	
	Title		
	Tag	0	
5	Widget Name	TextView	
	Frame	76 87 108 103	
	Resource ID	0	
	Flags	$00030002	
	Title		
	Tag	0	
6	Widget Name	TextView	
	Low X	76 68 108 84	
	Resource ID	0	
	Flags	$00030002	
	Title		
	Tag	0	
7	Widget Name	BtnView	Creates buttons—checkboxes, radio buttons, and icon buttons.
	Frame	6 49 116 63	
	Resource ID	0	
	Flags	$00050002	
	Title	Random rotation	
	Tag	0	

TABLE 8-5
Example
UIrz Resource
(continued)

Item	Field	Enter	What it does
8	Widget Name	BtnView	
	Frame	6 36 116 48	
	Resource ID	0	
	Flags	$00050002	
	Title	Random skewing	
	Tag	0	
9	Widget Name	TextView	
	Frame	1 106 40 122	
	Resource ID	0	
	Flags	$00800002	
	Title	Size:	
	Tag	0	
10	Widget Name	TextView	
	Frame	1 87 74 103	
	Resource ID	0	
	Flags	$00800002	
	Title	Spacing:	
	Tag	0	
11	Widget Name	TextView	
	Frame	1 68 74 84	
	Resource ID	0	
	Flags	$00800002	
	Title	Angle:	
	Tag	0	
12	Widget Name	TextView	
	Frame	108 68 120 84	
	Resource ID	0	
	Flags	$00000002	
	Title	°	
	Tag	0	

Item	Field	Enter	What it does
13	Widget Name	MUView	Draws a dotted line across the Inspector, separating different sections.
	Frame	0 136 121 137	
	Resource ID	0	
	Flags	$00002002	
	Title		
	Tag	0	
14	Widget Name	MUView	
	Frame	0 65 121 66	
	Resource ID	0	
	Flags	$00002002	
	Title		
	Tag	0	
15	Widget Name	MUView	
	Frame	0 32 121 33	
	Resource ID	0	
	Flags	$00002002	
	Title		
	Tag	0	
16	Widget Name	TextView	
	Frame	1 3 121 15	
	Resource ID	0	
	Flags	$00040002	
	Title	Real World FreeHand 8	Your message here
	Tag	0	
17	Widget Name	TextView	
	Frame	40 125 76 138	
	Resource ID	0	
	Flags	$00040002	
	Title	min:	
	Tag	0	

Item	Field	Enter	What it does
18	Widget Name	TextView	
	Frame	74 125 110 138	
	Resource ID	0	
	Flags	$00040002	
	Title	max:	
	Tag	0	

Item	Flag	What it means
Any	$00000002	Display text in nine-point Geneva
MUView	$00002000	Draw a gray line on either side of the text
ColorWell	$00010000	Color swatches can be dropped in
	$00020000	Color swatches can be dragged out
	$00080000	Display the color name to the right of the color well
TextView	$00008000	Left-align text
	$00040000	Center text
	$00800000	Right-align text
	$00010000	Draw a border around the text
	$00020000	Editable field
	$00400000	Italicize text
	$00080000	Make text bold
BtnView	$00010000	Button toggles when clicked (like a checkbox)
	$00040000	Button is a checkbox
	$00080000	Button is a radio button
	$00100000	Button is an icon button

Different flags can be added together. To produce a color well you can drag color swatches out of (00020000) or drop color swatches into (00010000), which also displays the name of the color to the right of the color well (00080000), and displays that name in nine-point Geneva (00000002), you'd enter 000B0002 ("B" because 8 + 2 + 1 = B in the hexadecimal universe—where you count 0, 1, 2, 3, 4, 5, 6, 7, 8, 9, A, B, C, D, E, F).

Creating a GnEf resource for a custom fill. You create GnEf resources for custom fills exactly as you would for a custom stroke effect (see "Creating a GnEf Resource," earlier in this chapter). For our example custom fill, enter the values shown in Table 8-7.

Now that we've got the code we need, it's time to create a new Post resource.

TABLE 8-7
Example GnEf

Field	What you enter	
Version	1	
CProc Type	2	
NumParms	9	
DB Name	boldX_f	
Name	boldX_f	
PostNeeded	1000	*Make sure you enter a space here.*
PostNeeded	1300	
PS Code	^1 ^2 ^3 ^4 ^5 ^7 ^6 ^8 ^0 boldX_f	
Res ID of editing UIrz	29360	

Field	Label	What you enter
UIrz item 1*	Type	0
	Minimum	0
	Maximum	0
	Default	1

* The GnEf resource refers to the UIrz controls in order and starts counting following the Frame item in the UIrz. In this case, the color well is UIrz item #1, UIrz items 2 and 3 set the minimum and maximum size of the "X," and UIrz items 5 and 6 are the checkboxes controlling random rotation and random skewing, respectively. When FreeHand uses the values from these items in the PostScript it sends to the printer (as directed by the GnEf), everything shifts down by one—the value in UIrz item 1 is plugged in for variable "^0", the value for UIrz item 2 is entered for "^1", and so on.

	Field	Label	What you enter
TABLE 8-7 Example GnEf (continued)	UIrz item 2	Type	3
		Minimum	65535
		Maximum	6553500
		Default	786432
	UIrz item 3	Type	3
		Minimum	65535
		Maximum	6553500
		Default	786432
	UIrz item 3	Type	3
		Minimum	65535
		Maximum	6553500
		Default	786432
	UIrz item 5	Type	4
		Minimum	-23592960
		Maximum	23592960
		Default	1966080
	UIrz item 6	Type	7
		Minimum	0
		Maximum	1
		Default	0
	UIrz Item 7	Type	7
		Minimum	0
		Maximum	1
		Default	0
	UIrz Item 8	Type	7
		Minimum	0
		Maximum	1
		Default	0
	UIrz Item 9	Type	7
		Minimum	0
		Maximum	1
		Default	0

1. Start ResEdit (if it's not already running) and open the external resource file you've been working on (if it's not already open).

2. Create two new Post resources with the ID numbers 2000 and 2300.

3. Copy the PostScript code from pages 659 to 663 (beginning with "%Real World FreeHand User Prep" and ending with "%end of rw_tile_f") and paste it into Post resource 2000. Copy the PostScript code defining the "boldX_f" fill effect from page 659 and paste it into Post resource 2300. Name the Post resource 2300 "boldX_f".

4. Save the resource file.

Add an Xvrs resource to the file (see "Adding an Xvrs Resource," earlier in this chapter) and save the file. The next time you start FreeHand, you should see a new menu item, "boldX_f," on FreeHand's list of custom fills in the Fill Inspector (see Figure 8-22). When you choose this item from the popup menu, FreeHand should display the controls for your new effect in the Inspector.

FIGURE 8-22
Your new custom
fill effect

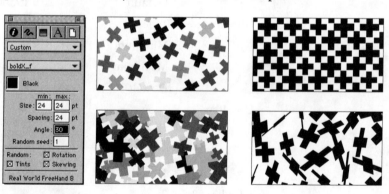

PostScript Postscript

Though this has been the hardest chapter in the book to write, it's also been the most fun. At the same time, I feel I've only scratched the surface of what you can do with FreeHand and PostScript. I know some of it looks a little intimidating, at first, but I urge you to give it a try. You'll learn how to create incredible special effect— and you'll learn a lot about how FreeHand works, too.

FreeHand and the Web

to fireworks @ 100%

Brushes and Fills

Brush | Fill | Effect

Pencil

Colored

Netscape: AE.FH8

Home   Search   Guide   Images   Print   Security

Volume 6 Number 1

▶ Letters

▶ Field Notes

▶ The French Conne

Ancient Egypt and the First
by Olav Martin Kvern

When the tired remnants of
Napoleon Bonaparte's Egyptia
expedition returned to France,
they brought with them more th
what you'll see in the Louvre...

▶ Khufu

Searching for scarabs at
a Parisian flea market...
by **Leslie Renee Simons**

▶ Dig This
    her adventures
    d Egyptologist...

Amateur Egyptologist

Back   Forward   Reload   Home

Location   file:///Tavia/amateur%20egyptologist/html/AE FH8001.html

that's a moiré

Layer 1

Scene 1   1   24.0 fps   0.0s

Controller

I think we'll look back on the 1990s as a revolutionary period in human communication. It's when we discovered a new publishing medium: the Web. We didn't *invent* it this decade—computer networks, including the Internet, had existed since the dawn of the computing age, predating even the microcomputers that sit on our desktops. What turned the little-known Internet into the ubiquitous Web was the development of a kind of page-description language, HTML (for Hypertext Markup Language) and programs capable of drawing HTML pages on computer screens (which, today, we refer to as "browsers").

The HTML/browser combination is to the Web as moveable type was to printing, or PostScript and PageMaker were to desktop publishing. By this I mean that the *idea* of the Web had existed for some time, but it took NCSA Mosaic and Netscape Navigator to make it a practical reality. In the space of a couple of years, the Web has become a legitimate publishing medium, just like putting ink on paper.

We're still working out ways to use this medium, just as early printers took some time to figure out what and how to publish using moveable type. It took around forty years—from the time Gutenberg printed his first Bible to the time Aldus Manutius printed his first book—for the paperback book to appear, for example. Things happen faster these days. Web publishing has already been through several generations of publishing technology—and the pace of change hasn't shown any sign of slowing down.

I have to admit that I'm a late comer to the Web. I don't know nearly as much about it as I do about putting ink on paper. I don't exactly "surf" the Web—I wade, and sometimes flounder. Still, I have learned a few things about preparing FreeHand graphics for use on Web sites and in Web pages.

Cast of Characters

If you're new to the Web, you're probably confused by the terminology. I know am. It seems that just as I learn a new file format or programming approach, another appears to take its place. What's Shockwave, or Flash, for that matter? What's a GIF, and when do you want to use one instead of a JPEG (whatever that is)? What are URLs, or "browser-safe" color palettes? I'll take a shot at explaining these buzzwords and concepts.

First, a URL (for Universal Resource Locator) is an address to something—a web page, a newsgroup, or a file—on the Web. URLs are the key to navigating the Web. Shockwave and Flash started life as separate beings, but are now merged into Shockwave Flash, a method for displaying vector (or "object") graphics and animation on the Web. GIF and JPEG are both bitmap formats, and are commonly used to display images in Web pages (each has advantages and disadvantages).

Why not just use TIFF and EPS? In printed publications, quality is king; on the Web, it's file size. The file size of the graphics you include in your web page determines the time it'll take for someone to download and view the page. What happens when graphics take too long to load? Your audience moves on—they hit the Back button, or the Stop button, in their browser. And you've lost them.

So the solution is to compress the graphics in your Web pages. Unfortunately, this compromises the quality of the images. Which also makes your audience wander.

It's another balancing act. You want the graphics you use to look as good as they possibly can, but take up as little space (and downloading time) as possible. The GIF and JPEG image formats give you different ways to reduce the size of the images you use, while Shockwave Flash gives you a way to include FreeHand's vector graphics in Web publications. All of these formats do their work in very little space.

First Things First   All browsers can display files saved in the GIF or JPEG formats. As I write this, you'll need to install the appropriate plug-in to view Shockwave Flash graphics or Acrobat PDF files, but I understand the next version of Netscape Navigator will include support for Flash animations.

Macromedia refers to "Shockwave-compatible" browsers. What do they mean? They mean Netscape Navigator or Microsoft Internet Explorer equipped with a plug-in (or plug-ins) for viewing Shockwave Flash files. Where can you get these plug-ins? You can get them from your FreeHand installation CD, but I'd recommend you go to Macromedia's web site at http://www.macromedia.com and download the most current version of the Shockwave Flash plug-in.

Which Format?   Which file format should you use? That depends on the type of graphic, and on your expectations of your audience.

◆ If you expect your audience has the Shockwave Flash plug-in installed (or won't mind downloading and installing it), you can export FreeHand objects in the Flash format.

◆ If the graphic you're dealing with is made up of FreeHand paths and you don't want to require that your audience have the Shockwave Flash plug-in installed, use GIF or PNG.

◆ If you're working with a natural image—say, a picture you scanned or any bitmap image that contains smooth gradations of color or a very large number of colors—use JPEG.

◆ If you're distributing an entire publication over the Web, or think that your audience might want to print the publication, export the publication as a PDF (see Chapter 4, "Importing and Exporting"). Your audience can then either view the PDF in their browser (if they have the Acrobat PDF plug-in installed), or download the PDF and view or print it using the Acrobat Reader (both the Reader and the plug-in are available from Adobe's Web site at http://www.adobe.com).

Why use GIF instead of JPEG? Because most FreeHand artwork (paths and text) contains a fairly small number of colors. GIFs use color palettes to store the colors used in the file—which means that you can make your file size smaller by reducing the number of colors in the palette. If you're only using four colors, your GIF's color palette should contain *only* those four colors. JPEG images, on the other hand, use RGB to specify the color value of every pixel in the image—which makes the file larger.

Why use PNG (pronounced "ping") instead of GIF? Many people (mostly software developers) are offended and/or inconvenienced by the fact that Unisys, the owner of the patent on the LZW compression scheme that is an integral part of GIF, wants anyone writing software that reads or writes GIF to pay them a license fee. At one point, Unisys seemed to expect a fee from anyone *using* the GIF images on their web sites, but they seem to have given up on that. In any case, PNG is a free (i.e., "legally unencumbered") alternative to GIF, offers a number of advantages over GIF, and is now supported by most web browsers. For more information on PNG, refer to the PNG specification at www.boutell.com/boutell/png or the PNG home page (it's funny) at www.cdrom.com/pub/png.

Exporting GIF Images

The process of exporting a GIF is shown in Chapter 4, "Importing and Exporting." In this chapter, I'll talk a little bit about the GIF Options dialog box—which you reach by clicking the More button in the Bitmap Export Defaults dialog box (see Figure 9-1).

Choose the palette you want to save in the exported GIF file from the Palette pop-up menu—the choice you make here affects the colors displayed in the palette preview window in the middle of the dialog box.

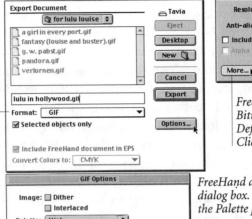

Choose Export from the File menu, choose GIF from the Formats pop-up menu, and then click the Options button in the Export Document dialog box.

FreeHand displays the Bitmap Export Defaults dialog box. Click the More button.

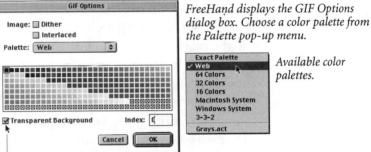

FreeHand displays the GIF Options dialog box. Choose a color palette from the Palette pop-up menu.

Available color palettes.

Turn on the Transparent Background option and choose the color you want to make transparent, if you want (215 is the white background of a FreeHand page).

Photoshop Color Table dialog box.

If you've chosen the Exact Palette option from the Palette pop-up menu, and have chosen to anti-alias the image (by choosing anything other than None in the Anti Aliasing pop-up menu)...

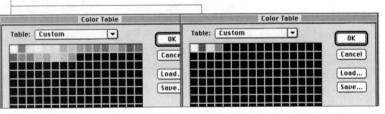

...the GIF image you export will have more colors in its palette...

...than the same image without anti-aliasing.

Choose Web to use the standard color lookup table used by most Web browsers (see "Color and the Web," later in this chapter). Choose "Exact Palette" to use only those colors actually used in the objects you're exporting. When you choose "Exact Palette," the palette preview disappears. The 64, 32, and 16-color palettes are all cut-down versions of the Web palette. Most of the time, choosing these palettes means you'll get a poor match between the colors in your FreeHand publication and the colors in the GIF—

choosing one of these palettes, on the other hand, reduces the size of the GIF file. The 3-3-2 palette is the color palette used by the FreeHand GIF Export Xtra.

If you don't see the color palette you need in the list of palettes, you can add palette files from Photoshop or xRes. Once you've created a palette file, save it in the Palettes folder inside the Macromedia folder inside your System folder (on the Macintosh), or in the ~:\Program Files\Macromedia\FH8\English\Xtras directory (in Windows). The palette appears on the Palettes pop-up menu in the GIF Options dialog box.

Turn on the Transparent Background option and click a color in the palette preview (or enter a value in the Index field) to define a color as transparent (see Figure 9-2). This does not work (for me, at least) unless you've turned on the Include Alpha Channel option in the Bitmap Export Defaults dialog box.

Finally, turn off the Dithering option unless you're exporting images you've imported into your FreeHand publication—you'll save lots of space.

FIGURE 9-2
Making the
background of a
GIF transparent

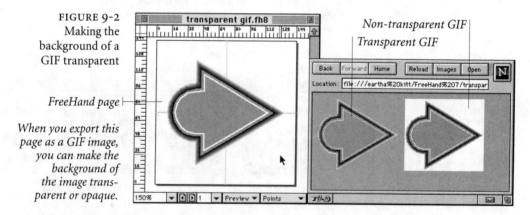

FreeHand page

When you export this page as a GIF image, you can make the background of the image transparent or opaque.

Non-transparent GIF
Transparent GIF

Creating Shockwave Flash Graphics

You can export FreeHand graphics in the Shockwave Flash format. Here are a few things you need to keep in mind.

◆ The Flash file you create is the same size (in pixels) as the FreeHand page is (in points).

◆ FreeHand won't export paths with line caps other than Butt Cap (the default) or Join settings of other than Miter Join (the default).

◆ Any URL references you've applied to FreeHand graphics are retained in the exported Flash file.

◆ PostScript, Patterned, Custom, and Textured fills won't appear in files you export using the Create Flash Image Xtra, nor will PostScript, Patterned, or Custom strokes.

◆ Clipping paths are not exported to the Flash format—the contents of the clipping path will be included, but they won't be pasted inside the path (it's as if you'd chosen "Cut Contents" before exporting).

◆ All colors in the exported artwork are converted to RGB. If the colors were defined as RGB in your FreeHand publication (as they will be if you use the "web safe" color library), they won't change—otherwise, they probably will. Remember to turn FreeHand's color management system off before you save Flash files.

◆ FreeHand's text effects (Strikethrough, Zoom Text, Underline, Shadow, Inline, and Highlight) are not exported to the Flash file format. Inline graphics, however, are exported.

To save FreeHand graphics as a Shockwave Flash graphic (or animation), follow these steps (see Figure 9-3).

1. Choose Export from the File menu. FreeHand displays the Export Document dialog box.

2. Choose Flash 2 SWF from the Format pop-up menu. FreeHand displays the Flash Export As dialog box.

3. Enter a name for the Flash file, if necessary, then click the Options button. FreeHand displays the Flash Export Options dialog box.

4. Use the options in the Flash Export Options dialog box to control the way your publication's is converted into the Flash format.

FIGURE 9-3
Creating
Flash graphics

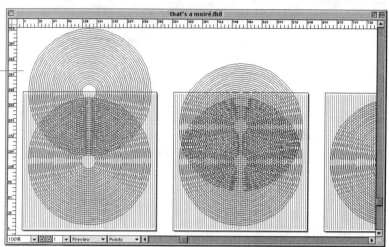

FreeHand pages

While this illustration shows FreeHand graphics being used in a Flash movie, you can also use the Flash format to create "still" pictures that look great (or at least better than their GIF or JPEG equivalents) on your web pages.

Press Command-Shift-R/Ctrl-Shift-R to display the Export Document dialog box.

Choose Flash 2 SWF from the Format pop-up menu, then click the Options button.

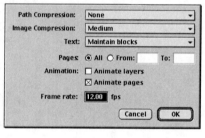

FreeHand displays the Flash Export Options dialog box. Set up the options the way you want them (for more details, see the body of the text), then click the OK button.

FreeHand returns you to me Export Document dialog box. Click the Export button to save the file.

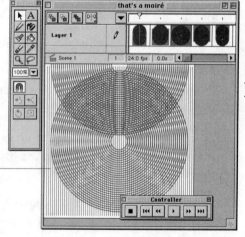

You can view Flash images in a Web browser (provided you've installed the Shock-wave Flash plug-in), or embed the movie (or frames from a movie) in an HTML file (treat them as you would any other graphic).

Movie open in Flash 3.

Select the amount of compression you want to apply to any paths from the Path Compression pop-up menu. This control is something like the Simplify path operation, and controls the number of points used to describe each path in the Flash file.

Choose the compression method and amount you want to apply to any images in your publication using the Image Compression pop-up menu.

Set the range of pages you want to export.

When you turn on the Animate Pages option or the Animate Layers option, each page or layer in the range of pages you're exporting becomes a separate frame in a Flash movie. When you turn on the both options, each page becomes a "scene" in Flash and each layer on the page becomes a frame inside that scene. With both option turned off, FreeHand exports each page in the range of pages you've chosen as a separate Flash SWF file.

Finally, set the frame rate you want to use in the Flash movie. Rates equal to or higher than 12 frames per second (fps) produce smooth animation.

4. Click the OK button to close the Flash Export Options dialog box, then click the Save button to save the pages you've specified as Flash files.

Embed the Flash graphic (or graphics) in your Web pages as you would any other type of graphic, or open and edit them using the Flash application.

Using the Release to Layers Xtra

It's clear from the above that you can create Flash movies one frame at a time by manipulating FreeHand's layers and pages. In addition, you can use the Release to Layers Xtra to automate some of that (potentially laborious) process. When you select a blend, a text block, or text on a path, FreeHand disassembles the object, placing each constituent part of the object on a separate layer (see Figure 9-4).

When you export the resulting objects and layers to a Flash animation, FreeHand produces a movie, playing the objects from the bottom to the top of the stack of layers, in order.

FIGURE 9-4
Release to Layers

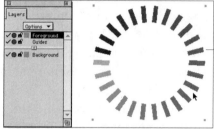

A blend joined to a circular path.

Choose Release to Layers from
the Animate submenu of the
Xtras menu.

FreeHand ungroups the blend
and moves each object in the
blend to its own layer.

New layer names
appear in the Layers
palette.

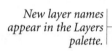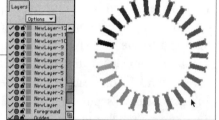

Export the page using
the Flash format.

When you open the file
in Flash, you'll see a
movie made up of the
objects in the blend.

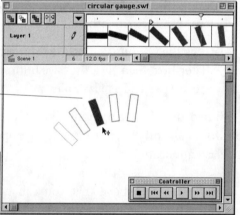

When you view the Flash
movie in a browser, you'll see
a movie of the objects in the
blend moving along a path.

What happens when you run the
Release to Layers Xtra on a text block?

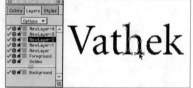

FreeHand converts the text to paths,
then moves each character to its own
layer.

From FreeHand to Fireworks

Fireworks is an amazing new web-oriented drawing and file processing program from Macromedia. It's a vector drawing program, like FreeHand, but you can apply "natural media" effects—such as brush strokes—to the paths you draw. It's something like working with an image editing program like MetaCreations Painter. The difference is that the paths *remain* paths—you don't have to convert them to images to get all the cool effects.

The best way to learn more about Fireworks is to get a demo copy from Macromedia's web site. It's not just a web drawing program, either—it can add great special effects to FreeHand publications you want to print on paper (see Figure 9-5).

FIGURE 9-5
Opening a FreeHand
file in Fireworks

*Save your
FreeHand file.*

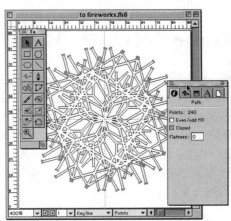
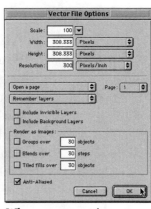

*When you open or import a
FreeHand file, Fireworks
displays the Vector File Options
dialog box.*

*After Fireworks converts
the objects in the
FreeHand file into
Fireworks paths, text,
and placed images, you
can have some fun with
Fireworks' special
effects.*

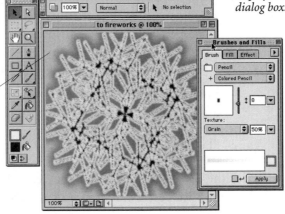

There's no real trick to getting FreeHand paths into Fireworks. You can copy and paste or drag and drop, but you'll get more control over the conversion process if you import or open your Free-Hand files. When you open or import a FreeHand file, Fireworks displays the Vector File Options dialog box (this dialog box doesn't appear if you copy and paste or drag and drop). Use the controls in the Vector File Options dialog box to specify what you want done with the various parts of the imported file (should invisible layers be included? how about background layers?). You can even choose to convert parts of the file into images as you import them.

Once you've opened the file, you can edit and format the objects in it just as you would any other Fireworks objects.

Attaching URLs to FreeHand Objects

Want to put nifty navigational controls in your Web page? Why not draw the controls in FreeHand, then attach a URL to each control? You can do this using FreeHand's URL Editor Xtra. When you export to Flash, or use the Insta.html Xtra to export your pages as HTML, your URL references are retained. You can't add Free-Hand's URL references to GIF or JPEG images you export. To attach a URL to an object in a FreeHand publication, follow these steps (see Figure 9-6).

1. Select an object (URLs cannot be applied to groups).

2. Display the URL Editor, if it's not already visible (choose URL Editor from the Xtras submenu of the Window menu).

3. Choose New from the URL Editor's Options pop-up menu. FreeHand displays the New URL dialog box.

4. Enter the URL in the field, then click the OK button to assign the URL to the selected object.

To apply an existing URL (that is, one you've already added to the list of URLs in the URL Editor) to an object, you can either click the URL when you have the object selected, or drag the URL from the URL Editor and drop it on the object.

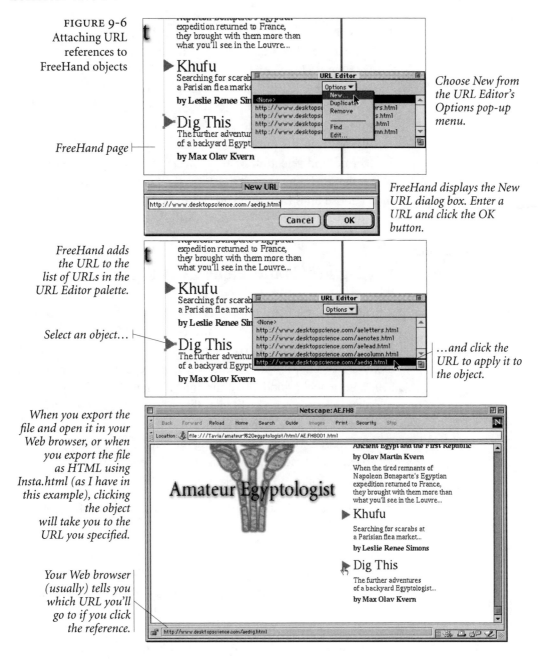

FIGURE 9-6
Attaching URL
references to
FreeHand objects

Choose New from
the URL Editor's
Options pop-up
menu.

FreeHand page

FreeHand displays the New
URL dialog box. Enter a
URL and click the OK
button.

FreeHand adds
the URL to the
list of URLs in the
URL Editor palette.

Select an object...

...and click the
URL to apply it to
the object.

When you export the
file and open it in your
Web browser, or when
you export the file
as HTML using
Insta.html (as I have in
this example), clicking
the object
will take you to the
URL you specified.

Your Web browser
(usually) tells you
which URL you'll
go to if you click
the reference.

To change the URL attached to an object, select the object, then choose Edit from the URL Editor's Options pop-up menu. Free-Hand displays the Edit URL dialog box. Enter the new URL name in the field and then click the OK button to apply the edited URL to the selected object. To remove any URL reference from an object, select the object and click "<None>" in the URL Editor's list of available URLs.

To remove a URL you've added to the URL Editor, select the URL from the list and choose Remove from the URL Editor's Options pop-up menu. This removes the URL reference from any Free-Hand objects in the publication.

To find and select all of the objects to which you've applied a particular URL, select the URL from the list in the URL Editor and then choose Find from the URL Editor's Options pop-up menu.

Saving FreeHand Pages as HTML

Want to save your FreeHand pages as HTML pages for use on your web site? Use the Insta.html Xtra (which I'll call "Insta" from here on out)—if you own the FreeHand Design in Motion suite, you've already got it; otherwise, you can download the Xtra from Macromedia's web site, try it, and, if you like, purchase it (for around $100). Insta does a good job of turning FreeHand layouts into HTML, converting graphics to web-friendly formats (JPEG, GIF, PNG, or Flash) as it does so. HTML files created with Insta also retain any URL references you've added using the URL Editor Xtra.

To export a FreeHand publication as a web page, save the publication, then follow these steps (see Figure 9-7).

1. Display the Insta palette by choosing Insta.html from the HTML submenu of the Xtras menu.

2. To set Insta's preferences, choose Preferences from the Export Options pop-up menu. Insta displays the Insta.html Preferences dialog box. In this dialog box, you can specify where you want Insta to save the HTML pages and their associated graphics. You can also choose the web browser you want to use—when you do this, Insta can direct the applications to open the pages you've exported (this saves you a step when you want to view the HTML pages). You can also choose the text editor you want to use when you enter custom HTML code (you can do this using a field in

FIGURE 9-7
Exporting as
HTML with Insta.html

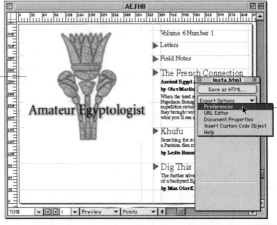

FreeHand page

*Choose Preferences
from the Export
Options pop-up
menu in the Insta
palette.*

*Insta displays the
Insta.html Preferences
dialog box. Set the
folders you've prepared
to receive the HTML
pages and graphics
exported by Insta.*

*You can also locate your text editor
and web browser, if you want. If
you do this, Insta will be able to
open them for you.*

*After you close the Insta.html
Preferences dialog box, click the
Export HTML button. Insta
displays the Save as HTML
dialog box.*

*After you set up your
export options and click
the Save button, Insta
exports the FreeHand
pages in the range
you've chosen as HTML
pages. If you've turned
on the Process Graphics
option, Insta also
exports graphics into
the folder you specified
in the Image Folder
field.*

*If you turned on the
View Result in Browser
option, Insta starts the
Web browser and
displays your Web pages.*

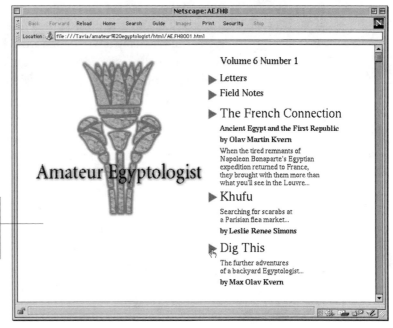

the Insta palette, but it's pretty small). When you've set the options you want, click the OK button to close the dialog box.

3. Click the Save as HTML button in the Insta palette. Insta displays the Save as HTML dialog box. Set the range of pages you want to export, and choose the type of HTML you want to use.

   Pages exported using DHTML (Dynamic HTML) will look more like your FreeHand pages (DHTML supports a wider range of font formatting options and provides for better graphic positioning), but can only be viewed using newer web browsers—mainly Netscape Navigator and Microsoft Internet Explorer versions 4 and above; pages exported in the HTML 3.2 format can be viewed using older and "off brand" web browsers, but won't look as much like your FreeHand pages.

   Choose GIF or Flash as the default image format. All web browsers can display images saved in the GIF format; most browsers will need the Flash plug-in to display images saved in the Flash format. I wouldn't worry about the need for a plug-in too much—paths drawn in FreeHand will look a lot better if you save them using the Flash format. The plug-in is free, and is easily downloaded from the Macromedia web site. You can also override the default image format for selected graphics using the Insta palette, as shown later in this chapter.

   Turn on the Process Images option to have Insta export the images it creates from your file to the folder you specified in the Insta.html Preferences dialog box; turn this option off if the images haven't changed since the last time you exported the pages (i.e., only the text in the pages has changed).

   Turn on the View Result in Browser option to have Insta launch your web browser and display the pages after it's through exporting the pages (nothing will happen if you haven't specified a web browser in the Insta.html Preferences dialog box).

4. Click the Save button to export the specified range of pages as HTML pages.

Setting image export options

What if you want Insta to export the paths in your publication using the Flash format, but export all of the images in the publication using the JPEG format? Use Insta's ability to assign file types to individual graphics. When you export the publication's pages as HTML, the file types you've assigned to the graphics override the default file types specified in the Save as HTML dialog box.

To assign a file type to an individual graphic, follow these steps (see Figure 9-8).

1. Select the graphic.

2. Display the Insta.html palette, if it's not already visible (choose Insta.html from the HTML submenu of the Xtras menu).

3. Choose the file type (GIF, JPEG, PNG, or Flash) you want to use from the Image Type pop-up menu. You can also use the controls in the palette to set the graphic's file name and ID, and choose an anti-aliasing level. The text you enter in the Alt(ernate) Text field is the text that will be displayed in place of the image in web browsers that can't display the image type you've chosen.

FIGURE 9-8
Setting export options for an individual graphic

Select a graphic...

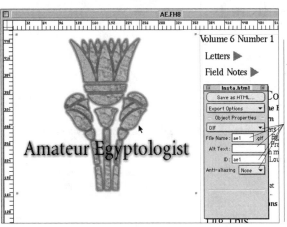

...then choose the file type, filename, and anti-aliasing level you want to use. You can also enter "alternate text" (what you see when your browser can't display an image) and an ID for use in JavaScript code you attach to the page.

Setting Document Options

When you export FreeHand pages as HTML, Insta creates a separate HTML page for each page in your FreeHand publication. Insta's Document Properties dialog box gives you a way to vary the filename, page name, background color, background image, and other page attributes between the HTML pages created from the pages of your FreeHand publication (see Figure 9-9).

To set the default properties for a series of pages, choose Document Properties from the Export Options pop-up menu. Insta displays the Document Properties dialog box. Choose Default from the Page Number pop-up menu, then use the controls in the dialog box to specify the default appearance and properties of the exported HTML pages. To vary any of these properties for a given page, choose the page number from the Page Number pop-up menu. When you do this, the Document Properties dialog box changes—specifically, a column of checkboxes appears to the right of the controls. Each checkbox corresponds to one of the attributes. To use something other than the default for an attribute, turn off (i.e., uncheck) the checkbox next to the relevant control, then change the control setting. If you want to use a different page title, for example, uncheck the checkbox next to the Page Title field, then enter a new name in the field.

FIGURE 9-9
Document Properties

Choose Default to set the properties for all of the pages in the publication.

Drag color swatches into these color wells to set the colors (you can drag from any Free-Hand color well).

To set options for an individual page, choose the page number...

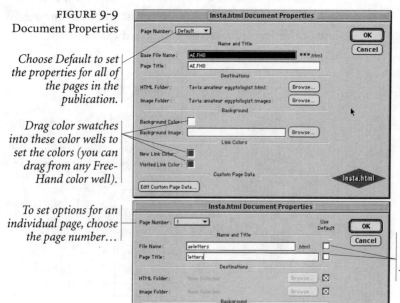

...then uncheck the Use Default checkbox for each control you want to change.

Color and the Web

Web browsers take the color values called for in the HTML code they're reading and display them on the screen. The way that the colors look, at that point, depends on the number of colors your computer's video system can display. This measurement is called *bit depth*, because it refers to the number of bits used to describe each pixel on your screen. With more bits per pixel, you get more colors. Eight-bit video systems are seen as the "lowest common denominator," and can display 256 colors.

If your system can display the color specified in the HTML code your browser is reading, you'll see the color on your screen. If your video system can't display the color, your web browser will display a dithered version of the color. Inside a scanned photograph, for example, dithering isn't particularly noticeable. When you have large areas of solid color, however, dithering can make you look bad—especially if you've applied a dithered color to type. "Plaid" was never meant to be a type style.

Because of the differences in video display systems among computer platforms, web browsers have taken it upon themselves to make sure that at least some colors will display without dithering. How do they do that? By carrying a set of colors—called a "color lookup table," or CLUT—with them. The 216 colors in the color lookup table display without dithering on any platform capable of displaying 256 or more colors at a time (that is, 8-bit, 16-bit, and 24-bit graphics systems). Pick a color in the color lookup table, and you're safe.

FreeHand comes with a color library containing the color palette used by Netscape Navigator and Microsoft Internet Explorer. To use it, follow these steps (see Figure 9-10).

1. Choose Websafe Color Library from the Colors palette's Options menu. FreeHand displays the Library dialog box.

2. Select the colors you want to use in the current publication, then click the OK button to add the colors to your Colors palette. FreeHand adds the colors to your publication.

If you don't want to use the color library, you can create the colors on your own using the RGB color model. When you define the colors, you can use the following values (for R, G, or B), in any combination: 0, 51, 102, 153, 204, and 255.

As long as you use only these values to specify RGB colors, and turn off FreeHand's color management system, you're guaranteed that the colors will match those in the color lookup tables used by today's popular Web browsers—which means you'll avoid unsightly dithering.

FIGURE 9-10
"Web-safe" colors

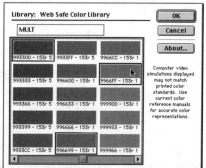

Choose Websafe Color Library from the Options pop-up menu...

...and FreeHand displays the Library dialog box. Select the colors you want to add to your Colors palette and click the OK button.

A Tangled Web

As I said earlier, I'm a Web neophyte. I hope my attempts to explain some of the features of our new publishing medium—and how and where FreeHand fits into it—haven't ended up confusing you. It comes with the territory, I guess—the Web is a wild place, and is changing even as I write this. At one point, I even thought this chapter was finished—only to have the appearance of Flash 3.0 force me to rethink some of what I'd already written.

Come next edition, maybe I'll just publish this—if not the entire book—on the Web. But I said that in the last edition, too.

Appendices

Index

Scripting

is a way of telling a program (an application, or a plug-in, or your system software) to do something without actually having to do it yourself. Instead of working with a program's user interface—clicking, dragging, and typing—to do what you need to do, you can have a script perform the same tasks and accomplish the same things. Scripting is what computing is supposed to be about: having your computer take over boring, repetitive tasks so that you can spend more time playing Duke Nukem 3D. I mean concentrating on your creative work.

What amazes me, therefore, is that scripting has never taken off—it's never seen as a "must have" feature such as, for example, tabbed palettes. Scripting is not universally supported by applications or system software and, when implemented, rarely follows any kind of standard. PageMaker features a fairly complete scripting system on both the Macintosh and Windows—but it only works in PageMaker and doesn't resemble the system-level scripting on either system (AppleScript and Visual Basic for Applications, or VBA, respectively). Quark XPress uses standard AppleScript methods on the Macintosh, but doesn't seem to offer scripting at all in Windows. The Actions palette in Photoshop gives people an easy-to-use way of recording commands, but has severe limitations.

It boggles my mind that a function this basic is so poorly understood, little used, and is presented in a bewildering and chaotic manner. What the heck, while I'm on my soapbox, I might as well tell software developers what I think they ought to do.

◆ Add scripting to your application, if it doesn't have it already. At the very least, your scripting system should be able to manipulate every user interface item in your program, just as a user would. If you want to add other nifty capabilities not available through the user interface, fine— just take care of the user interface items, first.

◆ Make it possible to save scripts as text-only documents that can be created and edited with any text editor.

◆ Make it possible to record user actions as a script.

◆ Make your scripting language look as much like English (or other human language) as possible.

◆ Your scripting system should be able to display dialog boxes containing simple controls (fields, buttons, checkboxes, and radio buttons) for user input.

◆ Support the system scripting standards: AppleScript on the Macintosh; VBA in Windows. Your scripting language doesn't have to support their control constructs and terminology, but it should be capable of sending messages to and receiving messages from these scripting methods.

◆ If your application runs in both the Macintosh and Windows environments, make your scripting system work the same way in either environment.

◆ Stop telling people scripting is hard, or that it's only for advanced users.

And now, back to the book.

Great Expectations

When friends at Macromedia told me that I'd be able to write and run scripts in FreeHand, I was thrilled. Now that I've worked with

FreeHand's scripting, I'm still excited—it's just that I'm more excited about the future than about the present. For the present, I have both good news and bad news. The bad news is that not all—very few, in fact—of FreeHand's capabilities are accessible through scripting. The good news is that the functions that *are* covered are ones that relate to tasks you're likely to *want* to automate—importing and exporting, and find and replace operations.

The method you use to write scripts for FreeHand varies, depending on the platform you're using:

◆ If you're using a Power Macintosh, you can choose to use scripts written in either AppleScript or Java.

◆ If you're using Windows, you can use scripts written in Java.

The capabilities of the different scripting approaches are the approximately the same, regardless of whether you use AppleScript or Java; the scripts you write, as you might expect, differ a great deal. Java programs written for the Windows version of FreeHand will run on the Power Macintosh. Learning to program in Java is harder than learning to write AppleScript, but the scripts you write in Java run faster.

Tip:
Java scripts and JavaScript

Java is a programming language (it's something like C++, which is something like C with a lot more annoying rules and regulations). JavaScript, as far as I can tell, is a scripting language for Web browsers. The FreeHand scripts you write using the Macromedia Script Editor are written in Java, not JavaScript.

Getting Started with Scripting

To install the Macromedia Script Editor and example Java scripts, open the XDK folder on your FreeHand installation CD. Use the installer you find there to install the software.

If you're using a Macintosh, you'll find AppleScript examples in the Scripting folder on the FreeHand installation CD. Copy them to your hard drive and start looking at them with the AppleScript Editor.

Using Java Scripts and the Macromedia Script Editor.

To start using or viewing the scripts installed with the Macromedia Script Editor, follow these steps.

1. In FreeHand, open the General Preferences dialog box and turn on the Enable Java Scripts option.

2. Quit FreeHand.

3. Restart FreeHand.

If everything's working, you'll see the Edit Scripts option at the bottom of the Xtras menu. To add the example scripts to the Xtras menu, move the Useful Scripts folder into your Xtras folder. The scripts will appear on the Useful Scripts submenu of the Xtras menu. You can run the scripts by choosing them from the menu—you don't have to start the Macromedia Script Editor application.

If you want to use the Macromedia Script Editor to look at the example scripts or to create your own scripts, choose Edit Scripts from the Xtras menu. FreeHand starts the Macromedia Script Editor and opens an untitled script (see Figure A-1). Lines preceded by "//" are comments.

Each script is made up of a number of methods. Typically, the first two methods (Imports, and Data Items) perform "housekeeping" tasks (they're something like the file "include" lists at the start of a standard C file) and are the same in all of the example scripts. The next method, Register, supplies the name of the script to FreeHand (see Figure A-2). When you create a new script, remember to enter the name of your script here (if you don't, it won't appear on the Xtras menu).

Any other methods you see in the script are the "active" part of the script—they're the code that makes things happen when you run the script (see Figure A-3).

The examples cover most of the things you can actually do with FreeHand's Java scripting—take a look at them, and you'll probably find one you can modify for your own purposes. I look forward to the future of FreeHand scripting using Java.

Working with AppleScript (Macintosh only)

If you'd rather write your scripts using AppleScript, you can. The same commands and functions available to Java scripting are available to AppleScript Scripts (more or less). In addition, you can use

FIGURE A-1
Starting the Macro-
media Script Editor

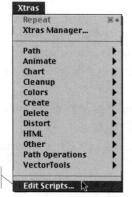

*Choose Edit Scripts
from the Xtras menu.*

*You can move from method to
method using this pop-up menu.*

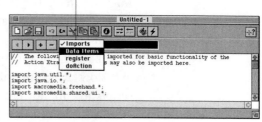

FreeHand starts the Macromedia Script Editor.

*To run the example
scripts, move the Useful
Scripts folder into the
Xtras folder. After you
do this, the Useful
Scripts submenu
appears on the Xtras
menu. To run a script,
select it from the menu.*

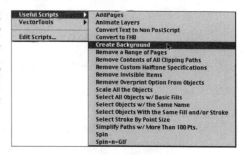

FIGURE A-2
Remember to fill in
the Register method

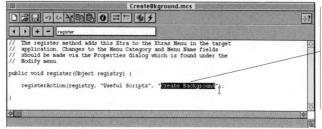

*Enter the
name for
your new
script here
(as you want
it to appear
on the Xtras
menu).*

FIGURE A-3
In most of the
examples, the doAction
method does most of
the work

```
CreateBkground.mcs
doAction
public void doAction() {

    Document doc = FreeHand.getCurrentDocument();

    // If there is no current document, exit the script.
    if (doc == null)
        return;

    MessageDialog.showMessage("about to get selection");
    Selection selection = doc.getSelection();
    MessageDialog.showMessage("got selection");
    Page page = doc.getCurrentPage();
```

*This is the start of the wacky CreateBackground script, which
duplicates the selected object and then pastes it at a random
position on the page, applying random scaling and rotation as
it does so. It's great for making geometric backgrounds.*

PreFab Player, an AppleScript programming extension that makes it possible to script actions that can manipulate FreeHand's user interface items (or those of any other program, for that matter). With Player, you can automate just about anything you can do in FreeHand.

What's the hitch? AppleScript is beautifully designed, rich, deep, and slow. If you're willing to put up with the time it takes your scripts to run, however, you can do some amazing things. And, as slow as it can be, it's still faster than you are.

What can you script using AppleScript without adding Player to your system? You can find it all in FreeHand's AppleScript dictionary. To view FreeHand's AppleScript dictionary, follow these steps (see Figure A-4).

1. Start the (Apple) Script Editor.

2. Choose Open Dictionary from the File menu. The Script Editor (after starting FreeHand, if necessary) displays the AppleScript commands FreeHand can respond to. You can view one command at a time, or click "FreeHand Suite" to see them all at once.

The Scripting folder on the FreeHand installation CD also includes a number of example scripts. To run any of the example scripts, double-clicking them in the Finder. Most of the sample scripts will bring FreeHand to the foreground as they execute.

Tip:
No Dictionary?

If you don't see FreeHand's AppleScript dictionary, it's probably because you haven't installed the AppleScript Xtra. FreeHand can't run AppleScript scripts without the AppleScript Xtra, so you'll have to find it and put it in your FreeHand Xtras folder.

To see an example use of each command, open the script files in the Syntax Examples folder (it's inside the Scripting folder on your FreeHand installation CD). In addition to showing you how to use the commands, some of the examples are actually useful.

Tip:
Keeping
Scripts Aloof

Store your AppleScript scripts for FreeHand anywhere but in the Xtras folder. If you store them there, FreeHand will rebuild the list of available Xtras every time you save a script. This can take some

FIGURE A-4
FreeHand's
AppleScript
dictionary

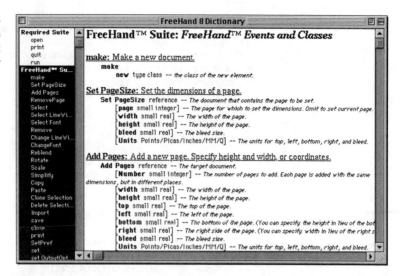

time, and, in some cases, cause scripts to fail. Putting the scripts in the Xtras folder won't make them appear on the Xtras menu, as Java scripts do.

FreeHand and Player. As I mentioned earlier, Player, from PreFab Software, is an AppleScript tool that makes it possible to script "unscriptable" applications. When you have Player running (it's a background application), you can tell Player to make menu choices, click buttons, enter text, or otherwise work with the user interface controls of the currently-running programs.

If the application you're controlling with Player uses "standard" Macintosh controls (dialog boxes, buttons, checkboxes, and fields), Player has little trouble finding and using the controls. Most of the controls in FreeHand aren't standard Macintosh controls. You can get around this problem by using pixel coordinates (relative to the lower-left corner of the window or dialog box you're working with) to click buttons, and by using keyboard shortcuts to move through fields and display other dialog boxes.

I often want to clone an object, rotate it, move it some distance, and scale it. This series of transformations is fairly simple—but suppose I wanted to do it 30 times? That's why I used AppleScript and Player to create a script (see Figure A-5). This example shows how to specify buttons for Player to click, and it also shows how to press modifier (i.e., command) keys and enter text.

FIGURE A-5
A script for
applying multiple
transformations

```
--this script requires Player from PreFab Software
tell application "FreeHand 8.0" to activate
--set up coordinates for Transform palette buttons
set moveButton to {13, 13}
set rotateButton to {39, 13}
set scaleButton to {62, 13}
set skewButton to {86, 13}
set reflectButton to {110, 13}
tell application "PreFab Player™"
        type "=" holding command
        set target window to "Transform"
        click dialog item rotateButton
        type "`" holding command
        type "5"
        --the Apply button is dialog item 1
        click dialog item 1
        click dialog item scaleButton
        type "`" holding command
        type "90" --assumes Uniform scaling
        click dialog item 1
        click dialog item moveButton
        type "`" holding command
        type "p12"
        type tab
        type "0"
        click dialog item 1
        repeat 9 times
          type "=" holding command
          set target window to "Transform"
          click dialog item rotateButton
          click dialog item 1
          click dialog item scaleButton
          click dialog item 1
          click dialog item moveButton
          click dialog item 1
        end repeat
end tell
```

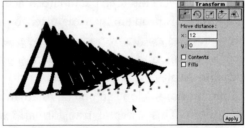

Why you (might) want to use this script.

While I do write, illustrate, and lay out the pages of this book, I am able to call on a small group of truly amazing people to help. Carl Juarez is my "intelligent updating agent"—he tests each illustration and procedure from the previous edition, then creates new screen shots where he sees that techniques or user interface items have changed. Someday I would like to publish the pages of notes on the physics of light that Jon Singer, my copy editor, wrote regarding the discussion of hue and saturation in Chapter 6 (I'm afraid, however, that I wasn't able to give Jon a reasonable amount of time this edition, and I take personal responsibility for all copy editing errors). Toby Malina pitched in with much-needed last-minute production help. ("Spell check. Replace ligatures. Update figure numbering. Print. Repeat.") And, as usual, Jan C. Wright, the queen of indexing, provided another superb index. When I look through an index in another computer book or manual I get mad. If *I* can afford to hire Jan to do the job right, why can't *they*?

James E. Talmage helped tremendously with his comments on the sections on perspective drawing and axonometric projection in Chapter 2 and Chapter 5. If he keeps this up, I'm going to have to put his name on the cover as a co-author. From the look of the FreeHand files he sent, he's a pretty hot technical illustrator, too.

I also want to thank Intergraph for the loan of one of their ExtremeZ graphics workstations—a Windows NT machine fast enough to keep up with the most complex Fireworks effects I could throw at it (even if they didn't make it into the book). Heck, it even made KPT Bryce seem like something reasonable to use (though what for is still open to question). The only hard part about having the machine around was having to give it back and return to my 150 Mhz Pentium running Windows 95.

I don't know how much longer it'll take, but, eventually (by the time you're reading this, I hope), you should be able to find more than a blank page at my web site www.desktopscience.com.

If you want any of the PostScript code and/or tools discussed in Chapter 8, "PostScript," please send me an email message at the address below. Let me know which platform you're using—this is one area where it makes quite a bit of difference.

I'm also (somewhat) available for customized FreeHand training and for custom FreeHand Xtra development (my company, Desktop Science, wrote many of the Xtras in the critically acclaimed VectorTools package from Extensis). Let me know if you're interested in more information on these services,

Finally, drop me a line—I'd love to know what you thought of the book (even if you didn't like it—I took my best shot, but I can't correct my aim unless I know I've missed). I'd also love to hear about any fabulous FreeHand tips and tricks you've come up with (so I can steal them for the next edition).

Olav Martin Kvern
4016 Francis Avenue North
Seattle, Washington 98103
(206) 285-7579 (office)
(206) 285-0308 (fax)
ole@desktopscience.com